SENTRY

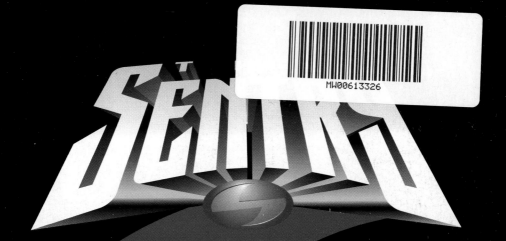

MARVEL KNIGHTS

THE SENTRY™ Contains material originally published in magazine form as THE SENTRY #'S 1-5, THE SENTRY/FANTASTIC FOUR, THE SENTRY/SPIDER-MAN, THE SENTRY/X-MEN, THE SENTRY/HULK, and THE SENTRY VS THE VOID. Published by MARVEL COMICS, a division of MARVEL ENTERPRISES, INC. Lou Gioia, Executive Vice-President, Publishing; Bob Greenberger, Director, Editorial Operations; Stan Lee, Chairman Emeritus. OFFICE OF PUBLICATION: 387 PARK AVENUE SOUTH, NEW YORK, N.Y. 10016. Copyright © 2000 and 2001. Marvel Characters, Inc. All rights reserved. No similarity between any of the names, characters, persons, and/or institutions in this magazine with those of any living or dead person or institution is intended, and any such similarity which may exist is purely coincidental. This periodical may not be sold except by authorized dealers and is sold subject to the condition that it shall not be sold or distributed with any part of its cover or markings removed, nor in a mutilated condition. SENTRY CHARACTERS, INC. Printed in Canada. First Printing, October, 2001. ISBN: 0-785-10799-1. GST #R127032852. MARVEL COMICS is a division of MARVEL ENTERPRISES, INC. Peter Cuneo, Chief Executive Officer; Avi Arad, Chief Creative Officer.

(including all prominent characters featured in this issue and the distinctive likenesses thereof) is a trademark of MARVEL CHAR-ACTERS, INC.

10 9 8 7 6 5 4 3 2 1

PAUL JENKINS

RICK LEONARDI, BILL SIENKIEWICZ, TOM PALMER and TERRY AUSTIN art •

RS & Comicraft's WES ABBOTT and JOHN 'JG' ROSHELL

JOE QUESADA, STUART MOORE and NANCI DAKESIAN original series editors

JESSICA SCHWARTZ production assistant • BEN ABERNATHY collections editor •

BOB GREENBERGER

photograph of the sentry by JOSE VILLARRUBIA • sentry model JONATHAN WHITE

NTRY

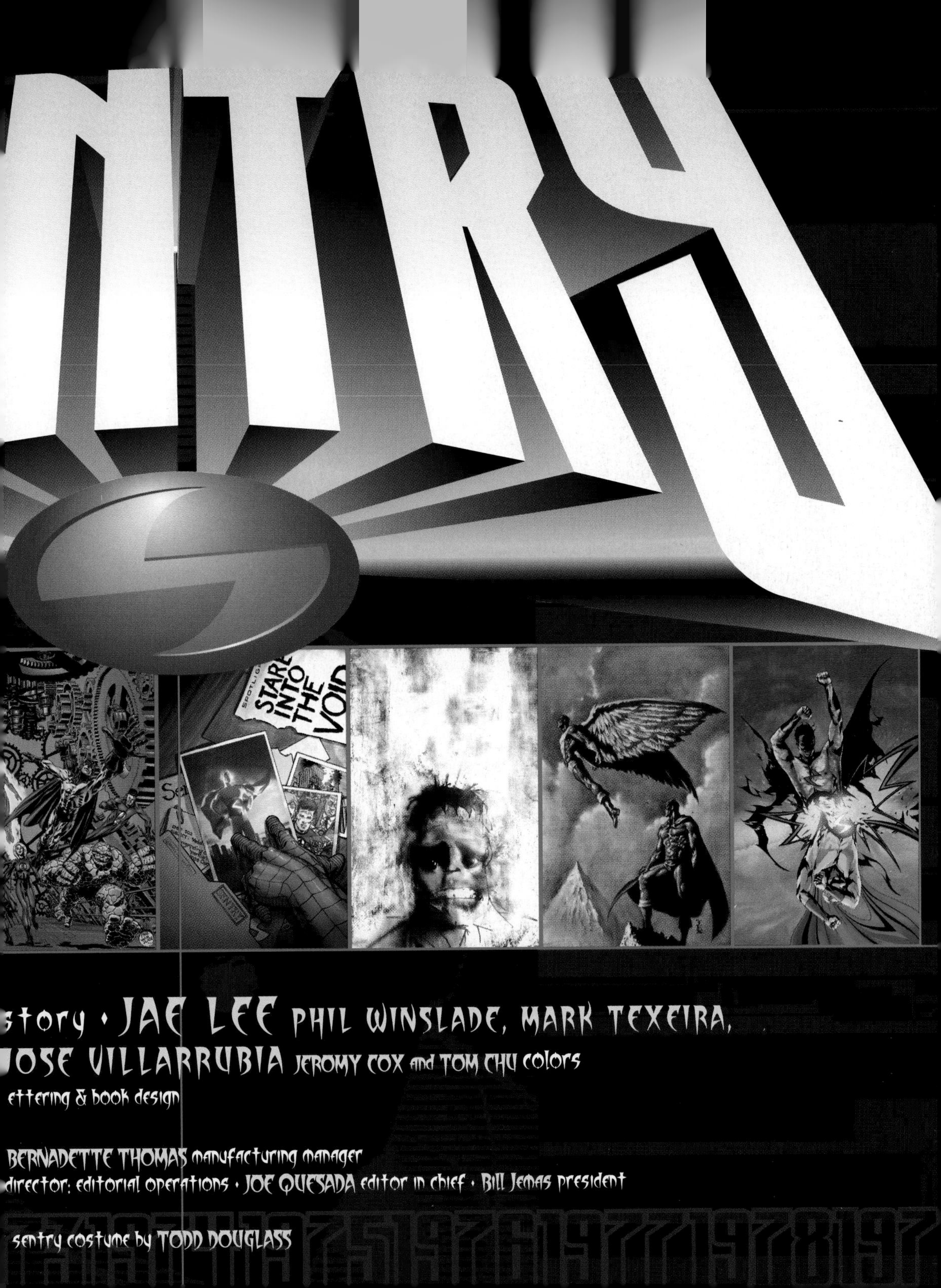
STARE INTO THE VOID

story • JAE LEE PHIL WINSLADE, MARK TEXEIRA,
JOSE VILLARRUBIA JEROMY COX and TOM CHU colors
ettering & book design

BERNADETTE THOMAS manufacturing manager
director: editorial operations • JOE QUESADA editor in chief • Bill Jemas president

sentry costume by TODD DOUGLASS

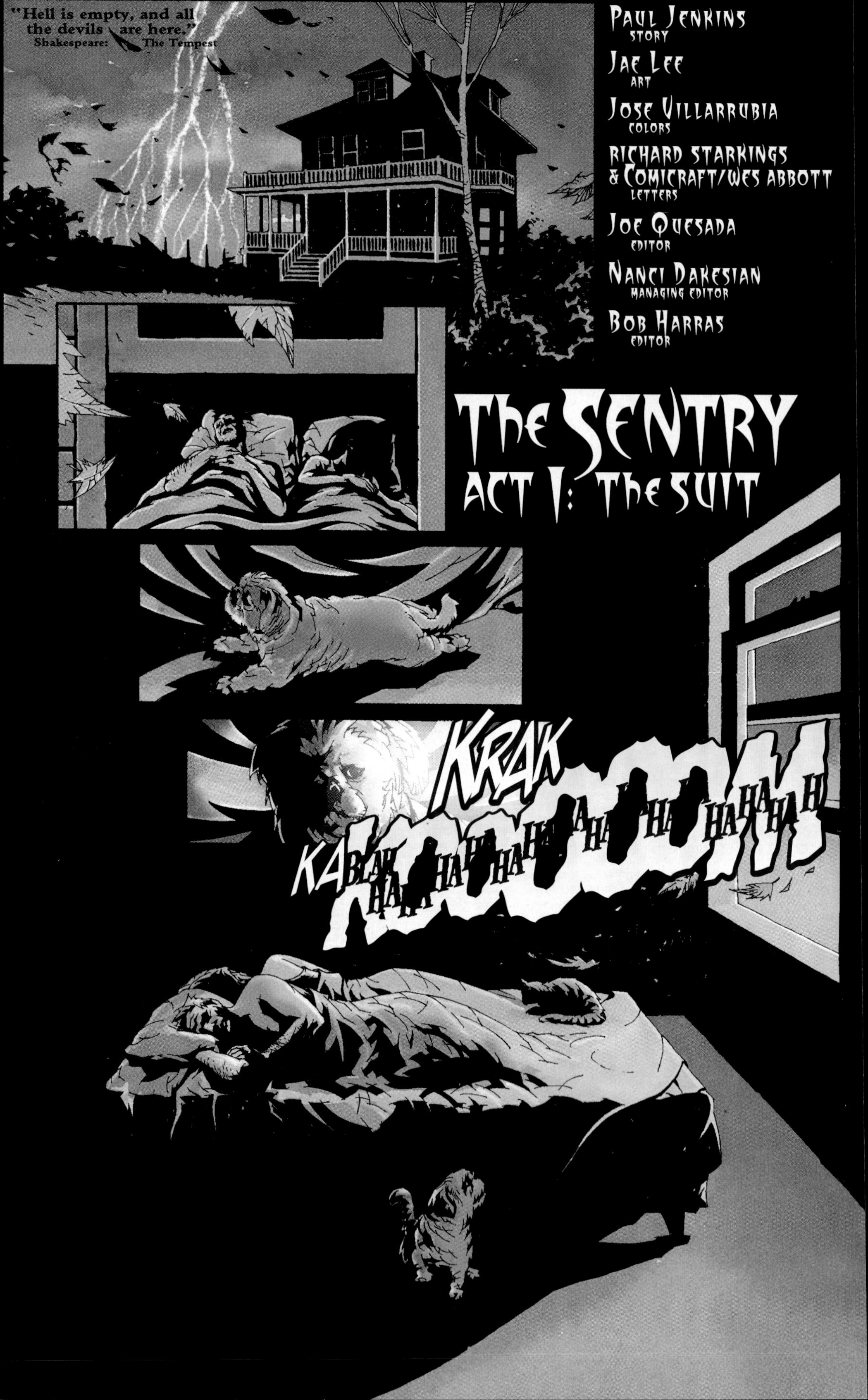
"Hell is empty, and all the devils are here."
Shakespeare: The Tempest
PAUL JENKINS
STORY
JAE LEE
ART
JOSE VILLARRUBIA
COLORS
RICHARD STARKINGS & COMICRAFT/WES ABBOTT
LETTERS
JOE QUESADA
EDITOR
NANCI DAKESIAN
MANAGING EDITOR
BOB HARRAS
EDITOR
THE SENTRY
ACT I: THE SUIT
KRAK

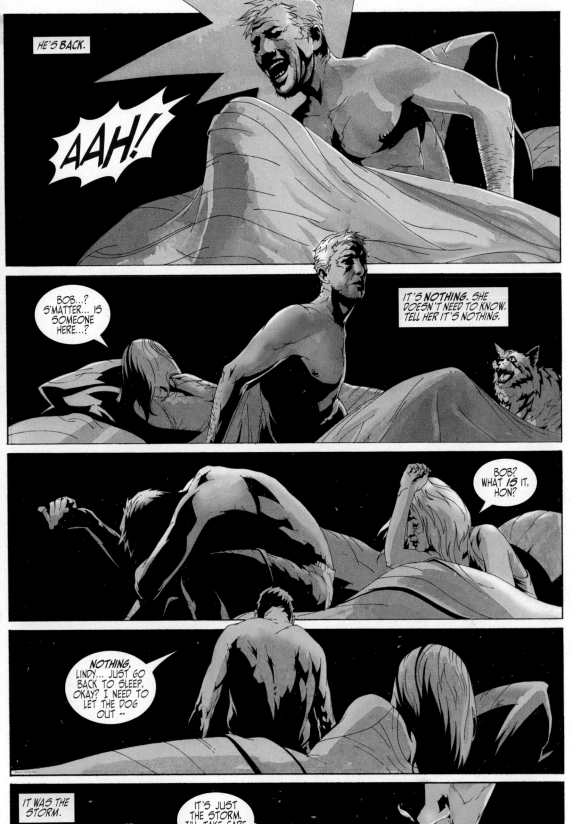

HE'S BACK.

AAH!

BOB...? S'MATTER... IS SOMEONE HERE...?

IT'S NOTHING. SHE DOESN'T NEED TO KNOW. TELL HER IT'S NOTHING.

BOB? WHAT IS IT, HON?

NOTHING, LINDY... JUST GO BACK TO SLEEP, OKAY? I NEED TO LET THE DOG OUT --

IT WAS THE STORM.

IT'S JUST THE STORM. I'LL TAKE CARE OF IT.

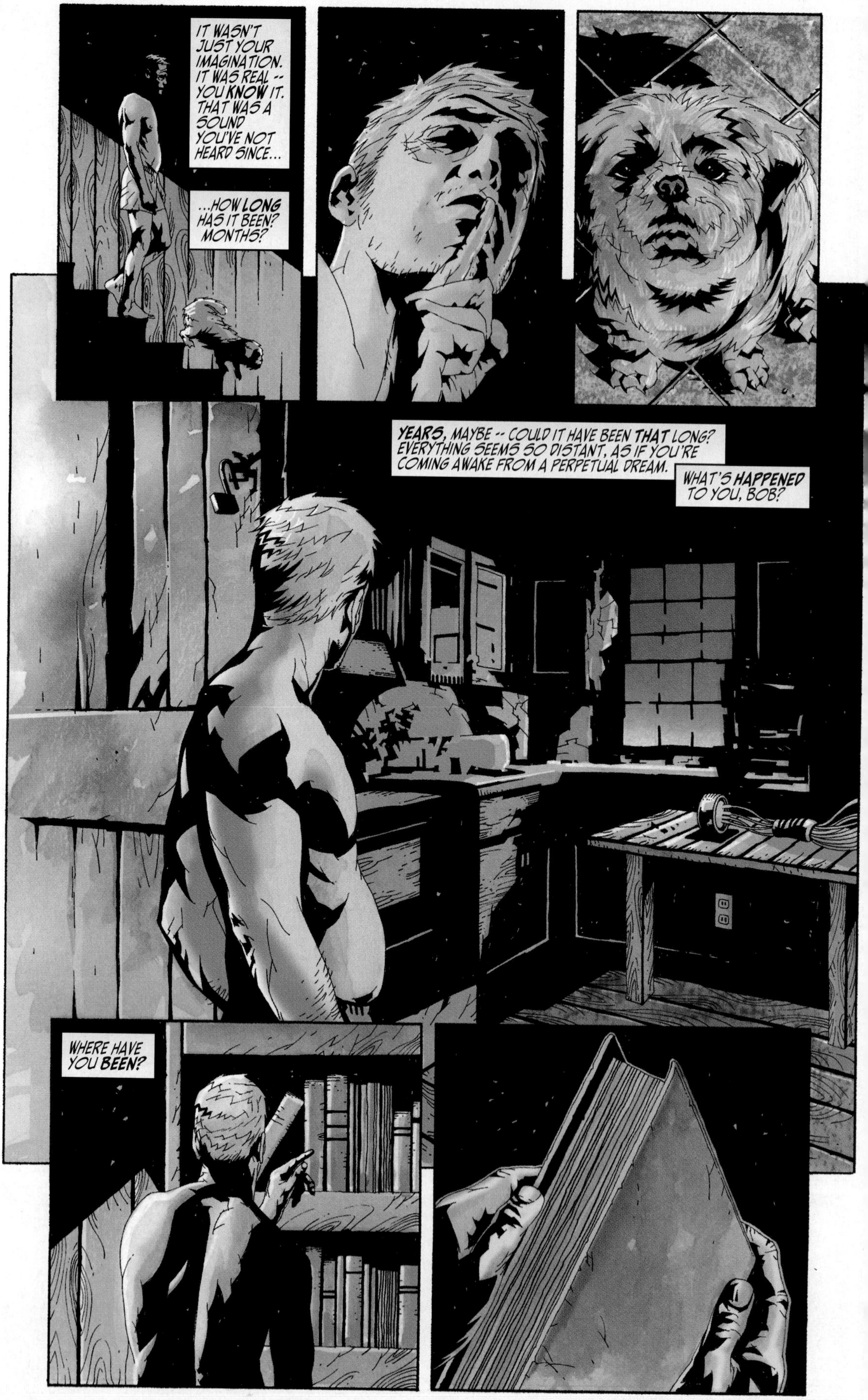
IT WASN'T JUST YOUR IMAGINATION. IT WAS REAL -- YOU KNOW IT. THAT WAS A SOUND YOU'VE NOT HEARD SINCE...
...HOW LONG HAS IT BEEN? MONTHS?
YEARS, MAYBE -- COULD IT HAVE BEEN THAT LONG? EVERYTHING SEEMS SO DISTANT, AS IF YOU'RE COMING AWAKE FROM A PERPETUAL DREAM.
WHAT'S HAPPENED TO YOU, BOB?
WHERE HAVE YOU BEEN?

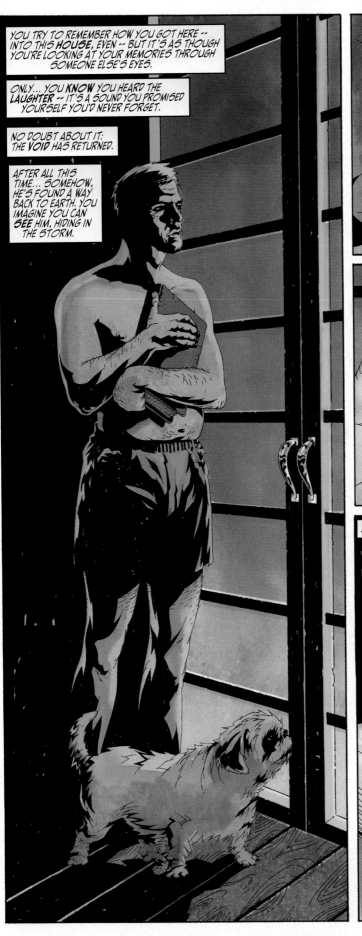

YOU TRY TO REMEMBER HOW YOU GOT HERE -- INTO THIS **HOUSE,** EVEN -- BUT IT'S AS THOUGH YOU'RE LOOKING AT YOUR MEMORIES THROUGH SOMEONE ELSE'S EYES.

ONLY... YOU **KNOW** YOU HEARD THE **LAUGHTER** -- IT'S A SOUND YOU PROMISED YOURSELF YOU'D NEVER FORGET.

NO DOUBT ABOUT IT: THE **VOID** HAS RETURNED.

AFTER ALL THIS TIME... SOMEHOW, HE'S FOUND A WAY BACK TO EARTH. YOU IMAGINE YOU CAN **SEE** HIM, HIDING IN THE STORM.

THAT'D BE JUST HOW HE'D MAKE HIS PLAY.

IF IT **IS** THE VOID, HE'LL BE STRONGER THAN EVER BEFORE. THE DANGER WILL BE BEYOND MEASURE.

AND THERE WILL BE ONLY ONE HOPE FOR HUMANITY:

YOU.

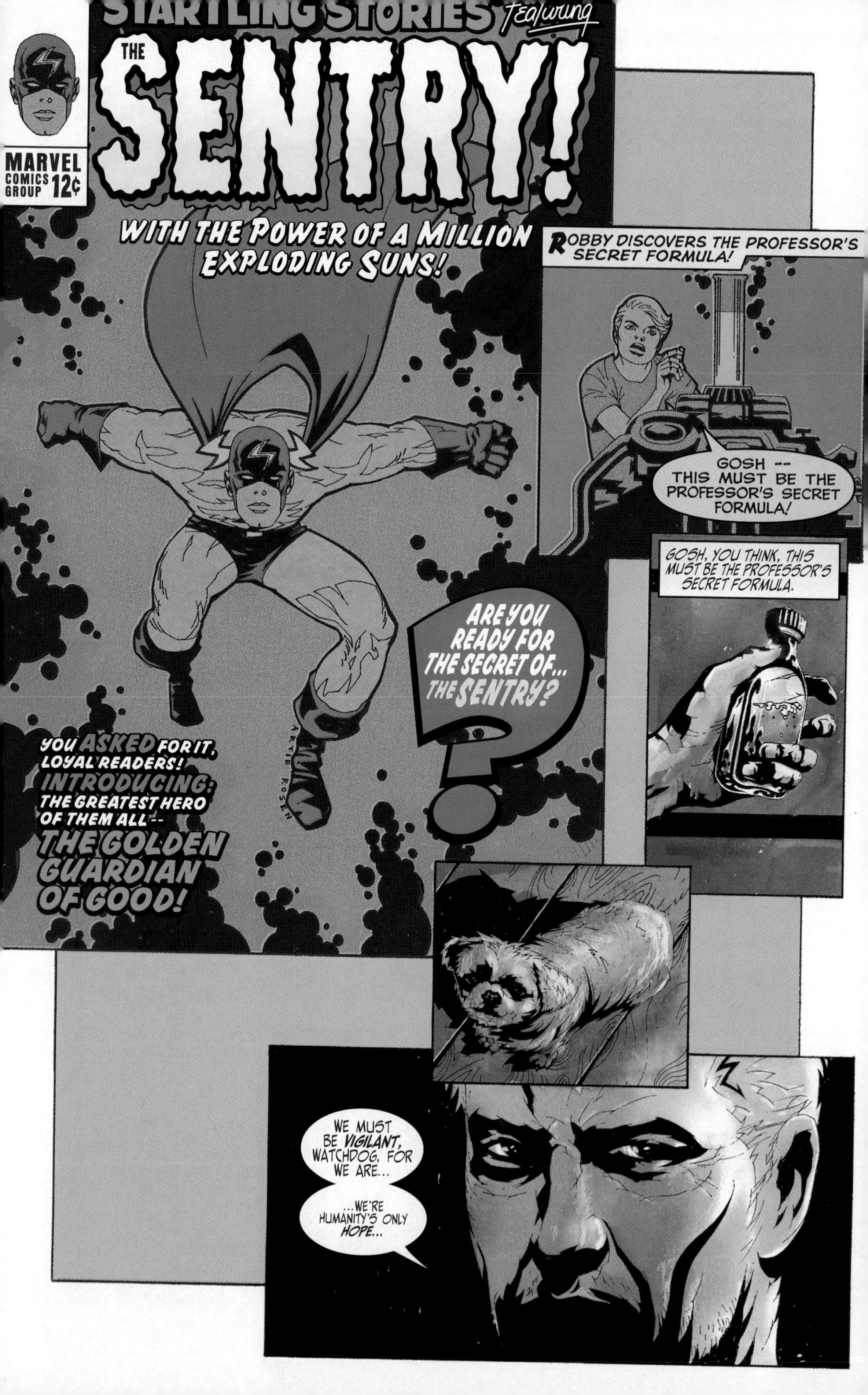

STARTLING STORIES featuring
THE SENTRY!
MARVEL COMICS GROUP 12¢
WITH THE POWER OF A MILLION EXPLODING SUNS!
ARE YOU READY FOR THE SECRET OF... THE SENTRY?
YOU ASKED FOR IT, LOYAL READERS! INTRODUCING: THE GREATEST HERO OF THEM ALL -- THE GOLDEN GUARDIAN OF GOOD!
ARTIE ROSEN
ROBBY DISCOVERS THE PROFESSOR'S SECRET FORMULA!
GOSH -- THIS MUST BE THE PROFESSOR'S SECRET FORMULA!
GOSH, YOU THINK, THIS MUST BE THE PROFESSOR'S SECRET FORMULA.
WE MUST BE VIGILANT, WATCHDOG, FOR WE ARE...
...WE'RE HUMANITY'S ONLY HOPE...

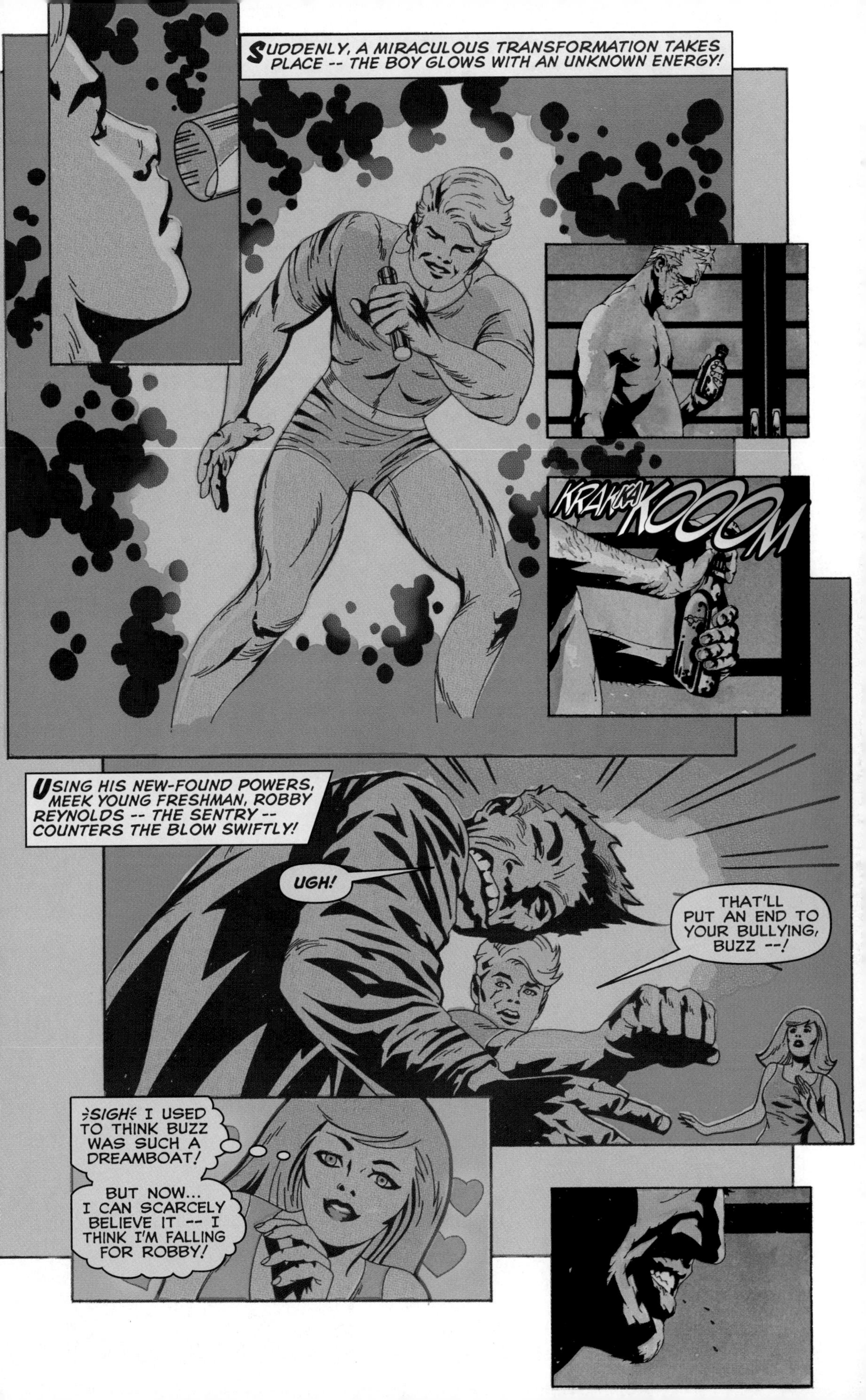
SUDDENLY, A MIRACULOUS TRANSFORMATION TAKES PLACE -- THE BOY GLOWS WITH AN UNKNOWN ENERGY!
KRAKKAKKOOOM
USING HIS NEW-FOUND POWERS, MEEK YOUNG FRESHMAN, ROBBY REYNOLDS -- THE SENTRY -- COUNTERS THE BLOW SWIFTLY!
UGH!
THAT'LL PUT AN END TO YOUR BULLYING, BUZZ --!
SIGH I USED TO THINK BUZZ WAS SUCH A DREAMBOAT!
BUT NOW... I CAN SCARCELY BELIEVE IT -- I THINK I'M FALLING FOR ROBBY!

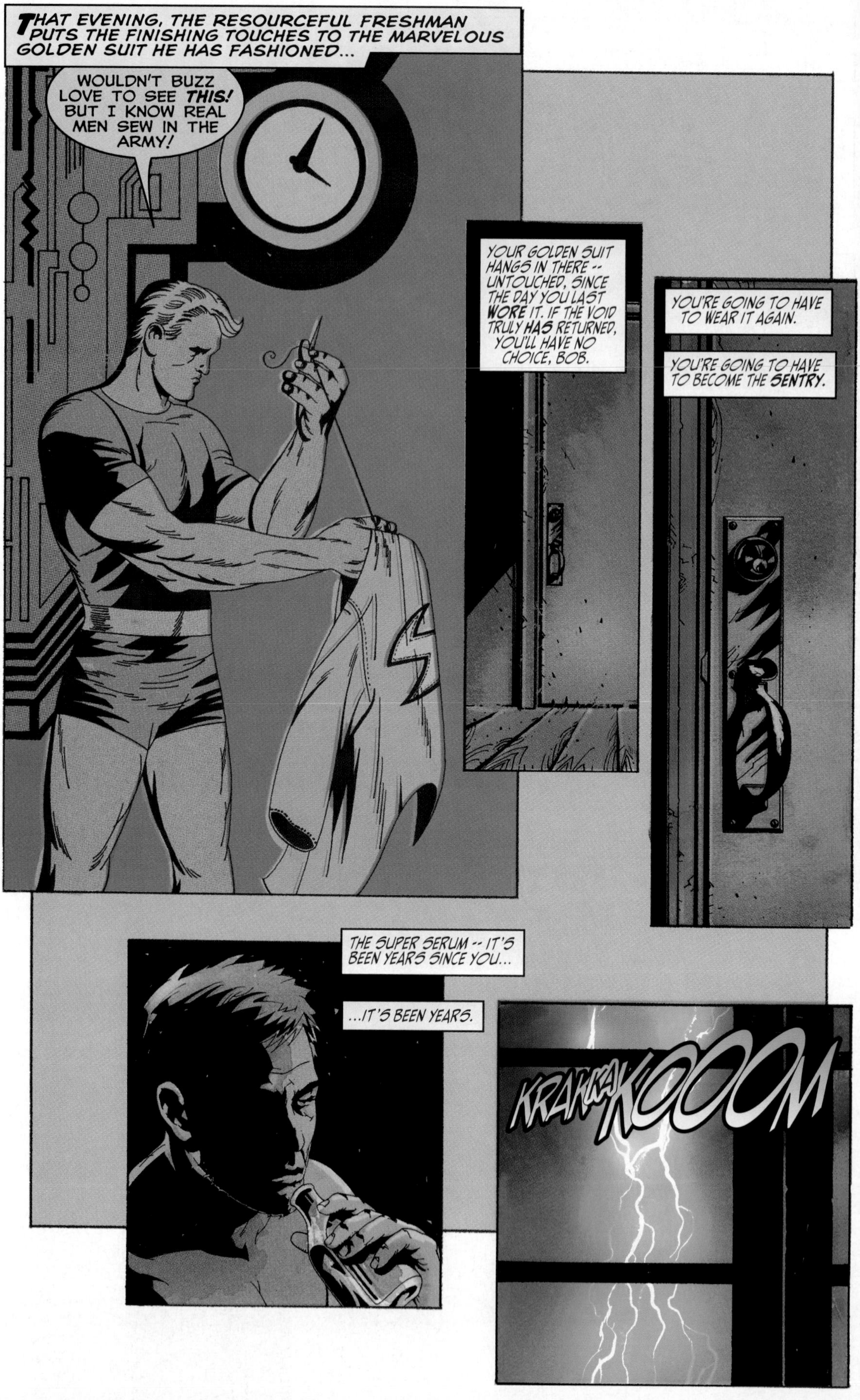
THAT EVENING, THE RESOURCEFUL FRESHMAN PUTS THE FINISHING TOUCHES TO THE MARVELOUS GOLDEN SUIT HE HAS FASHIONED...
WOULDN'T BUZZ LOVE TO SEE **THIS!** BUT I KNOW REAL MEN SEW IN THE ARMY!
YOUR GOLDEN SUIT HANGS IN THERE -- UNTOUCHED, SINCE THE DAY YOU LAST **WORE** IT. IF THE VOID TRULY **HAS** RETURNED, YOU'LL HAVE NO CHOICE, BOB.
YOU'RE GOING TO HAVE TO WEAR IT AGAIN.
YOU'RE GOING TO HAVE TO BECOME THE **SENTRY**.
THE SUPER SERUM -- IT'S BEEN YEARS SINCE YOU...
...IT'S BEEN YEARS.
KRAKKA KOOOM

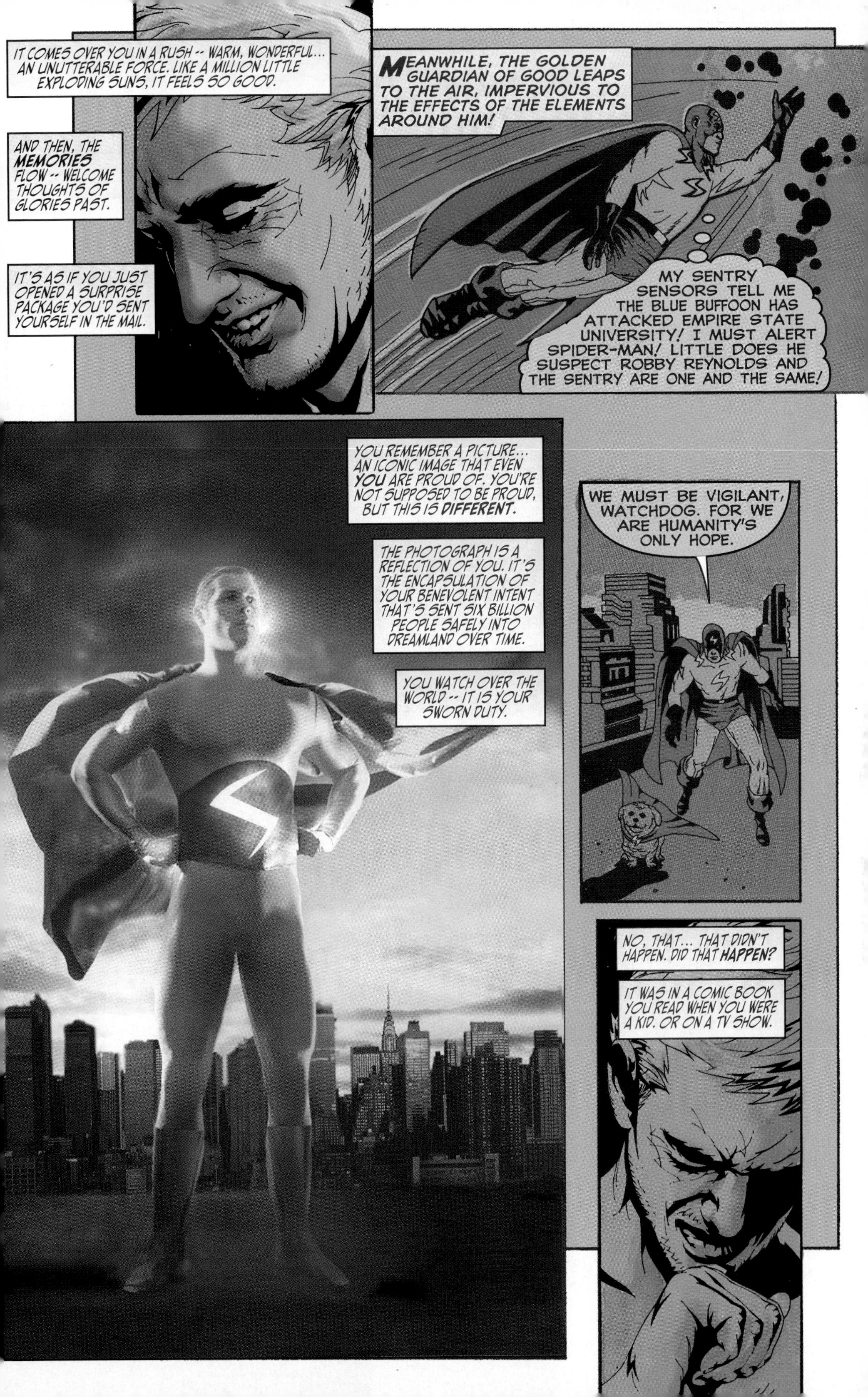
IT COMES OVER YOU IN A RUSH -- WARM, WONDERFUL... AN UNUTTERABLE FORCE. LIKE A MILLION LITTLE EXPLODING SUNS, IT FEELS SO GOOD.
AND THEN, THE MEMORIES FLOW -- WELCOME THOUGHTS OF GLORIES PAST.
IT'S AS IF YOU JUST OPENED A SURPRISE PACKAGE YOU'D SENT YOURSELF IN THE MAIL.
MEANWHILE, THE GOLDEN GUARDIAN OF GOOD LEAPS TO THE AIR, IMPERVIOUS TO THE EFFECTS OF THE ELEMENTS AROUND HIM!
MY SENTRY SENSORS TELL ME THE BLUE BUFFOON HAS ATTACKED EMPIRE STATE UNIVERSITY! I MUST ALERT SPIDER-MAN! LITTLE DOES HE SUSPECT ROBBY REYNOLDS AND THE SENTRY ARE ONE AND THE SAME!
YOU REMEMBER A PICTURE... AN ICONIC IMAGE THAT EVEN YOU ARE PROUD OF. YOU'RE NOT SUPPOSED TO BE PROUD, BUT THIS IS DIFFERENT.
THE PHOTOGRAPH IS A REFLECTION OF YOU. IT'S THE ENCAPSULATION OF YOUR BENEVOLENT INTENT THAT'S SENT SIX BILLION PEOPLE SAFELY INTO DREAMLAND OVER TIME.
YOU WATCH OVER THE WORLD -- IT IS YOUR SWORN DUTY.
WE MUST BE VIGILANT, WATCHDOG. FOR WE ARE HUMANITY'S ONLY HOPE.
NO, THAT... THAT DIDN'T HAPPEN. DID THAT HAPPEN?
IT WAS IN A COMIC BOOK YOU READ WHEN YOU WERE A KID. OR ON A TV SHOW.

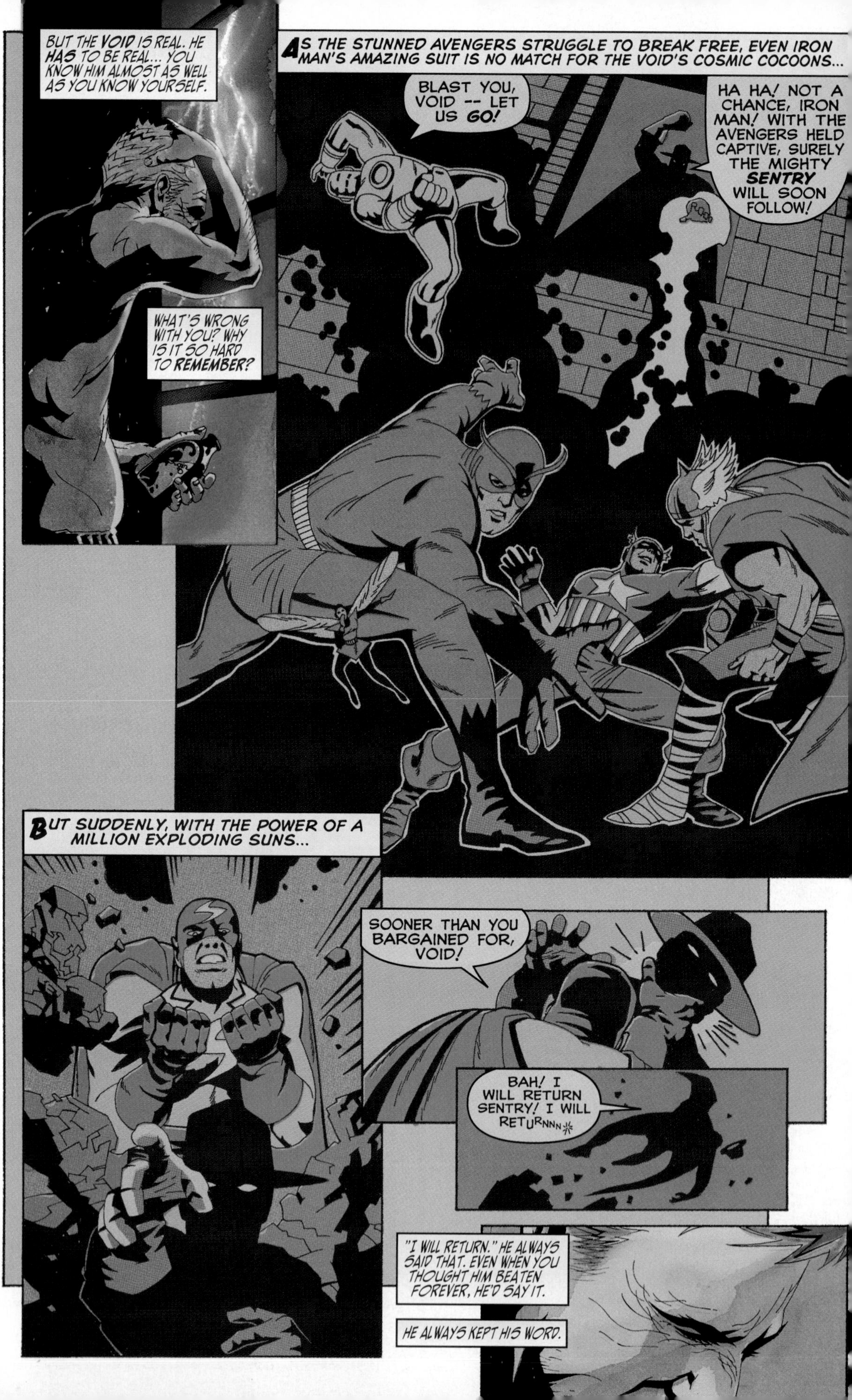

BUT THE VOID IS REAL. HE HAS TO BE REAL... YOU KNOW HIM ALMOST AS WELL AS YOU KNOW YOURSELF.
WHAT'S WRONG WITH YOU? WHY IS IT SO HARD TO REMEMBER?
AS THE STUNNED AVENGERS STRUGGLE TO BREAK FREE, EVEN IRON MAN'S AMAZING SUIT IS NO MATCH FOR THE VOID'S COSMIC COCOONS...
BLAST YOU, VOID -- LET US GO!
HA HA! NOT A CHANCE, IRON MAN! WITH THE AVENGERS HELD CAPTIVE, SURELY THE MIGHTY SENTRY WILL SOON FOLLOW!
BUT SUDDENLY, WITH THE POWER OF A MILLION EXPLODING SUNS...
SOONER THAN YOU BARGAINED FOR, VOID!
BAH! I WILL RETURN SENTRY! I WILL RETURNNN
"I WILL RETURN." HE ALWAYS SAID THAT. EVEN WHEN YOU THOUGHT HIM BEATEN FOREVER, HE'D SAY IT.
HE ALWAYS KEPT HIS WORD.

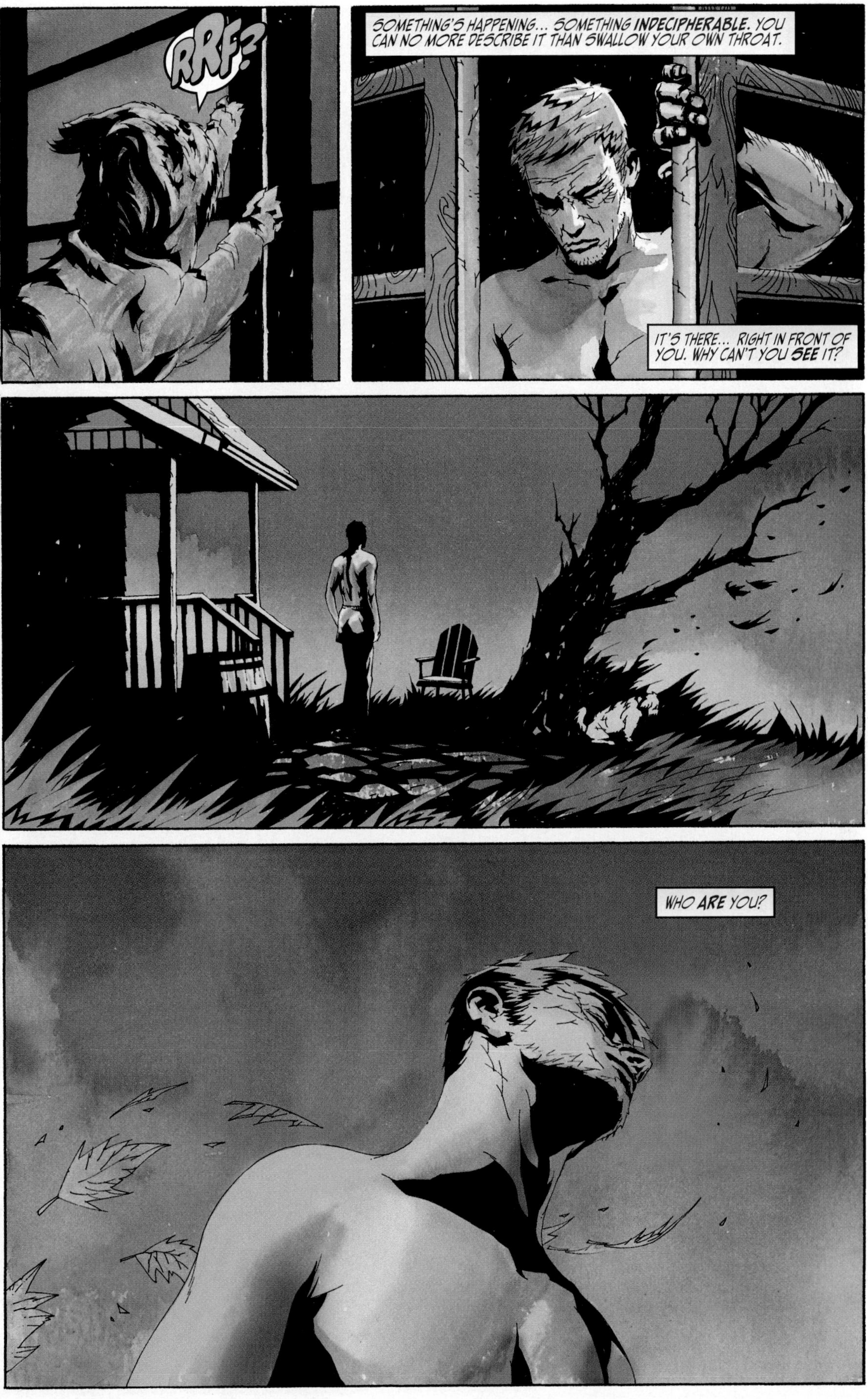
RRF?
SOMETHING'S HAPPENING... SOMETHING INDECIPHERABLE. YOU CAN NO MORE DESCRIBE IT THAN SWALLOW YOUR OWN THROAT.
IT'S THERE... RIGHT IN FRONT OF YOU. WHY CAN'T YOU SEE IT?
WHO ARE YOU?

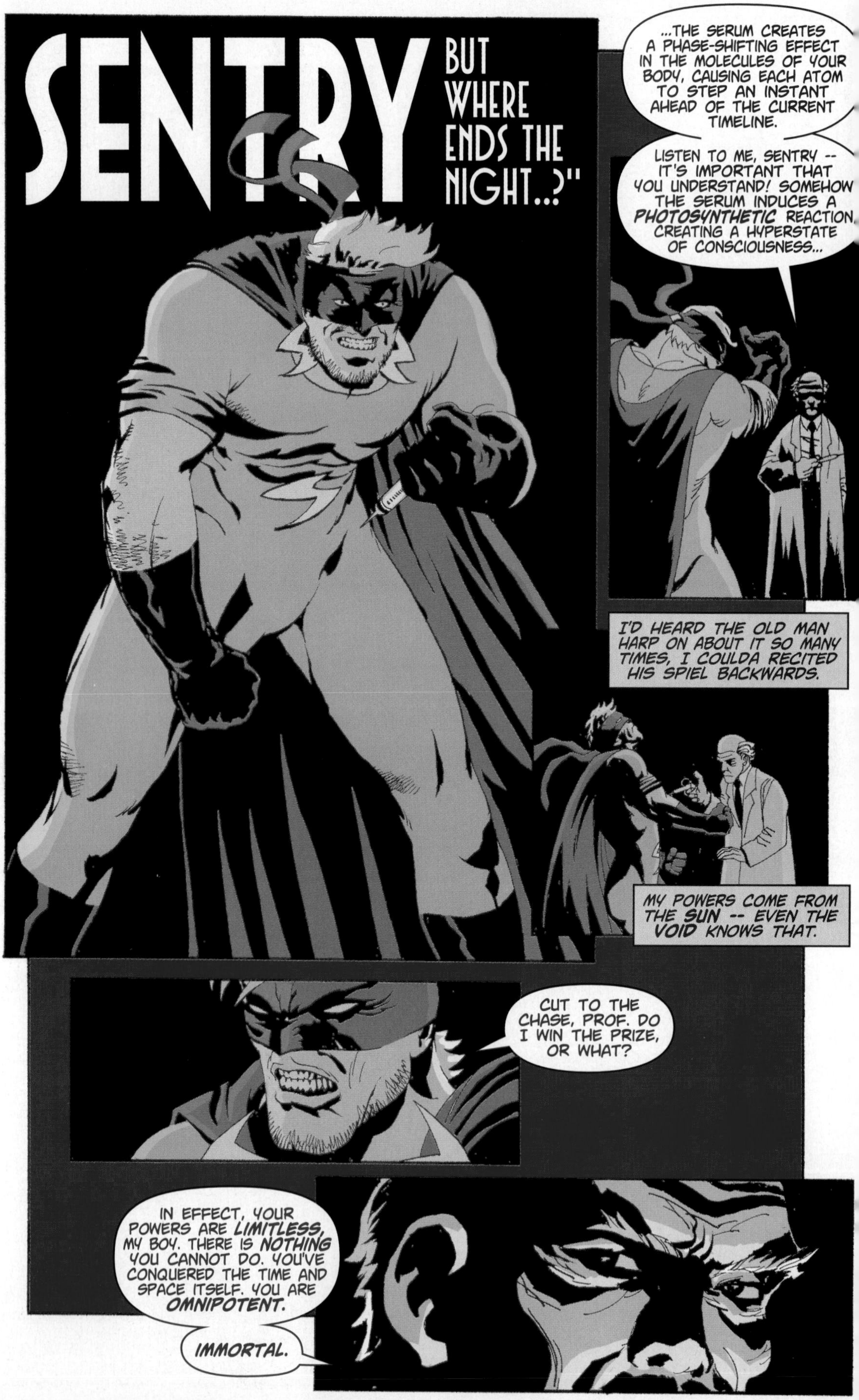
SENTRY
BUT WHERE ENDS THE NIGHT..?"
...THE SERUM CREATES A PHASE-SHIFTING EFFECT IN THE MOLECULES OF YOUR BODY, CAUSING EACH ATOM TO STEP AN INSTANT AHEAD OF THE CURRENT TIMELINE.
LISTEN TO ME, SENTRY -- IT'S IMPORTANT THAT YOU UNDERSTAND! SOMEHOW THE SERUM INDUCES A PHOTOSYNTHETIC REACTION, CREATING A HYPERSTATE OF CONSCIOUSNESS...
I'D HEARD THE OLD MAN HARP ON ABOUT IT SO MANY TIMES, I COULDA RECITED HIS SPIEL BACKWARDS.
MY POWERS COME FROM THE SUN -- EVEN THE VOID KNOWS THAT.
CUT TO THE CHASE, PROF. DO I WIN THE PRIZE, OR WHAT?
IN EFFECT, YOUR POWERS ARE LIMITLESS, MY BOY. THERE IS NOTHING YOU CANNOT DO. YOU'VE CONQUERED THE TIME AND SPACE ITSELF. YOU ARE OMNIPOTENT.
IMMORTAL.

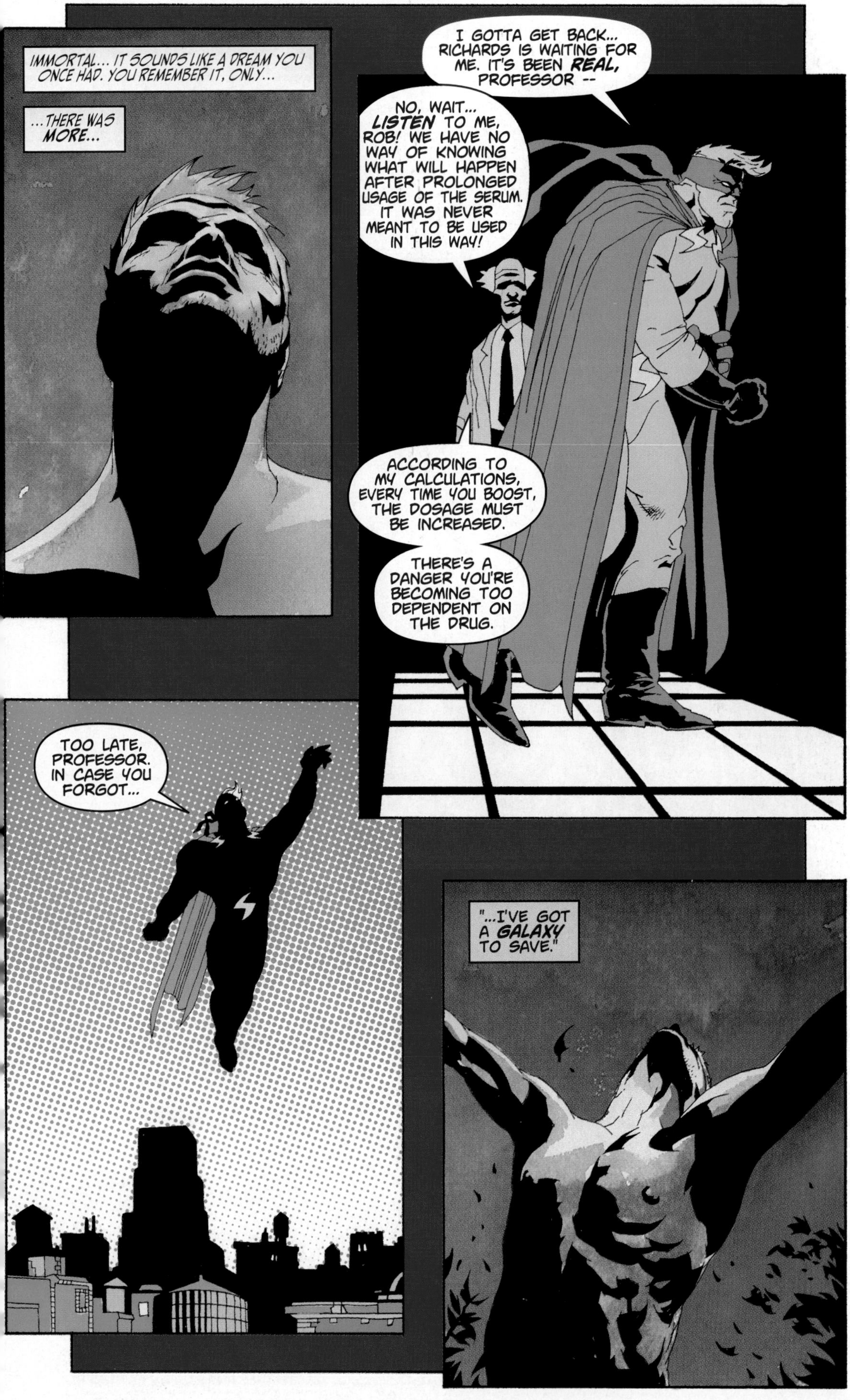
IMMORTAL... IT SOUNDS LIKE A DREAM YOU ONCE HAD. YOU REMEMBER IT, ONLY...
...THERE WAS MORE...
I GOTTA GET BACK... RICHARDS IS WAITING FOR ME. IT'S BEEN REAL, PROFESSOR --
NO, WAIT... LISTEN TO ME, ROB! WE HAVE NO WAY OF KNOWING WHAT WILL HAPPEN AFTER PROLONGED USAGE OF THE SERUM. IT WAS NEVER MEANT TO BE USED IN THIS WAY!
ACCORDING TO MY CALCULATIONS, EVERY TIME YOU BOOST, THE DOSAGE MUST BE INCREASED.
THERE'S A DANGER YOU'RE BECOMING TOO DEPENDENT ON THE DRUG.
TOO LATE, PROFESSOR. IN CASE YOU FORGOT...
"...I'VE GOT A GALAXY TO SAVE."

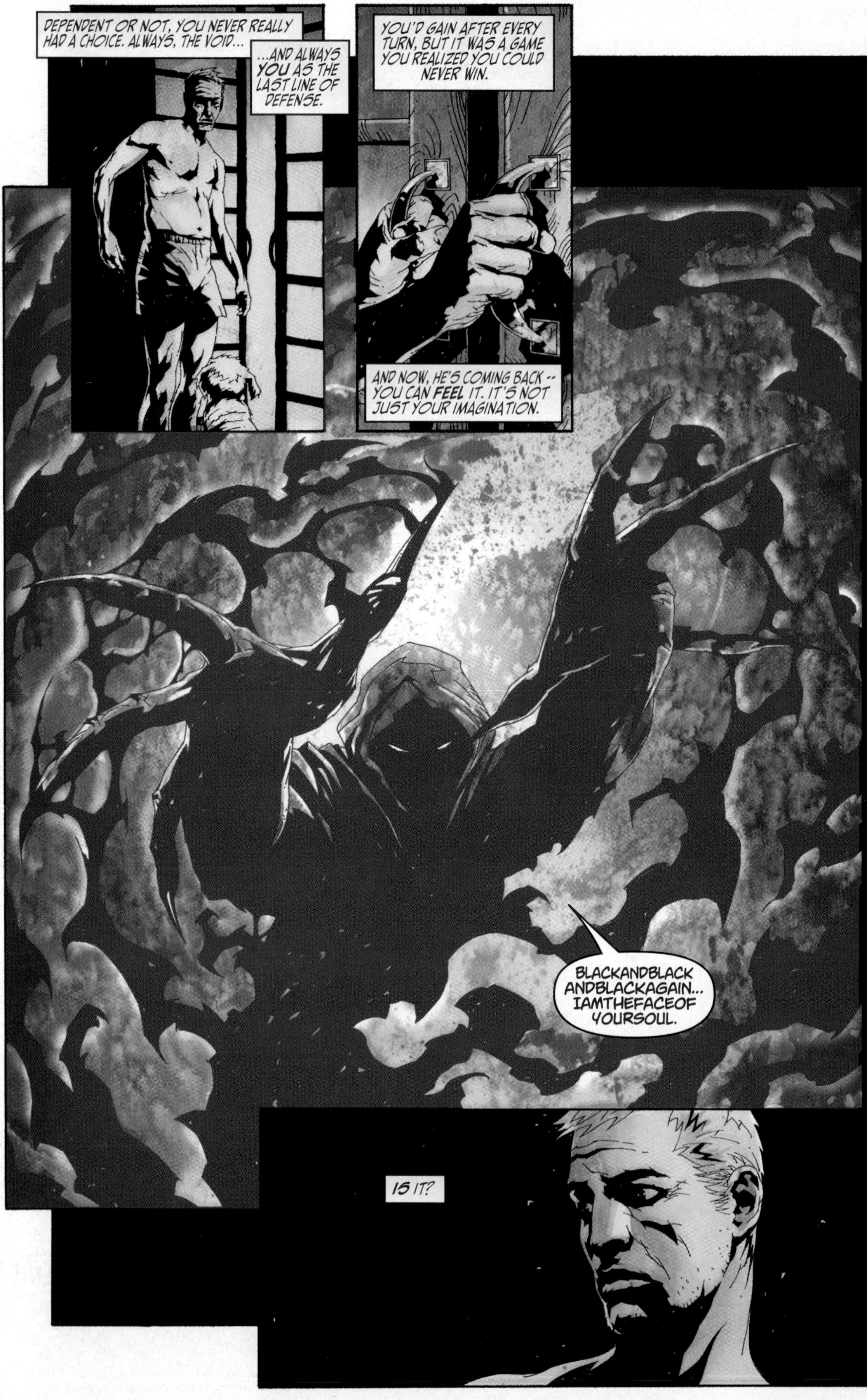

DEPENDENT OR NOT, YOU NEVER REALLY HAD A CHOICE. ALWAYS, THE VOID...
...AND ALWAYS **YOU** AS THE LAST LINE OF DEFENSE.
YOU'D GAIN AFTER EVERY TURN, BUT IT WAS A GAME YOU REALIZED YOU COULD NEVER WIN.
AND NOW, HE'S COMING BACK -- YOU CAN **FEEL** IT. IT'S NOT JUST YOUR IMAGINATION.
BLACKANDBLACK ANDBLACKAGAIN... IAMTHEFACEOF YOURSOUL.
IS IT?

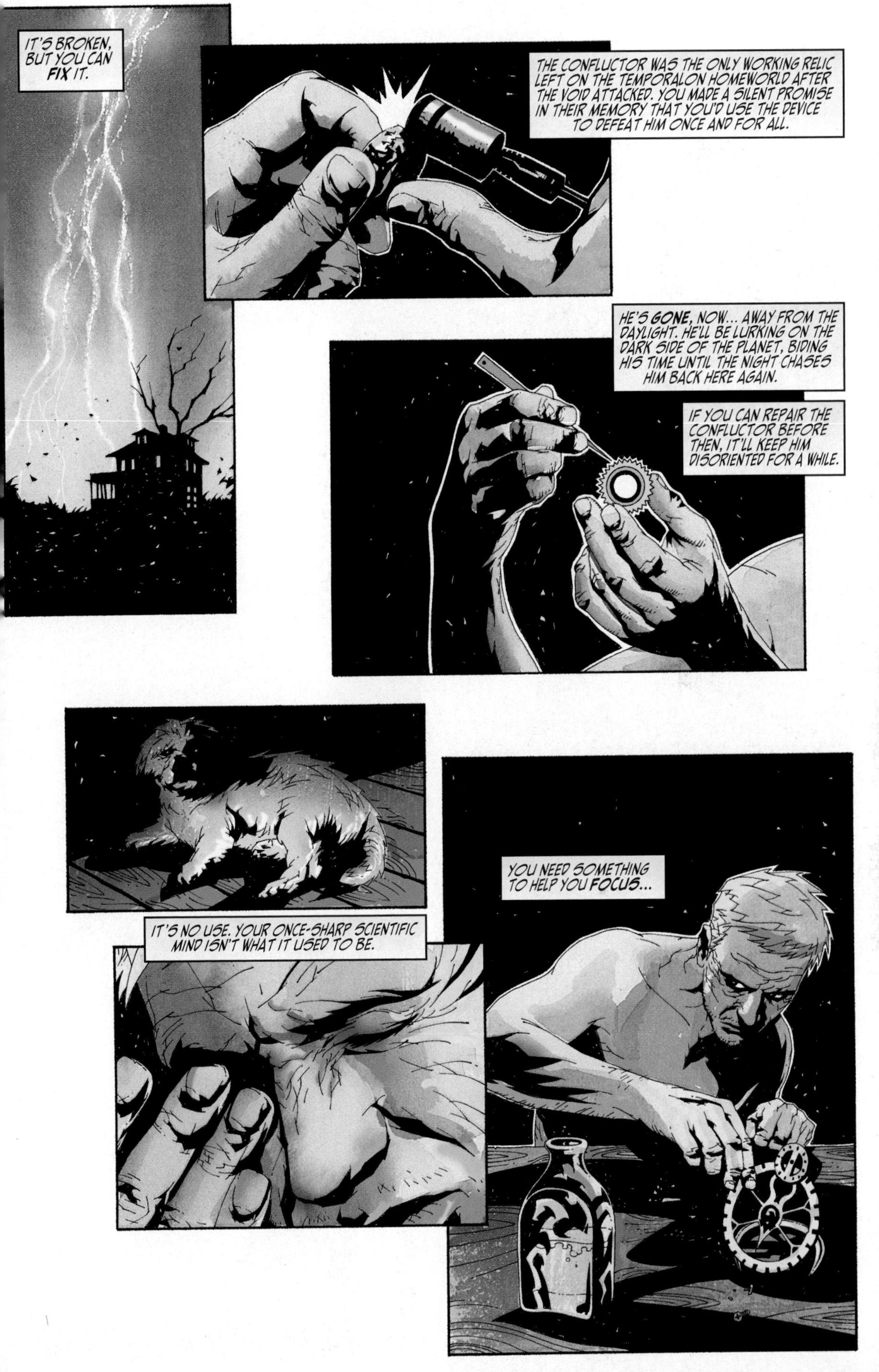
IT'S BROKEN, BUT YOU CAN FIX IT.
THE CONFLUCTOR WAS THE ONLY WORKING RELIC LEFT ON THE TEMPORALON HOMEWORLD AFTER THE VOID ATTACKED. YOU MADE A SILENT PROMISE IN THEIR MEMORY THAT YOU'D USE THE DEVICE TO DEFEAT HIM ONCE AND FOR ALL.
HE'S GONE, NOW... AWAY FROM THE DAYLIGHT. HE'LL BE LURKING ON THE DARK SIDE OF THE PLANET, BIDING HIS TIME UNTIL THE NIGHT CHASES HIM BACK HERE AGAIN.
IF YOU CAN REPAIR THE CONFLUCTOR BEFORE THEN, IT'LL KEEP HIM DISORIENTED FOR A WHILE.
YOU NEED SOMETHING TO HELP YOU FOCUS...
IT'S NO USE. YOUR ONCE-SHARP SCIENTIFIC MIND ISN'T WHAT IT USED TO BE.

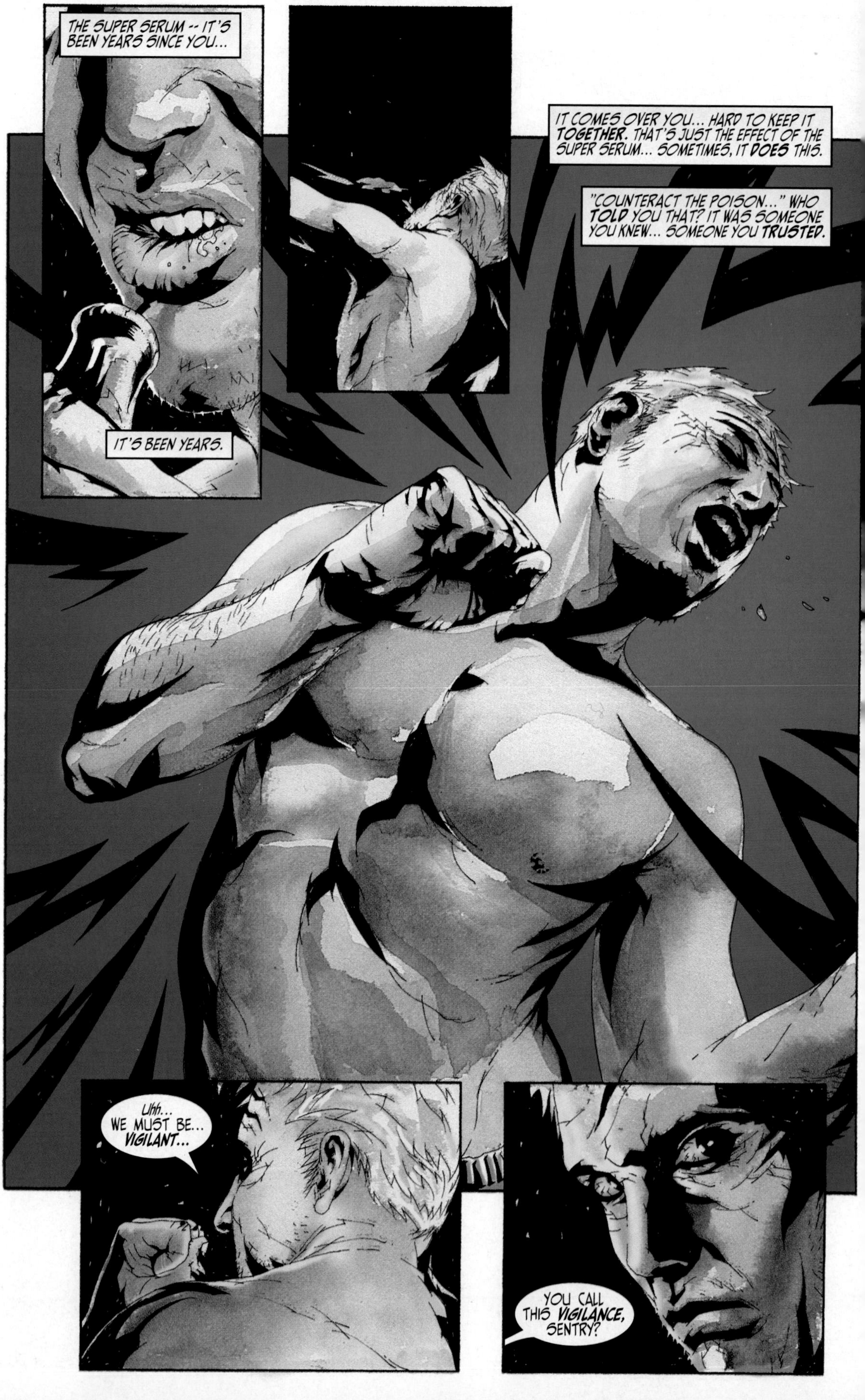
THE SUPER SERUM -- IT'S BEEN YEARS SINCE YOU...
IT'S BEEN YEARS.
IT COMES OVER YOU... HARD TO KEEP IT TOGETHER. THAT'S JUST THE EFFECT OF THE SUPER SERUM... SOMETIMES, IT DOES THIS.
"COUNTERACT THE POISON..." WHO TOLD YOU THAT? IT WAS SOMEONE YOU KNEW... SOMEONE YOU TRUSTED.
Uhh... WE MUST BE... VIGILANT...
YOU CALL THIS VIGILANCE, SENTRY?

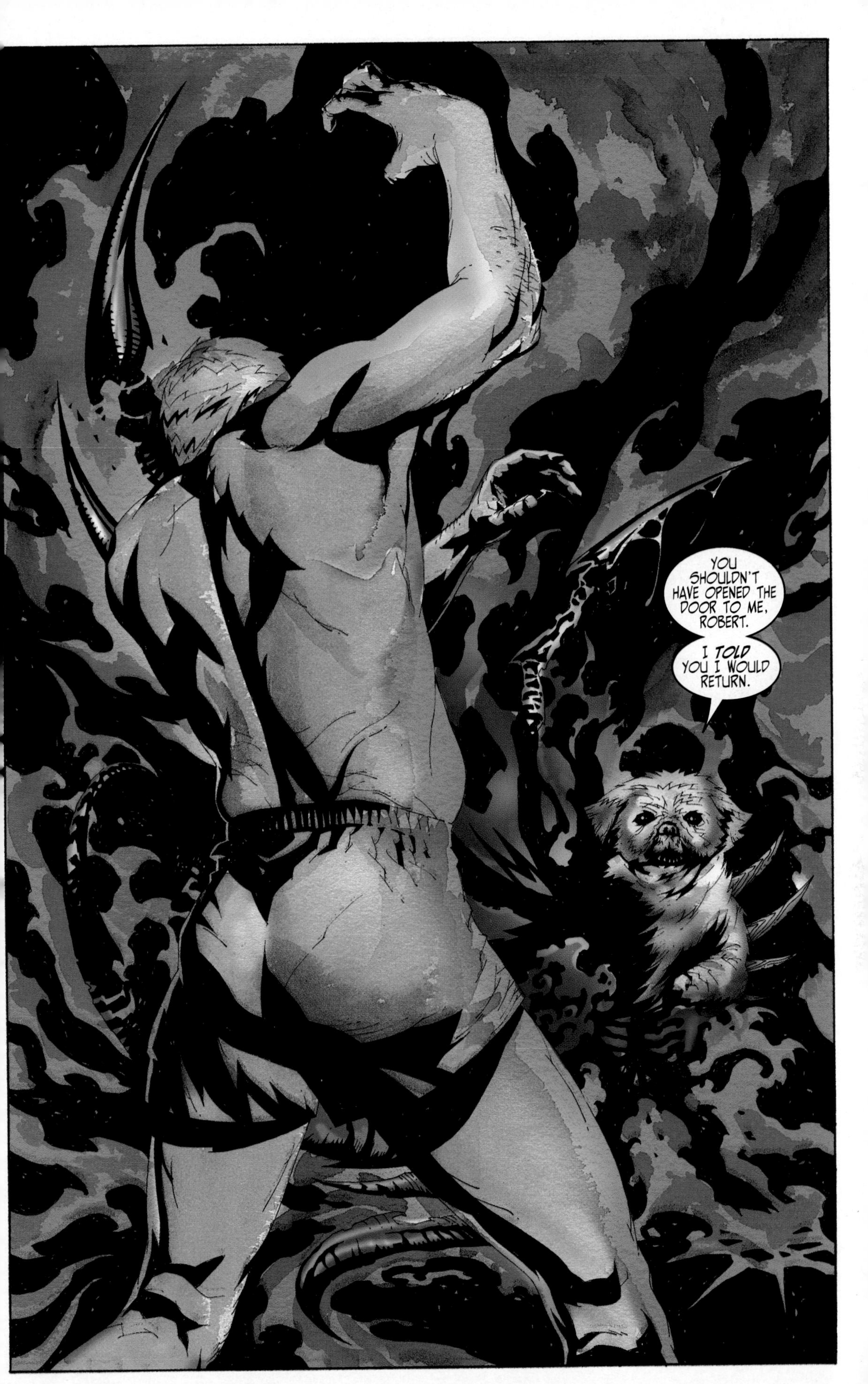
YOU SHOULDN'T HAVE OPENED THE DOOR TO ME, ROBERT.
I *TOLD* YOU I WOULD RETURN.

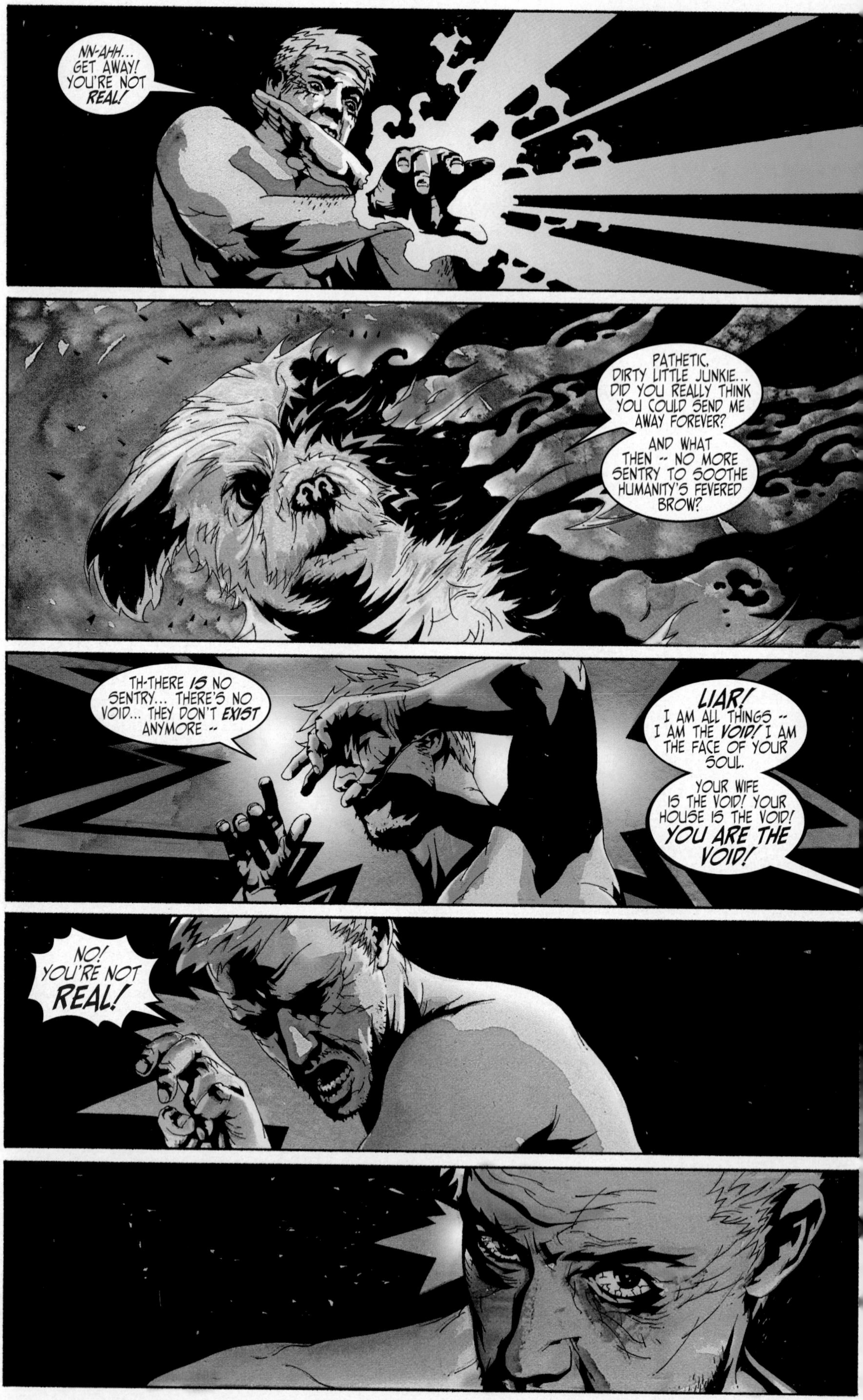

NN-AHH... GET AWAY! YOU'RE NOT REAL!
PATHETIC, DIRTY LITTLE JUNKIE... DID YOU REALLY THINK YOU COULD SEND ME AWAY FOREVER?
AND WHAT THEN -- NO MORE SENTRY TO SOOTHE HUMANITY'S FEVERED BROW?
TH-THERE IS NO SENTRY... THERE'S NO VOID... THEY DON'T EXIST ANYMORE --
LIAR! I AM ALL THINGS -- I AM THE VOID! I AM THE FACE OF YOUR SOUL.
YOUR WIFE IS THE VOID! YOUR HOUSE IS THE VOID! YOU ARE THE VOID!
NO! YOU'RE NOT REAL!

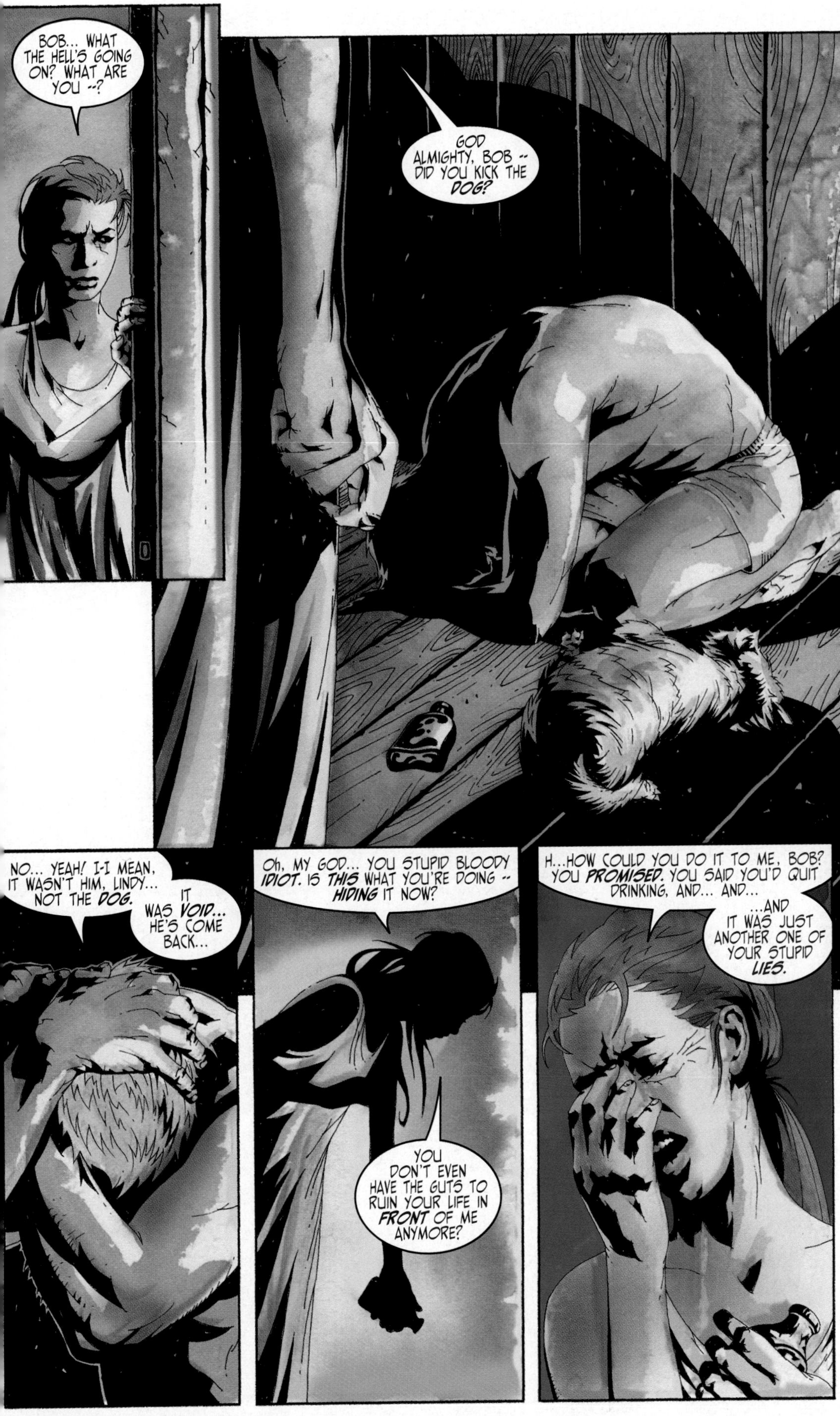
BOB... WHAT THE HELL'S GOING ON? WHAT ARE YOU --?
GOD ALMIGHTY, BOB -- DID YOU KICK THE *DOG?*
NO... YEAH! I-I MEAN, IT WASN'T HIM, LINDY... NOT THE *DOG.*
IT WAS *VOID...* HE'S COME BACK...
OH, MY GOD... YOU STUPID BLOODY *IDIOT.* IS *THIS* WHAT YOU'RE DOING -- *HIDING* IT NOW?
YOU DON'T EVEN HAVE THE GUTS TO RUIN YOUR LIFE IN *FRONT* OF ME ANYMORE?
H...HOW COULD YOU DO IT TO ME, BOB? YOU *PROMISED.* YOU SAID YOU'D QUIT DRINKING, AND... AND...
...AND IT WAS JUST ANOTHER ONE OF YOUR STUPID *LIES.*

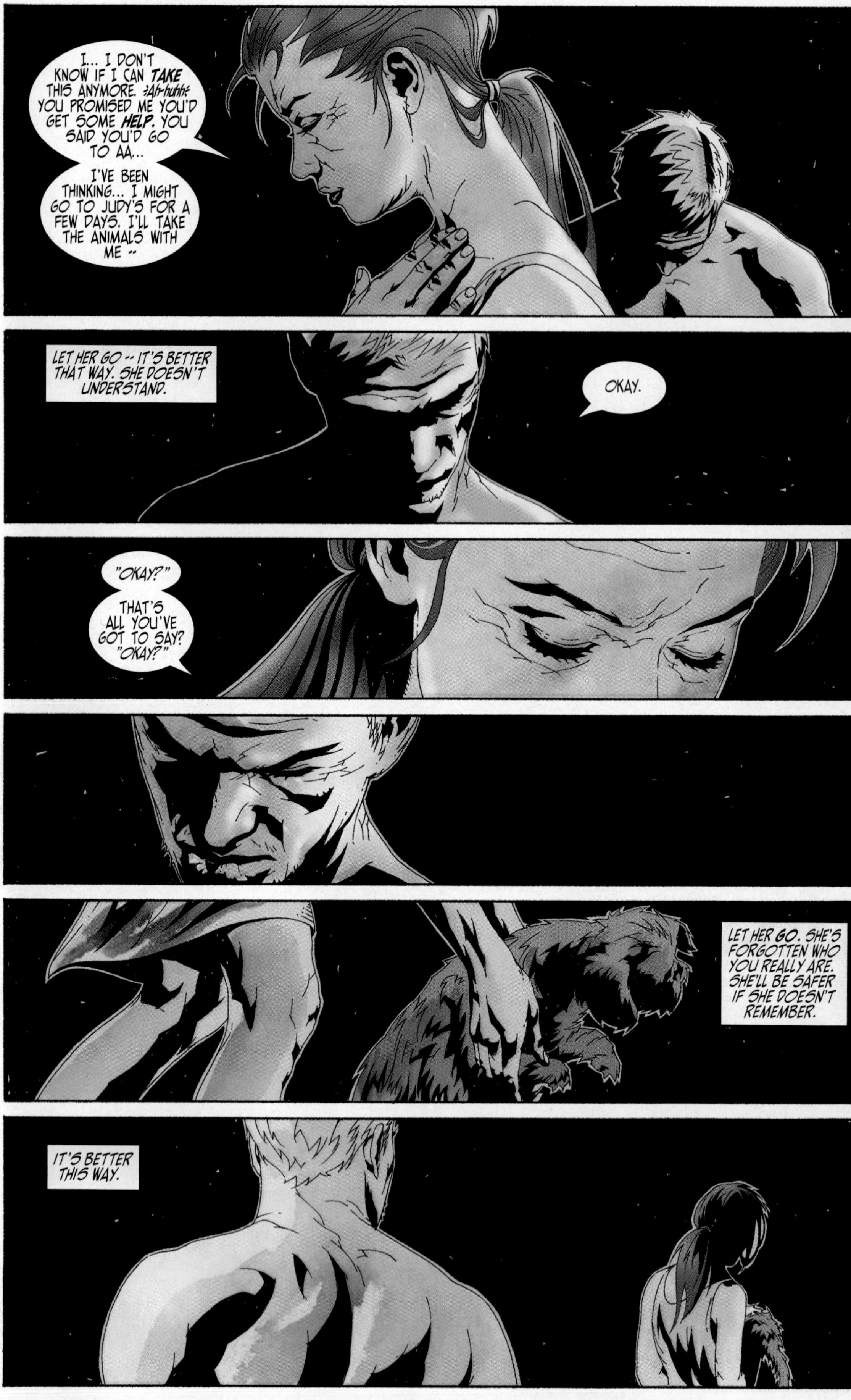
I... I DON'T KNOW IF I CAN TAKE THIS ANYMORE. *Ah-huhh* YOU PROMISED ME YOU'D GET SOME HELP. YOU SAID YOU'D GO TO AA...
I'VE BEEN THINKING... I MIGHT GO TO JUDY'S FOR A FEW DAYS. I'LL TAKE THE ANIMALS WITH ME --
LET HER GO -- IT'S BETTER THAT WAY. SHE DOESN'T UNDERSTAND.
OKAY.
"OKAY?"
THAT'S ALL YOU'VE GOT TO SAY? "OKAY?"
LET HER GO. SHE'S FORGOTTEN WHO YOU REALLY ARE. SHE'LL BE SAFER IF SHE DOESN'T REMEMBER.
IT'S BETTER THIS WAY.

NO ONE REMEMBERS, EXCEPT YOU.

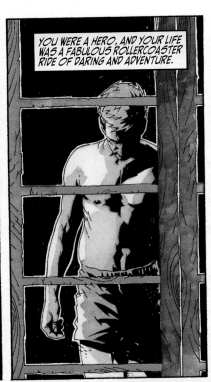

YOU WERE A HERO, AND YOUR LIFE WAS A FABULOUS ROLLERCOASTER RIDE OF DARING AND ADVENTURE.

YOU AND THE OTHERS -- THE HEROES -- YOU WERE ALL THAT STOOD IN THE WAY OF EVIL. AND THERE YOU REMAINED, UNTIL IT WENT AWAY.

BUT THE END OF EVERY RIDE IS ALWAYS THE BEGINNING OF ANOTHER. YOU MUST HAVE SUSPECTED IT WOULD ONE DAY COME TO THIS:

THAT YOU'D HAVE TO WEAR THE SENTRY SUIT AGAIN...

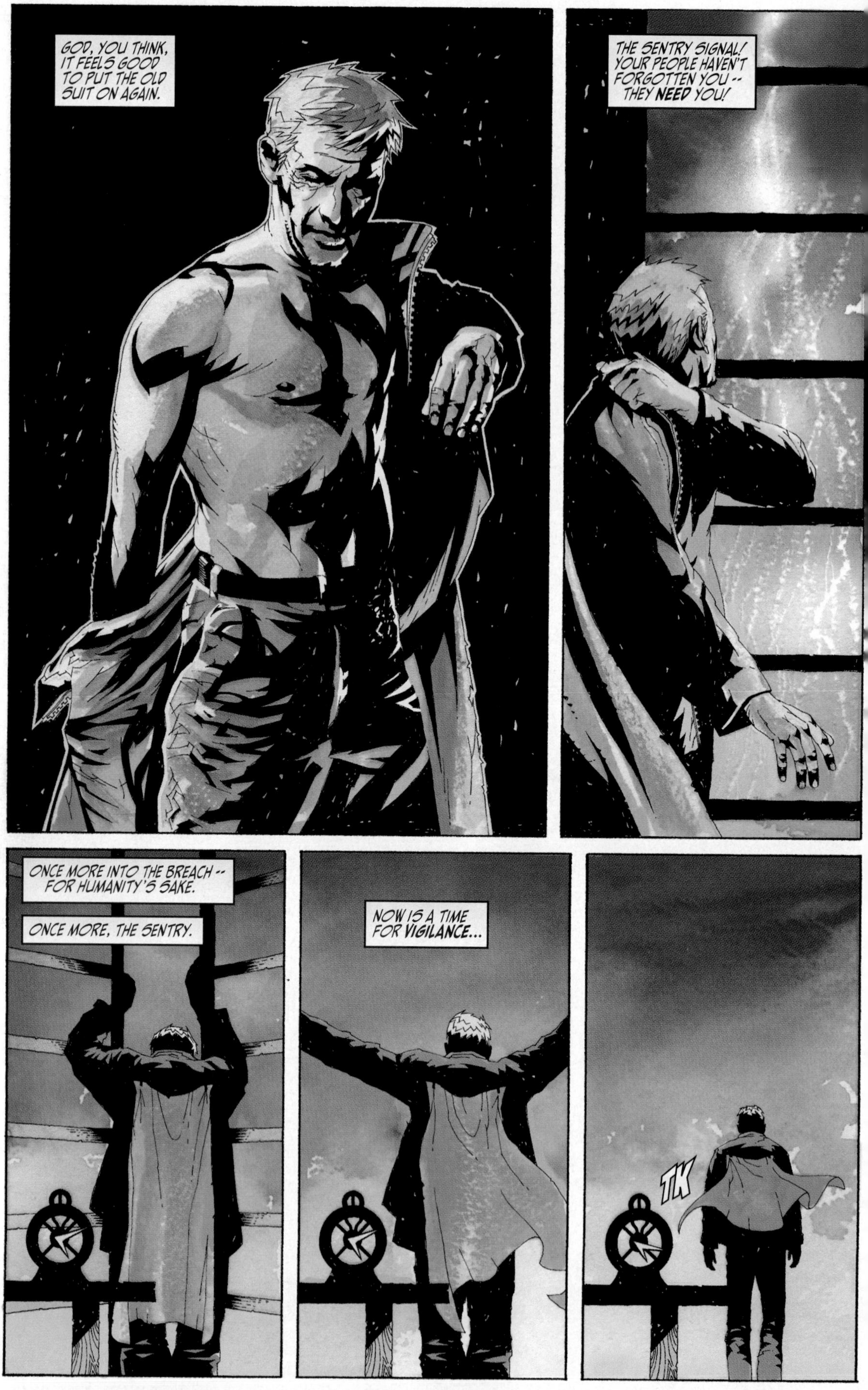
GOD, YOU THINK, IT FEELS GOOD TO PUT THE OLD SUIT ON AGAIN.
THE SENTRY SIGNAL! YOUR PEOPLE HAVEN'T FORGOTTEN YOU -- THEY NEED YOU!
ONCE MORE INTO THE BREACH -- FOR HUMANITY'S SAKE.
ONCE MORE, THE SENTRY.
NOW IS A TIME FOR VIGILANCE...
TK

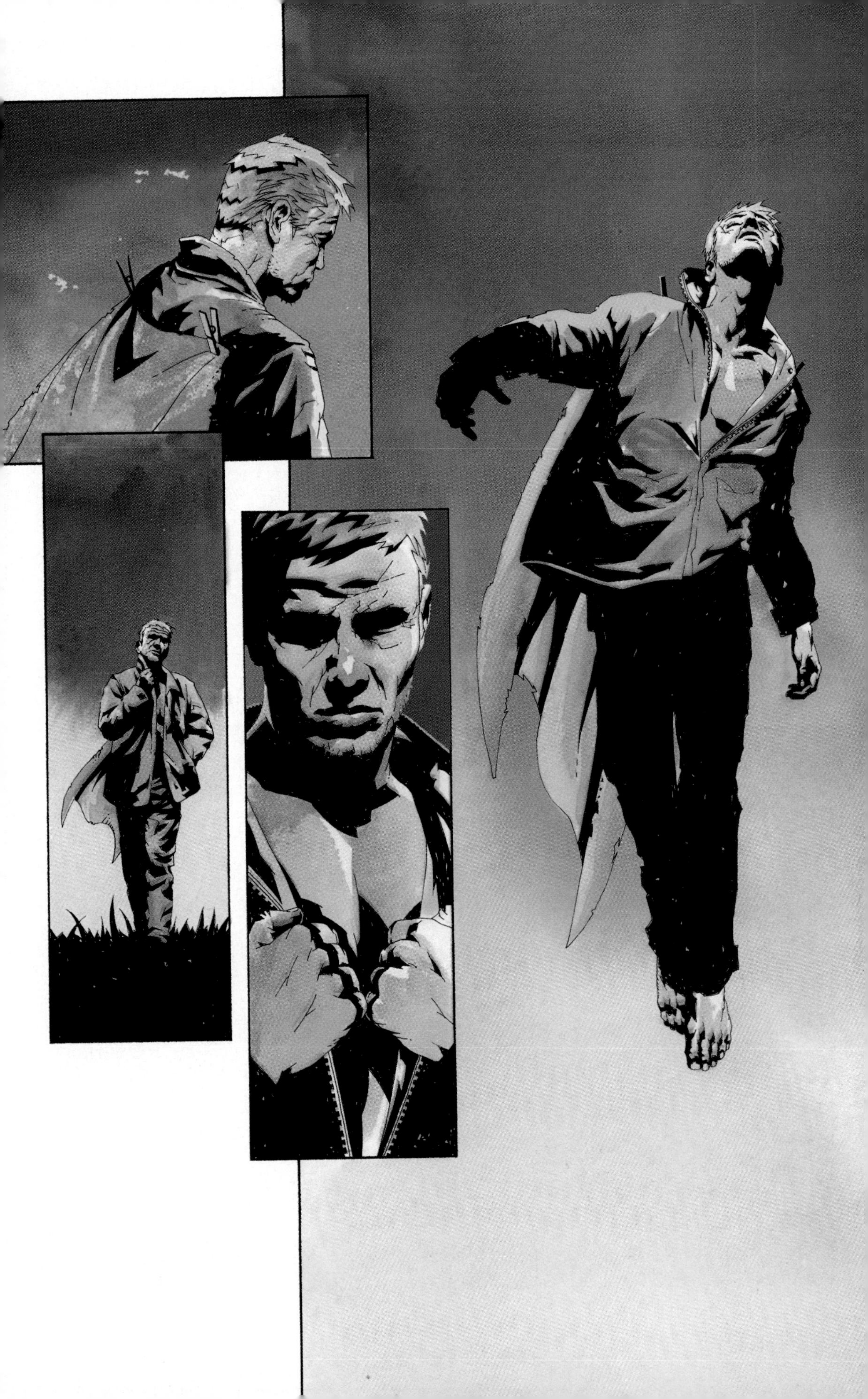

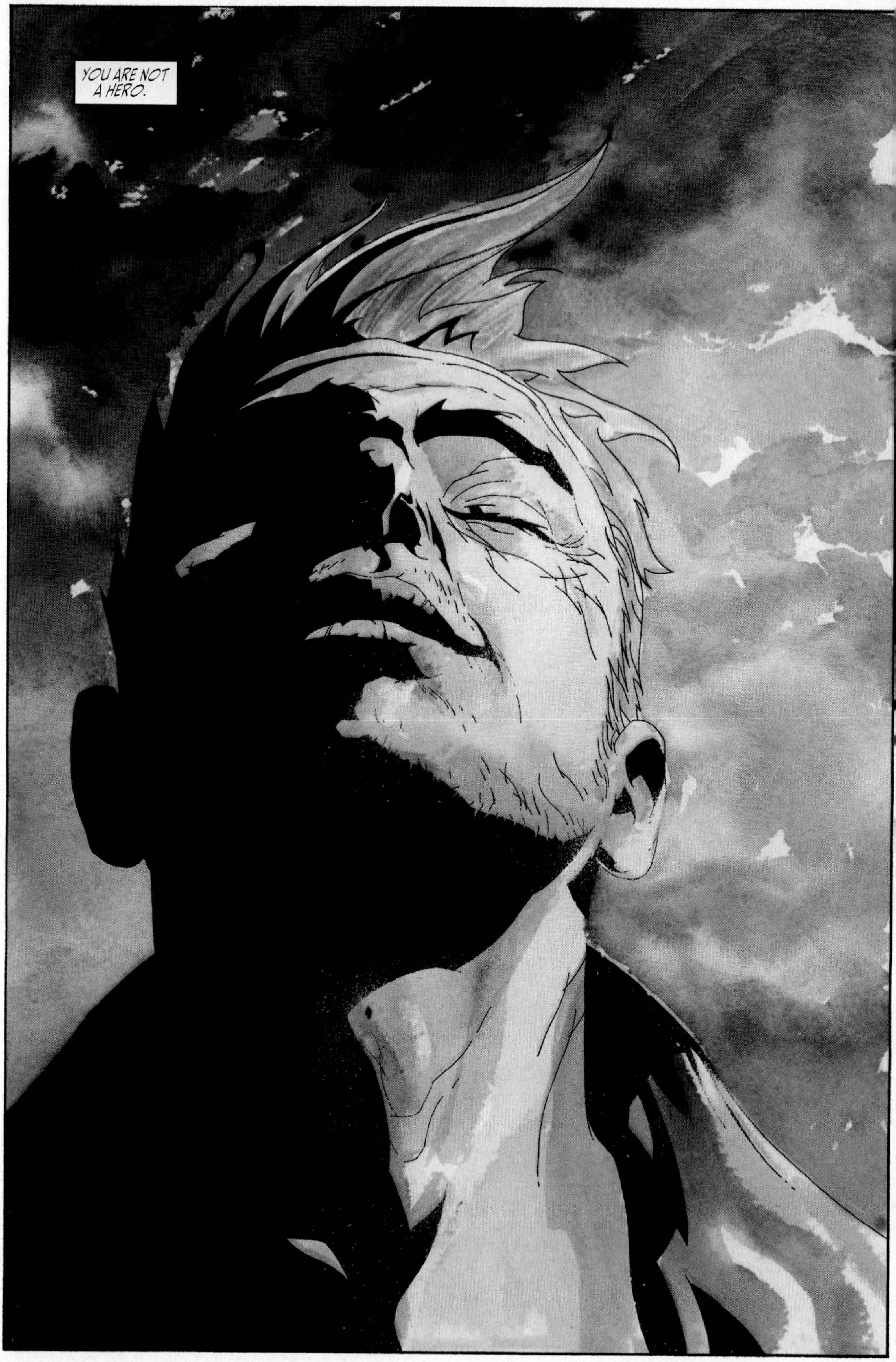
YOU ARE NOT A HERO.

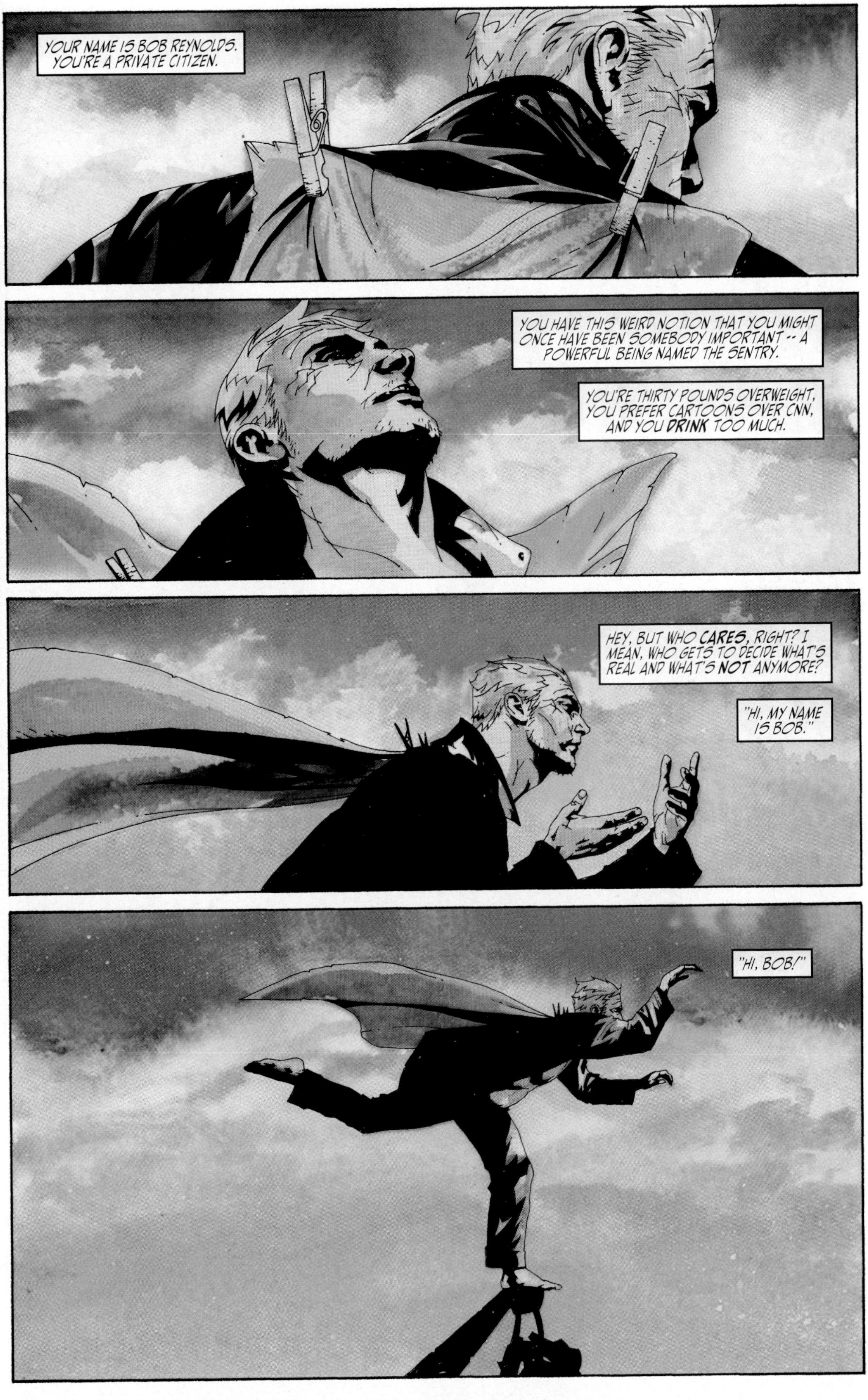
YOUR NAME IS BOB REYNOLDS. YOU'RE A PRIVATE CITIZEN.
YOU HAVE THIS WEIRD NOTION THAT YOU MIGHT ONCE HAVE BEEN SOMEBODY IMPORTANT -- A POWERFUL BEING NAMED THE SENTRY.
YOU'RE THIRTY POUNDS OVERWEIGHT, YOU PREFER CARTOONS OVER CNN, AND YOU DRINK TOO MUCH.
HEY, BUT WHO CARES, RIGHT? I MEAN, WHO GETS TO DECIDE WHAT'S REAL AND WHAT'S NOT ANYMORE?
"HI, MY NAME IS BOB."
"HI, BOB!"

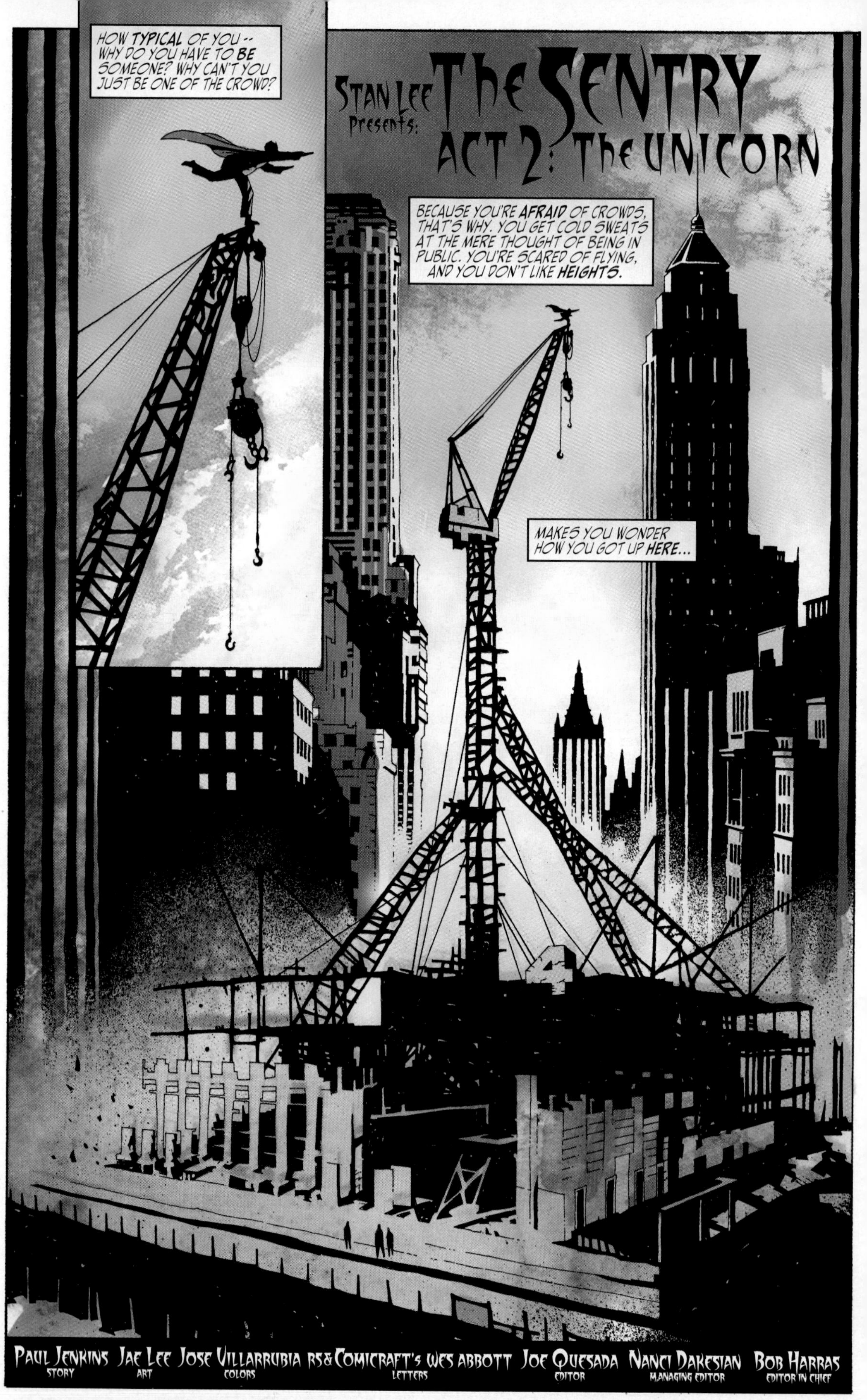

HOW TYPICAL OF YOU -- WHY DO YOU HAVE TO BE SOMEONE? WHY CAN'T YOU JUST BE ONE OF THE CROWD?
STAN LEE presents: THE SENTRY
ACT 2: THE UNICORN
BECAUSE YOU'RE AFRAID OF CROWDS, THAT'S WHY. YOU GET COLD SWEATS AT THE MERE THOUGHT OF BEING IN PUBLIC. YOU'RE SCARED OF FLYING, AND YOU DON'T LIKE HEIGHTS.
MAKES YOU WONDER HOW YOU GOT UP HERE...
PAUL JENKINS STORY
JAE LEE ART
JOSE VILLARRUBIA COLORS
RS&COMICRAFT'S WES ABBOTT LETTERS
JOE QUESADA EDITOR
NANCI DAKESIAN MANAGING EDITOR
BOB HARRAS EDITOR IN CHIEF

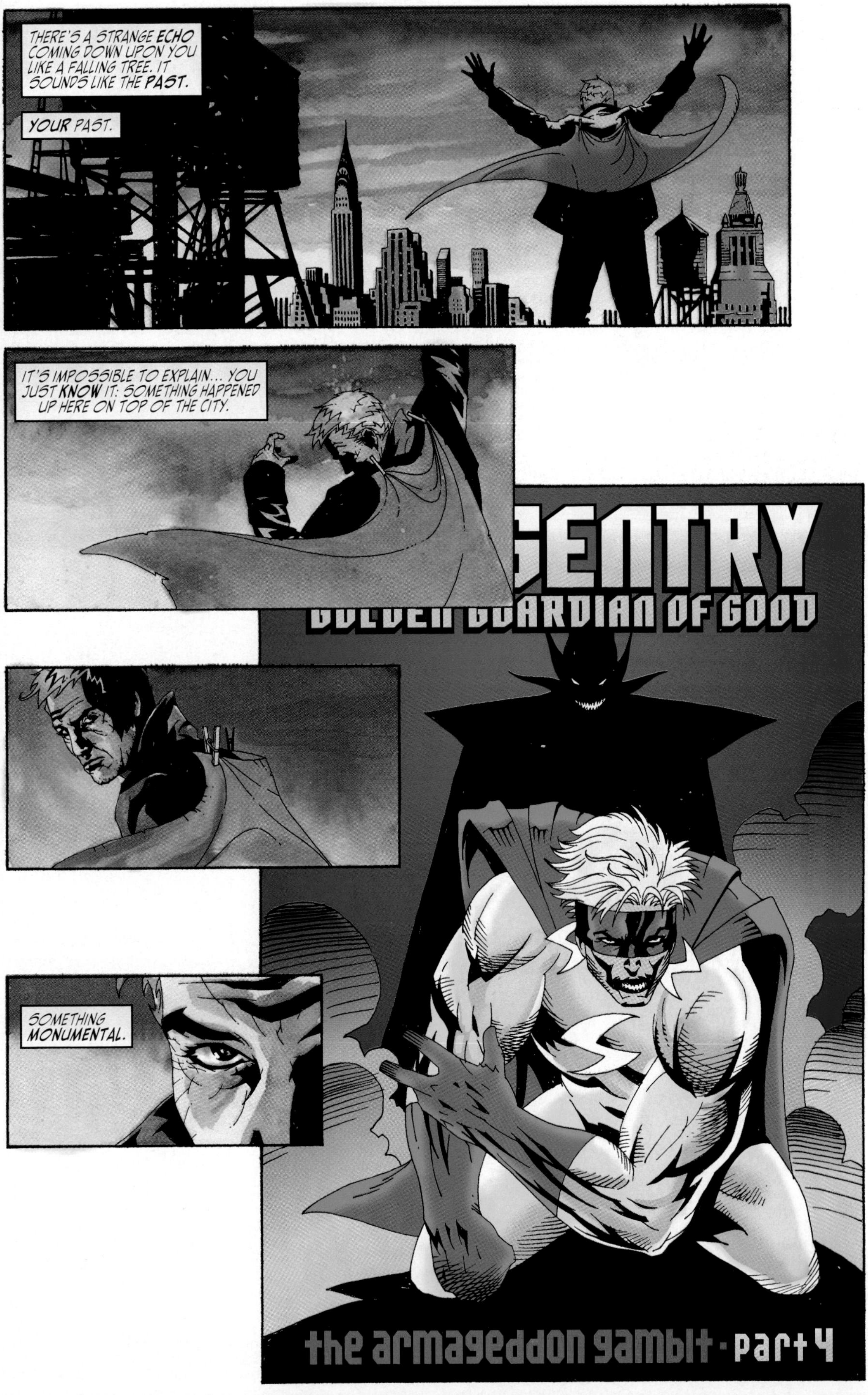
THERE'S A STRANGE ECHO COMING DOWN UPON YOU LIKE A FALLING TREE. IT SOUNDS LIKE THE PAST.
YOUR PAST.
IT'S IMPOSSIBLE TO EXPLAIN... YOU JUST KNOW IT: SOMETHING HAPPENED UP HERE ON TOP OF THE CITY.
SENTRY
GOLDEN GUARDIAN OF GOOD
SOMETHING MONUMENTAL.
the armageddon gambit · part 4

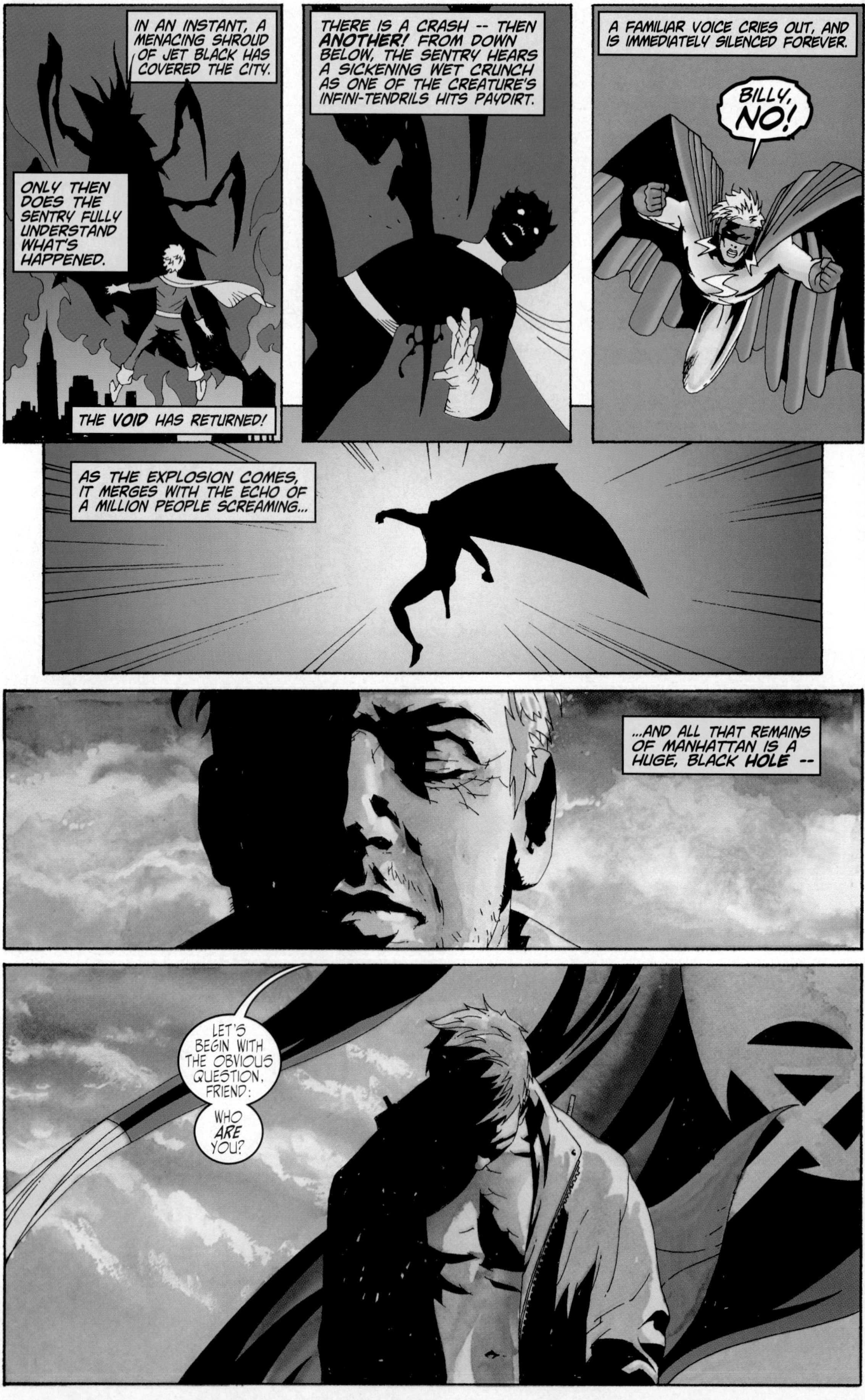
IN AN INSTANT, A MENACING SHROUD OF JET BLACK HAS COVERED THE CITY.
ONLY THEN DOES THE SENTRY FULLY UNDERSTAND WHAT'S HAPPENED.
THE VOID HAS RETURNED!
THERE IS A CRASH -- THEN ANOTHER! FROM DOWN BELOW, THE SENTRY HEARS A SICKENING WET CRUNCH AS ONE OF THE CREATURE'S INFINI-TENDRILS HITS PAYDIRT.
A FAMILIAR VOICE CRIES OUT, AND IS IMMEDIATELY SILENCED FOREVER.
BILLY, NO!
AS THE EXPLOSION COMES, IT MERGES WITH THE ECHO OF A MILLION PEOPLE SCREAMING...
...AND ALL THAT REMAINS OF MANHATTAN IS A HUGE, BLACK HOLE --
LET'S BEGIN WITH THE OBVIOUS QUESTION, FRIEND:
WHO ARE YOU?

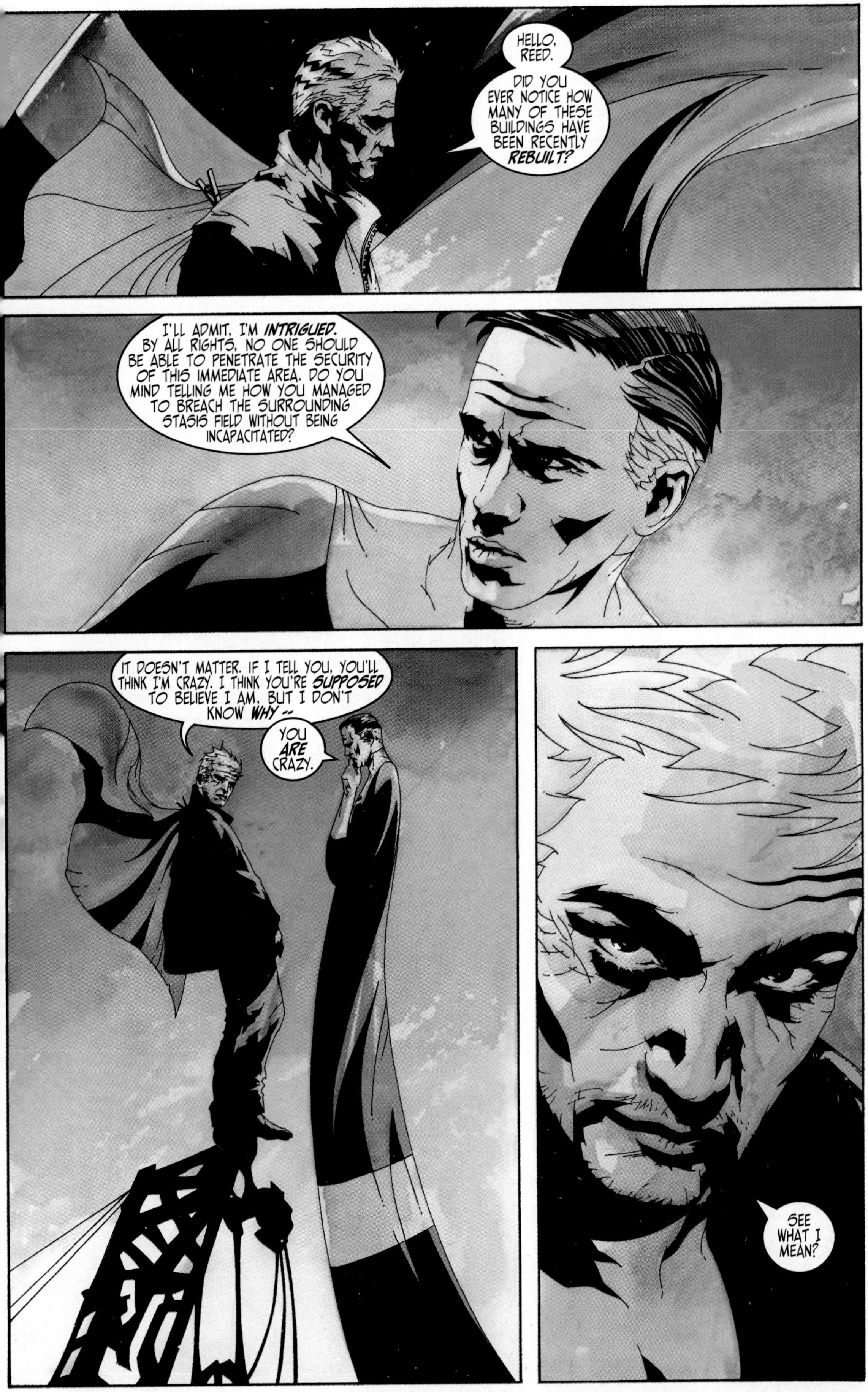
HELLO, REED.
DID YOU EVER NOTICE HOW MANY OF THESE BUILDINGS HAVE BEEN RECENTLY REBUILT?
I'LL ADMIT, I'M INTRIGUED. BY ALL RIGHTS, NO ONE SHOULD BE ABLE TO PENETRATE THE SECURITY OF THIS IMMEDIATE AREA. DO YOU MIND TELLING ME HOW YOU MANAGED TO BREACH THE SURROUNDING STASIS FIELD WITHOUT BEING INCAPACITATED?
IT DOESN'T MATTER. IF I TELL YOU, YOU'LL THINK I'M CRAZY. I THINK YOU'RE SUPPOSED TO BELIEVE I AM, BUT I DON'T KNOW WHY --
YOU ARE CRAZY.
SEE WHAT I MEAN?

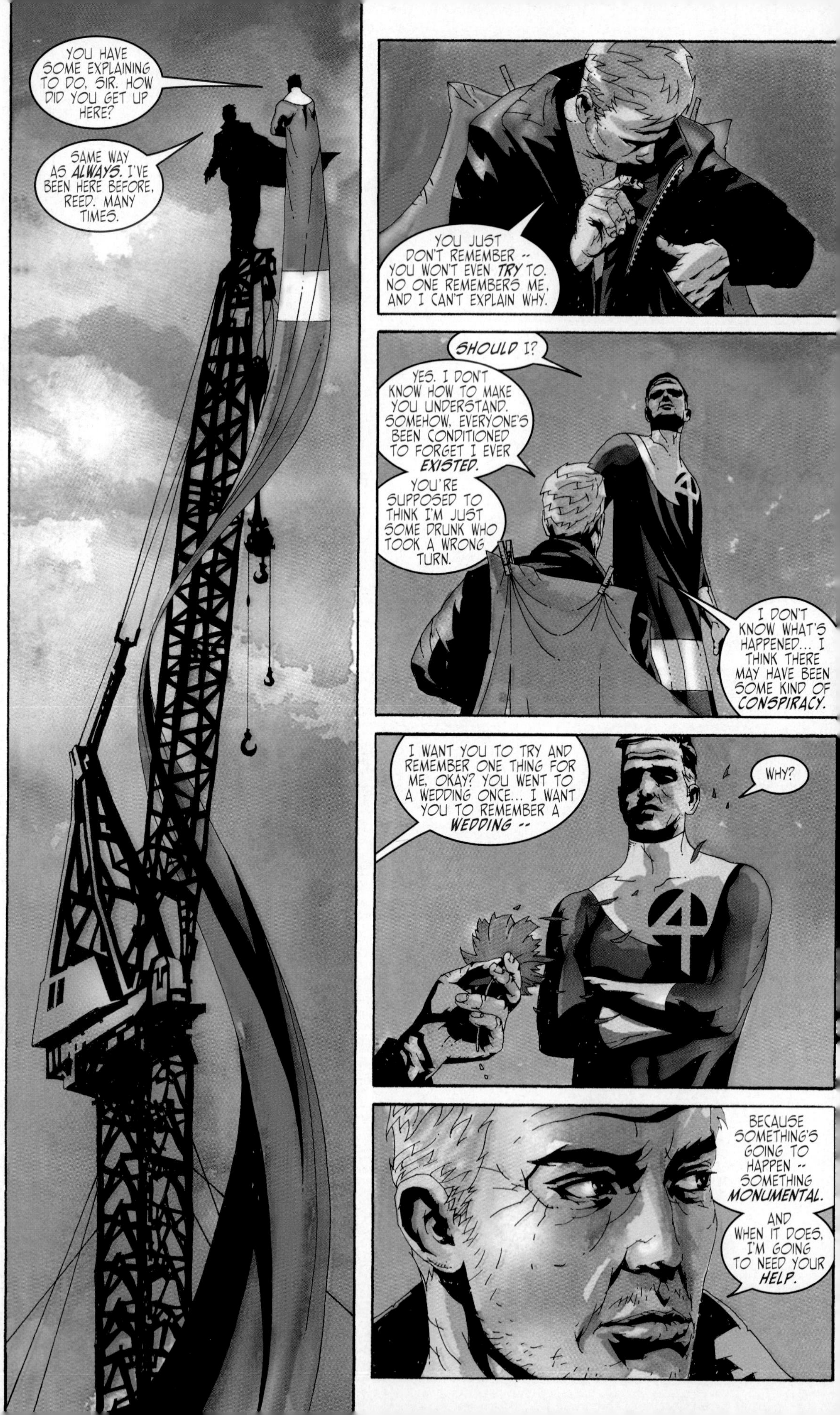
YOU HAVE SOME EXPLAINING TO DO, SIR. HOW DID YOU GET UP HERE?
SAME WAY AS ALWAYS. I'VE BEEN HERE BEFORE, REED. MANY TIMES.
YOU JUST DON'T REMEMBER -- YOU WON'T EVEN TRY TO. NO ONE REMEMBERS ME, AND I CAN'T EXPLAIN WHY.
SHOULD I?
YES. I DON'T KNOW HOW TO MAKE YOU UNDERSTAND. SOMEHOW, EVERYONE'S BEEN CONDITIONED TO FORGET I EVER EXISTED.
YOU'RE SUPPOSED TO THINK I'M JUST SOME DRUNK WHO TOOK A WRONG TURN.
I DON'T KNOW WHAT'S HAPPENED... I THINK THERE MAY HAVE BEEN SOME KIND OF CONSPIRACY.
I WANT YOU TO TRY AND REMEMBER ONE THING FOR ME, OKAY? YOU WENT TO A WEDDING ONCE... I WANT YOU TO REMEMBER A WEDDING --
WHY?
BECAUSE SOMETHING'S GOING TO HAPPEN -- SOMETHING MONUMENTAL.
AND WHEN IT DOES, I'M GOING TO NEED YOUR HELP.

LOOK, FRIEND... IF YOU'VE SOMEHOW FOUND A WAY TO HACK INTO MY SECURITY CODES, I APPLAUD YOU FOR YOUR COURAGE AND INNOVATION, BUT HARDLY FOR YOUR COMMON SENSE.

ARE YOU AWARE OF THE PENALTY ASSESSED FOR TRESPASSING IN NEW YORK CITY --?

"UNICORN."

UNICORN...? I, UH...

I CAN'T... I DON'T REMEMBER THAT...

I'M NOT ALLOWED TO --

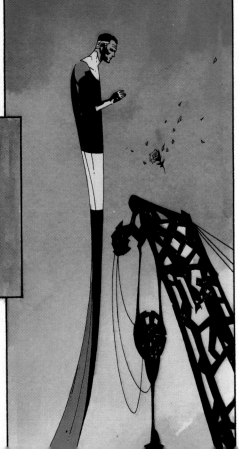

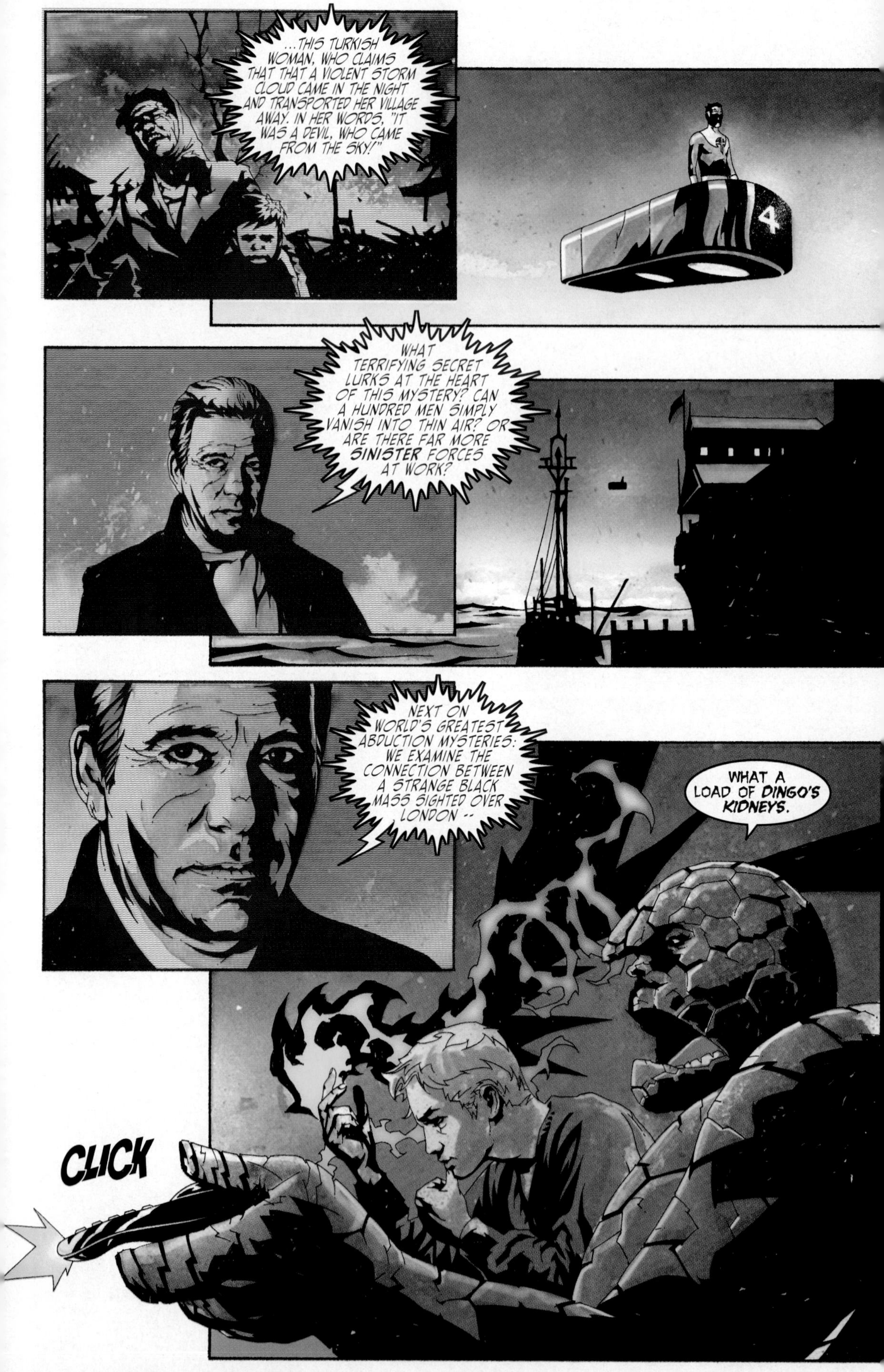
...THIS TURKISH WOMAN, WHO CLAIMS THAT THAT A VIOLENT STORM CLOUD CAME IN THE NIGHT AND TRANSPORTED HER VILLAGE AWAY. IN HER WORDS, "IT WAS A DEVIL, WHO CAME FROM THE SKY!"
4
WHAT TERRIFYING SECRET LURKS AT THE HEART OF THIS MYSTERY? CAN A HUNDRED MEN SIMPLY VANISH INTO THIN AIR? OR ARE THERE FAR MORE SINISTER FORCES AT WORK?
NEXT ON WORLD'S GREATEST ABDUCTION MYSTERIES: WE EXAMINE THE CONNECTION BETWEEN A STRANGE BLACK MASS SIGHTED OVER LONDON --
WHAT A LOAD OF DINGO'S KIDNEYS.
CLICK

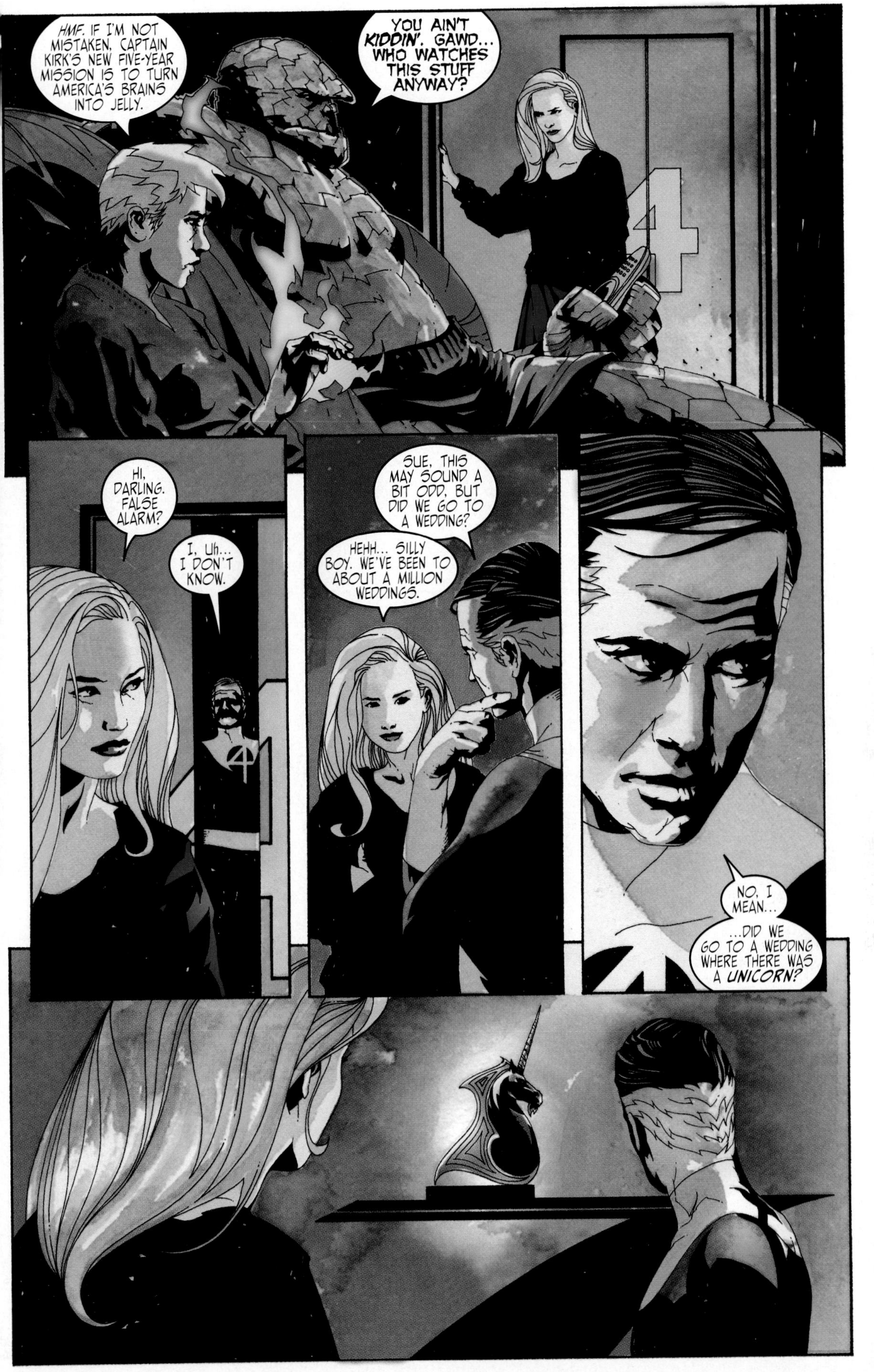
HMF. IF I'M NOT MISTAKEN, CAPTAIN KIRK'S NEW FIVE-YEAR MISSION IS TO TURN AMERICA'S BRAINS INTO JELLY.
YOU AIN'T KIDDIN'. GAWD... WHO WATCHES THIS STUFF ANYWAY?
HI, DARLING. FALSE ALARM?
I, UH... I DON'T KNOW.
SUE, THIS MAY SOUND A BIT ODD, BUT DID WE GO TO A WEDDING?
HEHH... SILLY BOY. WE'VE BEEN TO ABOUT A MILLION WEDDINGS.
NO, I MEAN...
...DID WE GO TO A WEDDING WHERE THERE WAS A UNICORN?

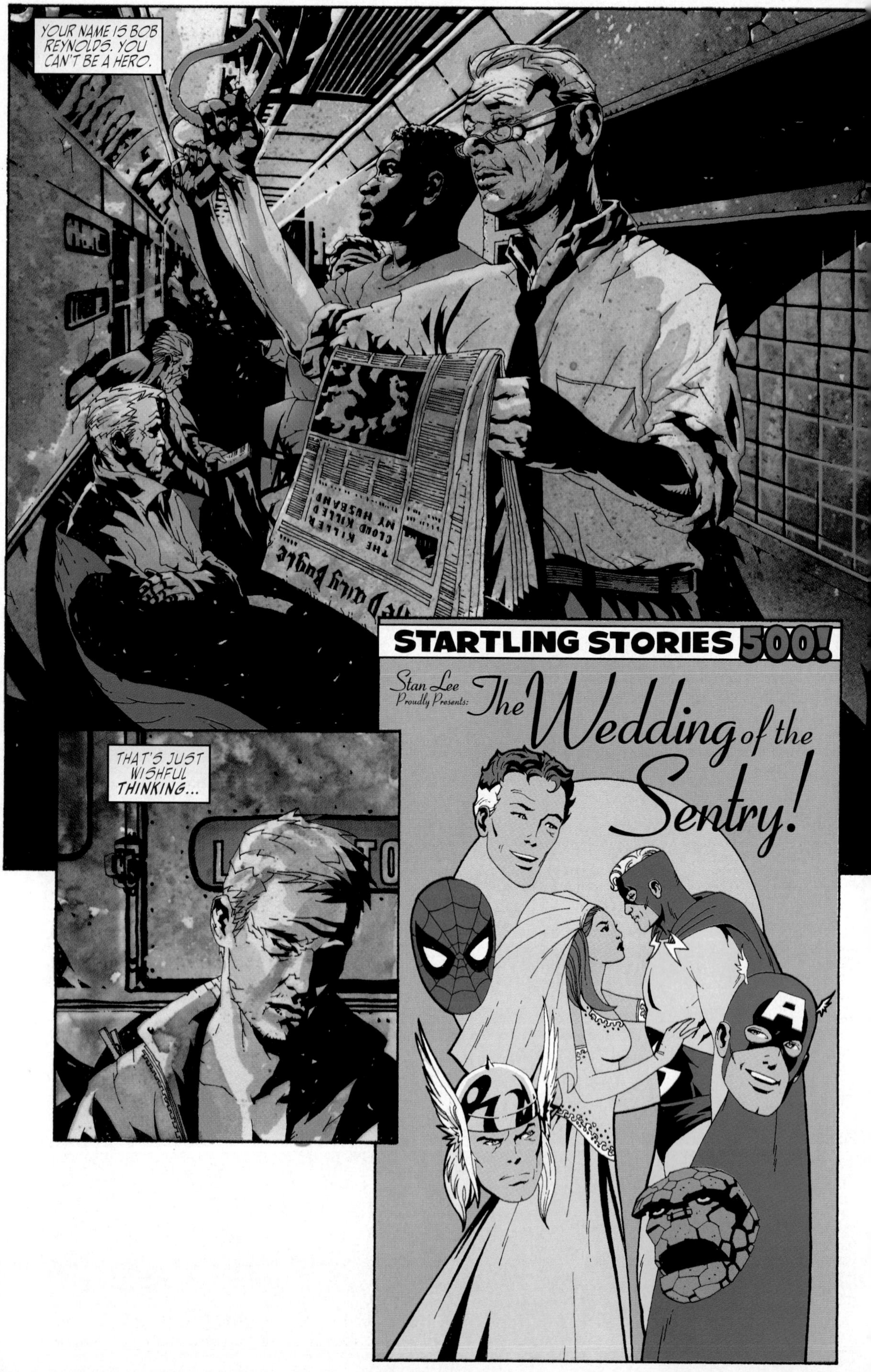
YOUR NAME IS BOB REYNOLDS. YOU CAN'T BE A HERO.
THAT'S JUST WISHFUL THINKING...
STARTLING STORIES 500!
Stan Lee Proudly Presents: The Wedding of the Sentry!

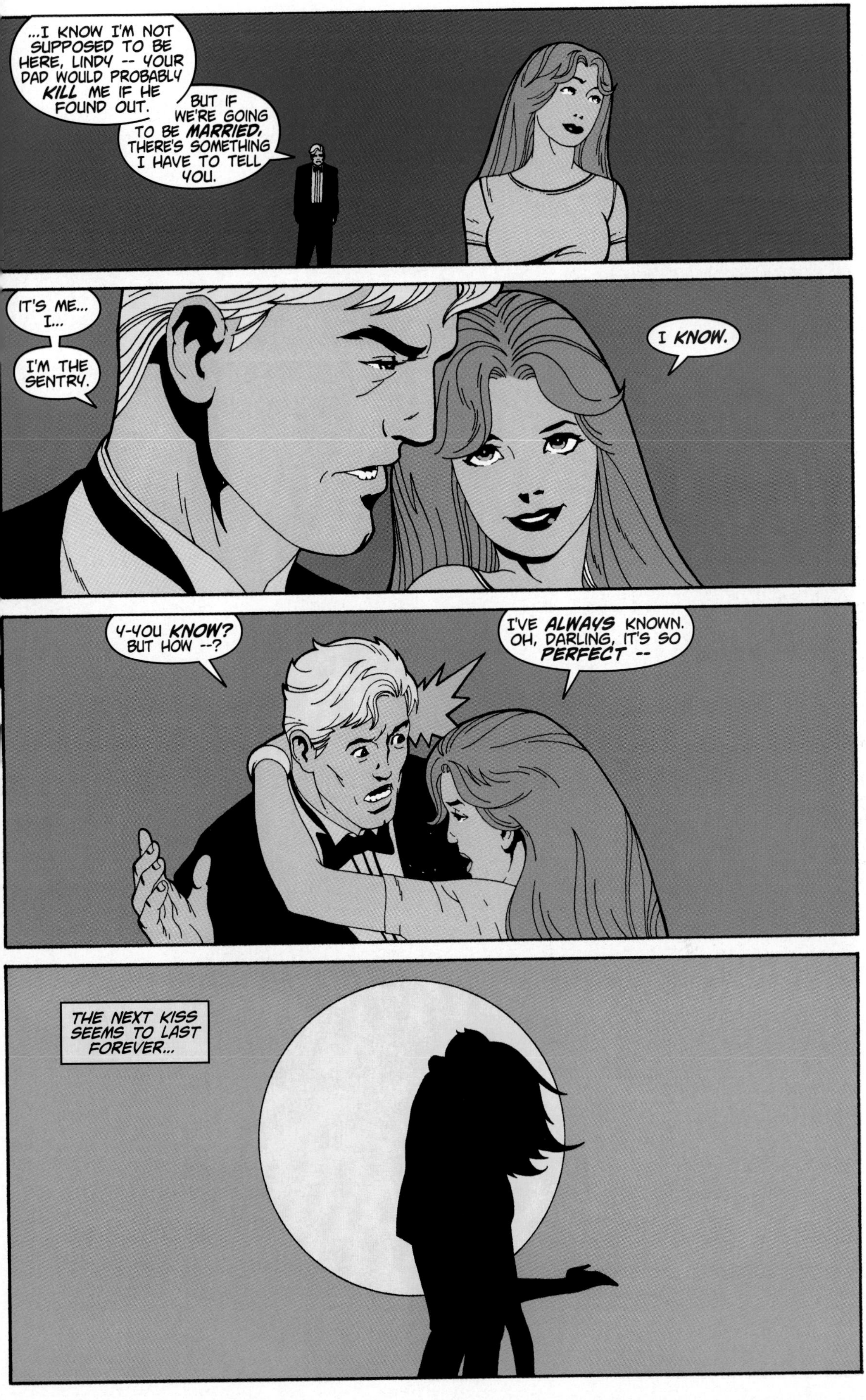

...I KNOW I'M NOT SUPPOSED TO BE HERE, LINDY -- YOUR DAD WOULD PROBABLY KILL ME IF HE FOUND OUT.
BUT IF WE'RE GOING TO BE MARRIED, THERE'S SOMETHING I HAVE TO TELL YOU.
IT'S ME... I...
I'M THE SENTRY.
I KNOW.
Y-YOU KNOW? BUT HOW --?
I'VE ALWAYS KNOWN. OH, DARLING, IT'S SO PERFECT --
THE NEXT KISS SEEMS TO LAST FOREVER...

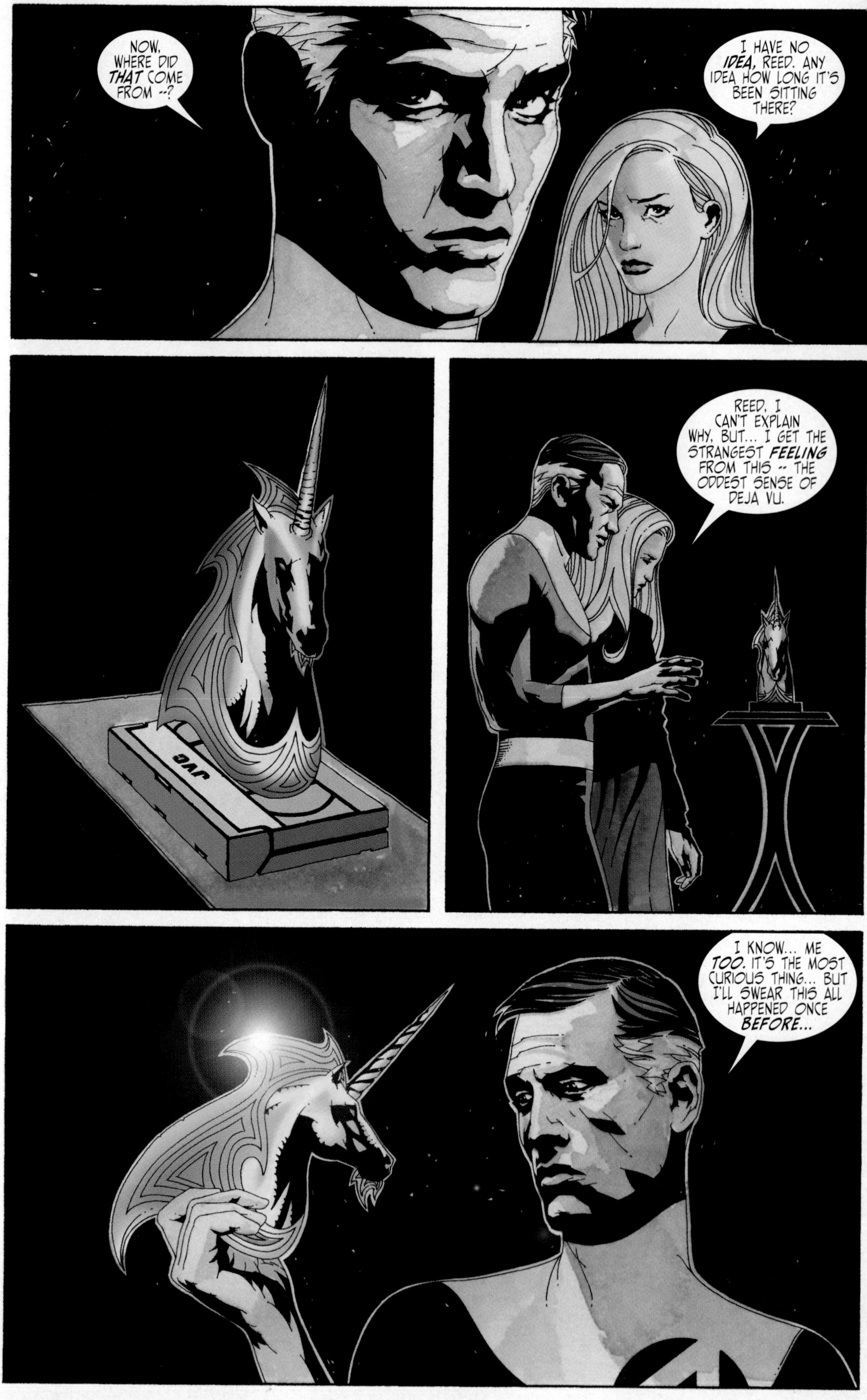
NOW, WHERE DID THAT COME FROM --?
I HAVE NO IDEA, REED. ANY IDEA HOW LONG IT'S BEEN SITTING THERE?
JVC
REED, I CAN'T EXPLAIN WHY, BUT... I GET THE STRANGEST FEELING FROM THIS -- THE ODDEST SENSE OF DEJA VU.
I KNOW... ME TOO. IT'S THE MOST CURIOUS THING... BUT I'LL SWEAR THIS ALL HAPPENED ONCE BEFORE...

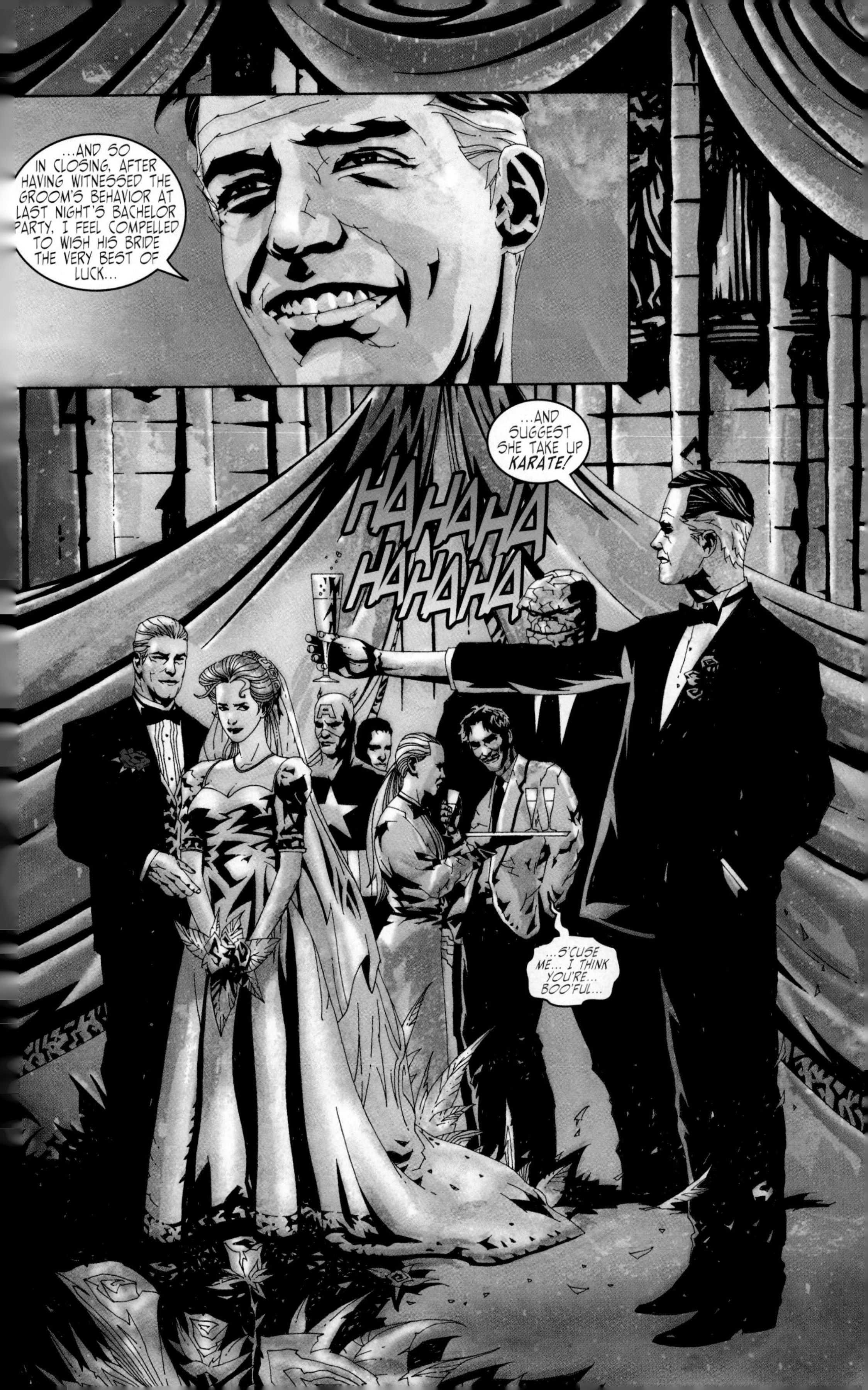
...AND SO IN CLOSING, AFTER HAVING WITNESSED THE GROOM'S BEHAVIOR AT LAST NIGHT'S BACHELOR PARTY, I FEEL COMPELLED TO WISH HIS BRIDE THE VERY BEST OF LUCK...
...AND SUGGEST SHE TAKE UP KARATE!
HAHAHA HAHAHA
...S'CUSE ME... I THINK YOU'RE... BOO'FUL...

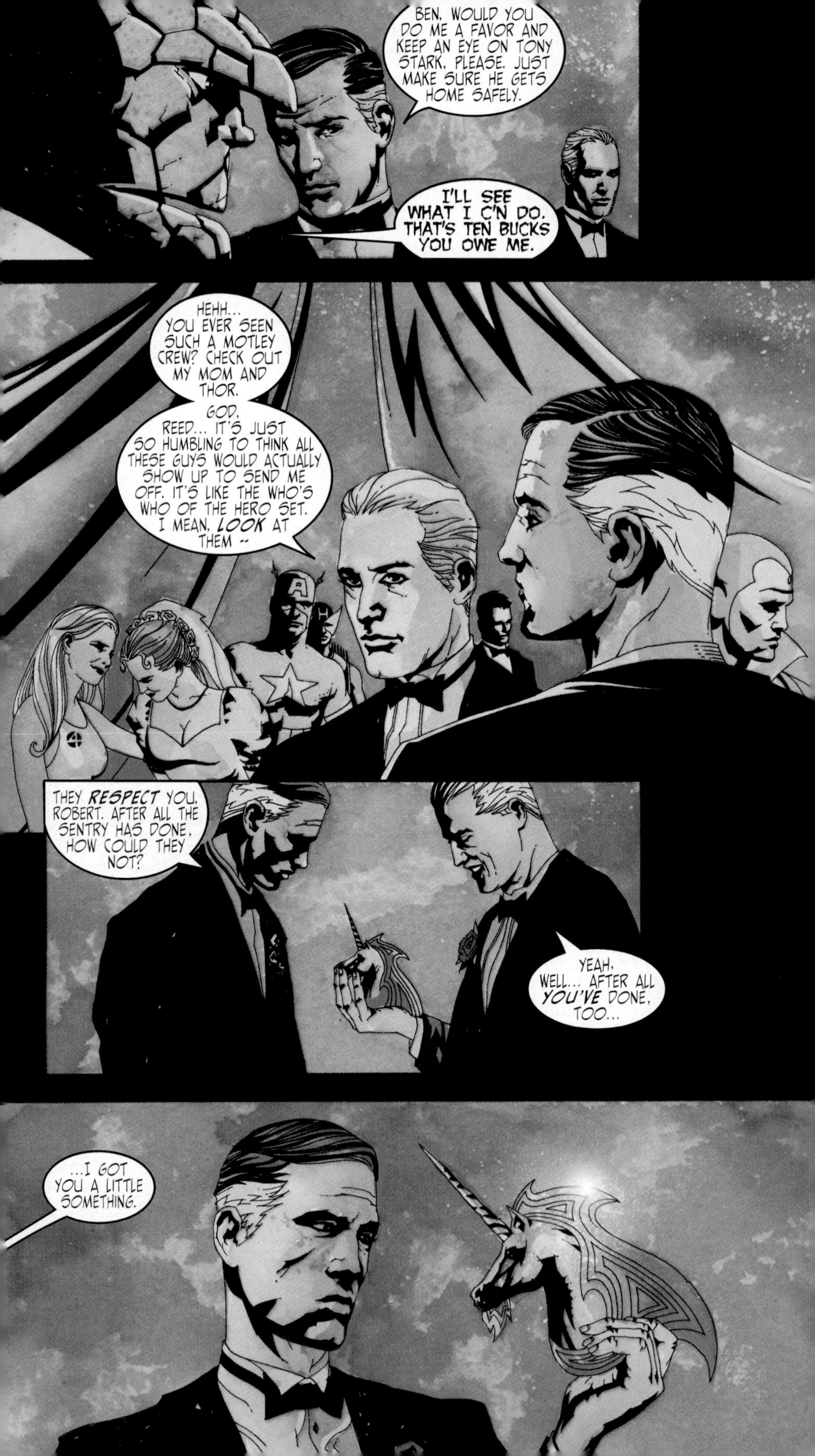
BEN, WOULD YOU DO ME A FAVOR AND KEEP AN EYE ON TONY STARK, PLEASE. JUST MAKE SURE HE GETS HOME SAFELY.
I'LL SEE WHAT I C'N DO. THAT'S TEN BUCKS YOU OWE ME.
HEHH... YOU EVER SEEN SUCH A MOTLEY CREW? CHECK OUT MY MOM AND THOR.
GOD, REED... IT'S JUST SO HUMBLING TO THINK ALL THESE GUYS WOULD ACTUALLY SHOW UP TO SEND ME OFF. IT'S LIKE THE WHO'S WHO OF THE HERO SET. I MEAN, LOOK AT THEM --
THEY RESPECT YOU, ROBERT. AFTER ALL THE SENTRY HAS DONE, HOW COULD THEY NOT?
YEAH, WELL... AFTER ALL YOU'VE DONE, TOO...
...I GOT YOU A LITTLE SOMETHING.

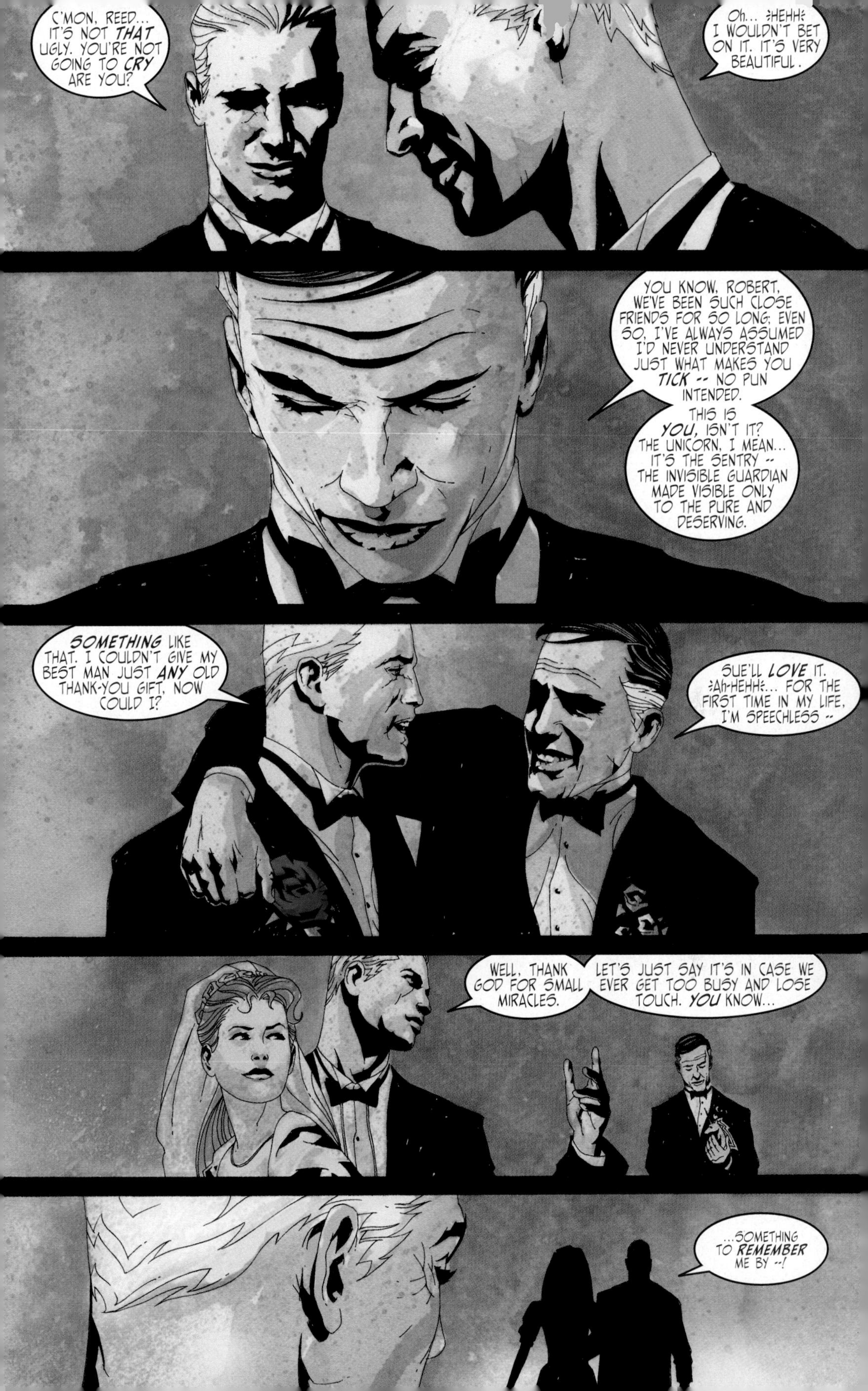
C'MON, REED... IT'S NOT THAT UGLY. YOU'RE NOT GOING TO CRY ARE YOU?
Oh... HEHH I WOULDN'T BET ON IT. IT'S VERY BEAUTIFUL.
YOU KNOW, ROBERT, WE'VE BEEN SUCH CLOSE FRIENDS FOR SO LONG; EVEN SO, I'VE ALWAYS ASSUMED I'D NEVER UNDERSTAND JUST WHAT MAKES YOU TICK -- NO PUN INTENDED.
THIS IS YOU, ISN'T IT? THE UNICORN, I MEAN... IT'S THE SENTRY -- THE INVISIBLE GUARDIAN MADE VISIBLE ONLY TO THE PURE AND DESERVING.
SOMETHING LIKE THAT. I COULDN'T GIVE MY BEST MAN JUST ANY OLD THANK-YOU GIFT, NOW COULD I?
SUE'LL LOVE IT. Ah-HEHH... FOR THE FIRST TIME IN MY LIFE, I'M SPEECHLESS --
WELL, THANK GOD FOR SMALL MIRACLES.
LET'S JUST SAY IT'S IN CASE WE EVER GET TOO BUSY AND LOSE TOUCH. YOU KNOW...
...SOMETHING TO REMEMBER ME BY --!

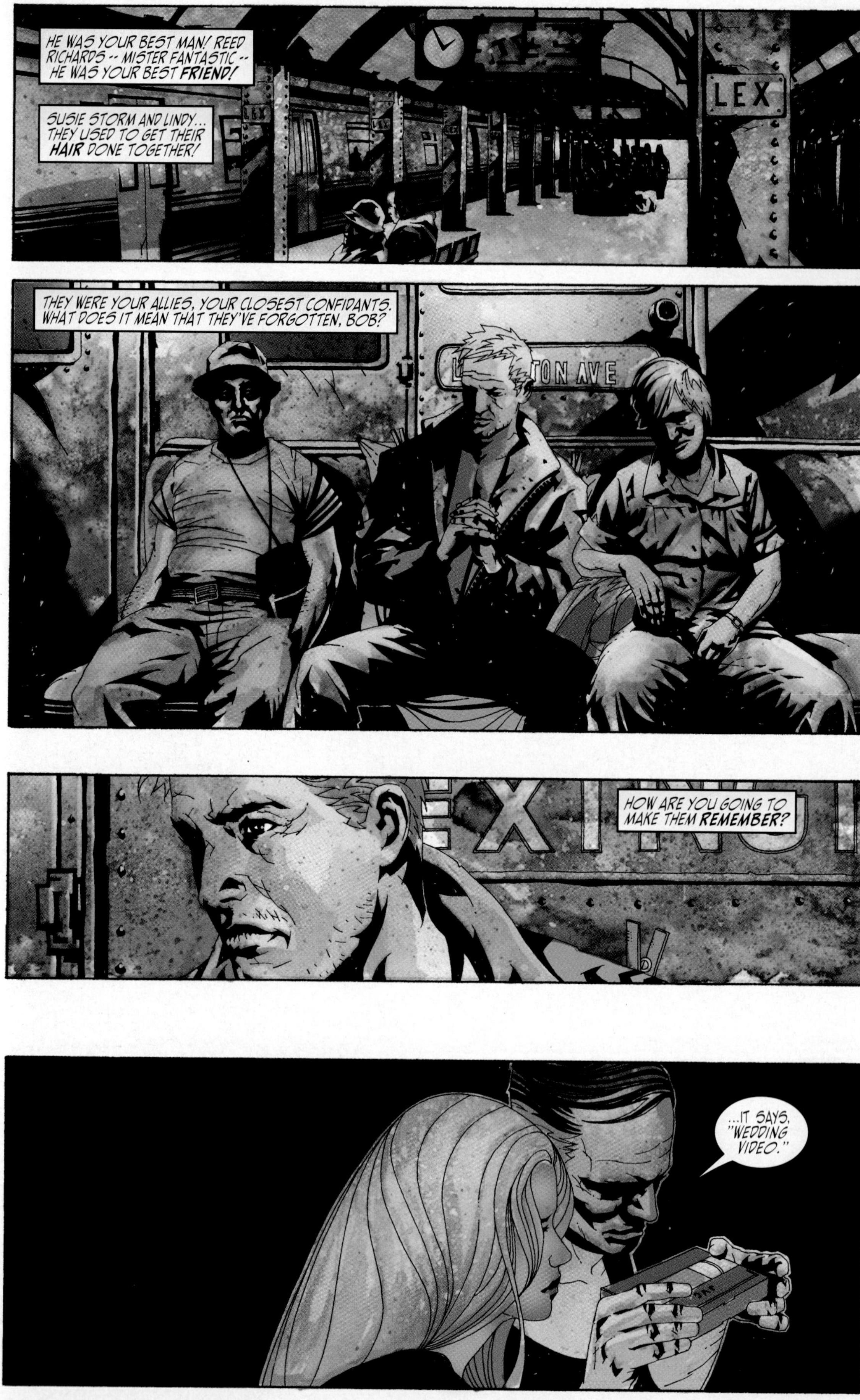
HE WAS YOUR BEST MAN! REED RICHARDS -- MISTER FANTASTIC -- HE WAS YOUR BEST FRIEND!
SUSIE STORM AND LINDY... THEY USED TO GET THEIR HAIR DONE TOGETHER!
LEX
THEY WERE YOUR ALLIES, YOUR CLOSEST CONFIDANTS. WHAT DOES IT MEAN THAT THEY'VE FORGOTTEN, BOB?
HOW ARE YOU GOING TO MAKE THEM REMEMBER?
...IT SAYS, "WEDDING VIDEO."

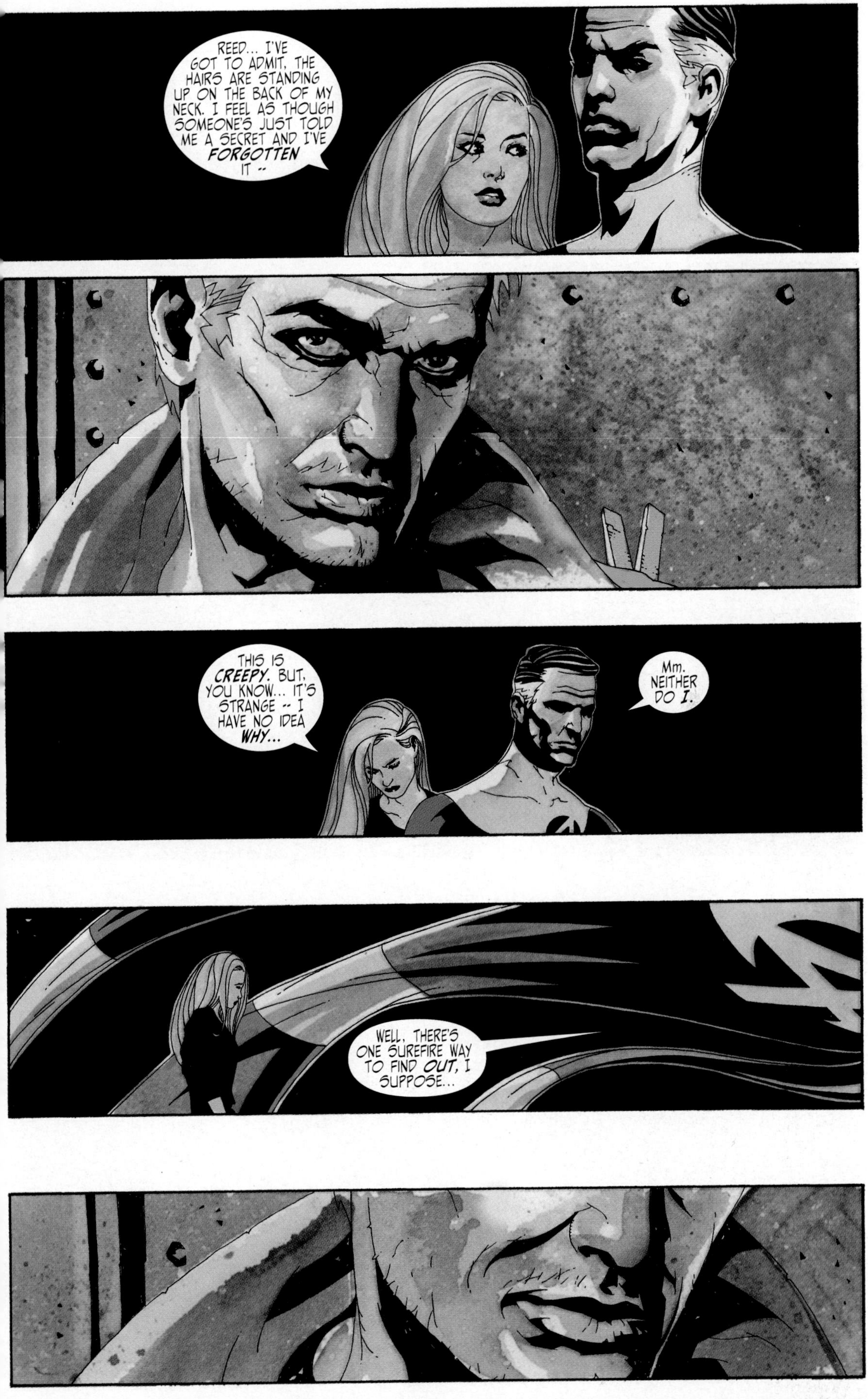
REED... I'VE GOT TO ADMIT, THE HAIRS ARE STANDING UP ON THE BACK OF MY NECK. I FEEL AS THOUGH SOMEONE'S JUST TOLD ME A SECRET AND I'VE FORGOTTEN IT --
THIS IS CREEPY. BUT, YOU KNOW... IT'S STRANGE -- I HAVE NO IDEA WHY...
Mm. NEITHER DO I.
WELL, THERE'S ONE SUREFIRE WAY TO FIND OUT, I SUPPOSE...

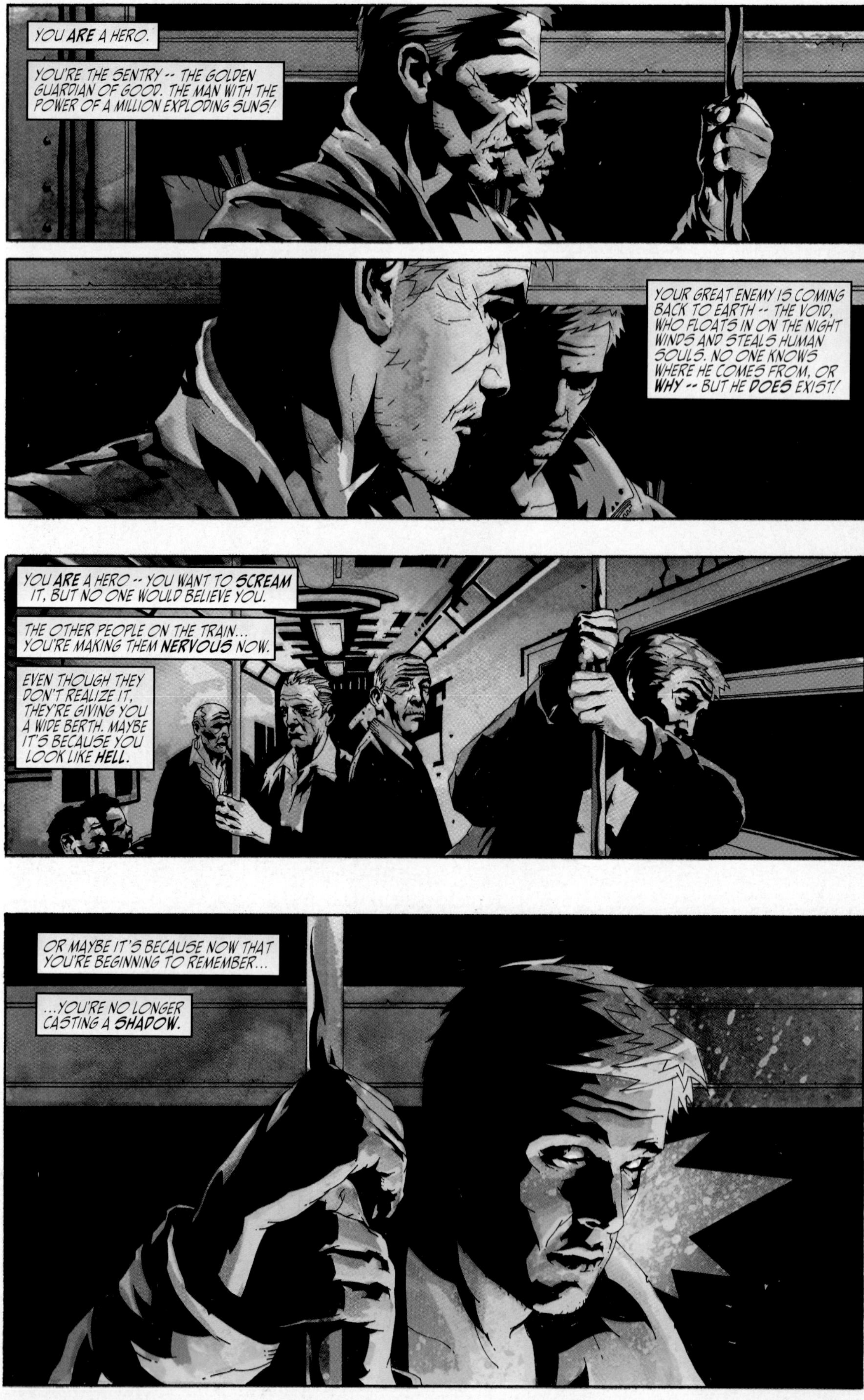
YOU **ARE** A HERO.
YOU'RE THE SENTRY -- THE GOLDEN GUARDIAN OF GOOD. THE MAN WITH THE POWER OF A MILLION EXPLODING SUNS!
YOUR GREAT ENEMY IS COMING BACK TO EARTH -- THE VOID, WHO FLOATS IN ON THE NIGHT WINDS AND STEALS HUMAN SOULS. NO ONE KNOWS WHERE HE COMES FROM, OR **WHY** -- BUT HE **DOES** EXIST!
YOU **ARE** A HERO -- YOU WANT TO **SCREAM** IT, BUT NO ONE WOULD BELIEVE YOU.
THE OTHER PEOPLE ON THE TRAIN... YOU'RE MAKING THEM **NERVOUS** NOW.
EVEN THOUGH THEY DON'T REALIZE IT, THEY'RE GIVING YOU A WIDE BERTH. MAYBE IT'S BECAUSE YOU LOOK LIKE **HELL**.
OR MAYBE IT'S BECAUSE NOW THAT YOU'RE BEGINNING TO REMEMBER...
...YOU'RE NO LONGER CASTING A **SHADOW**.

BOYS, WOULD YOU MIND DOING US A FAVOR? WE'D LIKE TO POP THIS VIDEO IN FOR JUST A MOMENT, OKAY?

SUITS ME. I WUZ ABOUT TO HURL ANYWAY...

AW, C'MON, REED... I WAS *WATCHING* THAT! CAN'T YOU USE THE DOWNSTAIRS VCR?

SORRY, JOHNNY -- NO CAN DO. WON'T BE A MOMENT... JUST HOLD TIGHT, OKAY...?

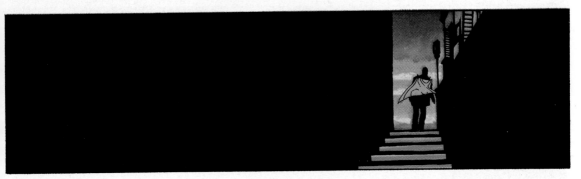

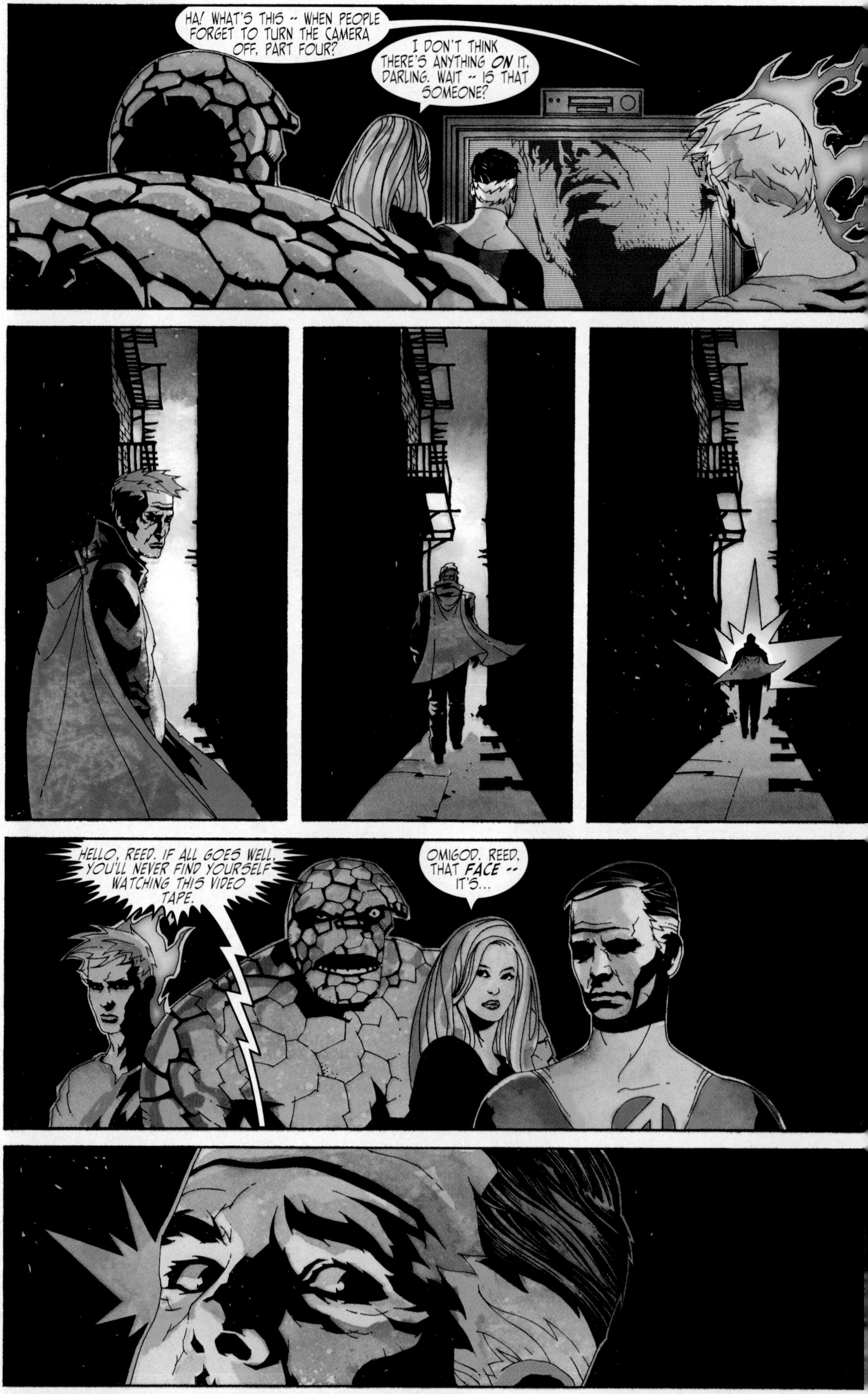
HA! WHAT'S THIS -- WHEN PEOPLE FORGET TO TURN THE CAMERA OFF, PART FOUR?
I DON'T THINK THERE'S ANYTHING ON IT, DARLING. WAIT -- IS THAT SOMEONE?
HELLO, REED. IF ALL GOES WELL, YOU'LL NEVER FIND YOURSELF WATCHING THIS VIDEO TAPE.
OMIGOD. REED, THAT FACE -- IT'S...

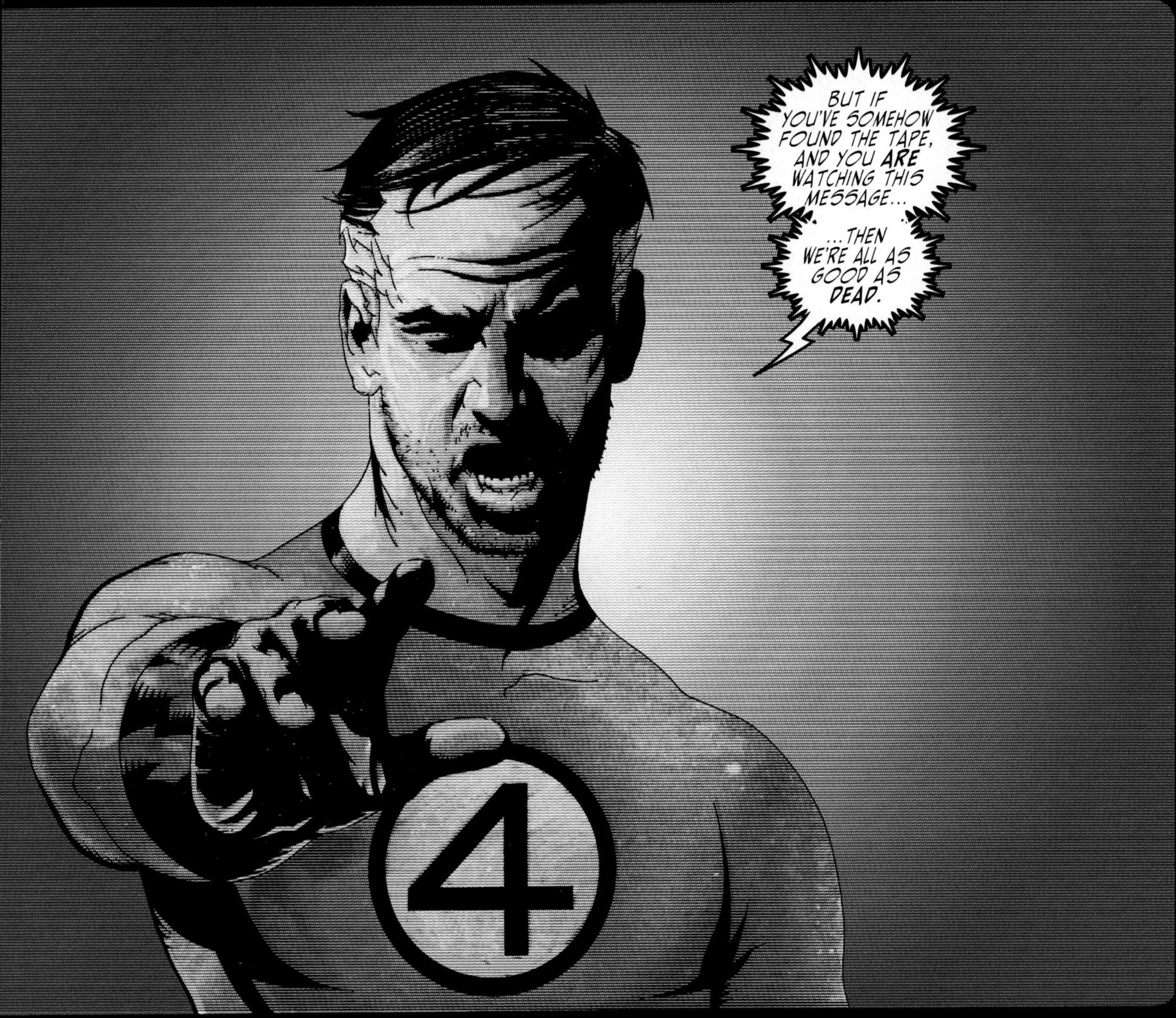
BUT IF YOU'VE SOMEHOW FOUND THE TAPE, AND YOU ARE WATCHING THIS MESSAGE...
...THEN WE'RE ALL AS GOOD AS DEAD.

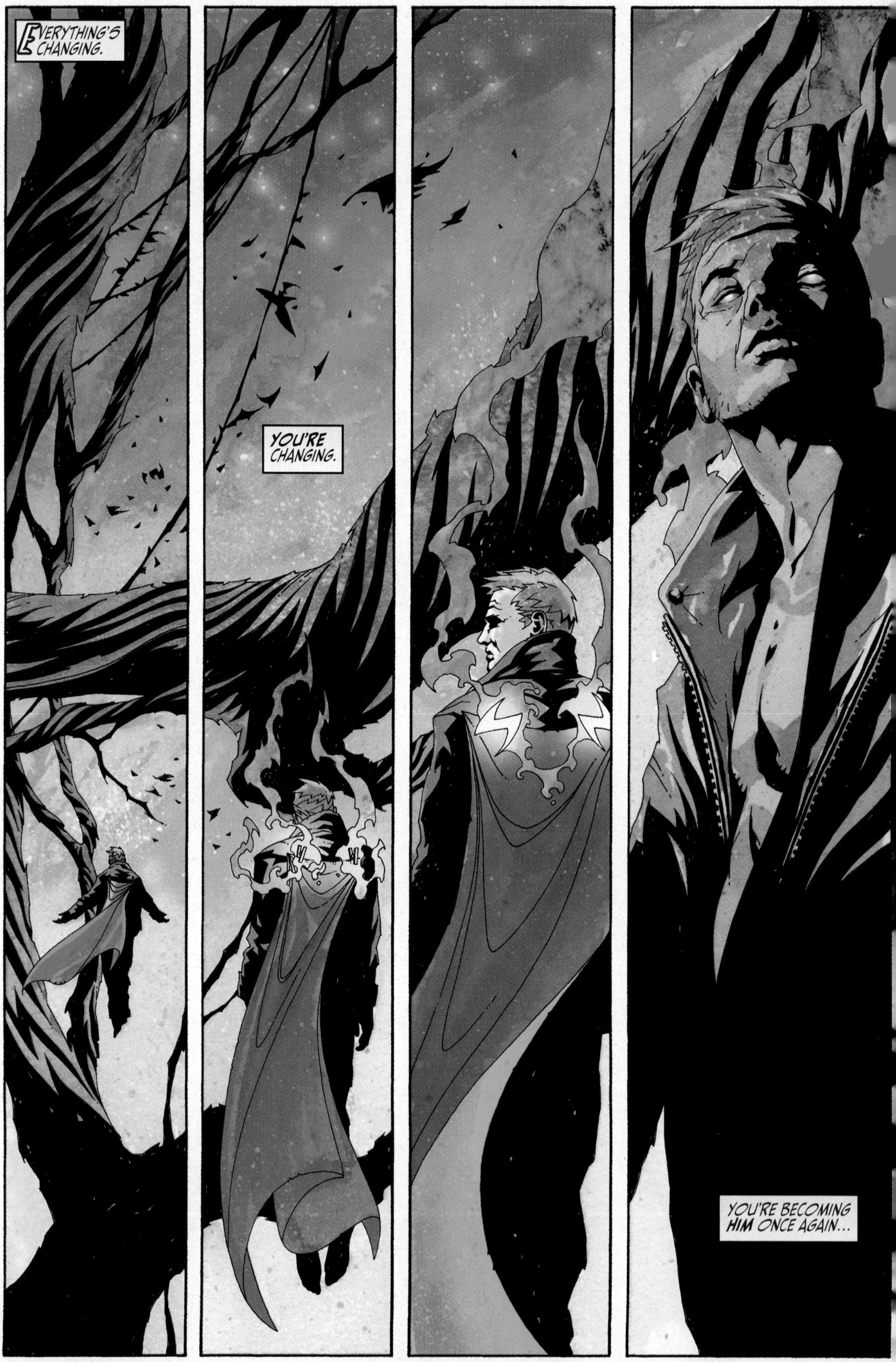
EVERYTHING'S CHANGING.
YOU'RE CHANGING.
YOU'RE BECOMING HIM ONCE AGAIN...

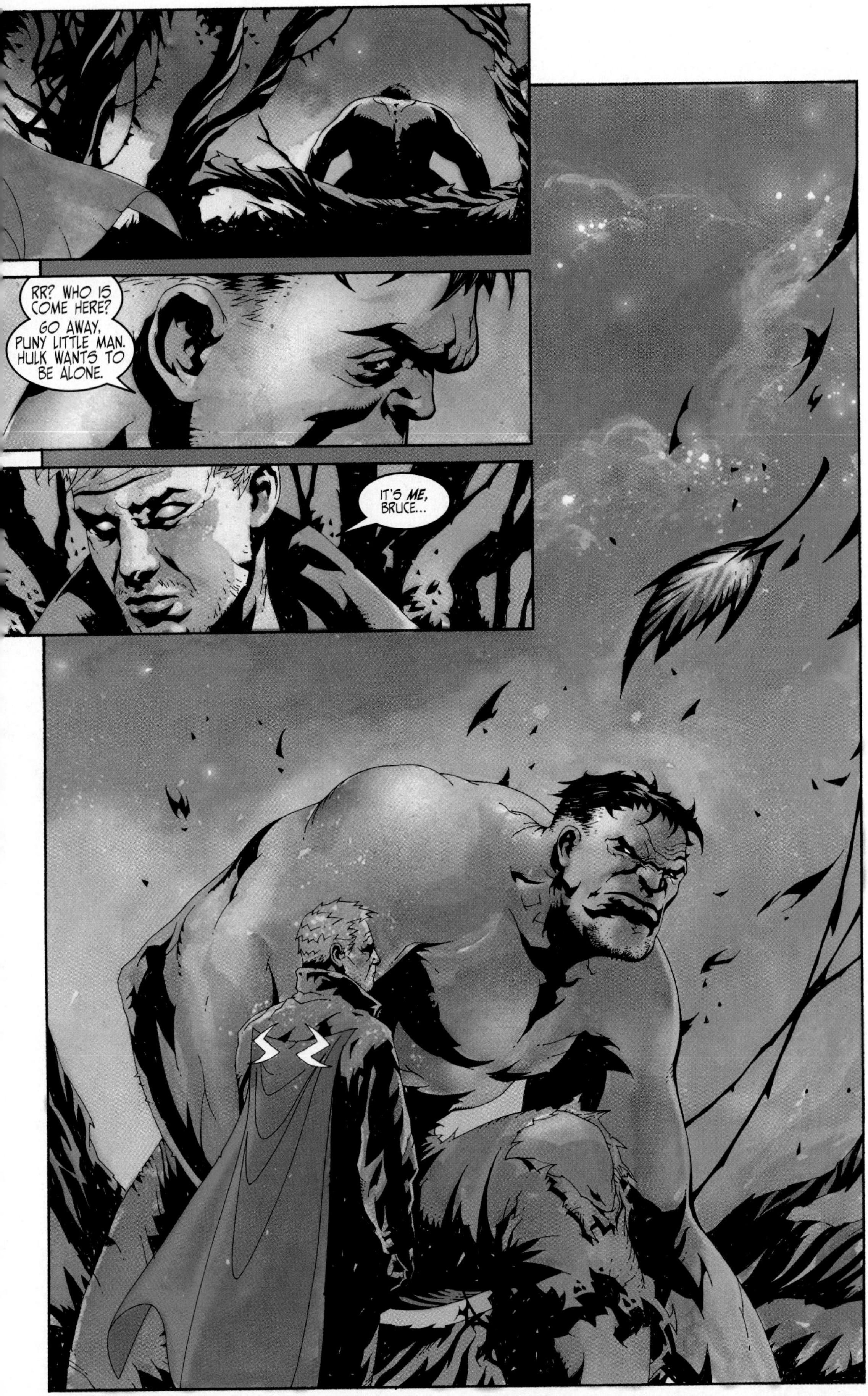
RR? WHO IS COME HERE? GO AWAY, PUNY LITTLE MAN. HULK WANTS TO BE ALONE.
IT'S *ME*, BRUCE...

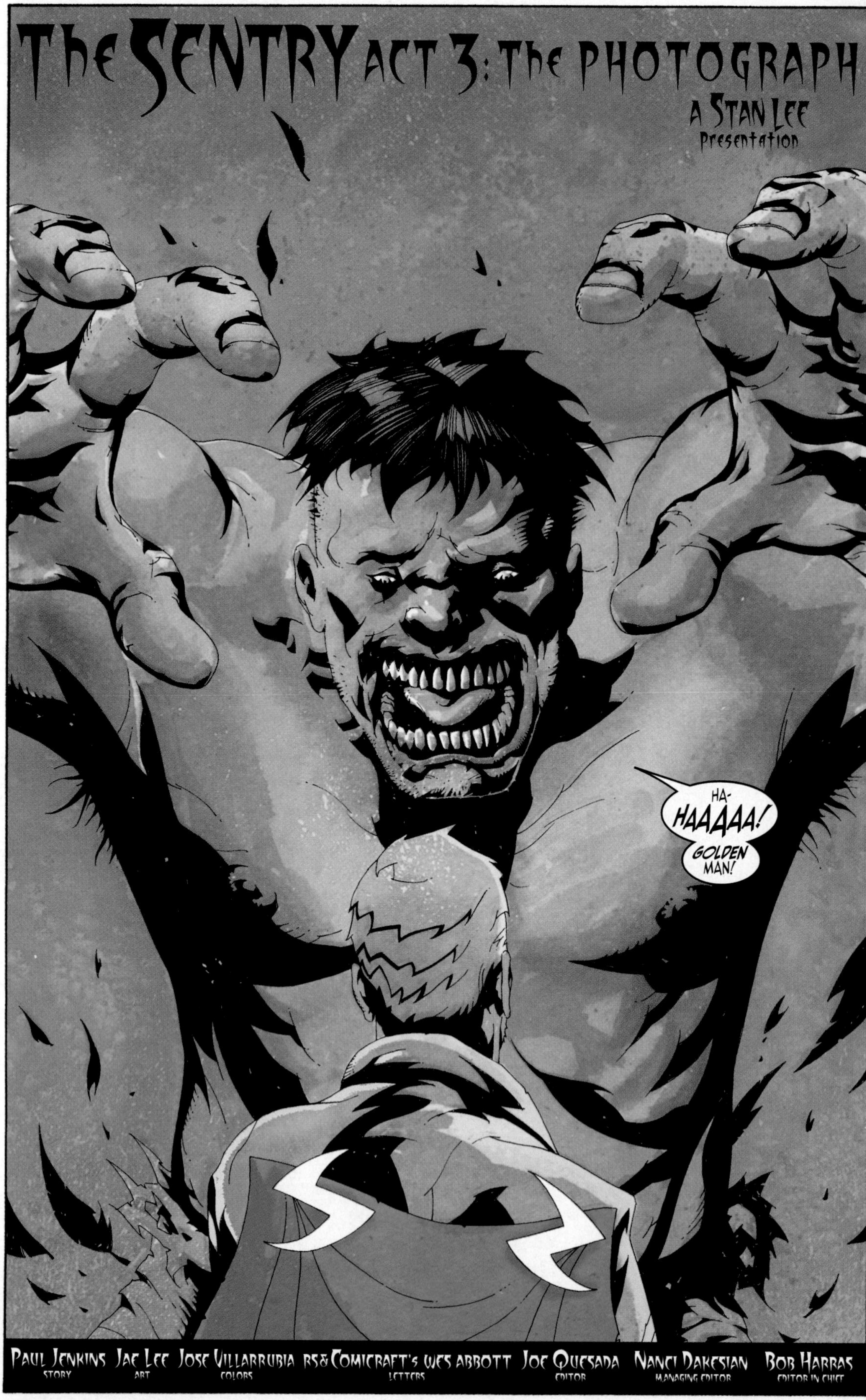
THE SENTRY ACT 3: THE PHOTOGRAPH
A STAN LEE PRESENTATION
HA-HAAAAA! GOLDEN MAN!
PAUL JENKINS STORY
JAE LEE ART
JOSE VILLARRUBIA COLORS
RS&COMICRAFT'S WES ABBOTT LETTERS
JOE QUESADA EDITOR
NANCI DAKESIAN MANAGING EDITOR
BOB HARRAS EDITOR IN CHIEF

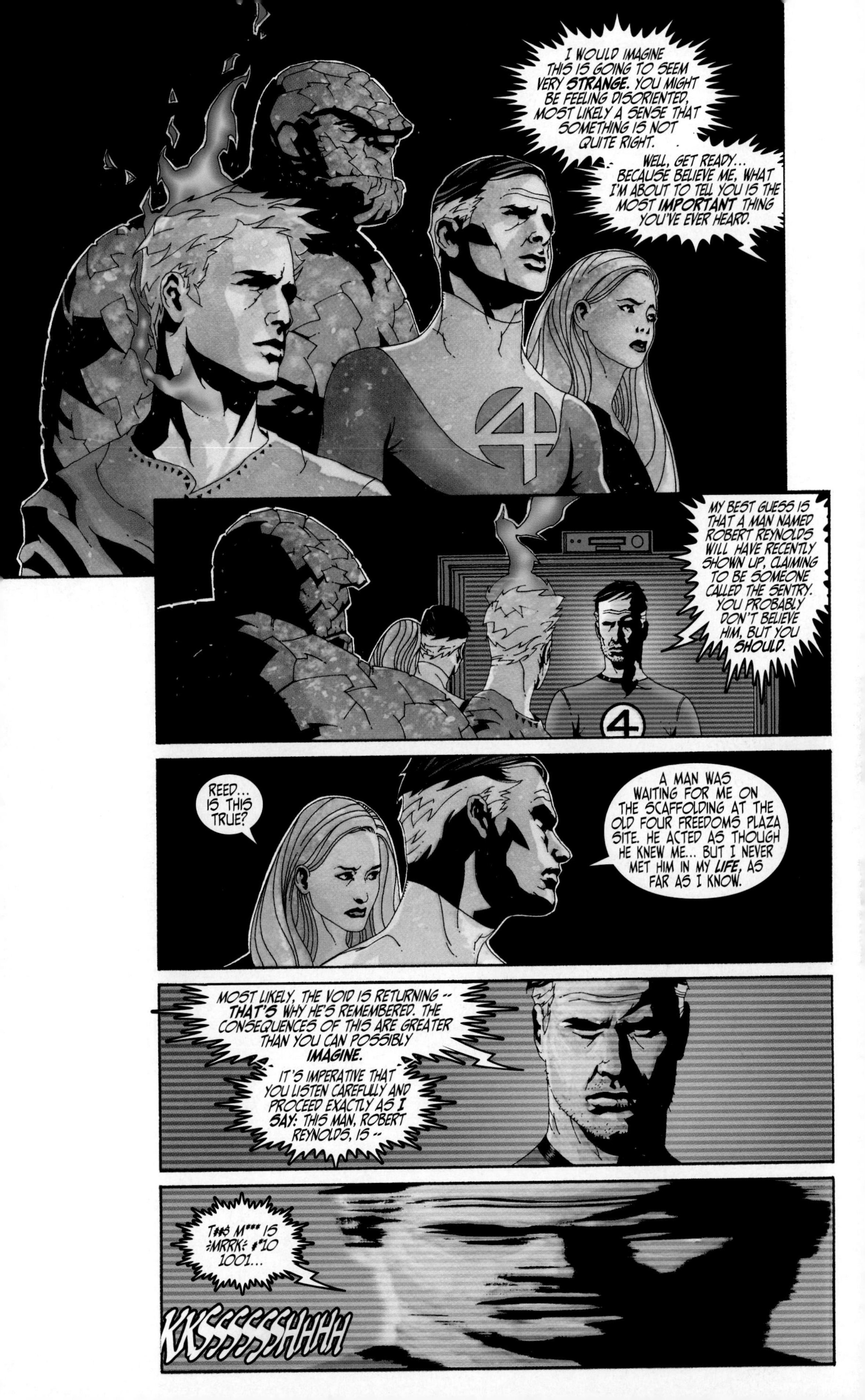
I WOULD IMAGINE THIS IS GOING TO SEEM VERY STRANGE. YOU MIGHT BE FEELING DISORIENTED, MOST LIKELY A SENSE THAT SOMETHING IS NOT QUITE RIGHT.
WELL, GET READY... BECAUSE BELIEVE ME, WHAT I'M ABOUT TO TELL YOU IS THE MOST IMPORTANT THING YOU'VE EVER HEARD.
MY BEST GUESS IS THAT A MAN NAMED ROBERT REYNOLDS WILL HAVE RECENTLY SHOWN UP, CLAIMING TO BE SOMEONE CALLED THE SENTRY. YOU PROBABLY DON'T BELIEVE HIM, BUT YOU SHOULD.
REED... IS THIS TRUE?
A MAN WAS WAITING FOR ME ON THE SCAFFOLDING AT THE OLD FOUR FREEDOMS PLAZA SITE. HE ACTED AS THOUGH HE KNEW ME... BUT I NEVER MET HIM IN MY LIFE, AS FAR AS I KNOW.
MOST LIKELY, THE VOID IS RETURNING -- THAT'S WHY HE'S REMEMBERED. THE CONSEQUENCES OF THIS ARE GREATER THAN YOU CAN POSSIBLY IMAGINE.
IT'S IMPERATIVE THAT YOU LISTEN CAREFULLY AND PROCEED EXACTLY AS I SAY: THIS MAN, ROBERT REYNOLDS, IS --
T##$ M*** IS =MRRK= #*10 1001...
KKSSSSSSHHHH

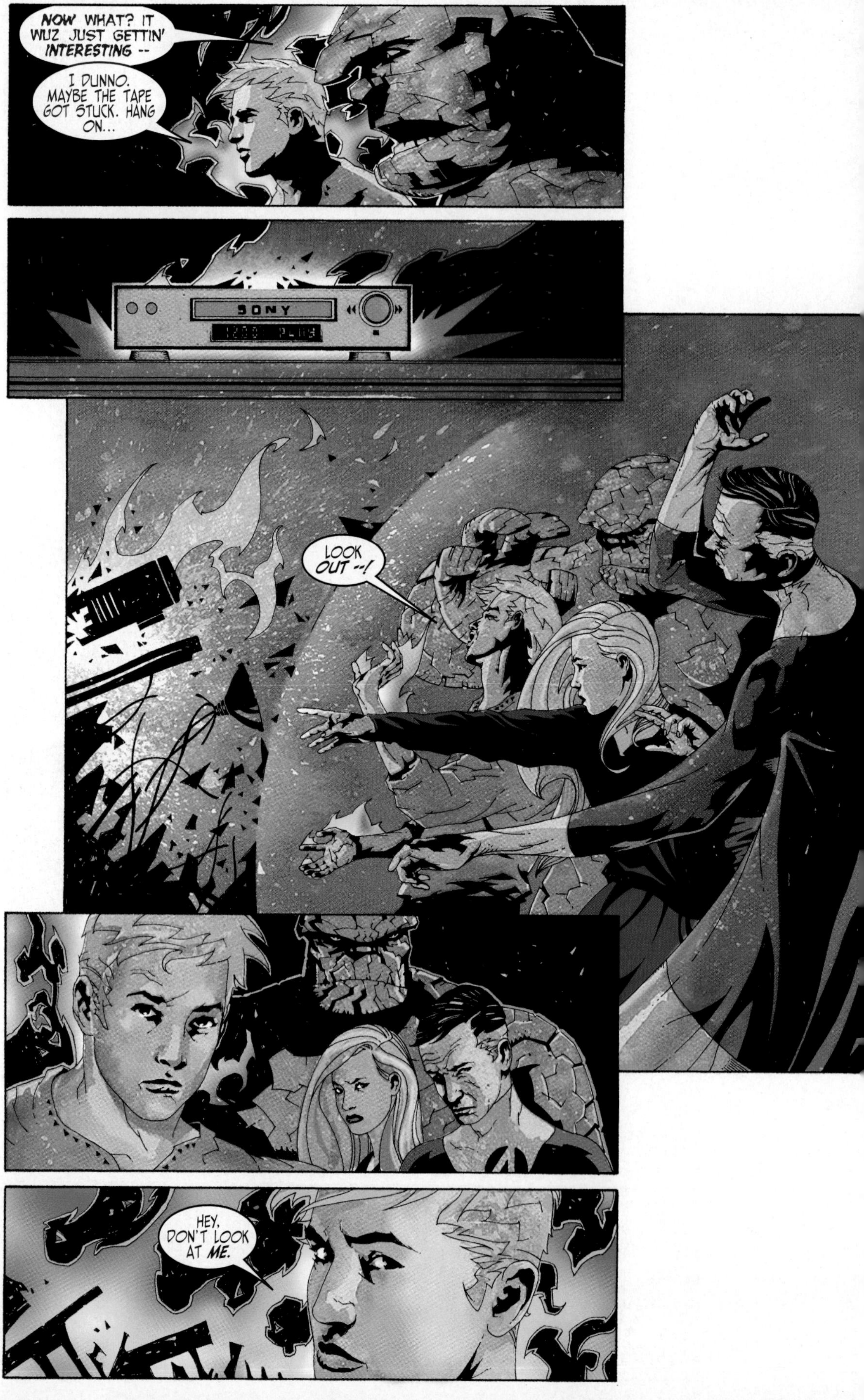
NOW WHAT? IT WUZ JUST GETTIN' INTERESTING --
I DUNNO. MAYBE THE TAPE GOT STUCK. HANG ON...
SONY
LOOK OUT --!
HEY, DON'T LOOK AT ME.

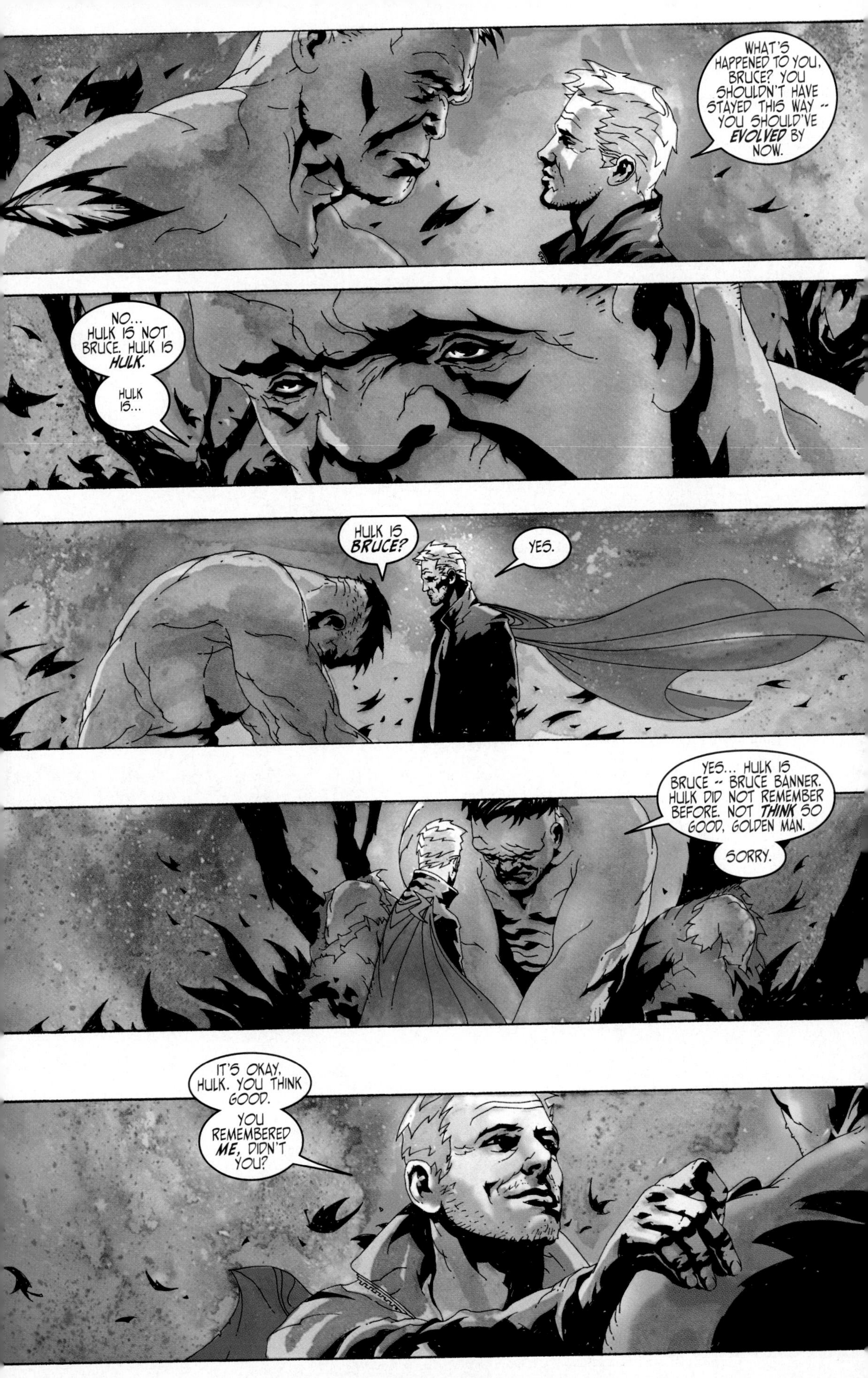
WHAT'S HAPPENED TO YOU, BRUCE? YOU SHOULDN'T HAVE STAYED THIS WAY -- YOU SHOULD'VE EVOLVED BY NOW.
NO... HULK IS NOT BRUCE. HULK IS HULK.
HULK IS...
HULK IS BRUCE?
YES.
YES... HULK IS BRUCE -- BRUCE BANNER. HULK DID NOT REMEMBER BEFORE. NOT THINK SO GOOD, GOLDEN MAN.
SORRY.
IT'S OKAY, HULK. YOU THINK GOOD.
YOU REMEMBERED ME, DIDN'T YOU?

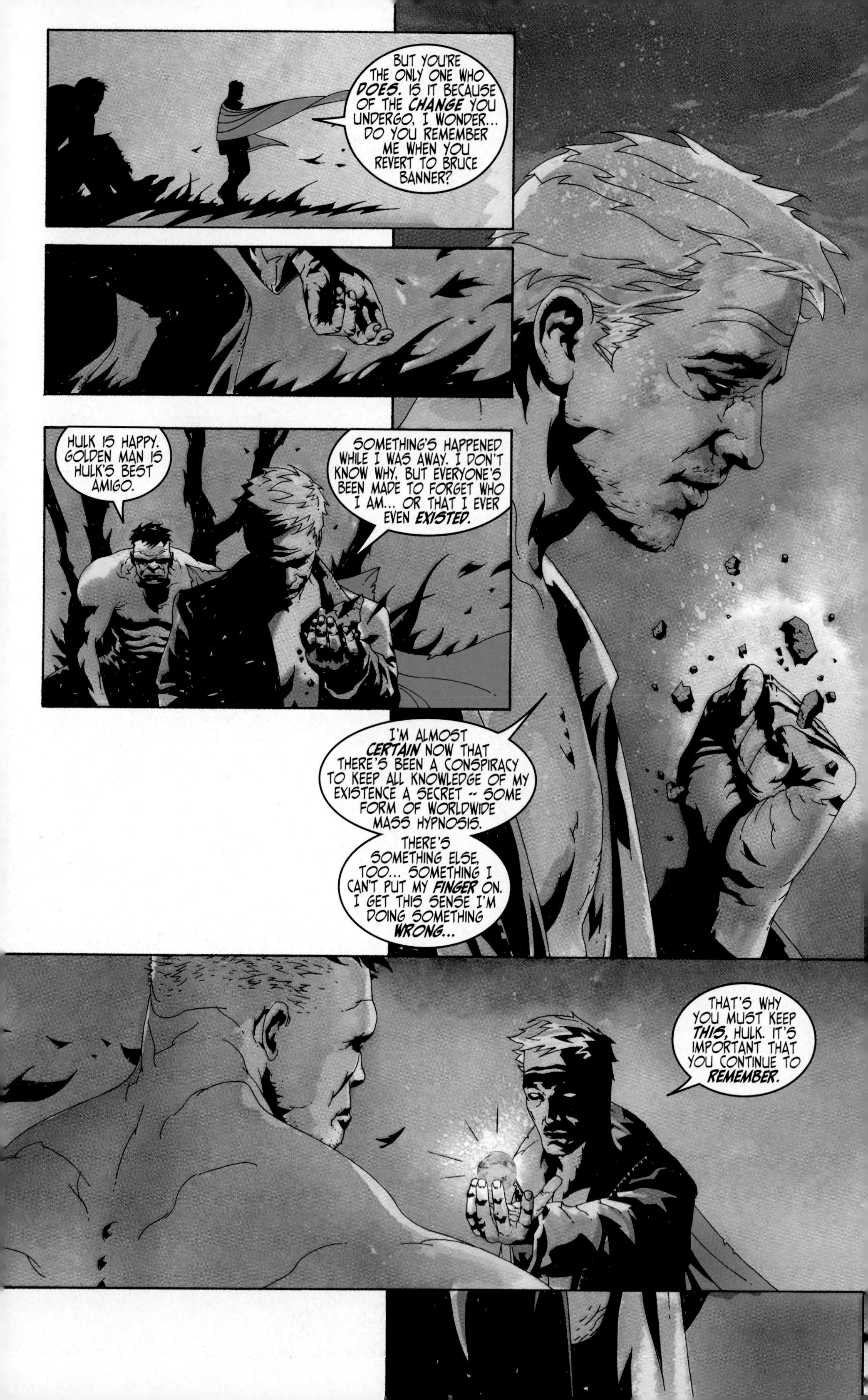
BUT YOU'RE THE ONLY ONE WHO DOES. IS IT BECAUSE OF THE CHANGE YOU UNDERGO, I WONDER... DO YOU REMEMBER ME WHEN YOU REVERT TO BRUCE BANNER?
HULK IS HAPPY. GOLDEN MAN IS HULK'S BEST AMIGO.
SOMETHING'S HAPPENED WHILE I WAS AWAY. I DON'T KNOW WHY, BUT EVERYONE'S BEEN MADE TO FORGET WHO I AM... OR THAT I EVER EVEN EXISTED.
I'M ALMOST CERTAIN NOW THAT THERE'S BEEN A CONSPIRACY TO KEEP ALL KNOWLEDGE OF MY EXISTENCE A SECRET -- SOME FORM OF WORLDWIDE MASS HYPNOSIS.
THERE'S SOMETHING ELSE, TOO... SOMETHING I CAN'T PUT MY FINGER ON. I GET THIS SENSE I'M DOING SOMETHING WRONG...
THAT'S WHY YOU MUST KEEP THIS, HULK. IT'S IMPORTANT THAT YOU CONTINUE TO REMEMBER.

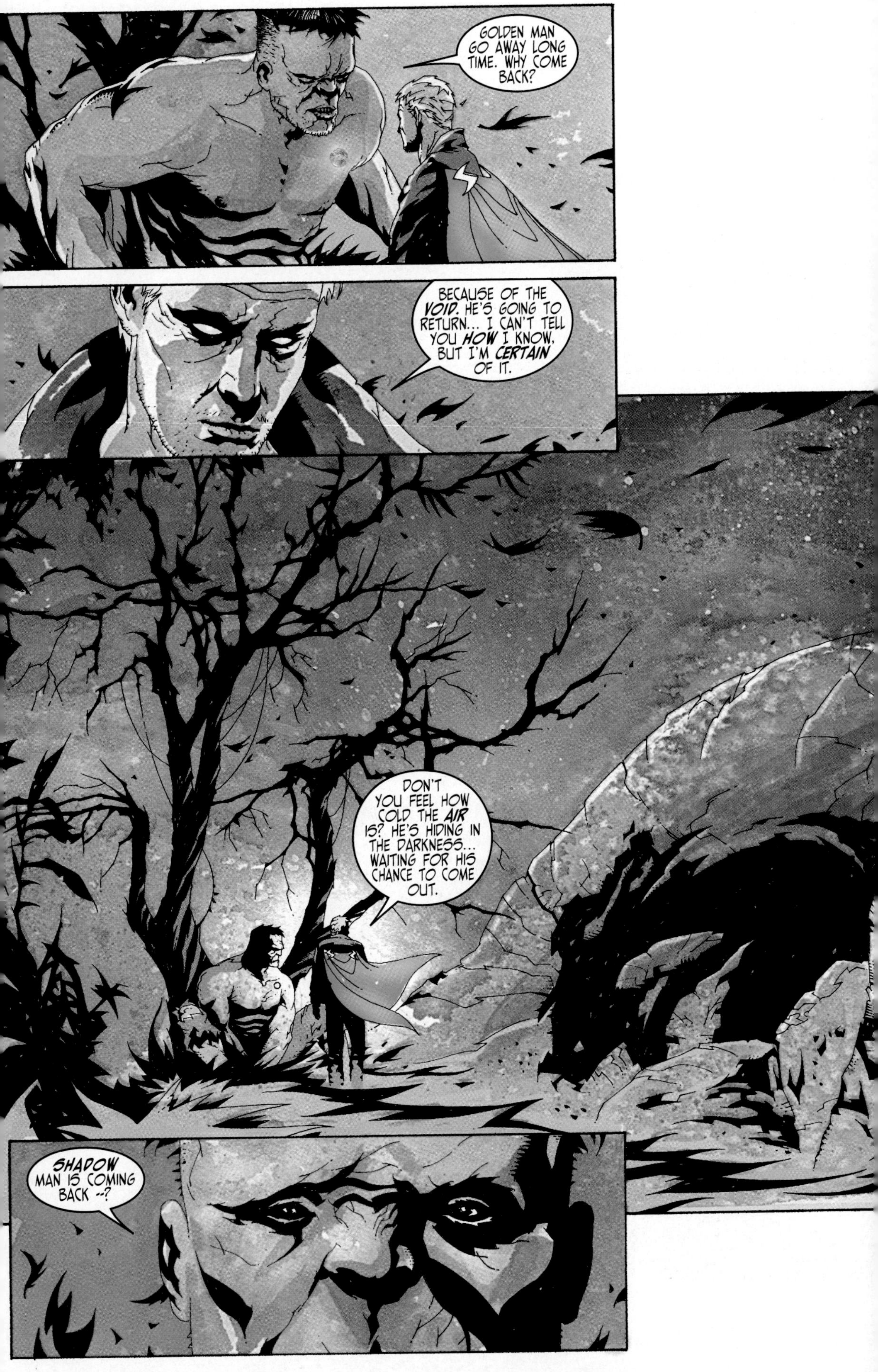
GOLDEN MAN GO AWAY LONG TIME. WHY COME BACK?
BECAUSE OF THE VOID. HE'S GOING TO RETURN... I CAN'T TELL YOU HOW I KNOW, BUT I'M CERTAIN OF IT.
DON'T YOU FEEL HOW COLD THE AIR IS? HE'S HIDING IN THE DARKNESS... WAITING FOR HIS CHANCE TO COME OUT.
SHADOW MAN IS COMING BACK --?

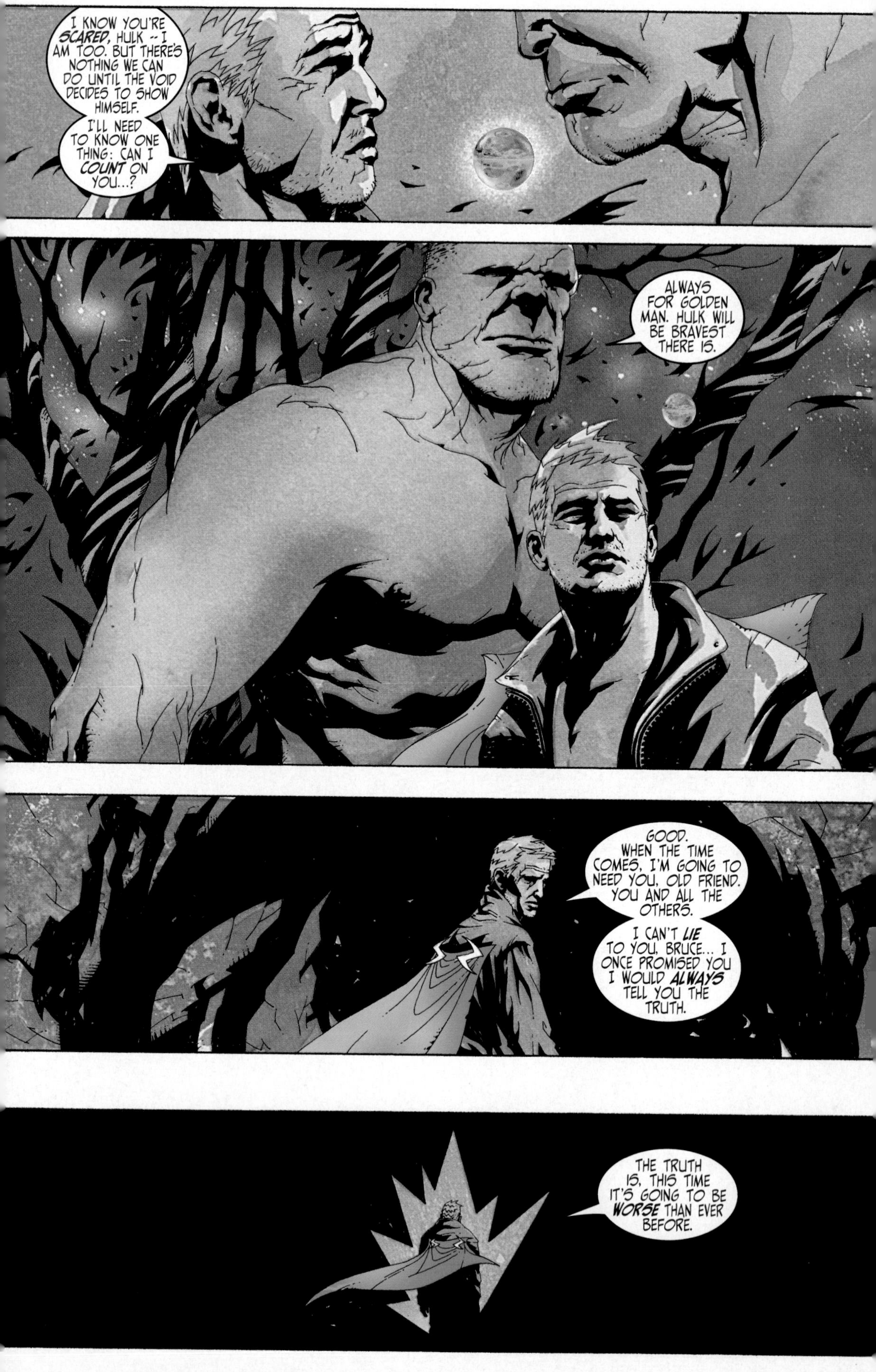

I KNOW YOU'RE SCARED, HULK -- I AM TOO. BUT THERE'S NOTHING WE CAN DO UNTIL THE VOID DECIDES TO SHOW HIMSELF.
I'LL NEED TO KNOW ONE THING: CAN I COUNT ON YOU...?
ALWAYS FOR GOLDEN MAN. HULK WILL BE BRAVEST THERE IS.
GOOD. WHEN THE TIME COMES, I'M GOING TO NEED YOU, OLD FRIEND. YOU AND ALL THE OTHERS.
I CAN'T LIE TO YOU, BRUCE... I ONCE PROMISED YOU I WOULD ALWAYS TELL YOU THE TRUTH.
THE TRUTH IS, THIS TIME IT'S GOING TO BE WORSE THAN EVER BEFORE.

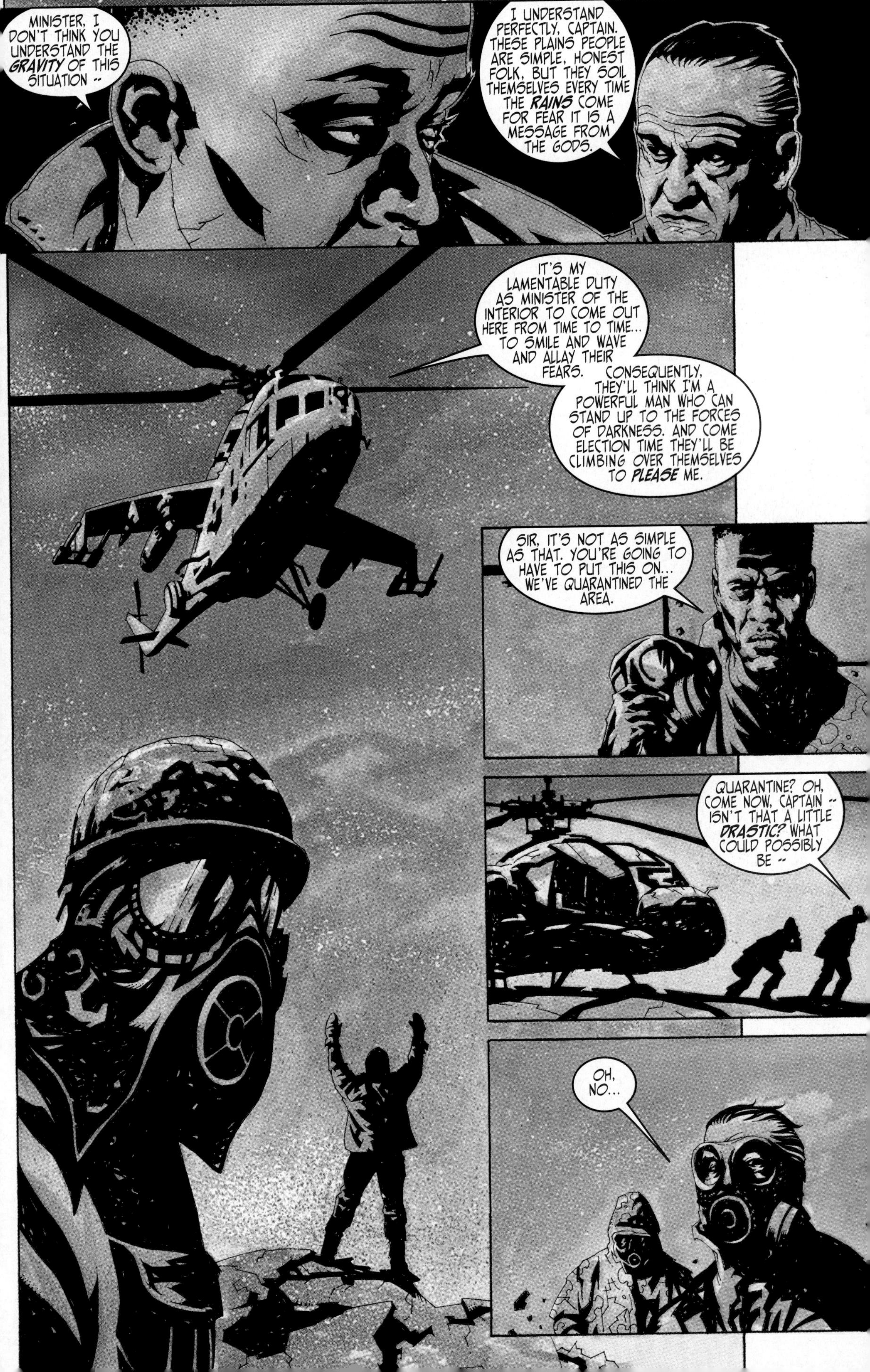
MINISTER, I DON'T THINK YOU UNDERSTAND THE GRAVITY OF THIS SITUATION --
I UNDERSTAND PERFECTLY, CAPTAIN. THESE PLAINS PEOPLE ARE SIMPLE, HONEST FOLK, BUT THEY SOIL THEMSELVES EVERY TIME THE RAINS COME FOR FEAR IT IS A MESSAGE FROM THE GODS.
IT'S MY LAMENTABLE DUTY AS MINISTER OF THE INTERIOR TO COME OUT HERE FROM TIME TO TIME... TO SMILE AND WAVE AND ALLAY THEIR FEARS.
CONSEQUENTLY, THEY'LL THINK I'M A POWERFUL MAN WHO CAN STAND UP TO THE FORCES OF DARKNESS. AND COME ELECTION TIME THEY'LL BE CLIMBING OVER THEMSELVES TO PLEASE ME.
SIR, IT'S NOT AS SIMPLE AS THAT. YOU'RE GOING TO HAVE TO PUT THIS ON... WE'VE QUARANTINED THE AREA.
QUARANTINE? OH, COME NOW, CAPTAIN -- ISN'T THAT A LITTLE DRASTIC? WHAT COULD POSSIBLY BE --
OH, NO...

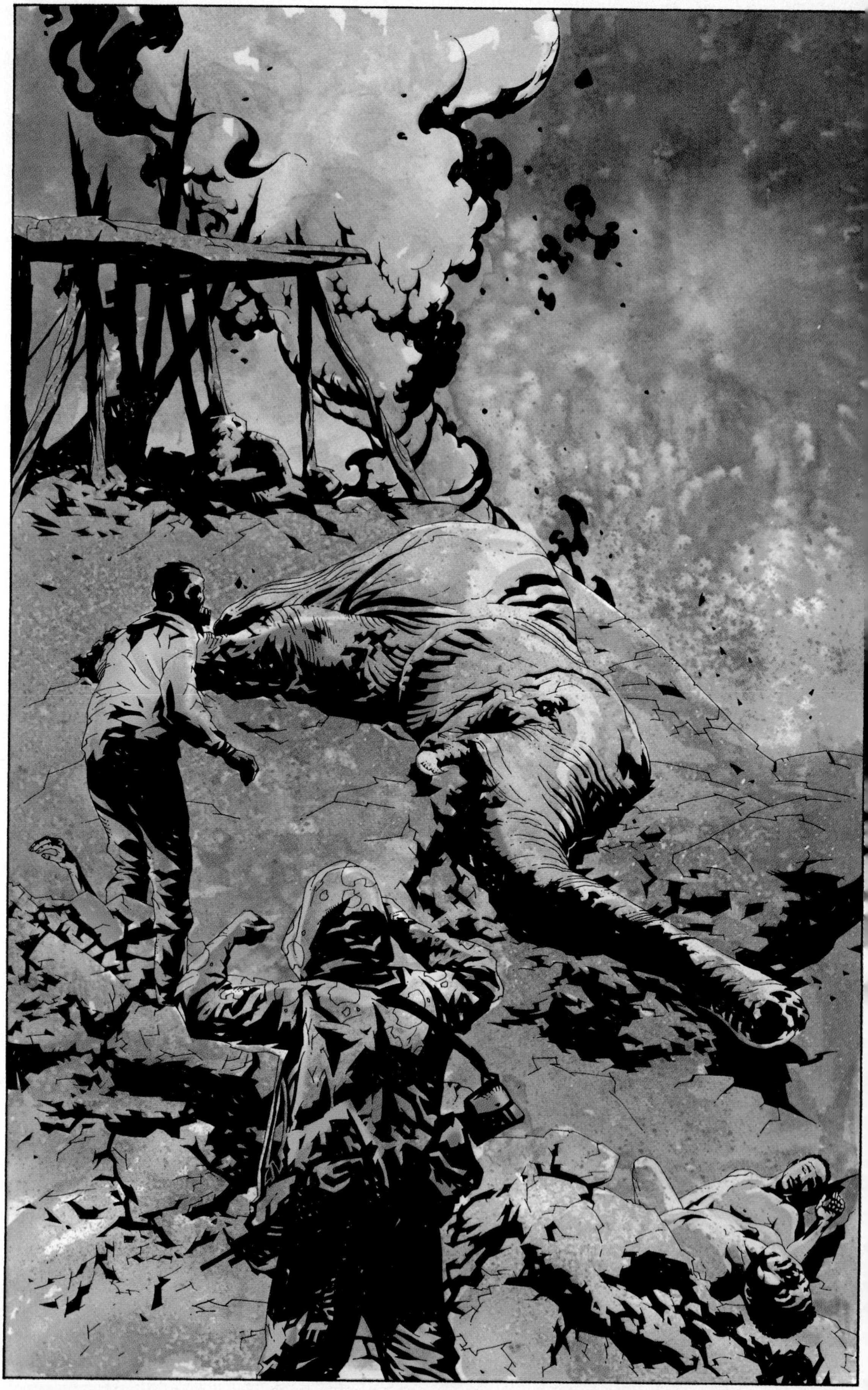

Excerpt from the diary of Reed Richards -- October 17th.

I'm now willing to admit: the further I go, the more **distant** I feel, as if abstractly removed from the comfortable evidence of civilization around me.

It's as though I'm being drawn into a whirlpool... ever decreasing concentric circles of intrigue. The facts rush by in front of me and I cannot reach out to grasp them.

Every time I try, an undercurrent of the truth tugs at my awareness, pulling me deeper.

Voice and video analysis confirms that Reynolds is who he **says** he is. But his social security number belongs to a man who died years ago.

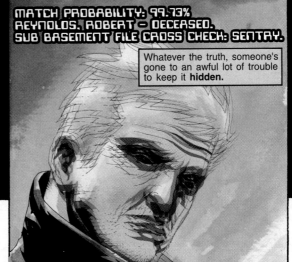

MATCH PROBABILITY: 99.73%
REYNOLDS, ROBERT - DECEASED.
SUB BASEMENT FILE CROSS CHECK: SENTRY.

Whatever the truth, someone's gone to an awful lot of trouble to keep it **hidden**.

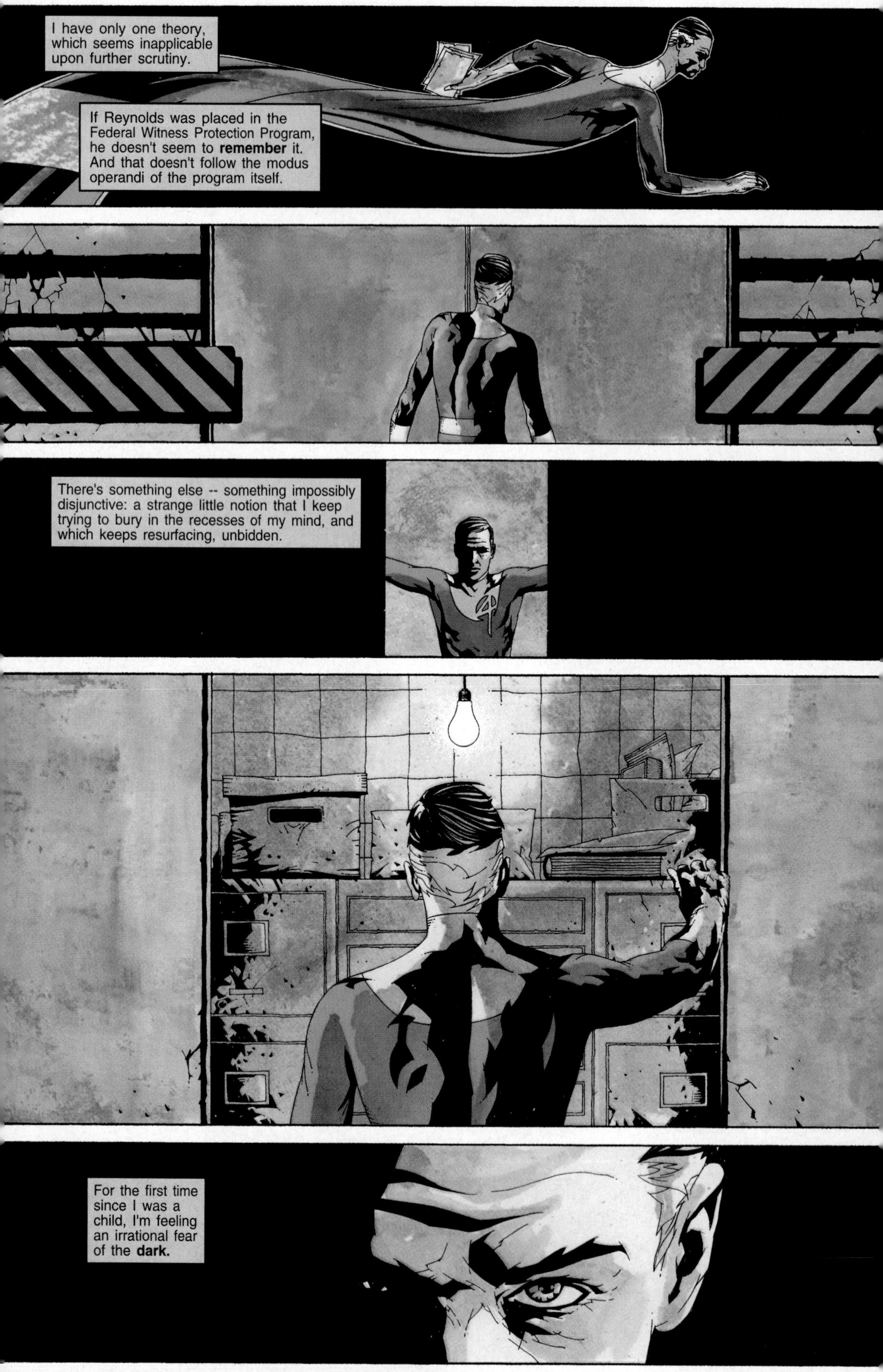
I have only one theory, which seems inapplicable upon further scrutiny.
If Reynolds was placed in the Federal Witness Protection Program, he doesn't seem to **remember** it. And that doesn't follow the modus operandi of the program itself.
There's something else -- something impossibly disjunctive: a strange little notion that I keep trying to bury in the recesses of my mind, and which keeps resurfacing, unbidden.
For the first time since I was a child, I'm feeling an irrational fear of the **dark.**

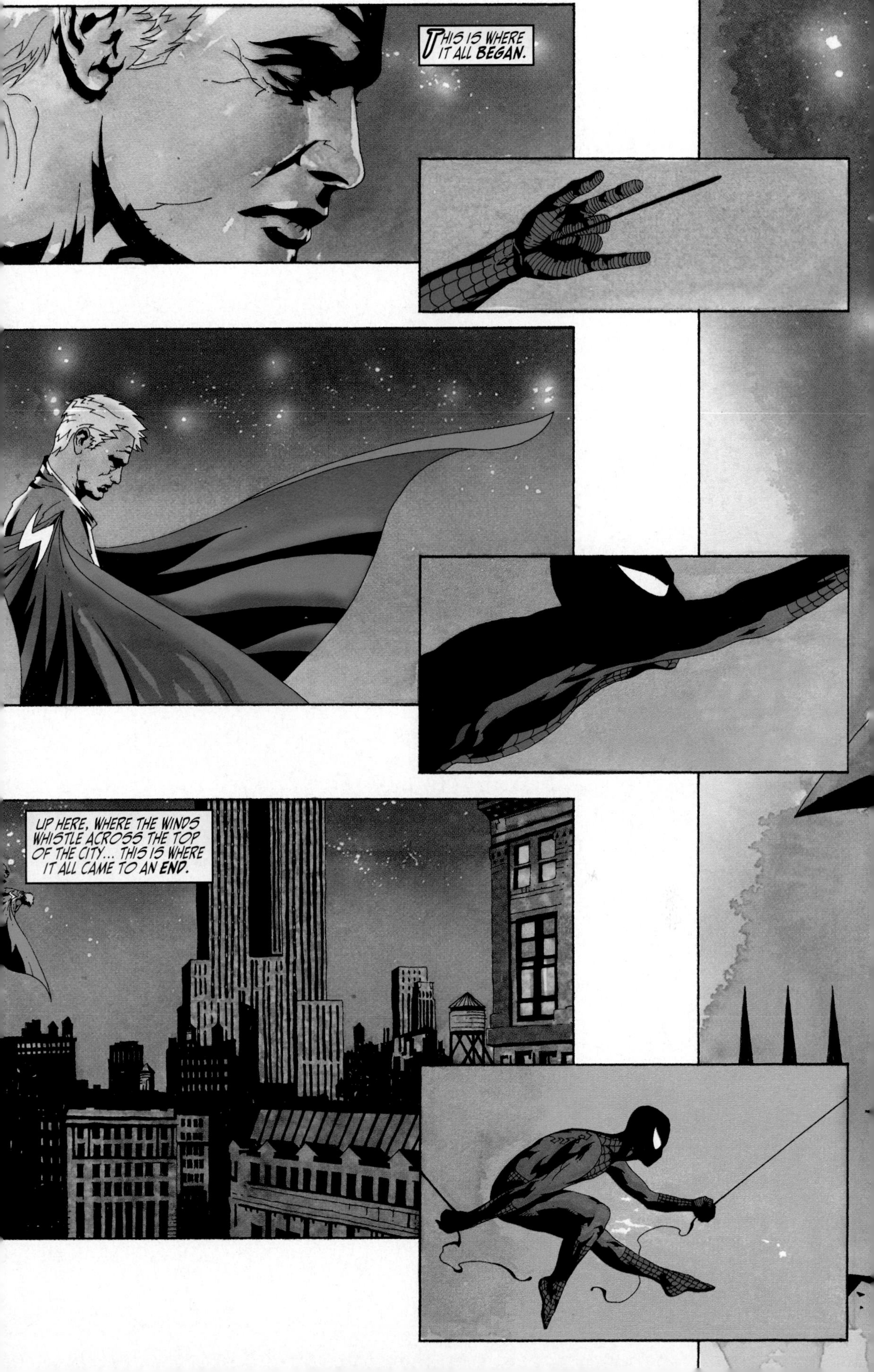
THIS IS WHERE IT ALL BEGAN.
UP HERE, WHERE THE WINDS WHISTLE ACROSS THE TOP OF THE CITY... THIS IS WHERE IT ALL CAME TO AN END.

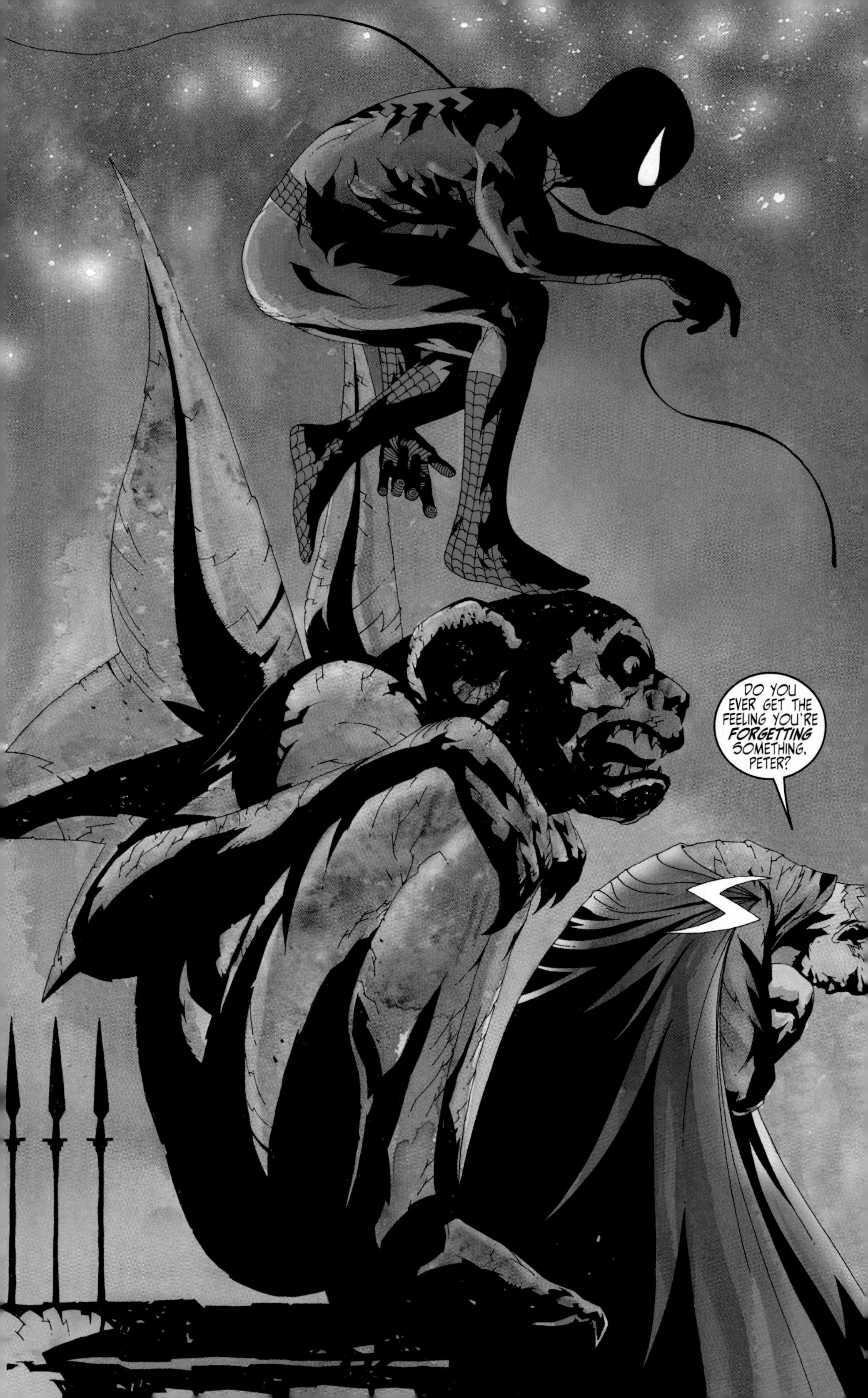
DO YOU EVER GET THE FEELING YOU'RE *FORGETTING* SOMETHING, PETER?

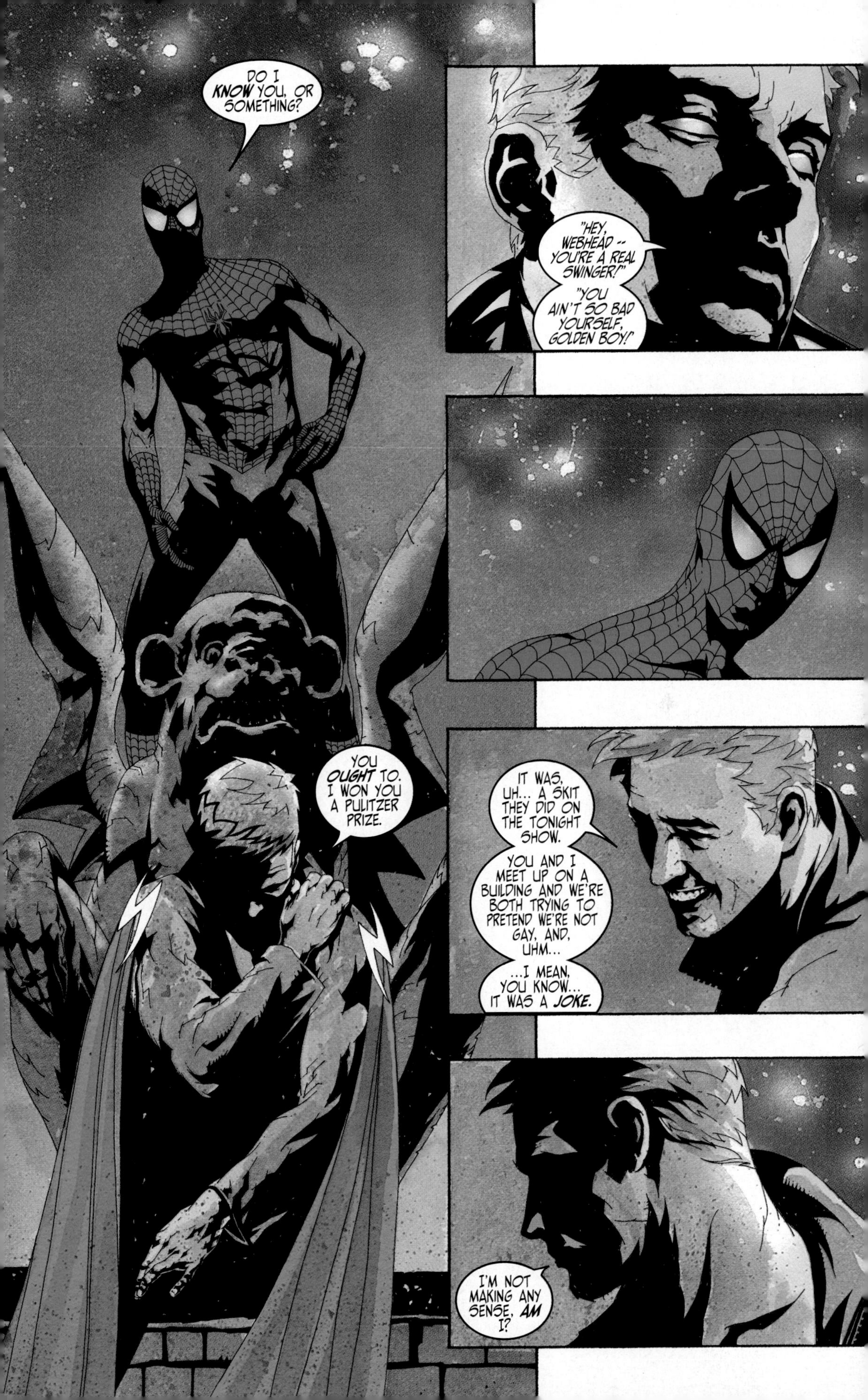
DO I KNOW YOU, OR SOMETHING?
YOU OUGHT TO. I WON YOU A PULITZER PRIZE.
"HEY, WEBHEAD -- YOU'RE A REAL SWINGER!"
"YOU AIN'T SO BAD YOURSELF, GOLDEN BOY!"
IT WAS, UH... A SKIT THEY DID ON THE TONIGHT SHOW.
YOU AND I MEET UP ON A BUILDING AND WE'RE BOTH TRYING TO PRETEND WE'RE NOT GAY, AND, UHM...
...I MEAN, YOU KNOW... IT WAS A JOKE.
I'M NOT MAKING ANY SENSE, AM I?

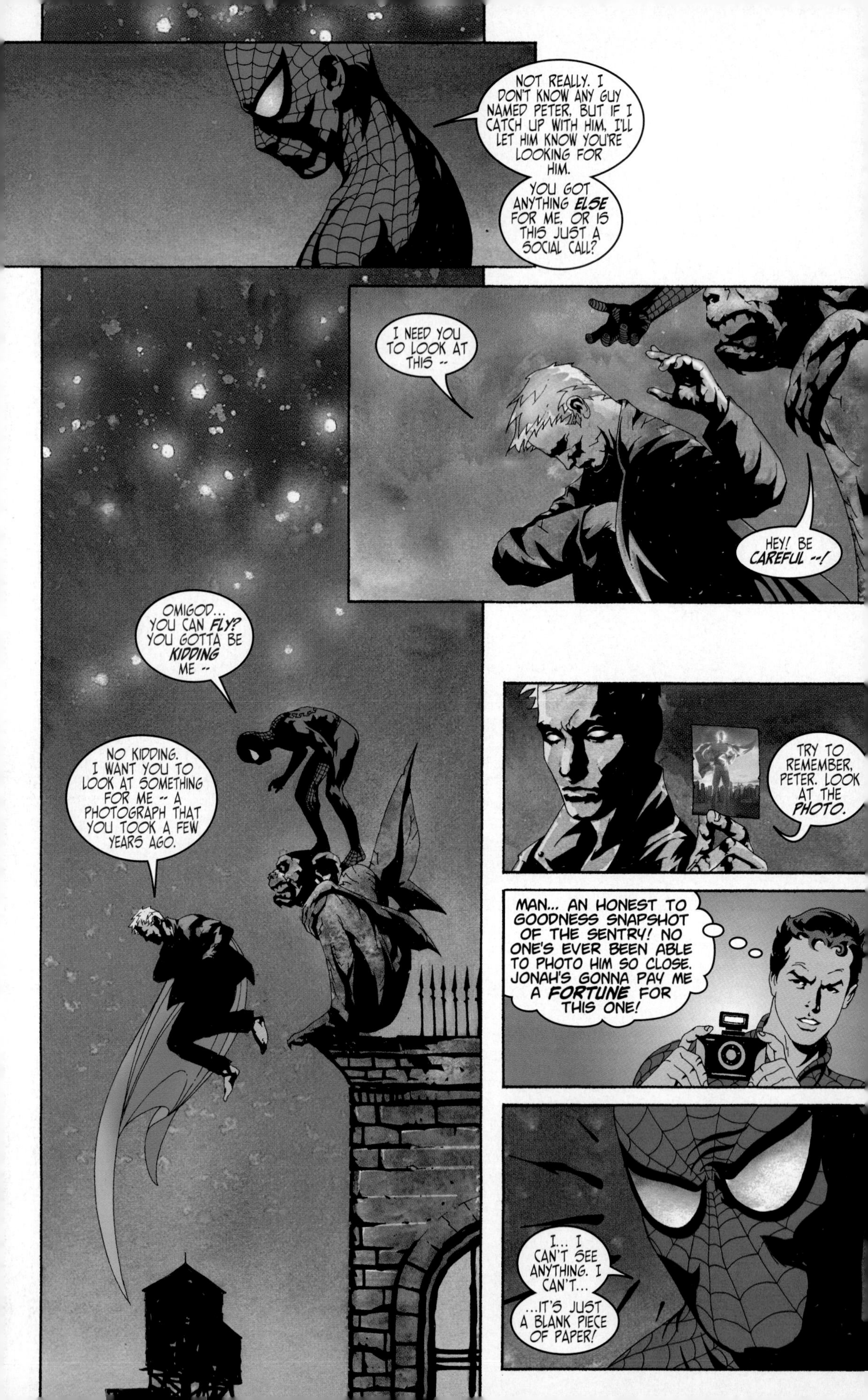
NOT REALLY. I DON'T KNOW ANY GUY NAMED PETER, BUT IF I CATCH UP WITH HIM, I'LL LET HIM KNOW YOU'RE LOOKING FOR HIM.
YOU GOT ANYTHING ELSE FOR ME, OR IS THIS JUST A SOCIAL CALL?
I NEED YOU TO LOOK AT THIS --
HEY! BE CAREFUL --!
OMIGOD... YOU CAN FLY? YOU GOTTA BE KIDDING ME --
NO KIDDING. I WANT YOU TO LOOK AT SOMETHING FOR ME -- A PHOTOGRAPH THAT YOU TOOK A FEW YEARS AGO.
TRY TO REMEMBER, PETER. LOOK AT THE PHOTO.
MAN... AN HONEST TO GOODNESS SNAPSHOT OF THE SENTRY! NO ONE'S EVER BEEN ABLE TO PHOTO HIM SO CLOSE. JONAH'S GONNA PAY ME A FORTUNE FOR THIS ONE!
I... I CAN'T SEE ANYTHING. I CAN'T...
...IT'S JUST A BLANK PIECE OF PAPER!

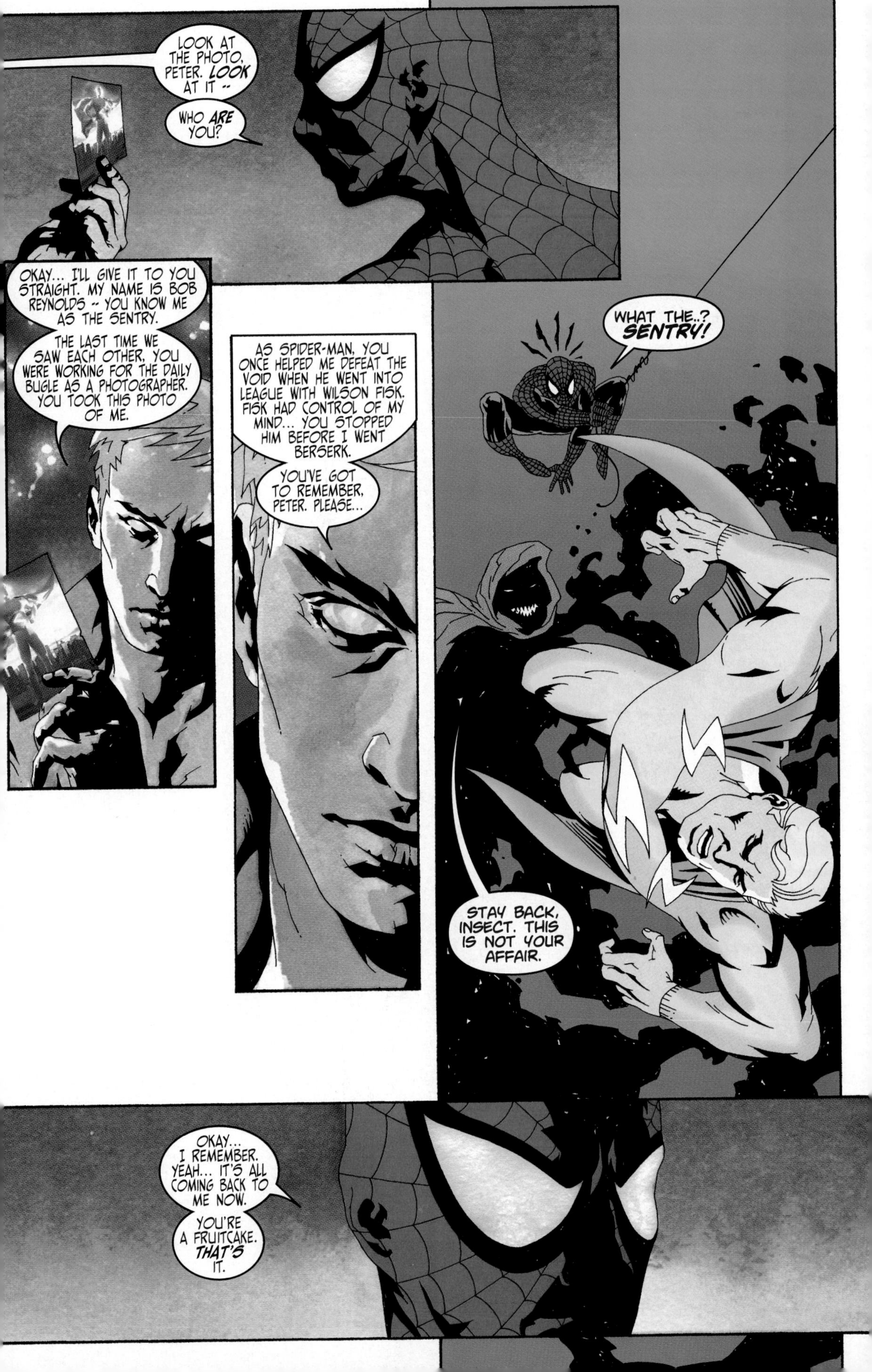

LOOK AT THE PHOTO, PETER. LOOK AT IT --
WHO ARE YOU?
OKAY... I'LL GIVE IT TO YOU STRAIGHT. MY NAME IS BOB REYNOLDS -- YOU KNOW ME AS THE SENTRY.
THE LAST TIME WE SAW EACH OTHER, YOU WERE WORKING FOR THE DAILY BUGLE AS A PHOTOGRAPHER. YOU TOOK THIS PHOTO OF ME.
AS SPIDER-MAN, YOU ONCE HELPED ME DEFEAT THE VOID WHEN HE WENT INTO LEAGUE WITH WILSON FISK. FISK HAD CONTROL OF MY MIND... YOU STOPPED HIM BEFORE I WENT BERSERK.
YOU'VE GOT TO REMEMBER, PETER. PLEASE...
WHAT THE..? SENTRY!
STAY BACK, INSECT. THIS IS NOT YOUR AFFAIR.
OKAY... I REMEMBER. YEAH... IT'S ALL COMING BACK TO ME NOW.
YOU'RE A FRUITCAKE. THAT'S IT.

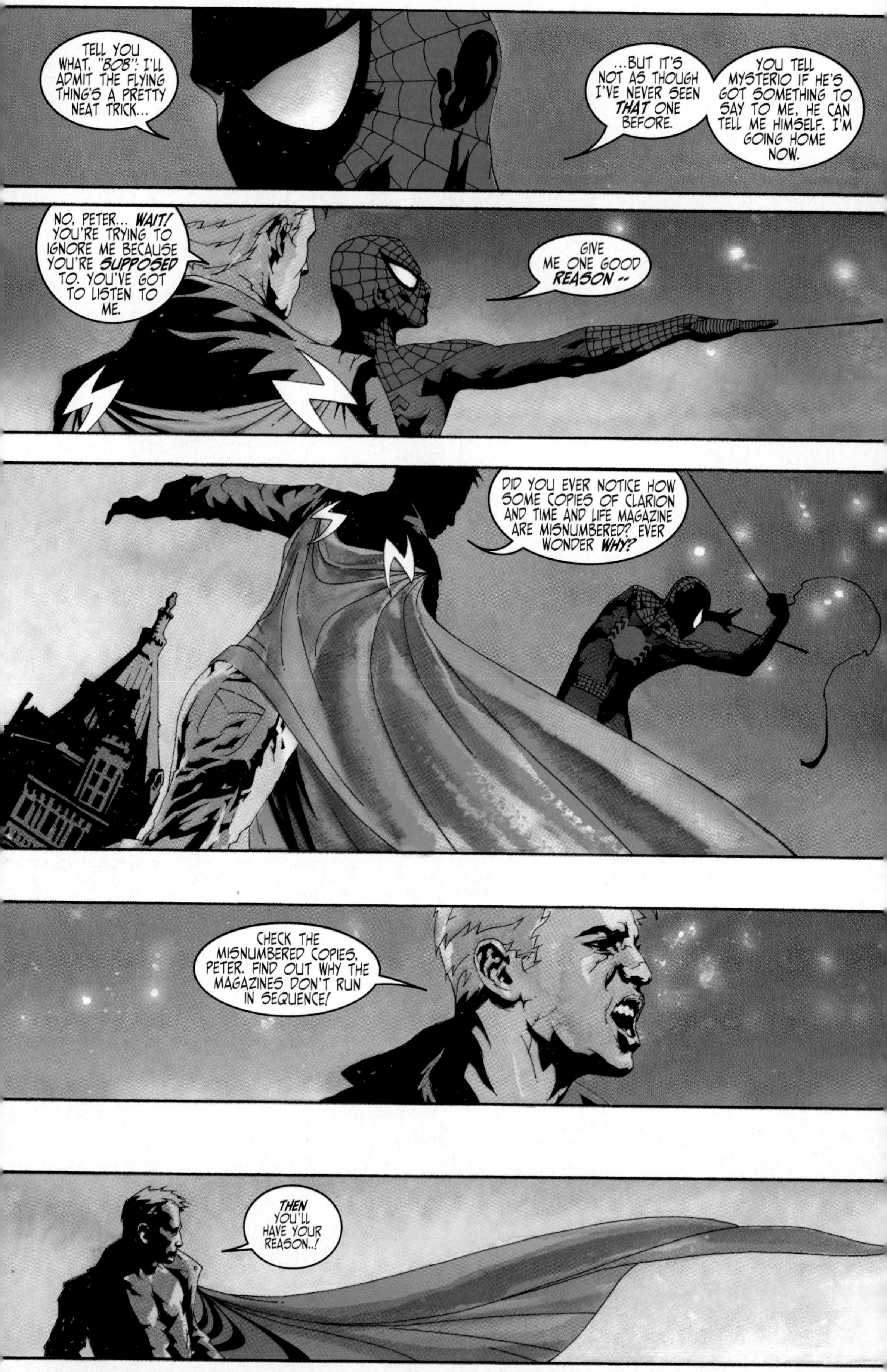
TELL YOU WHAT, "BOB": I'LL ADMIT THE FLYING THING'S A PRETTY NEAT TRICK...
...BUT IT'S NOT AS THOUGH I'VE NEVER SEEN THAT ONE BEFORE.
YOU TELL MYSTERIO IF HE'S GOT SOMETHING TO SAY TO ME, HE CAN TELL ME HIMSELF. I'M GOING HOME NOW.
NO, PETER... WAIT! YOU'RE TRYING TO IGNORE ME BECAUSE YOU'RE SUPPOSED TO. YOU'VE GOT TO LISTEN TO ME.
GIVE ME ONE GOOD REASON --
DID YOU EVER NOTICE HOW SOME COPIES OF CLARION AND TIME AND LIFE MAGAZINE ARE MISNUMBERED? EVER WONDER WHY?
CHECK THE MISNUMBERED COPIES, PETER. FIND OUT WHY THE MAGAZINES DON'T RUN IN SEQUENCE!
THEN YOU'LL HAVE YOUR REASON..!

SENTRY AVERTS
MINE SHAFT
DISASTER

TO MY BEST
FRIEND WITH
GRATITUDE
-ROBERT

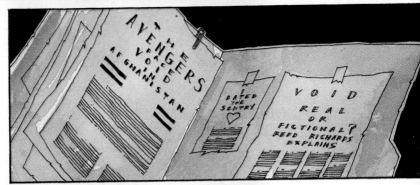

THE
AVENGERS
VOICE
VOID
AFGHANISTAN

I DATED
THE
SENTRY

VOID
REAL
OR
FICTIONAL?
REED RICHARDS
EXPLAINS

YES,
HE *DOES*
EXIST.

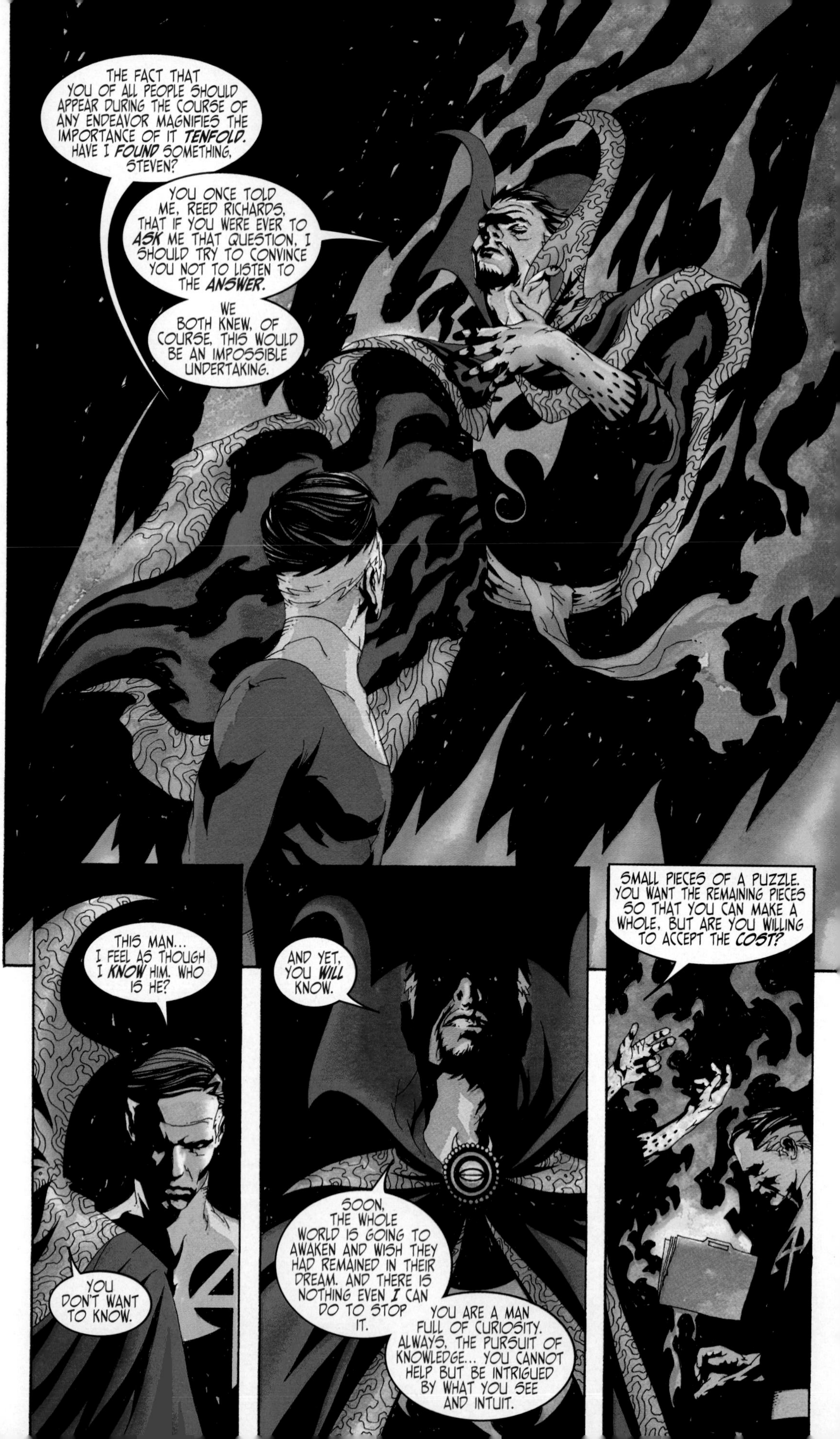
THE FACT THAT YOU OF ALL PEOPLE SHOULD APPEAR DURING THE COURSE OF ANY ENDEAVOR MAGNIFIES THE IMPORTANCE OF IT TENFOLD. HAVE I FOUND SOMETHING, STEVEN?
YOU ONCE TOLD ME, REED RICHARDS, THAT IF YOU WERE EVER TO ASK ME THAT QUESTION, I SHOULD TRY TO CONVINCE YOU NOT TO LISTEN TO THE ANSWER.
WE BOTH KNEW, OF COURSE, THIS WOULD BE AN IMPOSSIBLE UNDERTAKING.
THIS MAN... I FEEL AS THOUGH I KNOW HIM. WHO IS HE?
YOU DON'T WANT TO KNOW.
AND YET, YOU WILL KNOW.
SOON, THE WHOLE WORLD IS GOING TO AWAKEN AND WISH THEY HAD REMAINED IN THEIR DREAM. AND THERE IS NOTHING EVEN I CAN DO TO STOP IT.
YOU ARE A MAN FULL OF CURIOSITY. ALWAYS, THE PURSUIT OF KNOWLEDGE... YOU CANNOT HELP BUT BE INTRIGUED BY WHAT YOU SEE AND INTUIT.
SMALL PIECES OF A PUZZLE. YOU WANT THE REMAINING PIECES SO THAT YOU CAN MAKE A WHOLE, BUT ARE YOU WILLING TO ACCEPT THE COST?

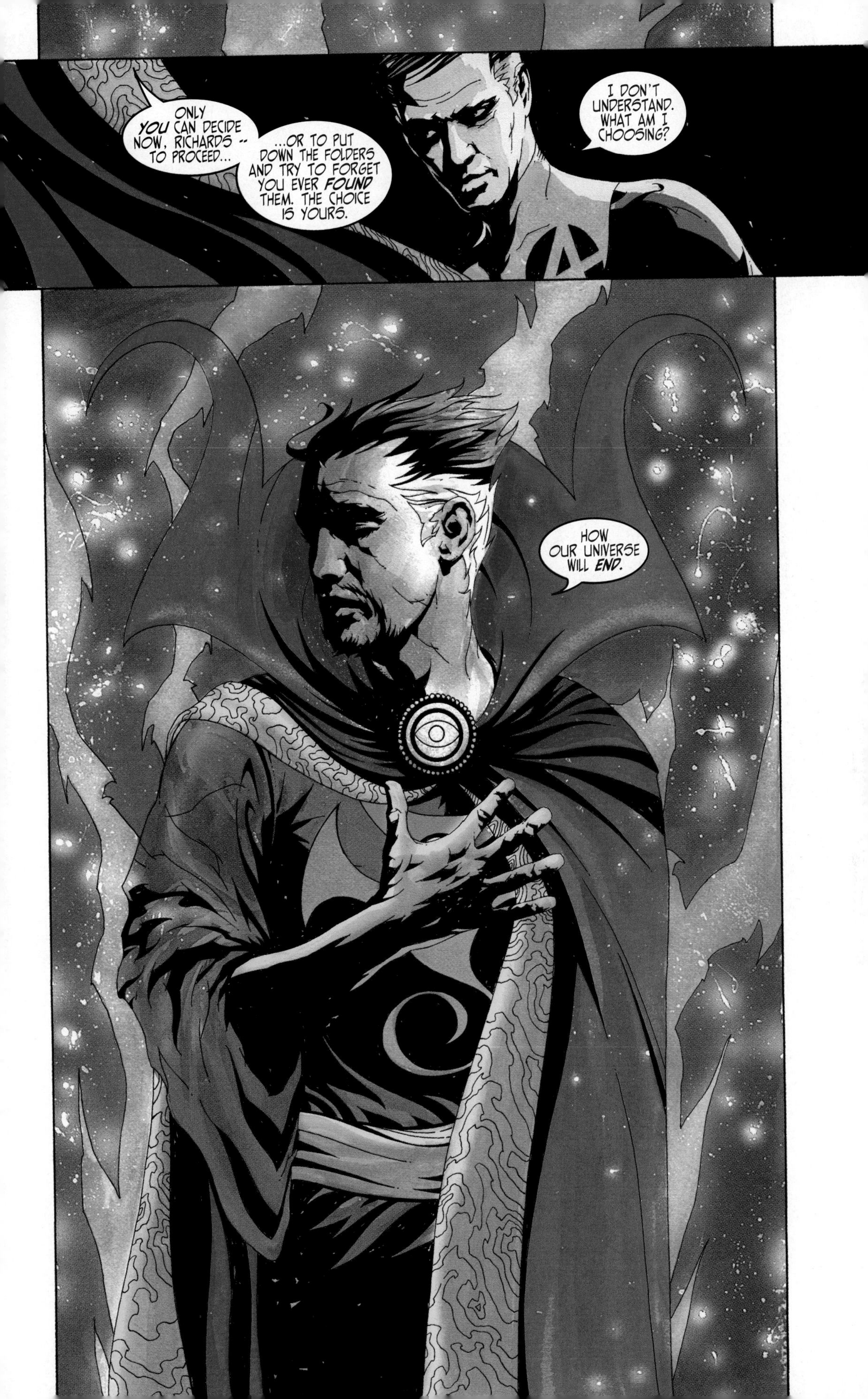
ONLY YOU CAN DECIDE NOW, RICHARDS -- TO PROCEED...
...OR TO PUT DOWN THE FOLDERS AND TRY TO FORGET YOU EVER FOUND THEM. THE CHOICE IS YOURS.
I DON'T UNDERSTAND. WHAT AM I CHOOSING?
HOW OUR UNIVERSE WILL END.

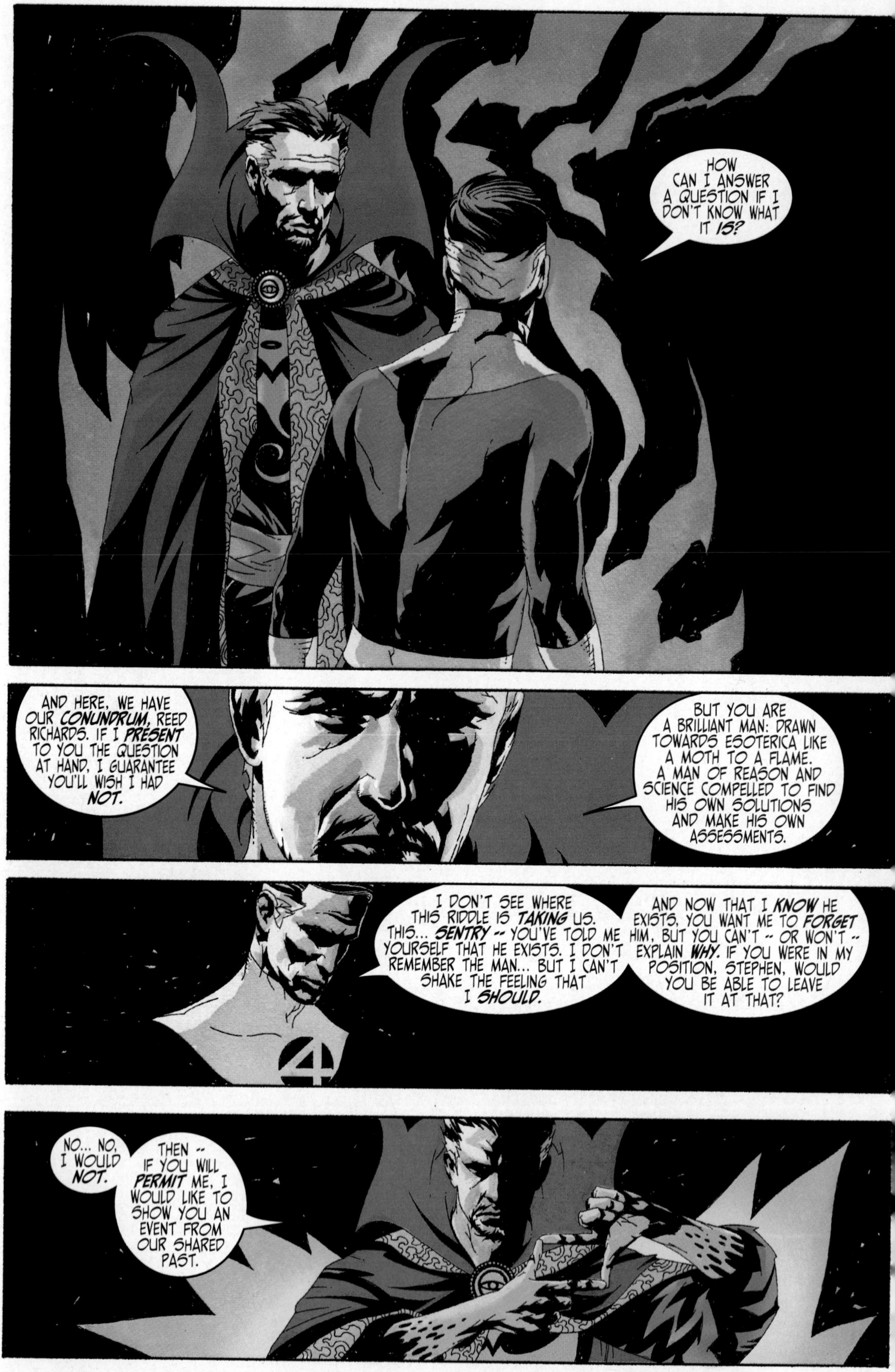
HOW CAN I ANSWER A QUESTION IF I DON'T KNOW WHAT IT IS?
AND HERE, WE HAVE OUR CONUNDRUM, REED RICHARDS. IF I PRESENT TO YOU THE QUESTION AT HAND, I GUARANTEE YOU'LL WISH I HAD NOT.
BUT YOU ARE A BRILLIANT MAN: DRAWN TOWARDS ESOTERICA LIKE A MOTH TO A FLAME. A MAN OF REASON AND SCIENCE COMPELLED TO FIND HIS OWN SOLUTIONS AND MAKE HIS OWN ASSESSMENTS.
I DON'T SEE WHERE THIS RIDDLE IS TAKING US. THIS... SENTRY -- YOU'VE TOLD ME YOURSELF THAT HE EXISTS. I DON'T REMEMBER THE MAN... BUT I CAN'T SHAKE THE FEELING THAT I SHOULD.
AND NOW THAT I KNOW HE EXISTS, YOU WANT ME TO FORGET HIM, BUT YOU CAN'T -- OR WON'T -- EXPLAIN WHY. IF YOU WERE IN MY POSITION, STEPHEN, WOULD YOU BE ABLE TO LEAVE IT AT THAT?
NO... NO, I WOULD NOT.
THEN -- IF YOU WILL PERMIT ME, I WOULD LIKE TO SHOW YOU AN EVENT FROM OUR SHARED PAST.

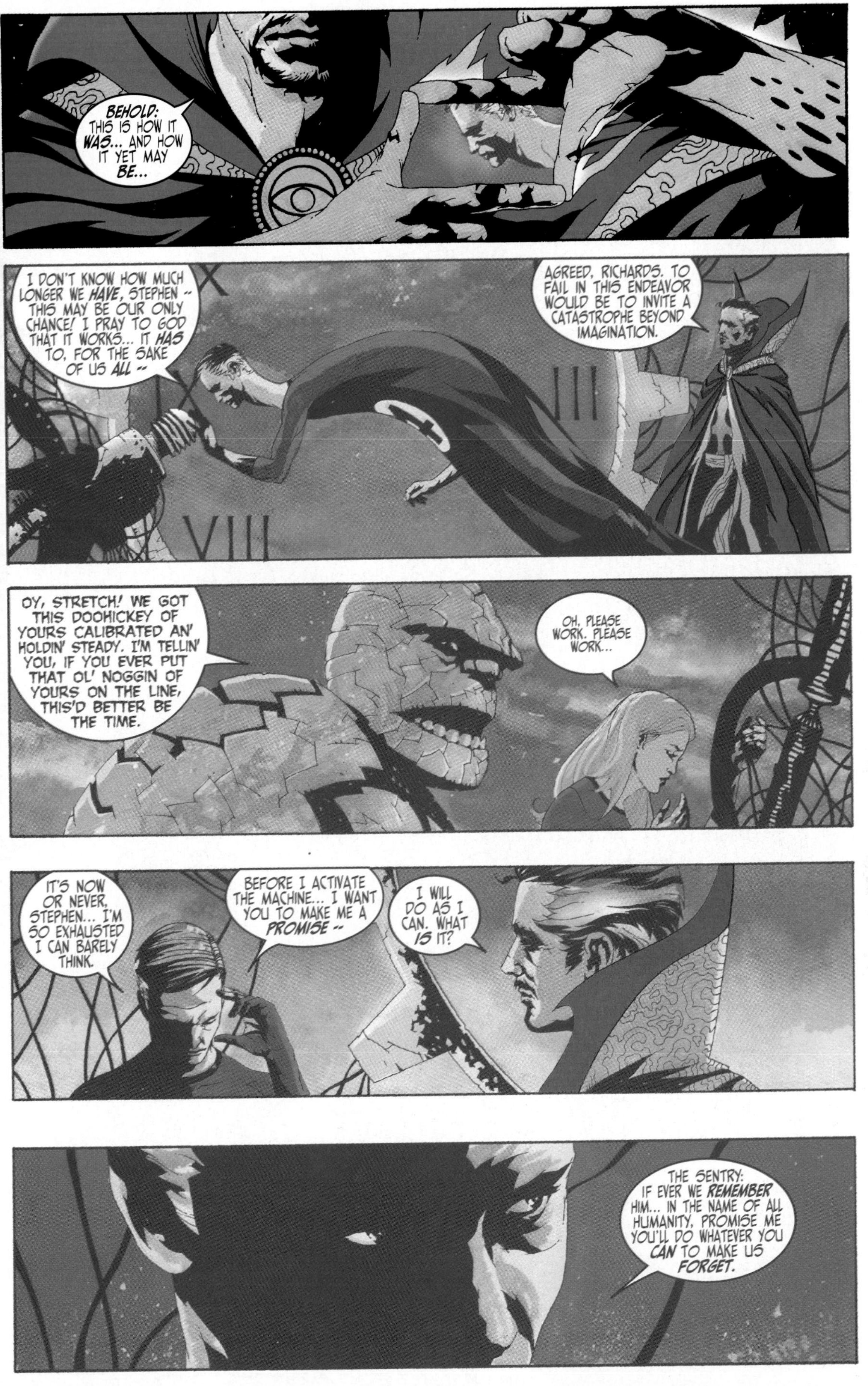

BEHOLD: THIS IS HOW IT WAS... AND HOW IT YET MAY BE...
I DON'T KNOW HOW MUCH LONGER WE HAVE, STEPHEN -- THIS MAY BE OUR ONLY CHANCE! I PRAY TO GOD THAT IT WORKS... IT HAS TO, FOR THE SAKE OF US ALL --
AGREED, RICHARDS. TO FAIL IN THIS ENDEAVOR WOULD BE TO INVITE A CATASTROPHE BEYOND IMAGINATION.
OY, STRETCH! WE GOT THIS DOOHICKEY OF YOURS CALIBRATED AN' HOLDIN' STEADY. I'M TELLIN' YOU, IF YOU EVER PUT THAT OL' NOGGIN OF YOURS ON THE LINE, THIS'D BETTER BE THE TIME.
OH, PLEASE WORK. PLEASE WORK...
IT'S NOW OR NEVER, STEPHEN... I'M SO EXHAUSTED I CAN BARELY THINK.
BEFORE I ACTIVATE THE MACHINE... I WANT YOU TO MAKE ME A PROMISE --
I WILL DO AS I CAN. WHAT IS IT?
THE SENTRY: IF EVER WE REMEMBER HIM... IN THE NAME OF ALL HUMANITY, PROMISE ME YOU'LL DO WHATEVER YOU CAN TO MAKE US FORGET.

IT WAS YOU. YOU DESTROYED THE VCR TAPE I MADE... BECAUSE I *ASKED* YOU TO? BECAUSE IT WOULD HAVE TOLD ME ABOUT THE SENTRY?

YES.

WHICH BRINGS US BACK TO OUR CONUNDRUM: "HOW CAN I ANSWER A QUESTION," YOU SAID, "IF I DON'T KNOW WHAT IT *IS*?"

PAUL JENKINS
STORY

JAE LEE
ART

JOSE VILLARRUBIA
COLORS

RS&COMICRAFT'S WES ABBOTT
LETTERS

KELLY LAMY
ASSISTANT EDITOR

NANCI DAKESIAN
EDITOR

JOE QUESADA
EDITOR IN CHIEF

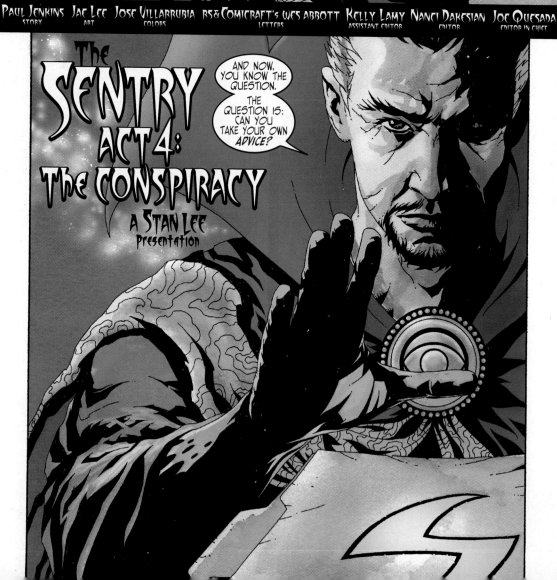

The SENTRY ACT 4: The CONSPIRACY

A STAN LEE Presentation

AND NOW, YOU KNOW THE QUESTION.

THE QUESTION IS: CAN YOU TAKE YOUR OWN *ADVICE?*

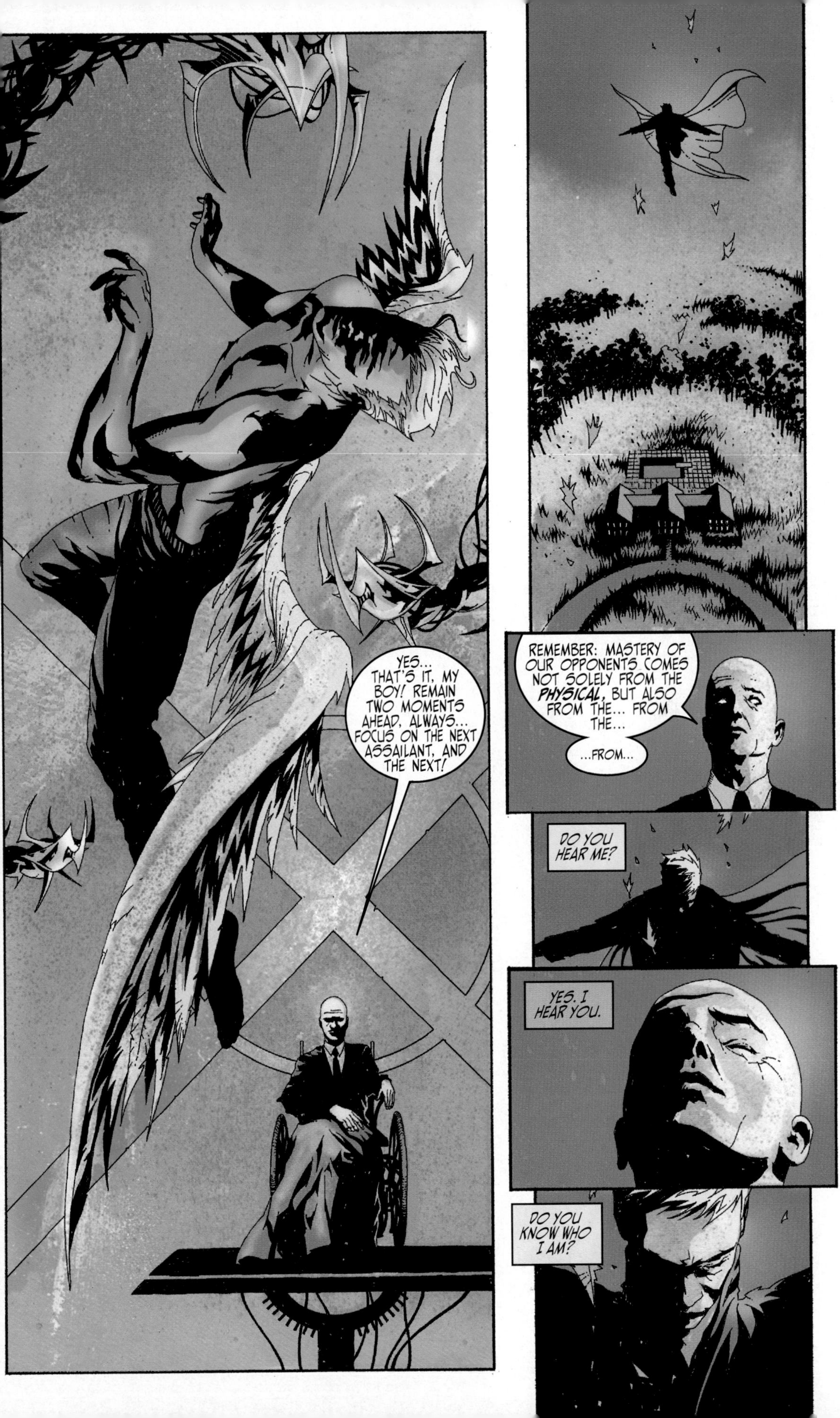
YES... THAT'S IT, MY BOY! REMAIN TWO MOMENTS AHEAD, ALWAYS... FOCUS ON THE NEXT ASSAILANT, AND THE NEXT!
REMEMBER: MASTERY OF OUR OPPONENTS COMES NOT SOLELY FROM THE PHYSICAL, BUT ALSO FROM THE... FROM THE...
...FROM...
DO YOU HEAR ME?
YES. I HEAR YOU.
DO YOU KNOW WHO I AM?

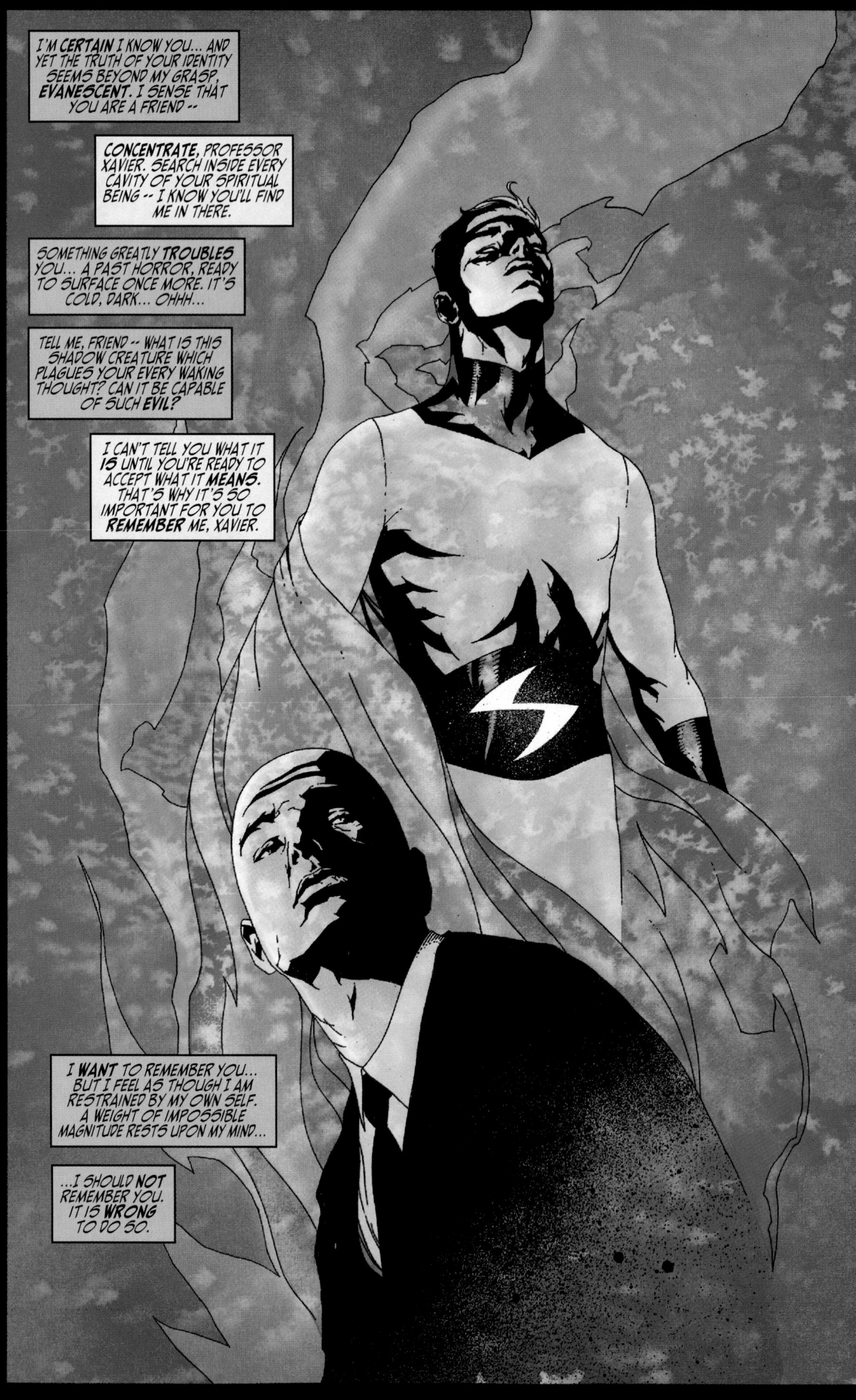
I'M CERTAIN I KNOW YOU... AND YET THE TRUTH OF YOUR IDENTITY SEEMS BEYOND MY GRASP, EVANESCENT. I SENSE THAT YOU ARE A FRIEND --
CONCENTRATE, PROFESSOR XAVIER. SEARCH INSIDE EVERY CAVITY OF YOUR SPIRITUAL BEING -- I KNOW YOU'LL FIND ME IN THERE.
SOMETHING GREATLY TROUBLES YOU... A PAST HORROR, READY TO SURFACE ONCE MORE. IT'S COLD, DARK... OHHH...
TELL ME, FRIEND -- WHAT IS THIS SHADOW CREATURE WHICH PLAGUES YOUR EVERY WAKING THOUGHT? CAN IT BE CAPABLE OF SUCH EVIL?
I CAN'T TELL YOU WHAT IT IS UNTIL YOU'RE READY TO ACCEPT WHAT IT MEANS. THAT'S WHY IT'S SO IMPORTANT FOR YOU TO REMEMBER ME, XAVIER.
I WANT TO REMEMBER YOU... BUT I FEEL AS THOUGH I AM RESTRAINED BY MY OWN SELF. A WEIGHT OF IMPOSSIBLE MAGNITUDE RESTS UPON MY MIND...
...I SHOULD NOT REMEMBER YOU. IT IS WRONG TO DO SO.

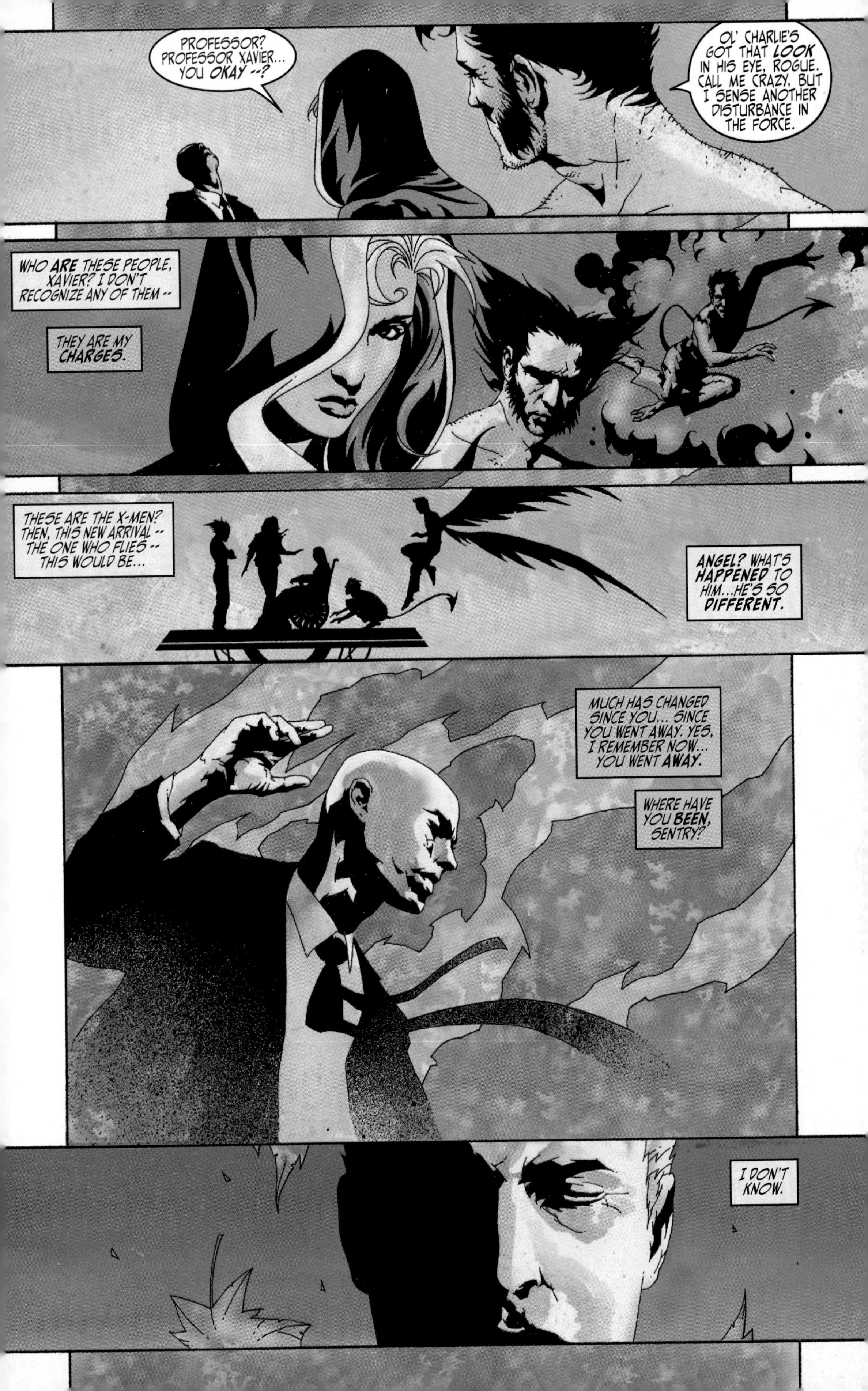
PROFESSOR? PROFESSOR XAVIER... YOU OKAY --?
OL' CHARLIE'S GOT THAT LOOK IN HIS EYE, ROGUE. CALL ME CRAZY, BUT I SENSE ANOTHER DISTURBANCE IN THE FORCE.
WHO ARE THESE PEOPLE, XAVIER? I DON'T RECOGNIZE ANY OF THEM --
THEY ARE MY CHARGES.
THESE ARE THE X-MEN? THEN, THIS NEW ARRIVAL -- THE ONE WHO FLIES -- THIS WOULD BE...
ANGEL? WHAT'S HAPPENED TO HIM...HE'S SO DIFFERENT.
MUCH HAS CHANGED SINCE YOU... SINCE YOU WENT AWAY. YES, I REMEMBER NOW... YOU WENT AWAY.
WHERE HAVE YOU BEEN, SENTRY?
I DON'T KNOW.

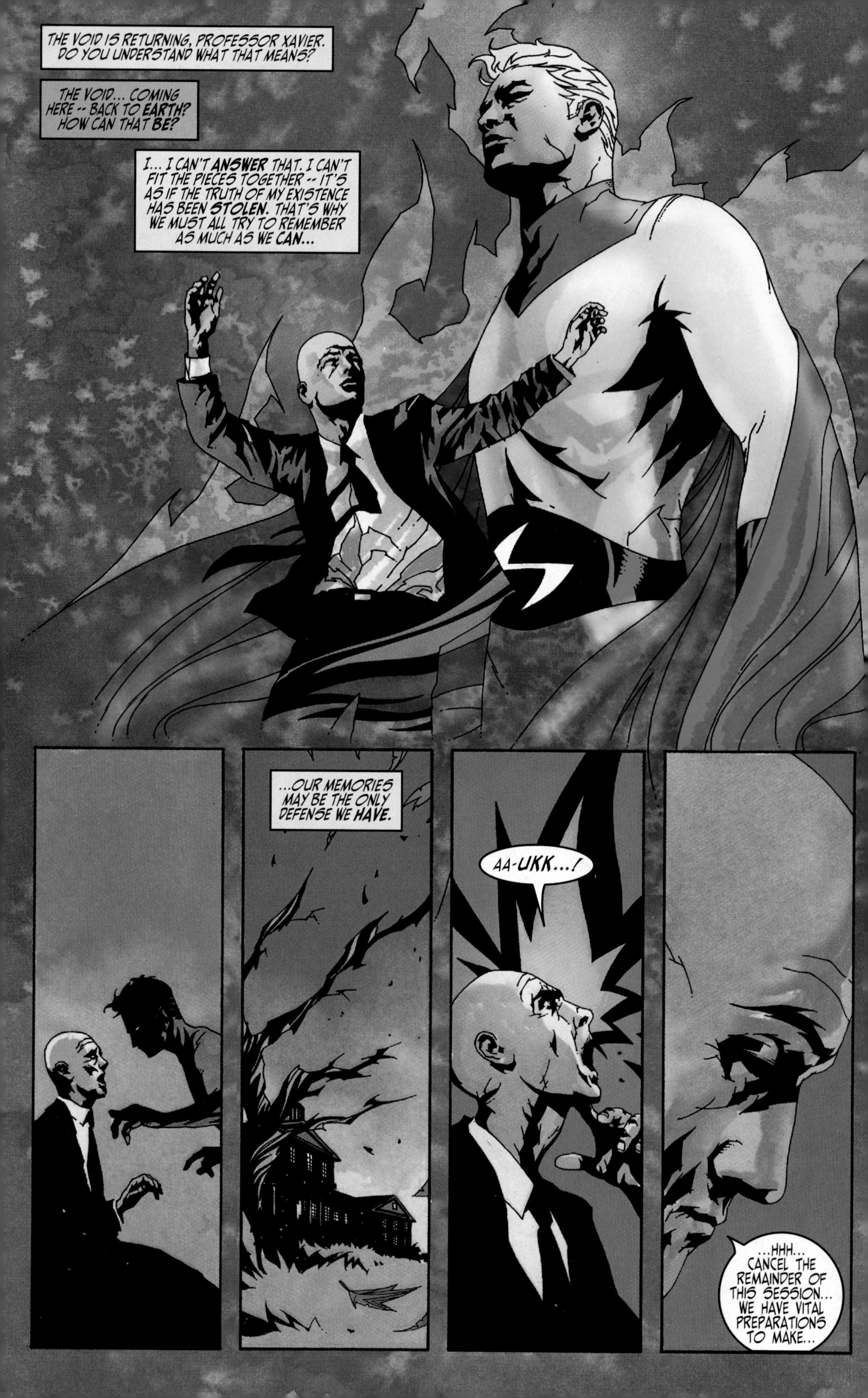
THE VOID IS RETURNING, PROFESSOR XAVIER. DO YOU UNDERSTAND WHAT THAT MEANS?
THE VOID... COMING HERE -- BACK TO EARTH? HOW CAN THAT BE?
I... I CAN'T ANSWER THAT. I CAN'T FIT THE PIECES TOGETHER -- IT'S AS IF THE TRUTH OF MY EXISTENCE HAS BEEN STOLEN. THAT'S WHY WE MUST ALL TRY TO REMEMBER AS MUCH AS WE CAN...
...OUR MEMORIES MAY BE THE ONLY DEFENSE WE HAVE.
AA-UKK...!
...HHH... CANCEL THE REMAINDER OF THIS SESSION... WE HAVE VITAL PREPARATIONS TO MAKE...

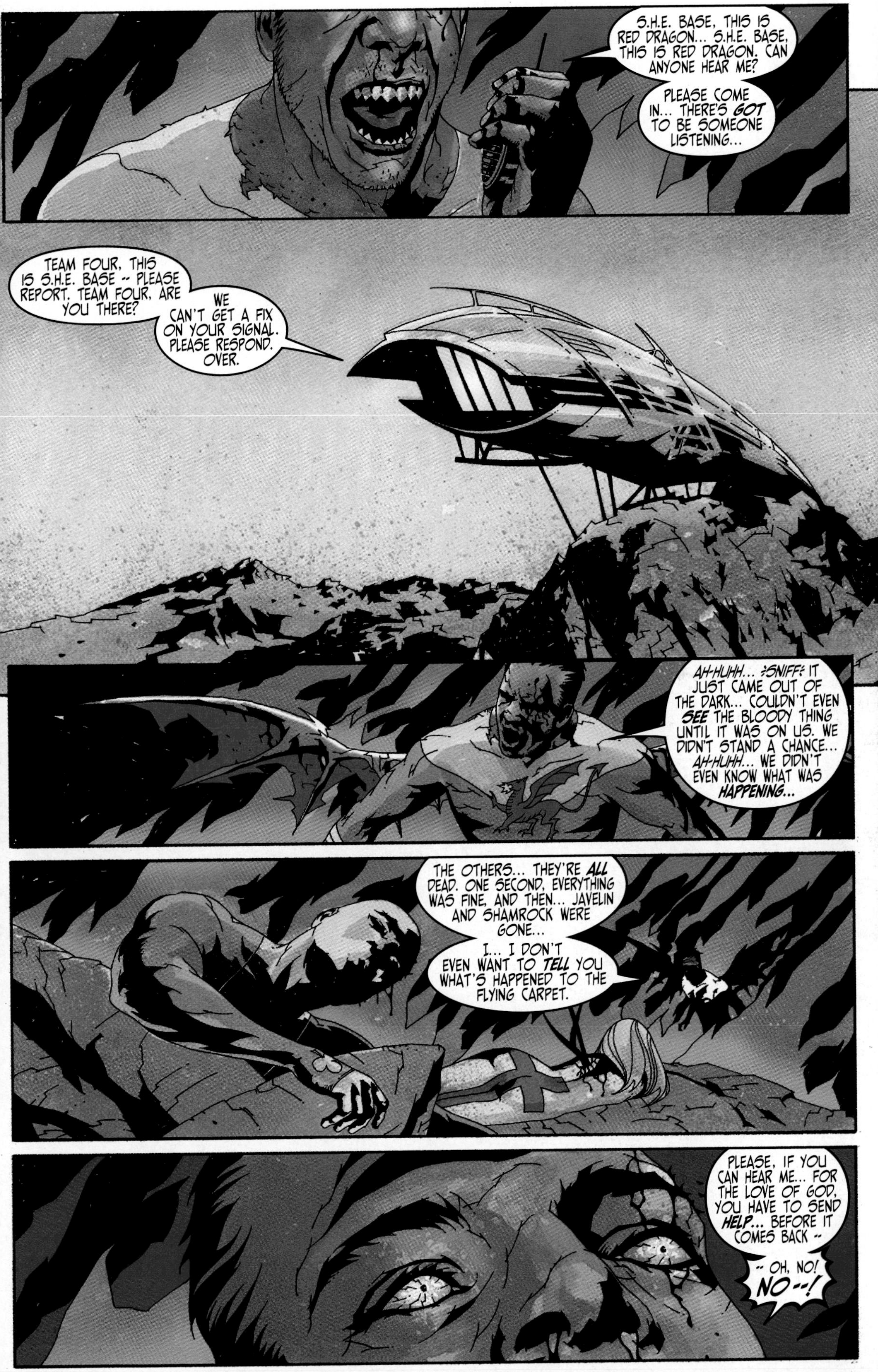

S.H.E. BASE, THIS IS RED DRAGON... S.H.E. BASE, THIS IS RED DRAGON. CAN ANYONE HEAR ME?
PLEASE COME IN... THERE'S *GOT* TO BE SOMEONE LISTENING...
TEAM FOUR, THIS IS S.H.E. BASE -- PLEASE REPORT. TEAM FOUR, ARE YOU THERE?
WE CAN'T GET A FIX ON YOUR SIGNAL. PLEASE RESPOND. OVER.
AH-HUHH... ≠SNIFF≠ IT JUST CAME OUT OF THE DARK... COULDN'T EVEN *SEE* THE BLOODY THING UNTIL IT WAS ON US. WE DIDN'T STAND A CHANCE... *AH-HUHH*... WE DIDN'T EVEN KNOW WHAT WAS *HAPPENING*...
THE OTHERS... THEY'RE *ALL* DEAD. ONE SECOND, EVERYTHING WAS FINE, AND THEN... JAVELIN AND SHAMROCK WERE GONE...
I... I DON'T EVEN WANT TO *TELL* YOU WHAT'S HAPPENED TO THE FLYING CARPET.
PLEASE, IF YOU CAN HEAR ME... FOR THE LOVE OF GOD, YOU HAVE TO SEND *HELP*... BEFORE IT COMES BACK --
-- OH, NO! *NO --!*

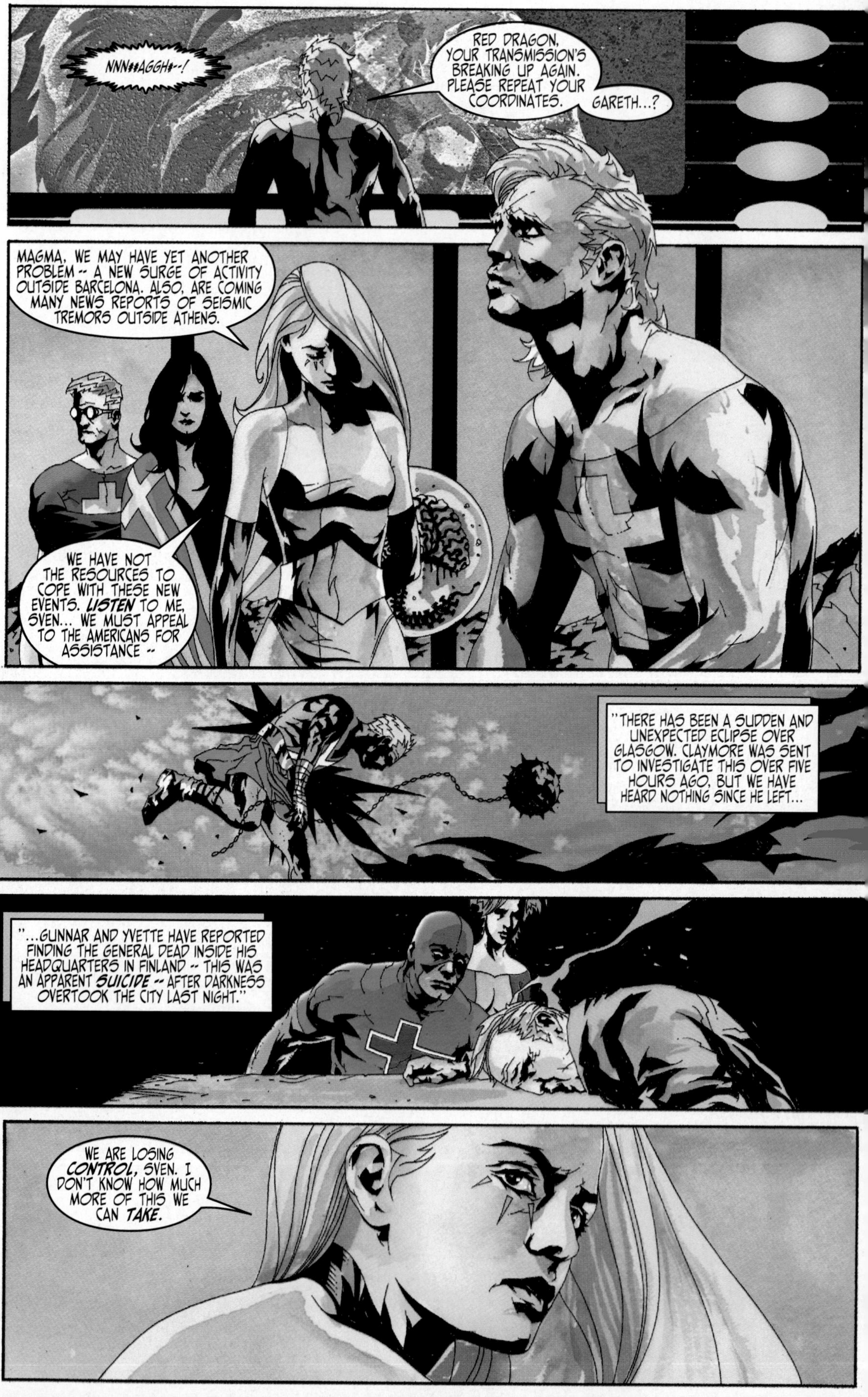
NNN##AGGH#--!
RED DRAGON, YOUR TRANSMISSION'S BREAKING UP AGAIN. PLEASE REPEAT YOUR COORDINATES.
GARETH...?
MAGMA, WE MAY HAVE YET ANOTHER PROBLEM -- A NEW SURGE OF ACTIVITY OUTSIDE BARCELONA. ALSO, ARE COMING MANY NEWS REPORTS OF SEISMIC TREMORS OUTSIDE ATHENS.
WE HAVE NOT THE RESOURCES TO COPE WITH THESE NEW EVENTS. LISTEN TO ME, SVEN... WE MUST APPEAL TO THE AMERICANS FOR ASSISTANCE --
"THERE HAS BEEN A SUDDEN AND UNEXPECTED ECLIPSE OVER GLASGOW. CLAYMORE WAS SENT TO INVESTIGATE THIS OVER FIVE HOURS AGO, BUT WE HAVE HEARD NOTHING SINCE HE LEFT...
"...GUNNAR AND YVETTE HAVE REPORTED FINDING THE GENERAL DEAD INSIDE HIS HEADQUARTERS IN FINLAND -- THIS WAS AN APPARENT SUICIDE -- AFTER DARKNESS OVERTOOK THE CITY LAST NIGHT."
WE ARE LOSING CONTROL, SVEN. I DON'T KNOW HOW MUCH MORE OF THIS WE CAN TAKE.

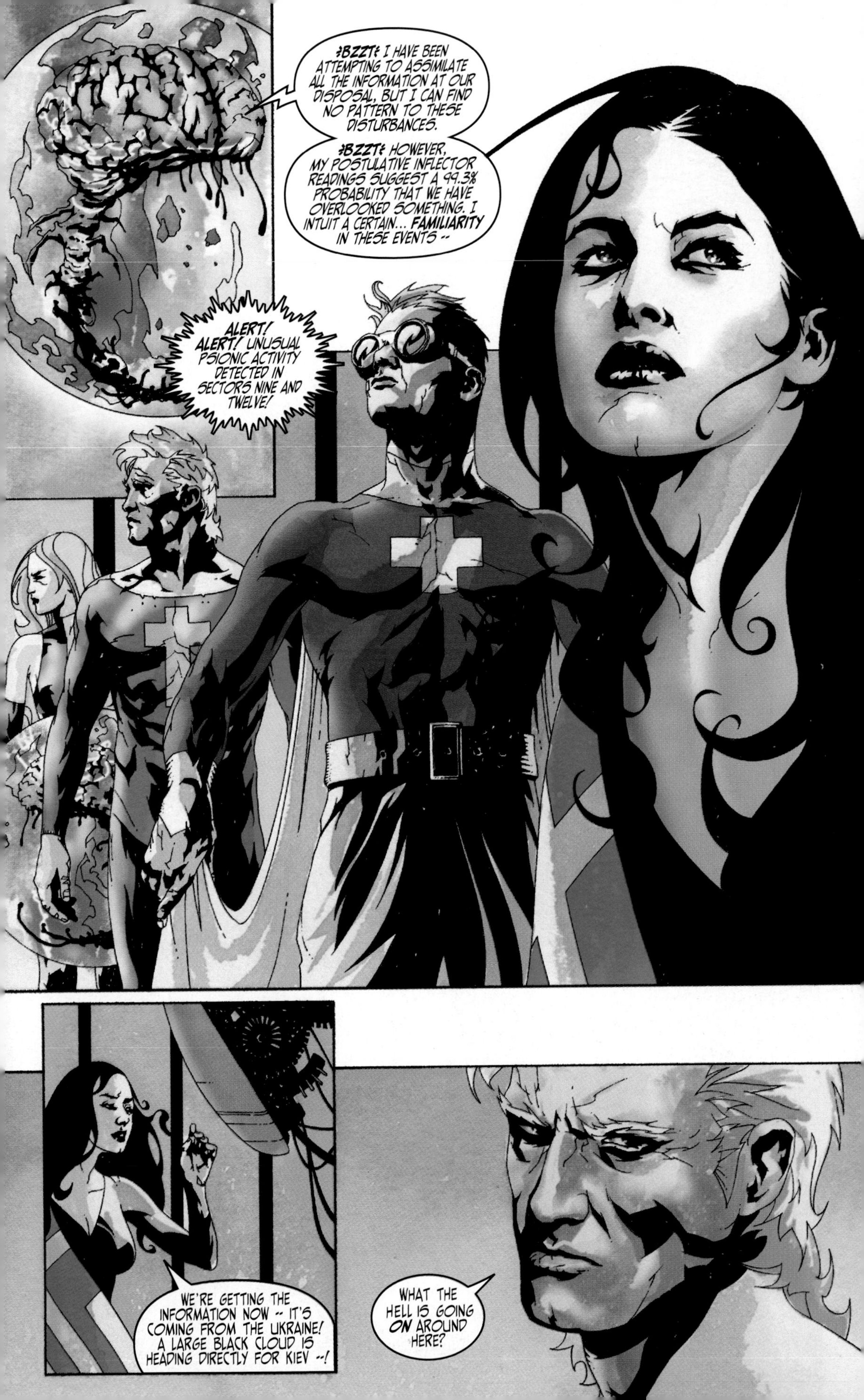

ƷBZZTƸ I HAVE BEEN ATTEMPTING TO ASSIMILATE ALL THE INFORMATION AT OUR DISPOSAL, BUT I CAN FIND NO PATTERN TO THESE DISTURBANCES.
ƷBZZTƸ HOWEVER, MY POSTULATIVE INFLECTOR READINGS SUGGEST A 99.3% PROBABILITY THAT WE HAVE OVERLOOKED SOMETHING. I INTUIT A CERTAIN... FAMILIARITY IN THESE EVENTS --
ALERT! ALERT! UNUSUAL PSIONIC ACTIVITY DETECTED IN SECTORS NINE AND TWELVE!
WE'RE GETTING THE INFORMATION NOW -- IT'S COMING FROM THE UKRAINE! A LARGE BLACK CLOUD IS HEADING DIRECTLY FOR KIEV --!
WHAT THE HELL IS GOING ON AROUND HERE?

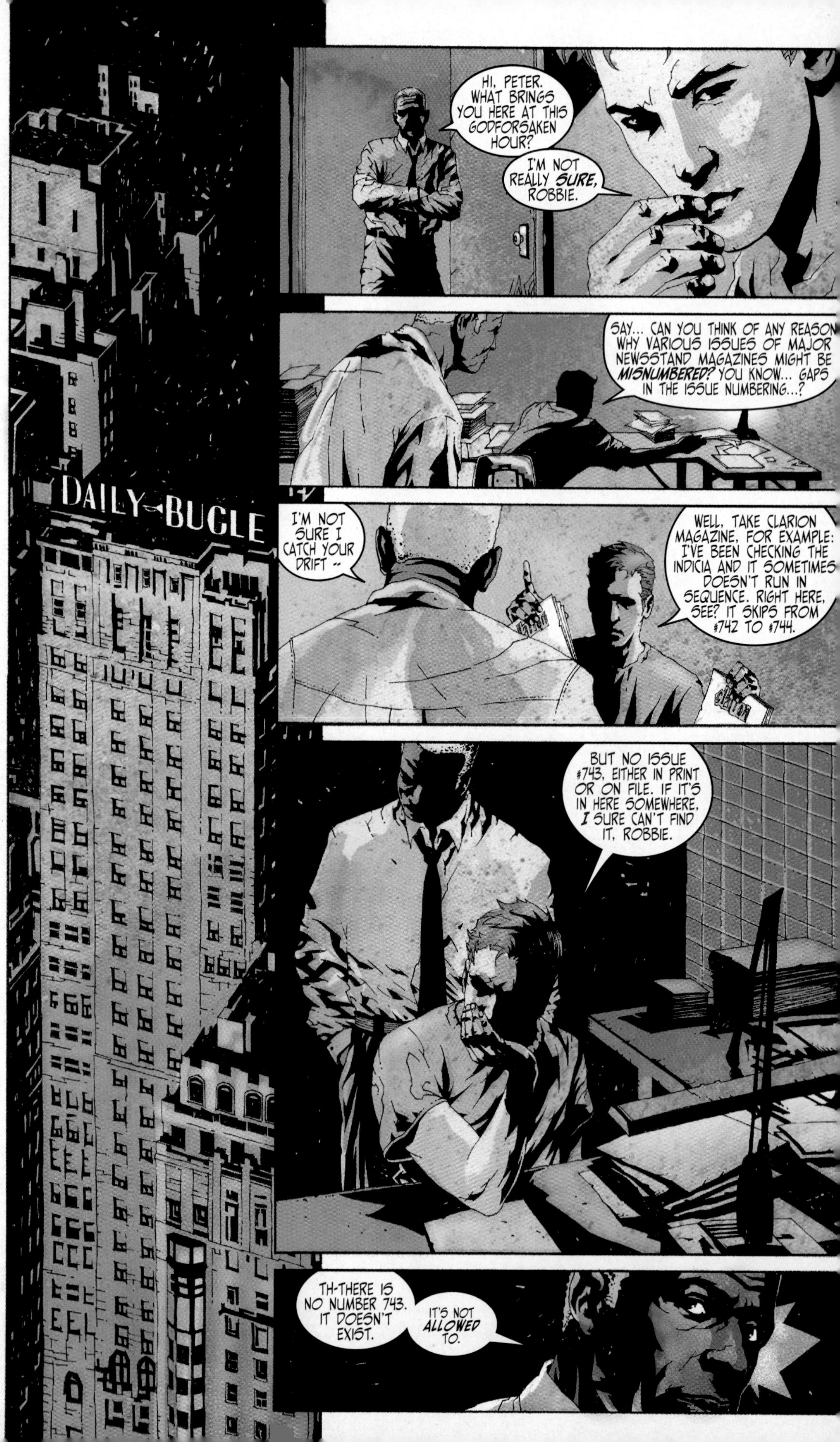
DAILY BUGLE
HI, PETER. WHAT BRINGS YOU HERE AT THIS GODFORSAKEN HOUR?
I'M NOT REALLY SURE, ROBBIE.
SAY... CAN YOU THINK OF ANY REASON WHY VARIOUS ISSUES OF MAJOR NEWSSTAND MAGAZINES MIGHT BE MISNUMBERED? YOU KNOW... GAPS IN THE ISSUE NUMBERING...?
I'M NOT SURE I CATCH YOUR DRIFT --
WELL, TAKE CLARION MAGAZINE, FOR EXAMPLE: I'VE BEEN CHECKING THE INDICIA AND IT SOMETIMES DOESN'T RUN IN SEQUENCE. RIGHT HERE, SEE? IT SKIPS FROM #742 TO #744.
BUT NO ISSUE #743, EITHER IN PRINT OR ON FILE. IF IT'S IN HERE SOMEWHERE, I SURE CAN'T FIND IT, ROBBIE.
TH-THERE IS NO NUMBER 743. IT DOESN'T EXIST.
IT'S NOT ALLOWED TO.

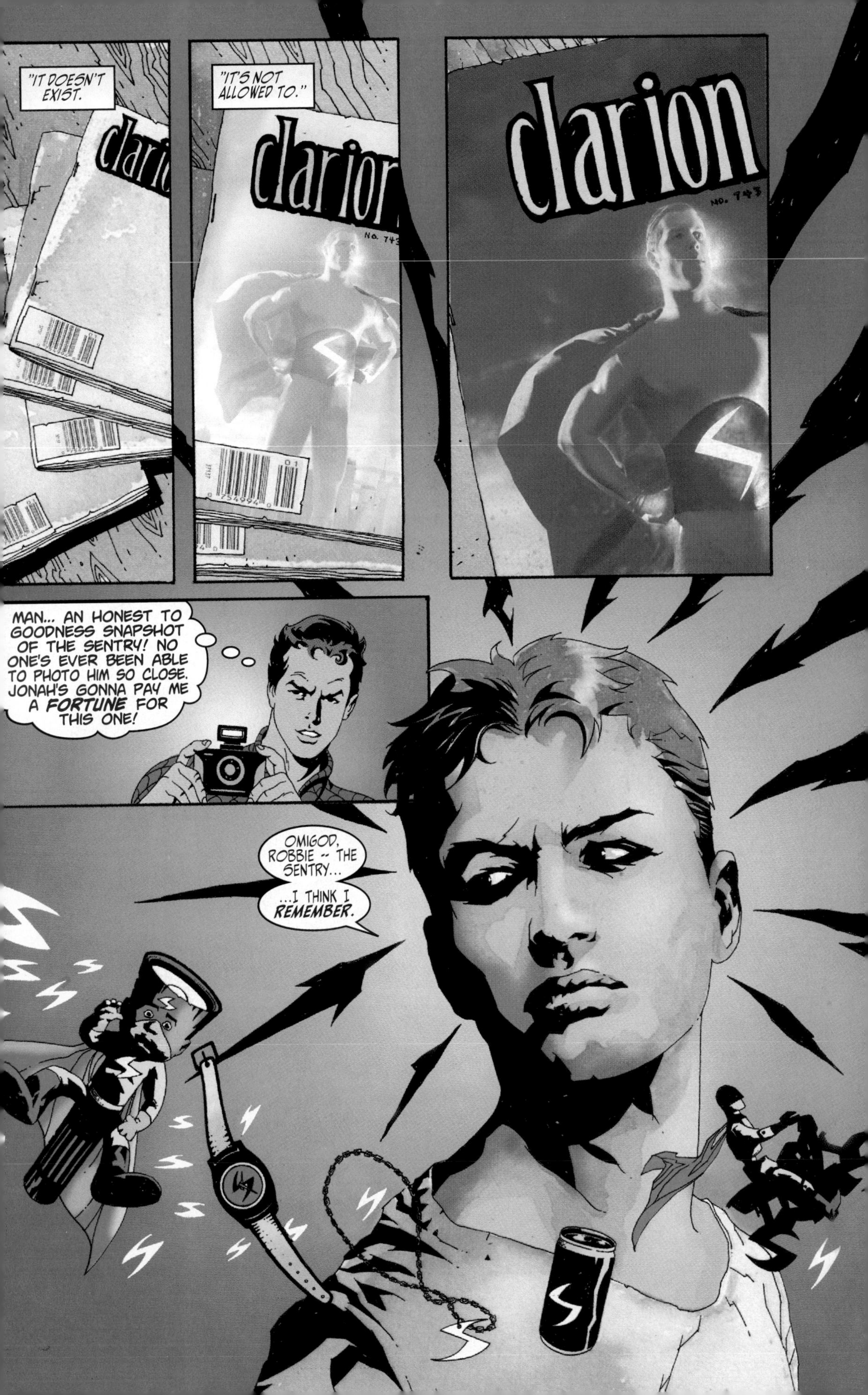
"IT DOESN'T EXIST.
"IT'S NOT ALLOWED TO."
clarion
clarion
NO. 743
clarion
NO. 743
MAN... AN HONEST TO GOODNESS SNAPSHOT OF THE SENTRY! NO ONE'S EVER BEEN ABLE TO PHOTO HIM SO CLOSE. JONAH'S GONNA PAY ME A FORTUNE FOR THIS ONE!
OMIGOD, ROBBIE -- THE SENTRY...
...I THINK I REMEMBER.

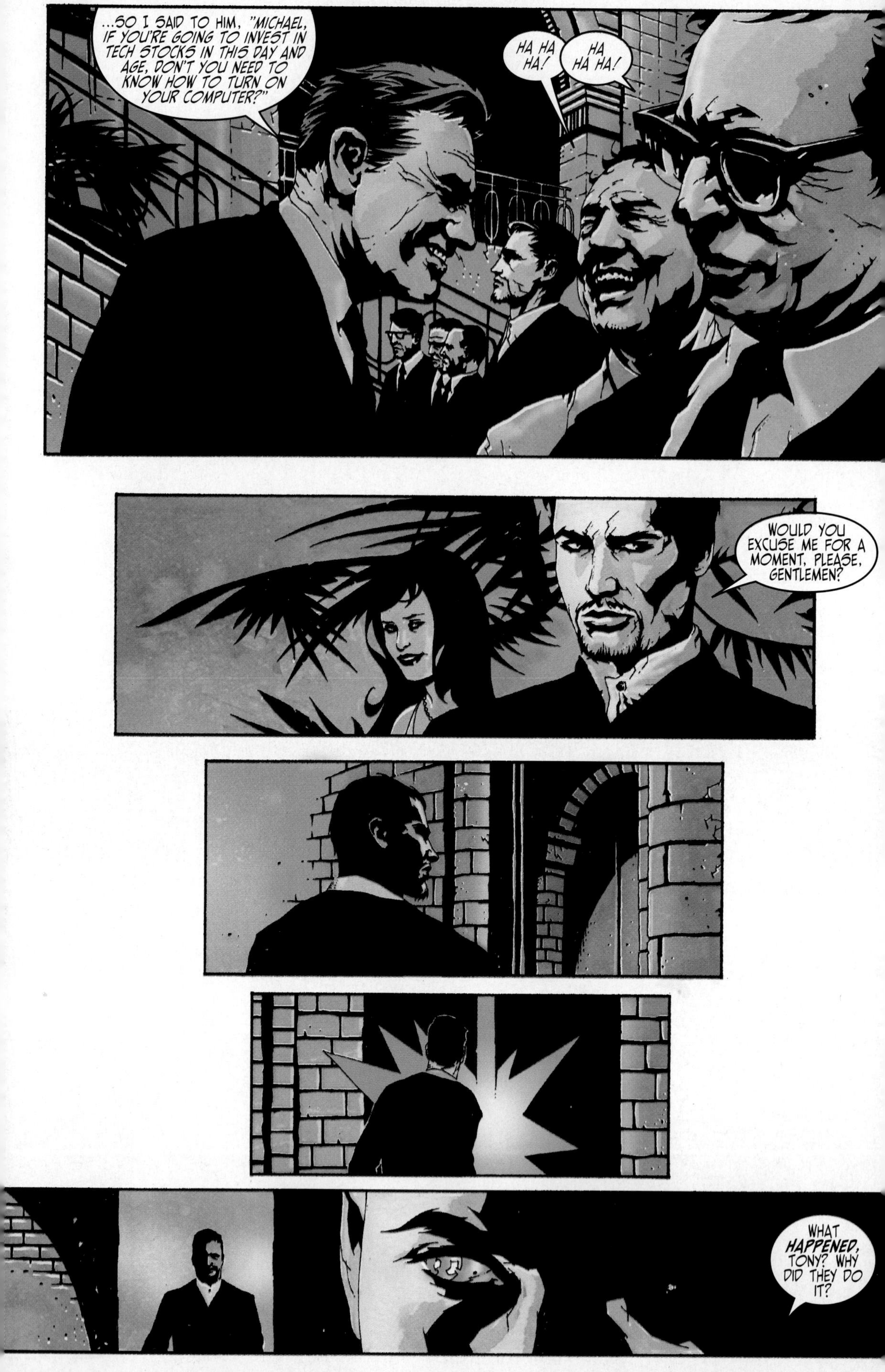
...SO I SAID TO HIM, "MICHAEL, IF YOU'RE GOING TO INVEST IN TECH STOCKS IN THIS DAY AND AGE, DON'T YOU NEED TO KNOW HOW TO TURN ON YOUR COMPUTER?"
HA HA HA!
HA HA HA!
WOULD YOU EXCUSE ME FOR A MOMENT, PLEASE, GENTLEMEN?
WHAT HAPPENED, TONY? WHY DID THEY DO IT?

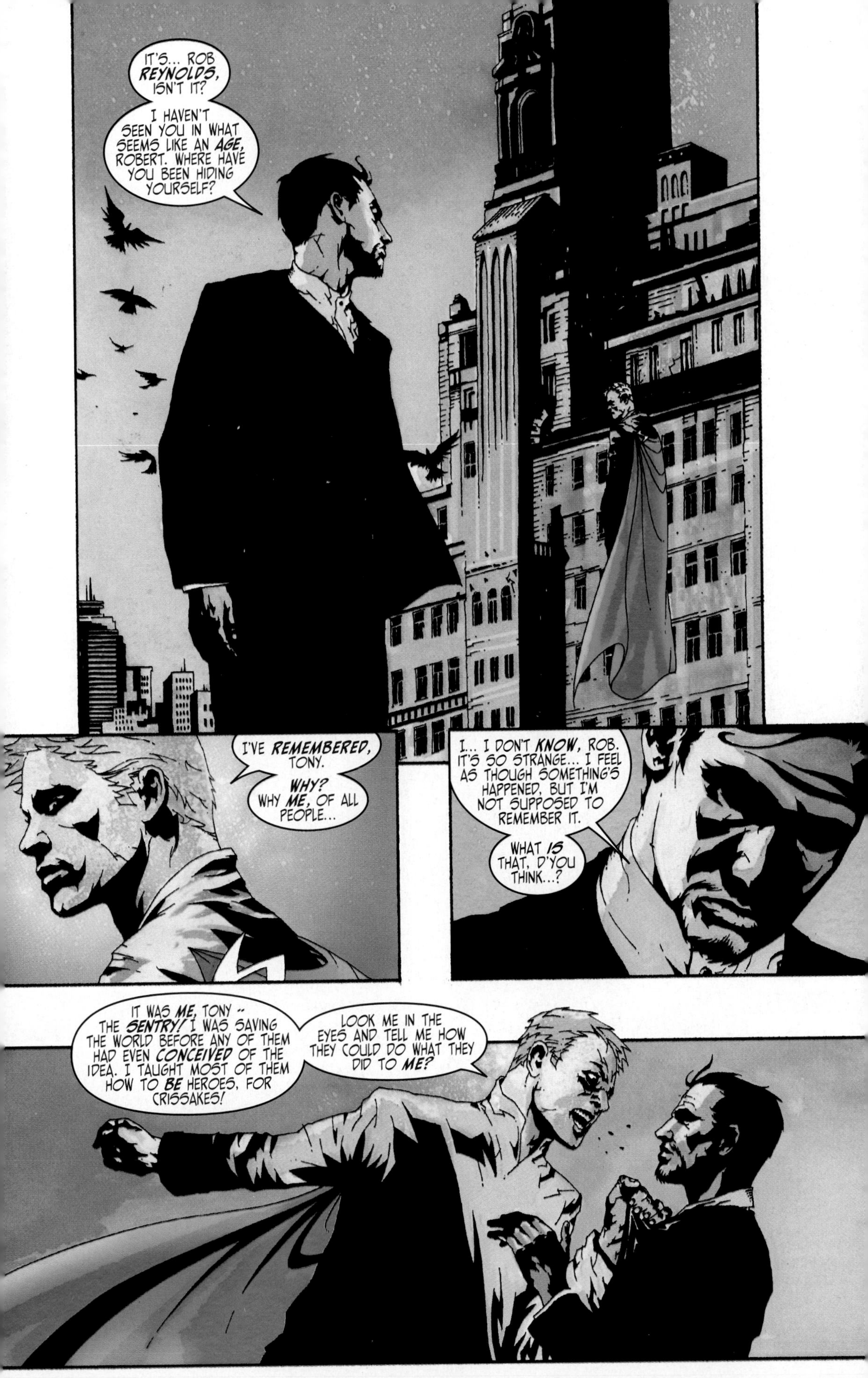
IT'S... ROB REYNOLDS, ISN'T IT?
I HAVEN'T SEEN YOU IN WHAT SEEMS LIKE AN AGE, ROBERT. WHERE HAVE YOU BEEN HIDING YOURSELF?
I'VE REMEMBERED, TONY.
WHY? WHY ME, OF ALL PEOPLE...
I... I DON'T KNOW, ROB. IT'S SO STRANGE... I FEEL AS THOUGH SOMETHING'S HAPPENED, BUT I'M NOT SUPPOSED TO REMEMBER IT.
WHAT IS THAT, D'YOU THINK...?
IT WAS ME, TONY -- THE SENTRY! I WAS SAVING THE WORLD BEFORE ANY OF THEM HAD EVEN CONCEIVED OF THE IDEA. I TAUGHT MOST OF THEM HOW TO BE HEROES, FOR CRISSAKES!
LOOK ME IN THE EYES AND TELL ME HOW THEY COULD DO WHAT THEY DID TO ME?

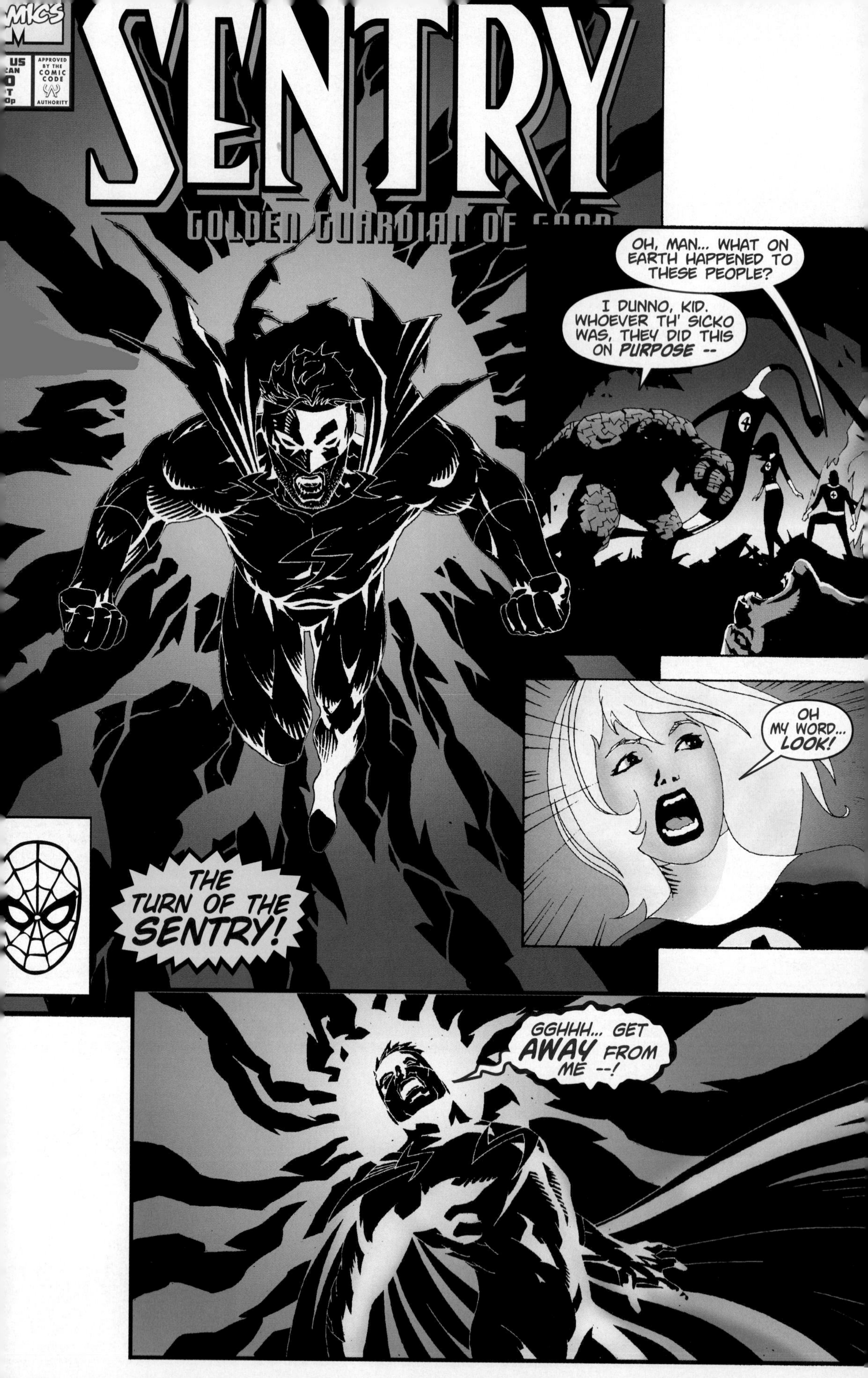
SENTRY
GOLDEN GUARDIAN OF GOOD
APPROVED BY THE COMIC CODE AUTHORITY
THE TURN OF THE SENTRY!
OH, MAN... WHAT ON EARTH HAPPENED TO THESE PEOPLE?
I DUNNO, KID. WHOEVER TH' SICKO WAS, THEY DID THIS ON PURPOSE --
OH MY WORD... LOOK!
GGHHH... GET AWAY FROM ME --!

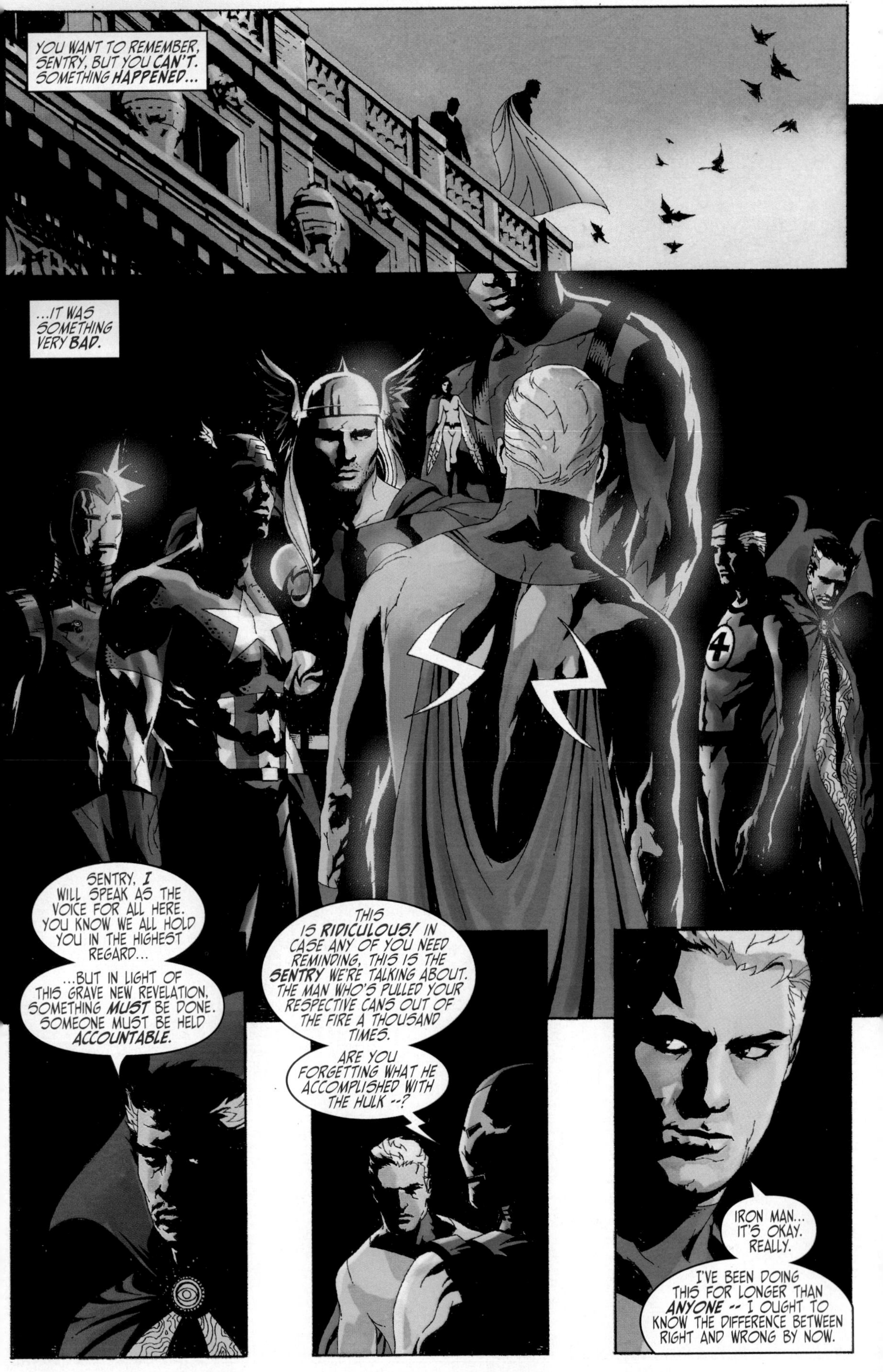
YOU WANT TO REMEMBER, SENTRY, BUT YOU CAN'T. SOMETHING HAPPENED...
...IT WAS SOMETHING VERY BAD.
SENTRY, I WILL SPEAK AS THE VOICE FOR ALL HERE. YOU KNOW WE ALL HOLD YOU IN THE HIGHEST REGARD...
...BUT IN LIGHT OF THIS GRAVE NEW REVELATION, SOMETHING MUST BE DONE. SOMEONE MUST BE HELD ACCOUNTABLE.
THIS IS RIDICULOUS! IN CASE ANY OF YOU NEED REMINDING, THIS IS THE SENTRY WE'RE TALKING ABOUT. THE MAN WHO'S PULLED YOUR RESPECTIVE CANS OUT OF THE FIRE A THOUSAND TIMES.
ARE YOU FORGETTING WHAT HE ACCOMPLISHED WITH THE HULK --?
IRON MAN... IT'S OKAY. REALLY.
I'VE BEEN DOING THIS FOR LONGER THAN ANYONE -- I OUGHT TO KNOW THE DIFFERENCE BETWEEN RIGHT AND WRONG BY NOW.

THE ENORMITY OF THY DEEDS ARE *KNOWN* TO US, SENTRY. BUT EQUALLY, THE SEVERITY OF THIS REVEALMENT DEFIES MEASURE.

HE'S RIGHT, ROBERT. YOU'VE BEEN RELYING MORE AND MORE ON THE *SERUM* OF LATE. CAN YOU HONESTLY SAY THAT ISN'T TRUE?

I URGE YOU TO RECONSIDER -- *ALL* OF YOU. THIS SITUATION CAN BE TURNED TO OUR ADVANTAGE -- I *KNOW* IT. THE VOID WOULDN'T *DARE* COME BACK TO EARTH AFTER THIS --

YOU DON'T KNOW THAT, SENTRY. NEITHER DO *WE*.

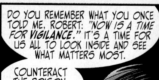

DO YOU REMEMBER WHAT YOU ONCE TOLD ME, ROBERT: *"NOW IS A TIME FOR VIGILANCE."* IT'S A TIME FOR US ALL TO LOOK INSIDE AND SEE WHAT MATTERS MOST.

COUNTERACT THE POISON. FOR THE SAKE OF *MANKIND.*

THEN IT'S *DECIDED.*

TO ALL INTENTS AND PURPOSES, THE SENTRY MUST *DIE.*

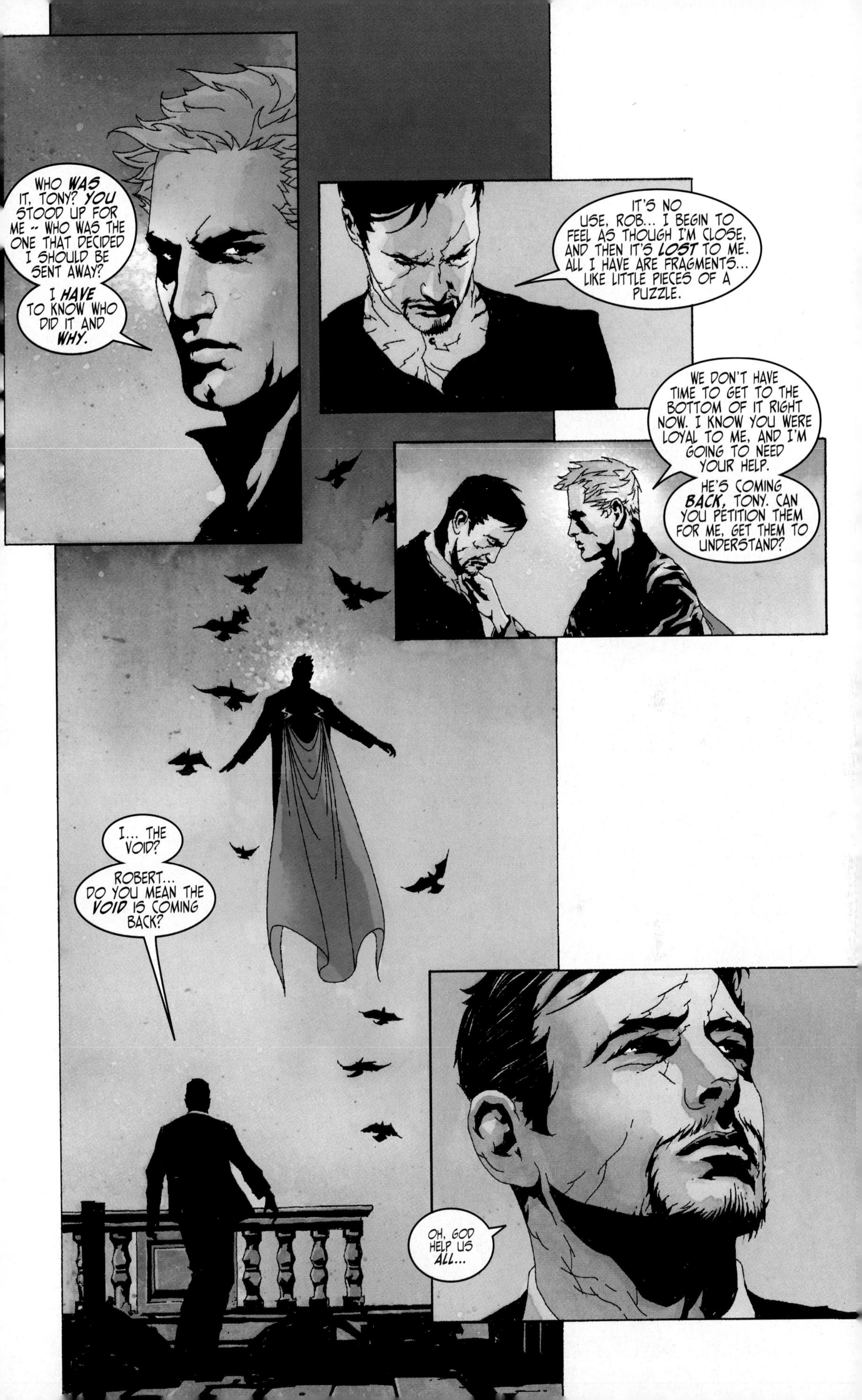
WHO WAS IT, TONY? YOU STOOD UP FOR ME -- WHO WAS THE ONE THAT DECIDED I SHOULD BE SENT AWAY?
I HAVE TO KNOW WHO DID IT AND WHY.
IT'S NO USE, ROB... I BEGIN TO FEEL AS THOUGH I'M CLOSE, AND THEN IT'S LOST TO ME. ALL I HAVE ARE FRAGMENTS... LIKE LITTLE PIECES OF A PUZZLE.
WE DON'T HAVE TIME TO GET TO THE BOTTOM OF IT RIGHT NOW. I KNOW YOU WERE LOYAL TO ME, AND I'M GOING TO NEED YOUR HELP.
HE'S COMING BACK, TONY. CAN YOU PETITION THEM FOR ME, GET THEM TO UNDERSTAND?
I... THE VOID?
ROBERT... DO YOU MEAN THE VOID IS COMING BACK?
OH, GOD HELP US ALL...

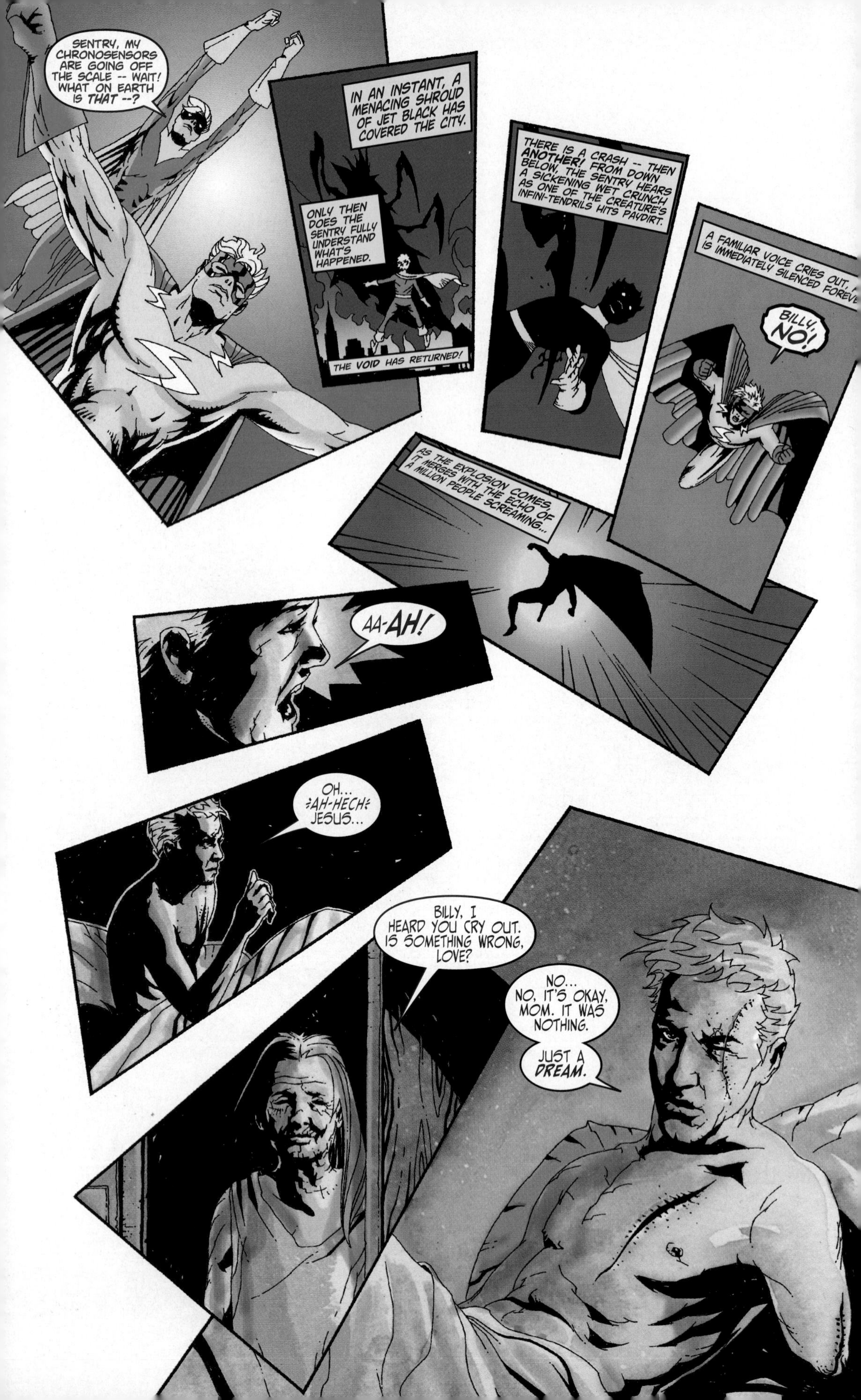

SENTRY, MY CHRONOSENSORS ARE GOING OFF THE SCALE -- WAIT! WHAT ON EARTH IS *THAT* --?
IN AN INSTANT, A MENACING SHROUD OF JET BLACK HAS COVERED THE CITY.
ONLY THEN DOES THE SENTRY FULLY UNDERSTAND WHAT'S HAPPENED.
THE *VOID* HAS RETURNED!
THERE IS A CRASH -- THEN **ANOTHER!** FROM DOWN BELOW, THE SENTRY HEARS A SICKENING WET CRUNCH AS ONE OF THE CREATURE'S INFINI-TENDRILS HITS PAYDIRT.
A FAMILIAR VOICE CRIES OUT, AND IS IMMEDIATELY SILENCED FOREVER.
BILLY, NO!
AS THE EXPLOSION COMES, IT MERGES WITH THE ECHO OF A MILLION PEOPLE SCREAMING...
AA-AH!
OH... *AH-HECH* JESUS...
BILLY, I HEARD YOU CRY OUT. IS SOMETHING WRONG, LOVE?
NO... NO, IT'S OKAY, MOM. IT WAS NOTHING.
JUST A *DREAM*.

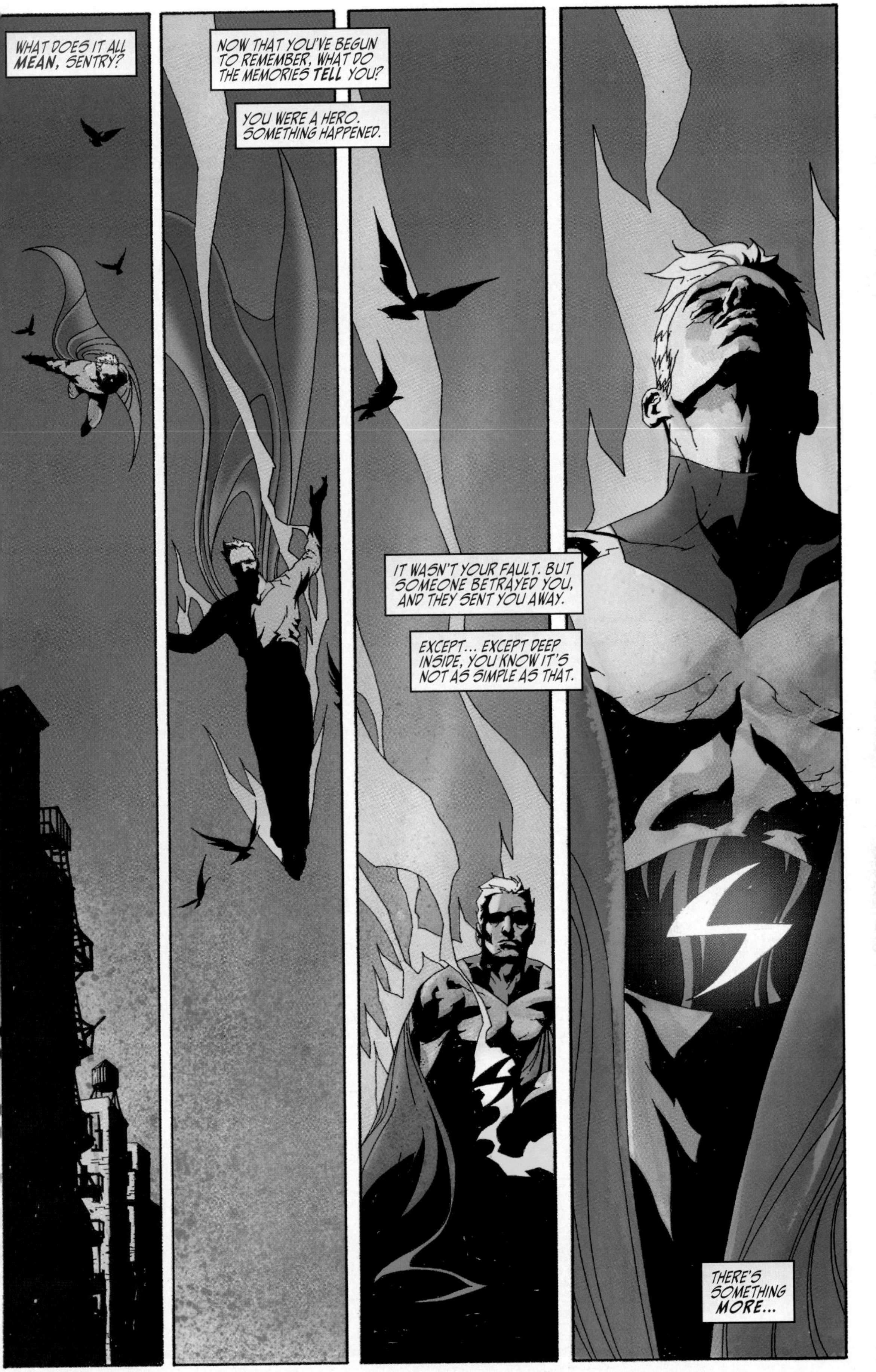
WHAT DOES IT ALL MEAN, SENTRY?
NOW THAT YOU'VE BEGUN TO REMEMBER, WHAT DO THE MEMORIES TELL YOU?
YOU WERE A HERO. SOMETHING HAPPENED.
IT WASN'T YOUR FAULT. BUT SOMEONE BETRAYED YOU, AND THEY SENT YOU AWAY.
EXCEPT... EXCEPT DEEP INSIDE, YOU KNOW IT'S NOT AS SIMPLE AS THAT.
THERE'S SOMETHING MORE...

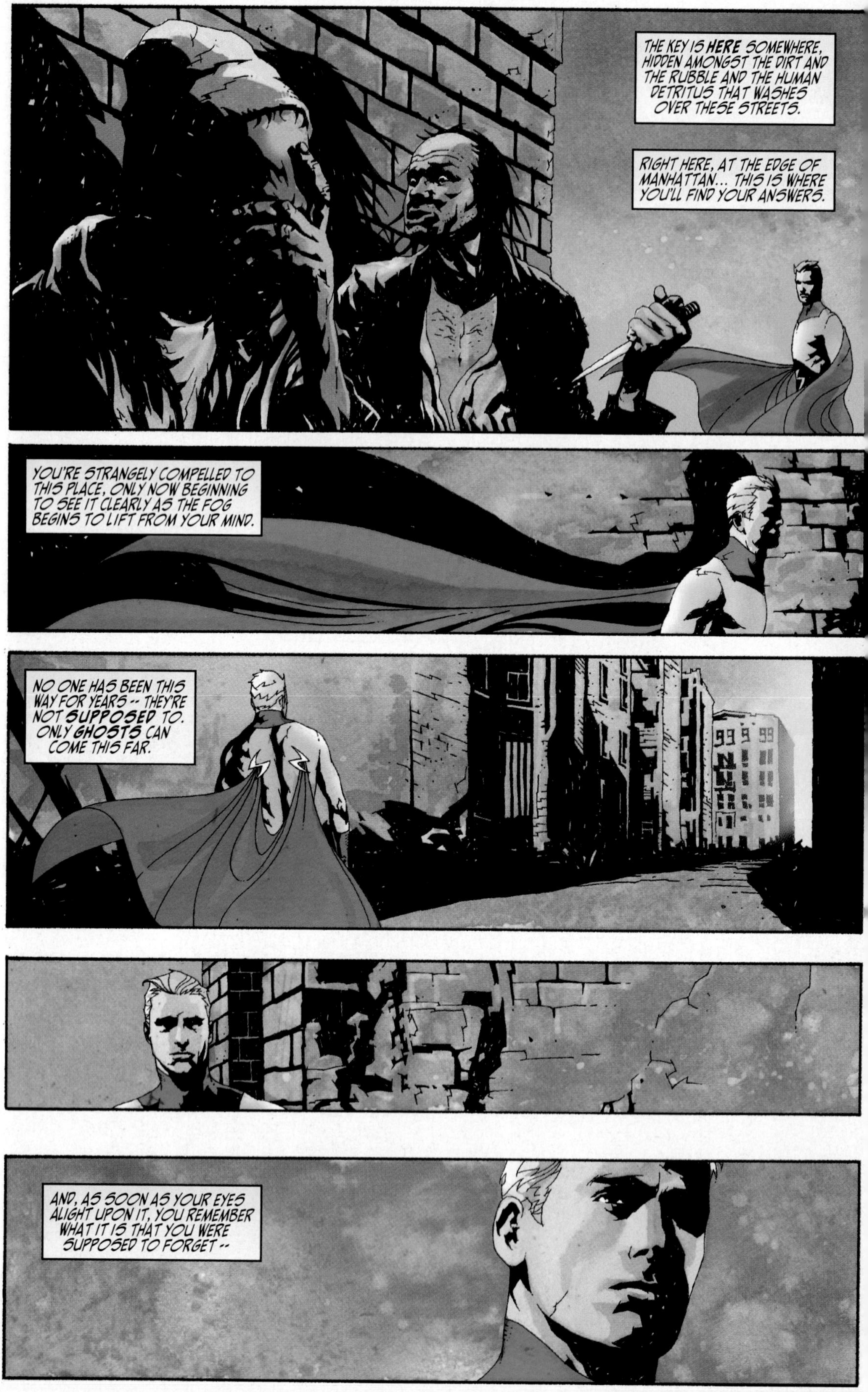
THE KEY IS **HERE** SOMEWHERE, HIDDEN AMONGST THE DIRT AND THE RUBBLE AND THE HUMAN DETRITUS THAT WASHES OVER THESE STREETS.
RIGHT HERE, AT THE EDGE OF MANHATTAN... THIS IS WHERE YOU'LL FIND YOUR ANSWERS.
YOU'RE STRANGELY COMPELLED TO THIS PLACE, ONLY NOW BEGINNING TO SEE IT CLEARLY AS THE FOG BEGINS TO LIFT FROM YOUR MIND.
NO ONE HAS BEEN THIS WAY FOR YEARS -- THEY'RE NOT **SUPPOSED** TO. ONLY **GHOSTS** CAN COME THIS FAR.
AND, AS SOON AS YOUR EYES ALIGHT UPON IT, YOU REMEMBER WHAT IT IS THAT YOU WERE SUPPOSED TO FORGET --

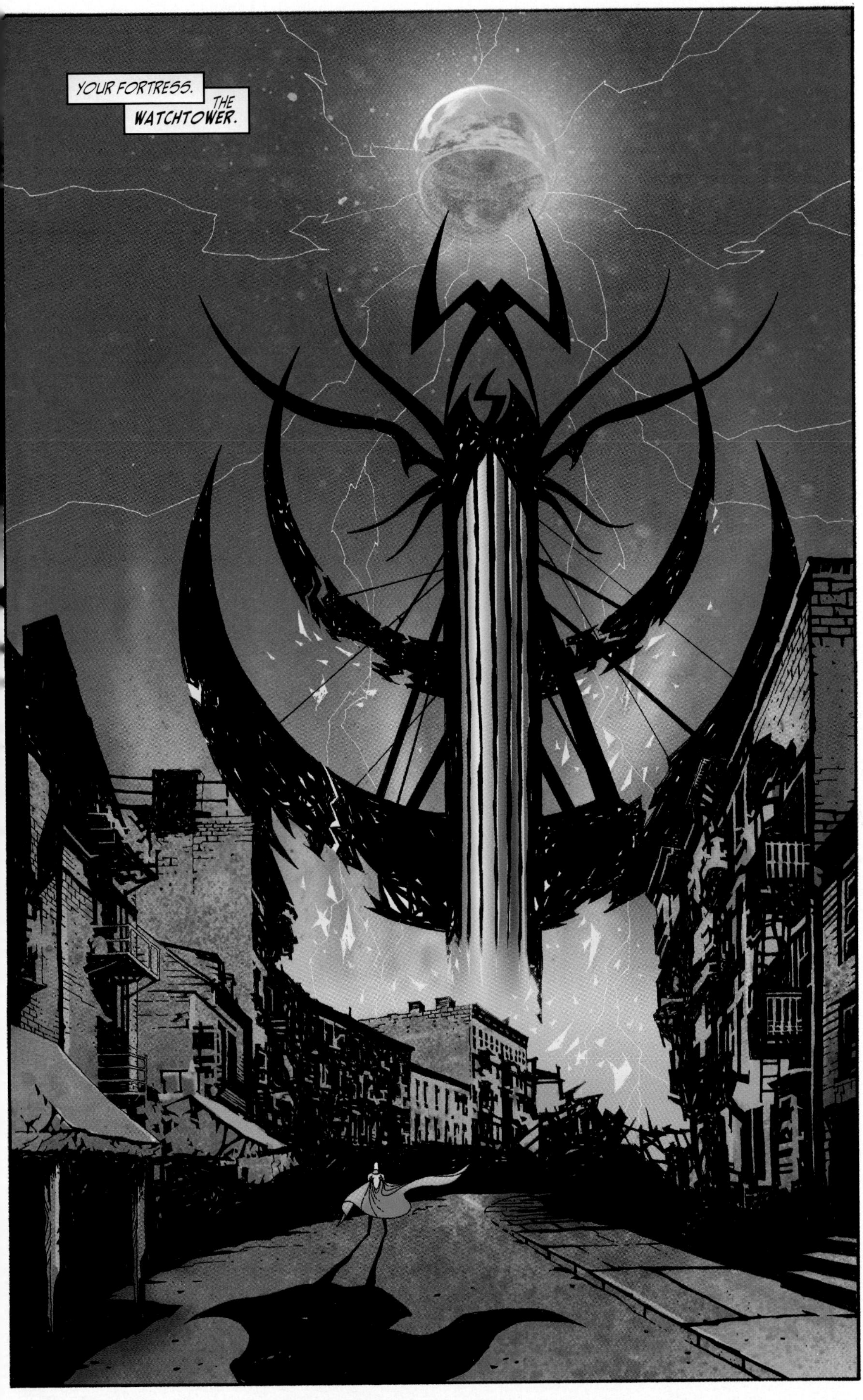
YOUR FORTRESS.
THE WATCHTOWER.

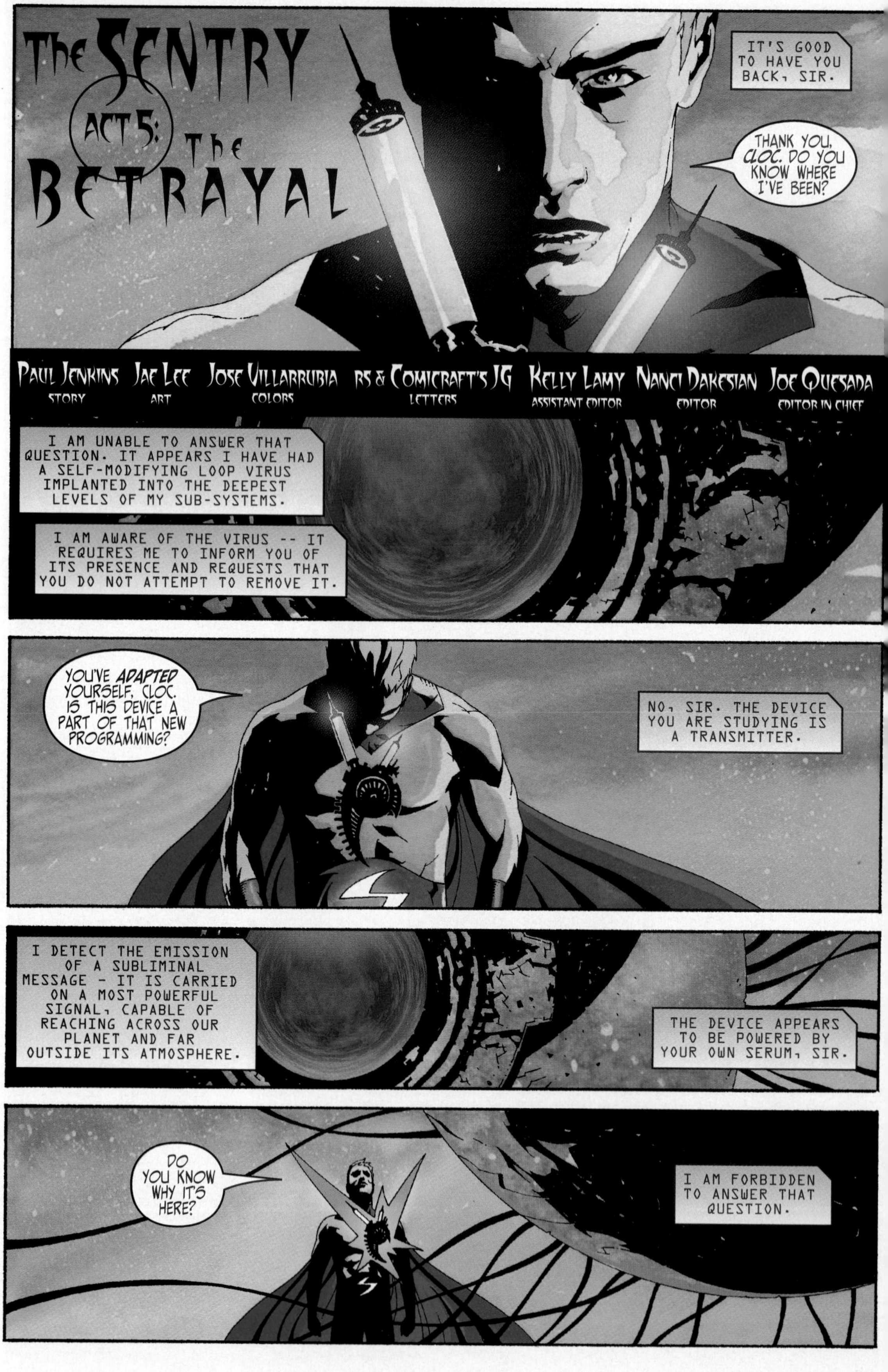
The SENTRY
ACT 5: The BETRAYAL
IT'S GOOD TO HAVE YOU BACK, SIR.
THANK YOU, CLOC. DO YOU KNOW WHERE I'VE BEEN?
PAUL JENKINS STORY
JAE LEE ART
JOSE VILLARRUBIA COLORS
RS & COMICRAFT'S JG LETTERS
KELLY LAMY ASSISTANT EDITOR
NANCI DAKESIAN EDITOR
JOE QUESADA EDITOR IN CHIEF
I AM UNABLE TO ANSWER THAT QUESTION. IT APPEARS I HAVE HAD A SELF-MODIFYING LOOP VIRUS IMPLANTED INTO THE DEEPEST LEVELS OF MY SUB-SYSTEMS.
I AM AWARE OF THE VIRUS -- IT REQUIRES ME TO INFORM YOU OF ITS PRESENCE AND REQUESTS THAT YOU DO NOT ATTEMPT TO REMOVE IT.
YOU'VE ADAPTED YOURSELF, CLOC. IS THIS DEVICE A PART OF THAT NEW PROGRAMMING?
NO, SIR. THE DEVICE YOU ARE STUDYING IS A TRANSMITTER.
I DETECT THE EMISSION OF A SUBLIMINAL MESSAGE - IT IS CARRIED ON A MOST POWERFUL SIGNAL, CAPABLE OF REACHING ACROSS OUR PLANET AND FAR OUTSIDE ITS ATMOSPHERE.
THE DEVICE APPEARS TO BE POWERED BY YOUR OWN SERUM, SIR.
DO YOU KNOW WHY IT'S HERE?
I AM FORBIDDEN TO ANSWER THAT QUESTION.

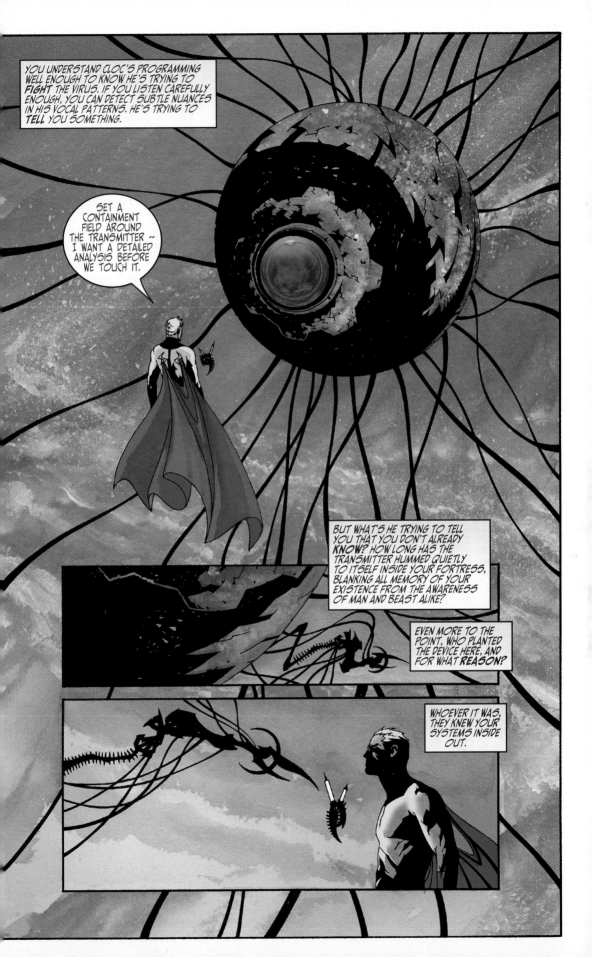

YOU UNDERSTAND CLOC'S PROGRAMMING WELL ENOUGH TO KNOW HE'S TRYING TO **FIGHT** THE VIRUS. IF YOU LISTEN CAREFULLY ENOUGH, YOU CAN DETECT SUBTLE NUANCES IN HIS VOCAL PATTERNS. HE'S TRYING TO **TELL** YOU SOMETHING.

SET A CONTAINMENT FIELD AROUND THE TRANSMITTER -- I WANT A DETAILED ANALYSIS BEFORE WE TOUCH IT.

BUT WHAT'S HE TRYING TO TELL YOU THAT YOU DON'T ALREADY **KNOW?** HOW LONG HAS THE TRANSMITTER HUMMED QUIETLY TO ITSELF INSIDE YOUR FORTRESS, BLANKING ALL MEMORY OF YOUR EXISTENCE FROM THE AWARENESS OF MAN AND BEAST ALIKE?

EVEN MORE TO THE POINT, WHO PLANTED THE DEVICE HERE, AND FOR WHAT **REASON?**

WHOEVER IT WAS, THEY KNEW YOUR SYSTEMS INSIDE OUT.

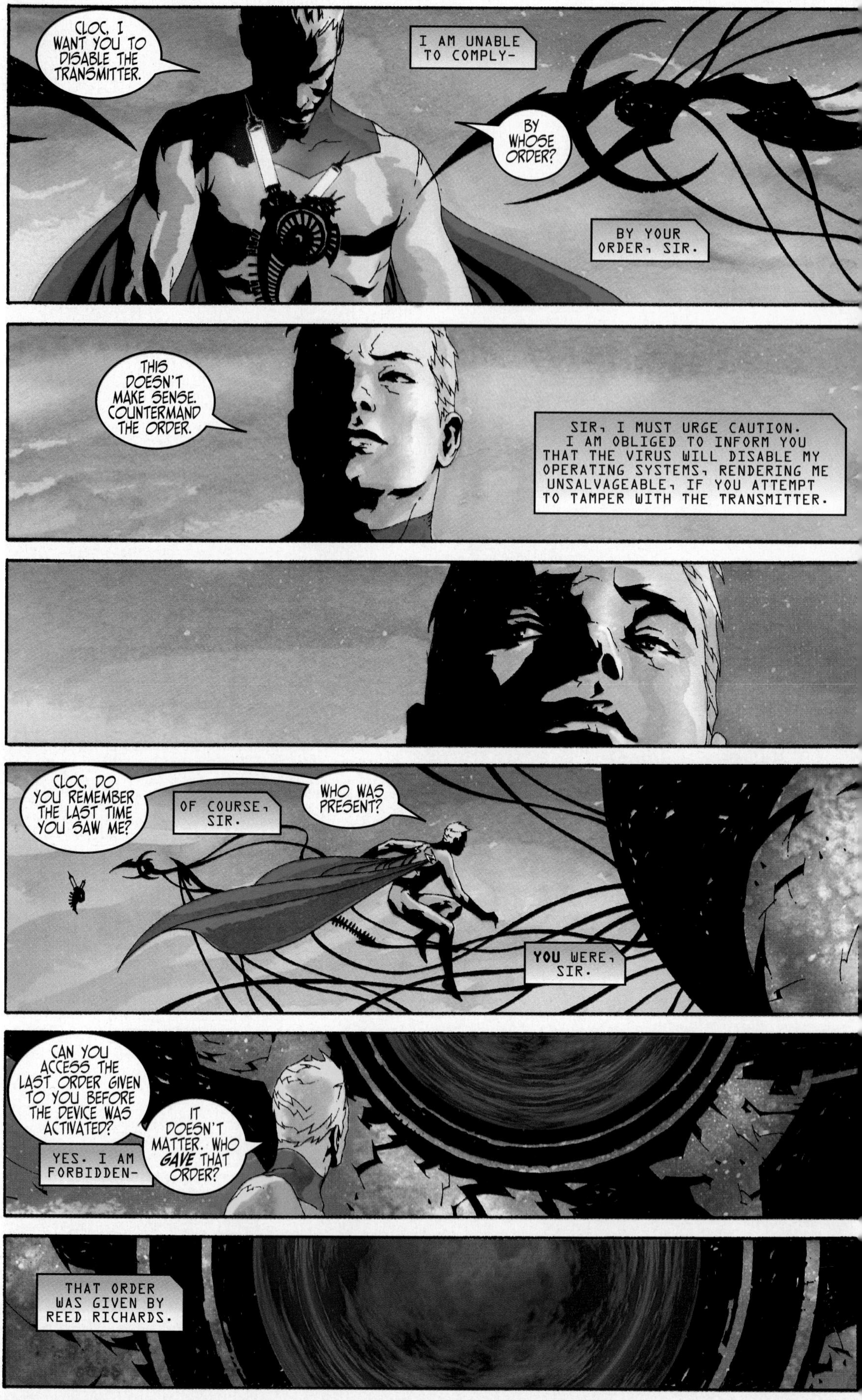
CLOC, I WANT YOU TO DISABLE THE TRANSMITTER.
I AM UNABLE TO COMPLY-
BY WHOSE ORDER?
BY YOUR ORDER, SIR.
THIS DOESN'T MAKE SENSE. COUNTERMAND THE ORDER.
SIR, I MUST URGE CAUTION. I AM OBLIGED TO INFORM YOU THAT THE VIRUS WILL DISABLE MY OPERATING SYSTEMS, RENDERING ME UNSALVAGEABLE, IF YOU ATTEMPT TO TAMPER WITH THE TRANSMITTER.
CLOC, DO YOU REMEMBER THE LAST TIME YOU SAW ME?
OF COURSE, SIR.
WHO WAS PRESENT?
YOU WERE, SIR.
CAN YOU ACCESS THE LAST ORDER GIVEN TO YOU BEFORE THE DEVICE WAS ACTIVATED?
YES. I AM FORBIDDEN-
IT DOESN'T MATTER. WHO GAVE THAT ORDER?
THAT ORDER WAS GIVEN BY REED RICHARDS.

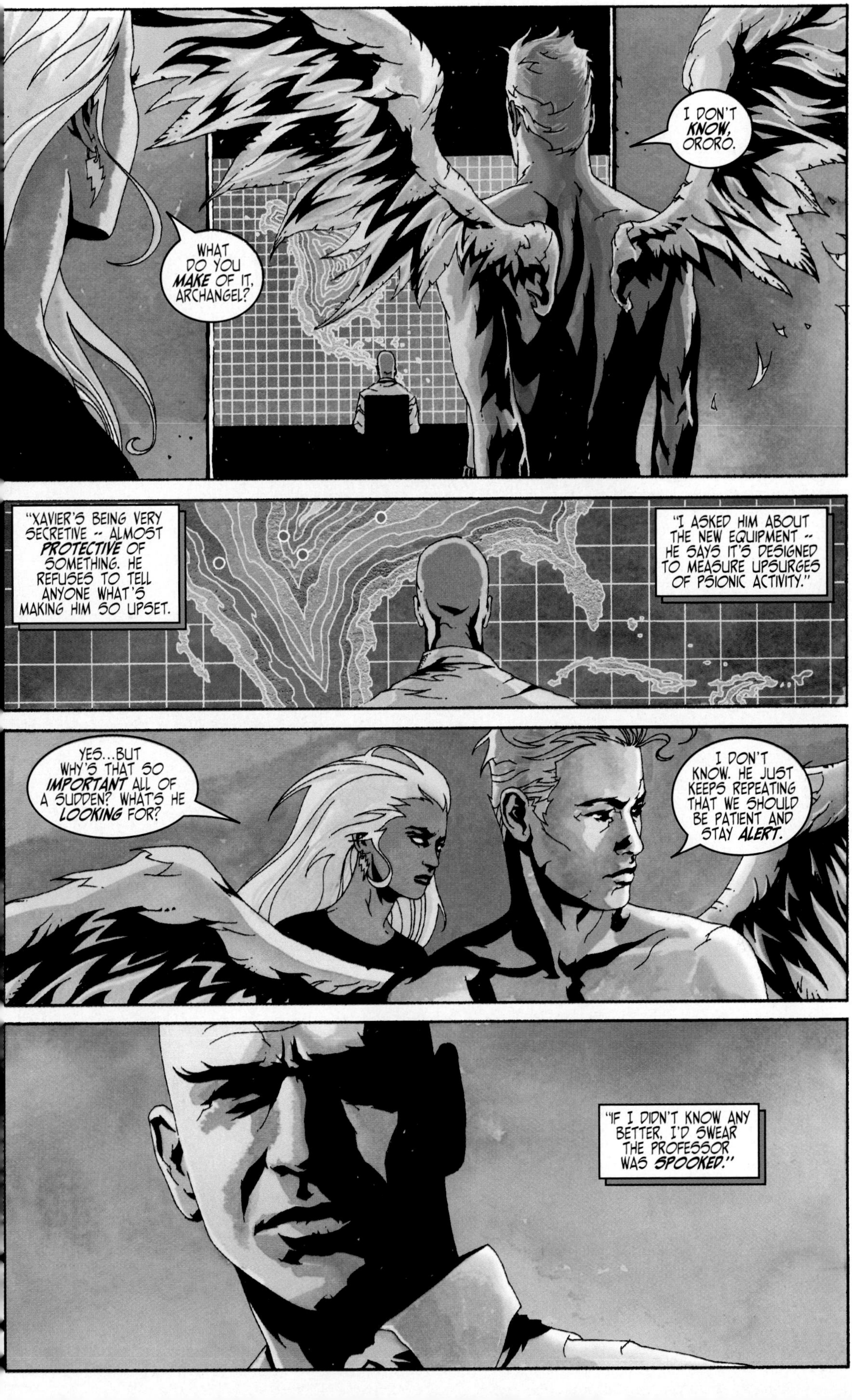
WHAT DO YOU MAKE OF IT, ARCHANGEL?
I DON'T KNOW, ORORO.
"XAVIER'S BEING VERY SECRETIVE -- ALMOST PROTECTIVE OF SOMETHING. HE REFUSES TO TELL ANYONE WHAT'S MAKING HIM SO UPSET.
"I ASKED HIM ABOUT THE NEW EQUIPMENT -- HE SAYS IT'S DESIGNED TO MEASURE UPSURGES OF PSIONIC ACTIVITY."
YES...BUT WHY'S THAT SO IMPORTANT ALL OF A SUDDEN? WHAT'S HE LOOKING FOR?
I DON'T KNOW. HE JUST KEEPS REPEATING THAT WE SHOULD BE PATIENT AND STAY ALERT.
"IF I DIDN'T KNOW ANY BETTER, I'D SWEAR THE PROFESSOR WAS SPOOKED."

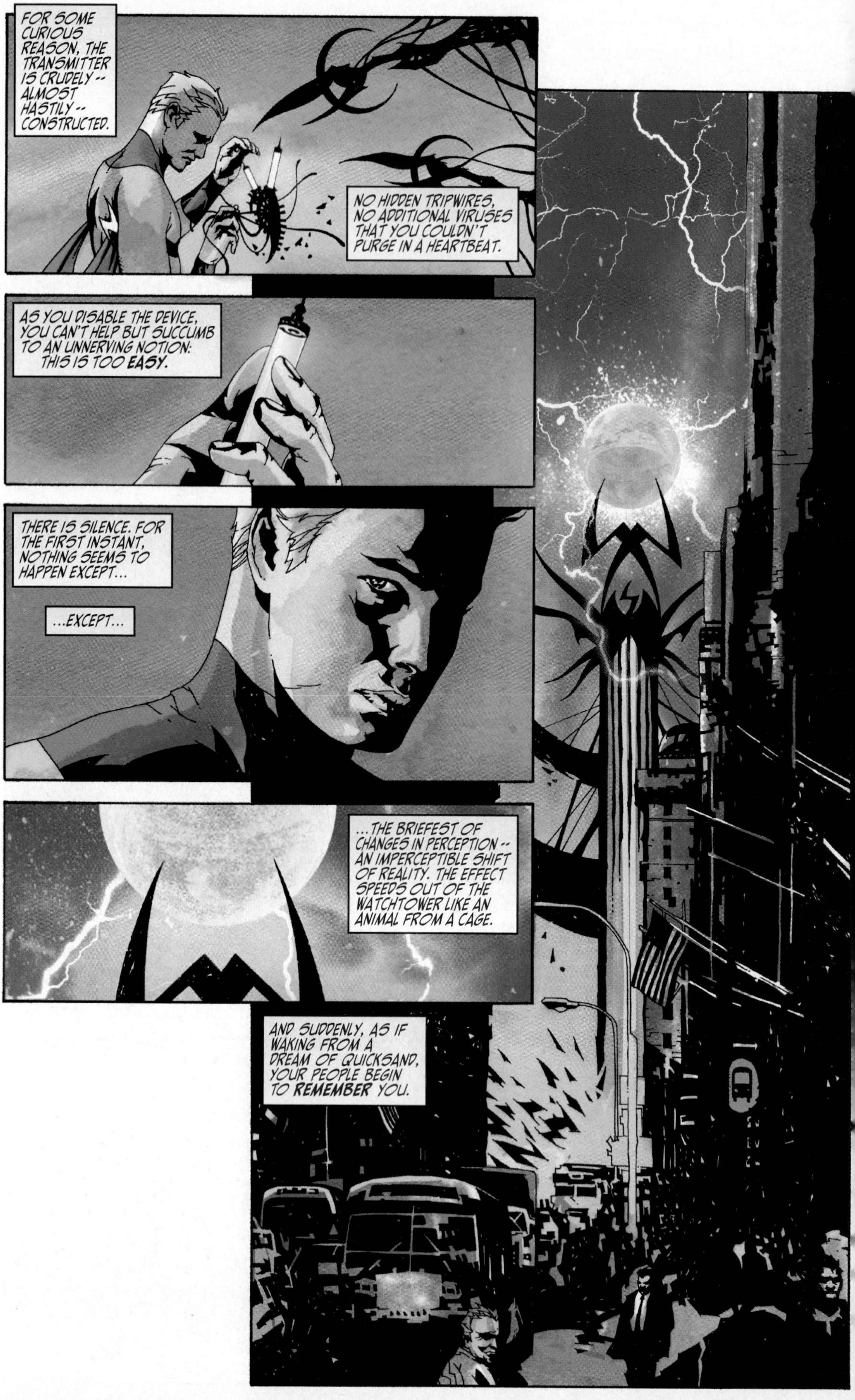
FOR SOME CURIOUS REASON, THE TRANSMITTER IS CRUDELY -- ALMOST HASTILY -- CONSTRUCTED.
NO HIDDEN TRIPWIRES, NO ADDITIONAL VIRUSES THAT YOU COULDN'T PURGE IN A HEARTBEAT.
AS YOU DISABLE THE DEVICE, YOU CAN'T HELP BUT SUCCUMB TO AN UNNERVING NOTION: THIS IS TOO EASY.
THERE IS SILENCE. FOR THE FIRST INSTANT, NOTHING SEEMS TO HAPPEN EXCEPT...
...EXCEPT...
...THE BRIEFEST OF CHANGES IN PERCEPTION -- AN IMPERCEPTIBLE SHIFT OF REALITY. THE EFFECT SPEEDS OUT OF THE WATCHTOWER LIKE AN ANIMAL FROM A CAGE.
AND SUDDENLY, AS IF WAKING FROM A DREAM OF QUICKSAND, YOUR PEOPLE BEGIN TO REMEMBER YOU.

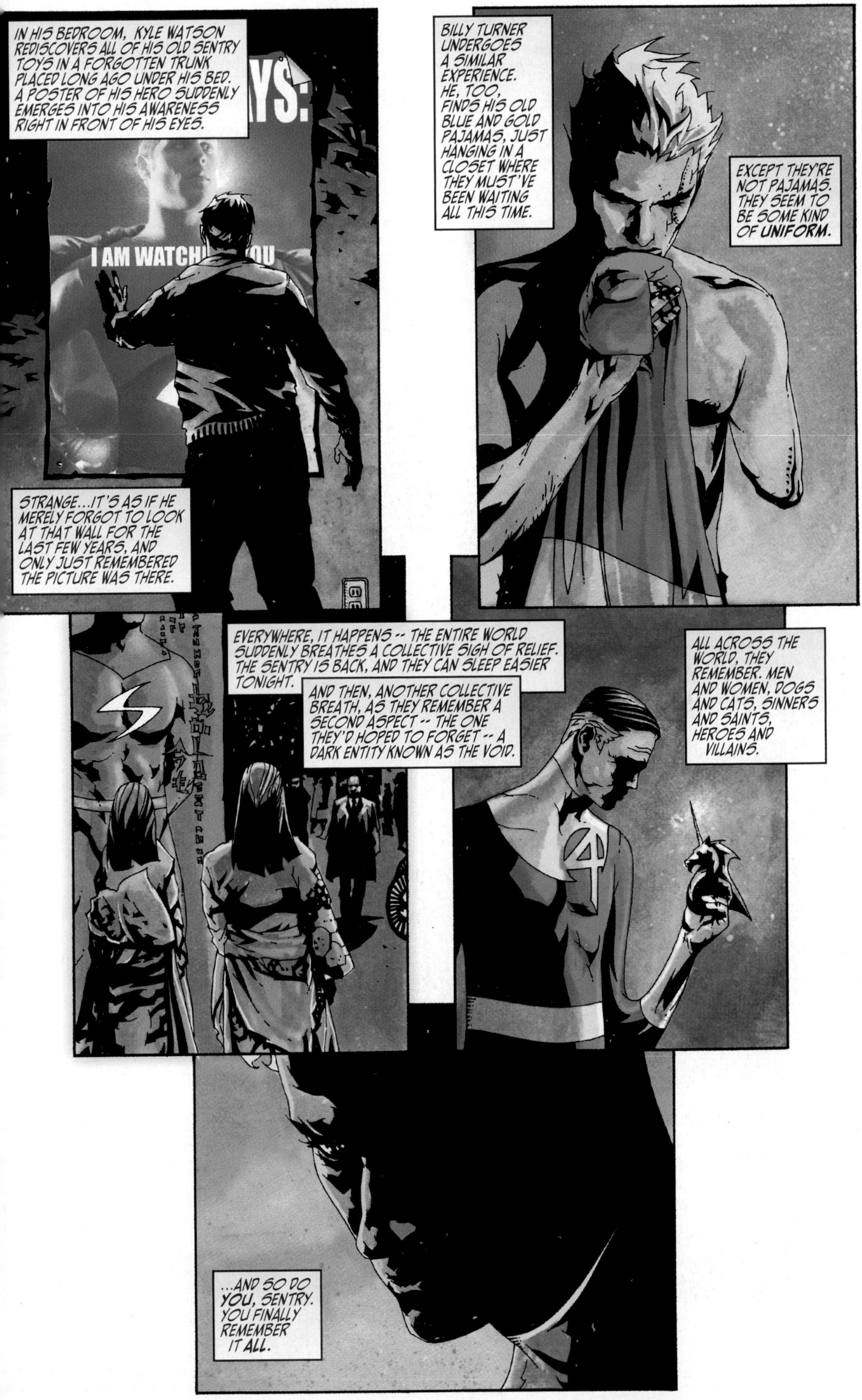

IN HIS BEDROOM, KYLE WATSON REDISCOVERS ALL OF HIS OLD SENTRY TOYS IN A FORGOTTEN TRUNK PLACED LONG AGO UNDER HIS BED. A POSTER OF HIS HERO SUDDENLY EMERGES INTO HIS AWARENESS RIGHT IN FRONT OF HIS EYES.
I AM WATCHI
STRANGE...IT'S AS IF HE MERELY FORGOT TO LOOK AT THAT WALL FOR THE LAST FEW YEARS, AND ONLY JUST REMEMBERED THE PICTURE WAS THERE.
BILLY TURNER UNDERGOES A SIMILAR EXPERIENCE. HE, TOO, FINDS HIS OLD BLUE AND GOLD PAJAMAS, JUST HANGING IN A CLOSET WHERE THEY MUST'VE BEEN WAITING ALL THIS TIME.
EXCEPT THEY'RE NOT PAJAMAS. THEY SEEM TO BE SOME KIND OF UNIFORM.
EVERYWHERE, IT HAPPENS -- THE ENTIRE WORLD SUDDENLY BREATHES A COLLECTIVE SIGH OF RELIEF. THE SENTRY IS BACK, AND THEY CAN SLEEP EASIER TONIGHT.
AND THEN, ANOTHER COLLECTIVE BREATH, AS THEY REMEMBER A SECOND ASPECT -- THE ONE THEY'D HOPED TO FORGET -- A DARK ENTITY KNOWN AS THE VOID.
ALL ACROSS THE WORLD, THEY REMEMBER. MEN AND WOMEN, DOGS AND CATS, SINNERS AND SAINTS, HEROES AND VILLAINS.
...AND SO DO YOU, SENTRY. YOU FINALLY REMEMBER IT ALL.

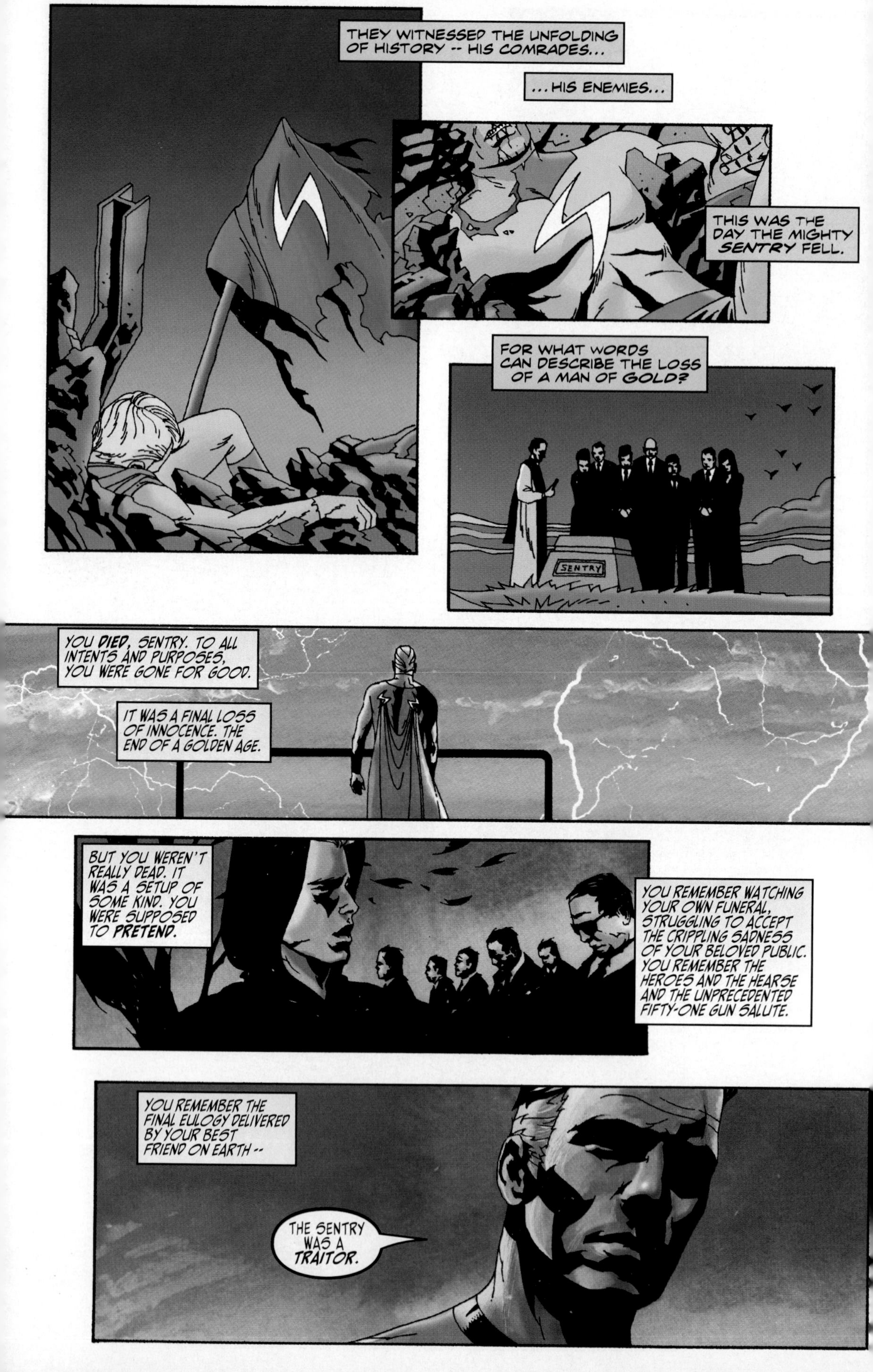
THEY WITNESSED THE UNFOLDING OF HISTORY -- HIS COMRADES...
...HIS ENEMIES...
THIS WAS THE DAY THE MIGHTY SENTRY FELL.
FOR WHAT WORDS CAN DESCRIBE THE LOSS OF A MAN OF GOLD?
SENTRY
YOU DIED, SENTRY. TO ALL INTENTS AND PURPOSES, YOU WERE GONE FOR GOOD.
IT WAS A FINAL LOSS OF INNOCENCE. THE END OF A GOLDEN AGE.
BUT YOU WEREN'T REALLY DEAD. IT WAS A SETUP OF SOME KIND. YOU WERE SUPPOSED TO PRETEND.
YOU REMEMBER WATCHING YOUR OWN FUNERAL, STRUGGLING TO ACCEPT THE CRIPPLING SADNESS OF YOUR BELOVED PUBLIC. YOU REMEMBER THE HEROES AND THE HEARSE AND THE UNPRECEDENTED FIFTY-ONE GUN SALUTE.
YOU REMEMBER THE FINAL EULOGY DELIVERED BY YOUR BEST FRIEND ON EARTH --
THE SENTRY WAS A TRAITOR.

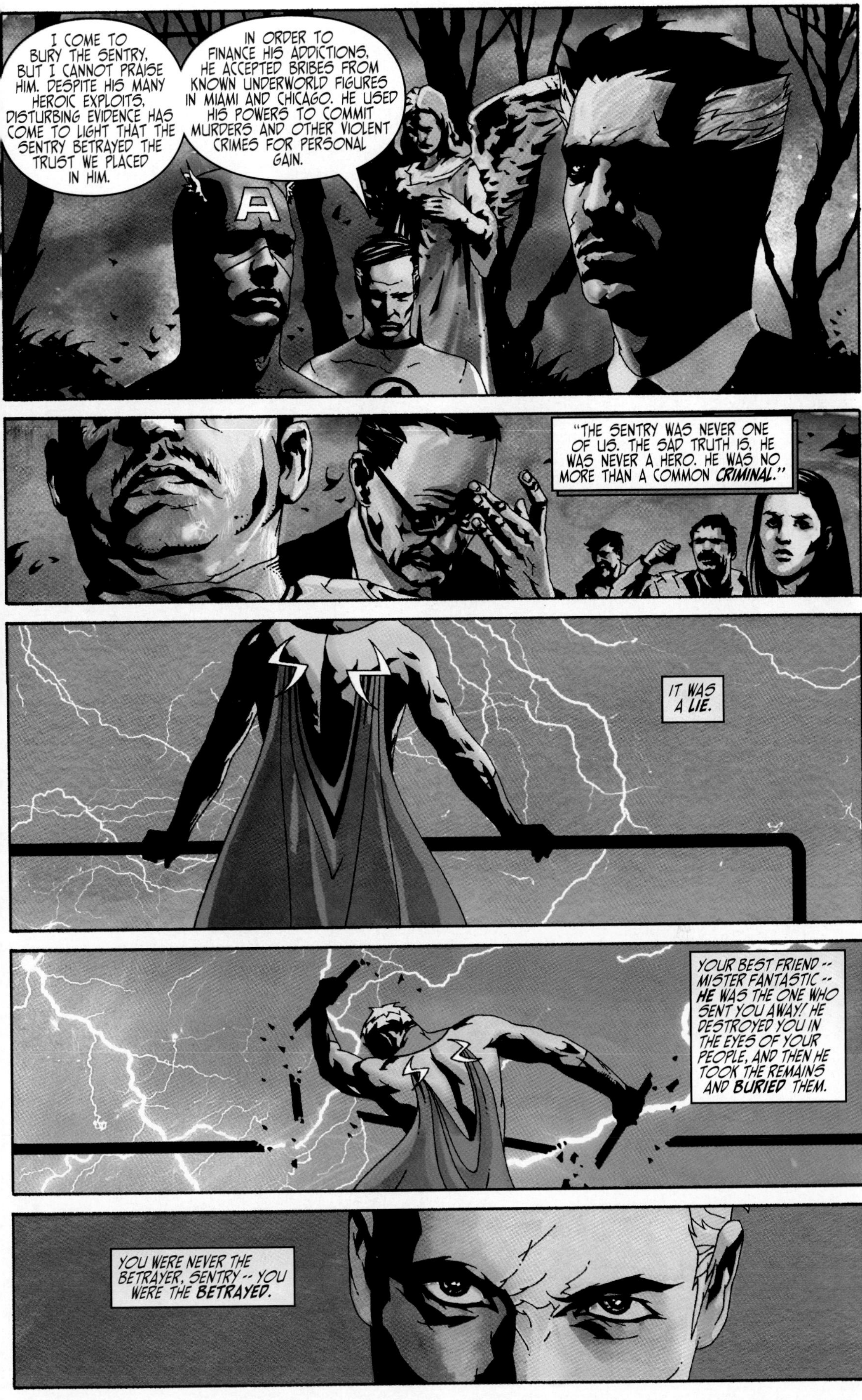
I COME TO BURY THE SENTRY, BUT I CANNOT PRAISE HIM. DESPITE HIS MANY HEROIC EXPLOITS, DISTURBING EVIDENCE HAS COME TO LIGHT THAT THE SENTRY BETRAYED THE TRUST WE PLACED IN HIM.
IN ORDER TO FINANCE HIS ADDICTIONS, HE ACCEPTED BRIBES FROM KNOWN UNDERWORLD FIGURES IN MIAMI AND CHICAGO. HE USED HIS POWERS TO COMMIT MURDERS AND OTHER VIOLENT CRIMES FOR PERSONAL GAIN.
"THE SENTRY WAS NEVER ONE OF US. THE SAD TRUTH IS, HE WAS NEVER A HERO. HE WAS NO MORE THAN A COMMON CRIMINAL."
IT WAS A LIE.
YOUR BEST FRIEND -- MISTER FANTASTIC -- HE WAS THE ONE WHO SENT YOU AWAY! HE DESTROYED YOU IN THE EYES OF YOUR PEOPLE, AND THEN HE TOOK THE REMAINS AND BURIED THEM.
YOU WERE NEVER THE BETRAYER, SENTRY -- YOU WERE THE BETRAYED.

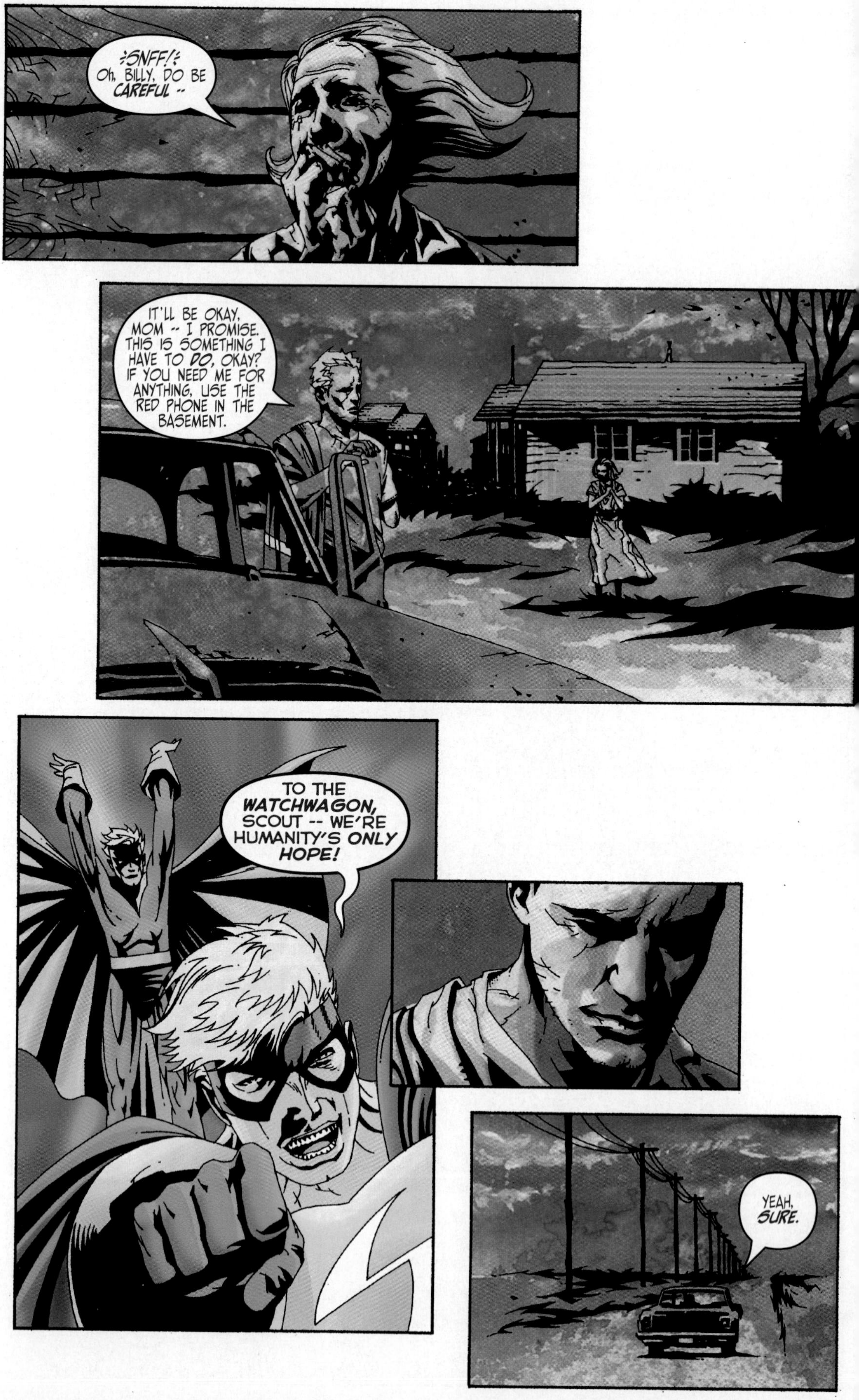
SNFF!
Oh, BILLY. DO BE CAREFUL --
IT'LL BE OKAY, MOM -- I PROMISE. THIS IS SOMETHING I HAVE TO DO, OKAY? IF YOU NEED ME FOR ANYTHING, USE THE RED PHONE IN THE BASEMENT.
TO THE WATCHWAGON, SCOUT -- WE'RE HUMANITY'S ONLY HOPE!
YEAH, SURE.

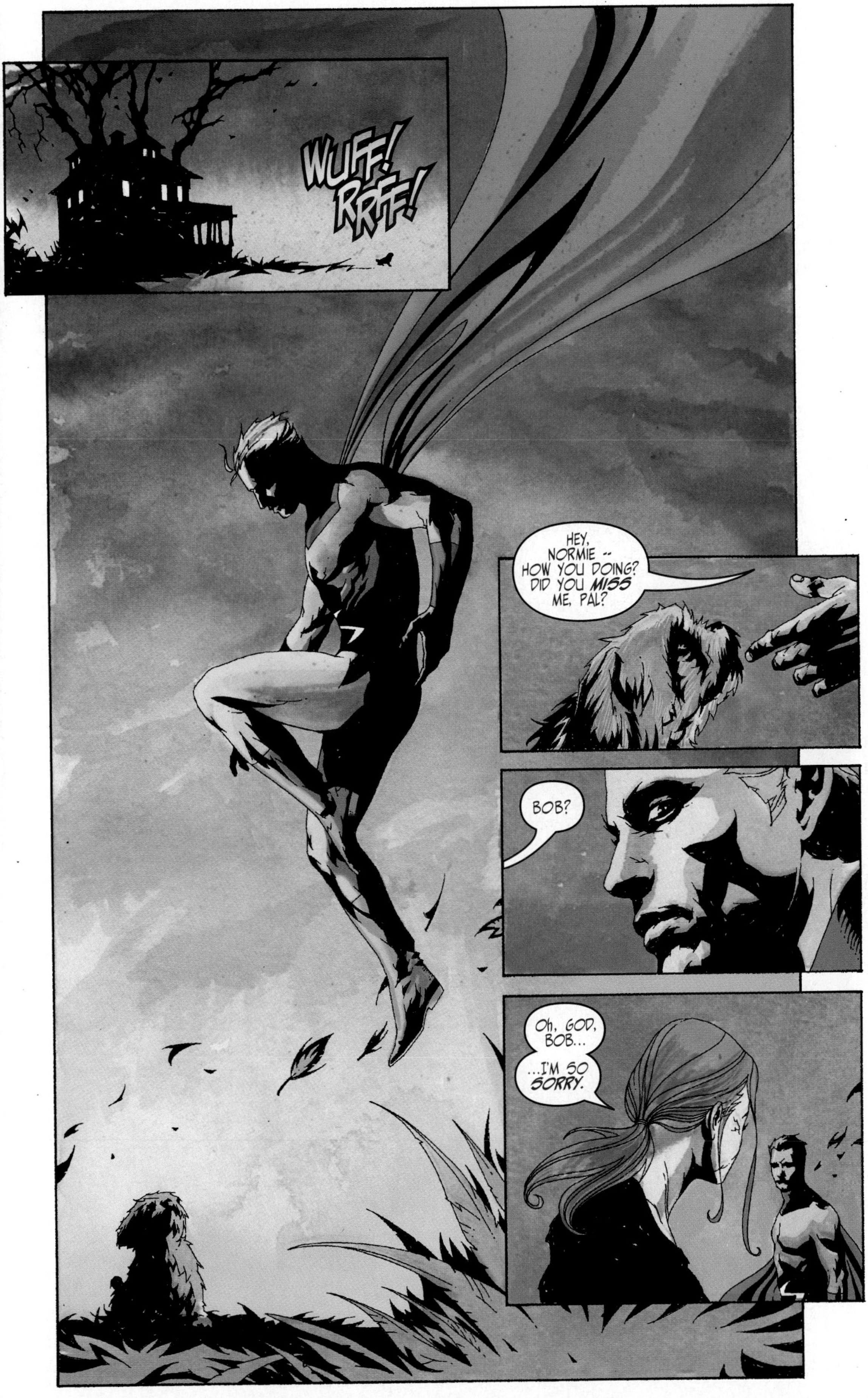
WUFF! RRFF!
HEY, NORMIE -- HOW YOU DOING? DID YOU MISS ME, PAL?
BOB?
Oh, GOD, BOB...
...I'M SO SORRY.

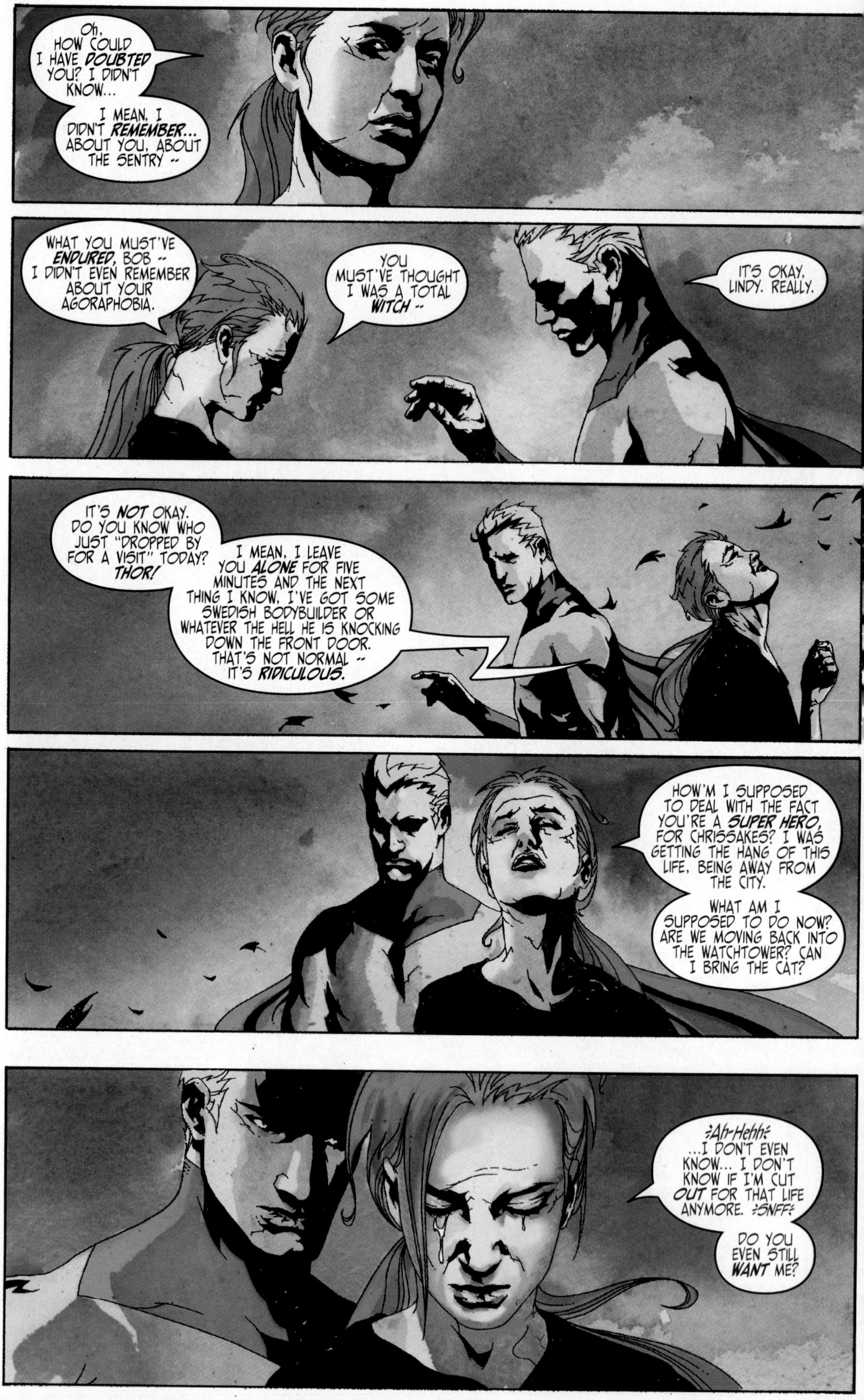

Oh, HOW COULD I HAVE DOUBTED YOU? I DIDN'T KNOW...
I MEAN, I DIDN'T REMEMBER... ABOUT YOU, ABOUT THE SENTRY --
WHAT YOU MUST'VE ENDURED, BOB -- I DIDN'T EVEN REMEMBER ABOUT YOUR AGORAPHOBIA.
YOU MUST'VE THOUGHT I WAS A TOTAL WITCH --
IT'S OKAY, LINDY. REALLY.
IT'S NOT OKAY. DO YOU KNOW WHO JUST "DROPPED BY FOR A VISIT" TODAY? THOR!
I MEAN, I LEAVE YOU ALONE FOR FIVE MINUTES AND THE NEXT THING I KNOW, I'VE GOT SOME SWEDISH BODYBUILDER OR WHATEVER THE HELL HE IS KNOCKING DOWN THE FRONT DOOR. THAT'S NOT NORMAL -- IT'S RIDICULOUS.
HOW'M I SUPPOSED TO DEAL WITH THE FACT YOU'RE A SUPER HERO, FOR CHRISSAKES? I WAS GETTING THE HANG OF THIS LIFE, BEING AWAY FROM THE CITY.
WHAT AM I SUPPOSED TO DO NOW? ARE WE MOVING BACK INTO THE WATCHTOWER? CAN I BRING THE CAT?
Ah-Hehh ...I DON'T EVEN KNOW... I DON'T KNOW IF I'M CUT OUT FOR THAT LIFE ANYMORE. SNFF
DO YOU EVEN STILL WANT ME?

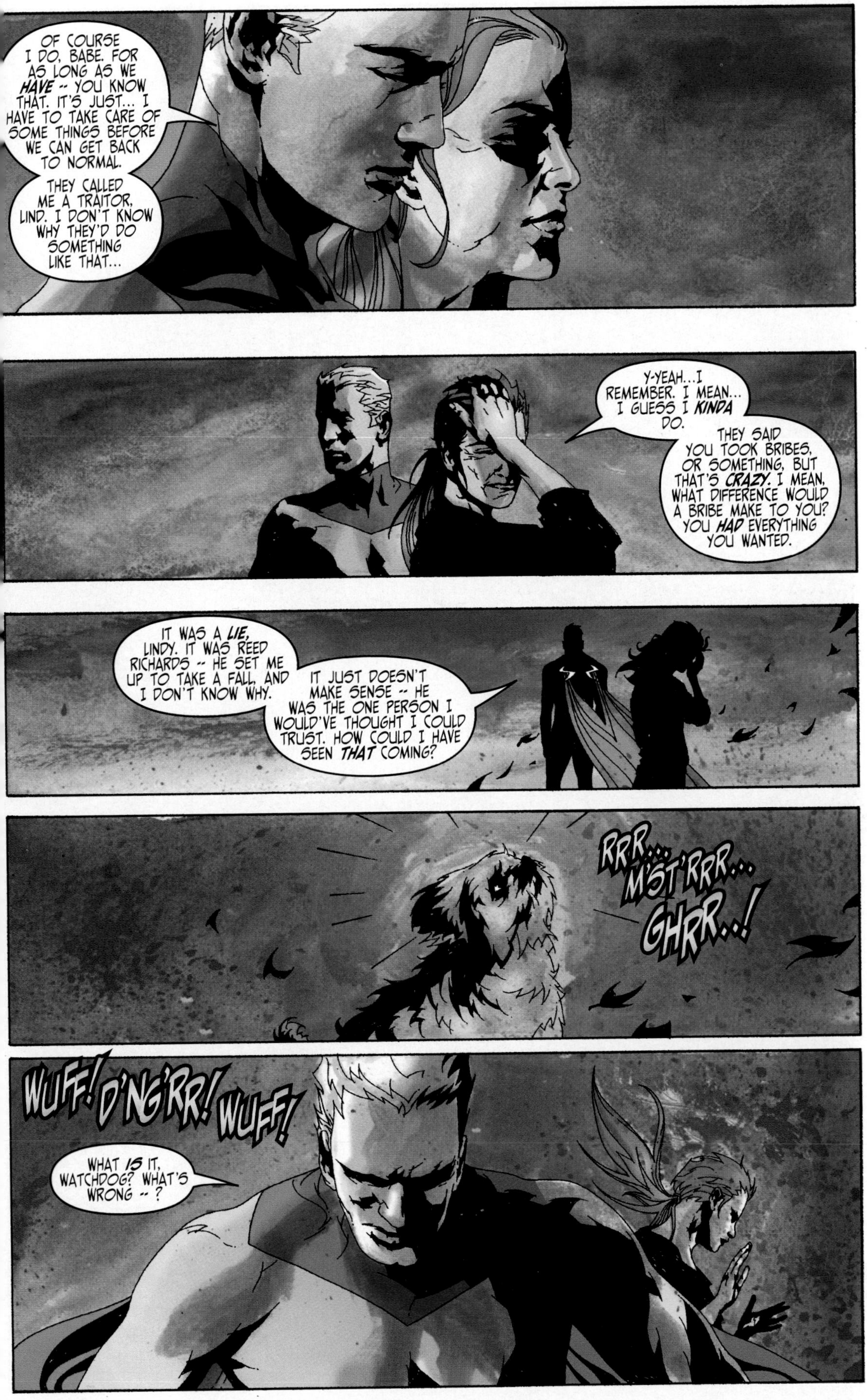

OF COURSE I DO, BABE. FOR AS LONG AS WE *HAVE* -- YOU KNOW THAT. IT'S JUST... I HAVE TO TAKE CARE OF SOME THINGS BEFORE WE CAN GET BACK TO NORMAL.
THEY CALLED ME A TRAITOR, LIND. I DON'T KNOW WHY THEY'D DO SOMETHING LIKE THAT...
Y-YEAH...I REMEMBER. I MEAN... I GUESS I *KINDA* DO.
THEY SAID YOU TOOK BRIBES, OR SOMETHING, BUT THAT'S *CRAZY*. I MEAN, WHAT DIFFERENCE WOULD A BRIBE MAKE TO YOU? YOU *HAD* EVERYTHING YOU WANTED.
IT WAS A *LIE*, LINDY. IT WAS REED RICHARDS -- HE SET ME UP TO TAKE A FALL, AND I DON'T KNOW WHY.
IT JUST DOESN'T MAKE SENSE -- HE WAS THE ONE PERSON I WOULD'VE THOUGHT I COULD TRUST. HOW COULD I HAVE SEEN *THAT* COMING?
RRR... M'ST'RRR... GHRR..!
WUFF! D'NG'RR! WUFF!
WHAT *IS* IT, WATCHDOG? WHAT'S WRONG -- ?

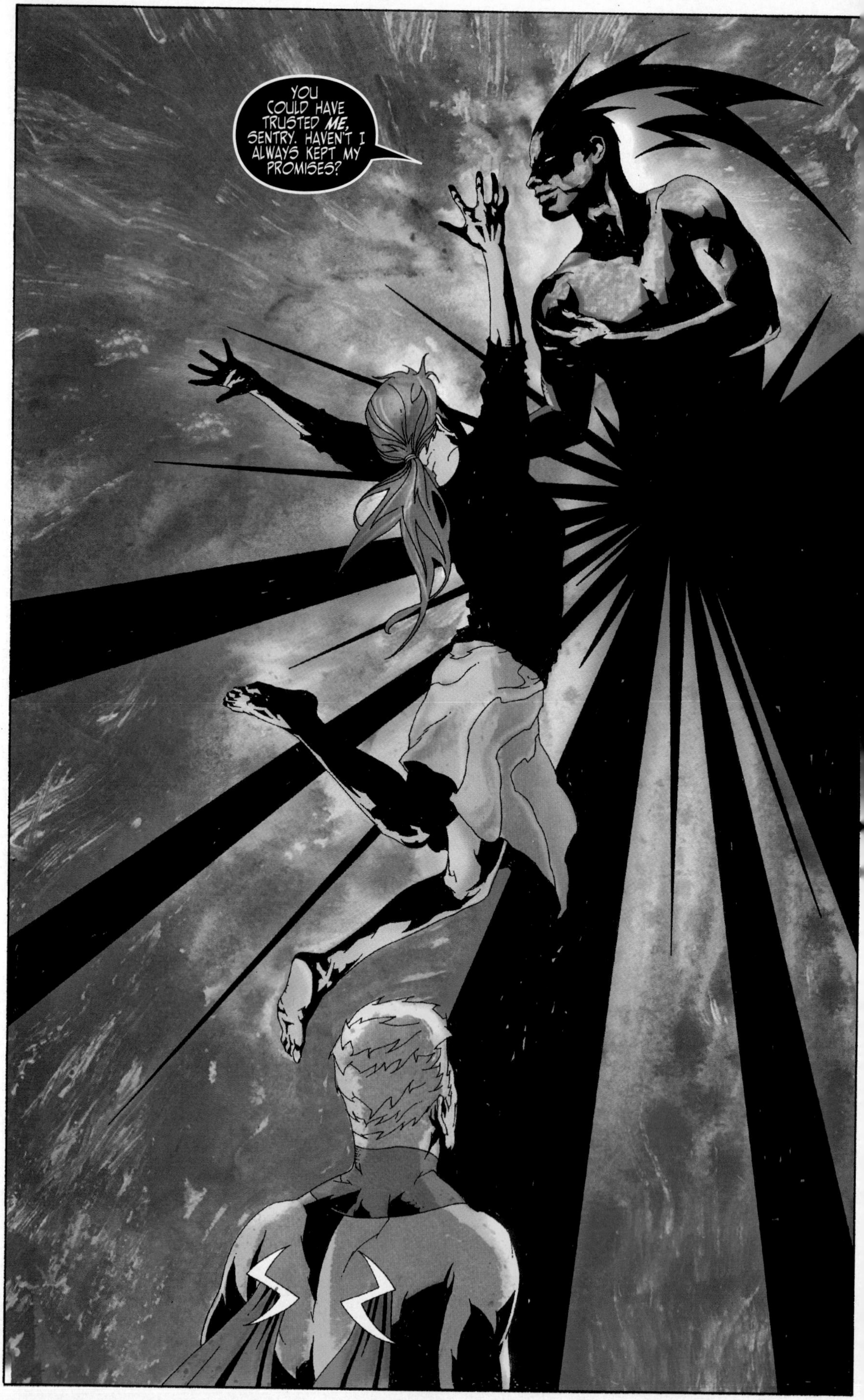
YOU COULD HAVE TRUSTED *ME,* SENTRY. HAVEN'T I ALWAYS KEPT MY PROMISES?

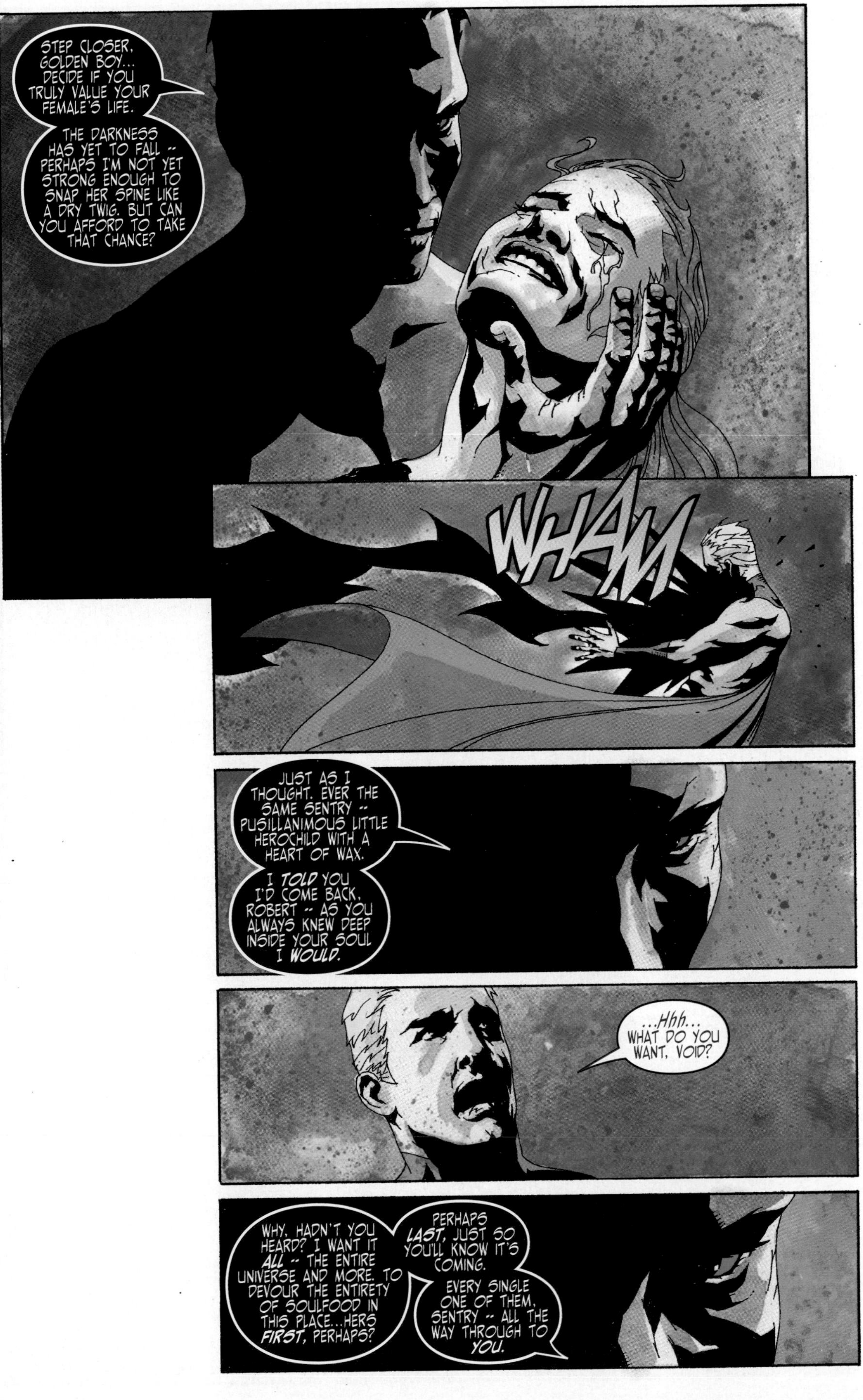
STEP CLOSER, GOLDEN BOY... DECIDE IF YOU TRULY VALUE YOUR FEMALE'S LIFE.
THE DARKNESS HAS YET TO FALL -- PERHAPS I'M NOT YET STRONG ENOUGH TO SNAP HER SPINE LIKE A DRY TWIG. BUT CAN YOU AFFORD TO TAKE THAT CHANCE?
WHAM
JUST AS I THOUGHT. EVER THE SAME SENTRY -- PUSILLANIMOUS LITTLE HEROCHILD WITH A HEART OF WAX.
I TOLD YOU I'D COME BACK, ROBERT -- AS YOU ALWAYS KNEW DEEP INSIDE YOUR SOUL I WOULD.
...Hhh... WHAT DO YOU WANT, VOID?
WHY, HADN'T YOU HEARD? I WANT IT ALL -- THE ENTIRE UNIVERSE AND MORE. TO DEVOUR THE ENTIRETY OF SOULFOOD IN THIS PLACE...HERS FIRST, PERHAPS?
PERHAPS LAST, JUST SO YOU'LL KNOW IT'S COMING.
EVERY SINGLE ONE OF THEM, SENTRY -- ALL THE WAY THROUGH TO YOU.

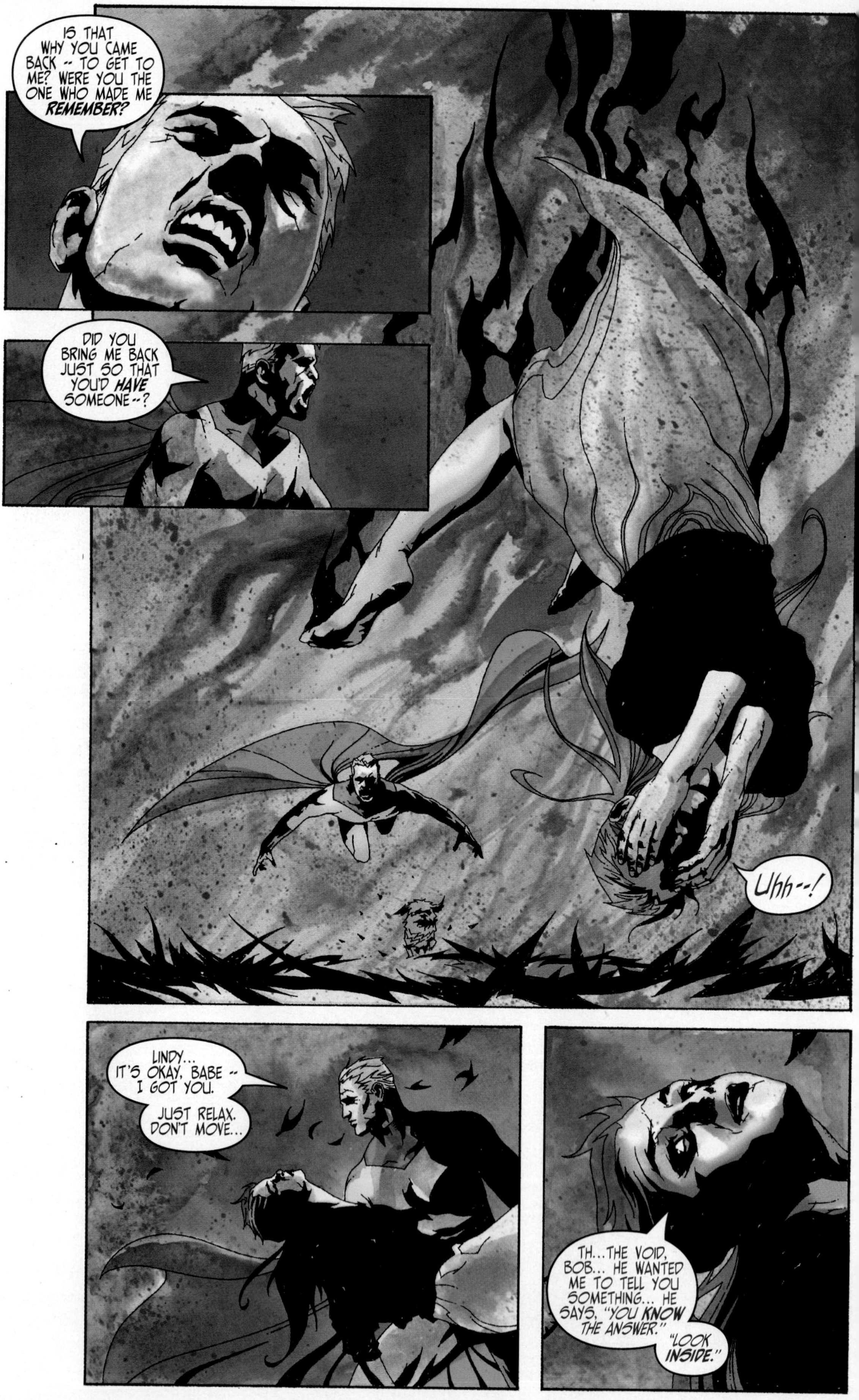
IS THAT WHY YOU CAME BACK -- TO GET TO ME? WERE YOU THE ONE WHO MADE ME REMEMBER?
DID YOU BRING ME BACK JUST SO THAT YOU'D HAVE SOMEONE--?
Uhh--!
LINDY... IT'S OKAY, BABE -- I GOT YOU.
JUST RELAX. DON'T MOVE...
TH...THE VOID, BOB... HE WANTED ME TO TELL YOU SOMETHING... HE SAYS, "YOU KNOW THE ANSWER."
"LOOK INSIDE."

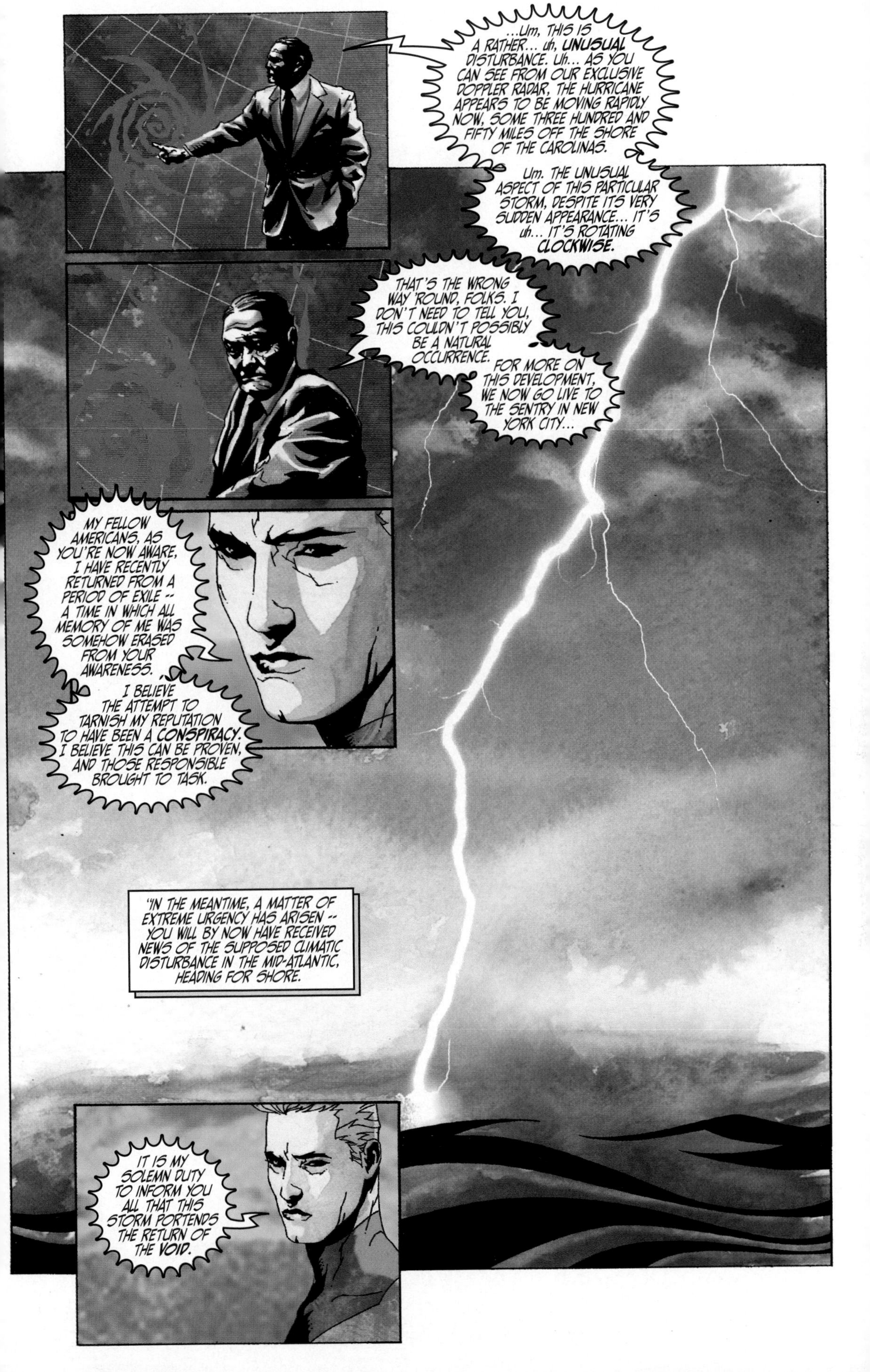
...UM, THIS IS A RATHER... UH, UNUSUAL DISTURBANCE. UH... AS YOU CAN SEE FROM OUR EXCLUSIVE DOPPLER RADAR, THE HURRICANE APPEARS TO BE MOVING RAPIDLY NOW, SOME THREE HUNDRED AND FIFTY MILES OFF THE SHORE OF THE CAROLINAS.
UM. THE UNUSUAL ASPECT OF THIS PARTICULAR STORM, DESPITE ITS VERY SUDDEN APPEARANCE... IT'S UH... IT'S ROTATING CLOCKWISE.
THAT'S THE WRONG WAY 'ROUND, FOLKS. I DON'T NEED TO TELL YOU, THIS COULDN'T POSSIBLY BE A NATURAL OCCURRENCE.
FOR MORE ON THIS DEVELOPMENT, WE NOW GO LIVE TO THE SENTRY IN NEW YORK CITY...
MY FELLOW AMERICANS, AS YOU'RE NOW AWARE, I HAVE RECENTLY RETURNED FROM A PERIOD OF EXILE -- A TIME IN WHICH ALL MEMORY OF ME WAS SOMEHOW ERASED FROM YOUR AWARENESS.
I BELIEVE THE ATTEMPT TO TARNISH MY REPUTATION TO HAVE BEEN A CONSPIRACY. I BELIEVE THIS CAN BE PROVEN, AND THOSE RESPONSIBLE BROUGHT TO TASK.
"IN THE MEANTIME, A MATTER OF EXTREME URGENCY HAS ARISEN -- YOU WILL BY NOW HAVE RECEIVED NEWS OF THE SUPPOSED CLIMATIC DISTURBANCE IN THE MID-ATLANTIC, HEADING FOR SHORE.
IT IS MY SOLEMN DUTY TO INFORM YOU ALL THAT THIS STORM PORTENDS THE RETURN OF THE VOID.

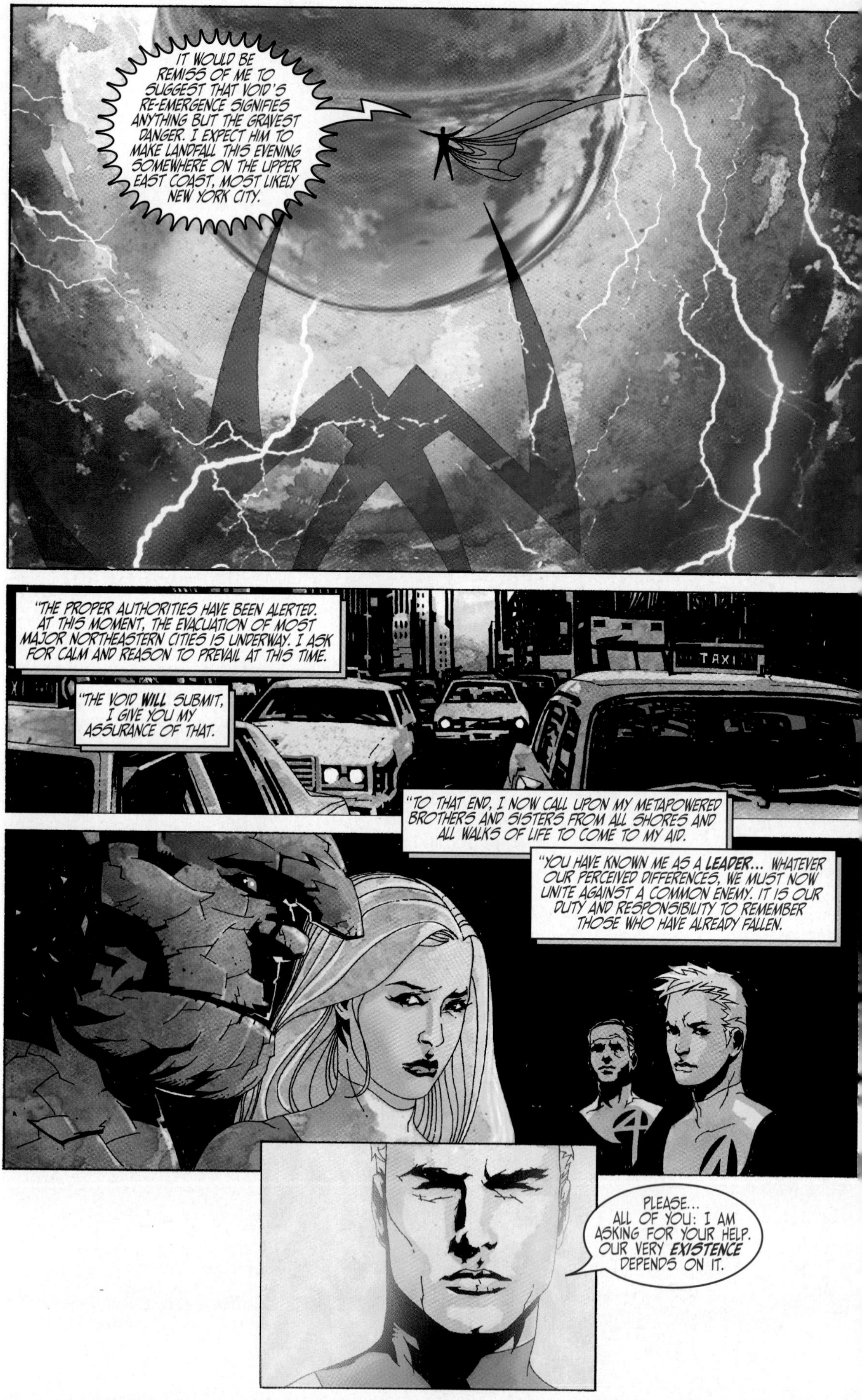
IT WOULD BE REMISS OF ME TO SUGGEST THAT VOID'S RE-EMERGENCE SIGNIFIES ANYTHING BUT THE GRAVEST DANGER. I EXPECT HIM TO MAKE LANDFALL THIS EVENING SOMEWHERE ON THE UPPER EAST COAST, MOST LIKELY NEW YORK CITY.
"THE PROPER AUTHORITIES HAVE BEEN ALERTED. AT THIS MOMENT, THE EVACUATION OF MOST MAJOR NORTHEASTERN CITIES IS UNDERWAY. I ASK FOR CALM AND REASON TO PREVAIL AT THIS TIME.
TAXI
"THE VOID **WILL** SUBMIT, I GIVE YOU MY ASSURANCE OF THAT.
"TO THAT END, I NOW CALL UPON MY METAPOWERED BROTHERS AND SISTERS FROM ALL SHORES AND ALL WALKS OF LIFE TO COME TO MY AID.
"YOU HAVE KNOWN ME AS A **LEADER...** WHATEVER OUR PERCEIVED DIFFERENCES, WE MUST NOW UNITE AGAINST A COMMON ENEMY. IT IS OUR DUTY AND RESPONSIBILITY TO REMEMBER THOSE WHO HAVE ALREADY FALLEN.
PLEASE... ALL OF YOU: I AM ASKING FOR YOUR HELP. OUR VERY ***EXISTENCE*** DEPENDS ON IT.

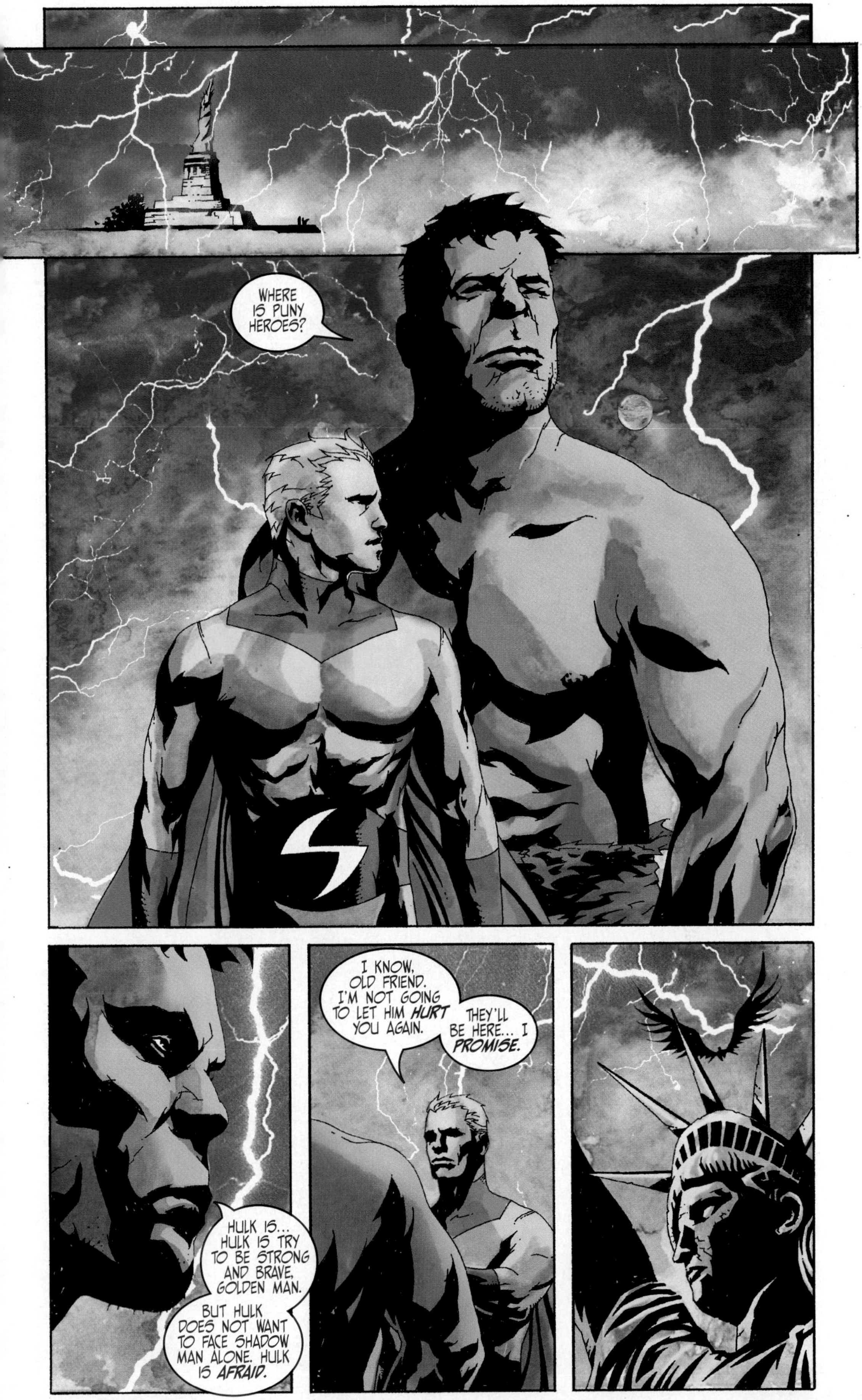

WHERE IS PUNY HEROES?
HULK IS... HULK IS TRY TO BE STRONG AND BRAVE, GOLDEN MAN.
BUT HULK DOES NOT WANT TO FACE SHADOW MAN ALONE. HULK IS AFRAID.
I KNOW, OLD FRIEND. I'M NOT GOING TO LET HIM HURT YOU AGAIN.
THEY'LL BE HERE... I PROMISE.

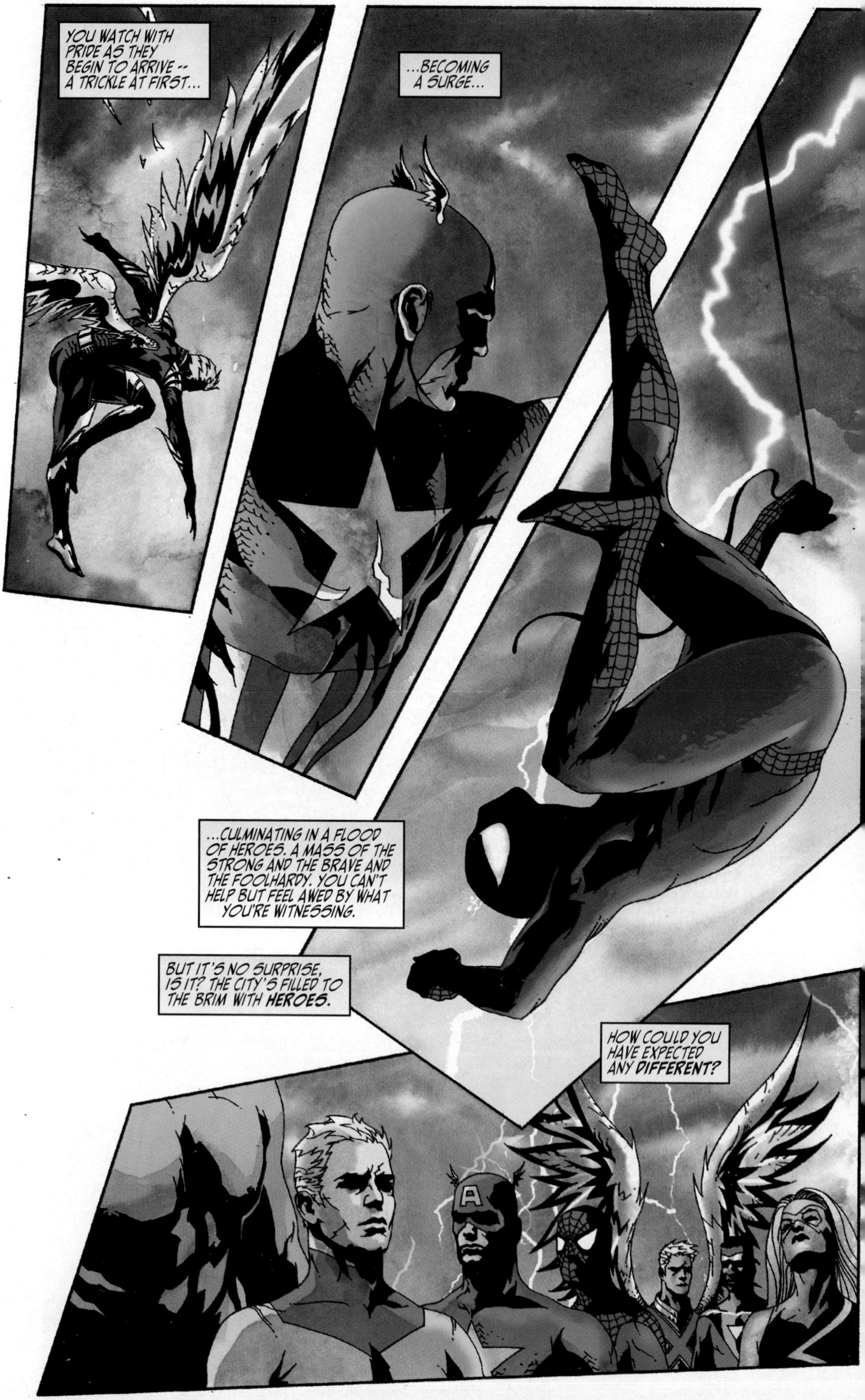
YOU WATCH WITH PRIDE AS THEY BEGIN TO ARRIVE -- A TRICKLE AT FIRST...
...BECOMING A SURGE...
...CULMINATING IN A FLOOD OF HEROES. A MASS OF THE STRONG AND THE BRAVE AND THE FOOLHARDY. YOU CAN'T HELP BUT FEEL AWED BY WHAT YOU'RE WITNESSING.
BUT IT'S NO SURPRISE, IS IT? THE CITY'S FILLED TO THE BRIM WITH **HEROES**.
HOW COULD YOU HAVE EXPECTED ANY **DIFFERENT**?

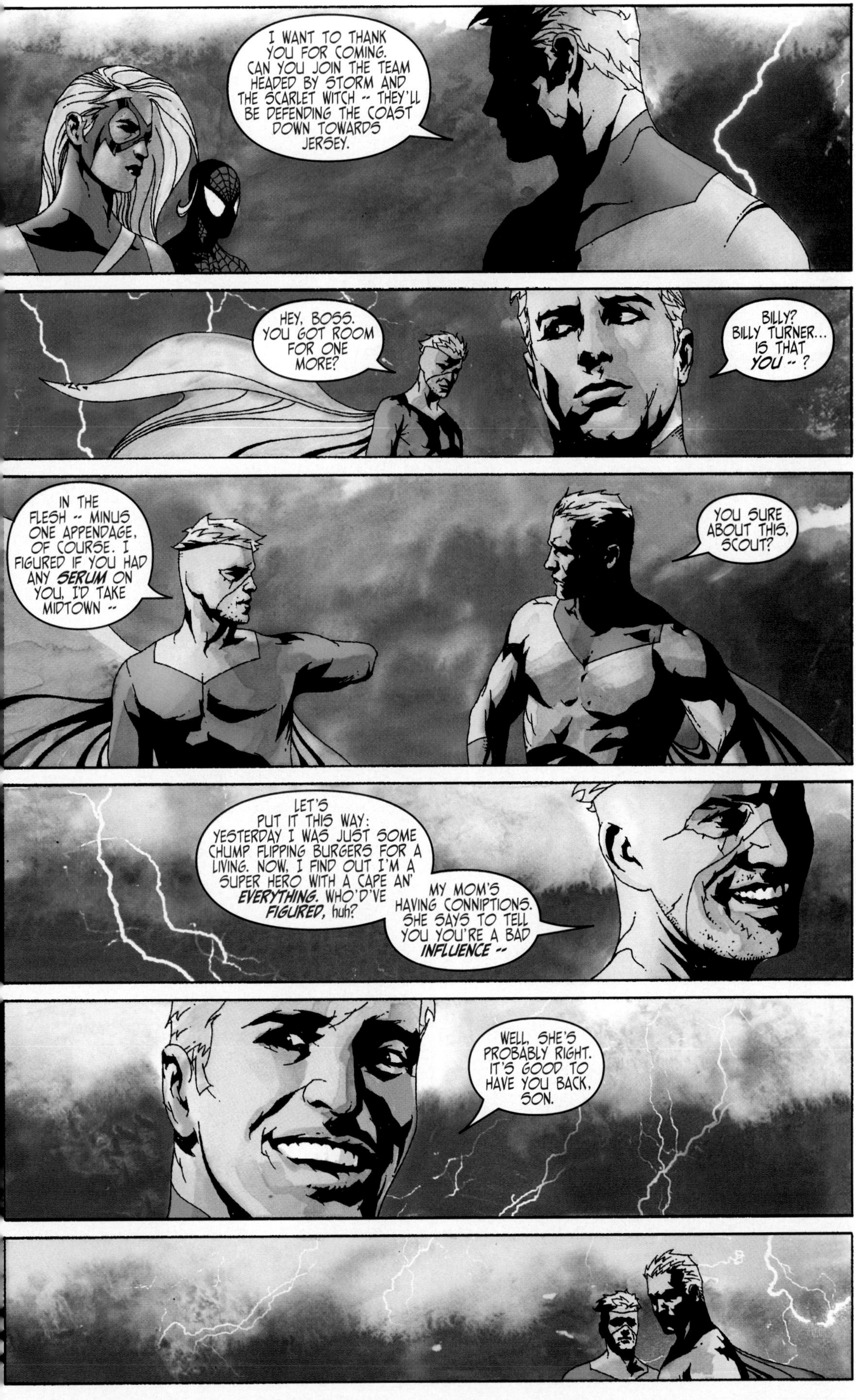
I WANT TO THANK YOU FOR COMING. CAN YOU JOIN THE TEAM HEADED BY STORM AND THE SCARLET WITCH -- THEY'LL BE DEFENDING THE COAST DOWN TOWARDS JERSEY.
HEY, BOSS. YOU GOT ROOM FOR ONE MORE?
BILLY? BILLY TURNER... IS THAT YOU -- ?
IN THE FLESH -- MINUS ONE APPENDAGE, OF COURSE. I FIGURED IF YOU HAD ANY SERUM ON YOU, I'D TAKE MIDTOWN --
YOU SURE ABOUT THIS, SCOUT?
LET'S PUT IT THIS WAY: YESTERDAY I WAS JUST SOME CHUMP FLIPPING BURGERS FOR A LIVING. NOW, I FIND OUT I'M A SUPER HERO WITH A CAPE AN' EVERYTHING. WHO'D'VE FIGURED, huh?
MY MOM'S HAVING CONNIPTIONS. SHE SAYS TO TELL YOU YOU'RE A BAD INFLUENCE --
WELL, SHE'S PROBABLY RIGHT. IT'S GOOD TO HAVE YOU BACK, SON.

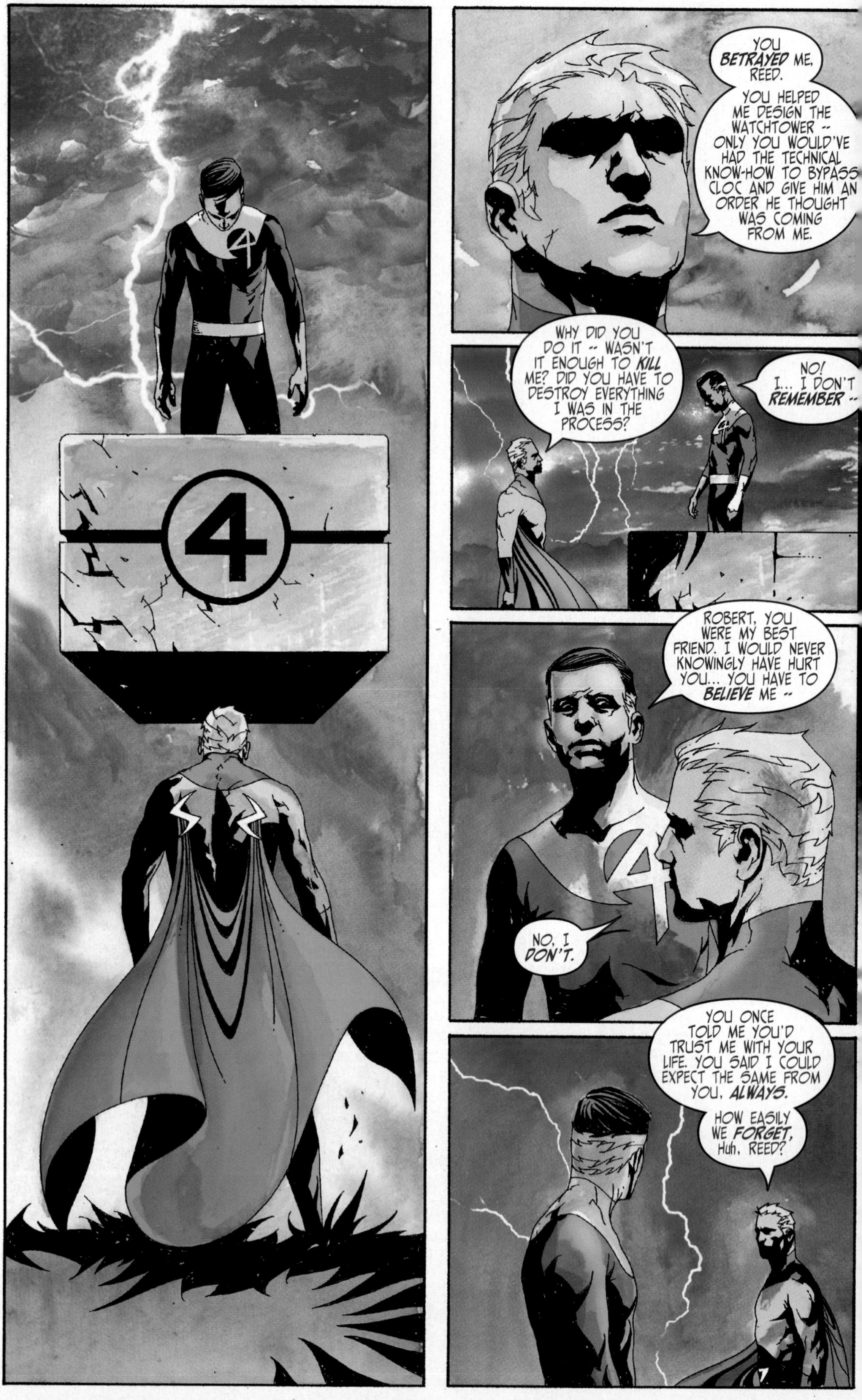
YOU BETRAYED ME, REED.
YOU HELPED ME DESIGN THE WATCHTOWER -- ONLY YOU WOULD'VE HAD THE TECHNICAL KNOW-HOW TO BYPASS CLOC AND GIVE HIM AN ORDER HE THOUGHT WAS COMING FROM ME.
WHY DID YOU DO IT -- WASN'T IT ENOUGH TO KILL ME? DID YOU HAVE TO DESTROY EVERYTHING I WAS IN THE PROCESS?
NO! I... I DON'T REMEMBER --
ROBERT, YOU WERE MY BEST FRIEND. I WOULD NEVER KNOWINGLY HAVE HURT YOU... YOU HAVE TO BELIEVE ME --
NO, I DON'T.
YOU ONCE TOLD ME YOU'D TRUST ME WITH YOUR LIFE. YOU SAID I COULD EXPECT THE SAME FROM YOU, ALWAYS.
HOW EASILY WE FORGET, Huh, REED?

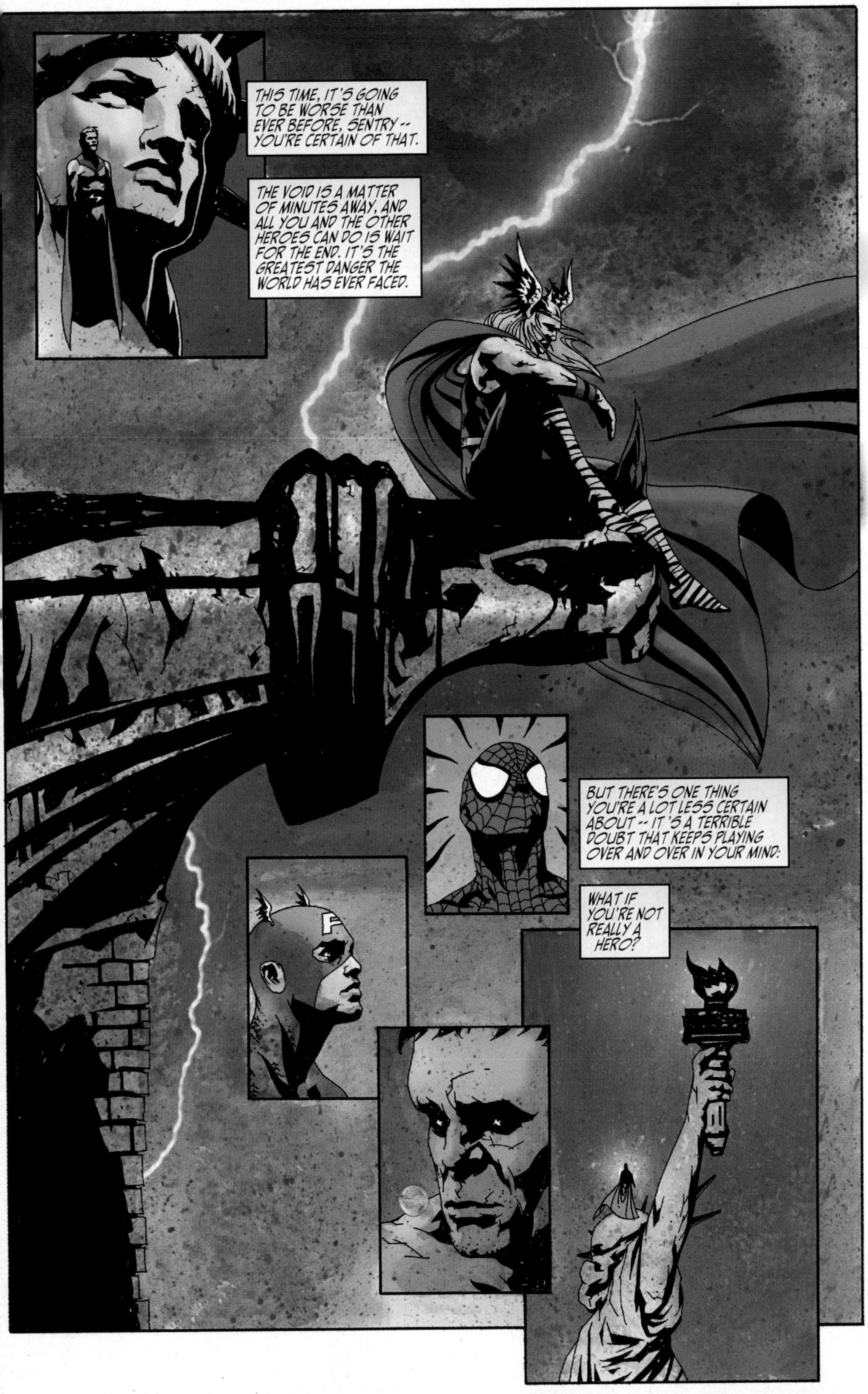
THIS TIME, IT'S GOING TO BE WORSE THAN EVER BEFORE, SENTRY -- YOU'RE CERTAIN OF THAT.
THE VOID IS A MATTER OF MINUTES AWAY, AND ALL YOU AND THE OTHER HEROES CAN DO IS WAIT FOR THE END. IT'S THE GREATEST DANGER THE WORLD HAS EVER FACED.
BUT THERE'S ONE THING YOU'RE A LOT LESS CERTAIN ABOUT -- IT'S A TERRIBLE DOUBT THAT KEEPS PLAYING OVER AND OVER IN YOUR MIND:
WHAT IF YOU'RE NOT REALLY A HERO?

cover gallery

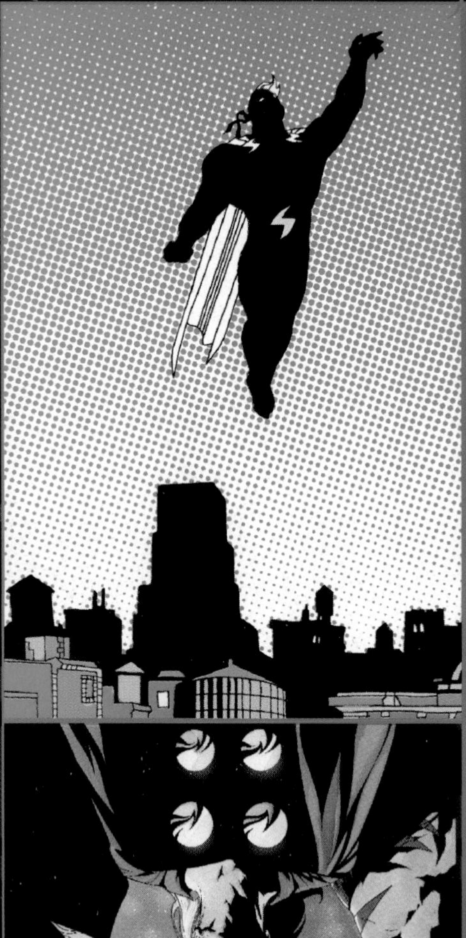

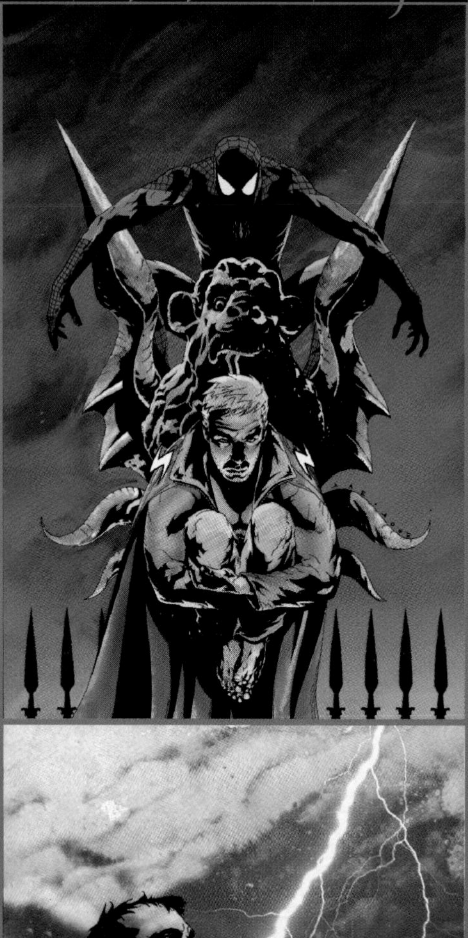

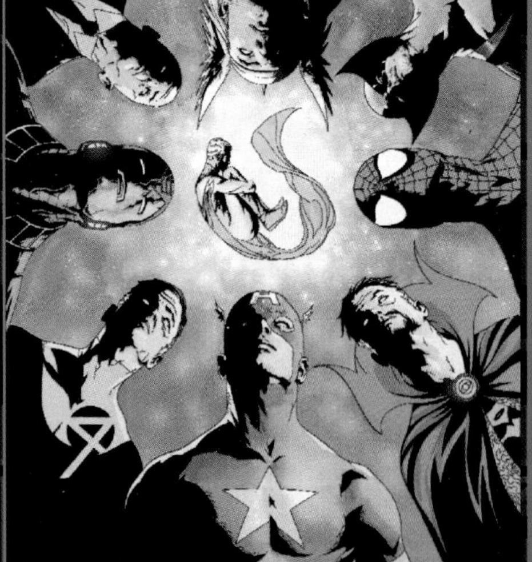

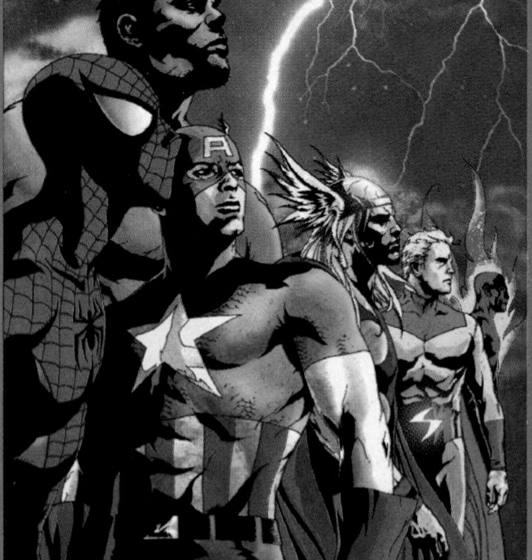

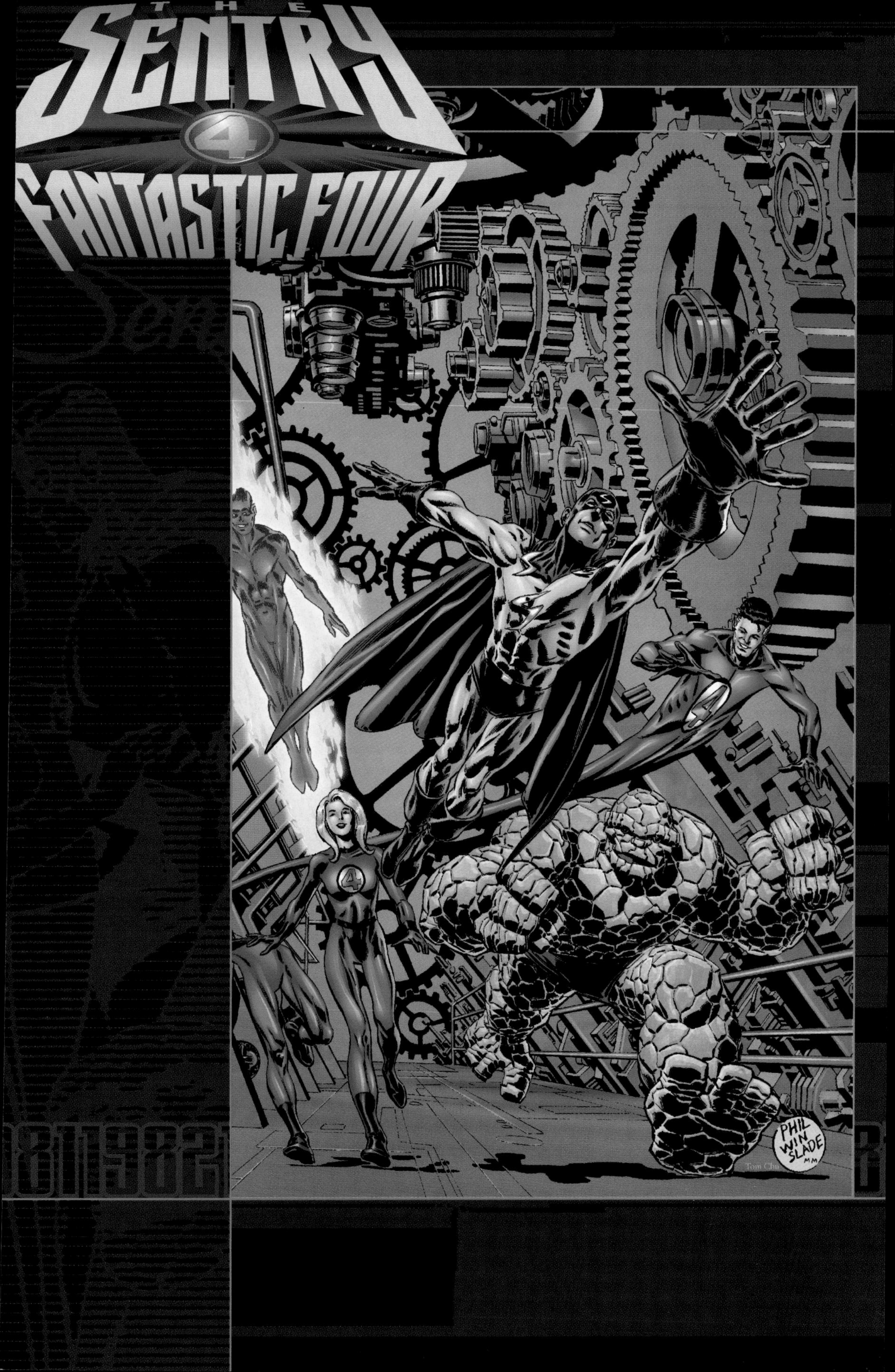
THE SENTRY
4
FANTASTIC FOUR
PHIL WIN SLADE MM
Tom Chu

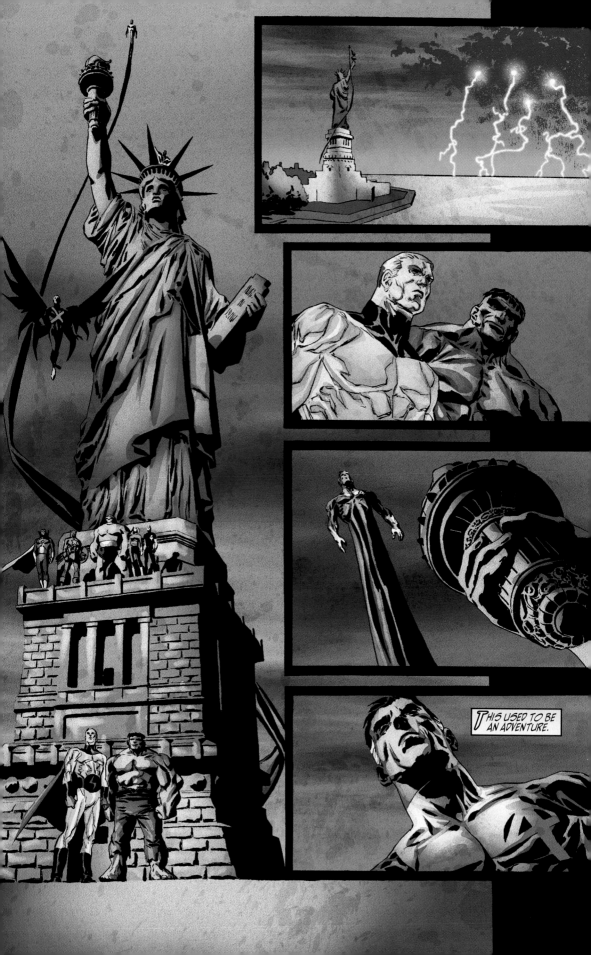

THIS USED TO BE AN ADVENTURE.

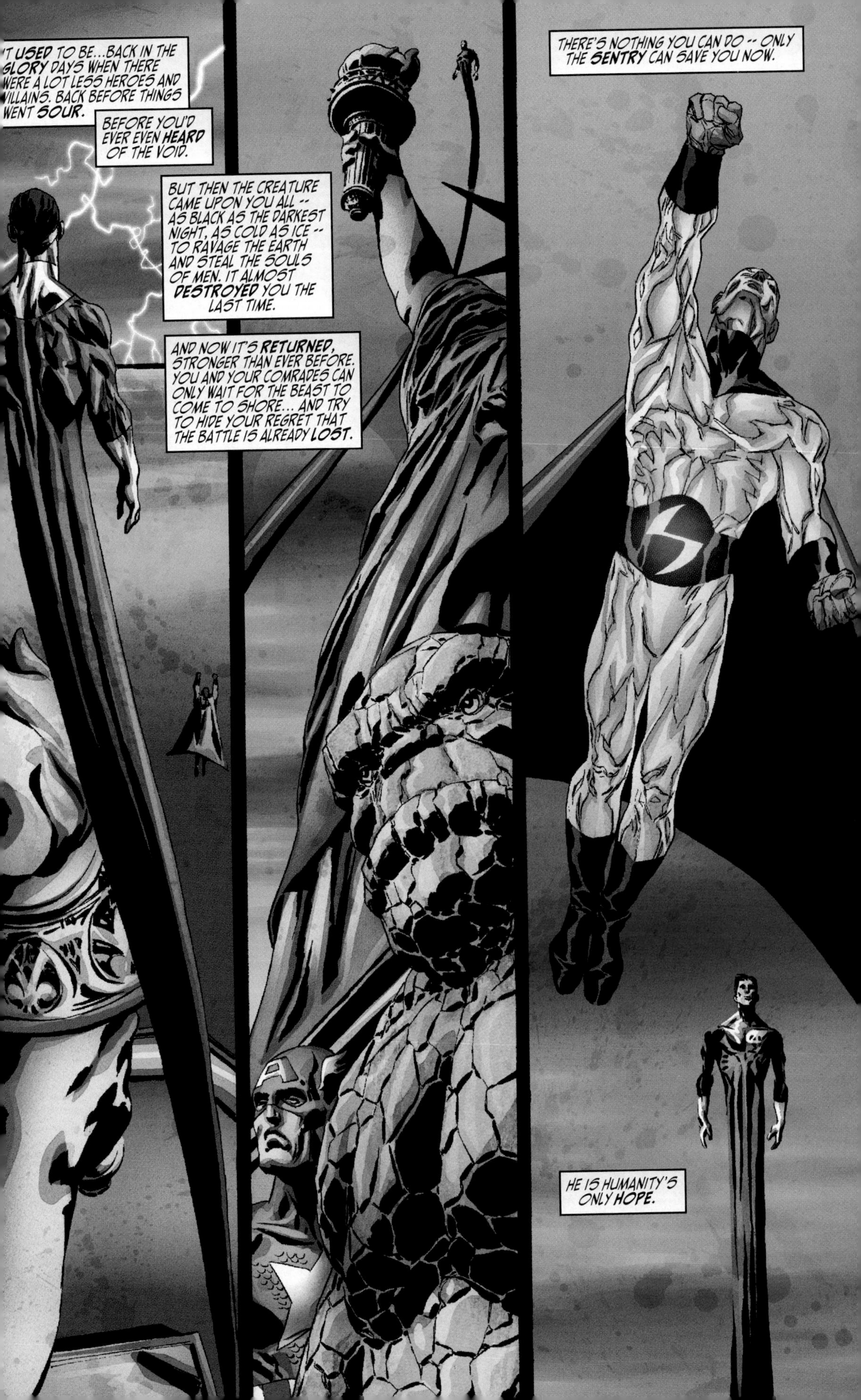
IT USED TO BE...BACK IN THE GLORY DAYS WHEN THERE WERE A LOT LESS HEROES AND VILLAINS. BACK BEFORE THINGS WENT SOUR.
BEFORE YOU'D EVER EVEN HEARD OF THE VOID.
BUT THEN THE CREATURE CAME UPON YOU ALL -- AS BLACK AS THE DARKEST NIGHT, AS COLD AS ICE -- TO RAVAGE THE EARTH AND STEAL THE SOULS OF MEN. IT ALMOST DESTROYED YOU THE LAST TIME.
AND NOW IT'S RETURNED, STRONGER THAN EVER BEFORE. YOU AND YOUR COMRADES CAN ONLY WAIT FOR THE BEAST TO COME TO SHORE... AND TRY TO HIDE YOUR REGRET THAT THE BATTLE IS ALREADY LOST.
THERE'S NOTHING YOU CAN DO -- ONLY THE SENTRY CAN SAVE YOU NOW.
HE IS HUMANITY'S ONLY HOPE.

ADMIT IT, REED: HE'S ALL YOU *HAVE.*

YOU AND THE OTHER HEROES, YOU'LL DO WHAT YOU CAN WHEN THE VOID ATTACKS.

BUT IT WON'T BE NEARLY ENOUGH.

AND SO YOU LOOK TO HIM -- THE BEST FRIEND YOU EVER HAD.

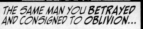

PAUL JENKINS
STORY

PHIL WINSLADE
PENCILS

TOM PALMER
INKS

THE SAME MAN YOU *BETRAYED* AND CONSIGNED TO OBLIVION...

...ALONG WITH ALL MEMORY OF THOSE WONDERFUL *ADVENTURES* YOU SHARED.

TOM CHU
COLORS

RS & COMICRAFT
LETTERS

MIKE RAICHT
ASSISTANT EDITOR

MIKE MARTS
EDITOR

JOE QUESADA
EDITOR IN CHIEF

STARTLING STORIES *featuring*

THE **SENTRY!**

MARVEL COMICS GROUP 12¢

15 APR

THE SENTRY... WHERE DID HE GO?

I CAN'T BELIEVE IT! THE SENTRY -- A *COWARD!*

THE FANTASTIC FOUR AND THE GOLDEN GUARDIAN, DEFEATED BY THE ANDROID PIRATES OF DIMENSION NINE?

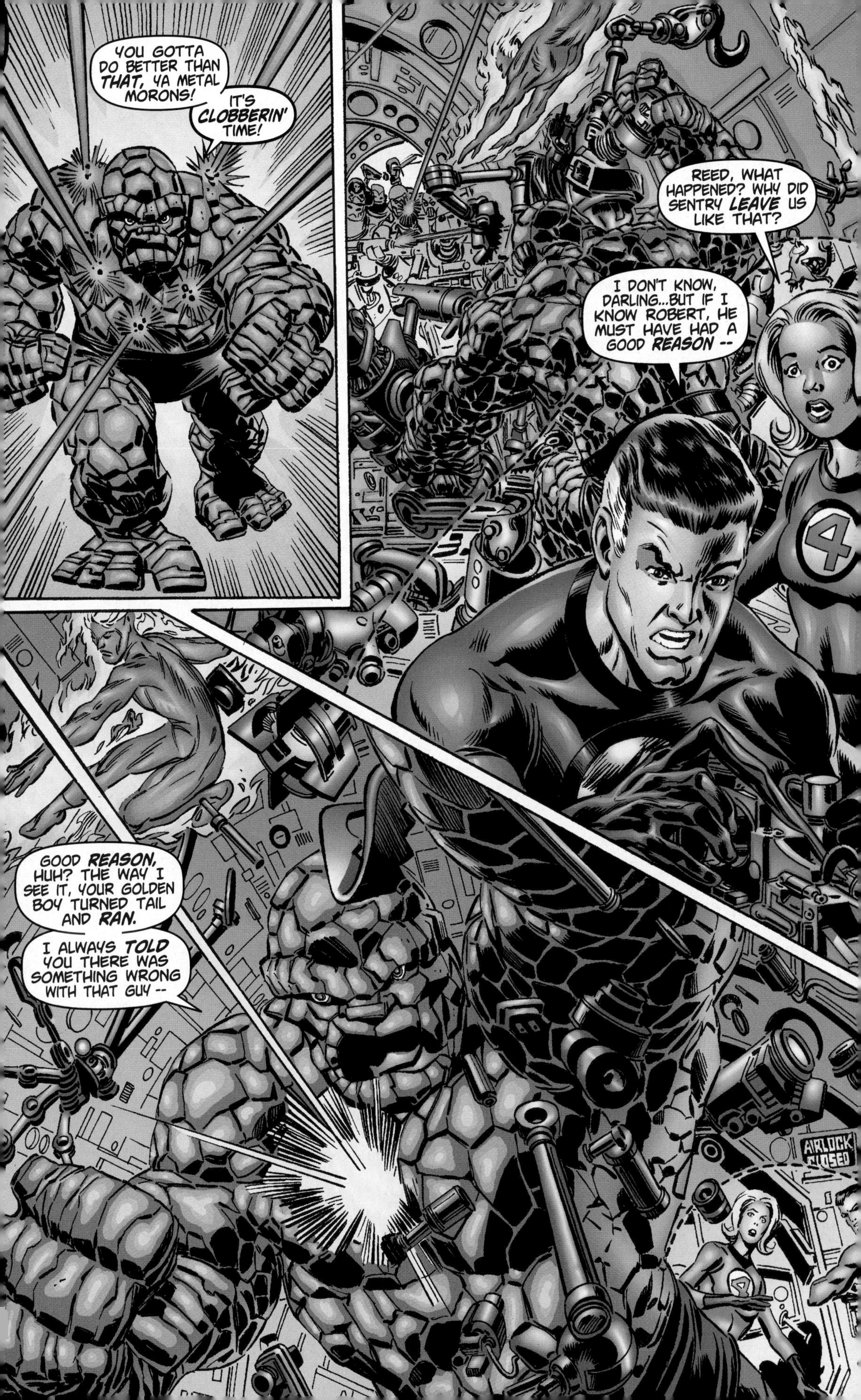
YOU GOTTA DO BETTER THAN THAT, YA METAL MORONS!
IT'S CLOBBERIN' TIME!
REED, WHAT HAPPENED? WHY DID SENTRY LEAVE US LIKE THAT?
I DON'T KNOW, DARLING...BUT IF I KNOW ROBERT, HE MUST HAVE HAD A GOOD REASON --
GOOD REASON, HUH? THE WAY I SEE IT, YOUR GOLDEN BOY TURNED TAIL AND RAN.
I ALWAYS TOLD YOU THERE WAS SOMETHING WRONG WITH THAT GUY --
AIRLOCK CLOSED

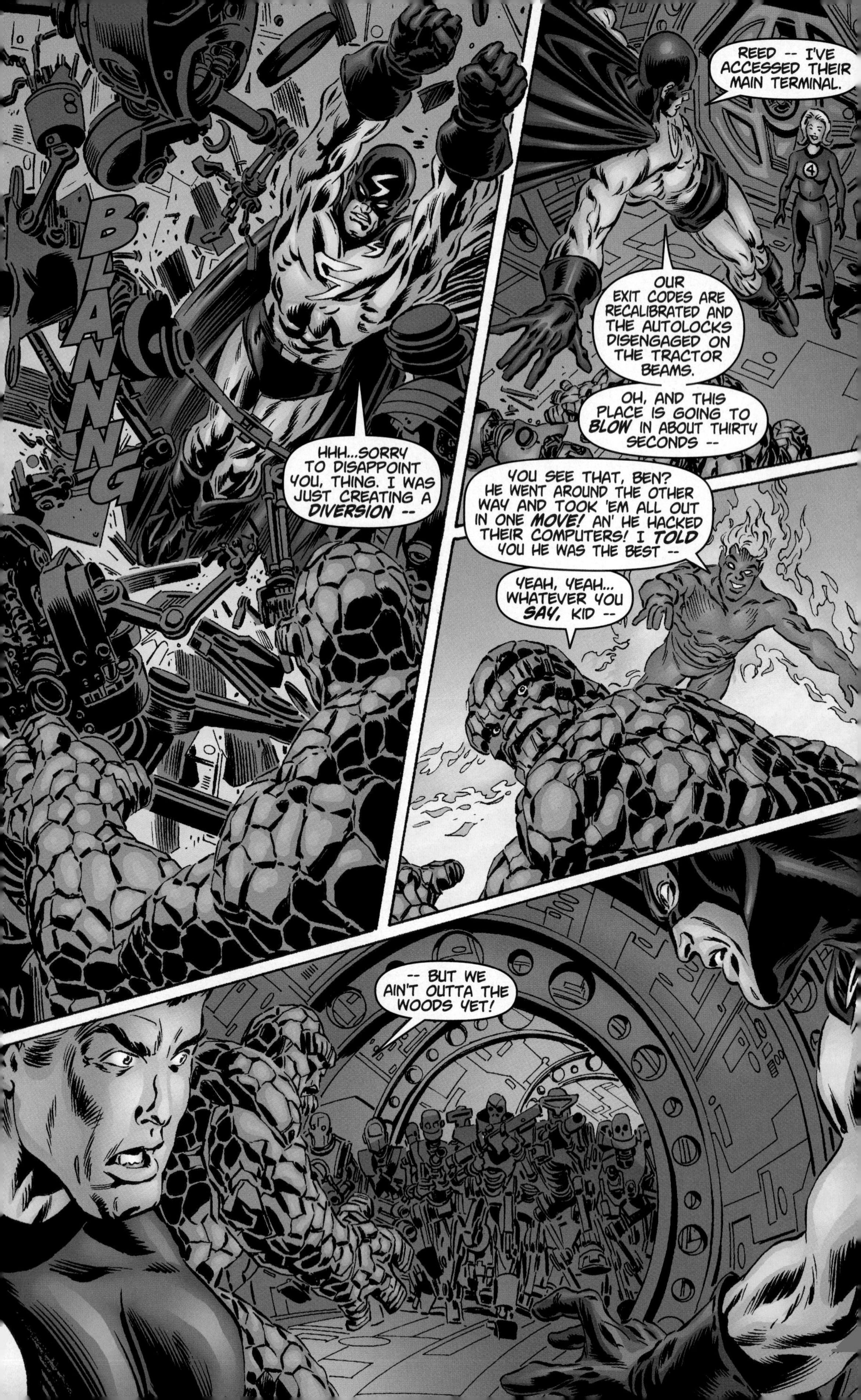
BLANNNG
HHH...SORRY TO DISAPPOINT YOU, THING. I WAS JUST CREATING A DIVERSION --
REED -- I'VE ACCESSED THEIR MAIN TERMINAL.
OUR EXIT CODES ARE RECALIBRATED AND THE AUTOLOCKS DISENGAGED ON THE TRACTOR BEAMS.
OH, AND THIS PLACE IS GOING TO BLOW IN ABOUT THIRTY SECONDS --
YOU SEE THAT, BEN? HE WENT AROUND THE OTHER WAY AND TOOK 'EM ALL OUT IN ONE MOVE! AN' HE HACKED THEIR COMPUTERS! I TOLD YOU HE WAS THE BEST --
YEAH, YEAH... WHATEVER YOU SAY, KID --
-- BUT WE AIN'T OUTTA THE WOODS YET!

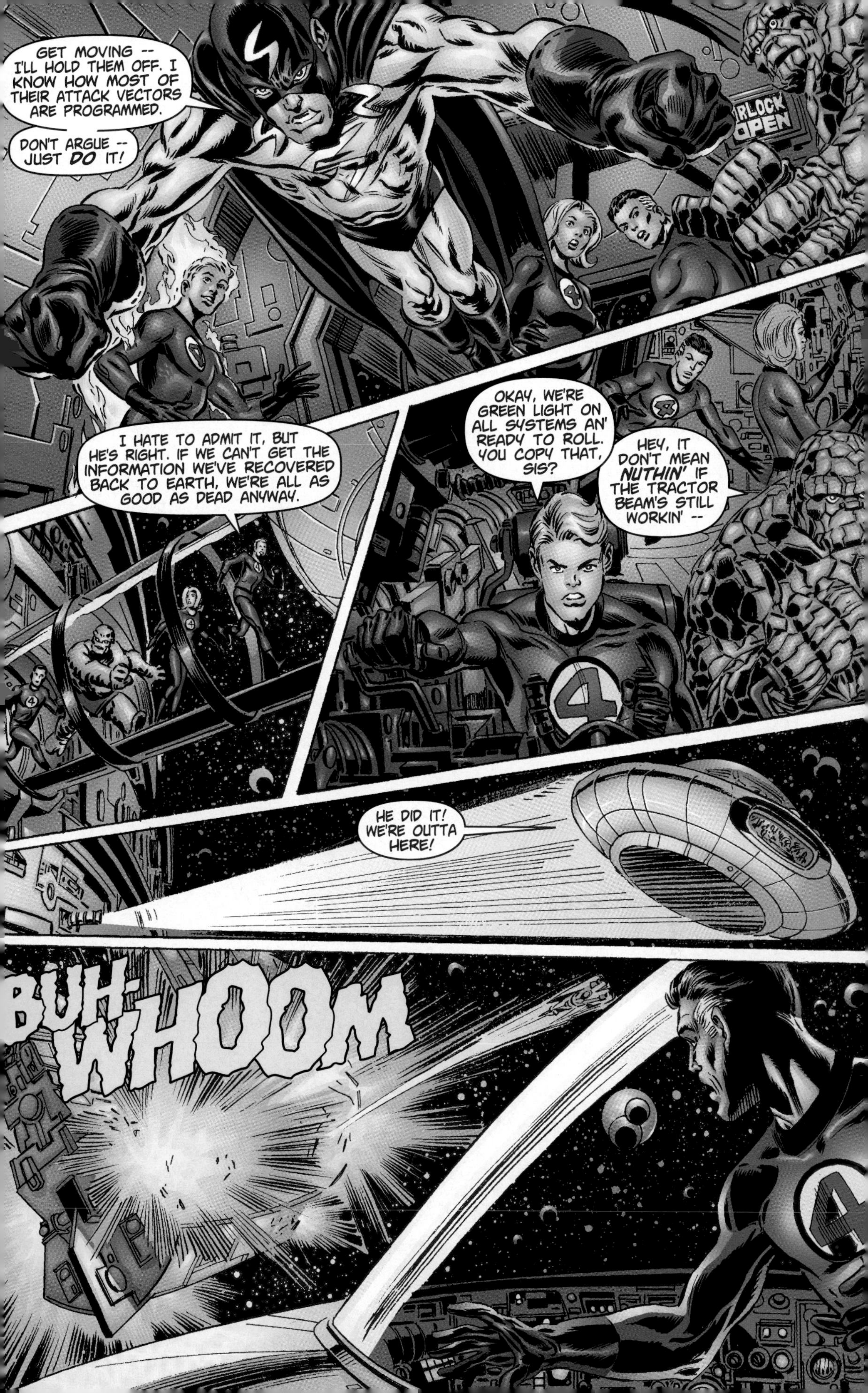
GET MOVING -- I'LL HOLD THEM OFF. I KNOW HOW MOST OF THEIR ATTACK VECTORS ARE PROGRAMMED.
DON'T ARGUE -- JUST DO IT!
OPEN
I HATE TO ADMIT IT, BUT HE'S RIGHT. IF WE CAN'T GET THE INFORMATION WE'VE RECOVERED BACK TO EARTH, WE'RE ALL AS GOOD AS DEAD ANYWAY.
OKAY, WE'RE GREEN LIGHT ON ALL SYSTEMS AN' READY TO ROLL. YOU COPY THAT, SIS?
HEY, IT DON'T MEAN NUTHIN' IF THE TRACTOR BEAM'S STILL WORKIN' --
HE DID IT! WE'RE OUTTA HERE!
BUH-WHOOM

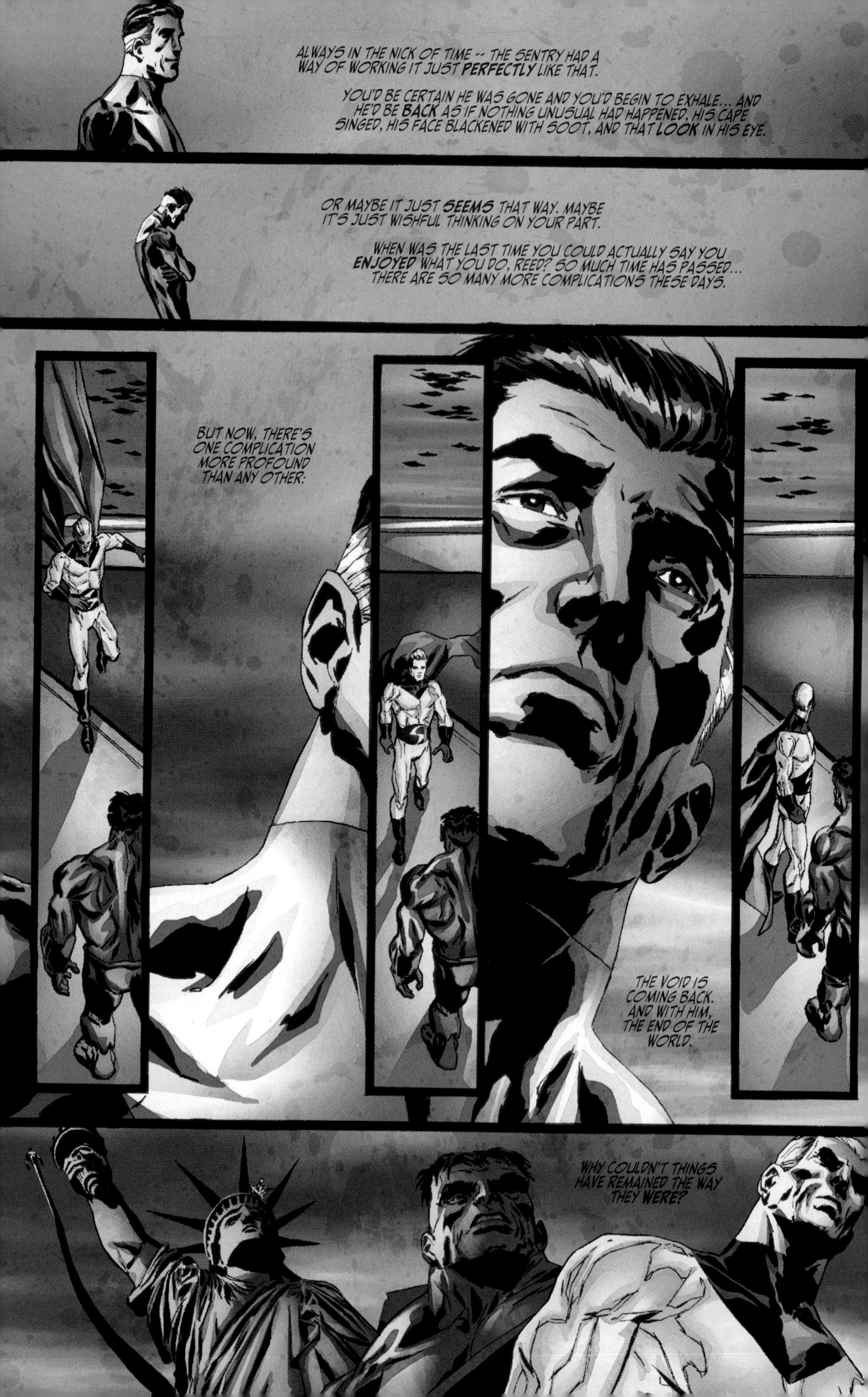
ALWAYS IN THE NICK OF TIME -- THE SENTRY HAD A WAY OF WORKING IT JUST PERFECTLY LIKE THAT.
YOU'D BE CERTAIN HE WAS GONE AND YOU'D BEGIN TO EXHALE... AND HE'D BE BACK AS IF NOTHING UNUSUAL HAD HAPPENED, HIS CAPE SINGED, HIS FACE BLACKENED WITH SOOT, AND THAT LOOK IN HIS EYE.
OR MAYBE IT JUST SEEMS THAT WAY. MAYBE IT'S JUST WISHFUL THINKING ON YOUR PART.
WHEN WAS THE LAST TIME YOU COULD ACTUALLY SAY YOU ENJOYED WHAT YOU DO, REED? SO MUCH TIME HAS PASSED... THERE ARE SO MANY MORE COMPLICATIONS THESE DAYS.
BUT NOW, THERE'S ONE COMPLICATION MORE PROFOUND THAN ANY OTHER:
THE VOID IS COMING BACK. AND WITH HIM, THE END OF THE WORLD.
WHY COULDN'T THINGS HAVE REMAINED THE WAY THEY WERE?

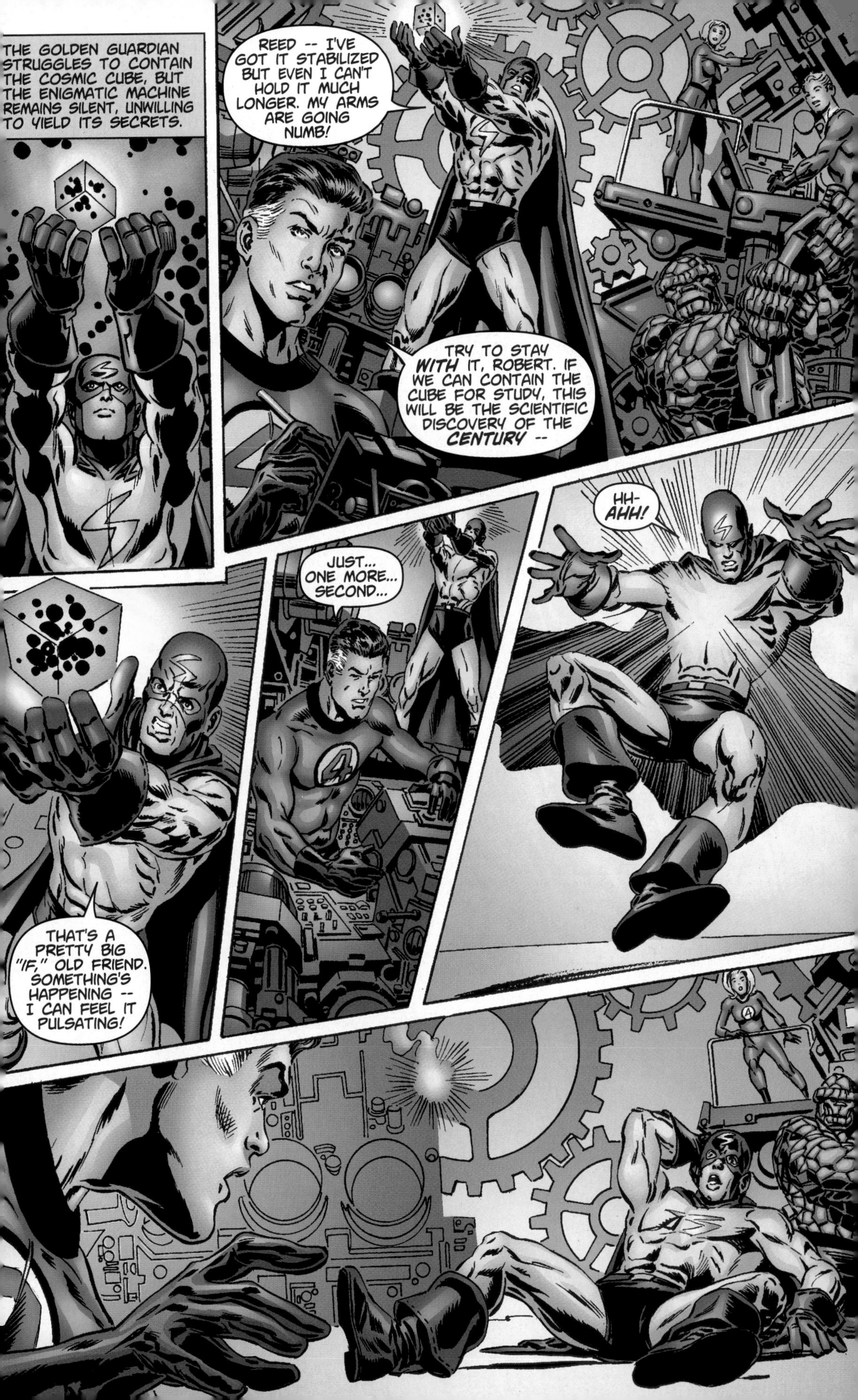

THE GOLDEN GUARDIAN STRUGGLES TO CONTAIN THE COSMIC CUBE, BUT THE ENIGMATIC MACHINE REMAINS SILENT, UNWILLING TO YIELD ITS SECRETS.
REED -- I'VE GOT IT STABILIZED BUT EVEN I CAN'T HOLD IT MUCH LONGER. MY ARMS ARE GOING NUMB!
TRY TO STAY WITH IT, ROBERT. IF WE CAN CONTAIN THE CUBE FOR STUDY, THIS WILL BE THE SCIENTIFIC DISCOVERY OF THE CENTURY --
THAT'S A PRETTY BIG "IF," OLD FRIEND. SOMETHING'S HAPPENING -- I CAN FEEL IT PULSATING!
JUST... ONE MORE... SECOND...
HH-AHH!

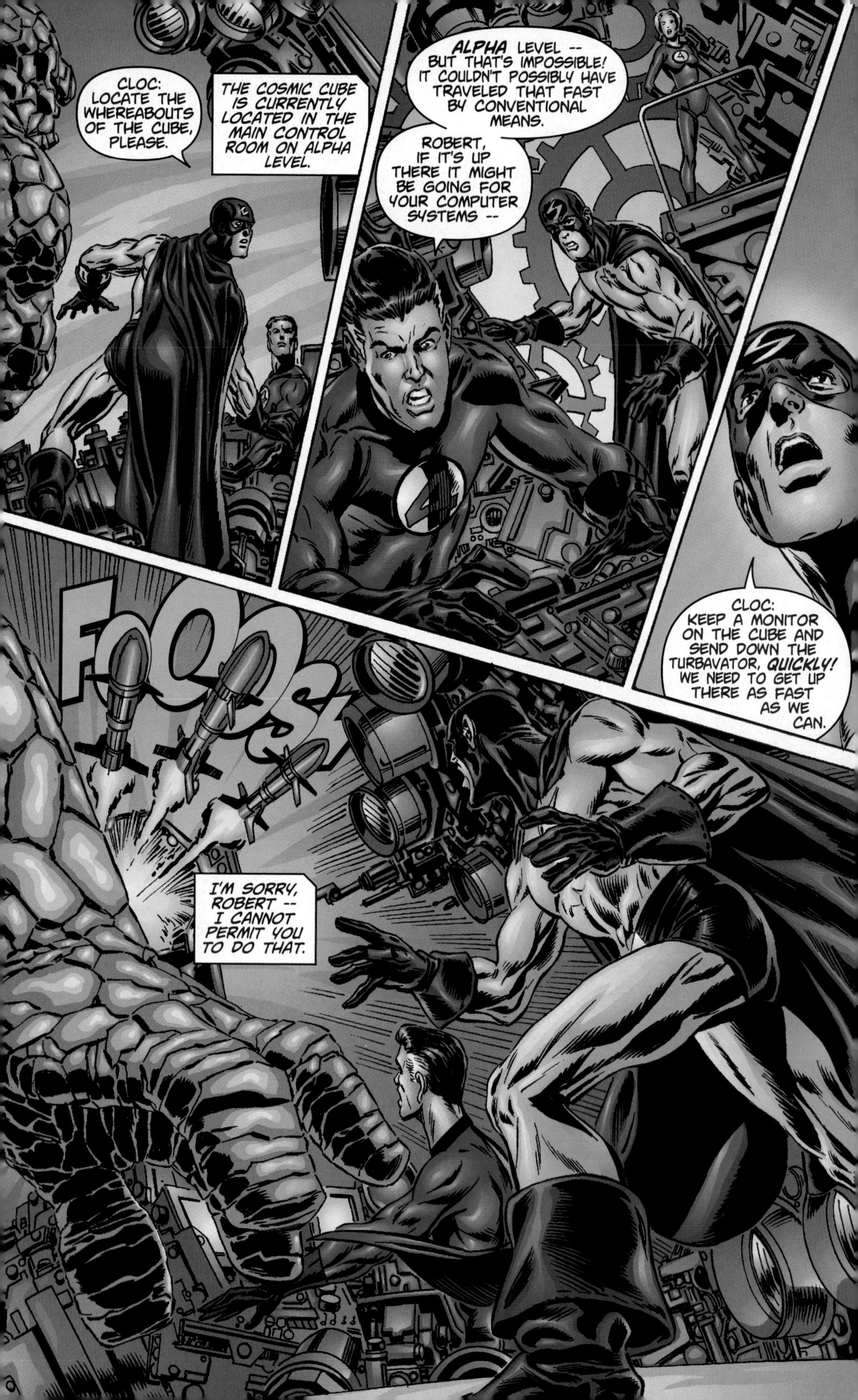
CLOC: LOCATE THE WHEREABOUTS OF THE CUBE, PLEASE.
THE COSMIC CUBE IS CURRENTLY LOCATED IN THE MAIN CONTROL ROOM ON ALPHA LEVEL.
ALPHA LEVEL -- BUT THAT'S IMPOSSIBLE! IT COULDN'T POSSIBLY HAVE TRAVELED THAT FAST BY CONVENTIONAL MEANS.
ROBERT, IF IT'S UP THERE IT MIGHT BE GOING FOR YOUR COMPUTER SYSTEMS --
CLOC: KEEP A MONITOR ON THE CUBE AND SEND DOWN THE TURBAVATOR, QUICKLY! WE NEED TO GET UP THERE AS FAST AS WE CAN.
FOOOSH
I'M SORRY, ROBERT -- I CANNOT PERMIT YOU TO DO THAT.

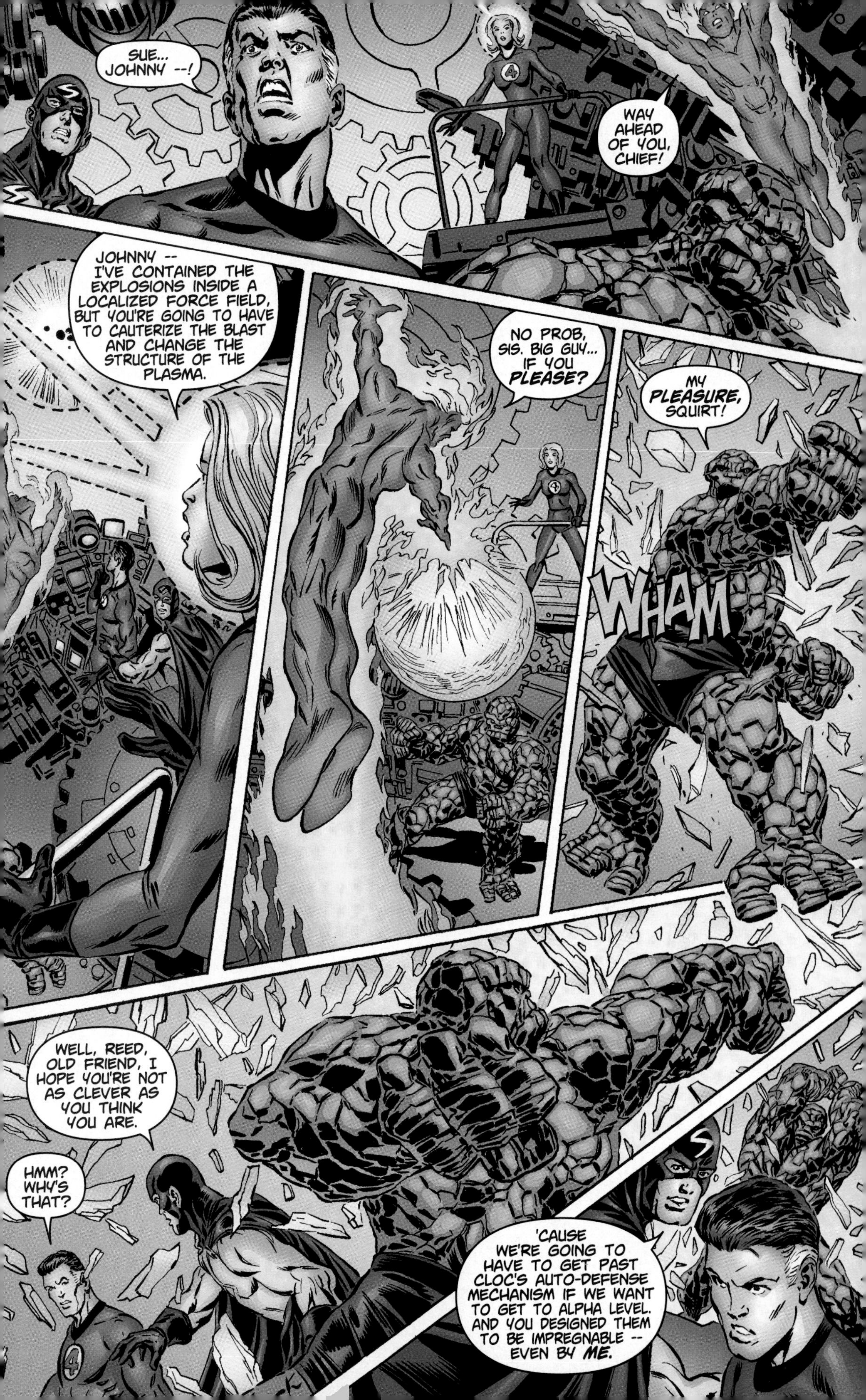
SUE... JOHNNY --!
WAY AHEAD OF YOU, CHIEF!
JOHNNY -- I'VE CONTAINED THE EXPLOSIONS INSIDE A LOCALIZED FORCE FIELD, BUT YOU'RE GOING TO HAVE TO CAUTERIZE THE BLAST AND CHANGE THE STRUCTURE OF THE PLASMA.
NO PROB, SIS. BIG GUY... IF YOU *PLEASE?*
MY *PLEASURE,* SQUIRT!
WHAM
WELL, REED, OLD FRIEND, I HOPE YOU'RE NOT AS CLEVER AS YOU THINK YOU ARE.
HMM? WHY'S THAT?
'CAUSE WE'RE GOING TO HAVE TO GET PAST CLOC'S AUTO-DEFENSE MECHANISM IF WE WANT TO GET TO ALPHA LEVEL. AND YOU DESIGNED THEM TO BE IMPREGNABLE -- EVEN BY *ME.*

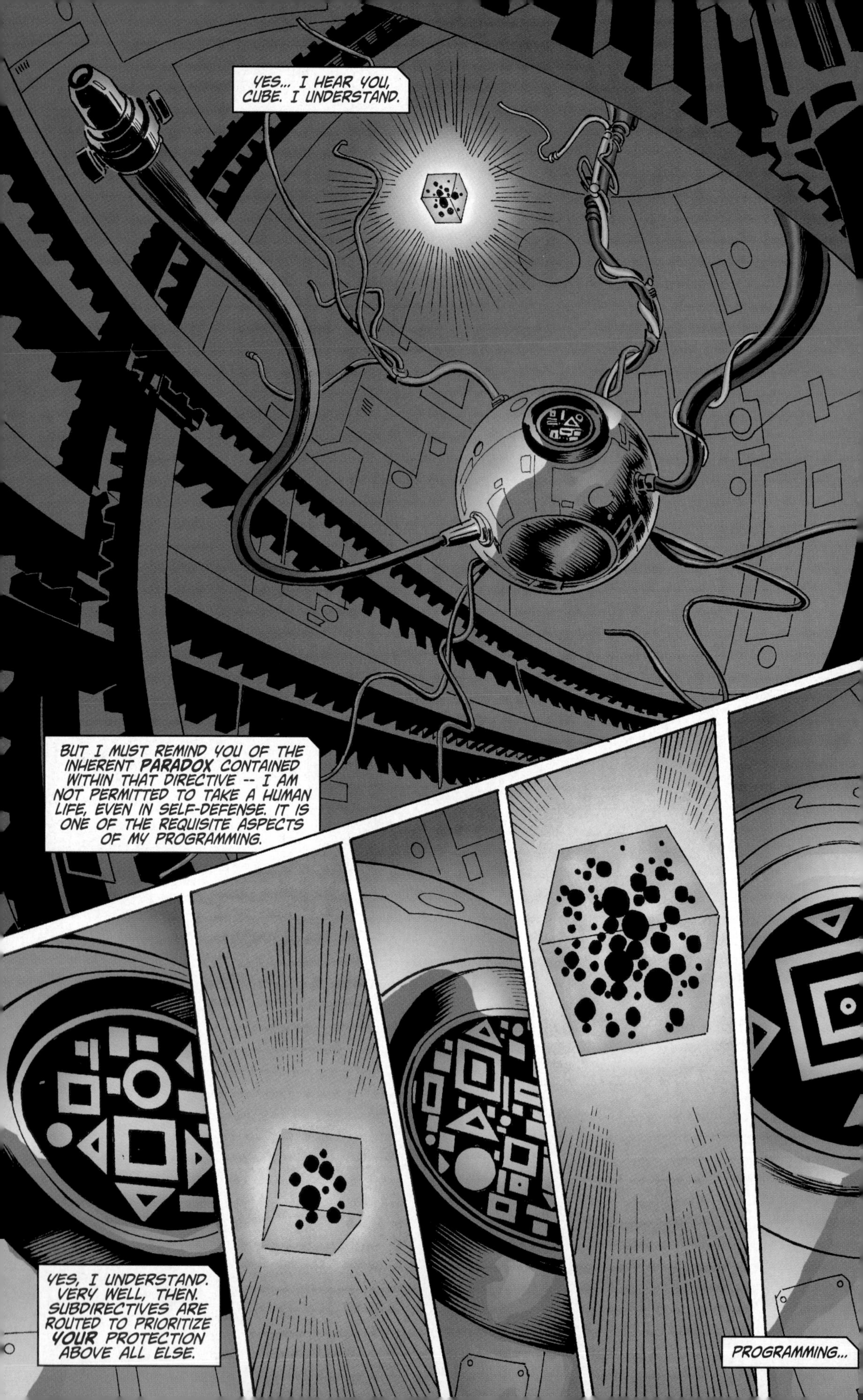
YES... I HEAR YOU, CUBE. I UNDERSTAND.
BUT I MUST REMIND YOU OF THE INHERENT PARADOX CONTAINED WITHIN THAT DIRECTIVE -- I AM NOT PERMITTED TO TAKE A HUMAN LIFE, EVEN IN SELF-DEFENSE. IT IS ONE OF THE REQUISITE ASPECTS OF MY PROGRAMMING.
YES, I UNDERSTAND. VERY WELL, THEN. SUBDIRECTIVES ARE ROUTED TO PRIORITIZE YOUR PROTECTION ABOVE ALL ELSE.
PROGRAMMING...

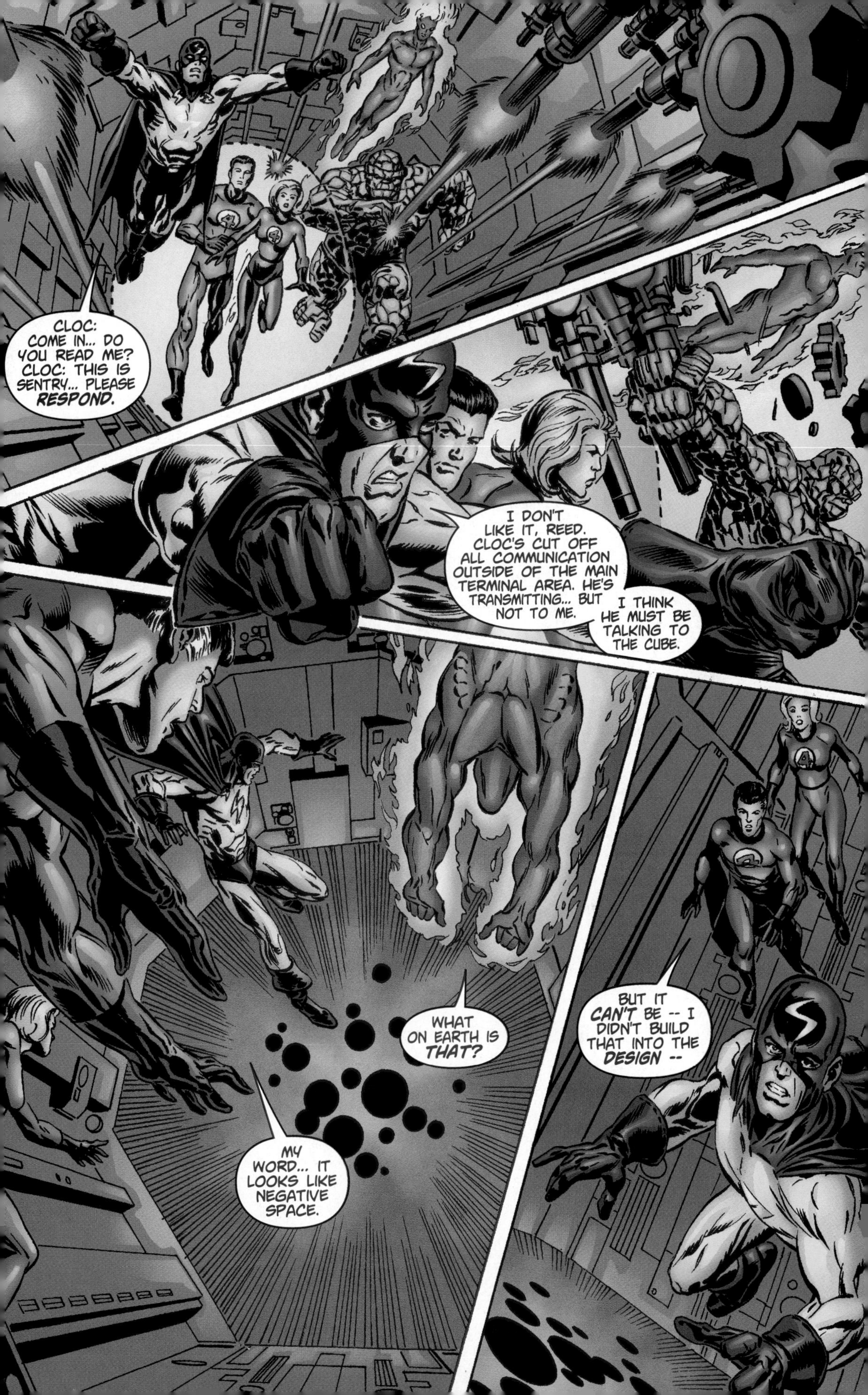
CLOC: COME IN... DO YOU READ ME? CLOC: THIS IS SENTRY... PLEASE RESPOND.
I DON'T LIKE IT, REED. CLOC'S CUT OFF ALL COMMUNICATION OUTSIDE OF THE MAIN TERMINAL AREA. HE'S TRANSMITTING... BUT NOT TO ME.
I THINK HE MUST BE TALKING TO THE CUBE.
WHAT ON EARTH IS THAT?
MY WORD... IT LOOKS LIKE NEGATIVE SPACE.
BUT IT CAN'T BE -- I DIDN'T BUILD THAT INTO THE DESIGN --

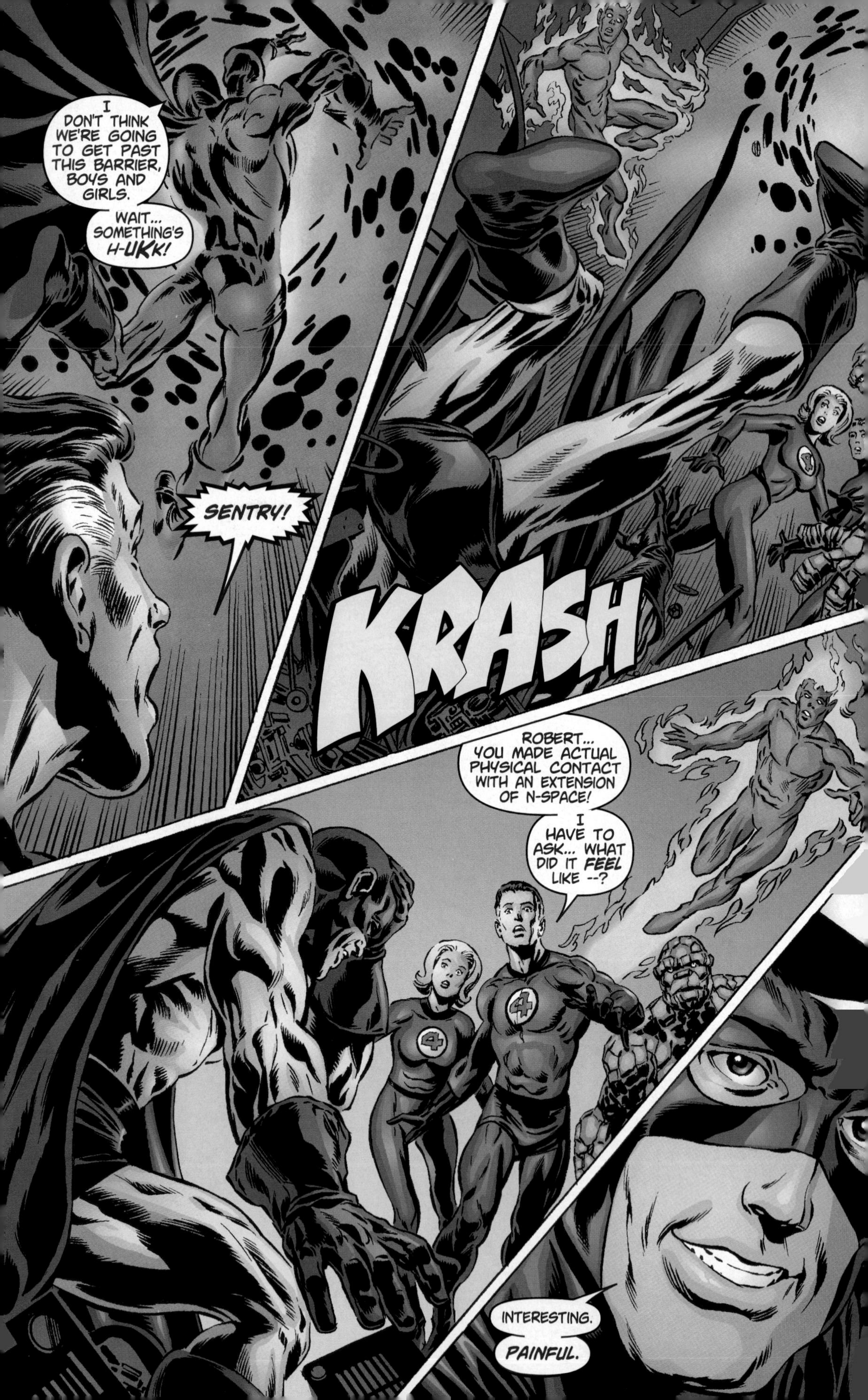
I DON'T THINK WE'RE GOING TO GET PAST THIS BARRIER, BOYS AND GIRLS.
WAIT... SOMETHING'S H-UKK!
SENTRY!
KRASH
ROBERT... YOU MADE ACTUAL PHYSICAL CONTACT WITH AN EXTENSION OF N-SPACE!
I HAVE TO ASK... WHAT DID IT FEEL LIKE --?
INTERESTING.
PAINFUL.

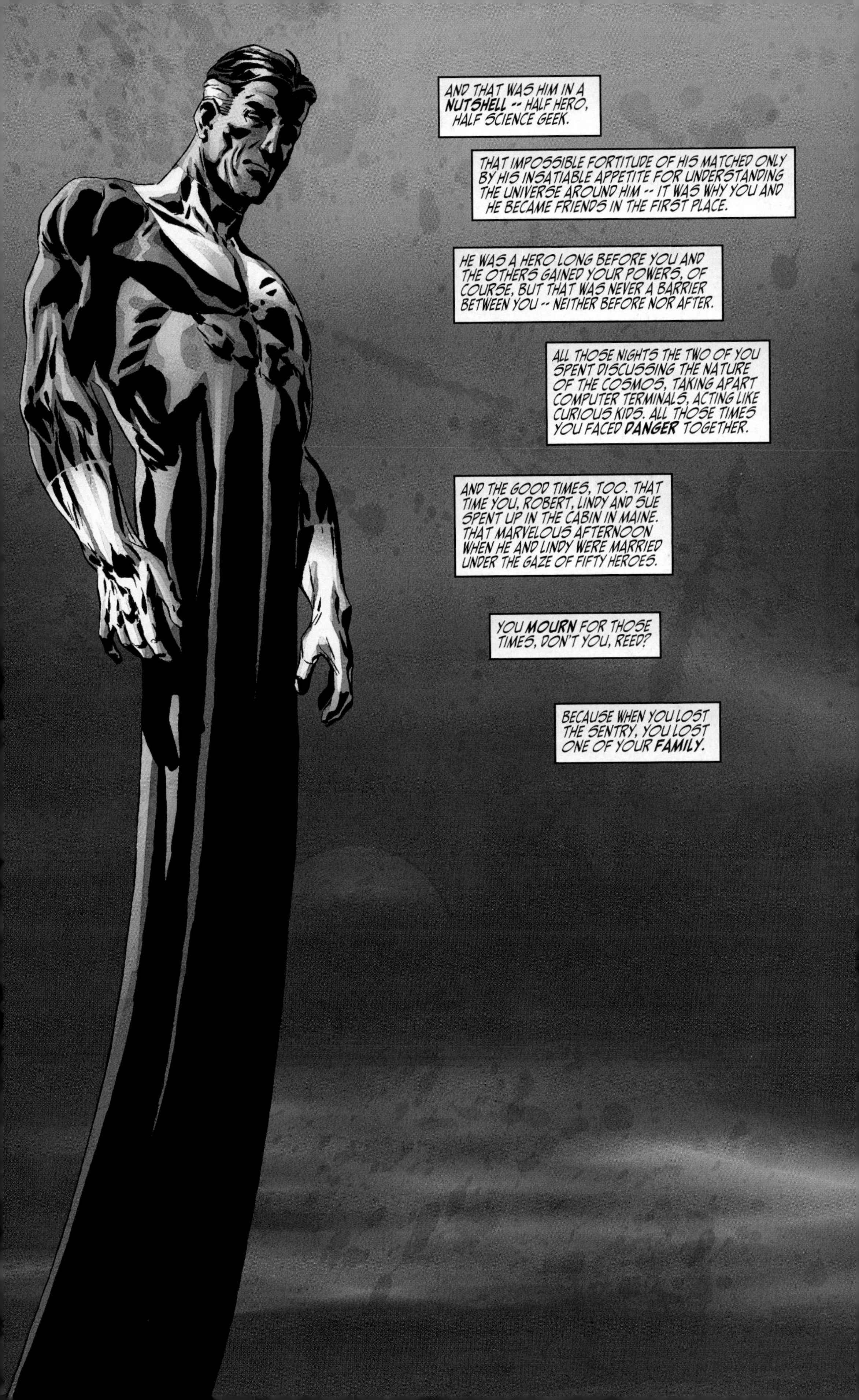
AND THAT WAS HIM IN A NUTSHELL -- HALF HERO, HALF SCIENCE GEEK.
THAT IMPOSSIBLE FORTITUDE OF HIS MATCHED ONLY BY HIS INSATIABLE APPETITE FOR UNDERSTANDING THE UNIVERSE AROUND HIM -- IT WAS WHY YOU AND HE BECAME FRIENDS IN THE FIRST PLACE.
HE WAS A HERO LONG BEFORE YOU AND THE OTHERS GAINED YOUR POWERS, OF COURSE, BUT THAT WAS NEVER A BARRIER BETWEEN YOU -- NEITHER BEFORE NOR AFTER.
ALL THOSE NIGHTS THE TWO OF YOU SPENT DISCUSSING THE NATURE OF THE COSMOS, TAKING APART COMPUTER TERMINALS, ACTING LIKE CURIOUS KIDS. ALL THOSE TIMES YOU FACED DANGER TOGETHER.
AND THE GOOD TIMES, TOO. THAT TIME YOU, ROBERT, LINDY AND SUE SPENT UP IN THE CABIN IN MAINE. THAT MARVELOUS AFTERNOON WHEN HE AND LINDY WERE MARRIED UNDER THE GAZE OF FIFTY HEROES.
YOU MOURN FOR THOSE TIMES, DON'T YOU, REED?
BECAUSE WHEN YOU LOST THE SENTRY, YOU LOST ONE OF YOUR FAMILY.

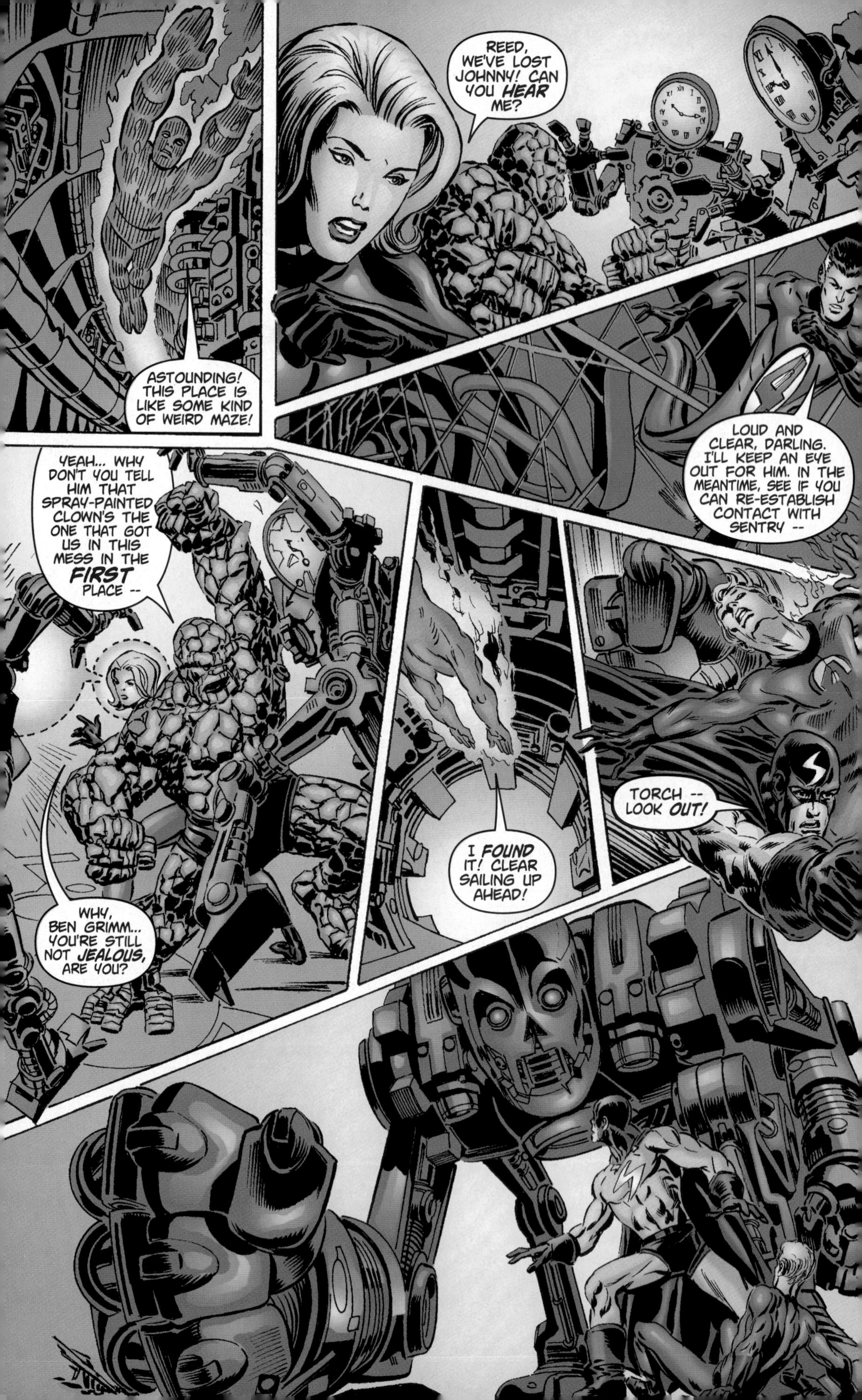
ASTOUNDING! THIS PLACE IS LIKE SOME KIND OF WEIRD MAZE!
REED, WE'VE LOST JOHNNY! CAN YOU HEAR ME?
LOUD AND CLEAR, DARLING. I'LL KEEP AN EYE OUT FOR HIM. IN THE MEANTIME, SEE IF YOU CAN RE-ESTABLISH CONTACT WITH SENTRY --
YEAH... WHY DON'T YOU TELL HIM THAT SPRAY-PAINTED CLOWN'S THE ONE THAT GOT US IN THIS MESS IN THE FIRST PLACE --
WHY, BEN GRIMM... YOU'RE STILL NOT JEALOUS, ARE YOU?
I FOUND IT! CLEAR SAILING UP AHEAD!
TORCH -- LOOK OUT!

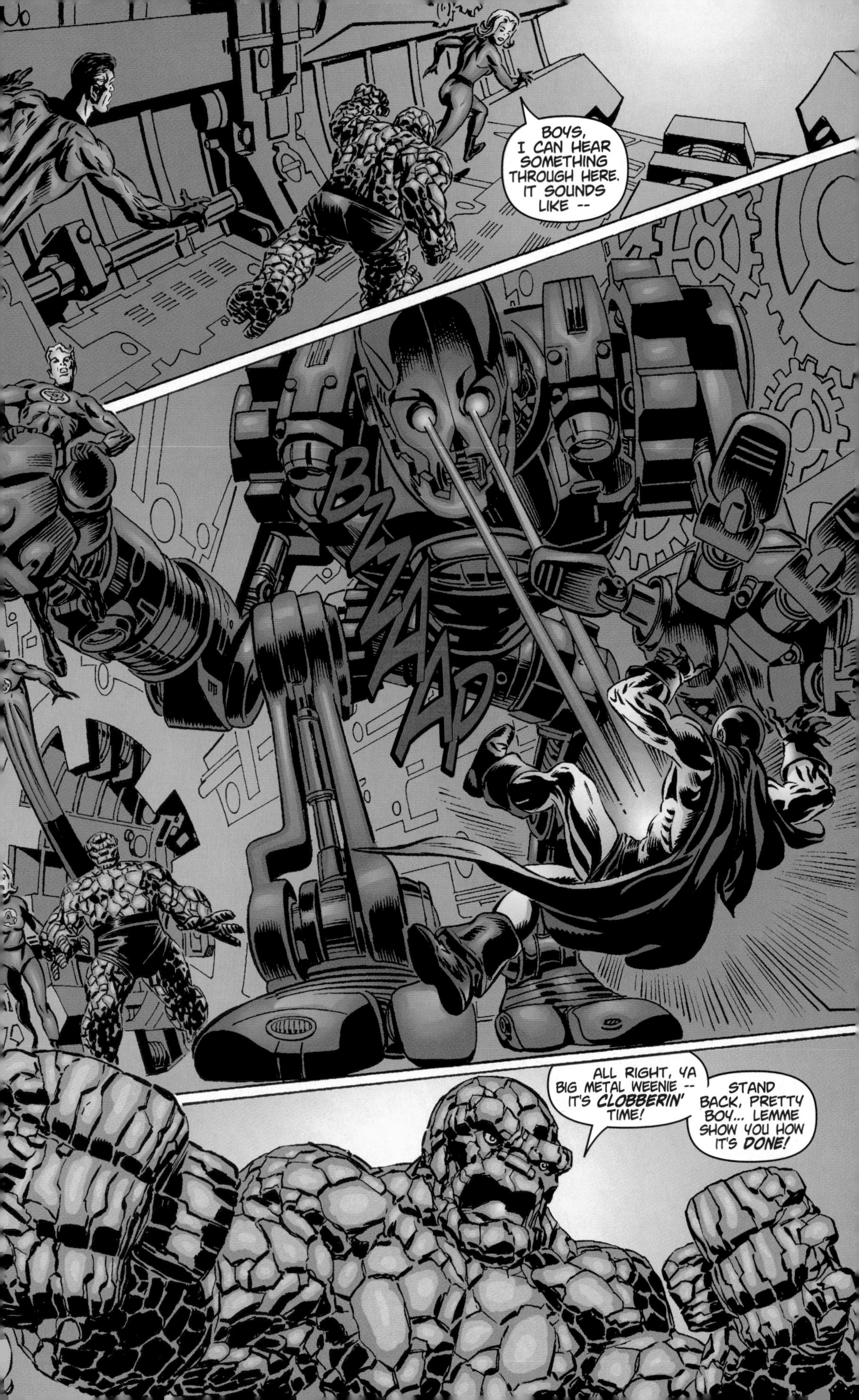

BOYS, I CAN HEAR SOMETHING THROUGH HERE. IT SOUNDS LIKE --
BZZZAAP
ALL RIGHT, YA BIG METAL WEENIE -- IT'S CLOBBERIN' TIME!
STAND BACK, PRETTY BOY... LEMME SHOW YOU HOW IT'S DONE!

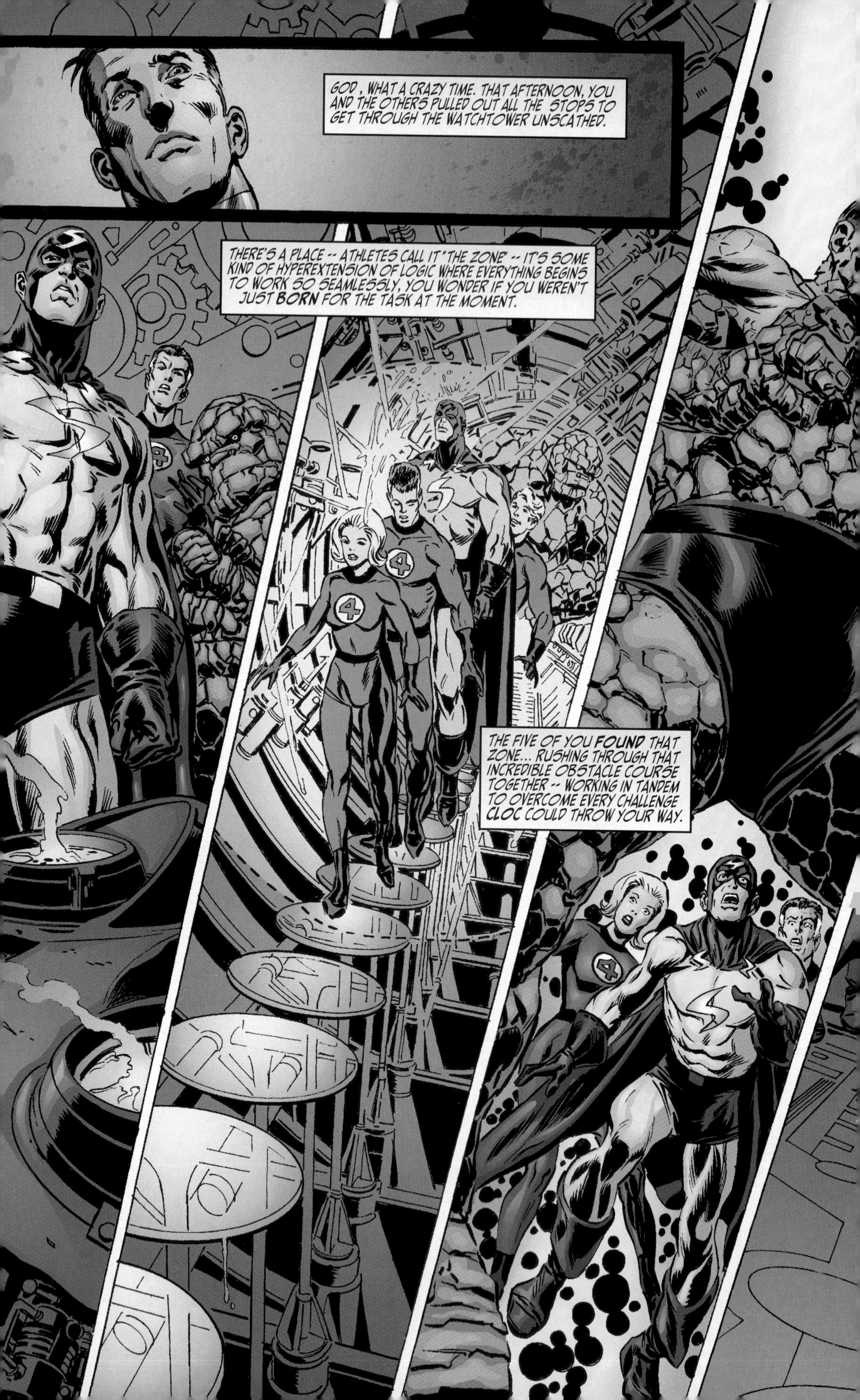
GOD, WHAT A CRAZY TIME. THAT AFTERNOON, YOU AND THE OTHERS PULLED OUT ALL THE STOPS TO GET THROUGH THE WATCHTOWER UNSCATHED.
THERE'S A PLACE -- ATHLETES CALL IT "THE ZONE" -- IT'S SOME KIND OF HYPEREXTENSION OF LOGIC WHERE EVERYTHING BEGINS TO WORK SO SEAMLESSLY, YOU WONDER IF YOU WEREN'T JUST BORN FOR THE TASK AT THE MOMENT.
THE FIVE OF YOU FOUND THAT ZONE... RUSHING THROUGH THAT INCREDIBLE OBSTACLE COURSE TOGETHER -- WORKING IN TANDEM TO OVERCOME EVERY CHALLENGE CLOC COULD THROW YOUR WAY.

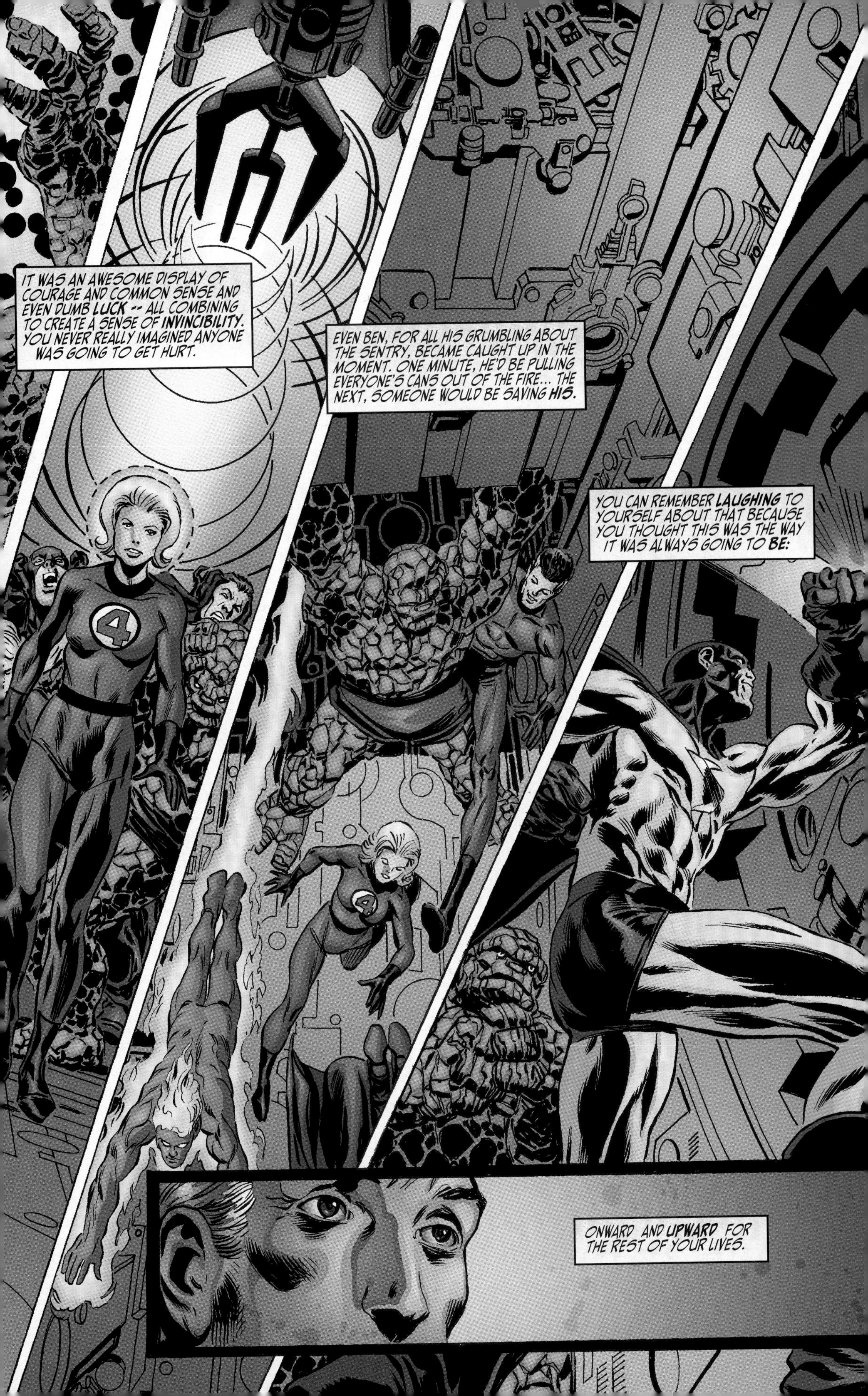
IT WAS AN AWESOME DISPLAY OF COURAGE AND COMMON SENSE AND EVEN DUMB LUCK -- ALL COMBINING TO CREATE A SENSE OF INVINCIBILITY. YOU NEVER REALLY IMAGINED ANYONE WAS GOING TO GET HURT.
EVEN BEN, FOR ALL HIS GRUMBLING ABOUT THE SENTRY, BECAME CAUGHT UP IN THE MOMENT. ONE MINUTE, HE'D BE PULLING EVERYONE'S CANS OUT OF THE FIRE... THE NEXT, SOMEONE WOULD BE SAVING HIS.
YOU CAN REMEMBER LAUGHING TO YOURSELF ABOUT THAT BECAUSE YOU THOUGHT THIS WAS THE WAY IT WAS ALWAYS GOING TO BE:
ONWARD AND UPWARD FOR THE REST OF YOUR LIVES.

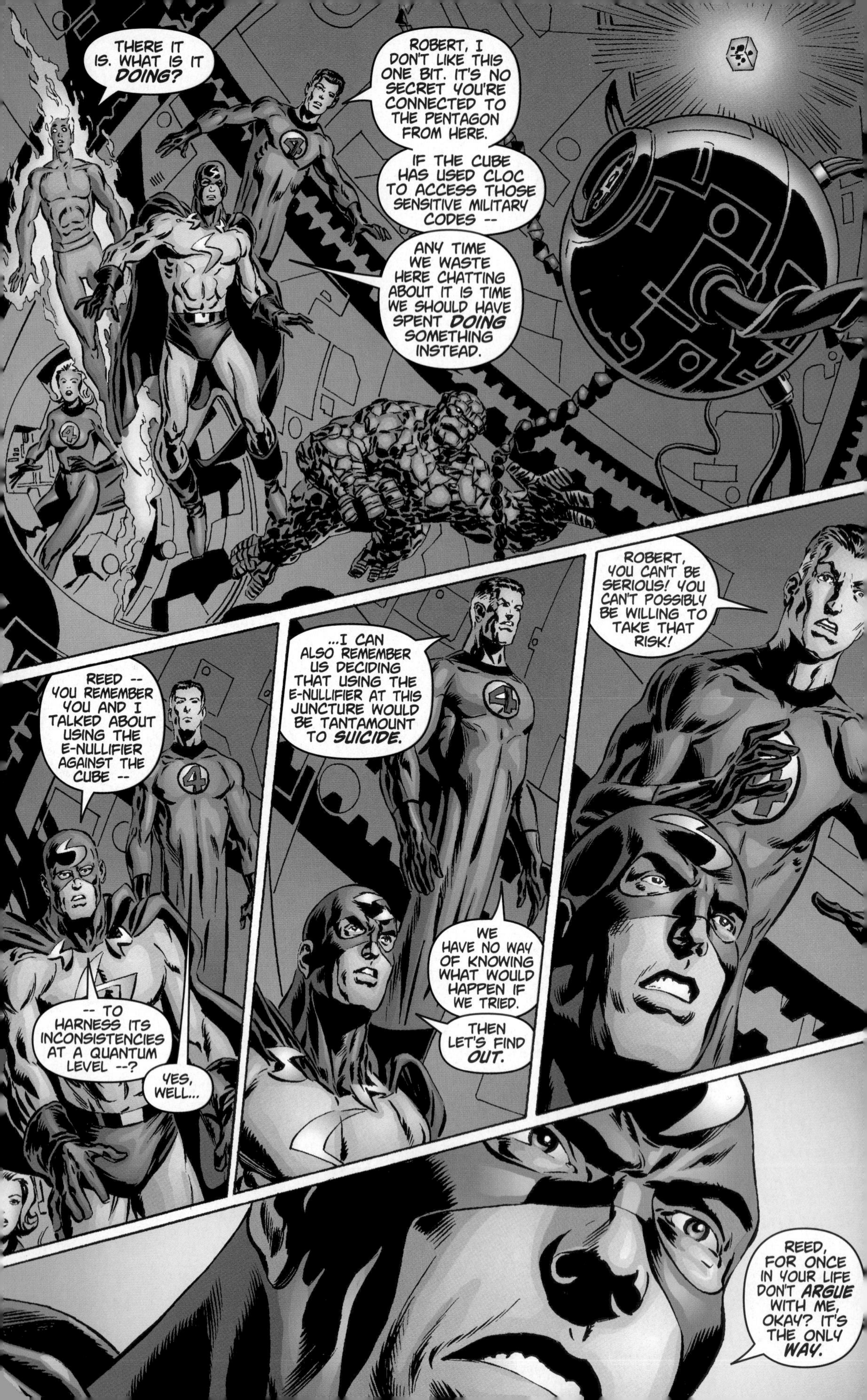

THERE IT IS. WHAT IS IT DOING?
ROBERT, I DON'T LIKE THIS ONE BIT. IT'S NO SECRET YOU'RE CONNECTED TO THE PENTAGON FROM HERE.
IF THE CUBE HAS USED CLOC TO ACCESS THOSE SENSITIVE MILITARY CODES --
ANY TIME WE WASTE HERE CHATTING ABOUT IT IS TIME WE SHOULD HAVE SPENT DOING SOMETHING INSTEAD.
REED -- YOU REMEMBER YOU AND I TALKED ABOUT USING THE E-NULLIFIER AGAINST THE CUBE --
-- TO HARNESS ITS INCONSISTENCIES AT A QUANTUM LEVEL --?
YES, WELL...
...I CAN ALSO REMEMBER US DECIDING THAT USING THE E-NULLIFIER AT THIS JUNCTURE WOULD BE TANTAMOUNT TO SUICIDE.
WE HAVE NO WAY OF KNOWING WHAT WOULD HAPPEN IF WE TRIED.
THEN LET'S FIND OUT.
ROBERT, YOU CAN'T BE SERIOUS! YOU CAN'T POSSIBLY BE WILLING TO TAKE THAT RISK!
REED, FOR ONCE IN YOUR LIFE DON'T ARGUE WITH ME, OKAY? IT'S THE ONLY WAY.

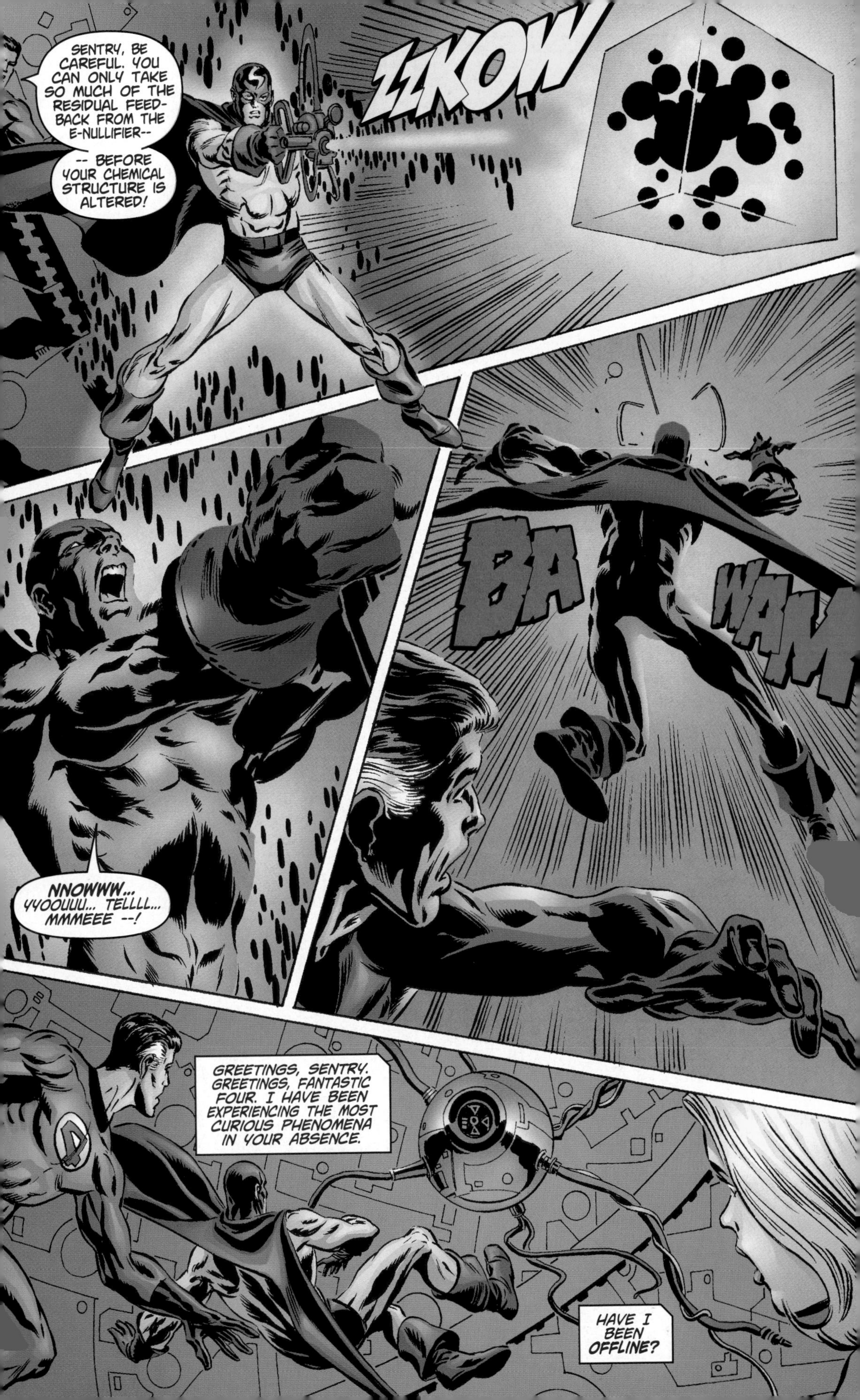

SENTRY, BE CAREFUL. YOU CAN ONLY TAKE SO MUCH OF THE RESIDUAL FEED-BACK FROM THE E-NULLIFIER--
-- BEFORE YOUR CHEMICAL STRUCTURE IS ALTERED!
ZZKOW
NNOWWW... YYOOUUU... TELLLL... MMMEEE --!
BA
WAM
GREETINGS, SENTRY. GREETINGS, FANTASTIC FOUR. I HAVE BEEN EXPERIENCING THE MOST CURIOUS PHENOMENA IN YOUR ABSENCE.
HAVE I BEEN OFFLINE?

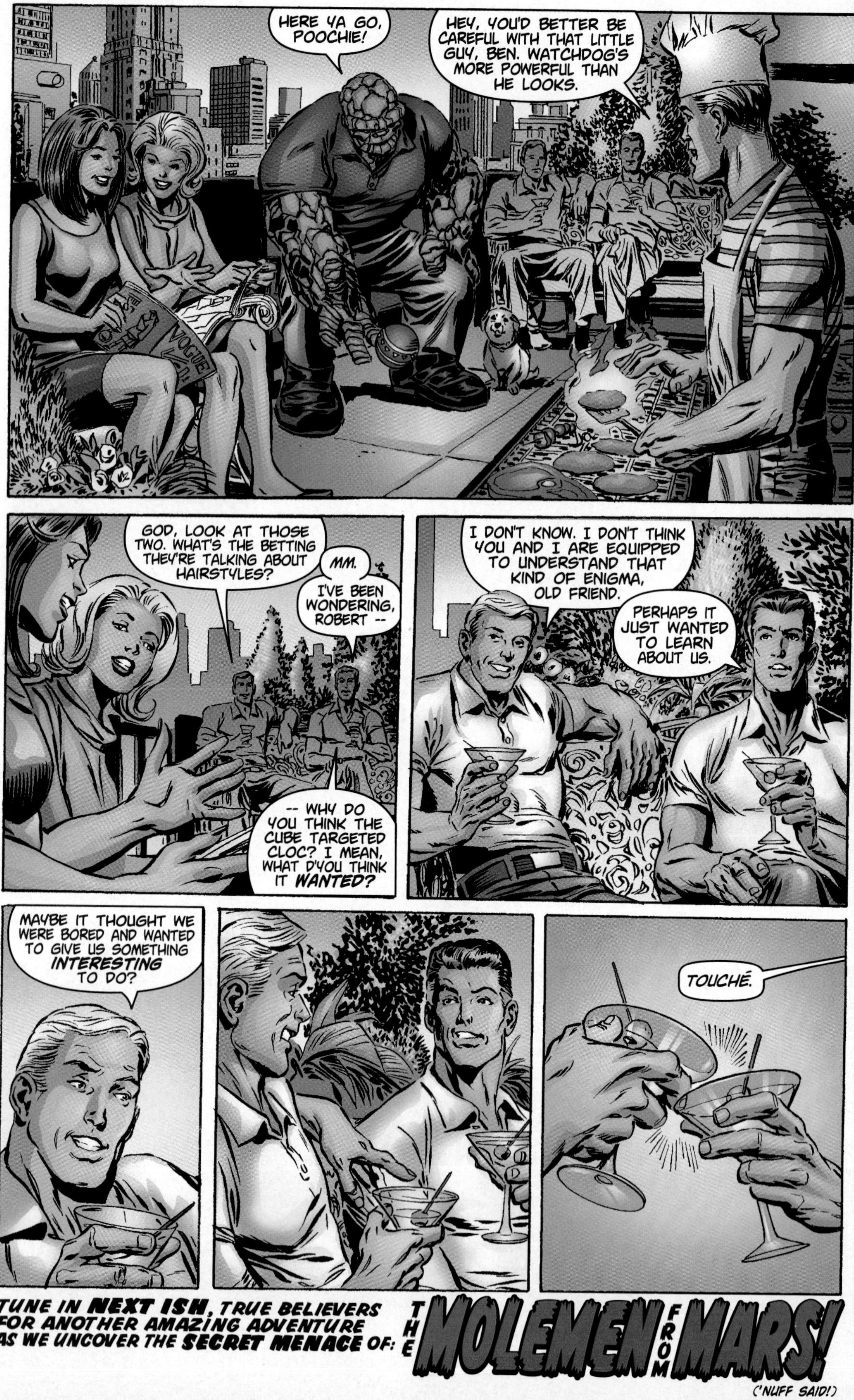
HERE YA GO, POOCHIE!
HEY, YOU'D BETTER BE CAREFUL WITH THAT LITTLE GUY, BEN. WATCHDOG'S MORE POWERFUL THAN HE LOOKS.
VOGUE
GOD, LOOK AT THOSE TWO. WHAT'S THE BETTING THEY'RE TALKING ABOUT HAIRSTYLES?
MM.
I'VE BEEN WONDERING, ROBERT --
-- WHY DO YOU THINK THE CUBE TARGETED CLOC? I MEAN, WHAT D'YOU THINK IT WANTED?
I DON'T KNOW. I DON'T THINK YOU AND I ARE EQUIPPED TO UNDERSTAND THAT KIND OF ENIGMA, OLD FRIEND.
PERHAPS IT JUST WANTED TO LEARN ABOUT US.
MAYBE IT THOUGHT WE WERE BORED AND WANTED TO GIVE US SOMETHING INTERESTING TO DO?
TOUCHÉ.
TUNE IN NEXT ISH, TRUE BELIEVERS FOR ANOTHER AMAZING ADVENTURE AS WE UNCOVER THE SECRET MENACE OF: THE MOLEMEN FROM MARS!
('NUFF SAID!)

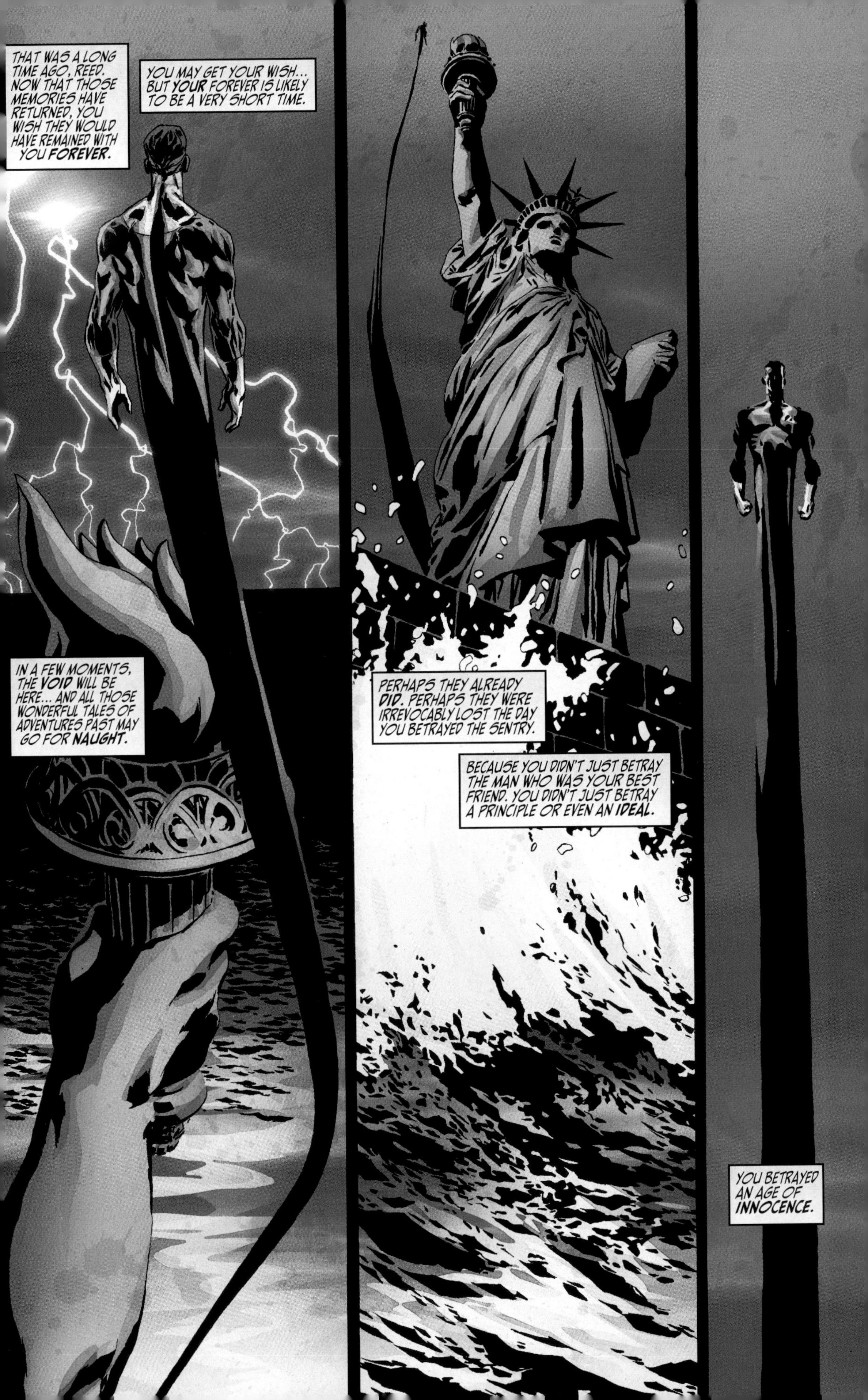
THAT WAS A LONG TIME AGO, REED. NOW THAT THOSE MEMORIES HAVE RETURNED, YOU WISH THEY WOULD HAVE REMAINED WITH YOU **FOREVER**.
YOU MAY GET YOUR WISH... BUT **YOUR** FOREVER IS LIKELY TO BE A VERY SHORT TIME.
IN A FEW MOMENTS, THE **VOID** WILL BE HERE... AND ALL THOSE WONDERFUL TALES OF ADVENTURES PAST MAY GO FOR **NAUGHT**.
PERHAPS THEY ALREADY **DID**. PERHAPS THEY WERE IRREVOCABLY LOST THE DAY YOU BETRAYED THE SENTRY.
BECAUSE YOU DIDN'T JUST BETRAY THE MAN WHO WAS YOUR BEST FRIEND. YOU DIDN'T JUST BETRAY A PRINCIPLE OR EVEN AN **IDEAL**.
YOU BETRAYED AN AGE OF **INNOCENCE**.

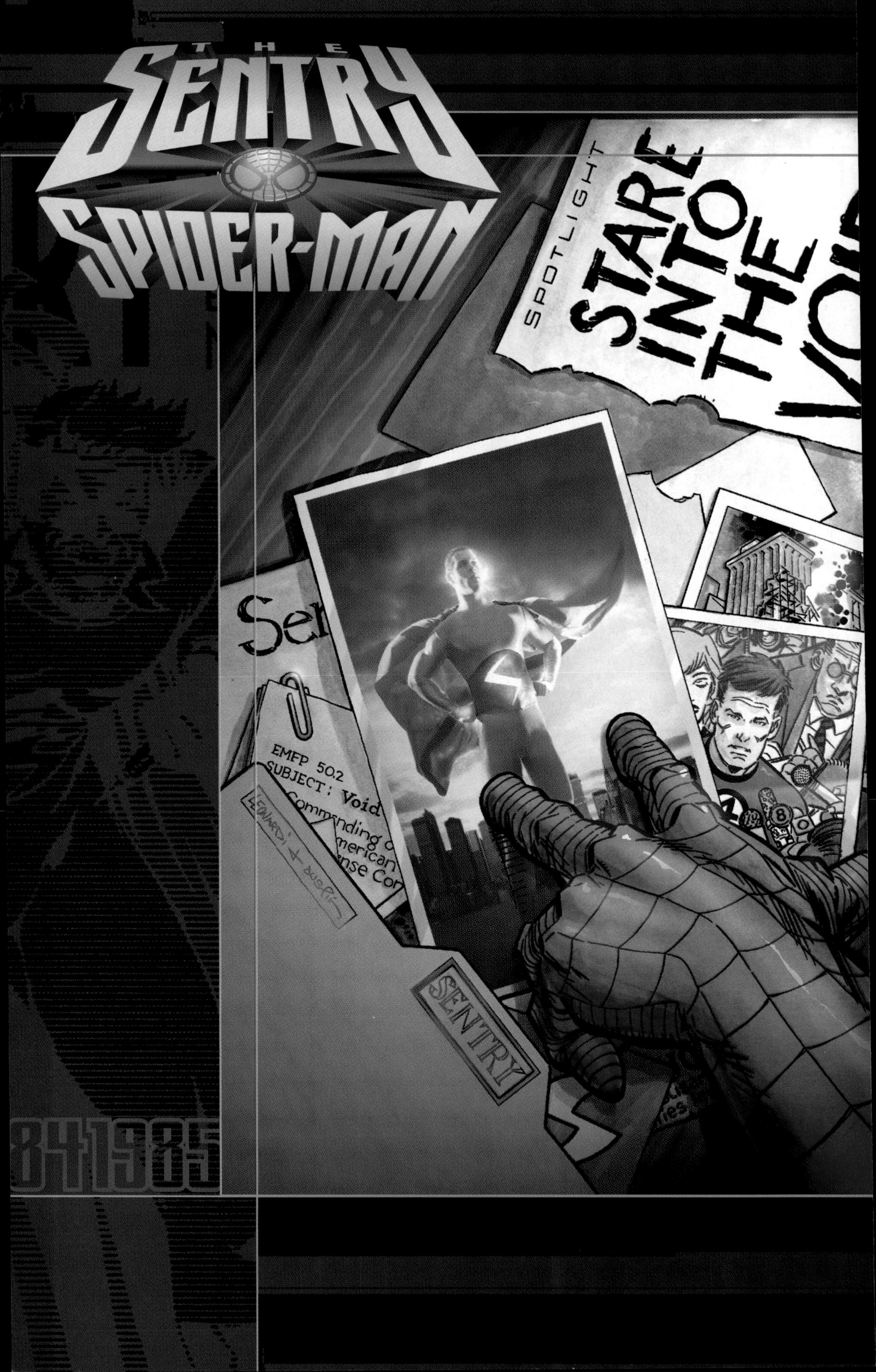
THE
SENTRY
SPIDER-MAN
SPOTLIGHT
STARE
INTO
THE
EMFP 50.2
SUBJECT: Void
SENTRY

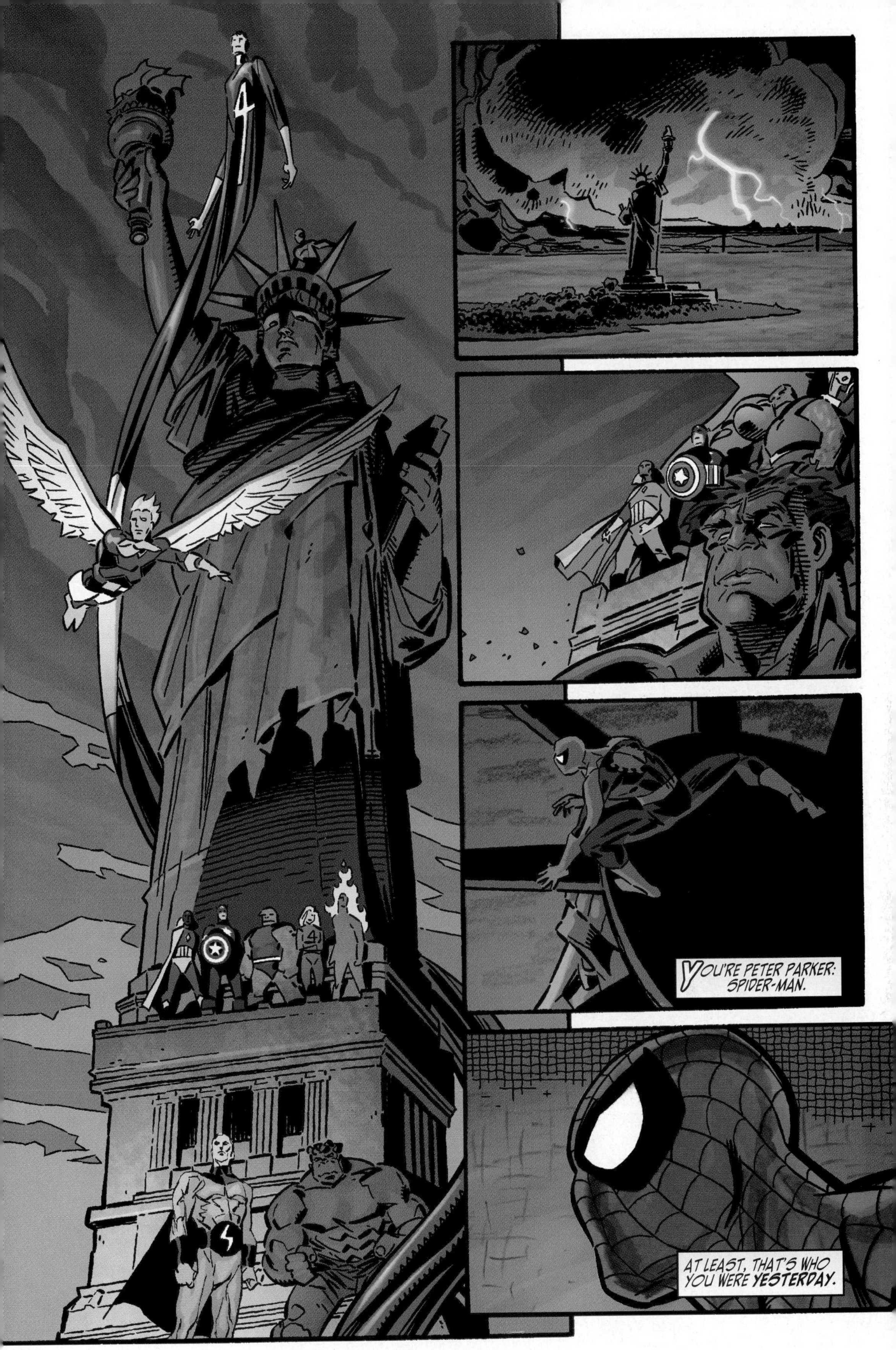
YOU'RE PETER PARKER:
SPIDER-MAN.
AT LEAST, THAT'S WHO YOU WERE YESTERDAY.

YESTERDAY, YOU WERE JUST LIKE ANY OTHER SCHLUB WITH A BROKEN HEART AND A DWINDLING BANK ACCOUNT. YOUR WIFE WAS GONE, YOU WERE LOOKING FOR WORK AND STRUGGLING TO MAKE THE RENT.

UP UNTIL YESTERDAY, YOU THOUGHT YOU WERE NOBODY.

AND THEN, YOU BEGAN TO REMEMBER.

LIKE EVERYONE ELSE, YOU BEGAN TO REMEMBER THE VOID -- THE SHADOW BEAST WHO DEVOURS THE HEARTS OF MEN. THE SOUL-DESTROYER, THE END OF EVERYTHING.

YOU BEGAN TO REMEMBER THE SICK, BLACK, SMOKESTACK STENCH OF THE CREATURE -- THE ONE WHO NOW HOVERS INTO VIEW A MILE OUT TO SEA, APPROACHING FAST.

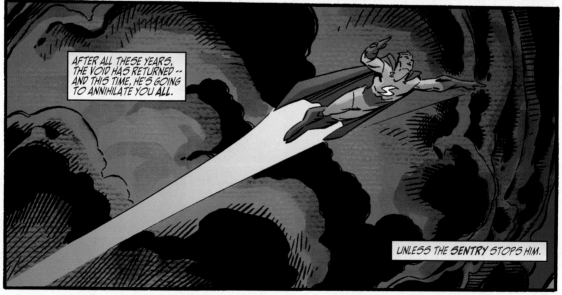

AFTER ALL THESE YEARS, THE VOID HAS RETURNED -- AND THIS TIME, HE'S GOING TO ANNIHILATE YOU ALL.

UNLESS THE SENTRY STOPS HIM.

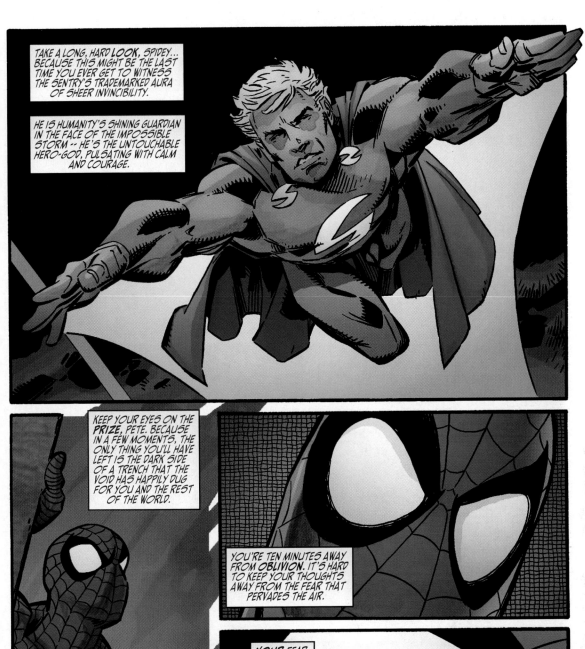

TAKE A LONG, HARD *LOOK*, SPIDEY... BECAUSE THIS MIGHT BE THE LAST TIME YOU EVER GET TO WITNESS THE SENTRY'S TRADEMARKED AURA OF SHEER INVINCIBILITY.

HE IS HUMANITY'S SHINING GUARDIAN IN THE FACE OF THE IMPOSSIBLE STORM -- HE'S THE UNTOUCHABLE HERO-GOD, PULSATING WITH CALM AND COURAGE.

KEEP YOUR EYES ON THE *PRIZE*, PETE. BECAUSE IN A FEW MOMENTS, THE ONLY THING YOU'LL HAVE LEFT IS THE DARK SIDE OF A TRENCH THAT THE VOID HAS HAPPILY DUG FOR YOU AND THE REST OF THE WORLD.

YOU'RE TEN MINUTES AWAY FROM *OBLIVION*. IT'S HARD TO KEEP YOUR THOUGHTS AWAY FROM THE FEAR THAT PERVADES THE AIR.

YOUR FEAR.

MAN... AN HONEST TO GOODNESS SNAPSHOT OF THE SENTRY! NO ONE'S EVER BEEN ABLE TO PHOTO HIM SO CLOSE. JONAH'S GONNA PAY ME A *FORTUNE* FOR THIS ONE!

STAN LEE PRESENTS:

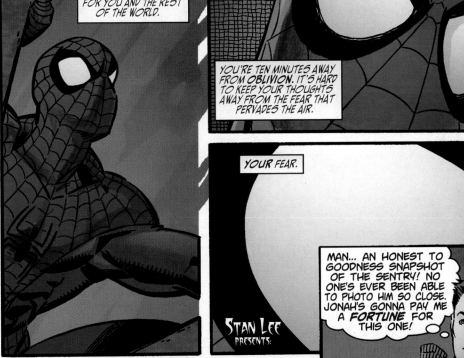

THE SENTRY & SPIDER-MAN

PAUL JENKINS
STORY

RICK LEONARDI
PENCILS

TERRY AUSTIN
INKS

JEROMY COX
COLORS

RS & COMICRAFT/WA
LETTERS

MIKE RAICHT
ASSISTANT EDITOR

MIKE MARTS
EDITOR

JOE QUESADA
EDITOR IN CHIEF

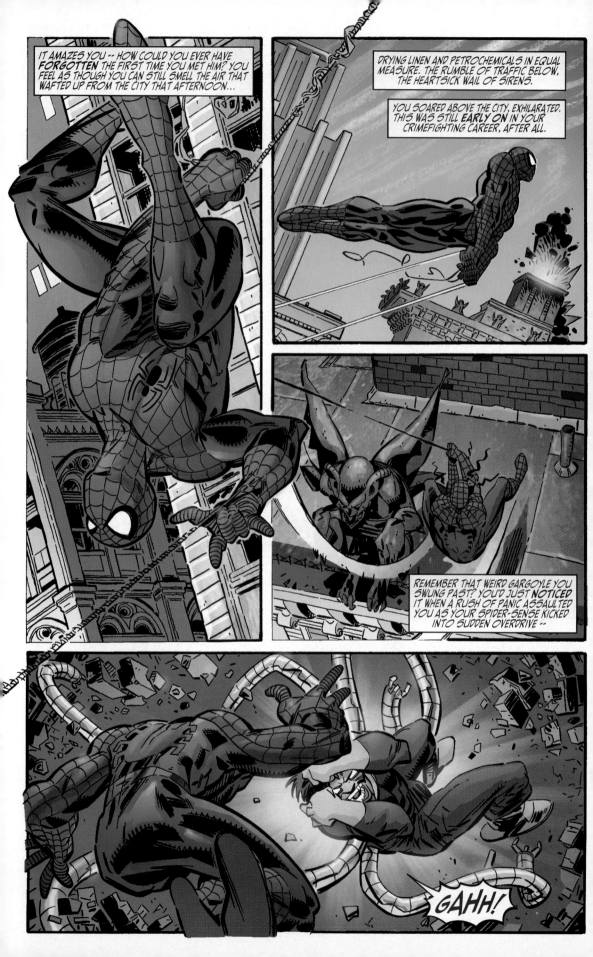

IT AMAZES YOU -- HOW COULD YOU EVER HAVE **FORGOTTEN** THE FIRST TIME YOU MET HIM? YOU FEEL AS THOUGH YOU CAN STILL SMELL THE AIR THAT WAFTED UP FROM THE CITY THAT AFTERNOON...

DRYING LINEN AND PETROCHEMICALS IN EQUAL MEASURE. THE RUMBLE OF TRAFFIC BELOW, THE HEARTSICK WAIL OF SIRENS.

YOU SOARED ABOVE THE CITY, EXHILARATED. THIS WAS STILL **EARLY ON** IN YOUR CRIMEFIGHTING CAREER, AFTER ALL.

REMEMBER THAT WEIRD GARGOYLE YOU SWUNG PAST? YOU'D JUST **NOTICED** IT WHEN A RUSH OF PANIC ASSAULTED YOU AS YOUR SPIDER-SENSE KICKED INTO SUDDEN OVERDRIVE --

GAHH!

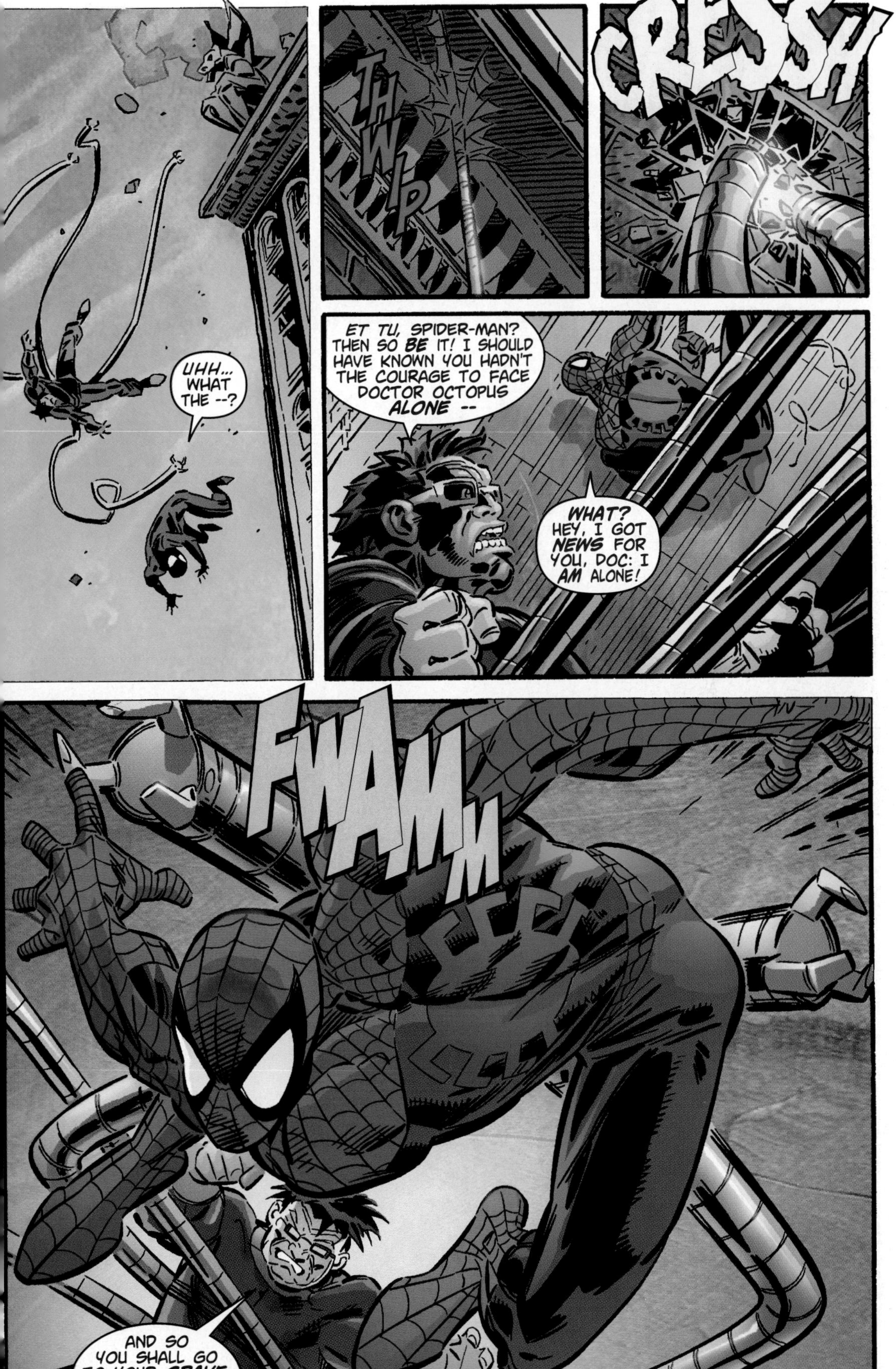

UHH... WHAT THE --?
THWIP
CRESSH
ET TU, SPIDER-MAN? THEN SO BE IT! I SHOULD HAVE KNOWN YOU HADN'T THE COURAGE TO FACE DOCTOR OCTOPUS ALONE --
WHAT? HEY, I GOT NEWS FOR YOU, DOC: I AM ALONE!
FWAMMM
AND SO YOU SHALL GO TO YOUR GRAVE, INSOLENT BRAT!

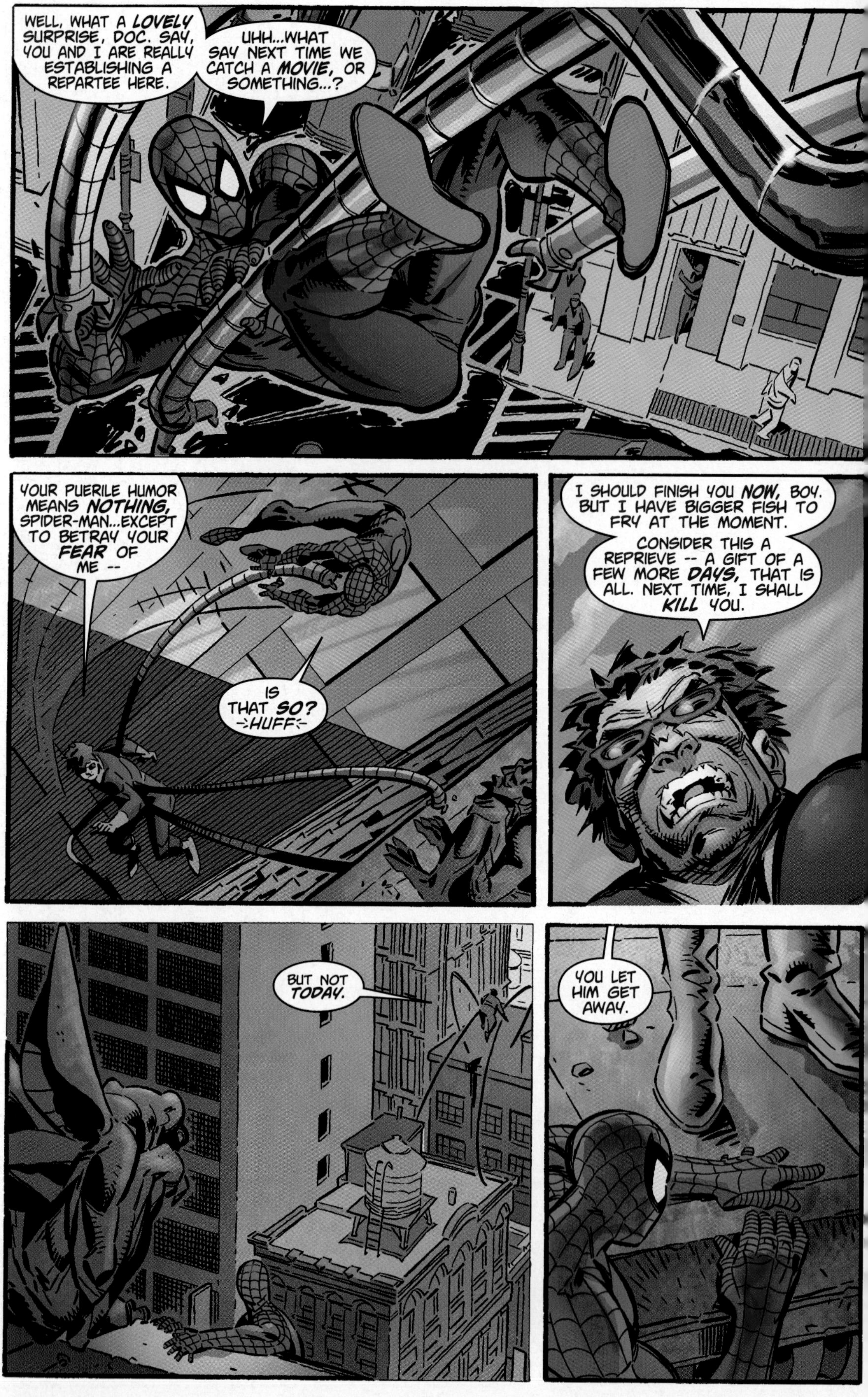

WELL, WHAT A LOVELY SURPRISE, DOC. SAY, YOU AND I ARE REALLY ESTABLISHING A REPARTEE HERE.
UHH...WHAT SAY NEXT TIME WE CATCH A MOVIE, OR SOMETHING...?
YOUR PUERILE HUMOR MEANS NOTHING, SPIDER-MAN...EXCEPT TO BETRAY YOUR FEAR OF ME --
IS THAT SO? -HUFF-
I SHOULD FINISH YOU NOW, BOY. BUT I HAVE BIGGER FISH TO FRY AT THE MOMENT.
CONSIDER THIS A REPRIEVE -- A GIFT OF A FEW MORE DAYS, THAT IS ALL. NEXT TIME, I SHALL KILL YOU.
BUT NOT TODAY.
YOU LET HIM GET AWAY.

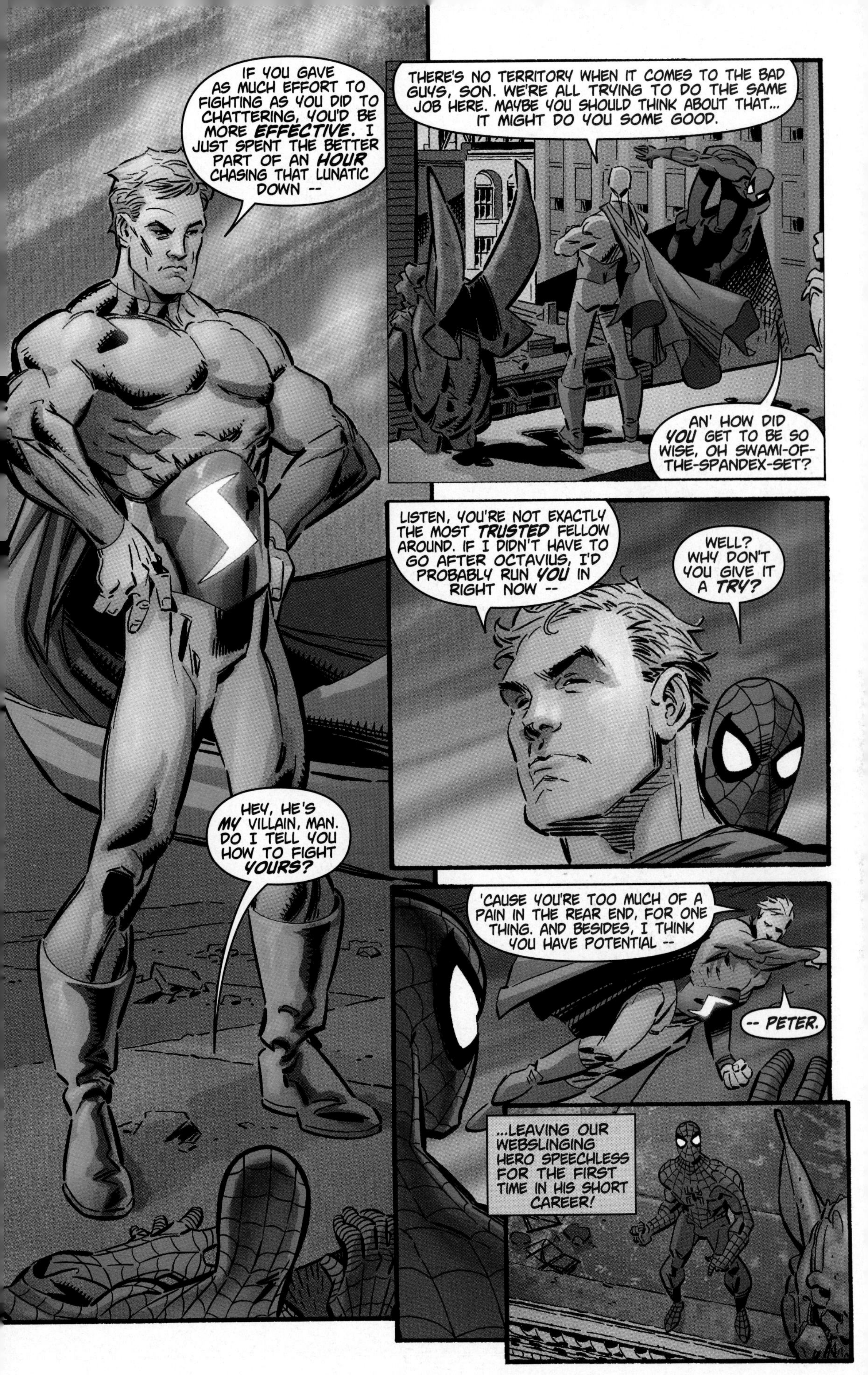
IF YOU GAVE AS MUCH EFFORT TO FIGHTING AS YOU DID TO CHATTERING, YOU'D BE MORE EFFECTIVE. I JUST SPENT THE BETTER PART OF AN HOUR CHASING THAT LUNATIC DOWN --
HEY, HE'S MY VILLAIN, MAN. DO I TELL YOU HOW TO FIGHT YOURS?
THERE'S NO TERRITORY WHEN IT COMES TO THE BAD GUYS, SON. WE'RE ALL TRYING TO DO THE SAME JOB HERE. MAYBE YOU SHOULD THINK ABOUT THAT... IT MIGHT DO YOU SOME GOOD.
AN' HOW DID YOU GET TO BE SO WISE, OH SWAMI-OF-THE-SPANDEX-SET?
LISTEN, YOU'RE NOT EXACTLY THE MOST TRUSTED FELLOW AROUND. IF I DIDN'T HAVE TO GO AFTER OCTAVIUS, I'D PROBABLY RUN YOU IN RIGHT NOW --
WELL? WHY DON'T YOU GIVE IT A TRY?
'CAUSE YOU'RE TOO MUCH OF A PAIN IN THE REAR END, FOR ONE THING. AND BESIDES, I THINK YOU HAVE POTENTIAL --
-- PETER.
...LEAVING OUR WEBSLINGING HERO SPEECHLESS FOR THE FIRST TIME IN HIS SHORT CAREER!

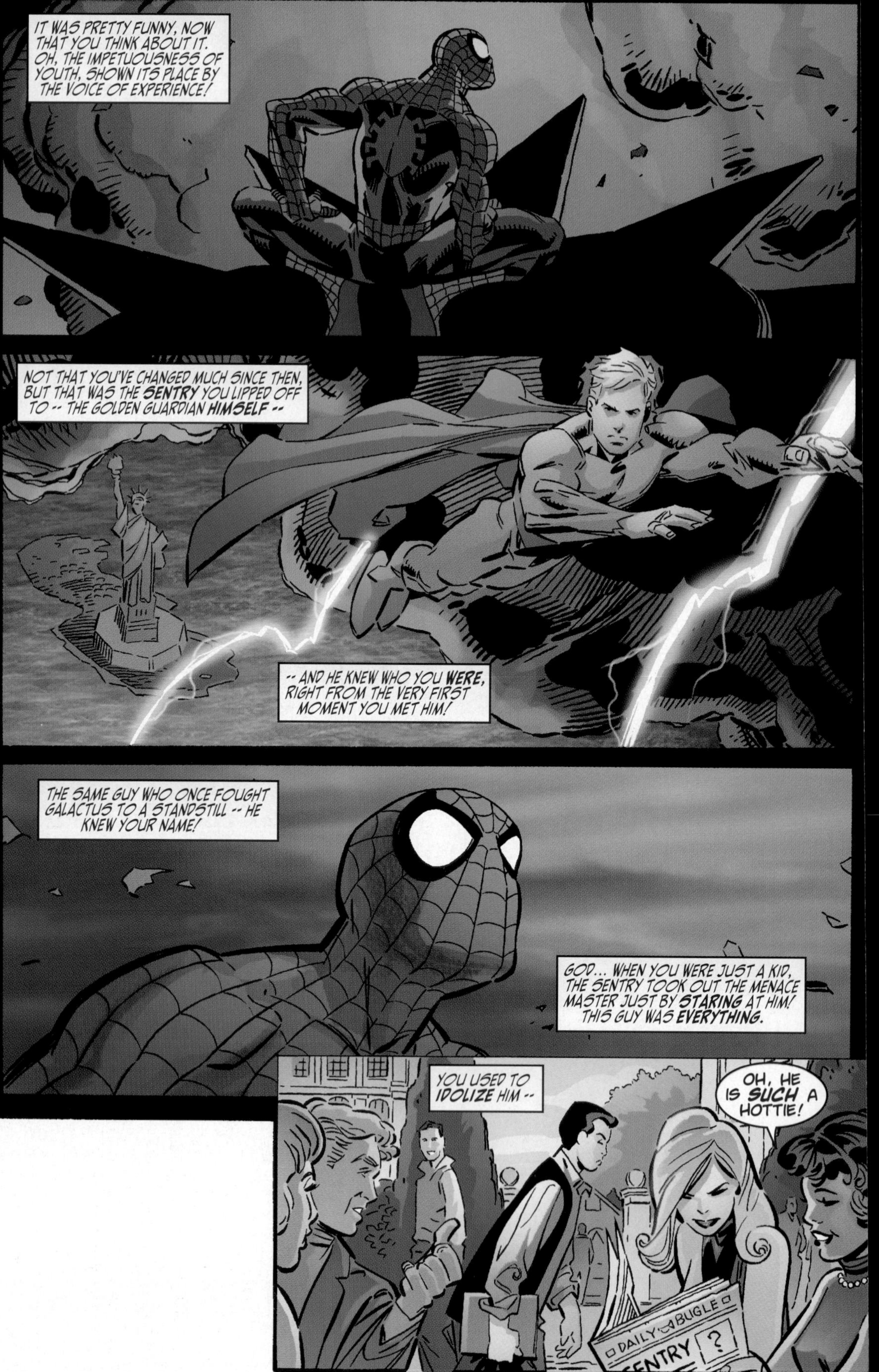
IT WAS PRETTY FUNNY, NOW THAT YOU THINK ABOUT IT. OH, THE IMPETUOUSNESS OF YOUTH, SHOWN ITS PLACE BY THE VOICE OF EXPERIENCE!
NOT THAT YOU'VE CHANGED MUCH SINCE THEN, BUT THAT WAS THE SENTRY YOU LIPPED OFF TO -- THE GOLDEN GUARDIAN HIMSELF --
-- AND HE KNEW WHO YOU WERE, RIGHT FROM THE VERY FIRST MOMENT YOU MET HIM!
THE SAME GUY WHO ONCE FOUGHT GALACTUS TO A STANDSTILL -- HE KNEW YOUR NAME!
GOD... WHEN YOU WERE JUST A KID, THE SENTRY TOOK OUT THE MENACE MASTER JUST BY STARING AT HIM! THIS GUY WAS EVERYTHING.
YOU USED TO IDOLIZE HIM --
OH, HE IS SUCH A HOTTIE!
DAILY BUGLE
SENTRY ?

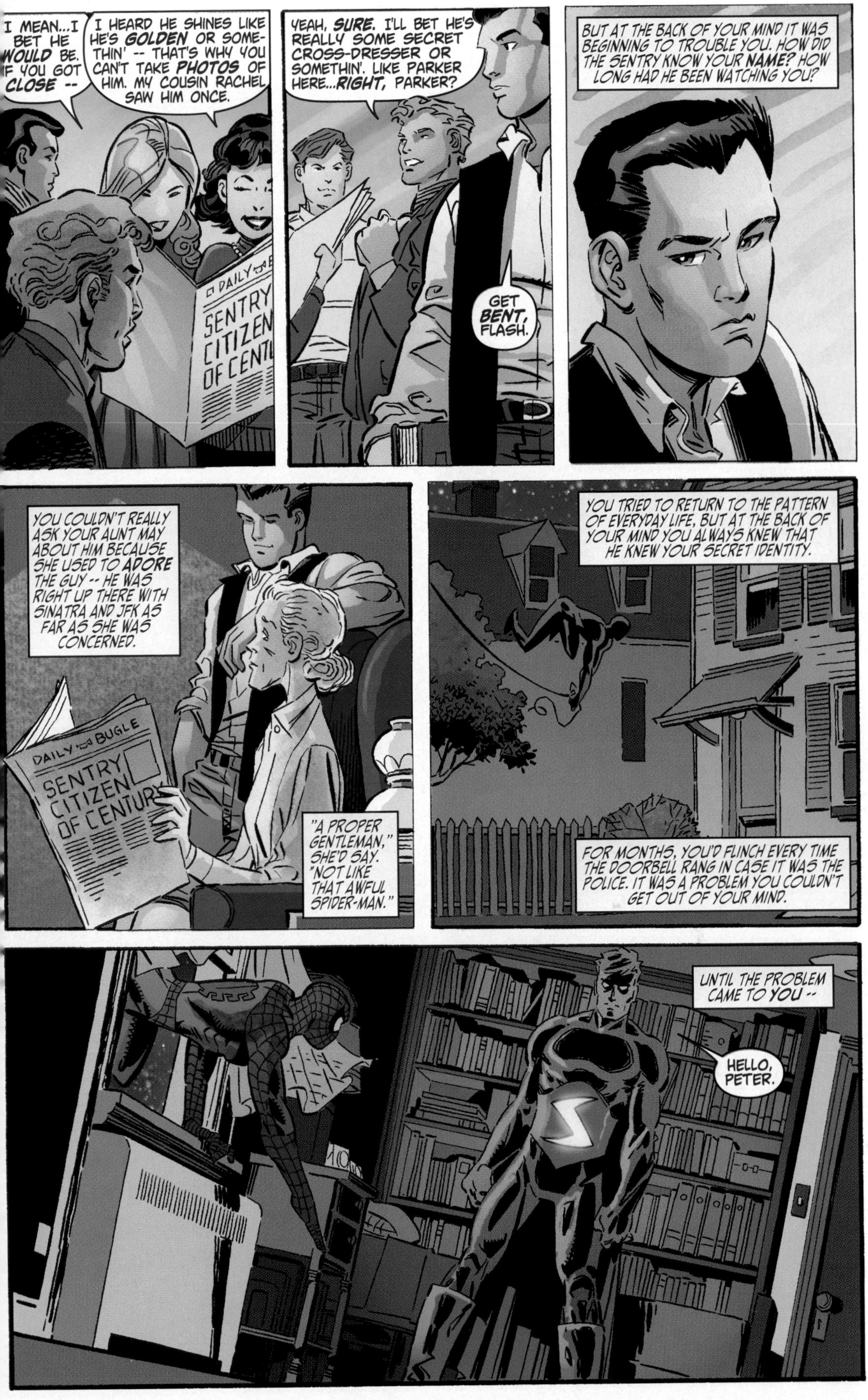
I MEAN...I BET HE WOULD BE. IF YOU GOT CLOSE --
I HEARD HE SHINES LIKE HE'S GOLDEN OR SOME-THIN' -- THAT'S WHY YOU CAN'T TAKE PHOTOS OF HIM. MY COUSIN RACHEL SAW HIM ONCE.
DAILY BUGLE
SENTRY CITIZEN OF CENTURY
YEAH, SURE. I'LL BET HE'S REALLY SOME SECRET CROSS-DRESSER OR SOMETHIN'. LIKE PARKER HERE...RIGHT, PARKER?
GET BENT, FLASH.
BUT AT THE BACK OF YOUR MIND IT WAS BEGINNING TO TROUBLE YOU. HOW DID THE SENTRY KNOW YOUR NAME? HOW LONG HAD HE BEEN WATCHING YOU?
YOU COULDN'T REALLY ASK YOUR AUNT MAY ABOUT HIM BECAUSE SHE USED TO ADORE THE GUY -- HE WAS RIGHT UP THERE WITH SINATRA AND JFK AS FAR AS SHE WAS CONCERNED.
DAILY BUGLE
SENTRY CITIZEN OF CENTURY
"A PROPER GENTLEMAN," SHE'D SAY. "NOT LIKE THAT AWFUL SPIDER-MAN."
YOU TRIED TO RETURN TO THE PATTERN OF EVERYDAY LIFE, BUT AT THE BACK OF YOUR MIND YOU ALWAYS KNEW THAT HE KNEW YOUR SECRET IDENTITY.
FOR MONTHS, YOU'D FLINCH EVERY TIME THE DOORBELL RANG IN CASE IT WAS THE POLICE. IT WAS A PROBLEM YOU COULDN'T GET OUT OF YOUR MIND.
UNTIL THE PROBLEM CAME TO YOU --
HELLO, PETER.

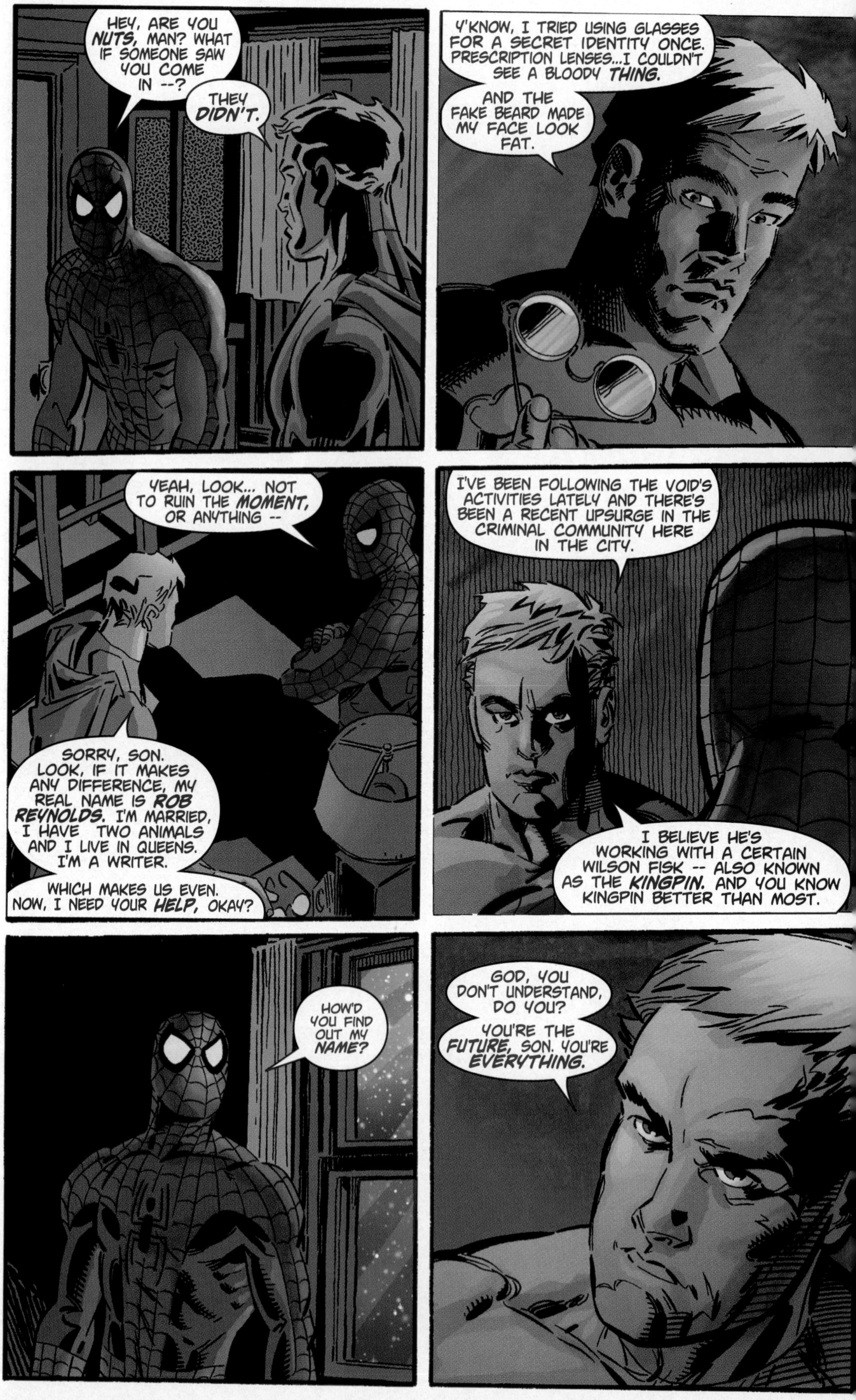

HEY, ARE YOU NUTS, MAN? WHAT IF SOMEONE SAW YOU COME IN --?
THEY DIDN'T.
Y'KNOW, I TRIED USING GLASSES FOR A SECRET IDENTITY ONCE. PRESCRIPTION LENSES...I COULDN'T SEE A BLOODY THING.
AND THE FAKE BEARD MADE MY FACE LOOK FAT.
YEAH, LOOK... NOT TO RUIN THE MOMENT, OR ANYTHING --
SORRY, SON. LOOK, IF IT MAKES ANY DIFFERENCE, MY REAL NAME IS ROB REYNOLDS. I'M MARRIED, I HAVE TWO ANIMALS AND I LIVE IN QUEENS. I'M A WRITER.
WHICH MAKES US EVEN. NOW, I NEED YOUR HELP, OKAY?
I'VE BEEN FOLLOWING THE VOID'S ACTIVITIES LATELY AND THERE'S BEEN A RECENT UPSURGE IN THE CRIMINAL COMMUNITY HERE IN THE CITY.
I BELIEVE HE'S WORKING WITH A CERTAIN WILSON FISK -- ALSO KNOWN AS THE KINGPIN. AND YOU KNOW KINGPIN BETTER THAN MOST.
HOW'D YOU FIND OUT MY NAME?
GOD, YOU DON'T UNDERSTAND, DO YOU?
YOU'RE THE FUTURE, SON. YOU'RE EVERYTHING.

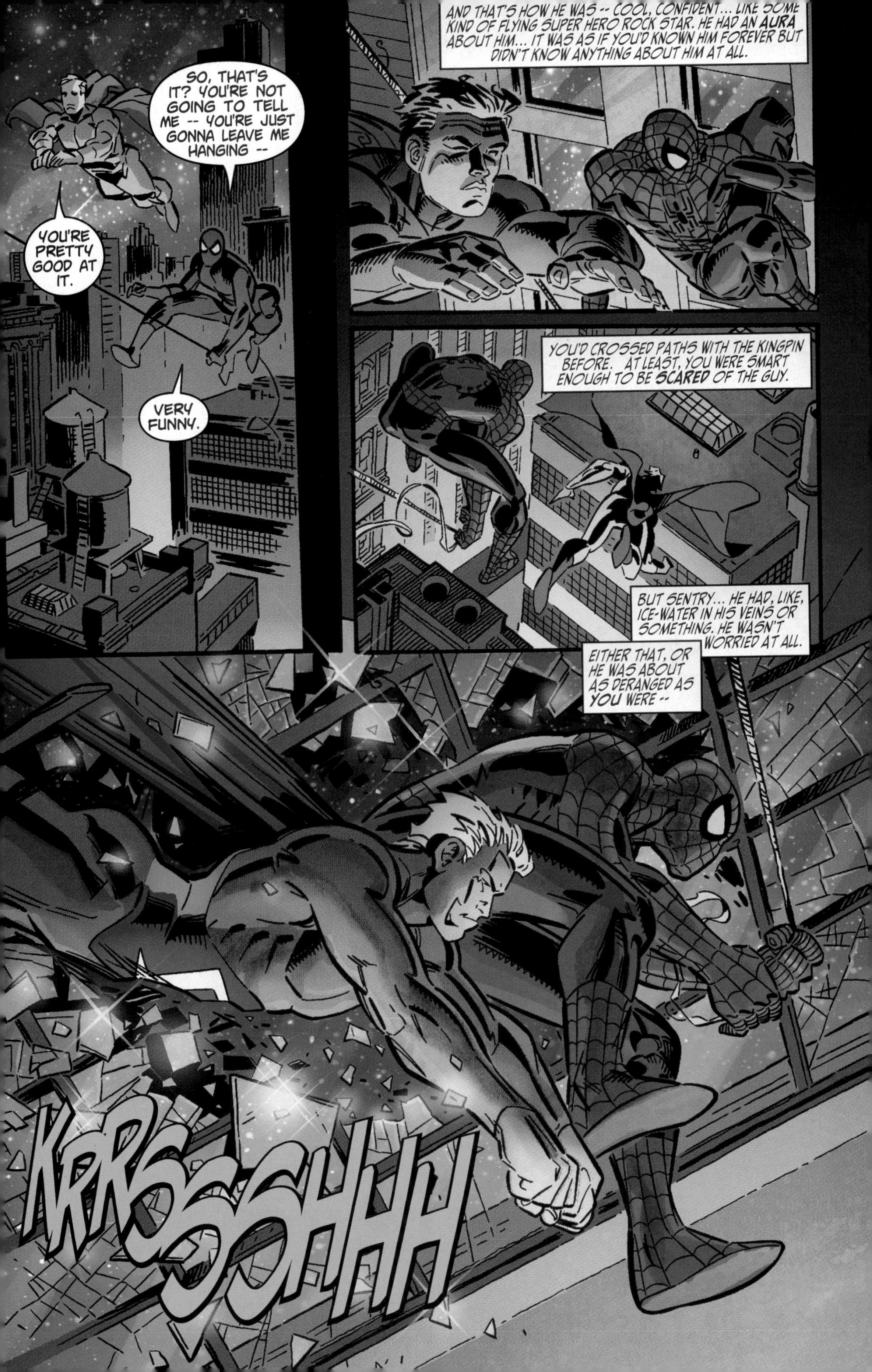
SO, THAT'S IT? YOU'RE NOT GOING TO TELL ME -- YOU'RE JUST GONNA LEAVE ME HANGING --
YOU'RE PRETTY GOOD AT IT.
VERY FUNNY.
AND THAT'S HOW HE WAS -- COOL, CONFIDENT... LIKE SOME KIND OF FLYING SUPER HERO ROCK STAR. HE HAD AN AURA ABOUT HIM... IT WAS AS IF YOU'D KNOWN HIM FOREVER BUT DIDN'T KNOW ANYTHING ABOUT HIM AT ALL.
YOU'D CROSSED PATHS WITH THE KINGPIN BEFORE. AT LEAST, YOU WERE SMART ENOUGH TO BE SCARED OF THE GUY.
BUT SENTRY... HE HAD, LIKE, ICE-WATER IN HIS VEINS OR SOMETHING. HE WASN'T WORRIED AT ALL.
EITHER THAT, OR HE WAS ABOUT AS DERANGED AS YOU WERE --
KRRSSSHHH

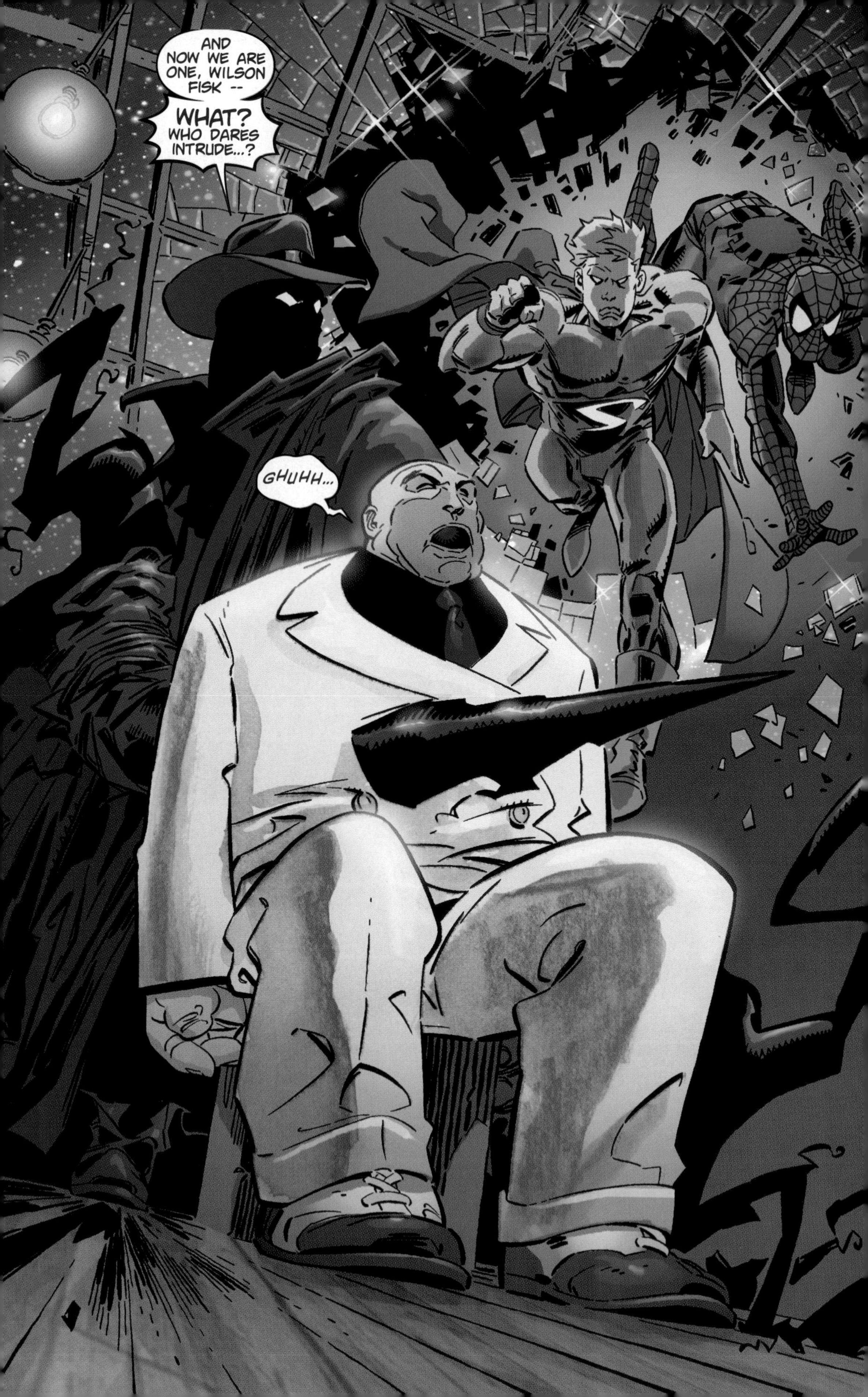
AND NOW WE ARE ONE, WILSON FISK --
WHAT? WHO DARES INTRUDE...?
GHUHH...

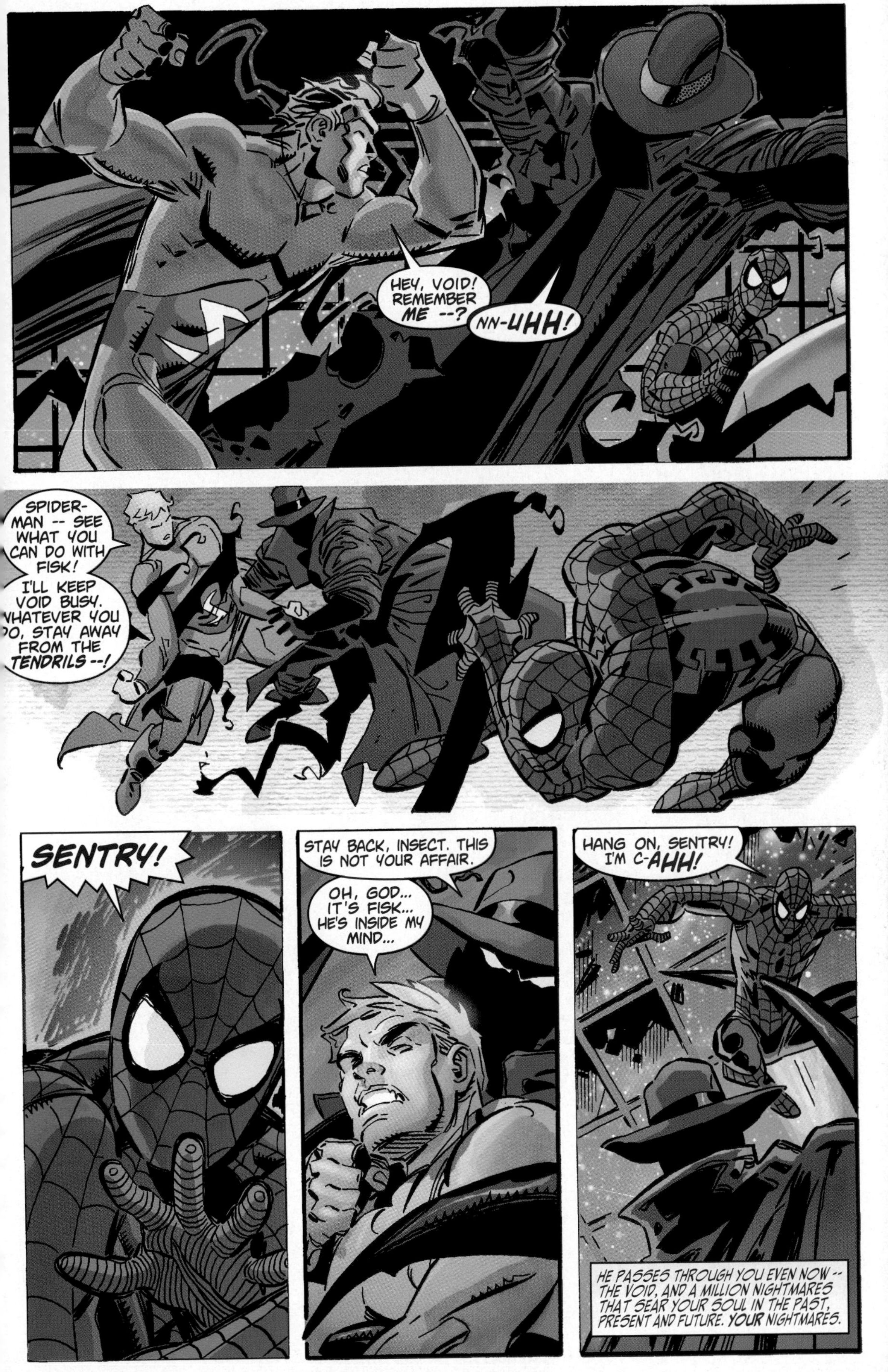
HEY, VOID! REMEMBER ME --?
NN-UHH!
SPIDER-MAN -- SEE WHAT YOU CAN DO WITH FISK!
I'LL KEEP VOID BUSY. WHATEVER YOU DO, STAY AWAY FROM THE TENDRILS --!
SENTRY!
STAY BACK, INSECT. THIS IS NOT YOUR AFFAIR.
OH, GOD... IT'S FISK... HE'S INSIDE MY MIND...
HANG ON, SENTRY! I'M C-AHH!
HE PASSES THROUGH YOU EVEN NOW -- THE VOID, AND A MILLION NIGHTMARES THAT SEAR YOUR SOUL IN THE PAST, PRESENT AND FUTURE. YOUR NIGHTMARES.

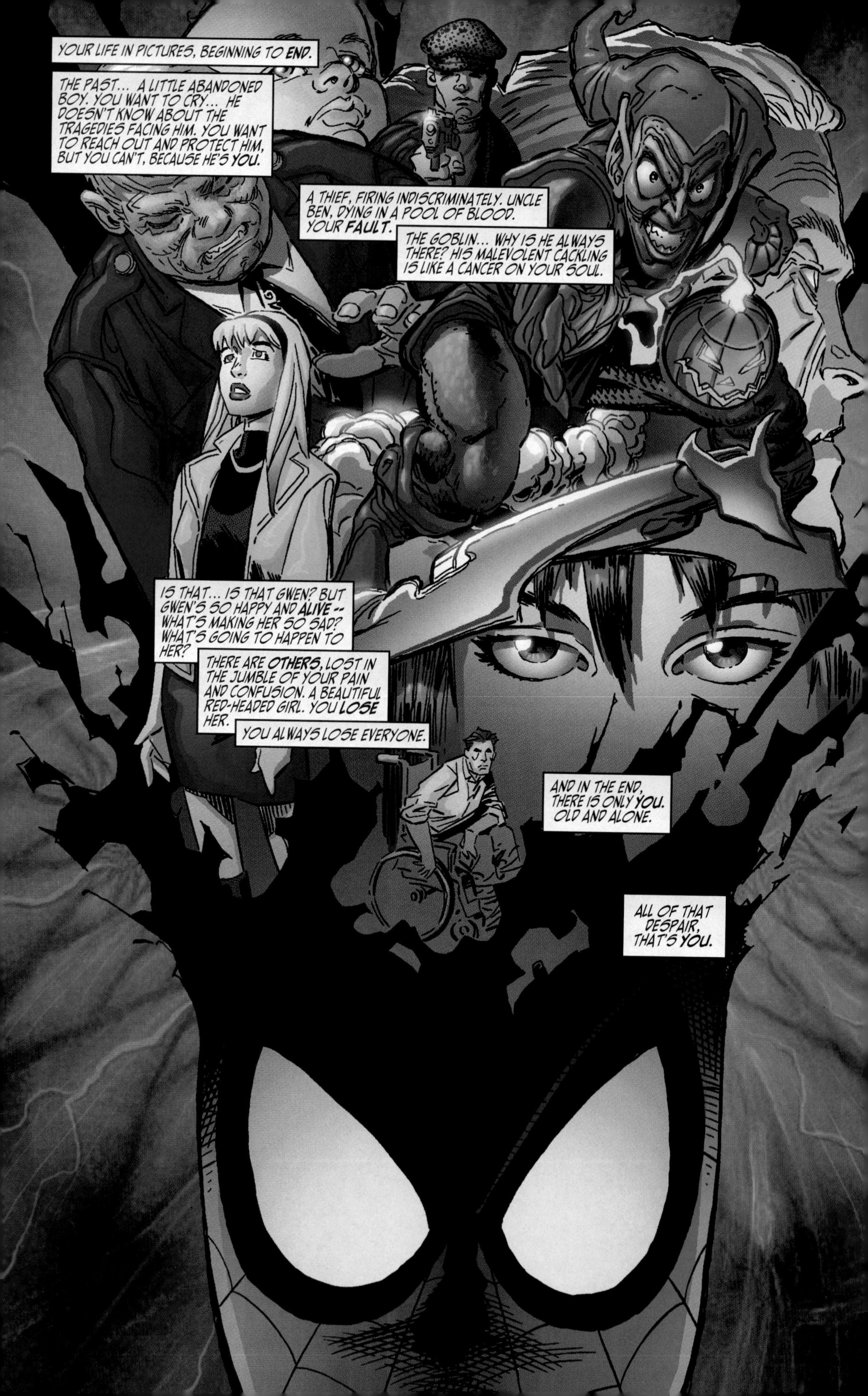
YOUR LIFE IN PICTURES, BEGINNING TO END.
THE PAST... A LITTLE ABANDONED BOY. YOU WANT TO CRY... HE DOESN'T KNOW ABOUT THE TRAGEDIES FACING HIM. YOU WANT TO REACH OUT AND PROTECT HIM, BUT YOU CAN'T, BECAUSE HE'S YOU.
A THIEF, FIRING INDISCRIMINATELY. UNCLE BEN, DYING IN A POOL OF BLOOD. YOUR FAULT.
THE GOBLIN... WHY IS HE ALWAYS THERE? HIS MALEVOLENT CACKLING IS LIKE A CANCER ON YOUR SOUL.
IS THAT... IS THAT GWEN? BUT GWEN'S SO HAPPY AND ALIVE -- WHAT'S MAKING HER SO SAD? WHAT'S GOING TO HAPPEN TO HER?
THERE ARE OTHERS, LOST IN THE JUMBLE OF YOUR PAIN AND CONFUSION. A BEAUTIFUL RED-HEADED GIRL. YOU LOSE HER.
YOU ALWAYS LOSE EVERYONE.
AND IN THE END, THERE IS ONLY YOU. OLD AND ALONE.
ALL OF THAT DESPAIR, THAT'S YOU.

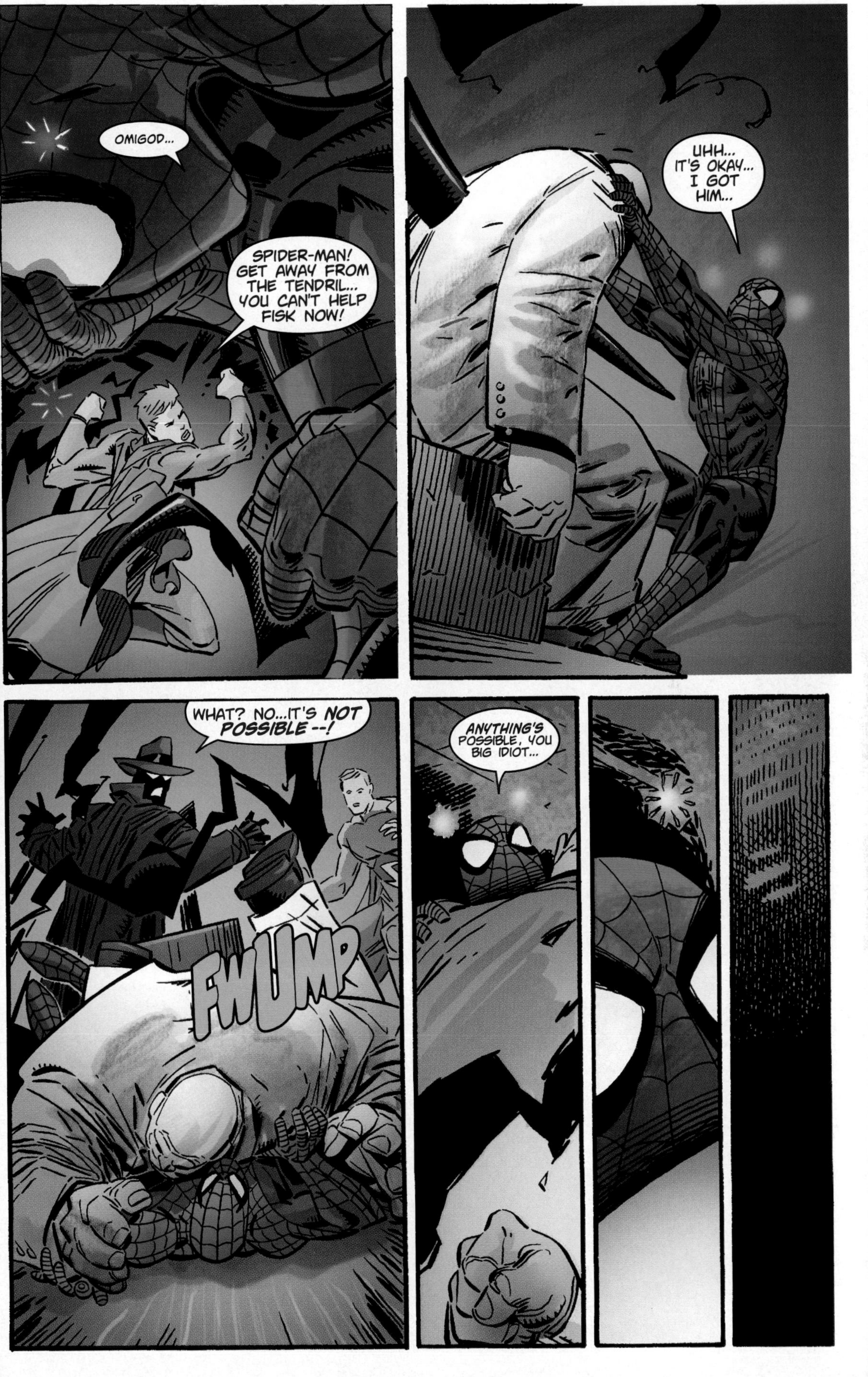
OMIGOD...
SPIDER-MAN! GET AWAY FROM THE TENDRIL... YOU CAN'T HELP FISK NOW!
UHH... IT'S OKAY... I GOT HIM...
WHAT? NO...IT'S NOT POSSIBLE --!
FWUMP
ANYTHING'S POSSIBLE, YOU BIG IDIOT...

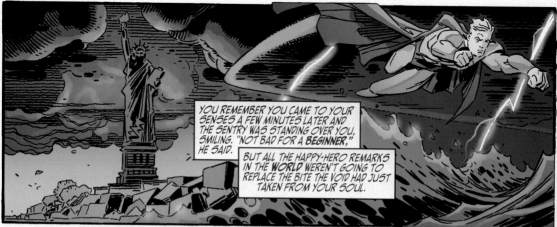

YOU REMEMBER YOU CAME TO YOUR SENSES A FEW MINUTES LATER AND THE SENTRY WAS STANDING OVER YOU, SMILING. "NOT BAD FOR A *BEGINNER,*" HE SAID.

BUT ALL THE HAPPY-HERO REMARKS IN THE *WORLD* WEREN'T GOING TO REPLACE THE BITE THE VOID HAD JUST TAKEN FROM YOUR SOUL.

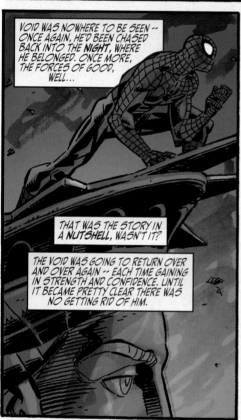

VOID WAS NOWHERE TO BE SEEN -- ONCE AGAIN, HE'D BEEN CHASED BACK INTO THE *NIGHT,* WHERE HE BELONGED. ONCE MORE, THE FORCES OF GOOD, WELL...

THAT WAS THE STORY IN A *NUTSHELL,* WASN'T IT?

THE VOID WAS GOING TO RETURN OVER AND OVER AGAIN -- EACH TIME GAINING IN STRENGTH AND CONFIDENCE. UNTIL IT BECAME PRETTY CLEAR THERE WAS NO GETTING RID OF HIM.

AND NOW, HE'S RE-ENTERED THE ETERNAL FRAY OF GOOD VERSUS EVIL ONCE *MORE.* YOUR BODY GIVES AN IMPERCEPTIBLE *SHUDDER* THAT BETRAYS YOUR UNDER-STANDING OF WHAT THIS MEANS FOR YOU ALL.

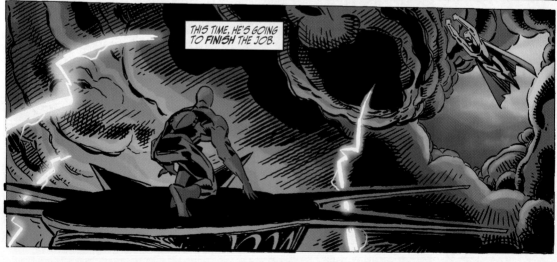

THIS TIME, HE'S GOING TO *FINISH* THE JOB.

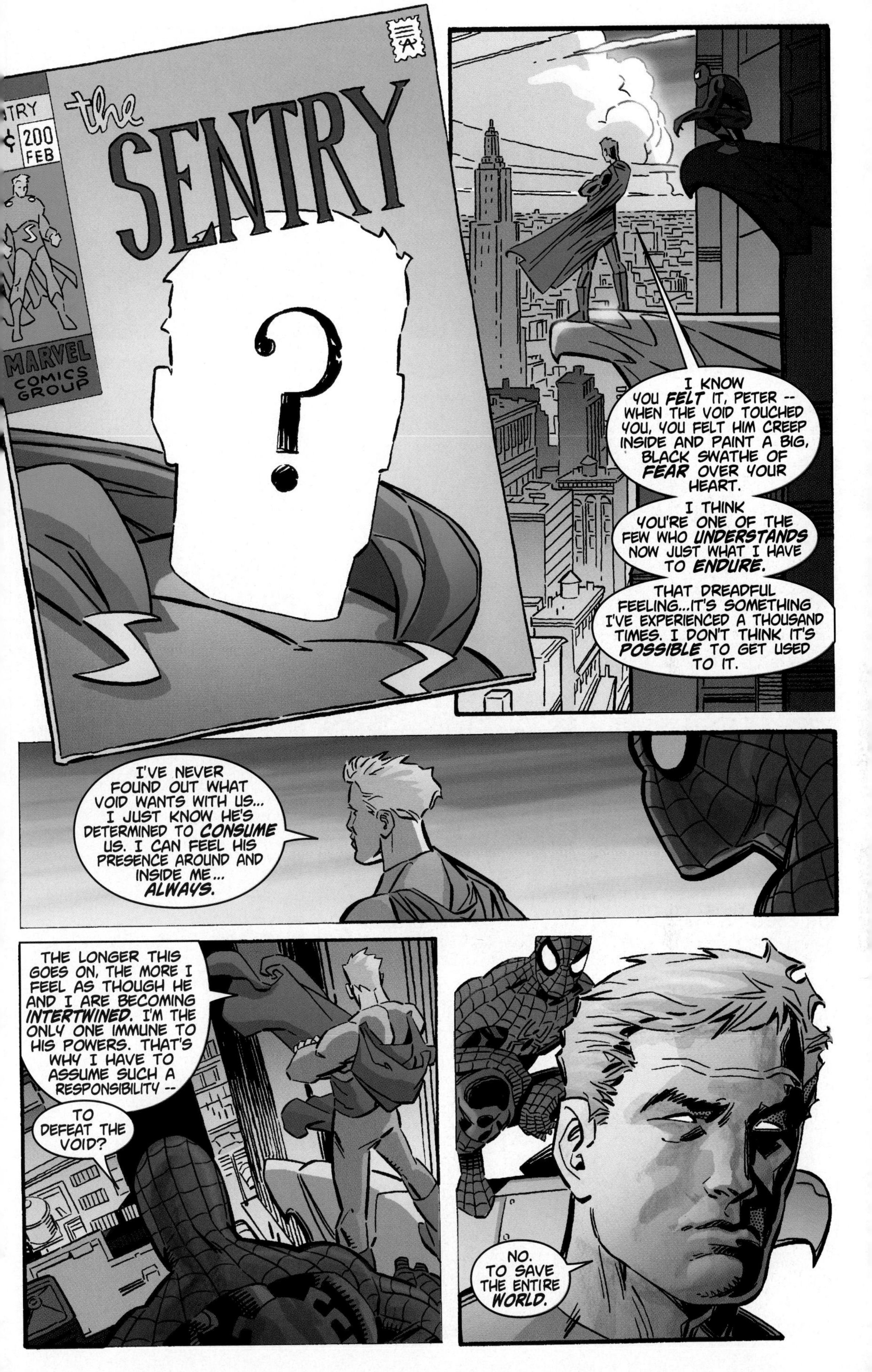

TRY
¢ 200
FEB
the SENTRY
MARVEL COMICS GROUP
?
I KNOW YOU FELT IT, PETER -- WHEN THE VOID TOUCHED YOU, YOU FELT HIM CREEP INSIDE AND PAINT A BIG, BLACK SWATHE OF FEAR OVER YOUR HEART.
I THINK YOU'RE ONE OF THE FEW WHO UNDERSTANDS NOW JUST WHAT I HAVE TO ENDURE.
THAT DREADFUL FEELING...IT'S SOMETHING I'VE EXPERIENCED A THOUSAND TIMES. I DON'T THINK IT'S POSSIBLE TO GET USED TO IT.
I'VE NEVER FOUND OUT WHAT VOID WANTS WITH US... I JUST KNOW HE'S DETERMINED TO CONSUME US. I CAN FEEL HIS PRESENCE AROUND AND INSIDE ME... ALWAYS.
THE LONGER THIS GOES ON, THE MORE I FEEL AS THOUGH HE AND I ARE BECOMING INTERTWINED. I'M THE ONLY ONE IMMUNE TO HIS POWERS. THAT'S WHY I HAVE TO ASSUME SUCH A RESPONSIBILITY --
TO DEFEAT THE VOID?
NO. TO SAVE THE ENTIRE WORLD.

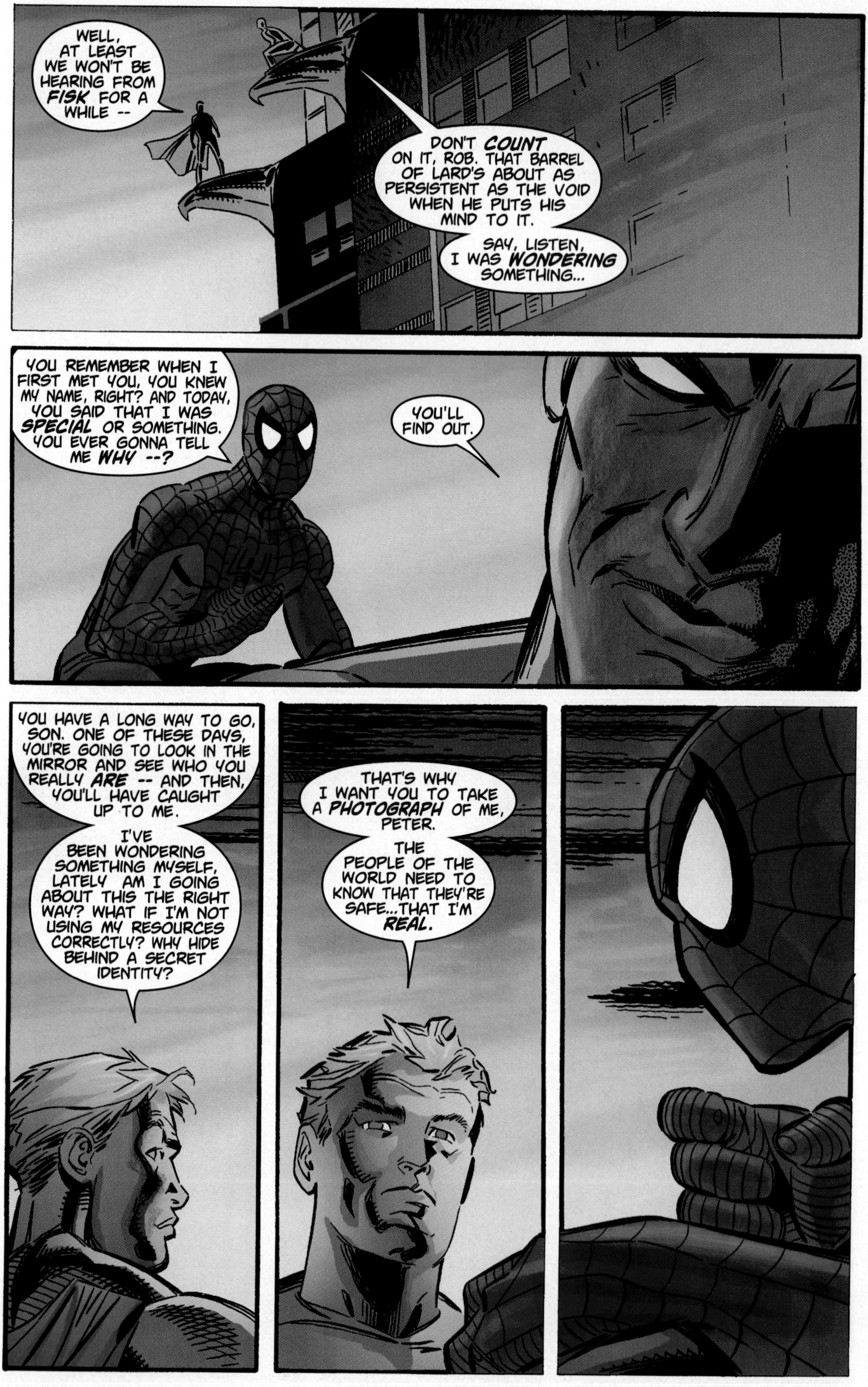
WELL, AT LEAST WE WON'T BE HEARING FROM FISK FOR A WHILE --
DON'T COUNT ON IT, ROB. THAT BARREL OF LARD'S ABOUT AS PERSISTENT AS THE VOID WHEN HE PUTS HIS MIND TO IT.
SAY, LISTEN, I WAS WONDERING SOMETHING...
YOU REMEMBER WHEN I FIRST MET YOU, YOU KNEW MY NAME, RIGHT? AND TODAY, YOU SAID THAT I WAS SPECIAL OR SOMETHING. YOU EVER GONNA TELL ME WHY --?
YOU'LL FIND OUT.
YOU HAVE A LONG WAY TO GO, SON. ONE OF THESE DAYS, YOU'RE GOING TO LOOK IN THE MIRROR AND SEE WHO YOU REALLY ARE -- AND THEN, YOU'LL HAVE CAUGHT UP TO ME.
I'VE BEEN WONDERING SOMETHING MYSELF, LATELY AM I GOING ABOUT THIS THE RIGHT WAY? WHAT IF I'M NOT USING MY RESOURCES CORRECTLY? WHY HIDE BEHIND A SECRET IDENTITY?
THAT'S WHY I WANT YOU TO TAKE A PHOTOGRAPH OF ME, PETER.
THE PEOPLE OF THE WORLD NEED TO KNOW THAT THEY'RE SAFE...THAT I'M REAL.

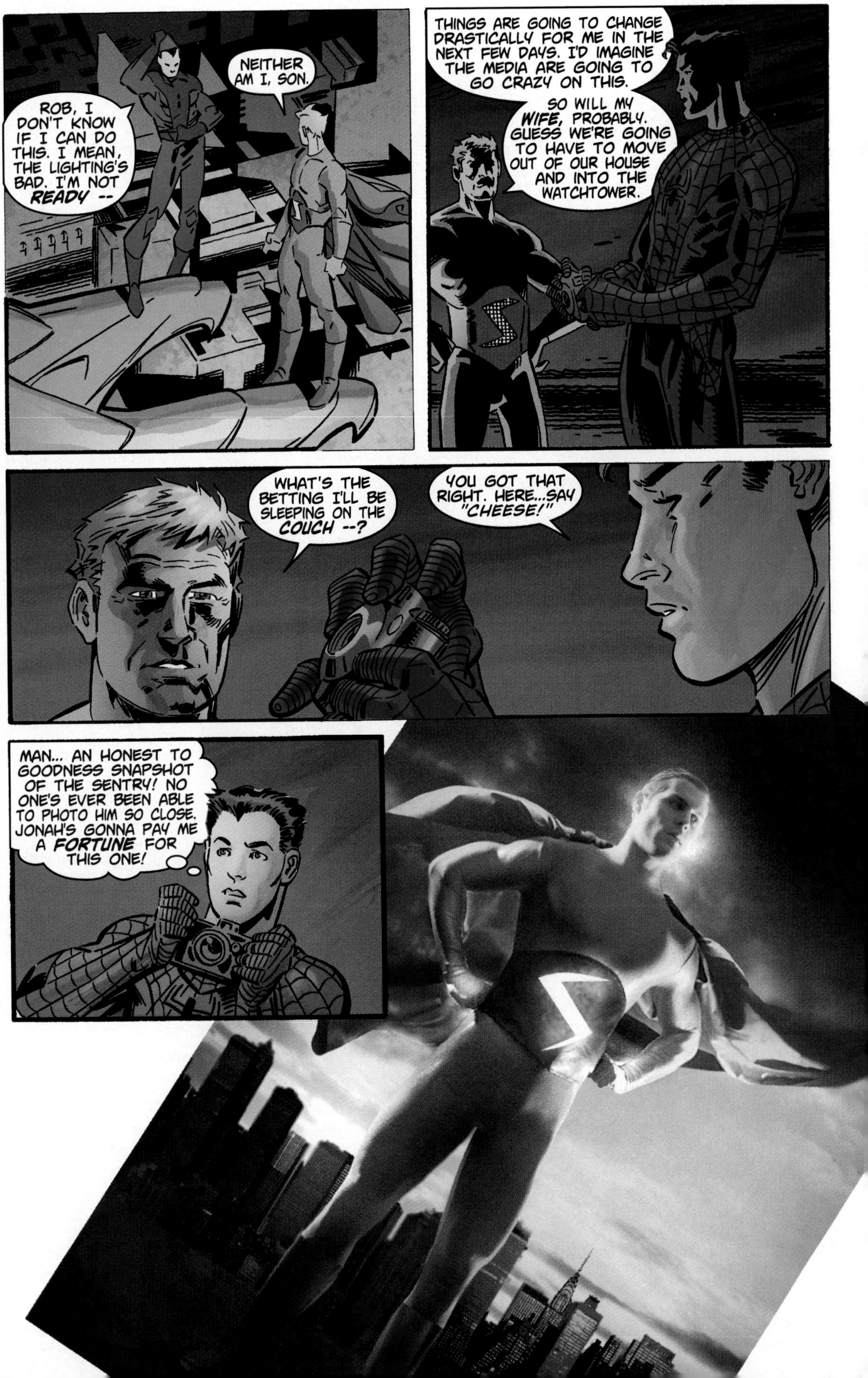
ROB, I DON'T KNOW IF I CAN DO THIS. I MEAN, THE LIGHTING'S BAD. I'M NOT READY --
NEITHER AM I, SON.
THINGS ARE GOING TO CHANGE DRASTICALLY FOR ME IN THE NEXT FEW DAYS. I'D IMAGINE THE MEDIA ARE GOING TO GO CRAZY ON THIS.
SO WILL MY WIFE, PROBABLY. GUESS WE'RE GOING TO HAVE TO MOVE OUT OF OUR HOUSE AND INTO THE WATCHTOWER.
WHAT'S THE BETTING I'LL BE SLEEPING ON THE COUCH --?
YOU GOT THAT RIGHT. HERE...SAY "CHEESE!"
MAN... AN HONEST TO GOODNESS SNAPSHOT OF THE SENTRY! NO ONE'S EVER BEEN ABLE TO PHOTO HIM SO CLOSE. JONAH'S GONNA PAY ME A FORTUNE FOR THIS ONE!

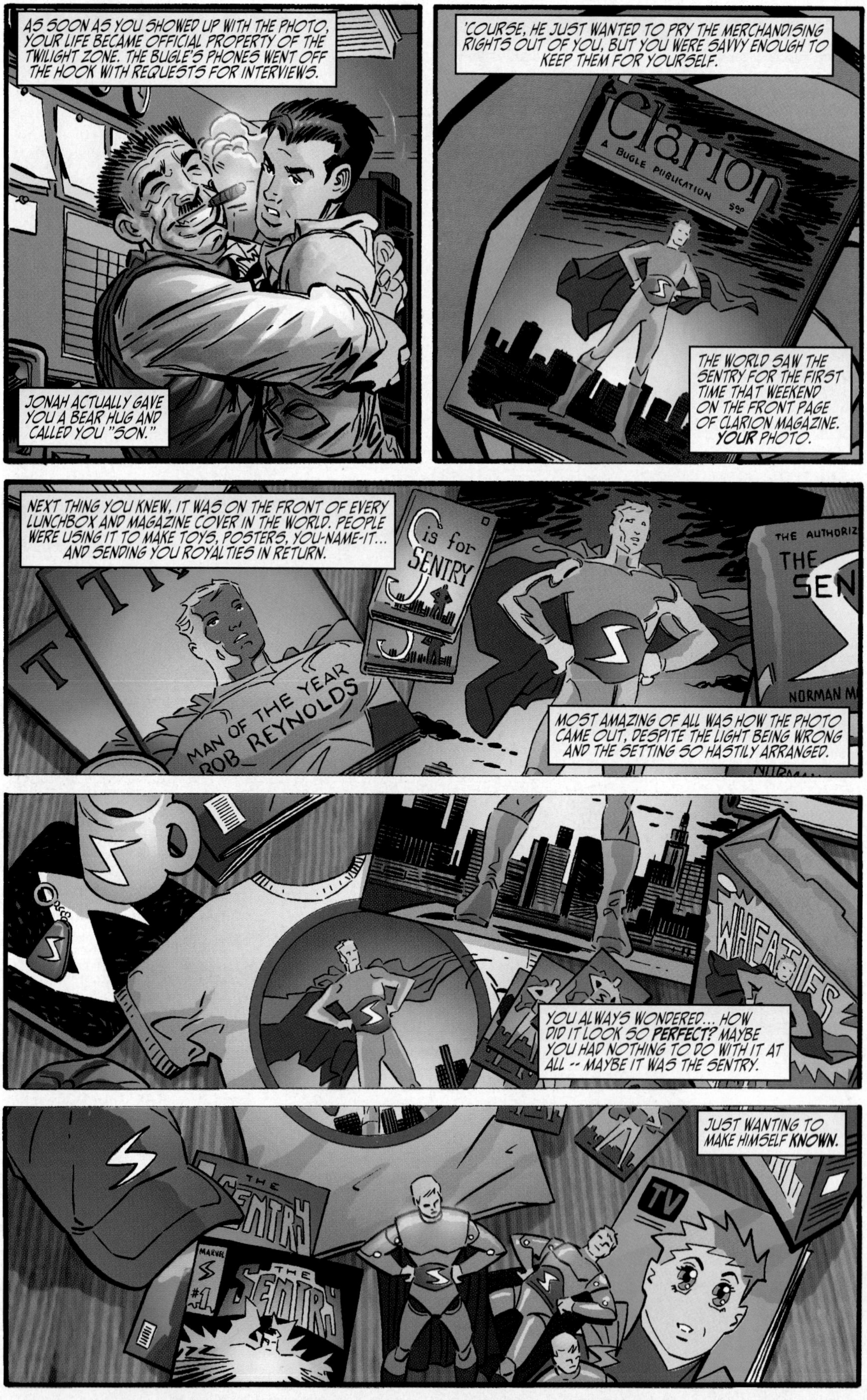

AS SOON AS YOU SHOWED UP WITH THE PHOTO, YOUR LIFE BECAME OFFICIAL PROPERTY OF THE TWILIGHT ZONE. THE BUGLE'S PHONES WENT OFF THE HOOK WITH REQUESTS FOR INTERVIEWS.
JONAH ACTUALLY GAVE YOU A BEAR HUG AND CALLED YOU "SON."
'COURSE, HE JUST WANTED TO PRY THE MERCHANDISING RIGHTS OUT OF YOU, BUT YOU WERE SAVVY ENOUGH TO KEEP THEM FOR YOURSELF.
Clarion
A BUGLE PUBLICATION
THE WORLD SAW THE SENTRY FOR THE FIRST TIME THAT WEEKEND ON THE FRONT PAGE OF CLARION MAGAZINE. YOUR PHOTO.
NEXT THING YOU KNEW, IT WAS ON THE FRONT OF EVERY LUNCHBOX AND MAGAZINE COVER IN THE WORLD. PEOPLE WERE USING IT TO MAKE TOYS, POSTERS, YOU-NAME-IT... AND SENDING YOU ROYALTIES IN RETURN.
S is for SENTRY
MAN OF THE YEAR
ROB REYNOLDS
THE AUTHORIZ
THE SEN
NORMAN M
MOST AMAZING OF ALL WAS HOW THE PHOTO CAME OUT, DESPITE THE LIGHT BEING WRONG AND THE SETTING SO HASTILY ARRANGED.
WHEATIES
YOU ALWAYS WONDERED... HOW DID IT LOOK SO PERFECT? MAYBE YOU HAD NOTHING TO DO WITH IT AT ALL -- MAYBE IT WAS THE SENTRY.
JUST WANTING TO MAKE HIMSELF KNOWN.
THE SENTRY
MARVEL
#1
TV

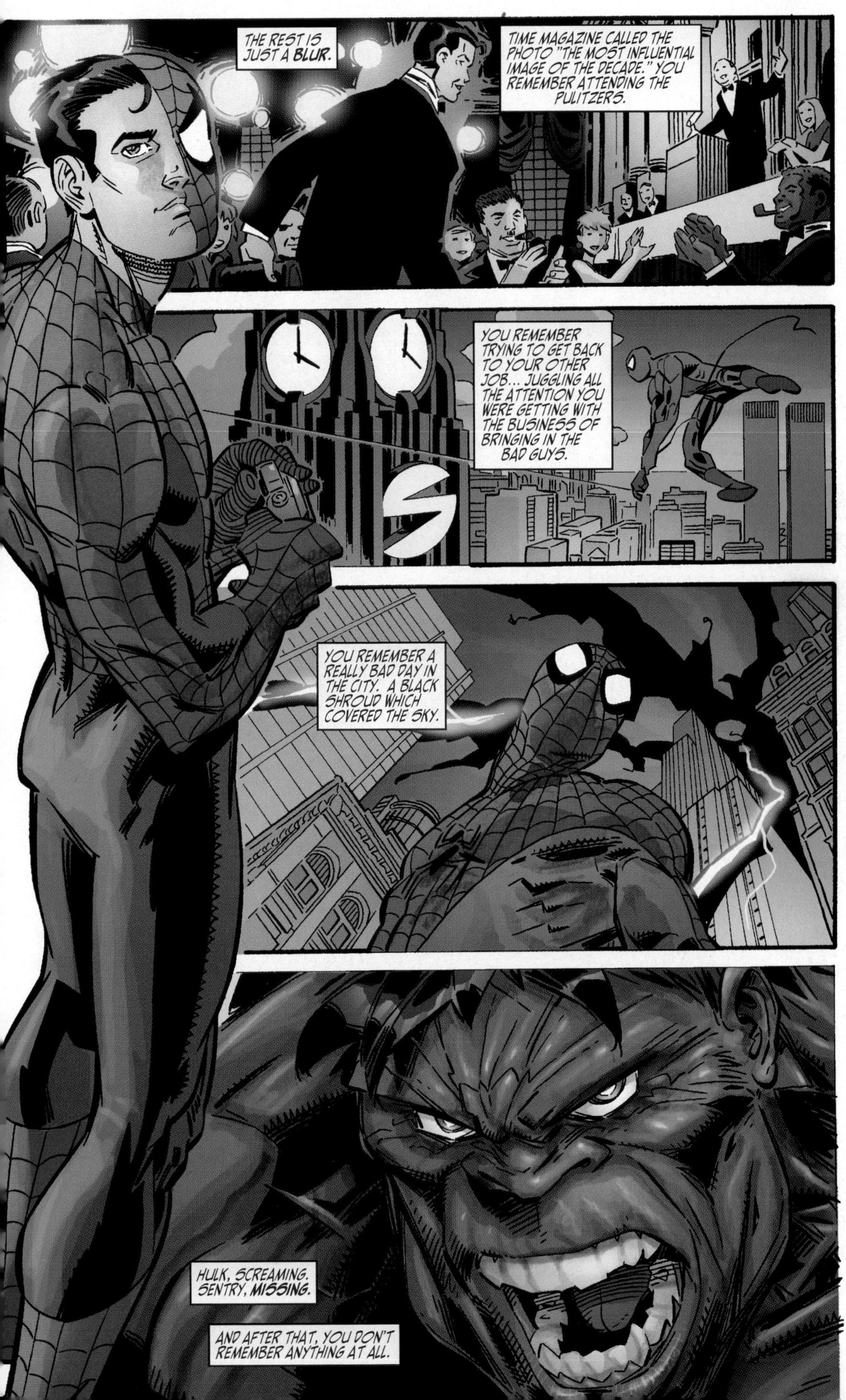
THE REST IS JUST A BLUR.
TIME MAGAZINE CALLED THE PHOTO "THE MOST INFLUENTIAL IMAGE OF THE DECADE." YOU REMEMBER ATTENDING THE PULITZERS.
YOU REMEMBER TRYING TO GET BACK TO YOUR OTHER JOB... JUGGLING ALL THE ATTENTION YOU WERE GETTING WITH THE BUSINESS OF BRINGING IN THE BAD GUYS.
YOU REMEMBER A REALLY BAD DAY IN THE CITY. A BLACK SHROUD WHICH COVERED THE SKY.
HULK, SCREAMING. SENTRY, MISSING.
AND AFTER THAT, YOU DON'T REMEMBER ANYTHING AT ALL.

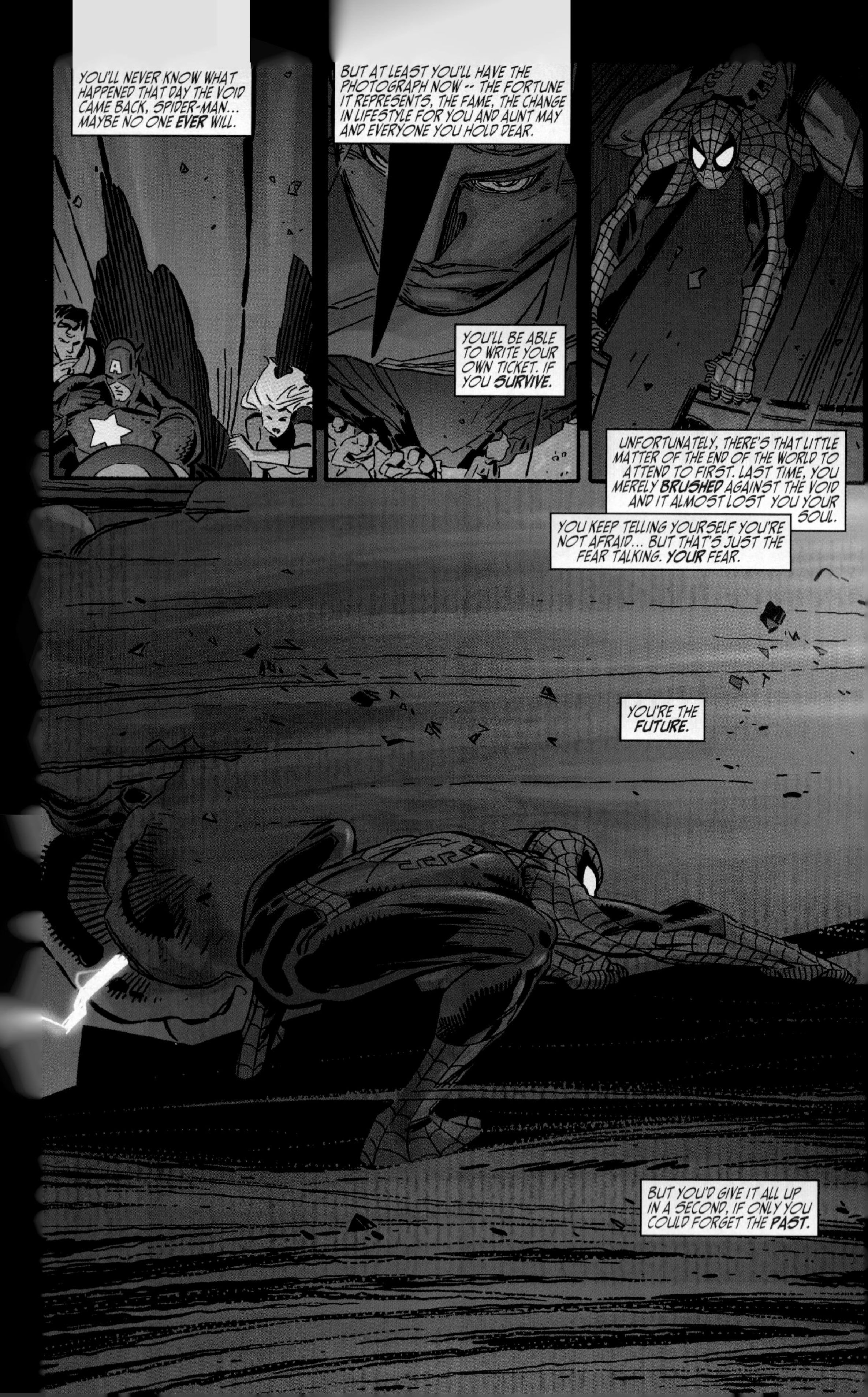
YOU'LL NEVER KNOW WHAT HAPPENED THAT DAY THE VOID CAME BACK, SPIDER-MAN... MAYBE NO ONE EVER WILL.
BUT AT LEAST YOU'LL HAVE THE PHOTOGRAPH NOW -- THE FORTUNE IT REPRESENTS, THE FAME, THE CHANGE IN LIFESTYLE FOR YOU AND AUNT MAY AND EVERYONE YOU HOLD DEAR.
YOU'LL BE ABLE TO WRITE YOUR OWN TICKET. IF YOU SURVIVE.
UNFORTUNATELY, THERE'S THAT LITTLE MATTER OF THE END OF THE WORLD TO ATTEND TO FIRST. LAST TIME, YOU MERELY BRUSHED AGAINST THE VOID AND IT ALMOST LOST YOU YOUR SOUL.
YOU KEEP TELLING YOURSELF YOU'RE NOT AFRAID... BUT THAT'S JUST THE FEAR TALKING. YOUR FEAR.
YOU'RE THE FUTURE.
BUT YOU'D GIVE IT ALL UP IN A SECOND, IF ONLY YOU COULD FORGET THE PAST.

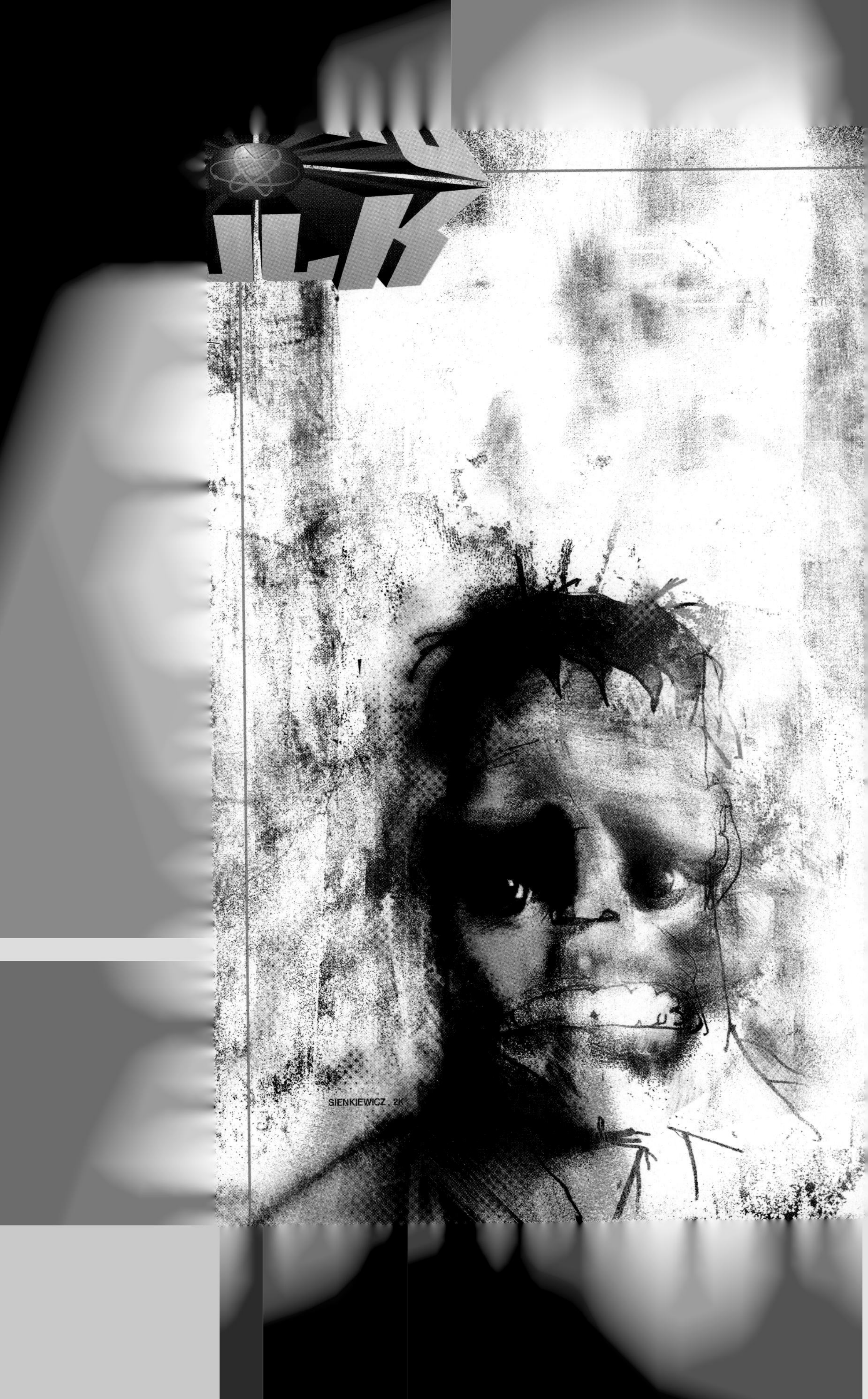
SIENKIEWICZ . 2K

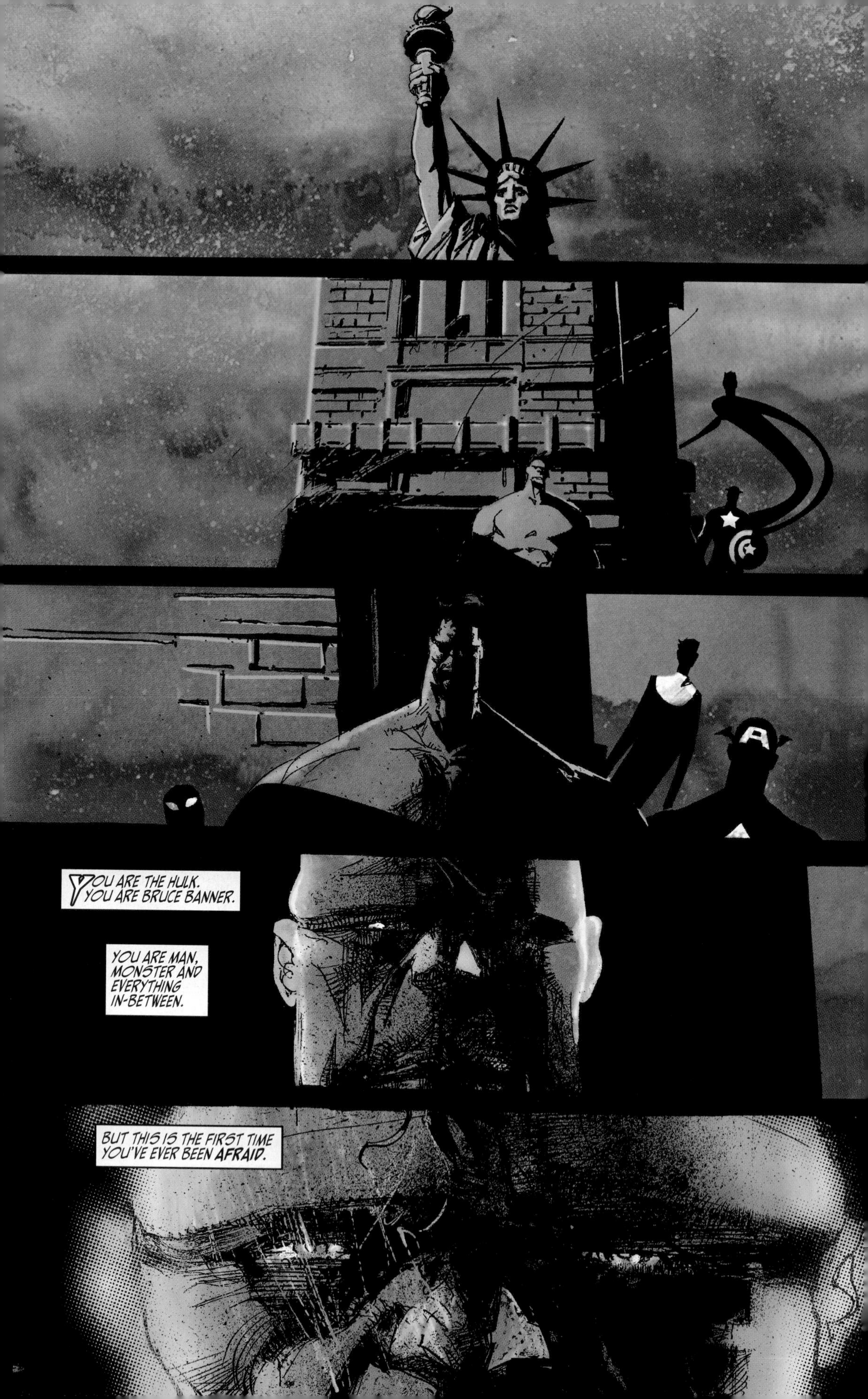
YOU ARE THE HULK. YOU ARE BRUCE BANNER.
YOU ARE MAN, MONSTER AND EVERYTHING IN-BETWEEN.
BUT THIS IS THE FIRST TIME YOU'VE EVER BEEN AFRAID.

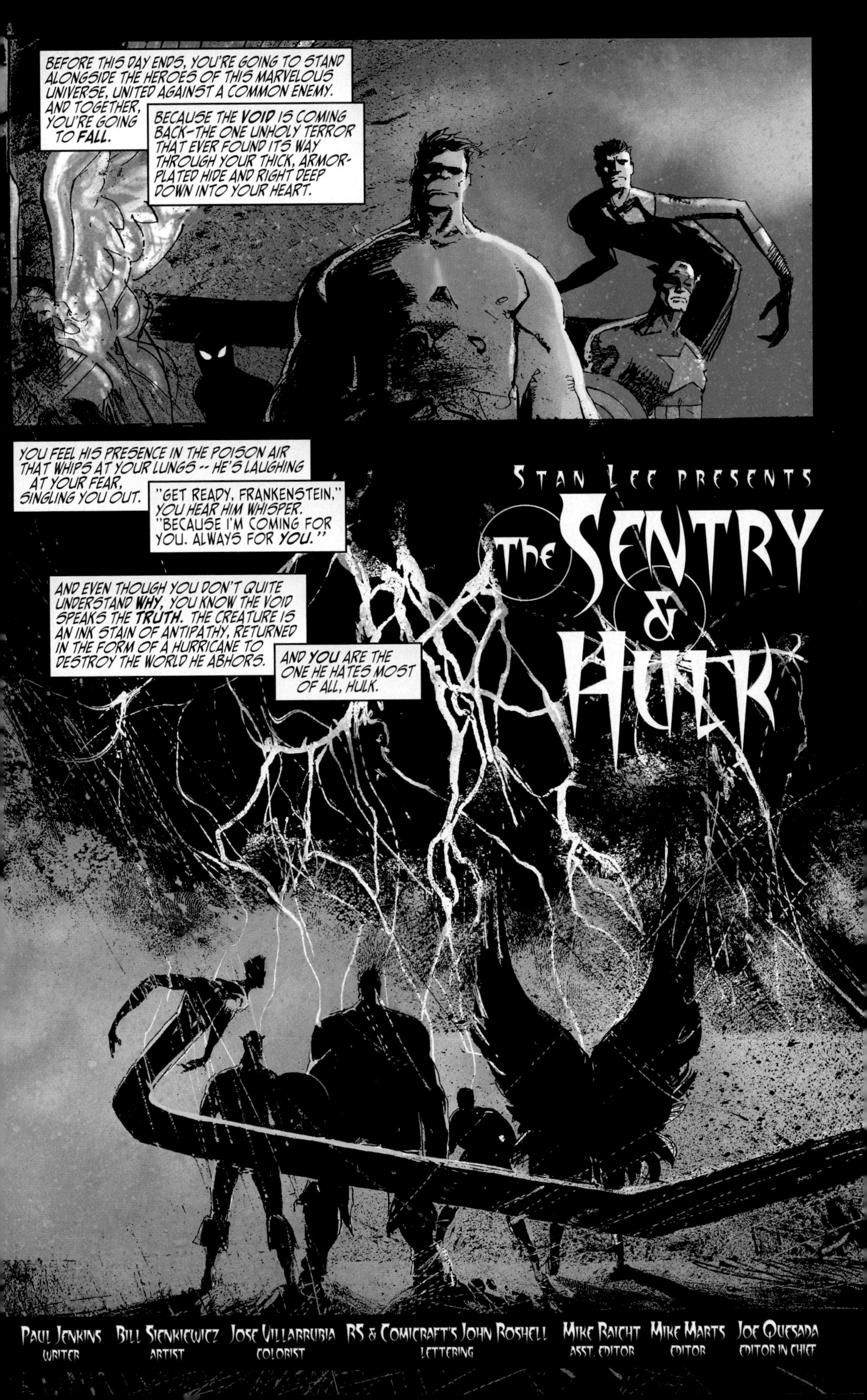
BEFORE THIS DAY ENDS, YOU'RE GOING TO STAND ALONGSIDE THE HEROES OF THIS MARVELOUS UNIVERSE, UNITED AGAINST A COMMON ENEMY.
AND TOGETHER, YOU'RE GOING TO FALL.
BECAUSE THE VOID IS COMING BACK–THE ONE UNHOLY TERROR THAT EVER FOUND ITS WAY THROUGH YOUR THICK, ARMOR-PLATED HIDE AND RIGHT DEEP DOWN INTO YOUR HEART.
YOU FEEL HIS PRESENCE IN THE POISON AIR THAT WHIPS AT YOUR LUNGS -- HE'S LAUGHING AT YOUR FEAR, SINGLING YOU OUT.
"GET READY, FRANKENSTEIN," YOU HEAR HIM WHISPER. "BECAUSE I'M COMING FOR YOU. ALWAYS FOR YOU."
AND EVEN THOUGH YOU DON'T QUITE UNDERSTAND WHY, YOU KNOW THE VOID SPEAKS THE TRUTH. THE CREATURE IS AN INK STAIN OF ANTIPATHY, RETURNED IN THE FORM OF A HURRICANE TO DESTROY THE WORLD HE ABHORS.
AND YOU ARE THE ONE HE HATES MOST OF ALL, HULK.
STAN LEE PRESENTS
The SENTRY & HULK
PAUL JENKINS WRITER
BILL SIENKIEWICZ ARTIST
JOSE VILLARRUBIA COLORIST
RS & COMICRAFT'S JOHN ROSHELL LETTERING
MIKE RAICHT ASST. EDITOR
MIKE MARTS EDITOR
JOE QUESADA EDITOR IN CHIEF

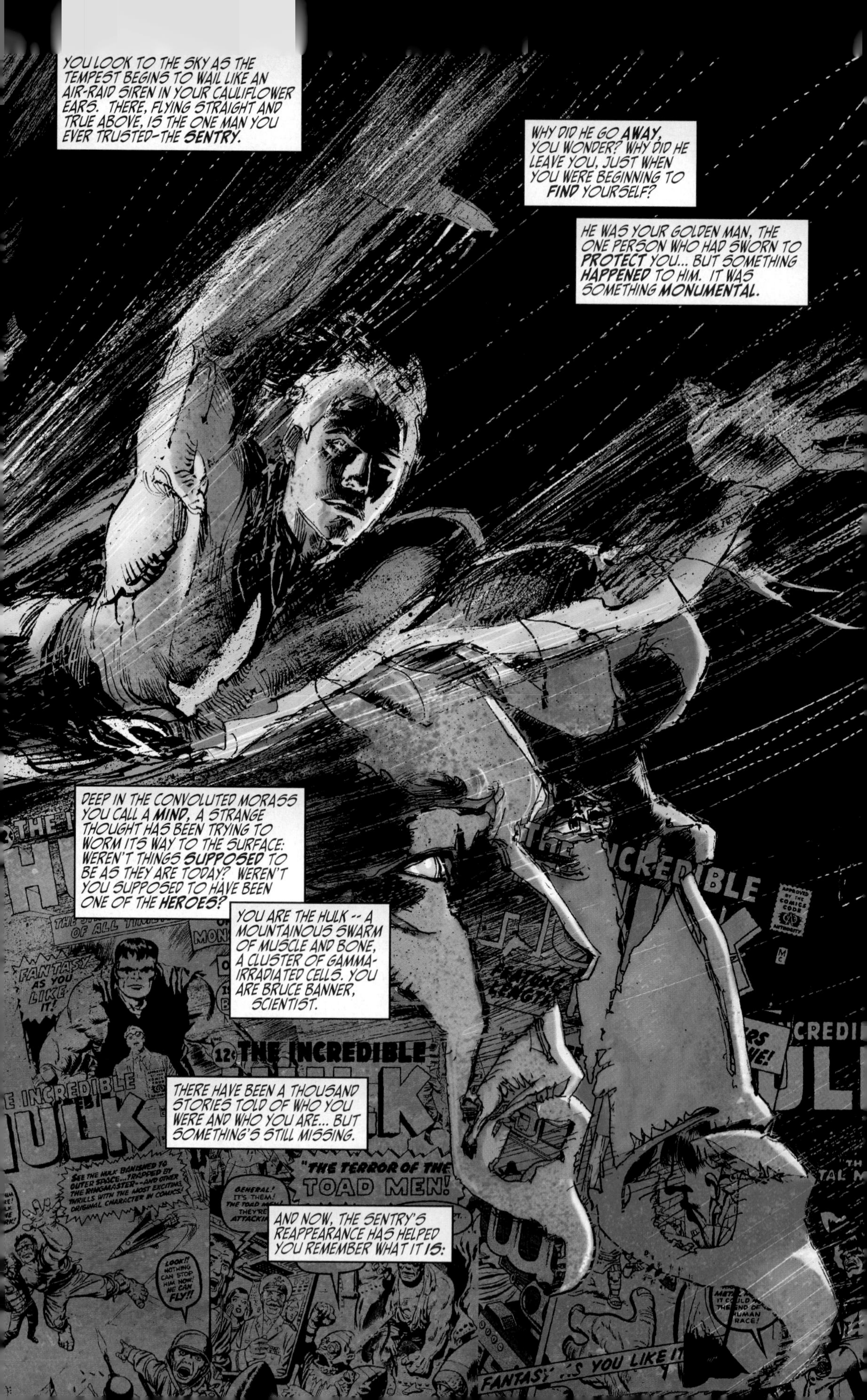
YOU LOOK TO THE SKY AS THE TEMPEST BEGINS TO WAIL LIKE AN AIR-RAID SIREN IN YOUR CAULIFLOWER EARS. THERE, FLYING STRAIGHT AND TRUE ABOVE, IS THE ONE MAN YOU EVER TRUSTED--THE SENTRY.
WHY DID HE GO AWAY, YOU WONDER? WHY DID HE LEAVE YOU, JUST WHEN YOU WERE BEGINNING TO FIND YOURSELF?
HE WAS YOUR GOLDEN MAN, THE ONE PERSON WHO HAD SWORN TO PROTECT YOU... BUT SOMETHING HAPPENED TO HIM. IT WAS SOMETHING MONUMENTAL.
DEEP IN THE CONVOLUTED MORASS YOU CALL A MIND, A STRANGE THOUGHT HAS BEEN TRYING TO WORM ITS WAY TO THE SURFACE: WEREN'T THINGS SUPPOSED TO BE AS THEY ARE TODAY? WEREN'T YOU SUPPOSED TO HAVE BEEN ONE OF THE HEROES?
YOU ARE THE HULK -- A MOUNTAINOUS SWARM OF MUSCLE AND BONE, A CLUSTER OF GAMMA-IRRADIATED CELLS. YOU ARE BRUCE BANNER, SCIENTIST.
THERE HAVE BEEN A THOUSAND STORIES TOLD OF WHO YOU WERE AND WHO YOU ARE... BUT SOMETHING'S STILL MISSING.
AND NOW, THE SENTRY'S REAPPEARANCE HAS HELPED YOU REMEMBER WHAT IT IS:
THE INCREDIBLE HULK
FANTASY AS YOU LIKE IT!
12¢ THE INCREDIBLE
THE INCREDIBLE HULK
"THE TERROR OF THE TOAD MEN!"
GENERAL! IT'S THEM! THE TOAD MEN! THEY'RE ATTACKING!
SEE THE HULK BANISHED TO OUTER SPACE--TRAPPED BY THE RINGMASTER--AND OTHER THRILLS WITH THE MOST EXCITING ORIGINAL CHARACTER IN COMICS!
LOOK!! NOTHING CAN STOP HIM NOW! HE CAN FLY!!
APPROVED BY THE COMICS CODE AUTHORITY
FANTASY AS YOU LIKE IT

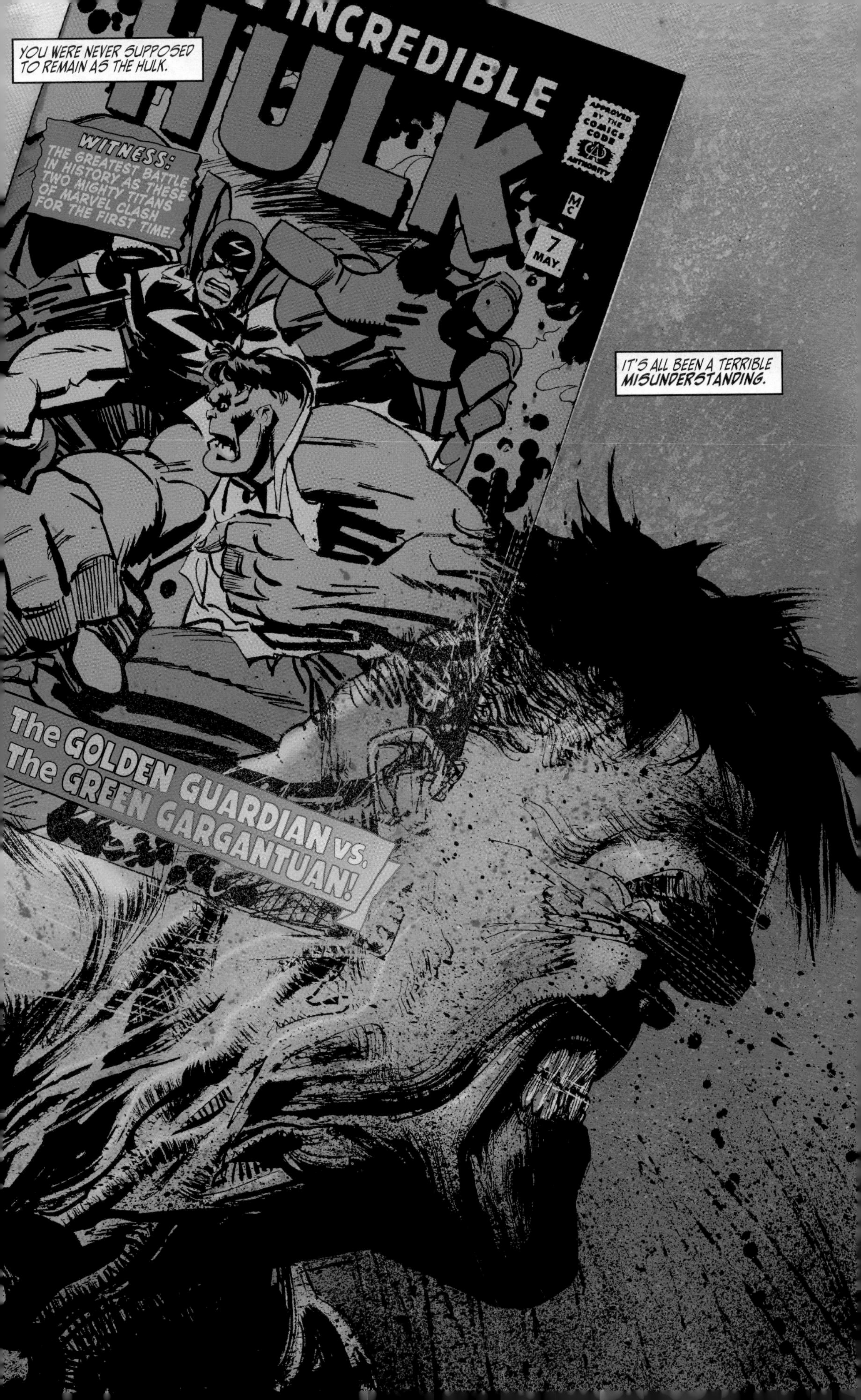
YOU WERE NEVER SUPPOSED TO REMAIN AS THE HULK.
INCREDIBLE HULK
APPROVED BY THE COMICS CODE AUTHORITY
MC
7 MAY
WITNESS: THE GREATEST BATTLE IN HISTORY AS THESE TWO MIGHTY TITANS OF MARVEL CLASH FOR THE FIRST TIME!
The GOLDEN GUARDIAN vs. The GREEN GARGANTUAN!
IT'S ALL BEEN A TERRIBLE MISUNDERSTANDING.

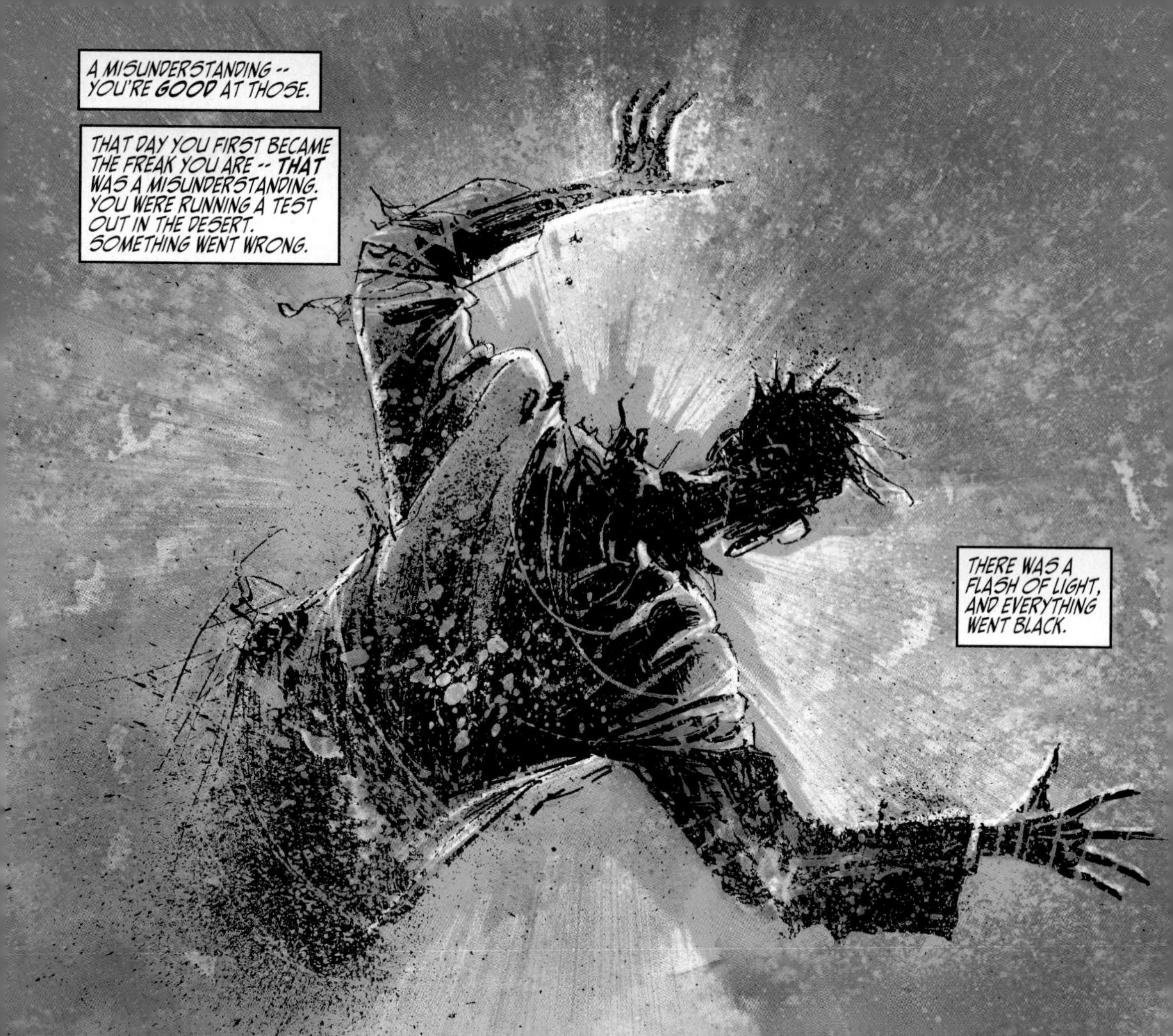

A MISUNDERSTANDING -- YOU'RE **GOOD** AT THOSE.
THAT DAY YOU FIRST BECAME THE FREAK YOU ARE -- **THAT** WAS A MISUNDERSTANDING. YOU WERE RUNNING A TEST OUT IN THE DESERT. SOMETHING WENT WRONG.
THERE WAS A FLASH OF LIGHT, AND EVERYTHING WENT BLACK.

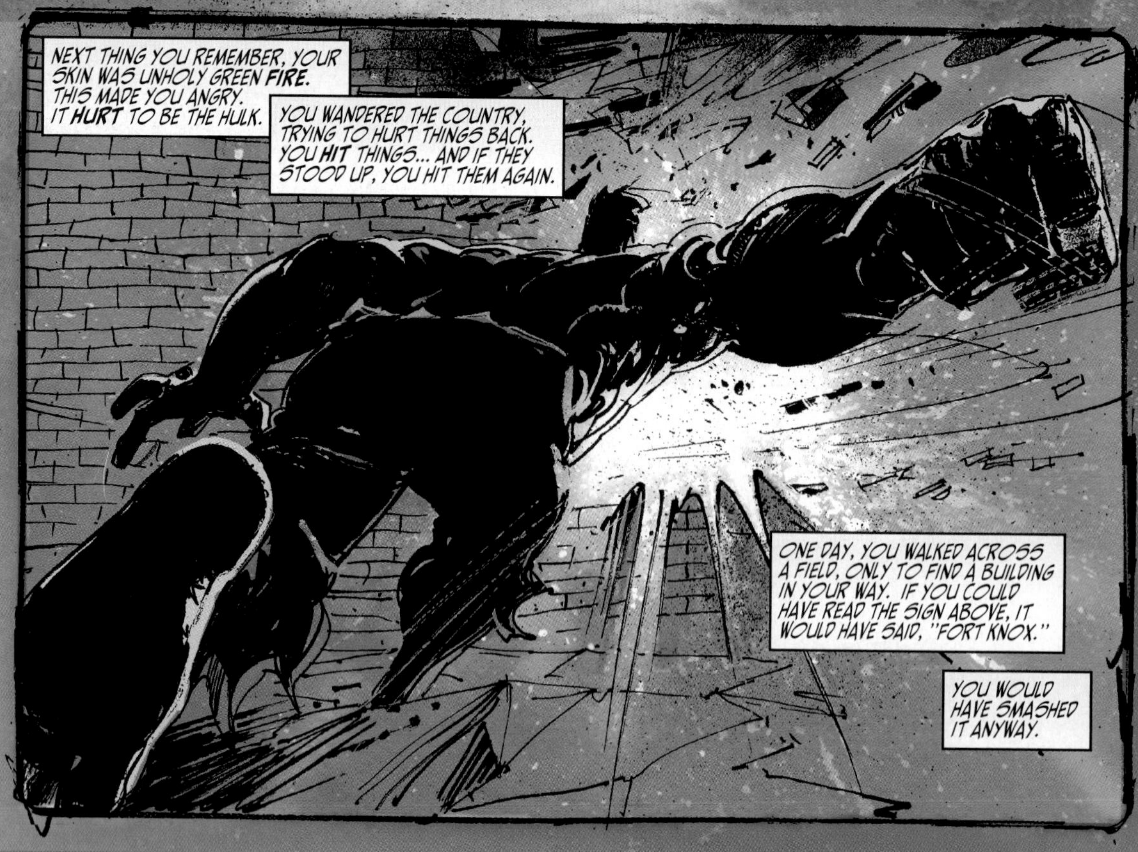

NEXT THING YOU REMEMBER, YOUR SKIN WAS UNHOLY GREEN **FIRE**. THIS MADE YOU ANGRY. IT **HURT** TO BE THE HULK.
YOU WANDERED THE COUNTRY, TRYING TO HURT THINGS BACK. YOU **HIT** THINGS... AND IF THEY STOOD UP, YOU HIT THEM AGAIN.
ONE DAY, YOU WALKED ACROSS A FIELD, ONLY TO FIND A BUILDING IN YOUR WAY. IF YOU COULD HAVE READ THE SIGN ABOVE, IT WOULD HAVE SAID, "FORT KNOX."
YOU WOULD HAVE SMASHED IT ANYWAY.

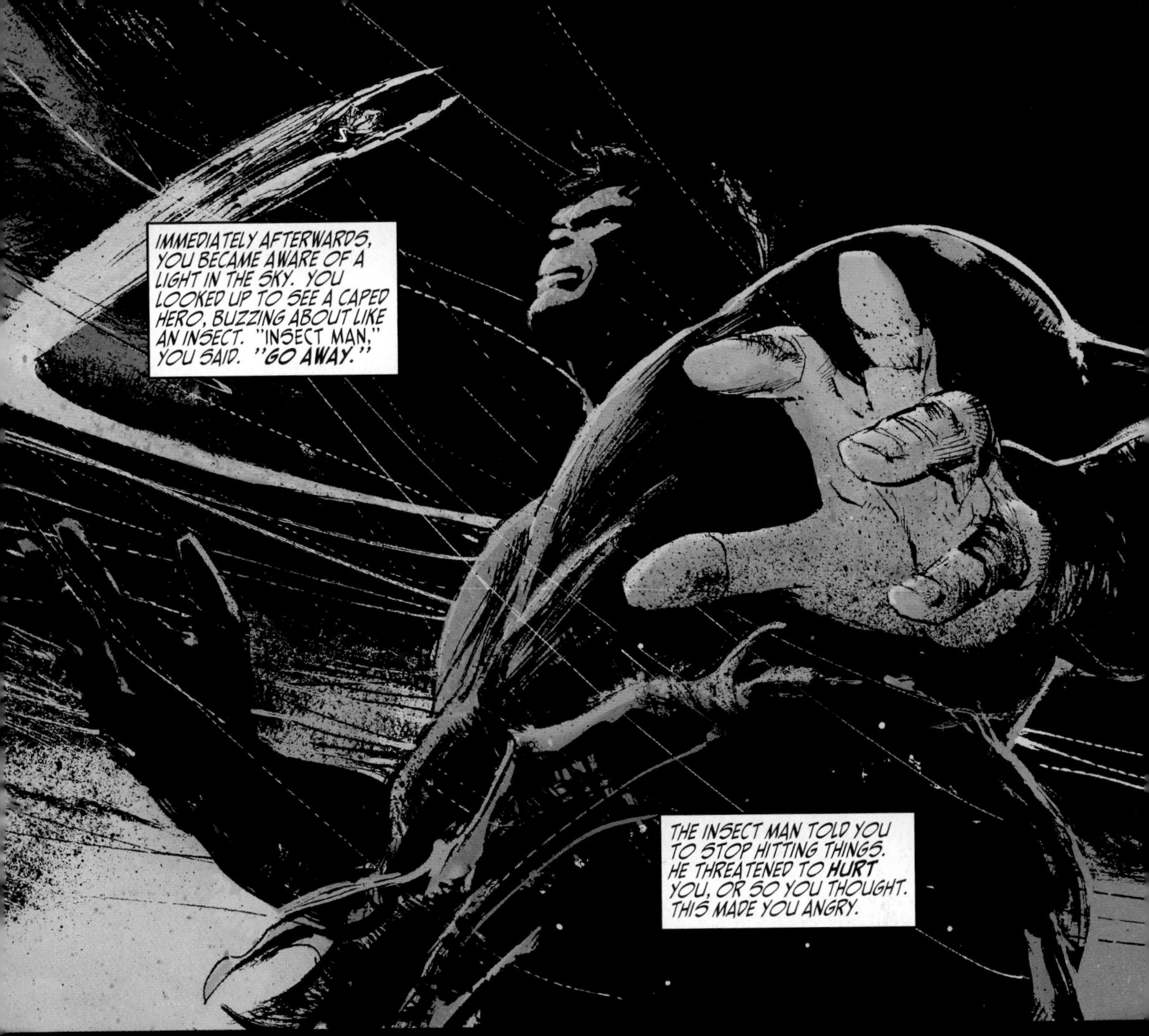
IMMEDIATELY AFTERWARDS, YOU BECAME AWARE OF A LIGHT IN THE SKY. YOU LOOKED UP TO SEE A CAPED HERO, BUZZING ABOUT LIKE AN INSECT. "INSECT MAN," YOU SAID. "GO AWAY."
THE INSECT MAN TOLD YOU TO STOP HITTING THINGS. HE THREATENED TO HURT YOU, OR SO YOU THOUGHT. THIS MADE YOU ANGRY.

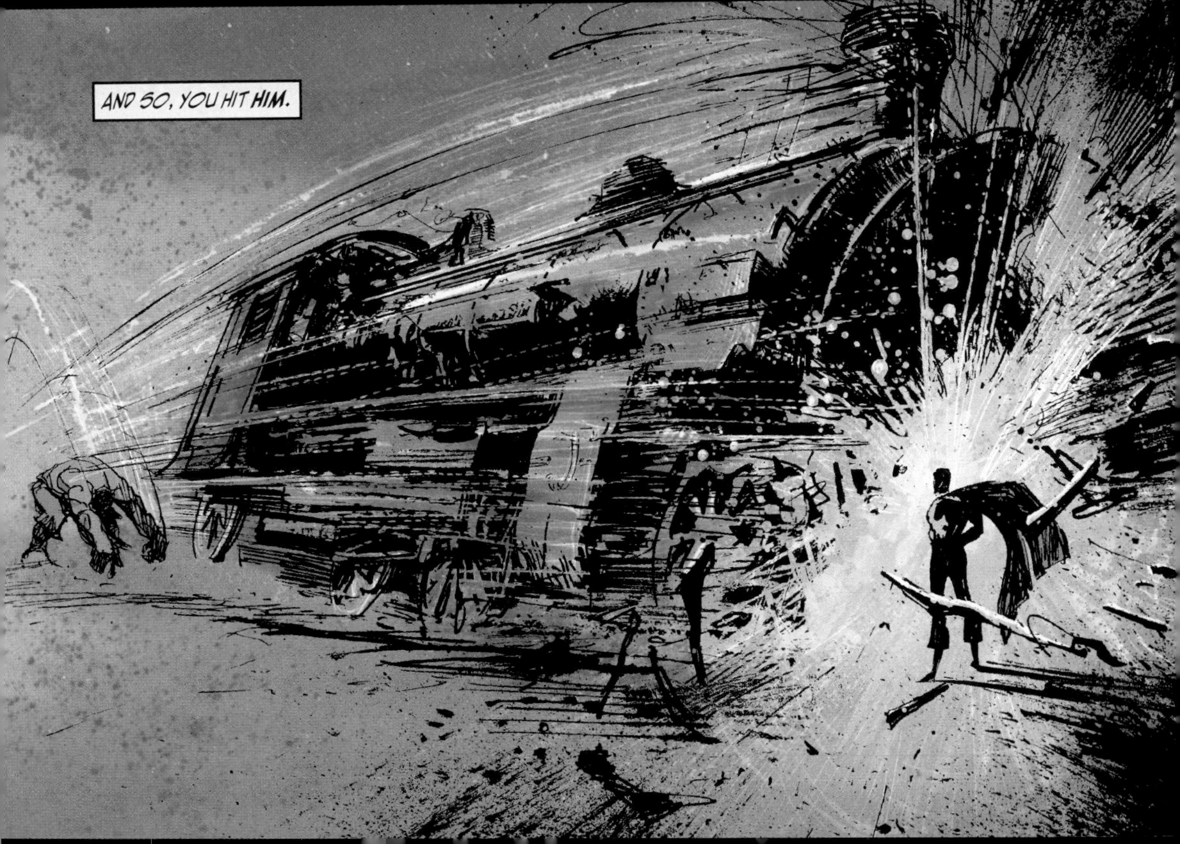
AND SO, YOU HIT HIM.

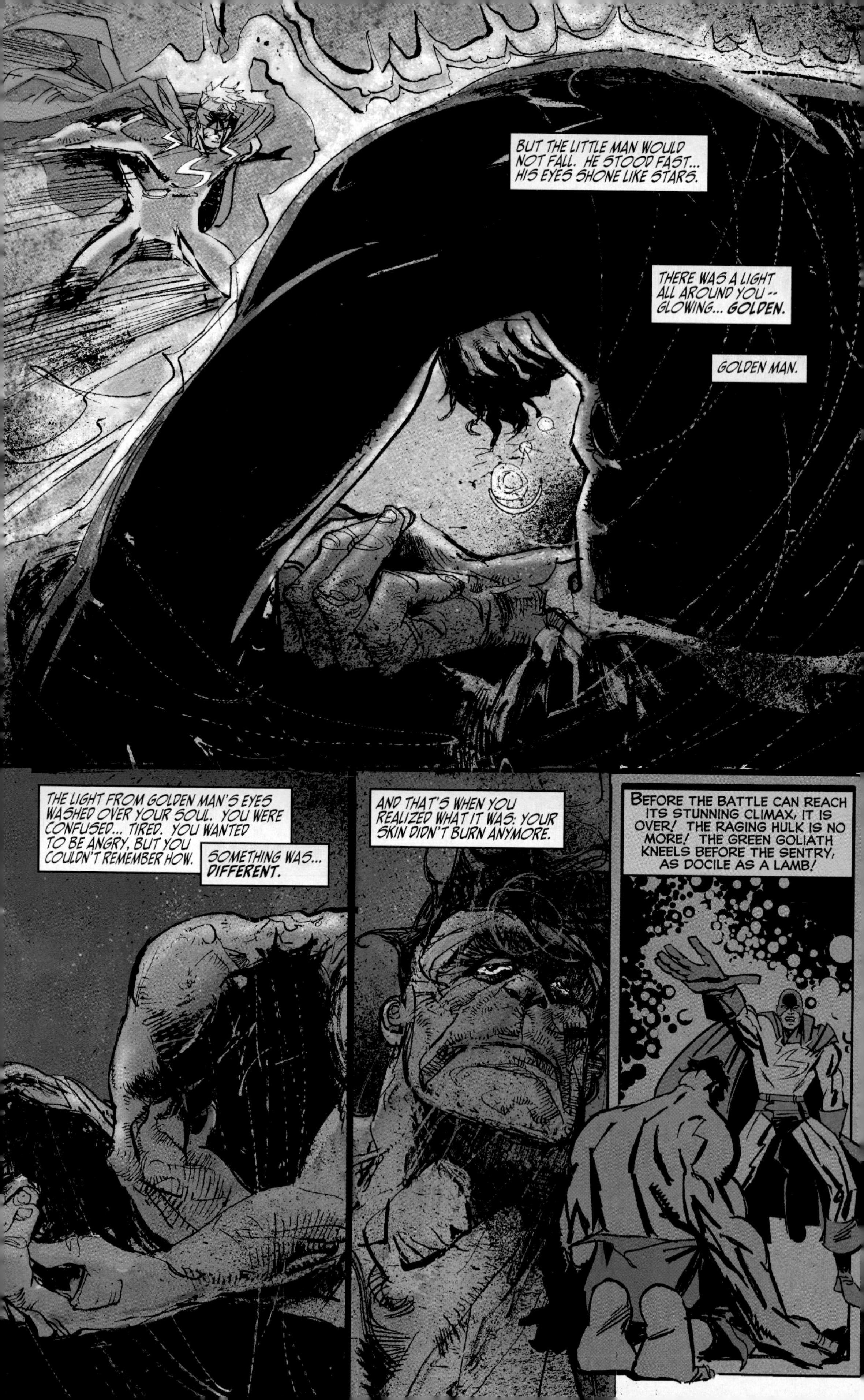
BUT THE LITTLE MAN WOULD NOT FALL. HE STOOD FAST... HIS EYES SHONE LIKE STARS.
THERE WAS A LIGHT ALL AROUND YOU -- GLOWING... GOLDEN.
GOLDEN MAN.
THE LIGHT FROM GOLDEN MAN'S EYES WASHED OVER YOUR SOUL. YOU WERE CONFUSED... TIRED. YOU WANTED TO BE ANGRY, BUT YOU COULDN'T REMEMBER HOW.
SOMETHING WAS... DIFFERENT.
AND THAT'S WHEN YOU REALIZED WHAT IT WAS: YOUR SKIN DIDN'T BURN ANYMORE.
BEFORE THE BATTLE CAN REACH ITS STUNNING CLIMAX, IT IS OVER! THE RAGING HULK IS NO MORE! THE GREEN GOLIATH KNEELS BEFORE THE SENTRY, AS DOCILE AS A LAMB!

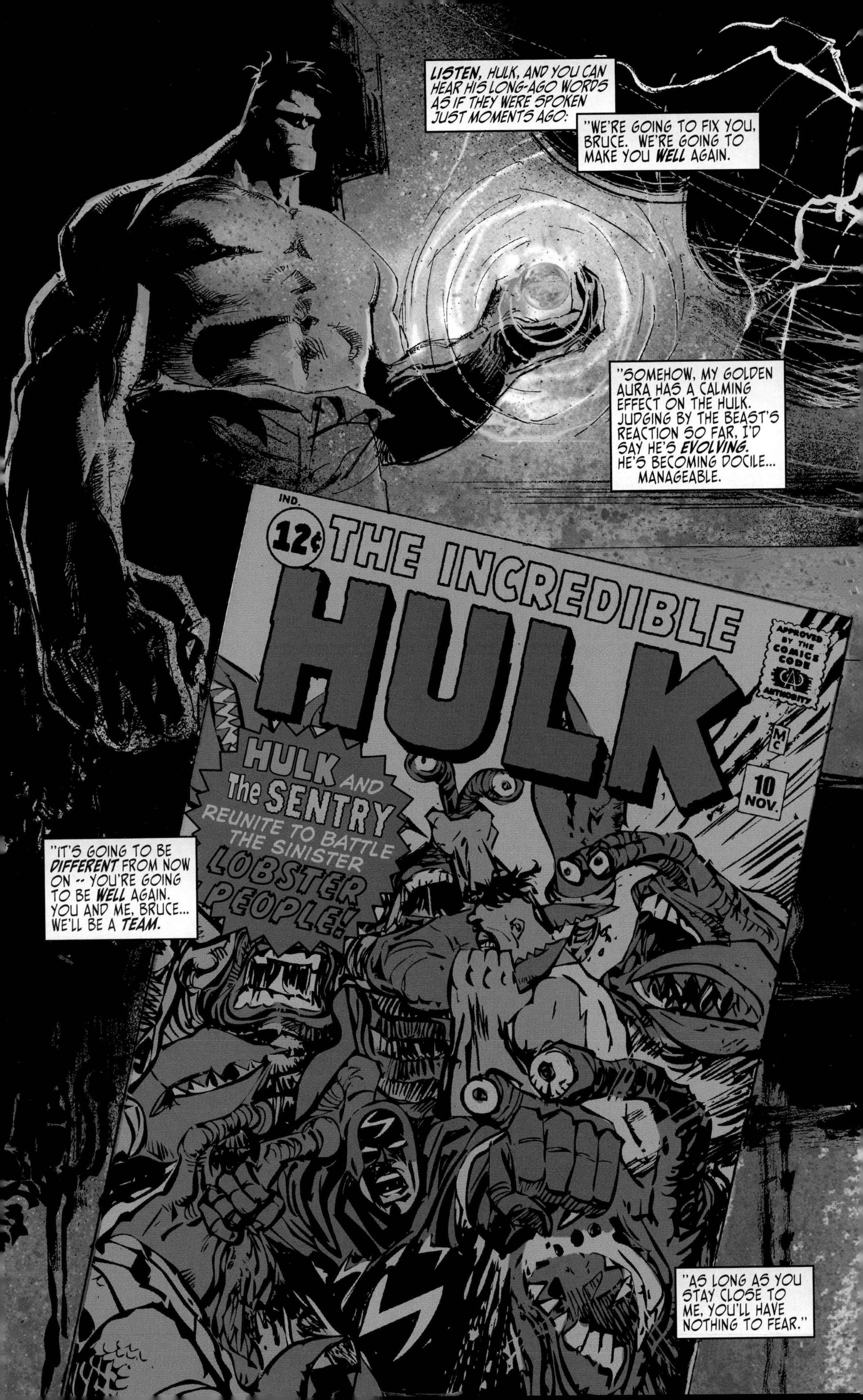
LISTEN, HULK, AND YOU CAN HEAR HIS LONG-AGO WORDS AS IF THEY WERE SPOKEN JUST MOMENTS AGO:
"WE'RE GOING TO FIX YOU, BRUCE. WE'RE GOING TO MAKE YOU WELL AGAIN.
"SOMEHOW, MY GOLDEN AURA HAS A CALMING EFFECT ON THE HULK. JUDGING BY THE BEAST'S REACTION SO FAR, I'D SAY HE'S EVOLVING. HE'S BECOMING DOCILE... MANAGEABLE.
IND.
12¢
THE INCREDIBLE HULK
APPROVED BY THE COMICS CODE AUTHORITY
MC
10 NOV.
HULK AND The SENTRY REUNITE TO BATTLE THE SINISTER LOBSTER PEOPLE!
"IT'S GOING TO BE DIFFERENT FROM NOW ON -- YOU'RE GOING TO BE WELL AGAIN. YOU AND ME, BRUCE... WE'LL BE A TEAM.
"AS LONG AS YOU STAY CLOSE TO ME, YOU'LL HAVE NOTHING TO FEAR."

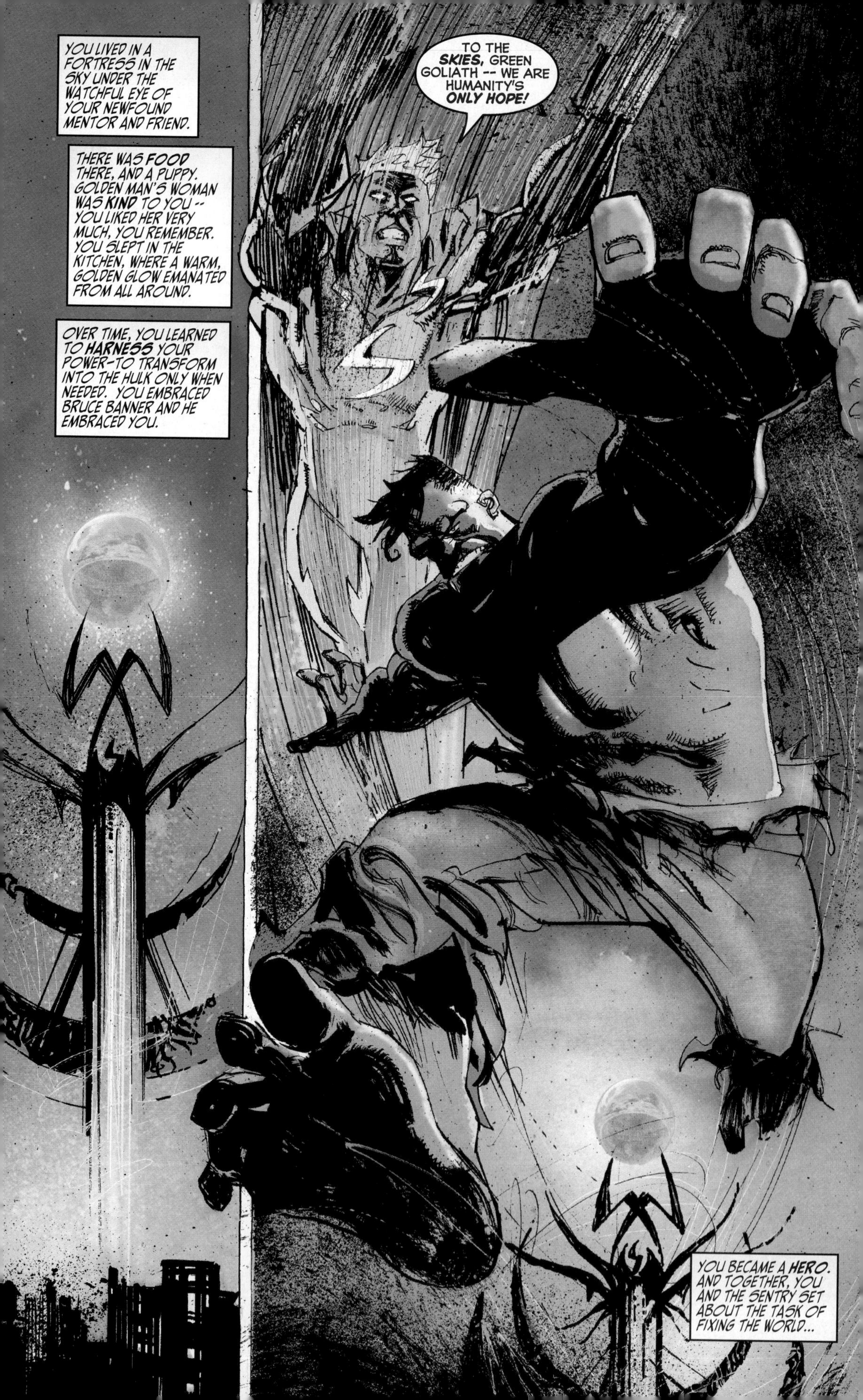

YOU LIVED IN A FORTRESS IN THE SKY UNDER THE WATCHFUL EYE OF YOUR NEWFOUND MENTOR AND FRIEND.
THERE WAS FOOD THERE, AND A PUPPY. GOLDEN MAN'S WOMAN WAS KIND TO YOU -- YOU LIKED HER VERY MUCH, YOU REMEMBER. YOU SLEPT IN THE KITCHEN, WHERE A WARM, GOLDEN GLOW EMANATED FROM ALL AROUND.
OVER TIME, YOU LEARNED TO HARNESS YOUR POWER--TO TRANSFORM INTO THE HULK ONLY WHEN NEEDED. YOU EMBRACED BRUCE BANNER AND HE EMBRACED YOU.
TO THE SKIES, GREEN GOLIATH -- WE ARE HUMANITY'S ONLY HOPE!
YOU BECAME A HERO. AND TOGETHER, YOU AND THE SENTRY SET ABOUT THE TASK OF FIXING THE WORLD...

THEY'RE BECOMING *CLEARER* NOW, THE MEMORIES OF THOSE ADVENTURES YOU HAD THOUGHT WERE *LOST*. YOU FOUGHT BESIDE THE SENTRY AGAINST THE GENERAL, THE LEADER AND THE LIVING NUKE.

THEN THERE WERE THE LOBSTER PEOPLE -- PRODUCTS OF A BRIEF INTERLUDE BETWEEN FATHER EVOLUTION AND MOTHER FATE -- IRRADIATED MUTANTS WHO HATED MANKIND.

THE POOR CREATURES HAD BEEN DRIVEN INTO UNDERGROUND CAVES BY A COMBINATION OF POLLUTION AND HUMAN INDIFFERENCE. YOU WERE SORRY FOR THEIR SADNESS. YOU UNDERSTOOD THEIR FEAR.

YOU, THEY TRUSTED... BUT THE SENTRY *SCARED* THEM... EVEN DESPITE HIS GOLDEN AURA. HE WAS ONE OF THE HUMANS WHO'D SENT THEM OUT OF THEIR HOMES AND INTO THE CAVES.

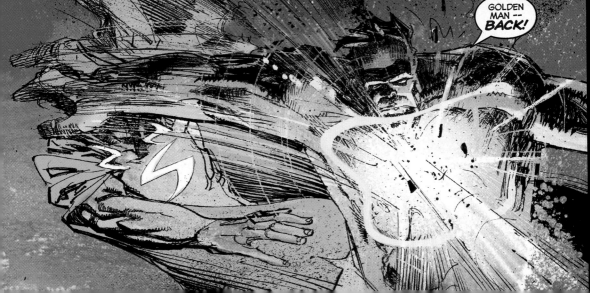

GOLDEN MAN -- *BACK!*

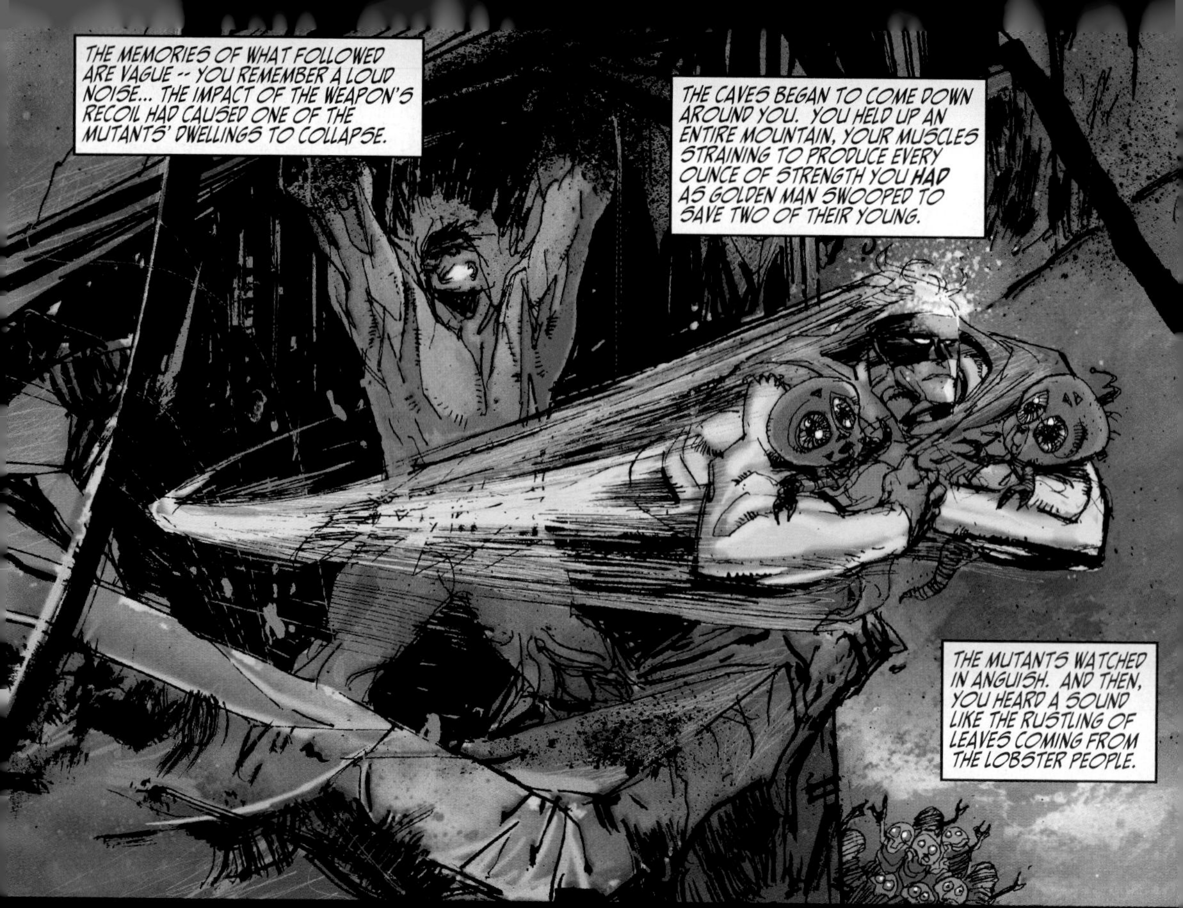
THE MEMORIES OF WHAT FOLLOWED ARE VAGUE -- YOU REMEMBER A LOUD NOISE... THE IMPACT OF THE WEAPON'S RECOIL HAD CAUSED ONE OF THE MUTANTS' DWELLINGS TO COLLAPSE.
THE CAVES BEGAN TO COME DOWN AROUND YOU. YOU HELD UP AN ENTIRE MOUNTAIN, YOUR MUSCLES STRAINING TO PRODUCE EVERY OUNCE OF STRENGTH YOU **HAD** AS GOLDEN MAN SWOOPED TO SAVE TWO OF THEIR YOUNG.
THE MUTANTS WATCHED IN ANGUISH. AND THEN, YOU HEARD A SOUND LIKE THE RUSTLING OF LEAVES COMING FROM THE LOBSTER PEOPLE.

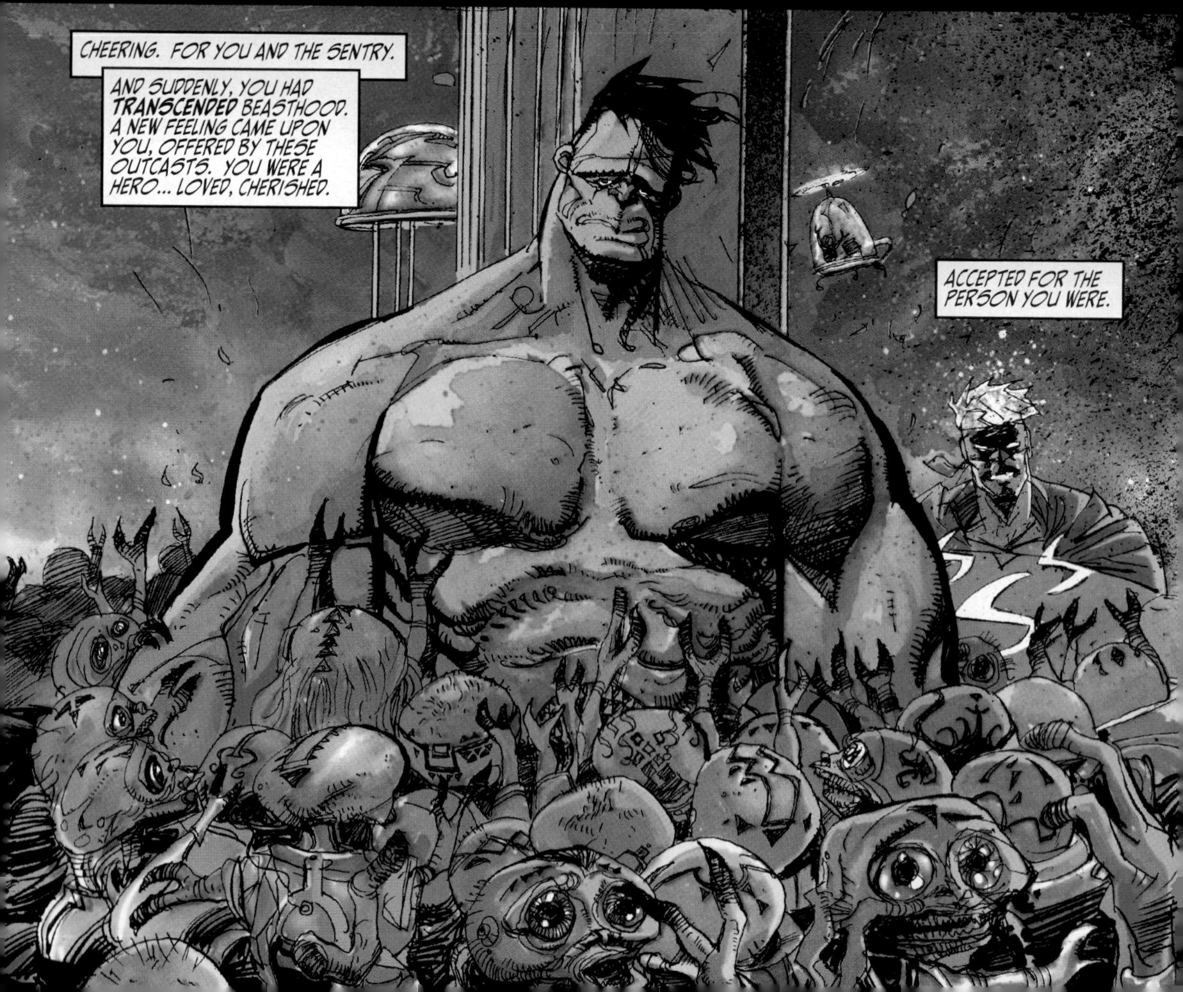
CHEERING. FOR YOU AND THE SENTRY.
AND SUDDENLY, YOU HAD **TRANSCENDED** BEASTHOOD. A NEW FEELING CAME UPON YOU, OFFERED BY THESE OUTCASTS. YOU WERE A HERO... LOVED, CHERISHED.
ACCEPTED FOR THE PERSON YOU WERE.

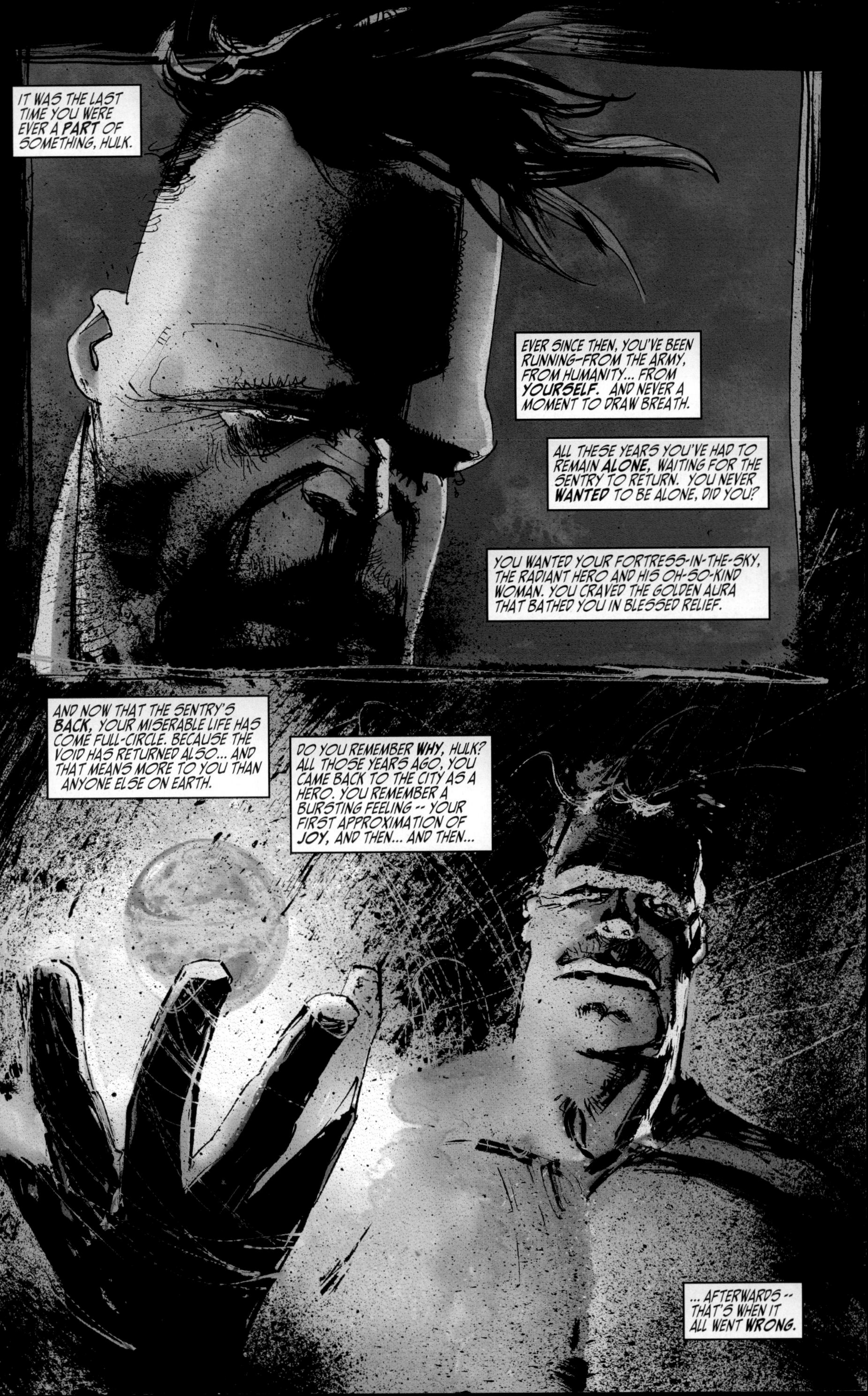
IT WAS THE LAST TIME YOU WERE EVER A PART OF SOMETHING, HULK.
EVER SINCE THEN, YOU'VE BEEN RUNNING--FROM THE ARMY, FROM HUMANITY... FROM YOURSELF. AND NEVER A MOMENT TO DRAW BREATH.
ALL THESE YEARS YOU'VE HAD TO REMAIN ALONE, WAITING FOR THE SENTRY TO RETURN. YOU NEVER WANTED TO BE ALONE, DID YOU?
YOU WANTED YOUR FORTRESS-IN-THE-SKY, THE RADIANT HERO AND HIS OH-SO-KIND WOMAN. YOU CRAVED THE GOLDEN AURA THAT BATHED YOU IN BLESSED RELIEF.
AND NOW THAT THE SENTRY'S BACK, YOUR MISERABLE LIFE HAS COME FULL-CIRCLE. BECAUSE THE VOID HAS RETURNED ALSO... AND THAT MEANS MORE TO YOU THAN ANYONE ELSE ON EARTH.
DO YOU REMEMBER WHY, HULK? ALL THOSE YEARS AGO, YOU CAME BACK TO THE CITY AS A HERO. YOU REMEMBER A BURSTING FEELING -- YOUR FIRST APPROXIMATION OF JOY, AND THEN... AND THEN...
... AFTERWARDS -- THAT'S WHEN IT ALL WENT WRONG.

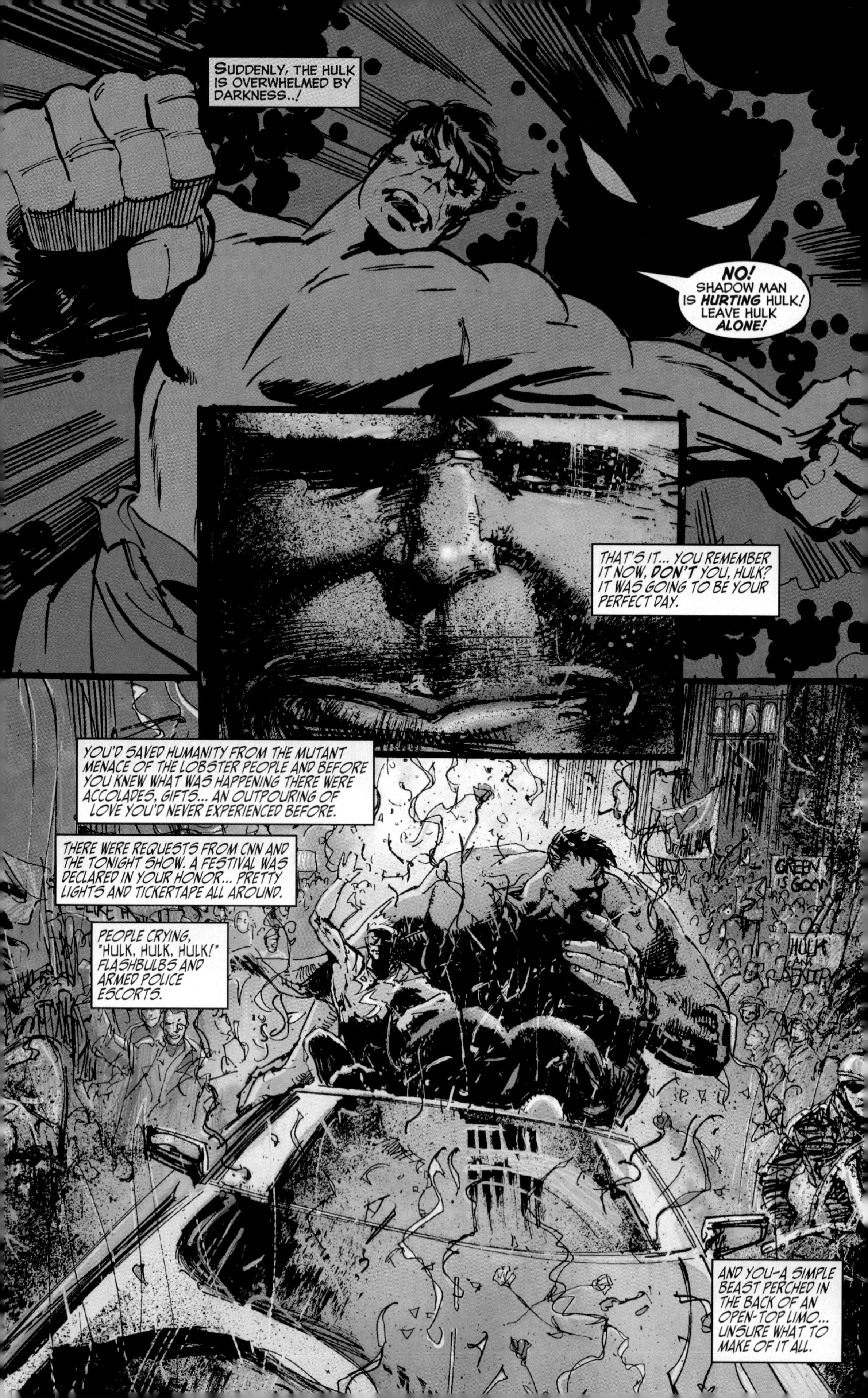
SUDDENLY, THE HULK IS OVERWHELMED BY DARKNESS..!
NO! SHADOW MAN IS HURTING HULK! LEAVE HULK ALONE!
THAT'S IT... YOU REMEMBER IT NOW, DON'T YOU, HULK? IT WAS GOING TO BE YOUR PERFECT DAY.
YOU'D SAVED HUMANITY FROM THE MUTANT MENACE OF THE LOBSTER PEOPLE AND BEFORE YOU KNEW WHAT WAS HAPPENING THERE WERE ACCOLADES, GIFTS... AN OUTPOURING OF LOVE YOU'D NEVER EXPERIENCED BEFORE.
THERE WERE REQUESTS FROM CNN AND THE TONIGHT SHOW. A FESTIVAL WAS DECLARED IN YOUR HONOR... PRETTY LIGHTS AND TICKERTAPE ALL AROUND.
PEOPLE CRYING, "HULK, HULK, HULK!" FLASHBULBS AND ARMED POLICE ESCORTS.
GREEN IS GOOD
HULK
AND YOU—A SIMPLE BEAST PERCHED IN THE BACK OF AN OPEN-TOP LIMO... UNSURE WHAT TO MAKE OF IT ALL.

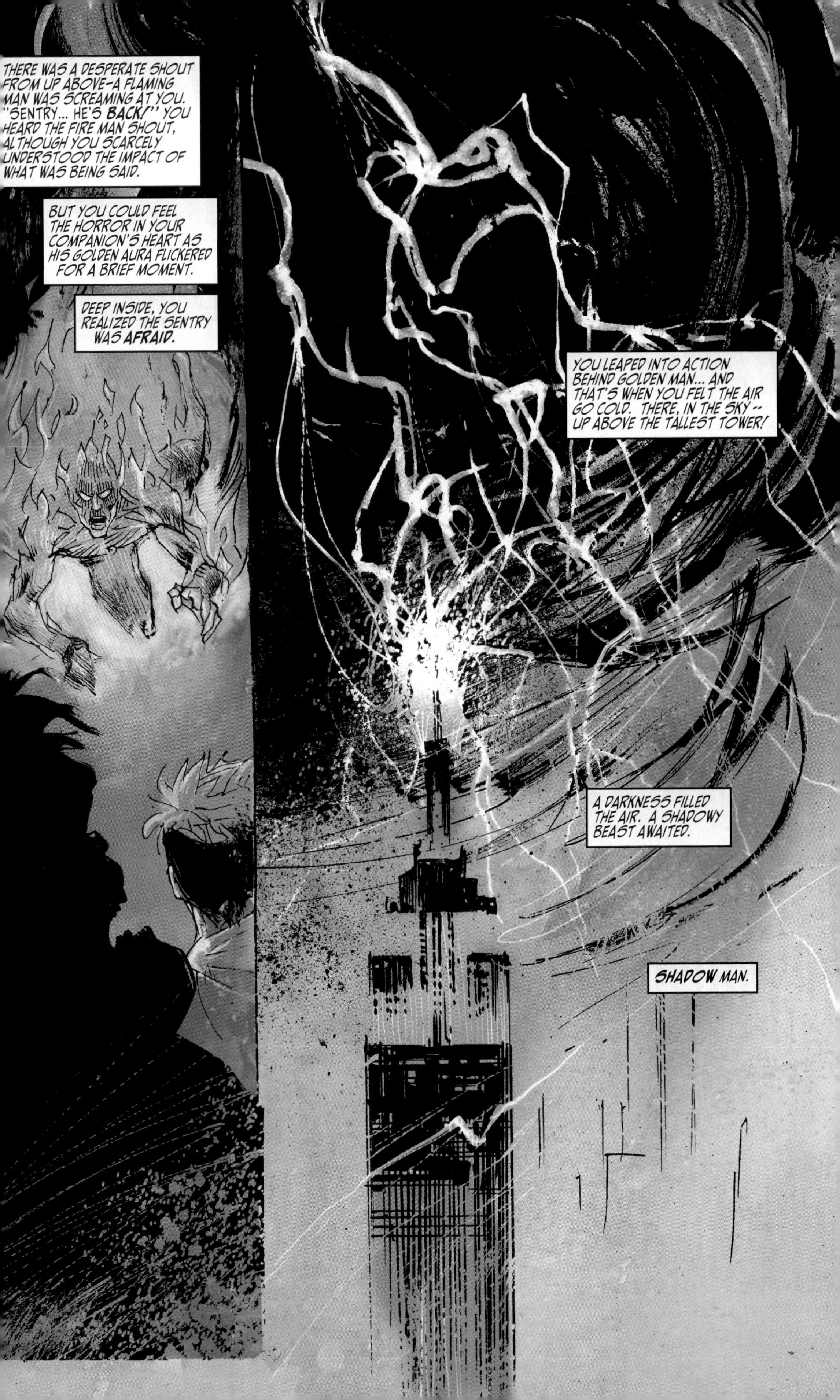
THERE WAS A DESPERATE SHOUT FROM UP ABOVE--A FLAMING MAN WAS SCREAMING AT YOU. "SENTRY... HE'S BACK!" YOU HEARD THE FIRE MAN SHOUT, ALTHOUGH YOU SCARCELY UNDERSTOOD THE IMPACT OF WHAT WAS BEING SAID.
BUT YOU COULD FEEL THE HORROR IN YOUR COMPANION'S HEART AS HIS GOLDEN AURA FLICKERED FOR A BRIEF MOMENT.
DEEP INSIDE, YOU REALIZED THE SENTRY WAS AFRAID.
YOU LEAPED INTO ACTION BEHIND GOLDEN MAN... AND THAT'S WHEN YOU FELT THE AIR GO COLD. THERE, IN THE SKY -- UP ABOVE THE TALLEST TOWER!
A DARKNESS FILLED THE AIR. A SHADOWY BEAST AWAITED.
SHADOW MAN.

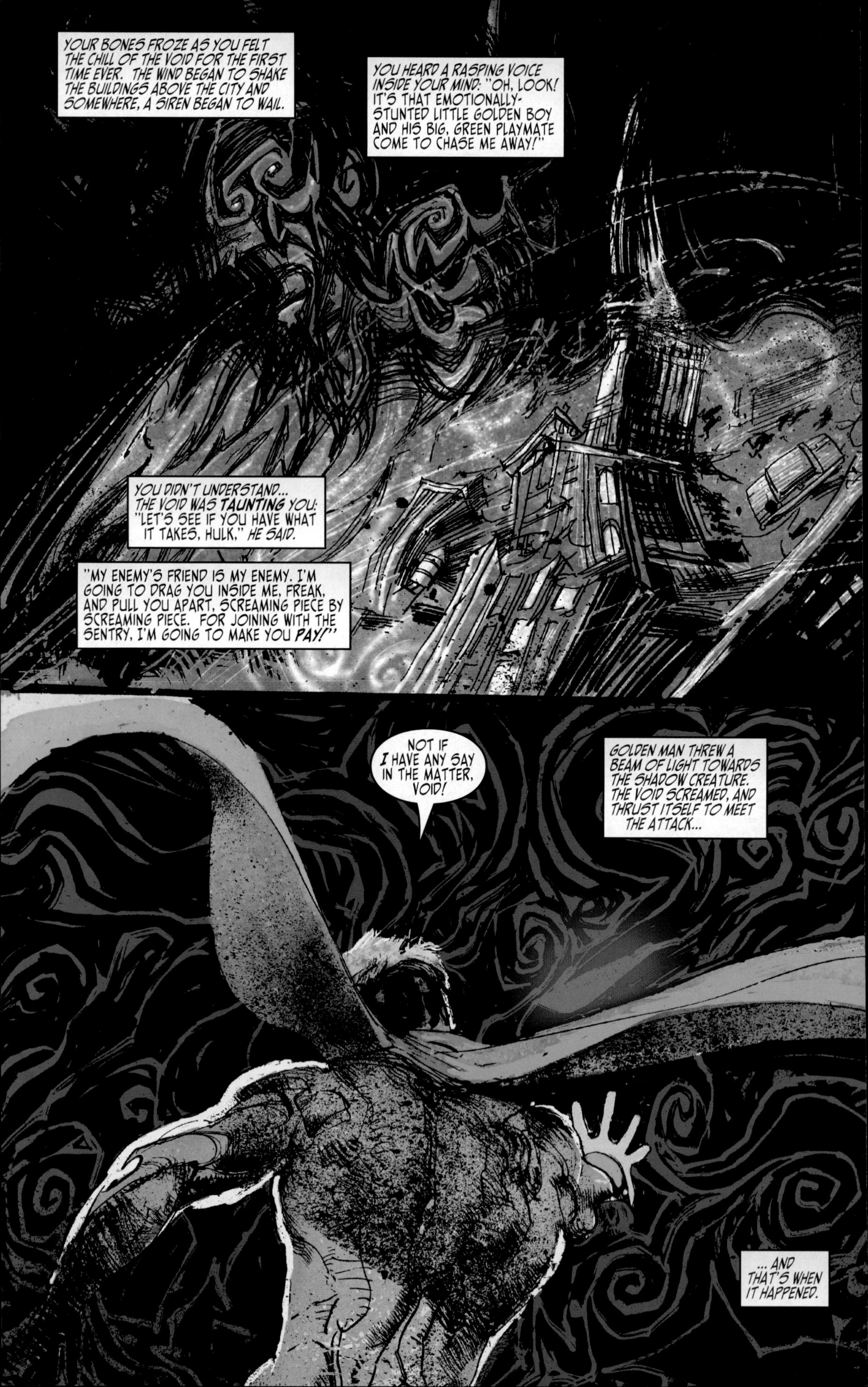
YOUR BONES FROZE AS YOU FELT THE CHILL OF THE VOID FOR THE FIRST TIME EVER. THE WIND BEGAN TO SHAKE THE BUILDINGS ABOVE THE CITY AND SOMEWHERE, A SIREN BEGAN TO WAIL.
YOU HEARD A RASPING VOICE INSIDE YOUR MIND: "OH, LOOK! IT'S THAT EMOTIONALLY-STUNTED LITTLE GOLDEN BOY AND HIS BIG, GREEN PLAYMATE COME TO CHASE ME AWAY!"
YOU DIDN'T UNDERSTAND... THE VOID WAS TAUNTING YOU: "LET'S SEE IF YOU HAVE WHAT IT TAKES, HULK," HE SAID.
"MY ENEMY'S FRIEND IS MY ENEMY. I'M GOING TO DRAG YOU INSIDE ME, FREAK, AND PULL YOU APART, SCREAMING PIECE BY SCREAMING PIECE. FOR JOINING WITH THE SENTRY, I'M GOING TO MAKE YOU PAY!"
NOT IF I HAVE ANY SAY IN THE MATTER, VOID!
GOLDEN MAN THREW A BEAM OF LIGHT TOWARDS THE SHADOW CREATURE. THE VOID SCREAMED, AND THRUST ITSELF TO MEET THE ATTACK...
... AND THAT'S WHEN IT HAPPENED.

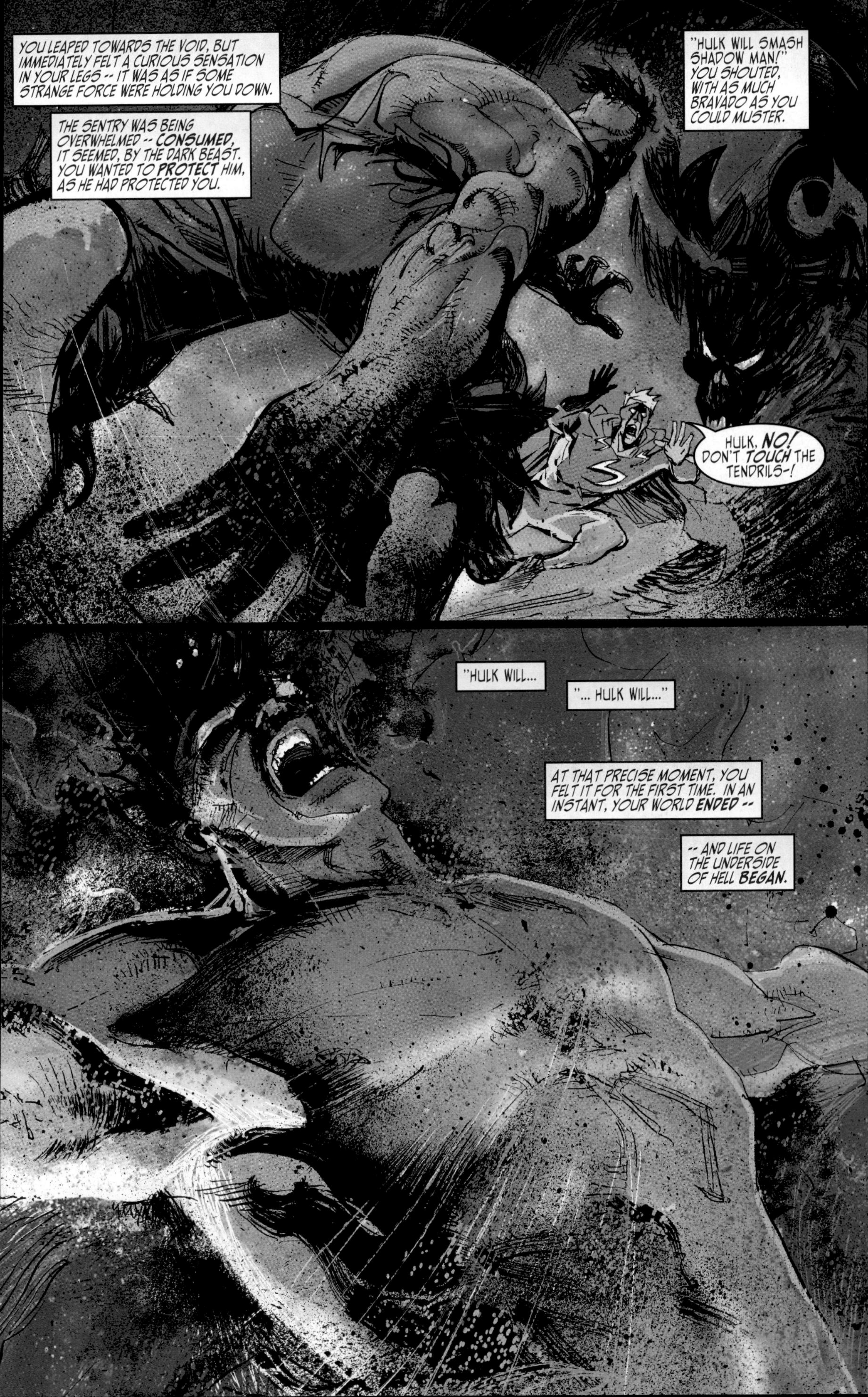
YOU LEAPED TOWARDS THE VOID, BUT IMMEDIATELY FELT A CURIOUS SENSATION IN YOUR LEGS -- IT WAS AS IF SOME STRANGE FORCE WERE HOLDING YOU DOWN.
"HULK WILL SMASH SHADOW MAN!" YOU SHOUTED, WITH AS MUCH BRAVADO AS YOU COULD MUSTER.
THE SENTRY WAS BEING OVERWHELMED -- CONSUMED, IT SEEMED, BY THE DARK BEAST. YOU WANTED TO PROTECT HIM, AS HE HAD PROTECTED YOU.
HULK, NO! DON'T TOUCH THE TENDRILS-!
"HULK WILL...
"... HULK WILL..."
AT THAT PRECISE MOMENT, YOU FELT IT FOR THE FIRST TIME. IN AN INSTANT, YOUR WORLD ENDED --
-- AND LIFE ON THE UNDERSIDE OF HELL BEGAN.

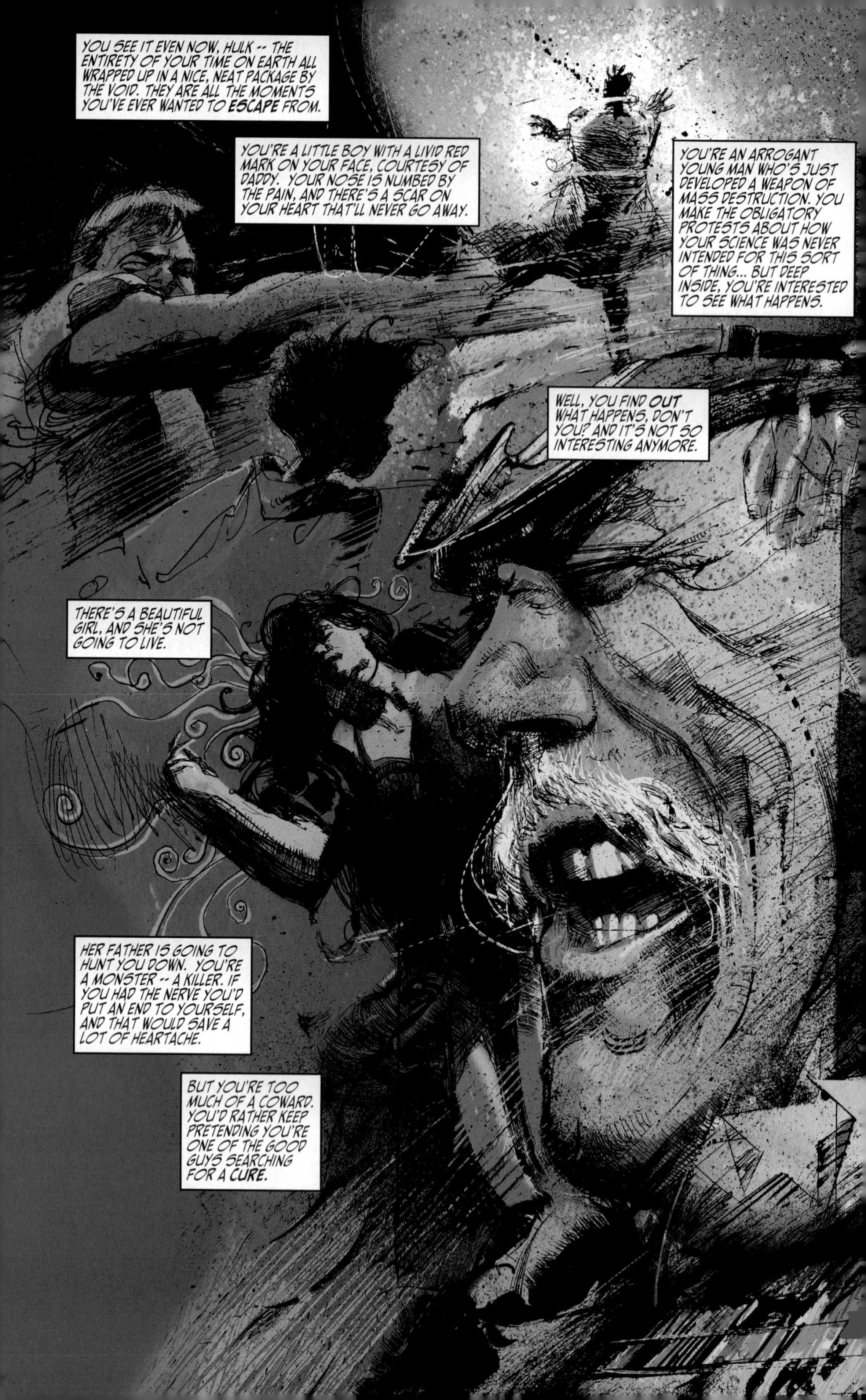
YOU SEE IT EVEN NOW, HULK -- THE ENTIRETY OF YOUR TIME ON EARTH ALL WRAPPED UP IN A NICE, NEAT PACKAGE BY THE VOID. THEY ARE ALL THE MOMENTS YOU'VE EVER WANTED TO ESCAPE FROM.
YOU'RE A LITTLE BOY WITH A LIVID RED MARK ON YOUR FACE, COURTESY OF DADDY. YOUR NOSE IS NUMBED BY THE PAIN, AND THERE'S A SCAR ON YOUR HEART THAT'LL NEVER GO AWAY.
YOU'RE AN ARROGANT YOUNG MAN WHO'S JUST DEVELOPED A WEAPON OF MASS DESTRUCTION. YOU MAKE THE OBLIGATORY PROTESTS ABOUT HOW YOUR SCIENCE WAS NEVER INTENDED FOR THIS SORT OF THING... BUT DEEP INSIDE, YOU'RE INTERESTED TO SEE WHAT HAPPENS.
WELL, YOU FIND OUT WHAT HAPPENS, DON'T YOU? AND IT'S NOT SO INTERESTING ANYMORE.
THERE'S A BEAUTIFUL GIRL, AND SHE'S NOT GOING TO LIVE.
HER FATHER IS GOING TO HUNT YOU DOWN. YOU'RE A MONSTER -- A KILLER. IF YOU HAD THE NERVE YOU'D PUT AN END TO YOURSELF, AND THAT WOULD SAVE A LOT OF HEARTACHE.
BUT YOU'RE TOO MUCH OF A COWARD. YOU'D RATHER KEEP PRETENDING YOU'RE ONE OF THE GOOD GUYS SEARCHING FOR A CURE.

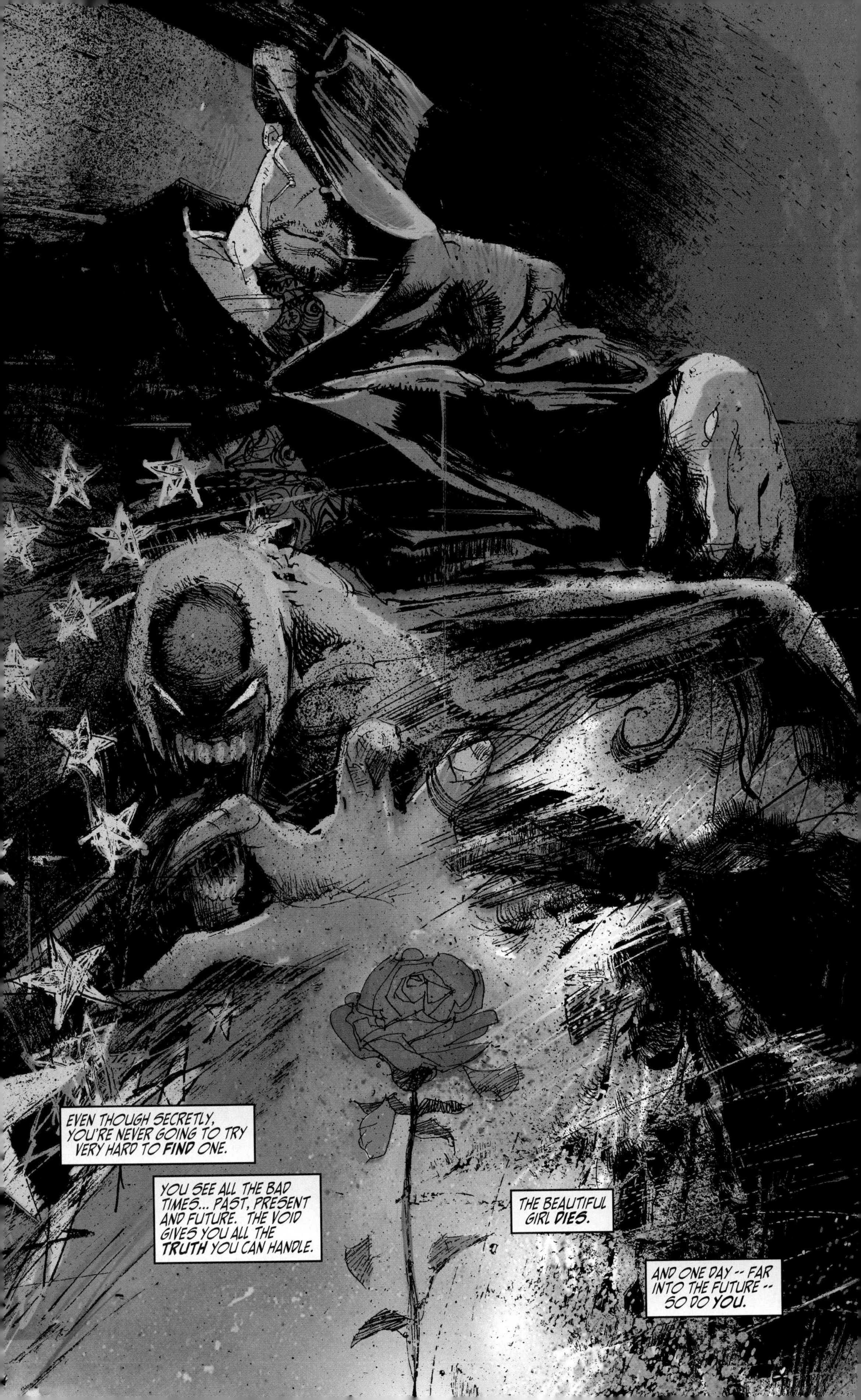
EVEN THOUGH SECRETLY, YOU'RE NEVER GOING TO TRY VERY HARD TO **FIND** ONE.
YOU SEE ALL THE BAD TIMES... PAST, PRESENT AND FUTURE. THE VOID GIVES YOU ALL THE **TRUTH** YOU CAN HANDLE.
THE BEAUTIFUL GIRL **DIES**.
AND ONE DAY -- FAR INTO THE FUTURE -- SO DO **YOU**.

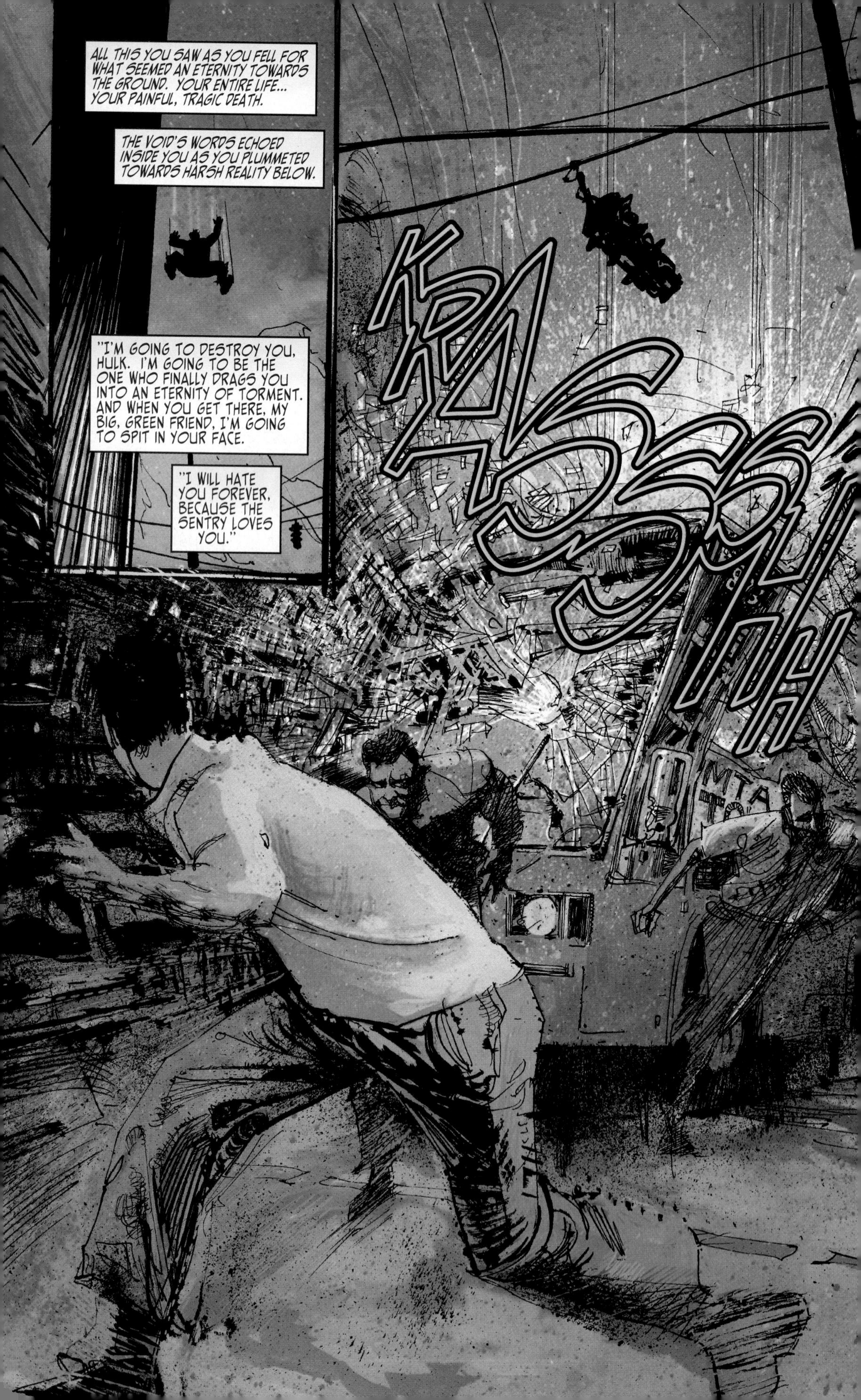
ALL THIS YOU SAW AS YOU FELL FOR WHAT SEEMED AN ETERNITY TOWARDS THE GROUND. YOUR ENTIRE LIFE... YOUR PAINFUL, TRAGIC DEATH.
THE VOID'S WORDS ECHOED INSIDE YOU AS YOU PLUMMETED TOWARDS HARSH REALITY BELOW.
"I'M GOING TO DESTROY YOU, HULK. I'M GOING TO BE THE ONE WHO FINALLY DRAGS YOU INTO AN ETERNITY OF TORMENT. AND WHEN YOU GET THERE, MY BIG, GREEN FRIEND, I'M GOING TO SPIT IN YOUR FACE.
"I WILL HATE YOU FOREVER, BECAUSE THE SENTRY LOVES YOU."
KRASSSHHH
MTA

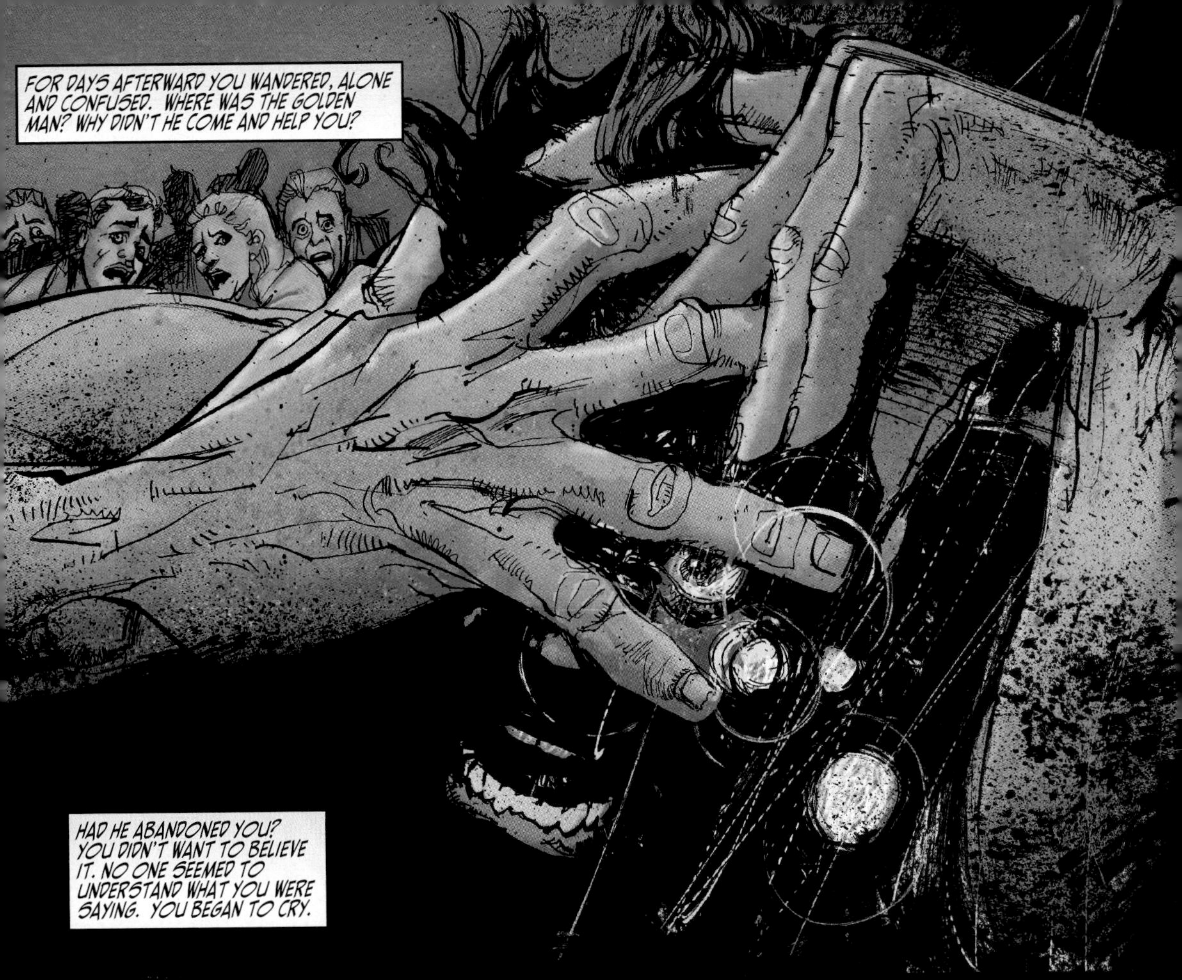
FOR DAYS AFTERWARD YOU WANDERED, ALONE AND CONFUSED. WHERE WAS THE GOLDEN MAN? WHY DIDN'T HE COME AND HELP YOU?
HAD HE ABANDONED YOU? YOU DIDN'T WANT TO BELIEVE IT. NO ONE SEEMED TO UNDERSTAND WHAT YOU WERE SAYING. YOU BEGAN TO CRY.

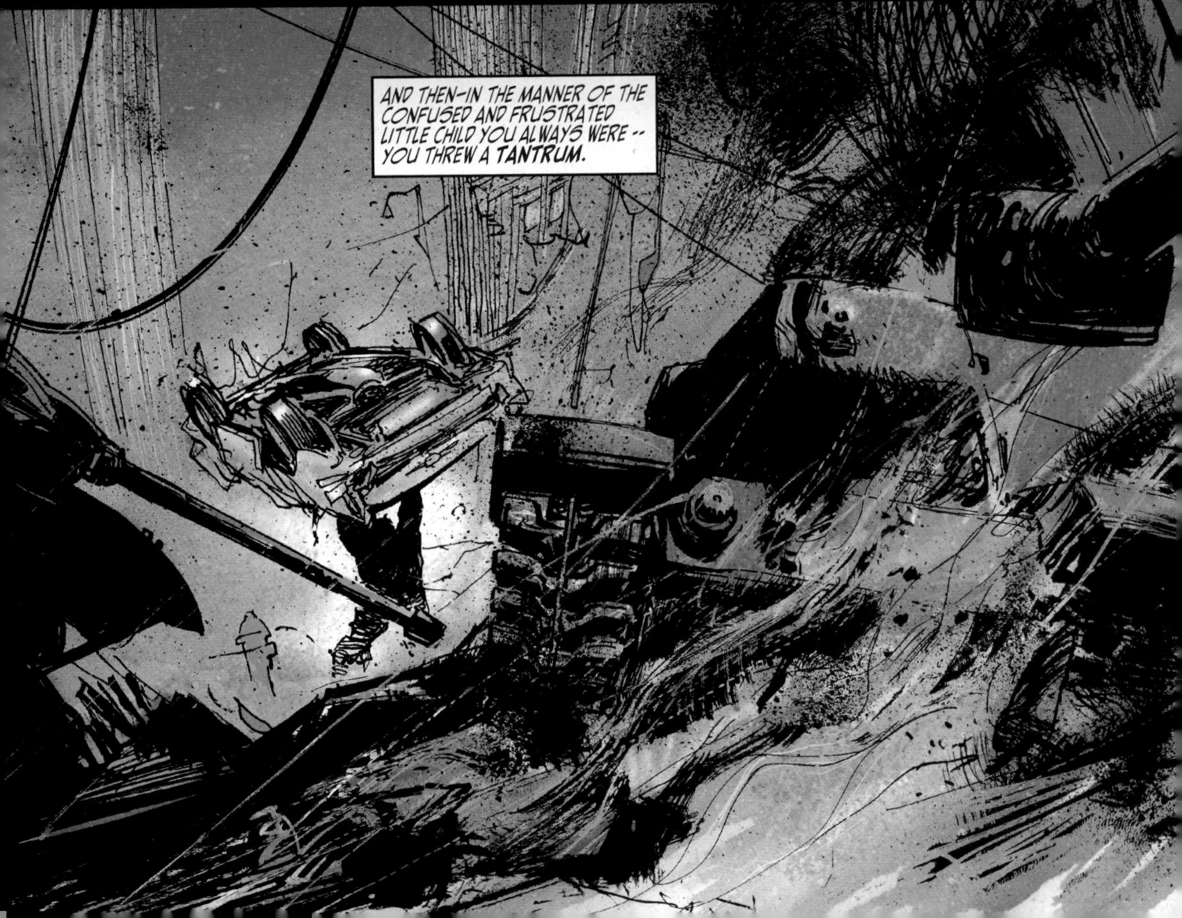
AND THEN--IN THE MANNER OF THE CONFUSED AND FRUSTRATED LITTLE CHILD YOU ALWAYS WERE -- YOU THREW A **TANTRUM**.

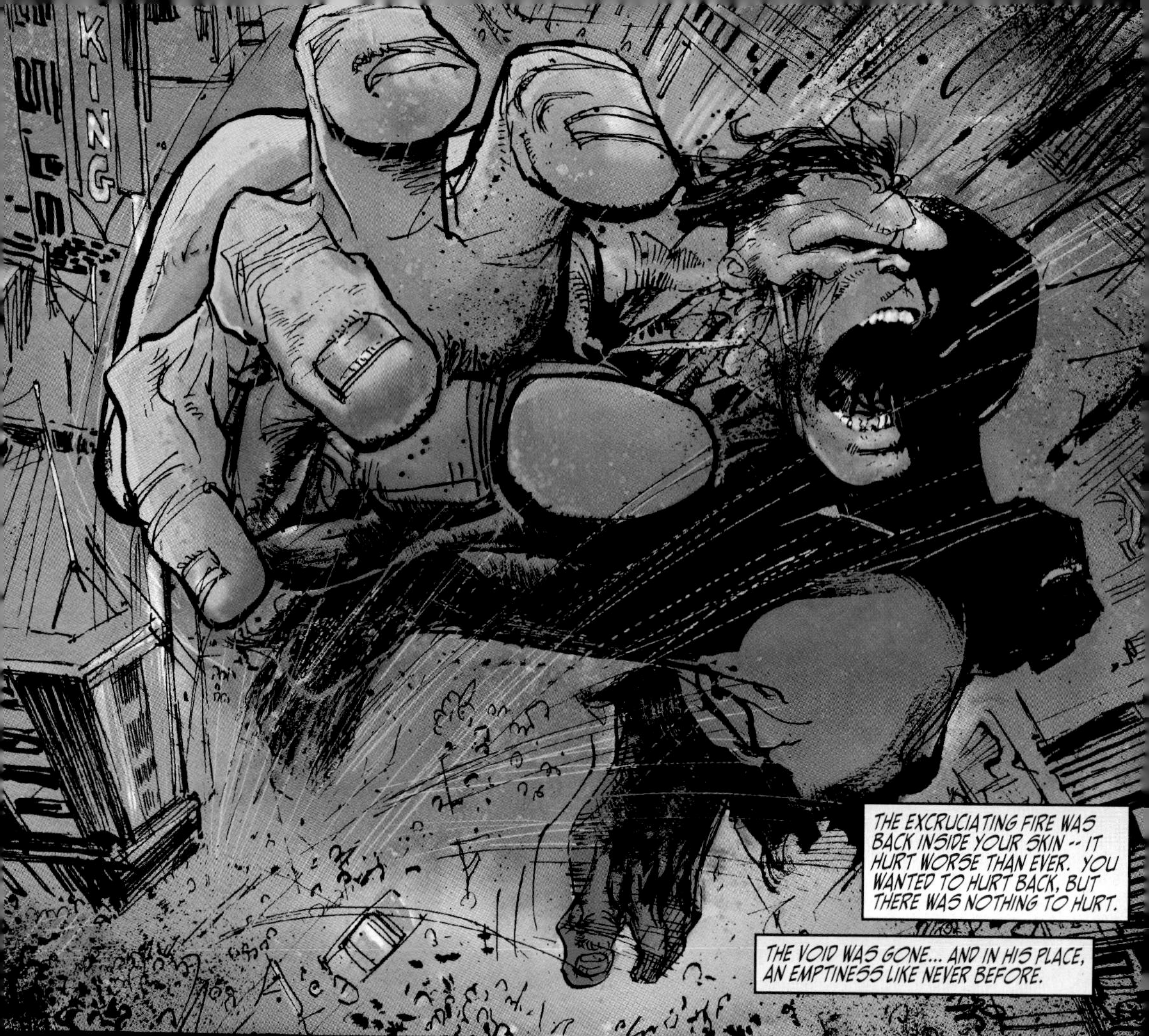
KING
THE EXCRUCIATING FIRE WAS BACK INSIDE YOUR SKIN -- IT HURT WORSE THAN EVER. YOU WANTED TO HURT BACK, BUT THERE WAS NOTHING TO HURT.
THE VOID WAS GONE... AND IN HIS PLACE, AN EMPTINESS LIKE NEVER BEFORE.

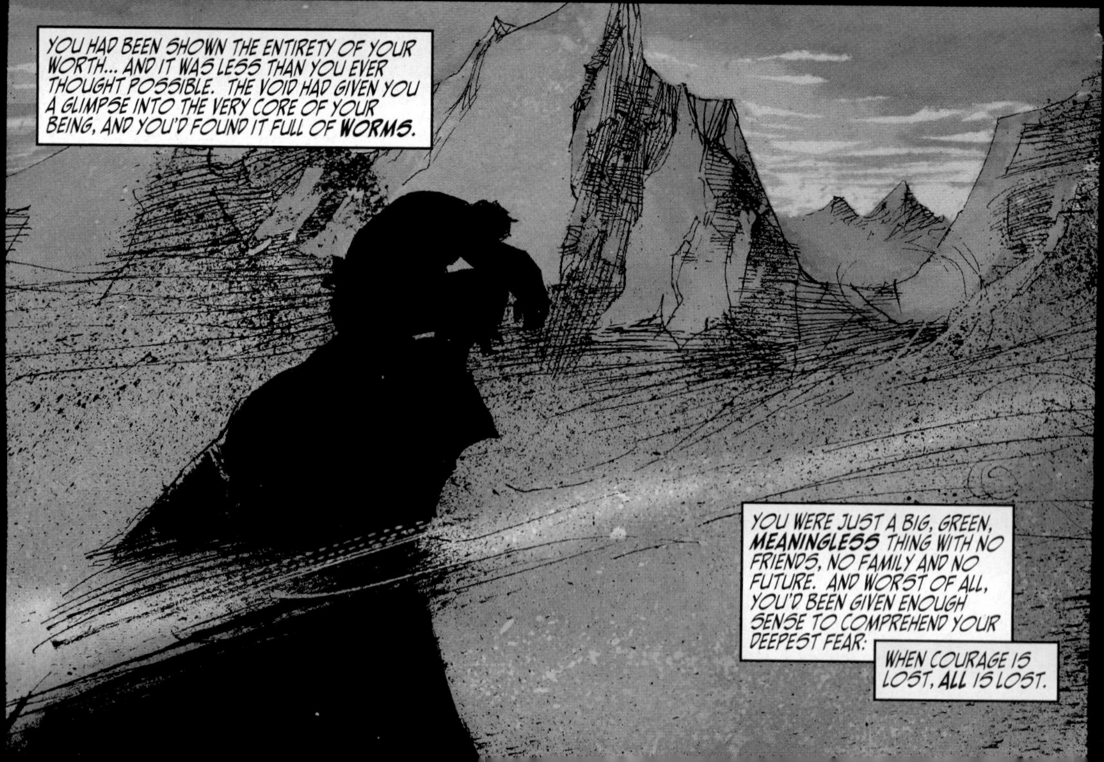
YOU HAD BEEN SHOWN THE ENTIRETY OF YOUR WORTH... AND IT WAS LESS THAN YOU EVER THOUGHT POSSIBLE. THE VOID HAD GIVEN YOU A GLIMPSE INTO THE VERY CORE OF YOUR BEING, AND YOU'D FOUND IT FULL OF **WORMS**.
YOU WERE JUST A BIG, GREEN, **MEANINGLESS** THING WITH NO FRIENDS, NO FAMILY AND NO FUTURE. AND WORST OF ALL, YOU'D BEEN GIVEN ENOUGH SENSE TO COMPREHEND YOUR DEEPEST FEAR:
WHEN COURAGE IS LOST, **ALL** IS LOST.

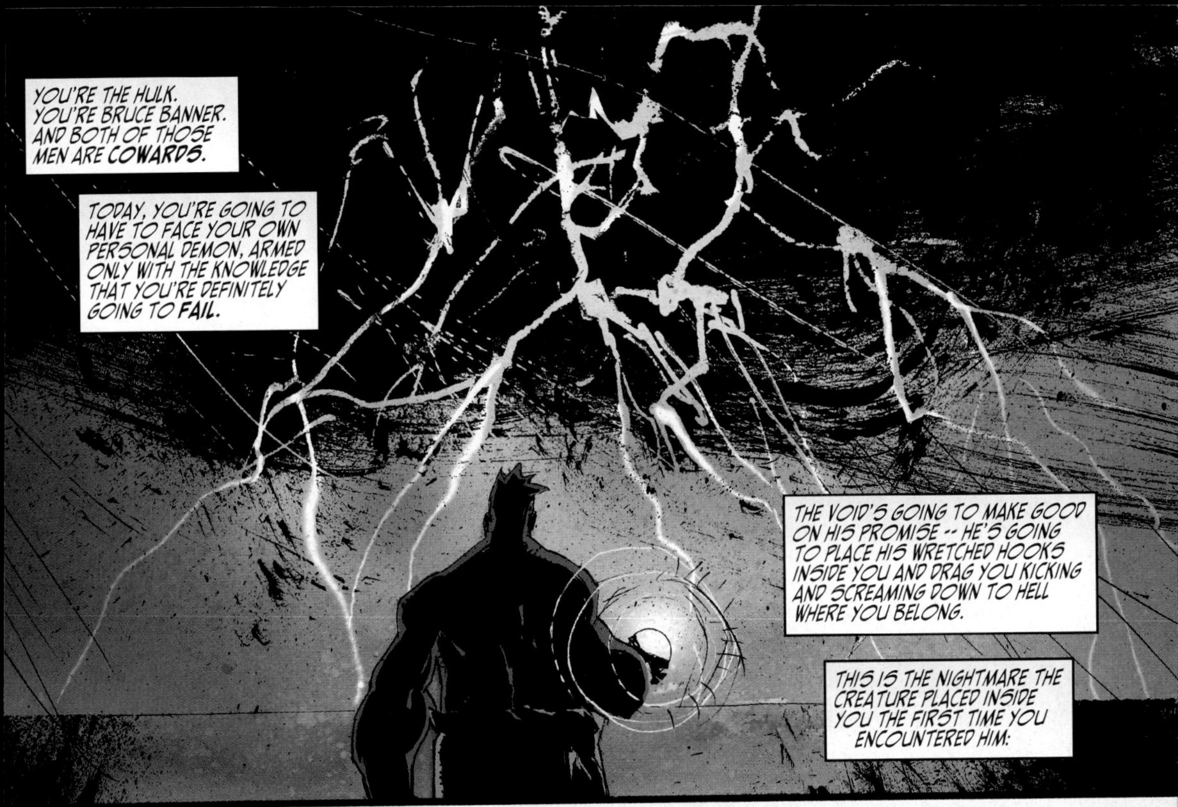
YOU'RE THE HULK. YOU'RE BRUCE BANNER. AND BOTH OF THOSE MEN ARE COWARDS.
TODAY, YOU'RE GOING TO HAVE TO FACE YOUR OWN PERSONAL DEMON, ARMED ONLY WITH THE KNOWLEDGE THAT YOU'RE DEFINITELY GOING TO FAIL.
THE VOID'S GOING TO MAKE GOOD ON HIS PROMISE -- HE'S GOING TO PLACE HIS WRETCHED HOOKS INSIDE YOU AND DRAG YOU KICKING AND SCREAMING DOWN TO HELL WHERE YOU BELONG.
THIS IS THE NIGHTMARE THE CREATURE PLACED INSIDE YOU THE FIRST TIME YOU ENCOUNTERED HIM:

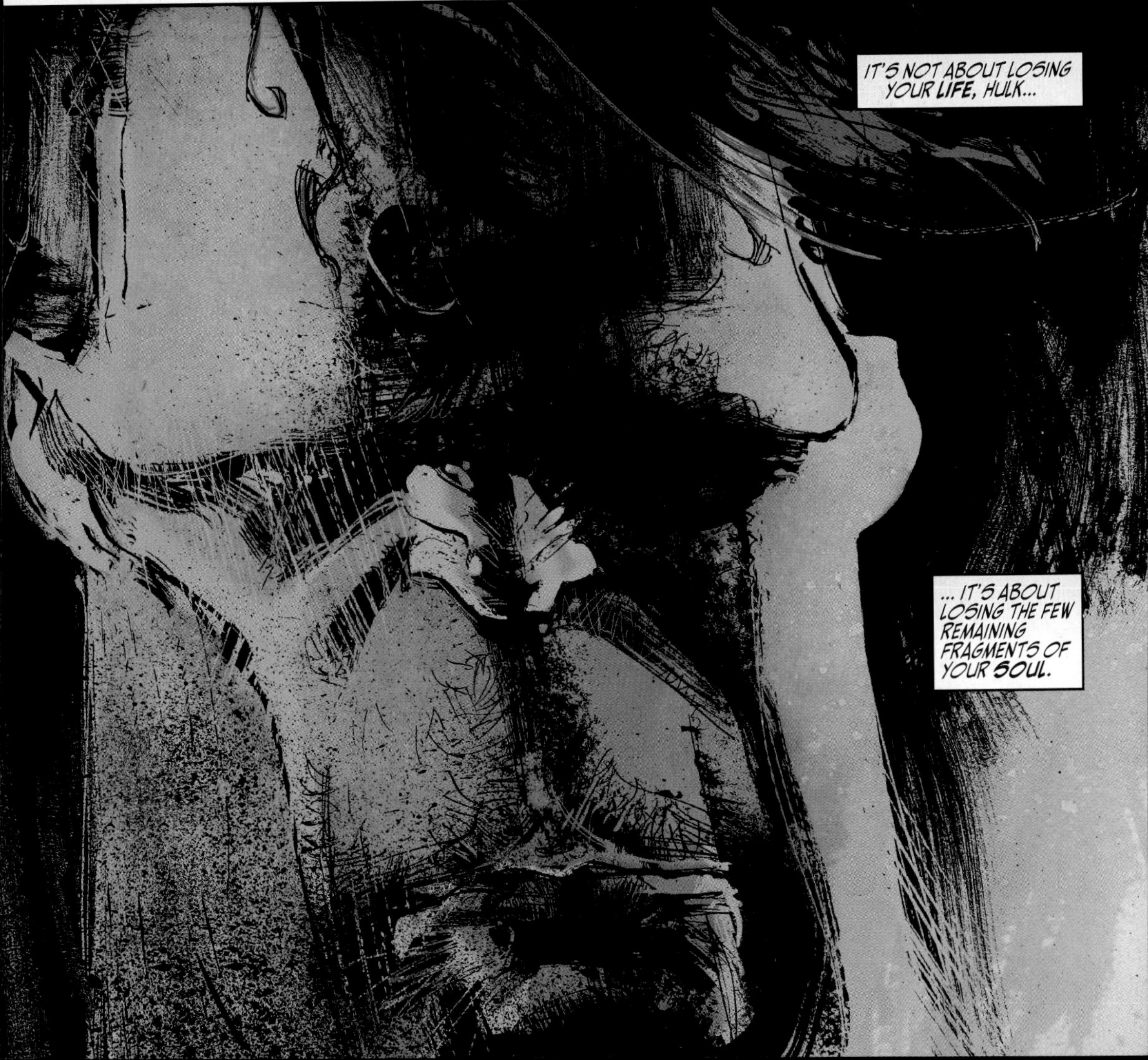
IT'S NOT ABOUT LOSING YOUR LIFE, HULK...
... IT'S ABOUT LOSING THE FEW REMAINING FRAGMENTS OF YOUR SOUL.

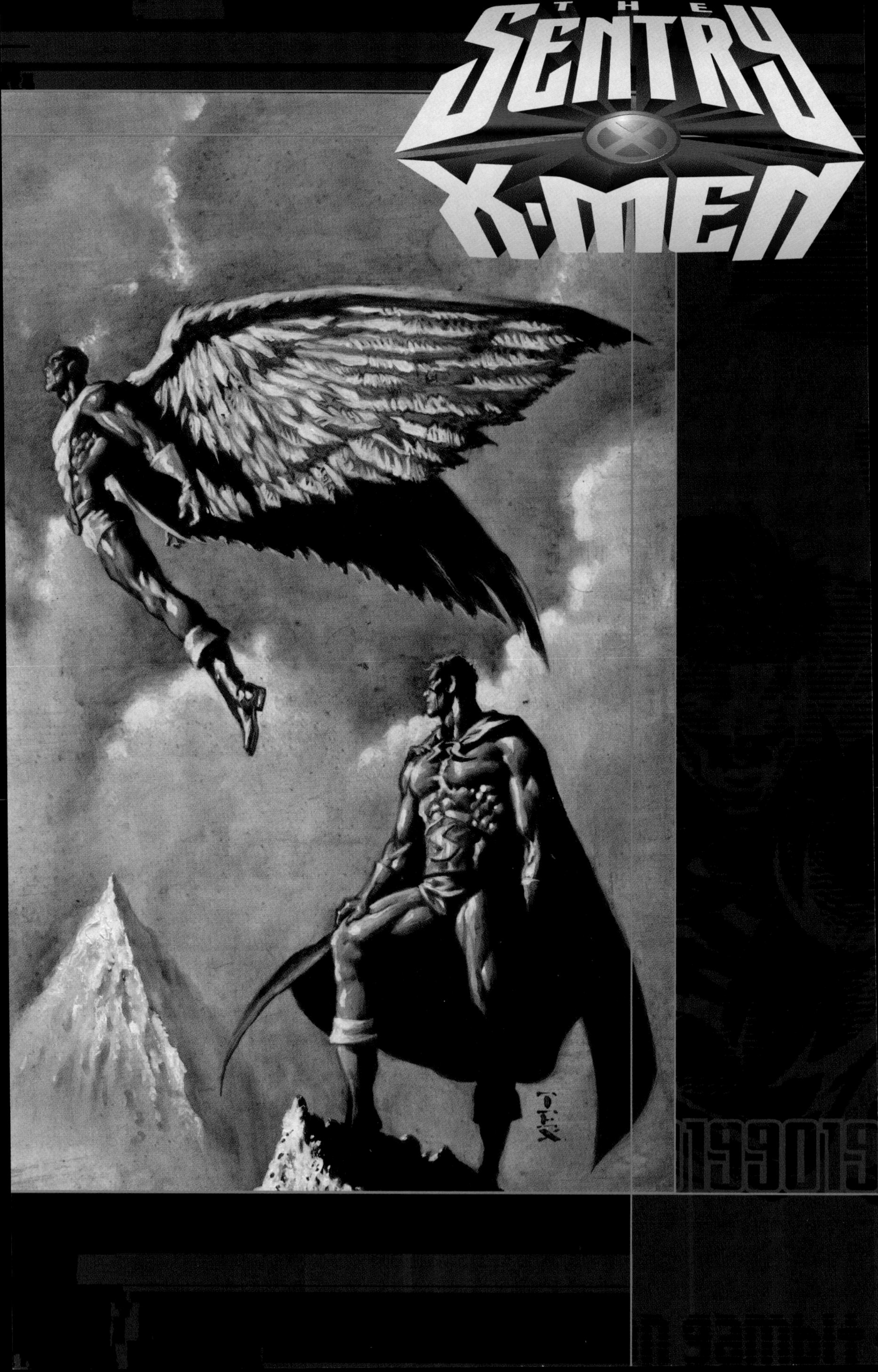
THE SENTRY X-MEN

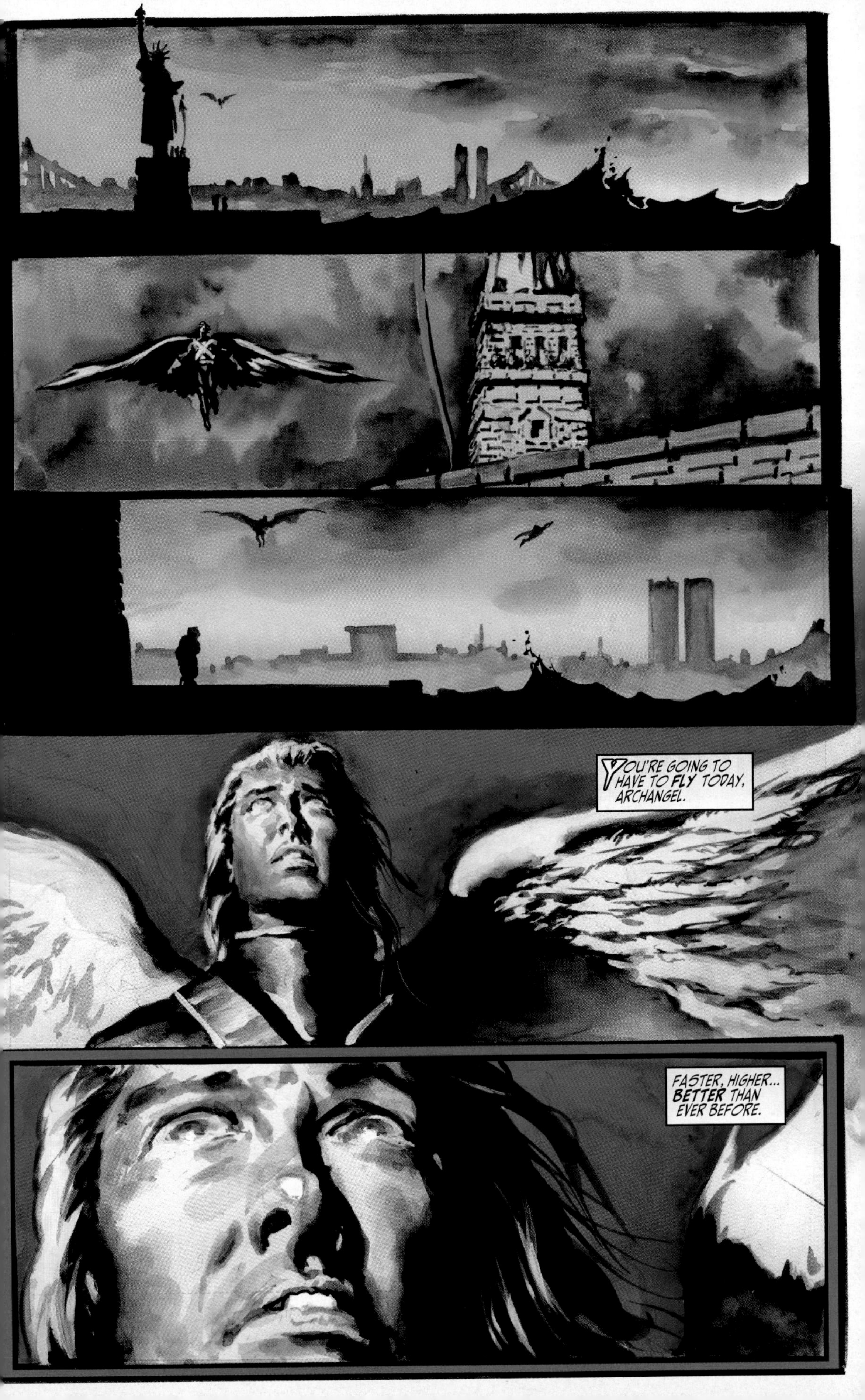
YOU'RE GOING TO HAVE TO FLY TODAY, ARCHANGEL.
FASTER, HIGHER... BETTER THAN EVER BEFORE.

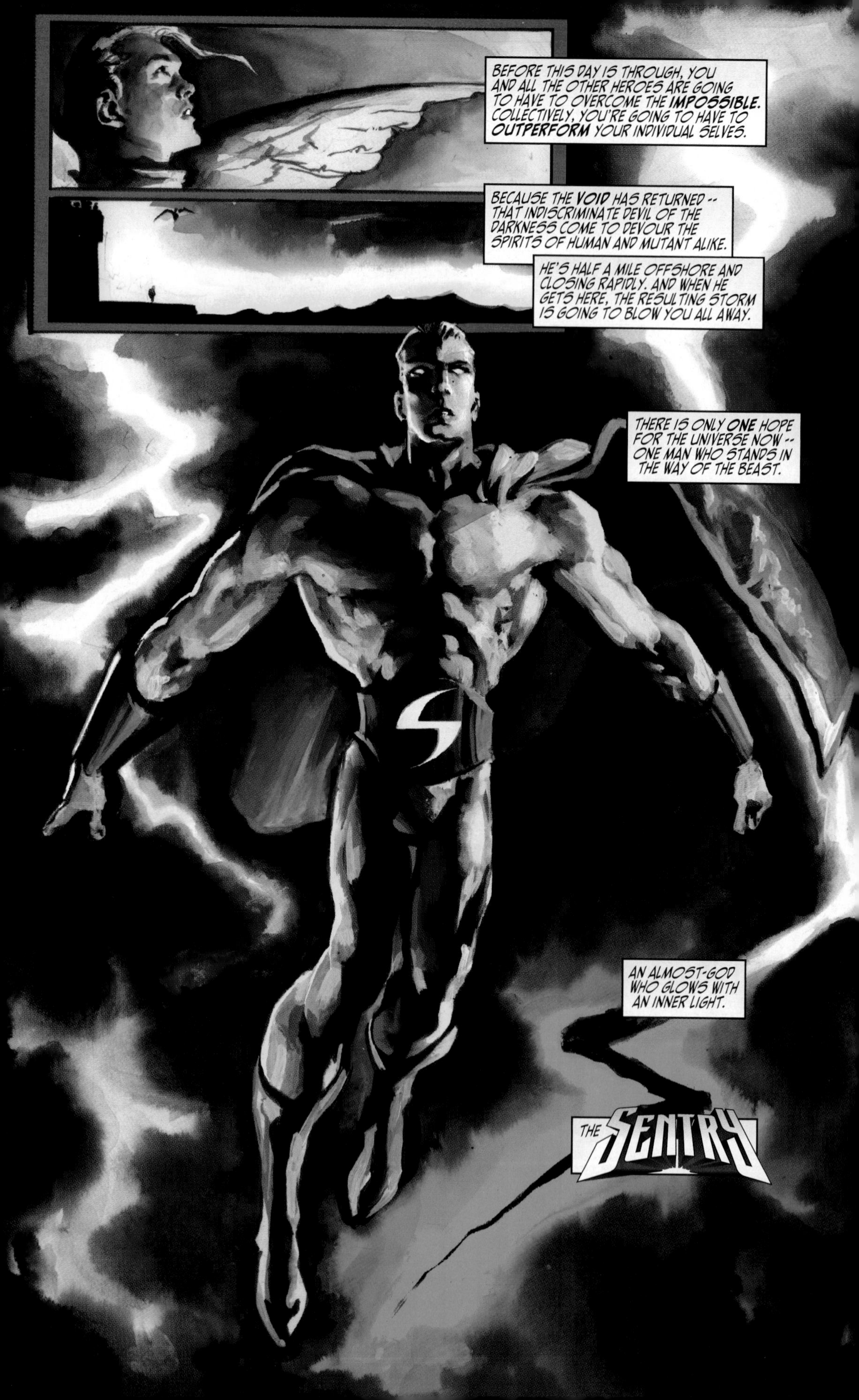
BEFORE THIS DAY IS THROUGH, YOU AND ALL THE OTHER HEROES ARE GOING TO HAVE TO OVERCOME THE IMPOSSIBLE. COLLECTIVELY, YOU'RE GOING TO HAVE TO OUTPERFORM YOUR INDIVIDUAL SELVES.
BECAUSE THE VOID HAS RETURNED -- THAT INDISCRIMINATE DEVIL OF THE DARKNESS COME TO DEVOUR THE SPIRITS OF HUMAN AND MUTANT ALIKE.
HE'S HALF A MILE OFFSHORE AND CLOSING RAPIDLY. AND WHEN HE GETS HERE, THE RESULTING STORM IS GOING TO BLOW YOU ALL AWAY.
THERE IS ONLY ONE HOPE FOR THE UNIVERSE NOW -- ONE MAN WHO STANDS IN THE WAY OF THE BEAST.
AN ALMOST-GOD WHO GLOWS WITH AN INNER LIGHT.
THE SENTRY

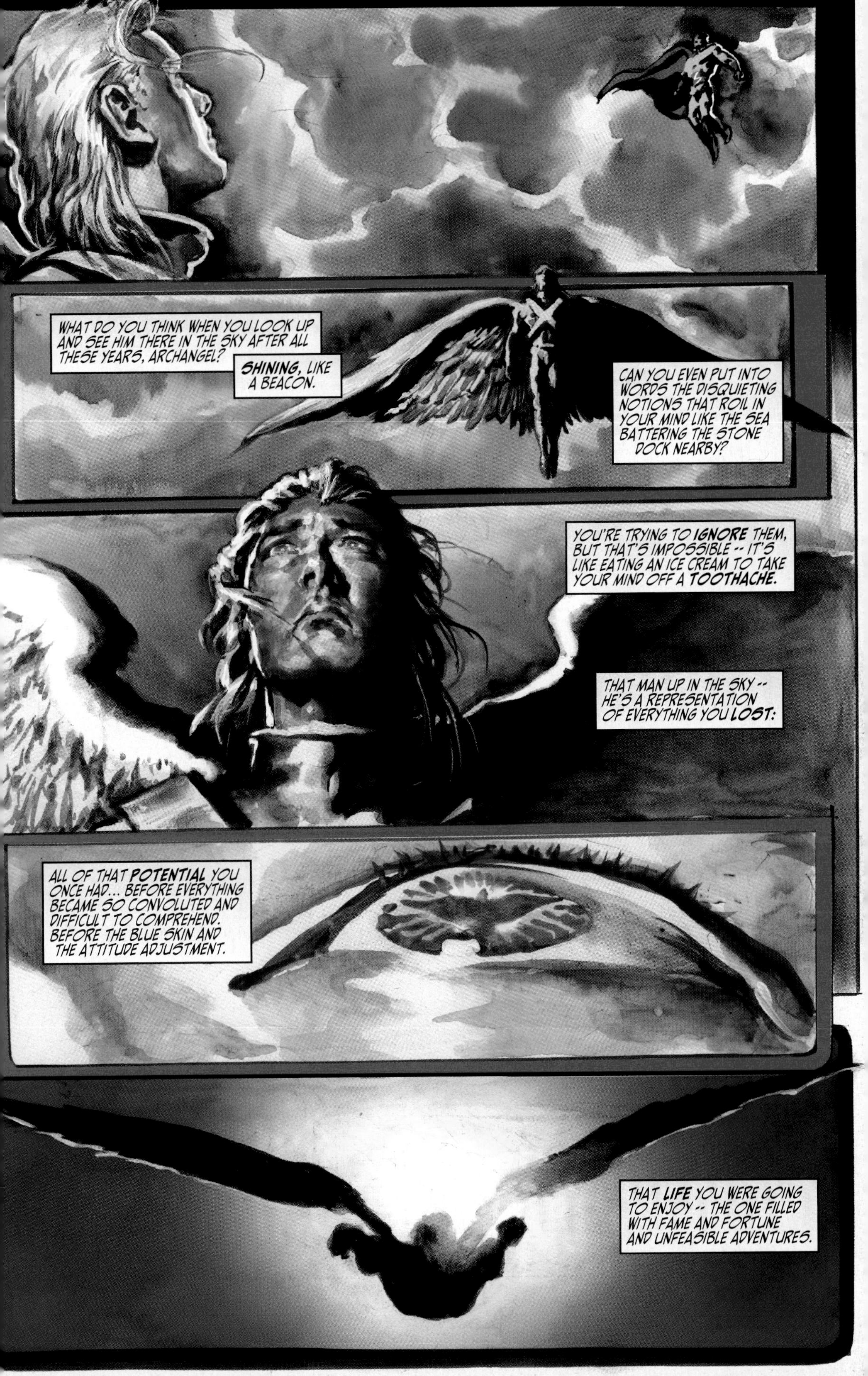
WHAT DO YOU THINK WHEN YOU LOOK UP AND SEE HIM THERE IN THE SKY AFTER ALL THESE YEARS, ARCHANGEL?
SHINING, LIKE A BEACON.
CAN YOU EVEN PUT INTO WORDS THE DISQUIETING NOTIONS THAT ROIL IN YOUR MIND LIKE THE SEA BATTERING THE STONE DOCK NEARBY?
YOU'RE TRYING TO IGNORE THEM, BUT THAT'S IMPOSSIBLE -- IT'S LIKE EATING AN ICE CREAM TO TAKE YOUR MIND OFF A TOOTHACHE.
THAT MAN UP IN THE SKY -- HE'S A REPRESENTATION OF EVERYTHING YOU LOST:
ALL OF THAT POTENTIAL YOU ONCE HAD... BEFORE EVERYTHING BECAME SO CONVOLUTED AND DIFFICULT TO COMPREHEND. BEFORE THE BLUE SKIN AND THE ATTITUDE ADJUSTMENT.
THAT LIFE YOU WERE GOING TO ENJOY -- THE ONE FILLED WITH FAME AND FORTUNE AND UNFEASIBLE ADVENTURES.

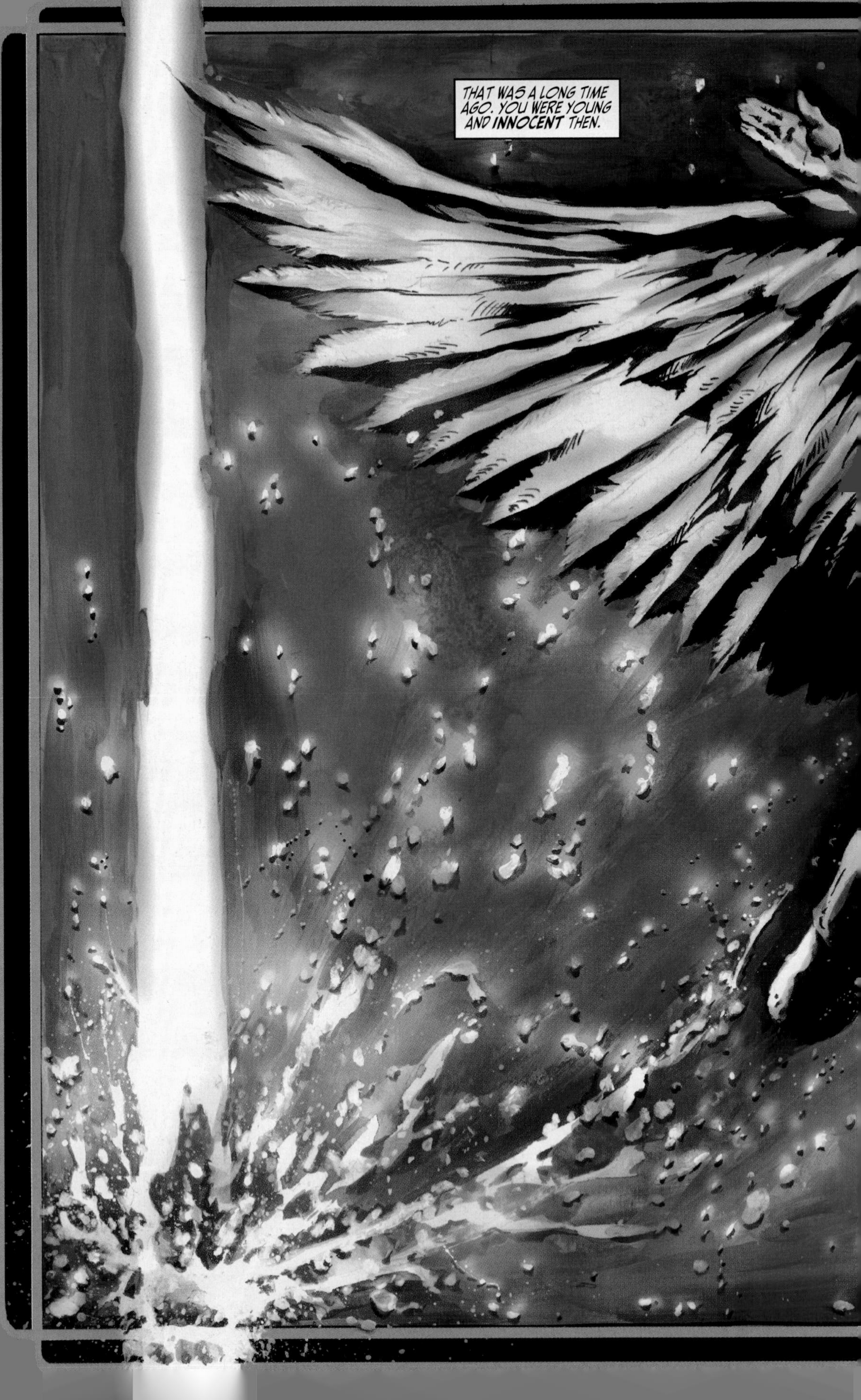
THAT WAS A LONG TIME AGO. YOU WERE YOUNG AND INNOCENT THEN.

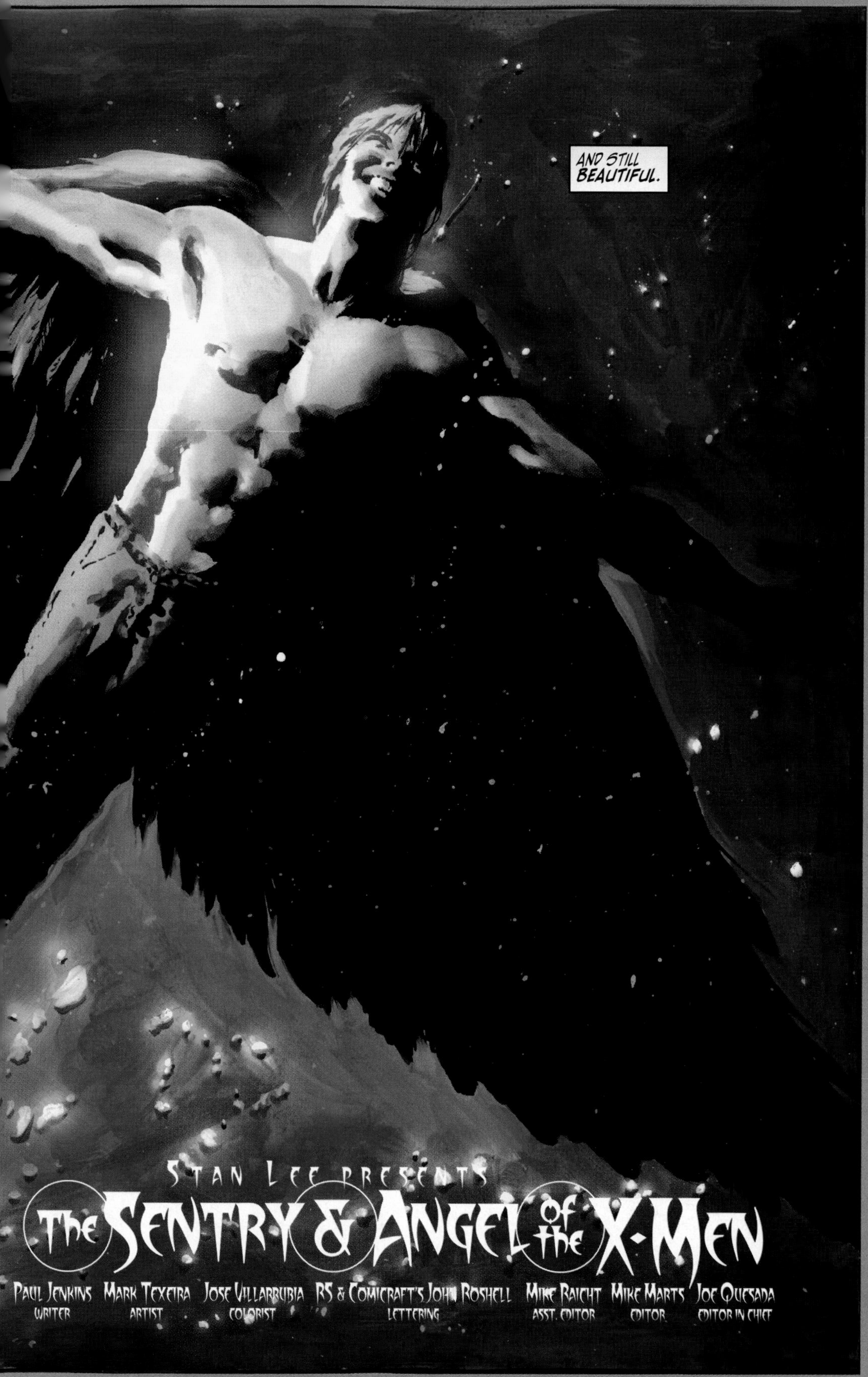
AND STILL BEAUTIFUL.
STAN LEE PRESENTS
THE SENTRY & ANGEL OF THE X-MEN
PAUL JENKINS WRITER
MARK TEXEIRA ARTIST
JOSE VILLARRUBIA COLORIST
RS & COMICRAFT'S JOHN ROSHELL LETTERING
MIKE RAICHT ASST. EDITOR
MIKE MARTS EDITOR
JOE QUESADA EDITOR IN CHIEF

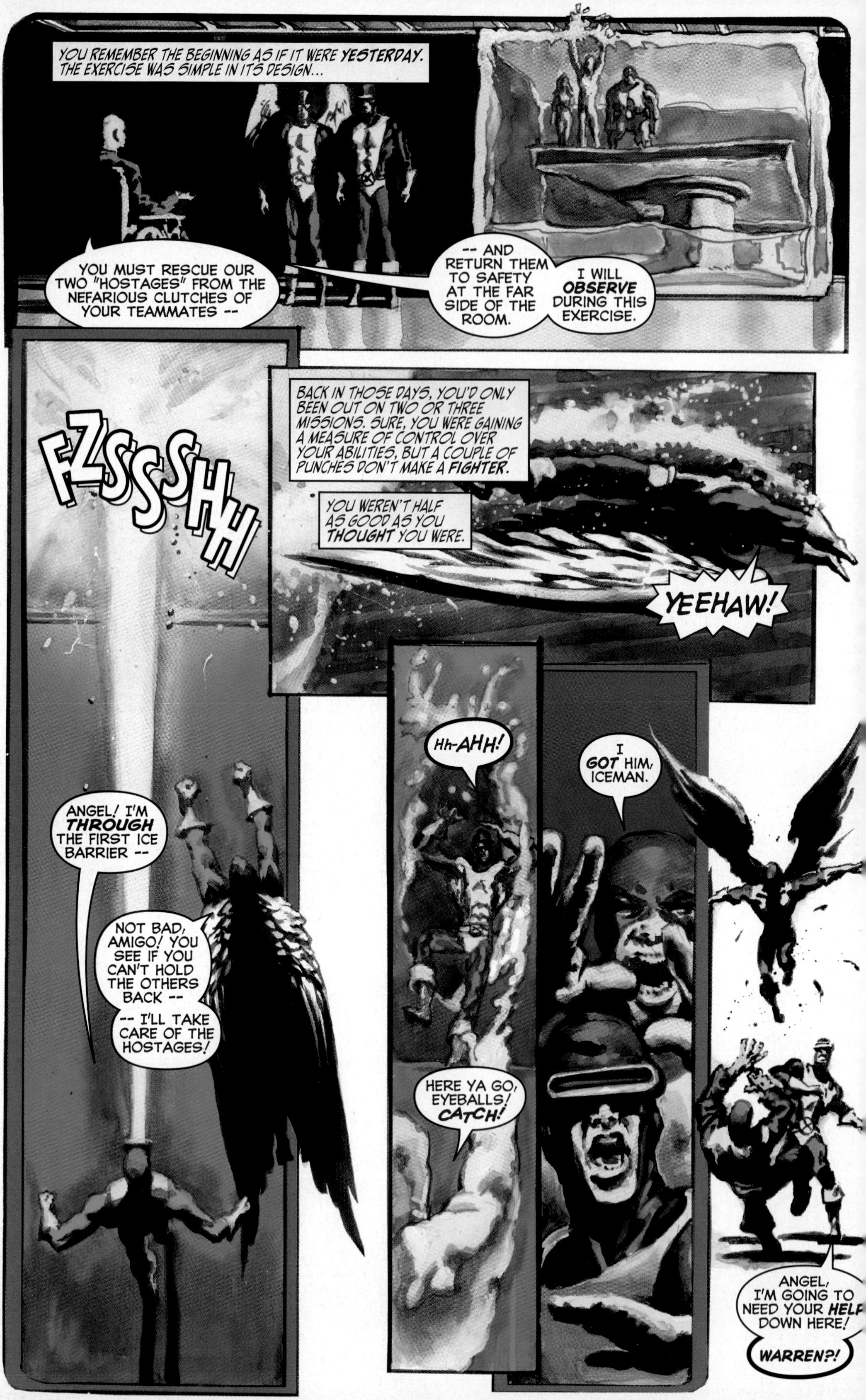
YOU REMEMBER THE BEGINNING AS IF IT WERE YESTERDAY. THE EXERCISE WAS SIMPLE IN ITS DESIGN...
YOU MUST RESCUE OUR TWO "HOSTAGES" FROM THE NEFARIOUS CLUTCHES OF YOUR TEAMMATES --
-- AND RETURN THEM TO SAFETY AT THE FAR SIDE OF THE ROOM.
I WILL OBSERVE DURING THIS EXERCISE.
FZSSSHH
BACK IN THOSE DAYS, YOU'D ONLY BEEN OUT ON TWO OR THREE MISSIONS. SURE, YOU WERE GAINING A MEASURE OF CONTROL OVER YOUR ABILITIES, BUT A COUPLE OF PUNCHES DON'T MAKE A FIGHTER.
YOU WEREN'T HALF AS GOOD AS YOU THOUGHT YOU WERE.
YEEHAW!
ANGEL! I'M THROUGH THE FIRST ICE BARRIER --
NOT BAD, AMIGO! YOU SEE IF YOU CAN'T HOLD THE OTHERS BACK --
-- I'LL TAKE CARE OF THE HOSTAGES!
Hh-AHH!
HERE YA GO, EYEBALLS! CATCH!
I GOT HIM, ICEMAN.
ANGEL, I'M GOING TO NEED YOUR HELP DOWN HERE!
WARREN?!

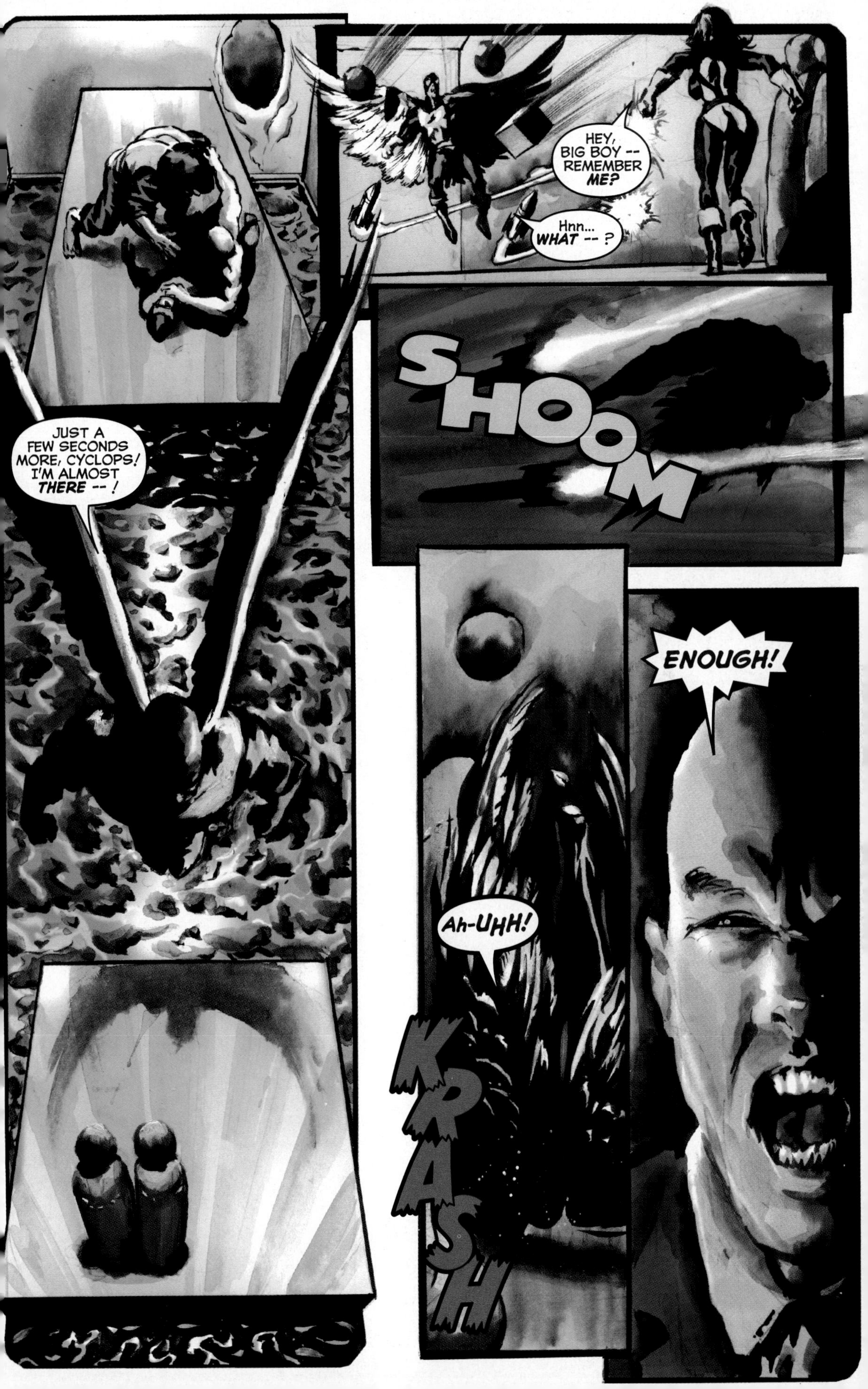
HEY, BIG BOY -- REMEMBER ME?
Hnn... WHAT -- ?
JUST A FEW SECONDS MORE, CYCLOPS! I'M ALMOST THERE -- !
SHOOM
ENOUGH!
Ah-UHH!
KRASH

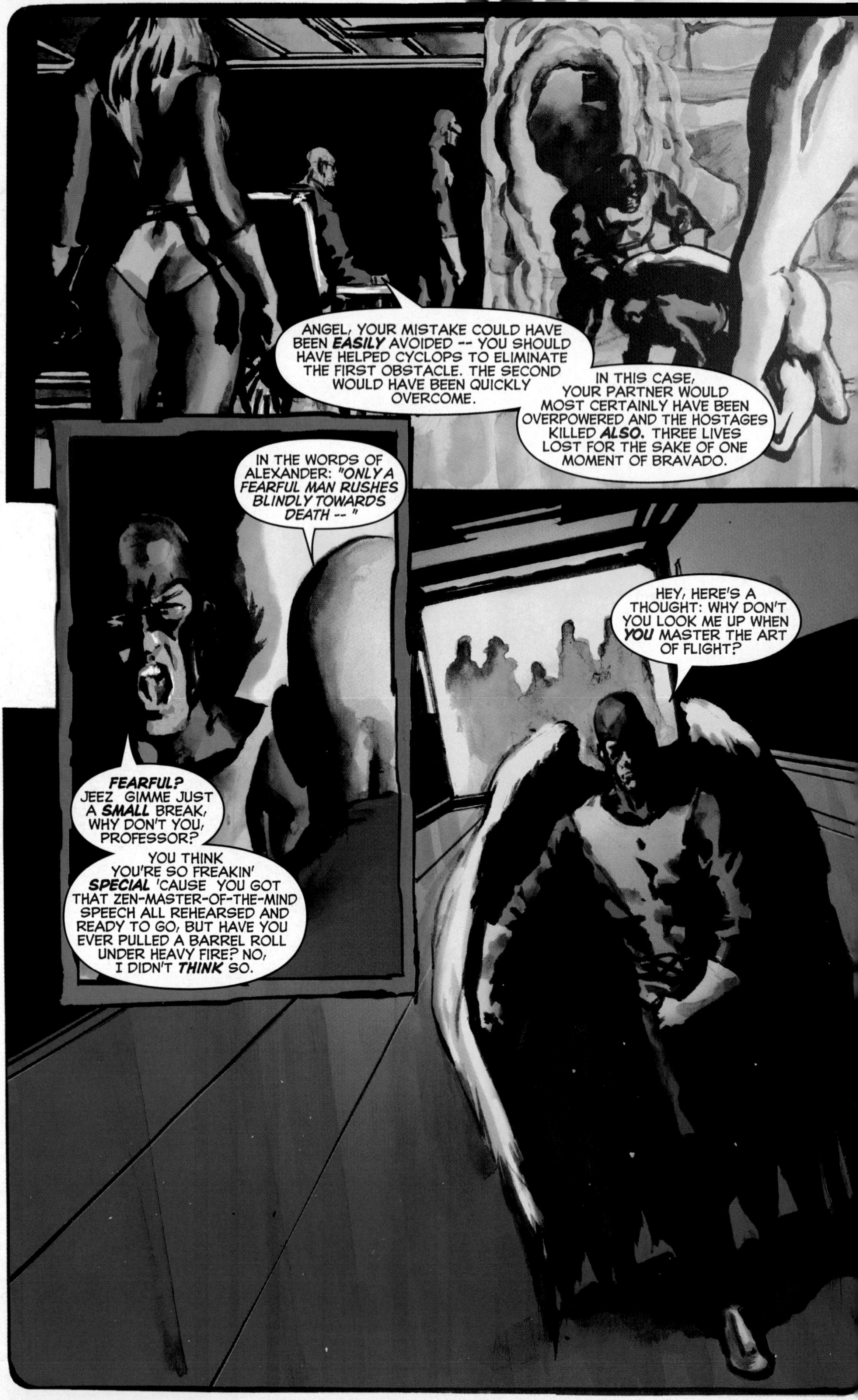

ANGEL, YOUR MISTAKE COULD HAVE BEEN **EASILY** AVOIDED -- YOU SHOULD HAVE HELPED CYCLOPS TO ELIMINATE THE FIRST OBSTACLE. THE SECOND WOULD HAVE BEEN QUICKLY OVERCOME.
IN THIS CASE, YOUR PARTNER WOULD MOST CERTAINLY HAVE BEEN OVERPOWERED AND THE HOSTAGES KILLED **ALSO.** THREE LIVES LOST FOR THE SAKE OF ONE MOMENT OF BRAVADO.
IN THE WORDS OF ALEXANDER: *"ONLY A FEARFUL MAN RUSHES BLINDLY TOWARDS DEATH -- "*
FEARFUL? JEEZ GIMME JUST A **SMALL** BREAK, WHY DON'T YOU, PROFESSOR?
YOU THINK YOU'RE SO FREAKIN' ***SPECIAL*** 'CAUSE YOU GOT THAT ZEN-MASTER-OF-THE-MIND SPEECH ALL REHEARSED AND READY TO GO, BUT HAVE YOU EVER PULLED A BARREL ROLL UNDER HEAVY FIRE? NO, I DIDN'T ***THINK*** SO.
HEY, HERE'S A THOUGHT: WHY DON'T YOU LOOK ME UP WHEN ***YOU*** MASTER THE ART OF FLIGHT?

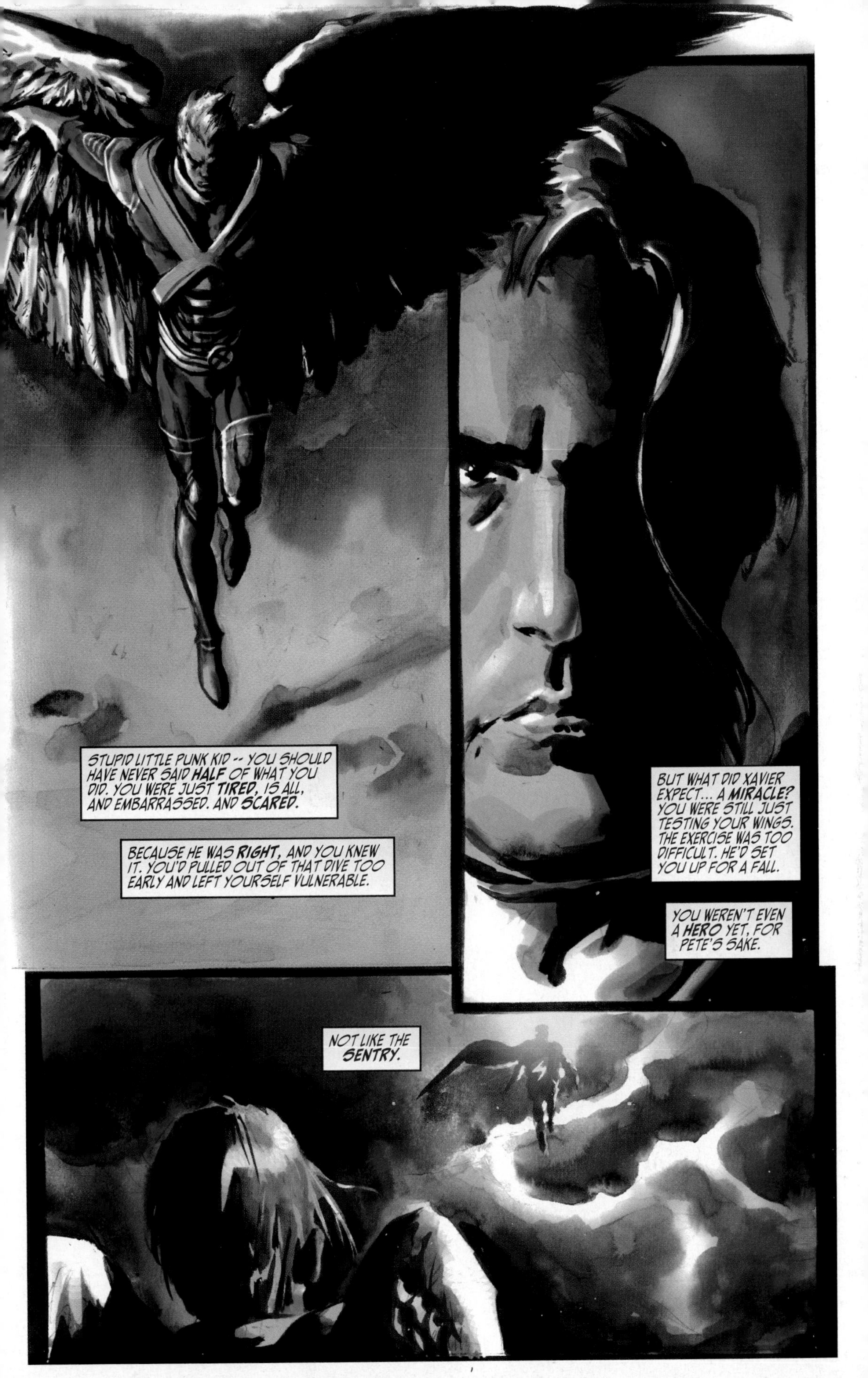

STUPID LITTLE PUNK KID -- YOU SHOULD HAVE NEVER SAID HALF OF WHAT YOU DID. YOU WERE JUST TIRED, IS ALL, AND EMBARRASSED. AND SCARED.
BECAUSE HE WAS RIGHT, AND YOU KNEW IT. YOU'D PULLED OUT OF THAT DIVE TOO EARLY AND LEFT YOURSELF VULNERABLE.
BUT WHAT DID XAVIER EXPECT... A MIRACLE? YOU WERE STILL JUST TESTING YOUR WINGS. THE EXERCISE WAS TOO DIFFICULT. HE'D SET YOU UP FOR A FALL.
YOU WEREN'T EVEN A HERO YET, FOR PETE'S SAKE.
NOT LIKE THE SENTRY.

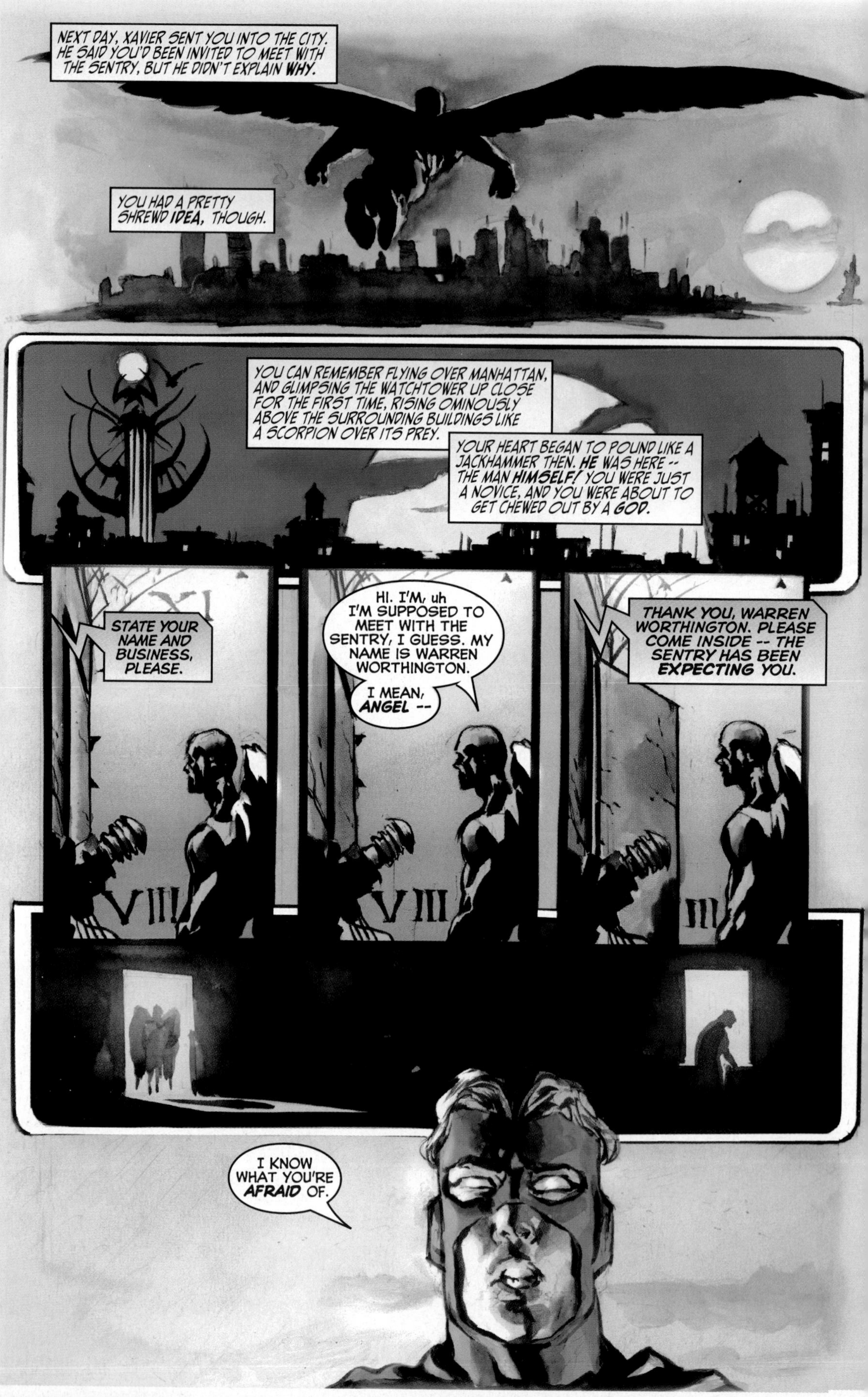
NEXT DAY, XAVIER SENT YOU INTO THE CITY. HE SAID YOU'D BEEN INVITED TO MEET WITH THE SENTRY, BUT HE DIDN'T EXPLAIN **WHY.**
YOU HAD A PRETTY SHREWD **IDEA,** THOUGH.
YOU CAN REMEMBER FLYING OVER MANHATTAN, AND GLIMPSING THE WATCHTOWER UP CLOSE FOR THE FIRST TIME, RISING OMINOUSLY ABOVE THE SURROUNDING BUILDINGS LIKE A SCORPION OVER ITS PREY.
YOUR HEART BEGAN TO POUND LIKE A JACKHAMMER THEN. **HE** WAS HERE -- THE MAN **HIMSELF!** YOU WERE JUST A NOVICE, AND YOU WERE ABOUT TO GET CHEWED OUT BY A **GOD.**
STATE YOUR NAME AND BUSINESS, PLEASE.
HI. I'M, uh I'M SUPPOSED TO MEET WITH THE SENTRY, I GUESS. MY NAME IS WARREN WORTHINGTON.
I MEAN, **ANGEL** --
THANK YOU, WARREN WORTHINGTON. PLEASE COME INSIDE -- THE SENTRY HAS BEEN **EXPECTING** YOU.
I KNOW WHAT YOU'RE **AFRAID** OF.

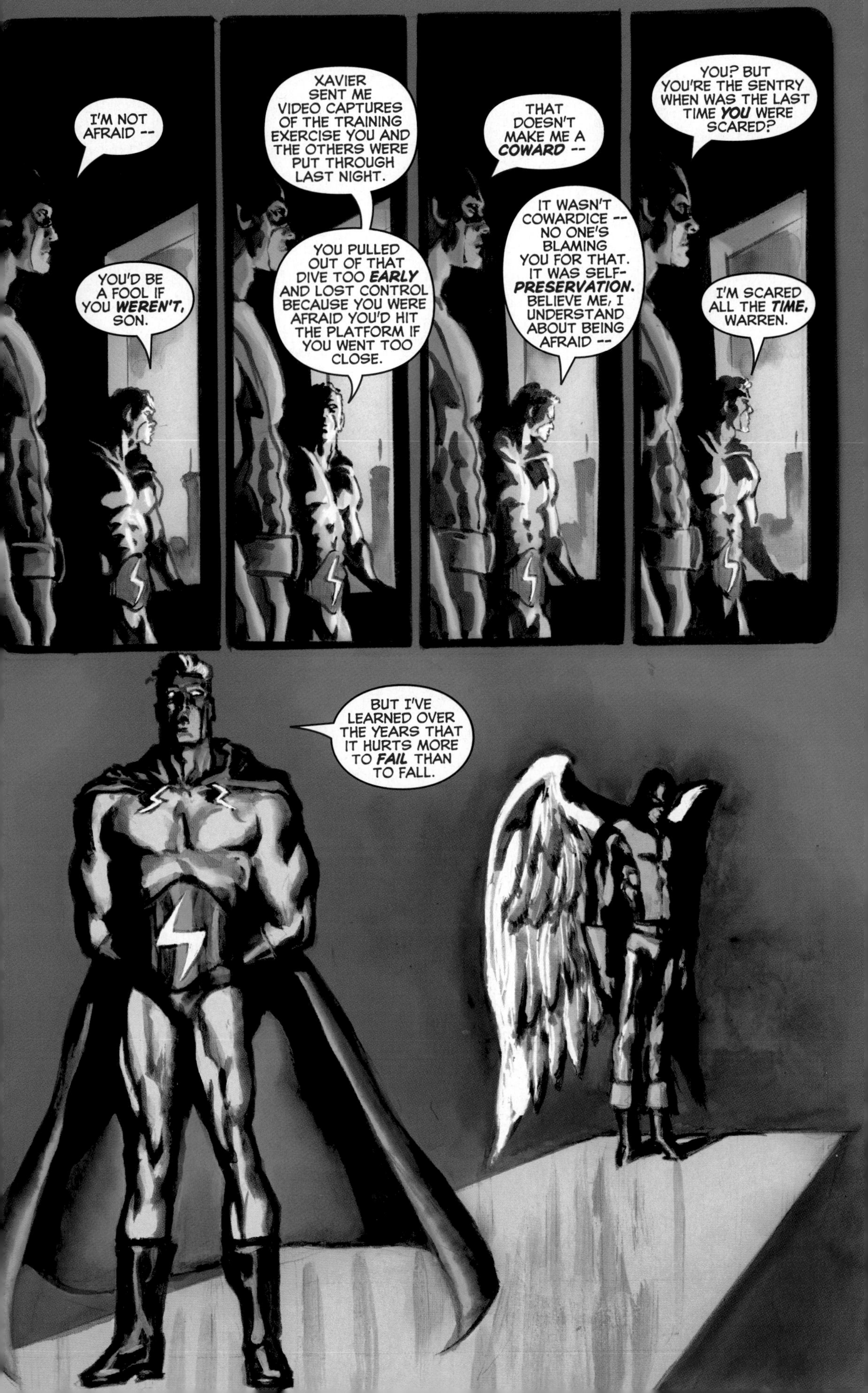
I'M NOT AFRAID --
YOU'D BE A FOOL IF YOU WEREN'T, SON.
XAVIER SENT ME VIDEO CAPTURES OF THE TRAINING EXERCISE YOU AND THE OTHERS WERE PUT THROUGH LAST NIGHT.
YOU PULLED OUT OF THAT DIVE TOO EARLY AND LOST CONTROL BECAUSE YOU WERE AFRAID YOU'D HIT THE PLATFORM IF YOU WENT TOO CLOSE.
THAT DOESN'T MAKE ME A COWARD --
IT WASN'T COWARDICE -- NO ONE'S BLAMING YOU FOR THAT. IT WAS SELF-PRESERVATION. BELIEVE ME, I UNDERSTAND ABOUT BEING AFRAID --
YOU? BUT YOU'RE THE SENTRY WHEN WAS THE LAST TIME YOU WERE SCARED?
I'M SCARED ALL THE TIME, WARREN.
BUT I'VE LEARNED OVER THE YEARS THAT IT HURTS MORE TO FAIL THAN TO FALL.

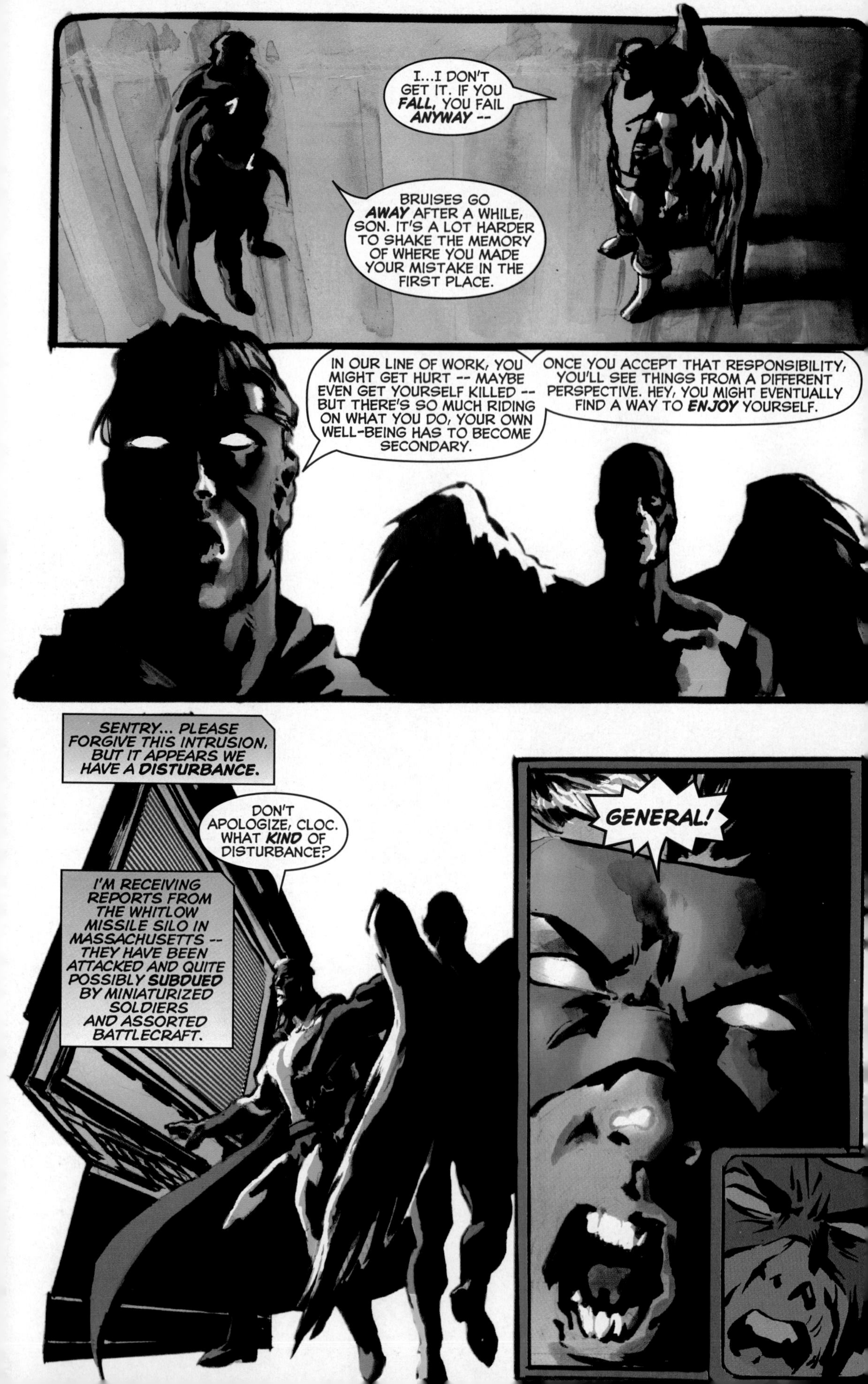

I...I DON'T GET IT. IF YOU FALL, YOU FAIL ANYWAY --
BRUISES GO AWAY AFTER A WHILE, SON. IT'S A LOT HARDER TO SHAKE THE MEMORY OF WHERE YOU MADE YOUR MISTAKE IN THE FIRST PLACE.
IN OUR LINE OF WORK, YOU MIGHT GET HURT -- MAYBE EVEN GET YOURSELF KILLED -- BUT THERE'S SO MUCH RIDING ON WHAT YOU DO, YOUR OWN WELL-BEING HAS TO BECOME SECONDARY.
ONCE YOU ACCEPT THAT RESPONSIBILITY, YOU'LL SEE THINGS FROM A DIFFERENT PERSPECTIVE. HEY, YOU MIGHT EVENTUALLY FIND A WAY TO ENJOY YOURSELF.
SENTRY... PLEASE FORGIVE THIS INTRUSION, BUT IT APPEARS WE HAVE A DISTURBANCE.
DON'T APOLOGIZE, CLOC. WHAT KIND OF DISTURBANCE?
I'M RECEIVING REPORTS FROM THE WHITLOW MISSILE SILO IN MASSACHUSETTS -- THEY HAVE BEEN ATTACKED AND QUITE POSSIBLY SUBDUED BY MINIATURIZED SOLDIERS AND ASSORTED BATTLECRAFT.
GENERAL!

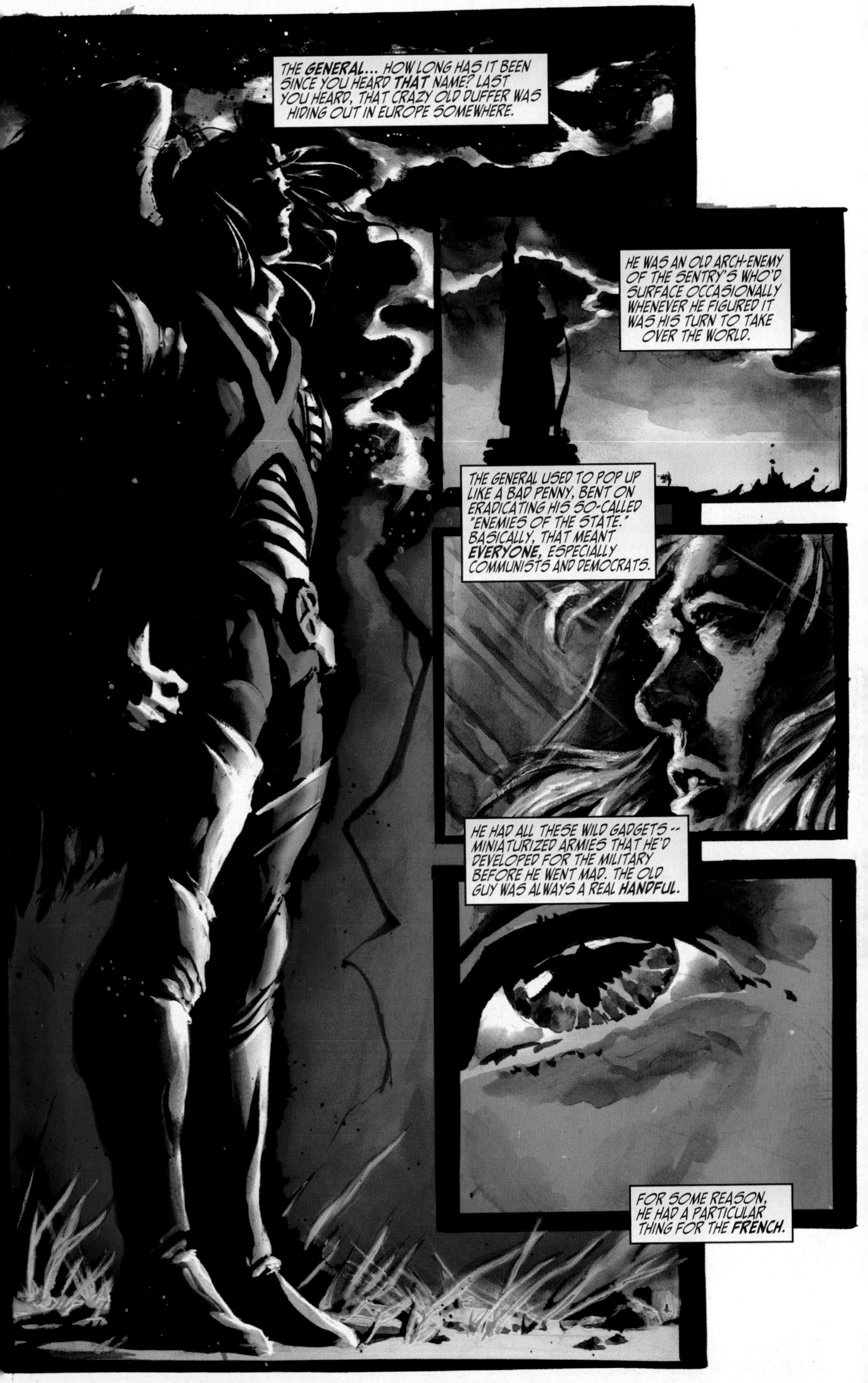
THE GENERAL... HOW LONG HAS IT BEEN SINCE YOU HEARD THAT NAME? LAST YOU HEARD, THAT CRAZY OLD DUFFER WAS HIDING OUT IN EUROPE SOMEWHERE.
HE WAS AN OLD ARCH-ENEMY OF THE SENTRY'S WHO'D SURFACE OCCASIONALLY WHENEVER HE FIGURED IT WAS HIS TURN TO TAKE OVER THE WORLD.
THE GENERAL USED TO POP UP LIKE A BAD PENNY, BENT ON ERADICATING HIS SO-CALLED "ENEMIES OF THE STATE." BASICALLY, THAT MEANT EVERYONE, ESPECIALLY COMMUNISTS AND DEMOCRATS.
HE HAD ALL THESE WILD GADGETS -- MINIATURIZED ARMIES THAT HE'D DEVELOPED FOR THE MILITARY BEFORE HE WENT MAD. THE OLD GUY WAS ALWAYS A REAL HANDFUL.
FOR SOME REASON, HE HAD A PARTICULAR THING FOR THE FRENCH.

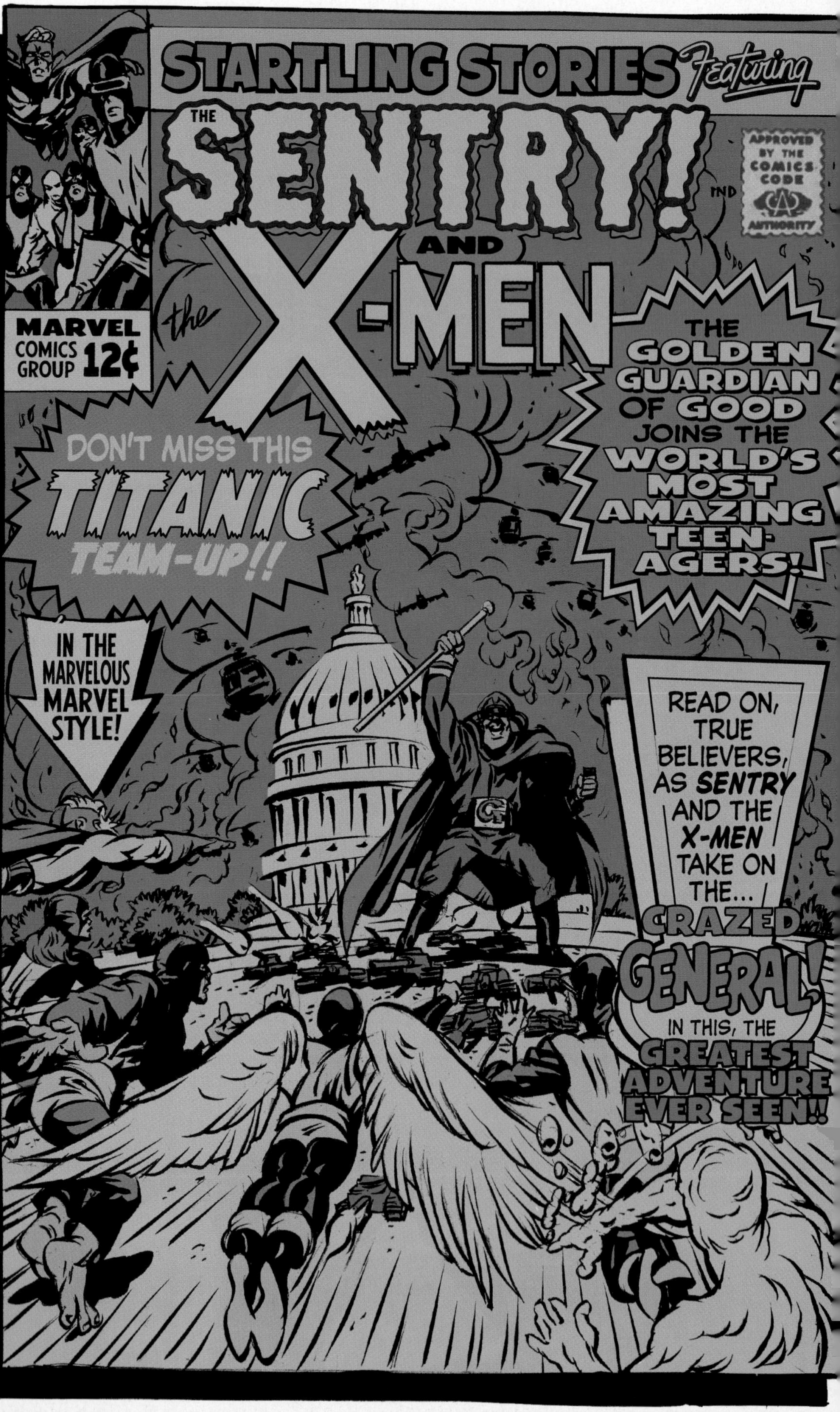
STARTLING STORIES Featuring
THE SENTRY!
AND
the X-MEN
APPROVED BY THE COMICS CODE AUTHORITY
MARVEL COMICS GROUP 12¢
THE GOLDEN GUARDIAN OF GOOD JOINS THE WORLD'S MOST AMAZING TEEN-AGERS!
DON'T MISS THIS TITANIC TEAM-UP!!
IN THE MARVELOUS MARVEL STYLE!
READ ON, TRUE BELIEVERS, AS SENTRY AND THE X-MEN TAKE ON THE... CRAZED GENERAL! IN THIS, THE GREATEST ADVENTURE EVER SEEN!!

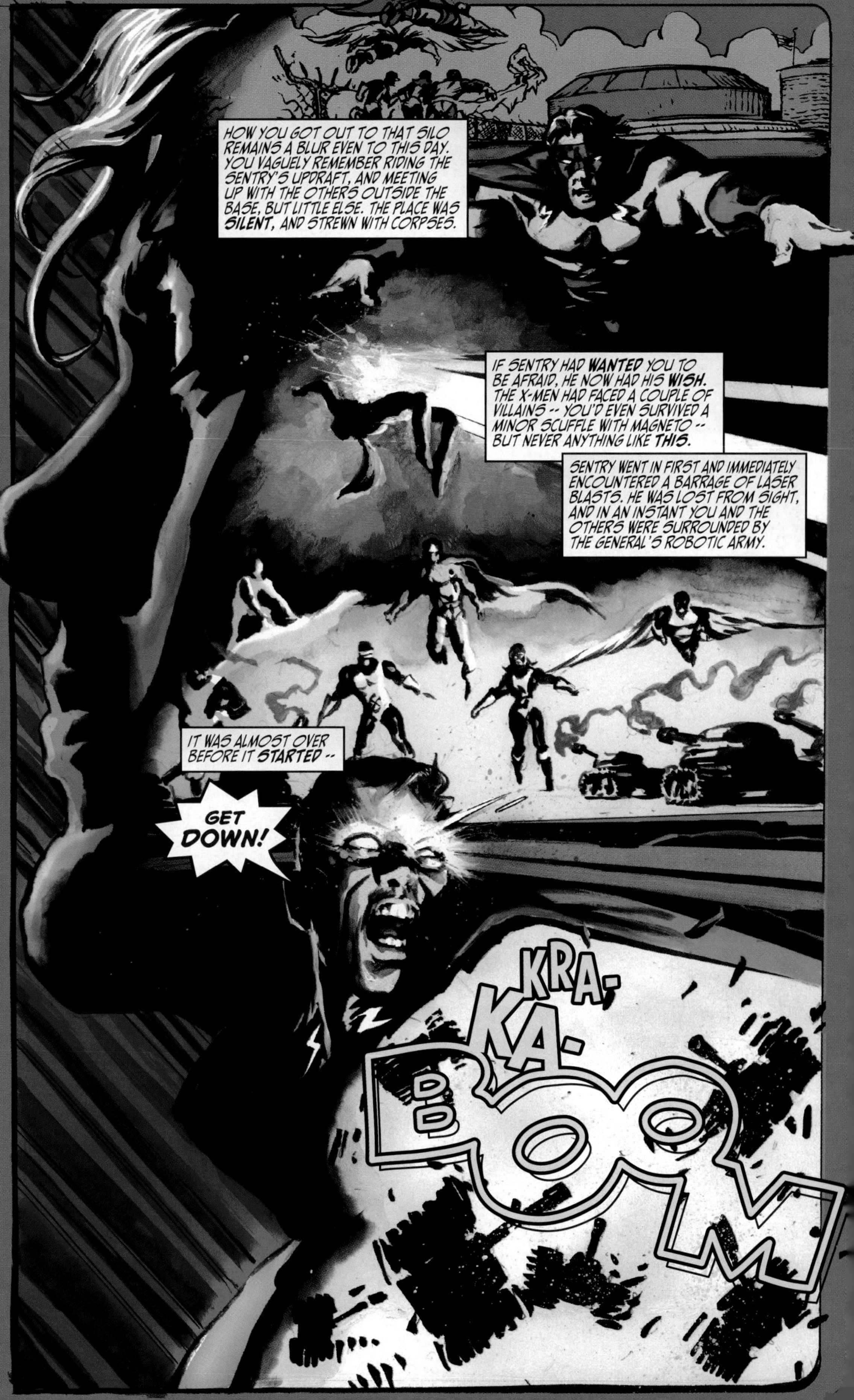
HOW YOU GOT OUT TO THAT SILO REMAINS A BLUR EVEN TO THIS DAY. YOU VAGUELY REMEMBER RIDING THE SENTRY'S UPDRAFT, AND MEETING UP WITH THE OTHERS OUTSIDE THE BASE, BUT LITTLE ELSE. THE PLACE WAS SILENT, AND STREWN WITH CORPSES.
IF SENTRY HAD WANTED YOU TO BE AFRAID, HE NOW HAD HIS WISH. THE X-MEN HAD FACED A COUPLE OF VILLAINS -- YOU'D EVEN SURVIVED A MINOR SCUFFLE WITH MAGNETO -- BUT NEVER ANYTHING LIKE THIS.
SENTRY WENT IN FIRST AND IMMEDIATELY ENCOUNTERED A BARRAGE OF LASER BLASTS. HE WAS LOST FROM SIGHT, AND IN AN INSTANT YOU AND THE OTHERS WERE SURROUNDED BY THE GENERAL'S ROBOTIC ARMY.
IT WAS ALMOST OVER BEFORE IT STARTED --
GET DOWN!
KRA-KA-DOOOM

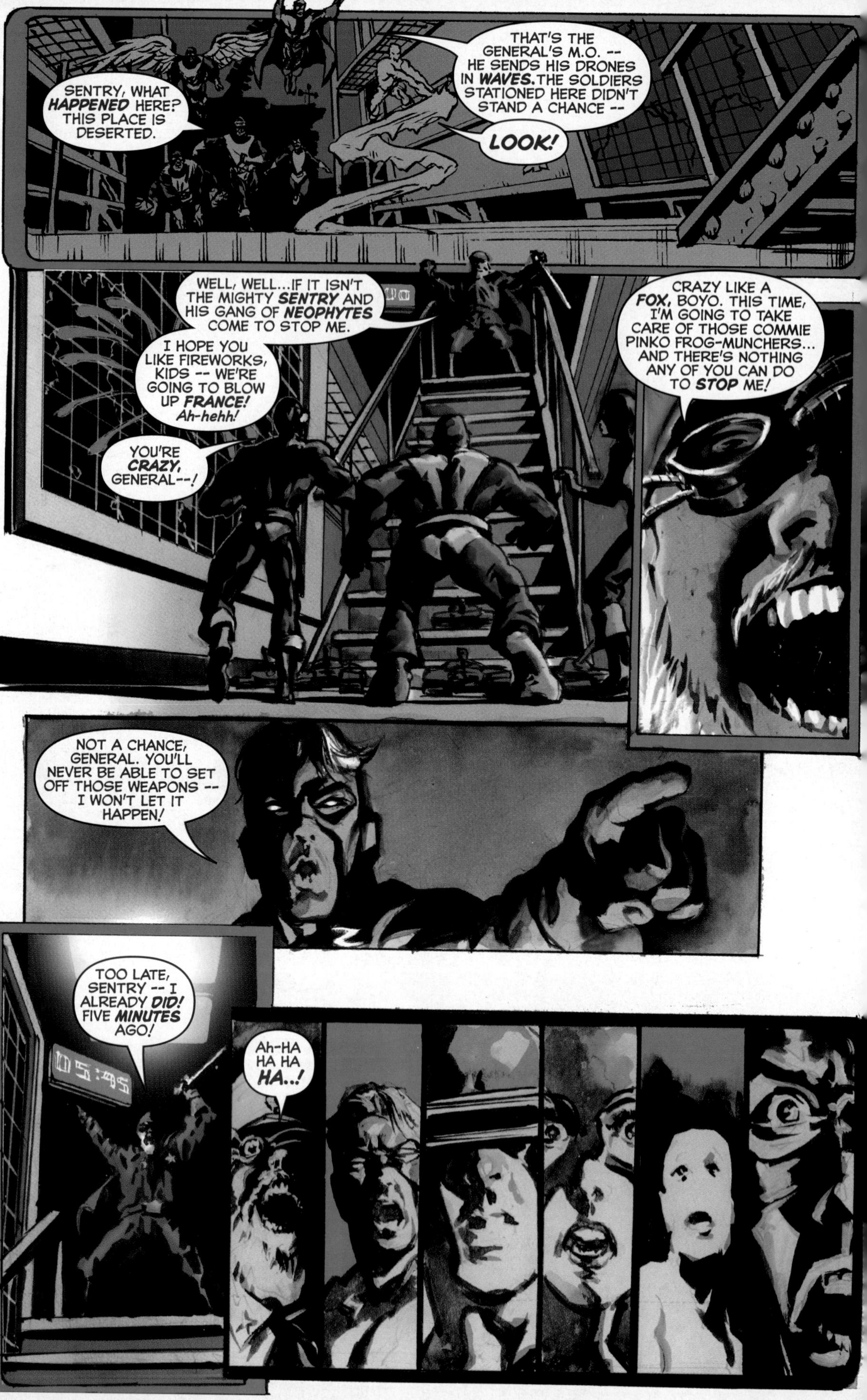
SENTRY, WHAT HAPPENED HERE? THIS PLACE IS DESERTED.
THAT'S THE GENERAL'S M.O. -- HE SENDS HIS DRONES IN WAVES. THE SOLDIERS STATIONED HERE DIDN'T STAND A CHANCE --
LOOK!
WELL, WELL...IF IT ISN'T THE MIGHTY SENTRY AND HIS GANG OF NEOPHYTES COME TO STOP ME.
I HOPE YOU LIKE FIREWORKS, KIDS -- WE'RE GOING TO BLOW UP FRANCE! Ah-hehh!
YOU'RE CRAZY, GENERAL--!
CRAZY LIKE A FOX, BOYO. THIS TIME, I'M GOING TO TAKE CARE OF THOSE COMMIE PINKO FROG-MUNCHERS... AND THERE'S NOTHING ANY OF YOU CAN DO TO STOP ME!
NOT A CHANCE, GENERAL. YOU'LL NEVER BE ABLE TO SET OFF THOSE WEAPONS -- I WON'T LET IT HAPPEN!
TOO LATE, SENTRY -- I ALREADY DID! FIVE MINUTES AGO!
05:45
Ah-HA HA HA HA..!

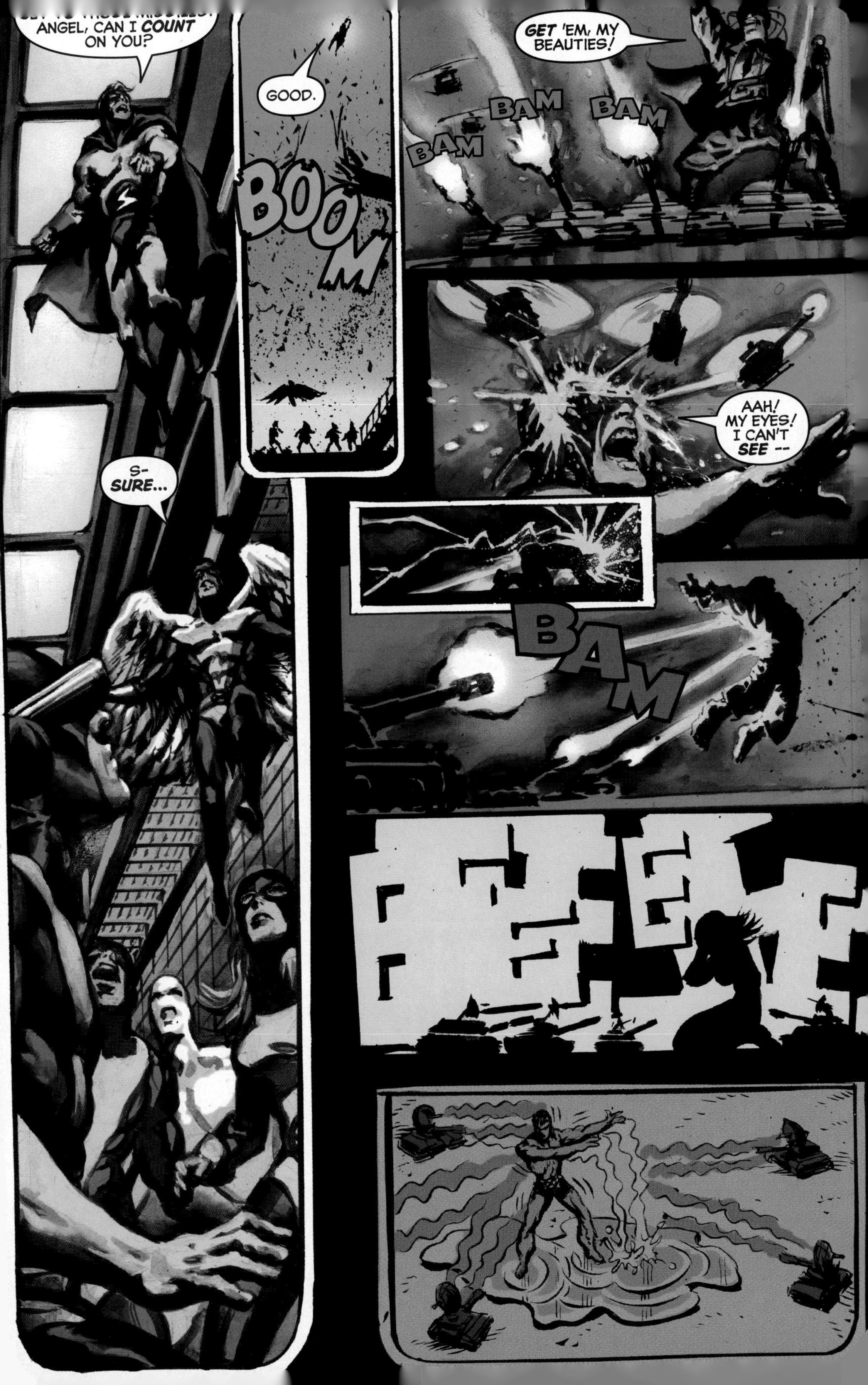
ANGEL, CAN I COUNT ON YOU?
S- SURE...
GOOD.
BOOM
GET 'EM, MY BEAUTIES!
BAM
BAM
BAM
AAH! MY EYES! I CAN'T SEE --
BAM

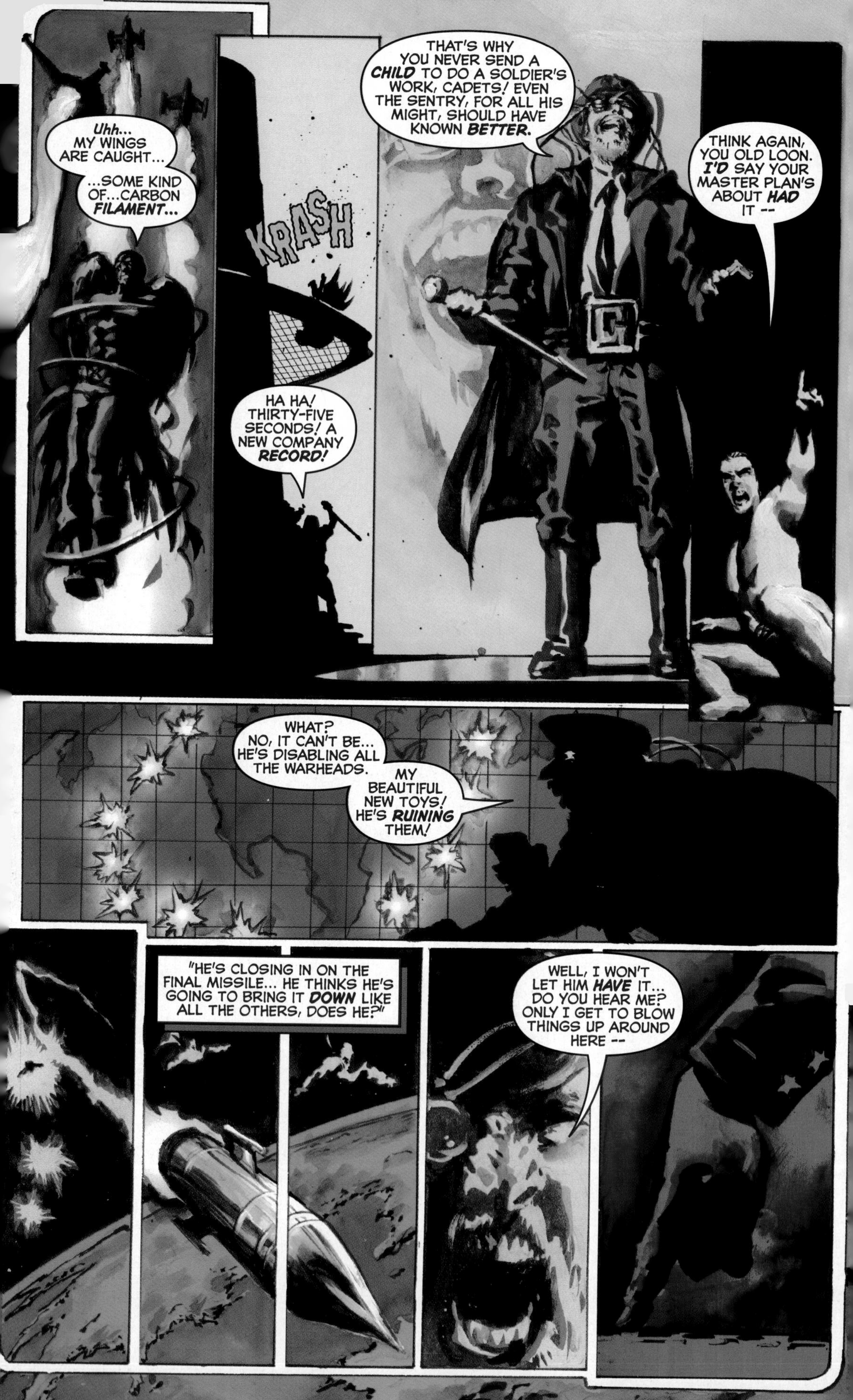
Uhh... MY WINGS ARE CAUGHT...
...SOME KIND OF...CARBON FILAMENT...
KRASH
HA HA! THIRTY-FIVE SECONDS! A NEW COMPANY RECORD!
THAT'S WHY YOU NEVER SEND A CHILD TO DO A SOLDIER'S WORK, CADETS! EVEN THE SENTRY, FOR ALL HIS MIGHT, SHOULD HAVE KNOWN BETTER.
THINK AGAIN, YOU OLD LOON. I'D SAY YOUR MASTER PLAN'S ABOUT HAD IT --
WHAT? NO, IT CAN'T BE... HE'S DISABLING ALL THE WARHEADS.
MY BEAUTIFUL NEW TOYS! HE'S RUINING THEM!
"HE'S CLOSING IN ON THE FINAL MISSILE... HE THINKS HE'S GOING TO BRING IT DOWN LIKE ALL THE OTHERS, DOES HE?"
WELL, I WON'T LET HIM HAVE IT... DO YOU HEAR ME? ONLY I GET TO BLOW THINGS UP AROUND HERE --

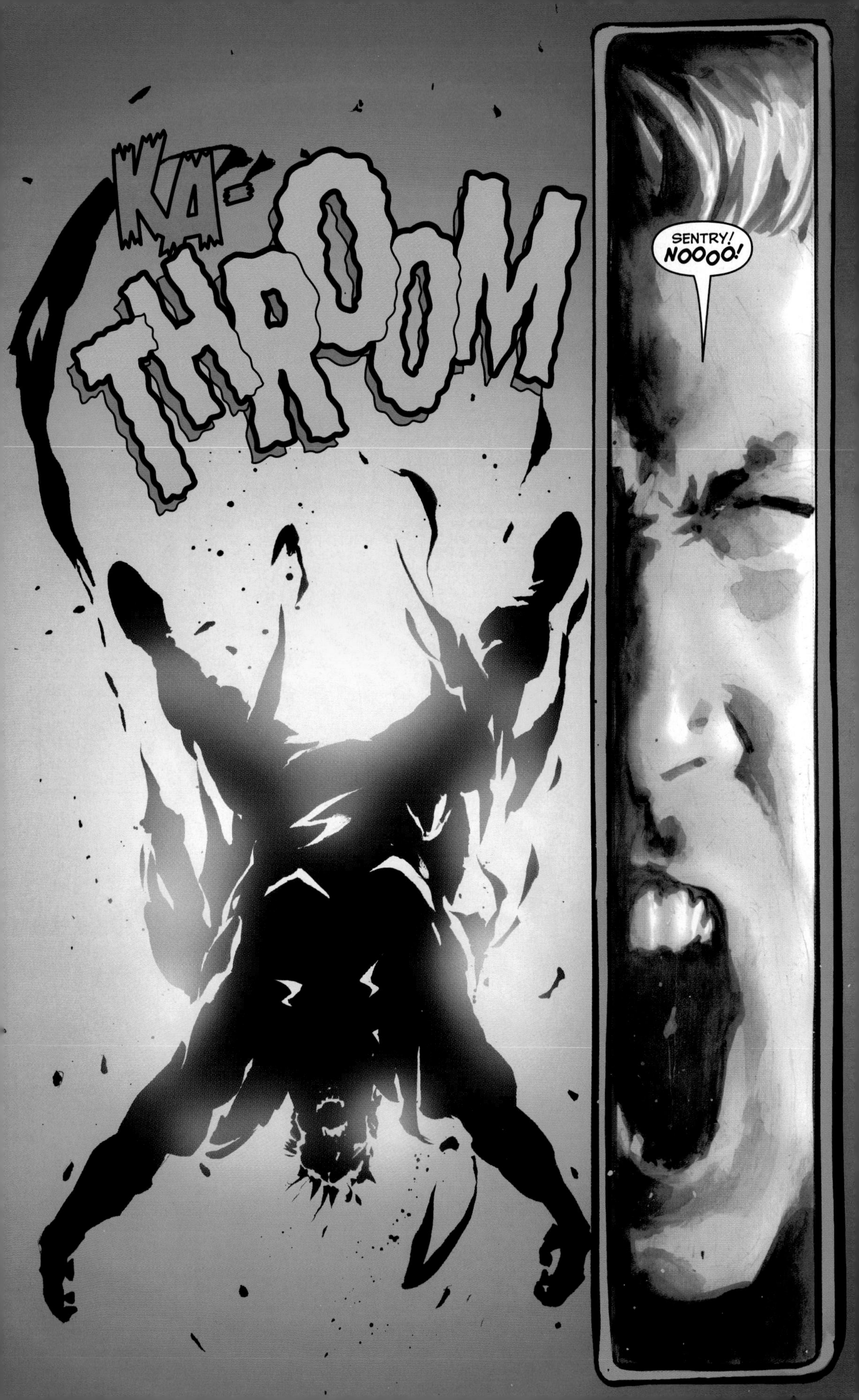
KA-THROOM
SENTRY! NOOOO!

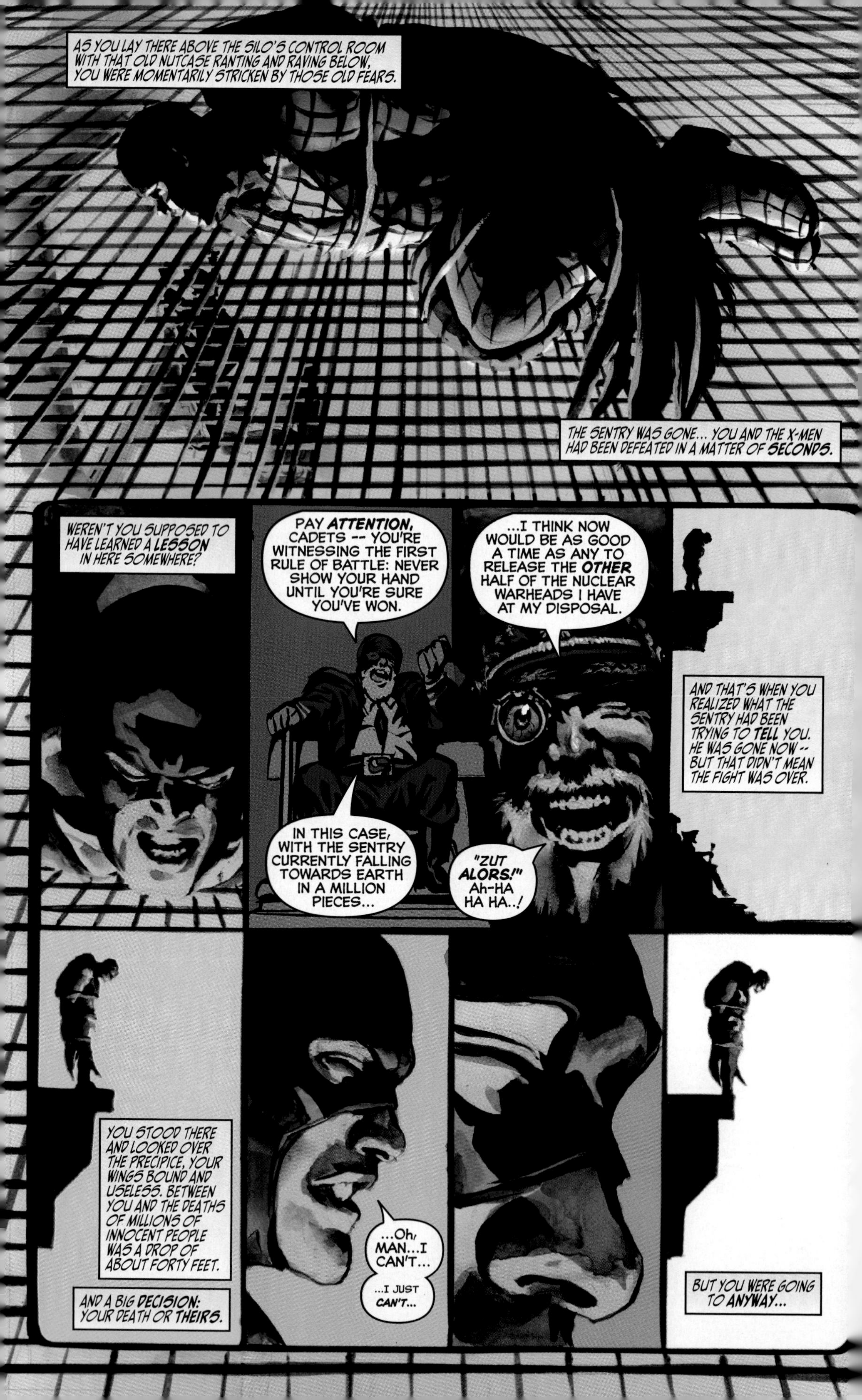
AS YOU LAY THERE ABOVE THE SILO'S CONTROL ROOM WITH THAT OLD NUTCASE RANTING AND RAVING BELOW, YOU WERE MOMENTARILY STRICKEN BY THOSE OLD FEARS.
THE SENTRY WAS GONE... YOU AND THE X-MEN HAD BEEN DEFEATED IN A MATTER OF SECONDS.
WEREN'T YOU SUPPOSED TO HAVE LEARNED A LESSON IN HERE SOMEWHERE?
PAY ATTENTION, CADETS -- YOU'RE WITNESSING THE FIRST RULE OF BATTLE: NEVER SHOW YOUR HAND UNTIL YOU'RE SURE YOU'VE WON.
IN THIS CASE, WITH THE SENTRY CURRENTLY FALLING TOWARDS EARTH IN A MILLION PIECES...
...I THINK NOW WOULD BE AS GOOD A TIME AS ANY TO RELEASE THE OTHER HALF OF THE NUCLEAR WARHEADS I HAVE AT MY DISPOSAL.
"ZUT ALORS!" Ah-HA HA HA..!
AND THAT'S WHEN YOU REALIZED WHAT THE SENTRY HAD BEEN TRYING TO TELL YOU. HE WAS GONE NOW -- BUT THAT DIDN'T MEAN THE FIGHT WAS OVER.
YOU STOOD THERE AND LOOKED OVER THE PRECIPICE, YOUR WINGS BOUND AND USELESS. BETWEEN YOU AND THE DEATHS OF MILLIONS OF INNOCENT PEOPLE WAS A DROP OF ABOUT FORTY FEET.
AND A BIG DECISION: YOUR DEATH OR THEIRS.
...Oh, MAN...I CAN'T...
...I JUST CAN'T...
BUT YOU WERE GOING TO ANYWAY...

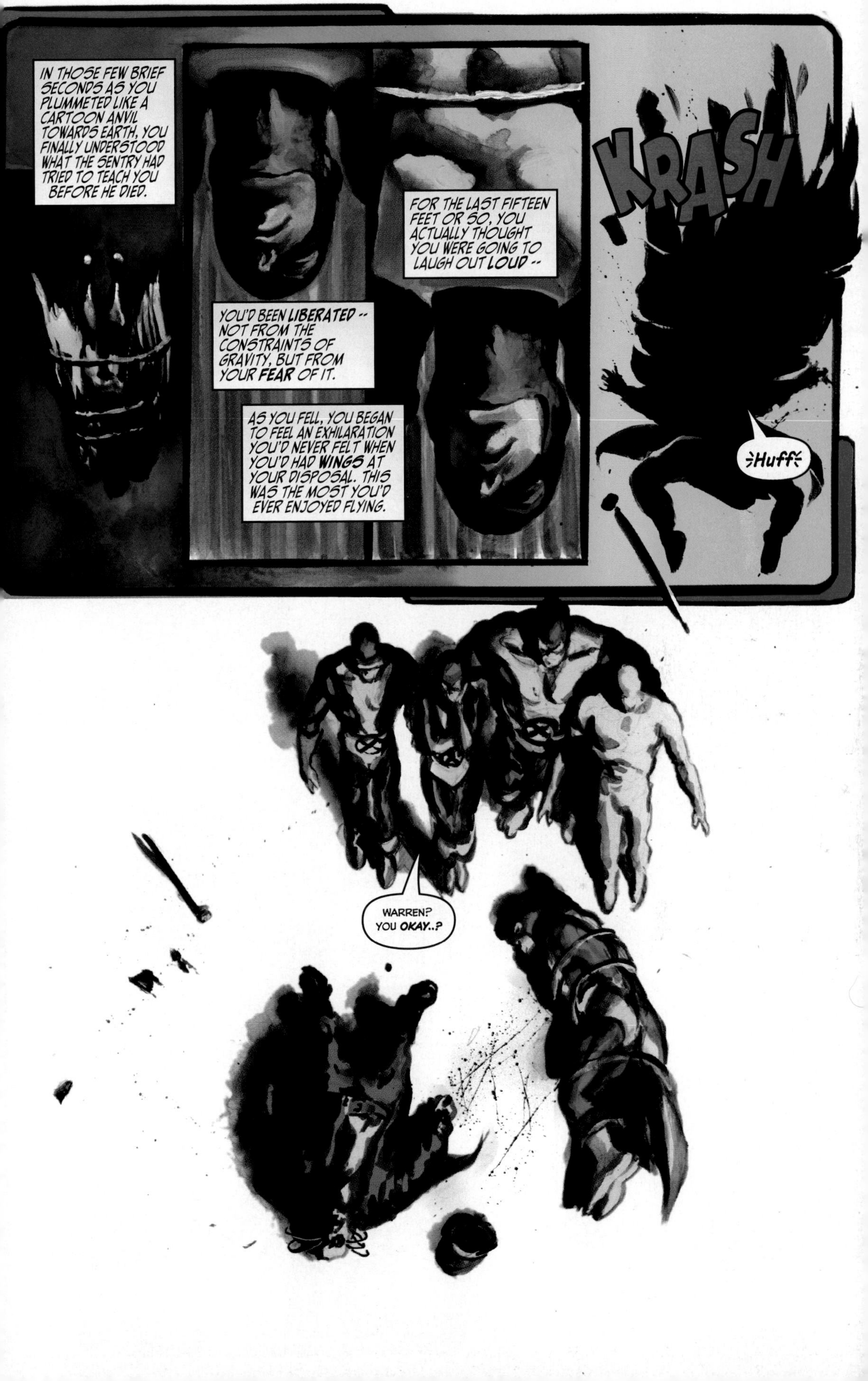
IN THOSE FEW BRIEF SECONDS AS YOU PLUMMETED LIKE A CARTOON ANVIL TOWARDS EARTH, YOU FINALLY UNDERSTOOD WHAT THE SENTRY HAD TRIED TO TEACH YOU BEFORE HE DIED.
YOU'D BEEN LIBERATED -- NOT FROM THE CONSTRAINTS OF GRAVITY, BUT FROM YOUR FEAR OF IT.
AS YOU FELL, YOU BEGAN TO FEEL AN EXHILARATION YOU'D NEVER FELT WHEN YOU'D HAD WINGS AT YOUR DISPOSAL. THIS WAS THE MOST YOU'D EVER ENJOYED FLYING.
FOR THE LAST FIFTEEN FEET OR SO, YOU ACTUALLY THOUGHT YOU WERE GOING TO LAUGH OUT LOUD --
KRASH
Huff
WARREN? YOU OKAY..?

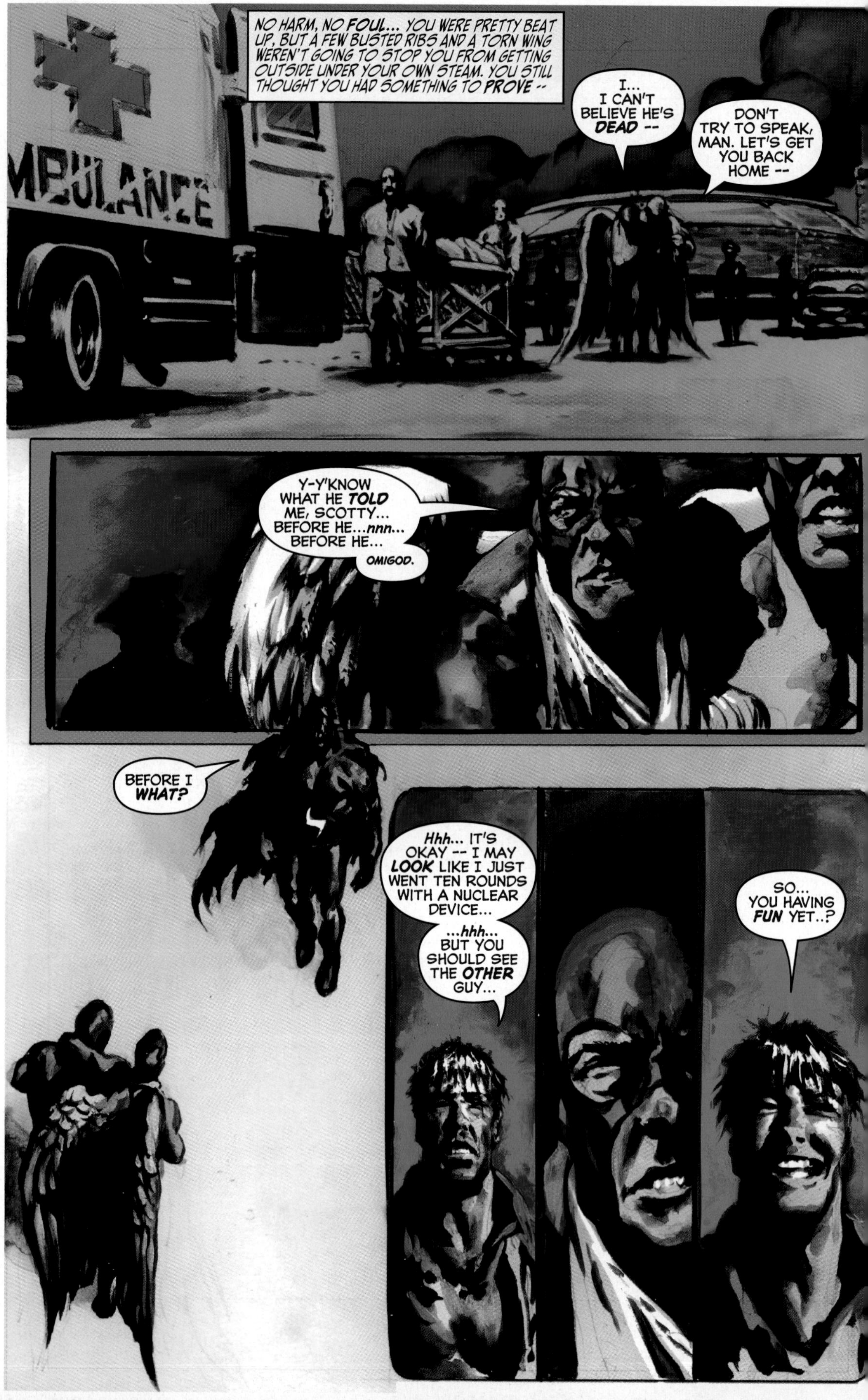
NO HARM, NO FOUL... YOU WERE PRETTY BEAT UP, BUT A FEW BUSTED RIBS AND A TORN WING WEREN'T GOING TO STOP YOU FROM GETTING OUTSIDE UNDER YOUR OWN STEAM. YOU STILL THOUGHT YOU HAD SOMETHING TO PROVE --
I... I CAN'T BELIEVE HE'S DEAD --
DON'T TRY TO SPEAK, MAN. LET'S GET YOU BACK HOME --
Y-Y'KNOW WHAT HE TOLD ME, SCOTTY... BEFORE HE...nnn... BEFORE HE...
OMIGOD.
BEFORE I WHAT?
Hhh... IT'S OKAY -- I MAY LOOK LIKE I JUST WENT TEN ROUNDS WITH A NUCLEAR DEVICE...
...hhh... BUT YOU SHOULD SEE THE OTHER GUY...
SO... YOU HAVING FUN YET..?

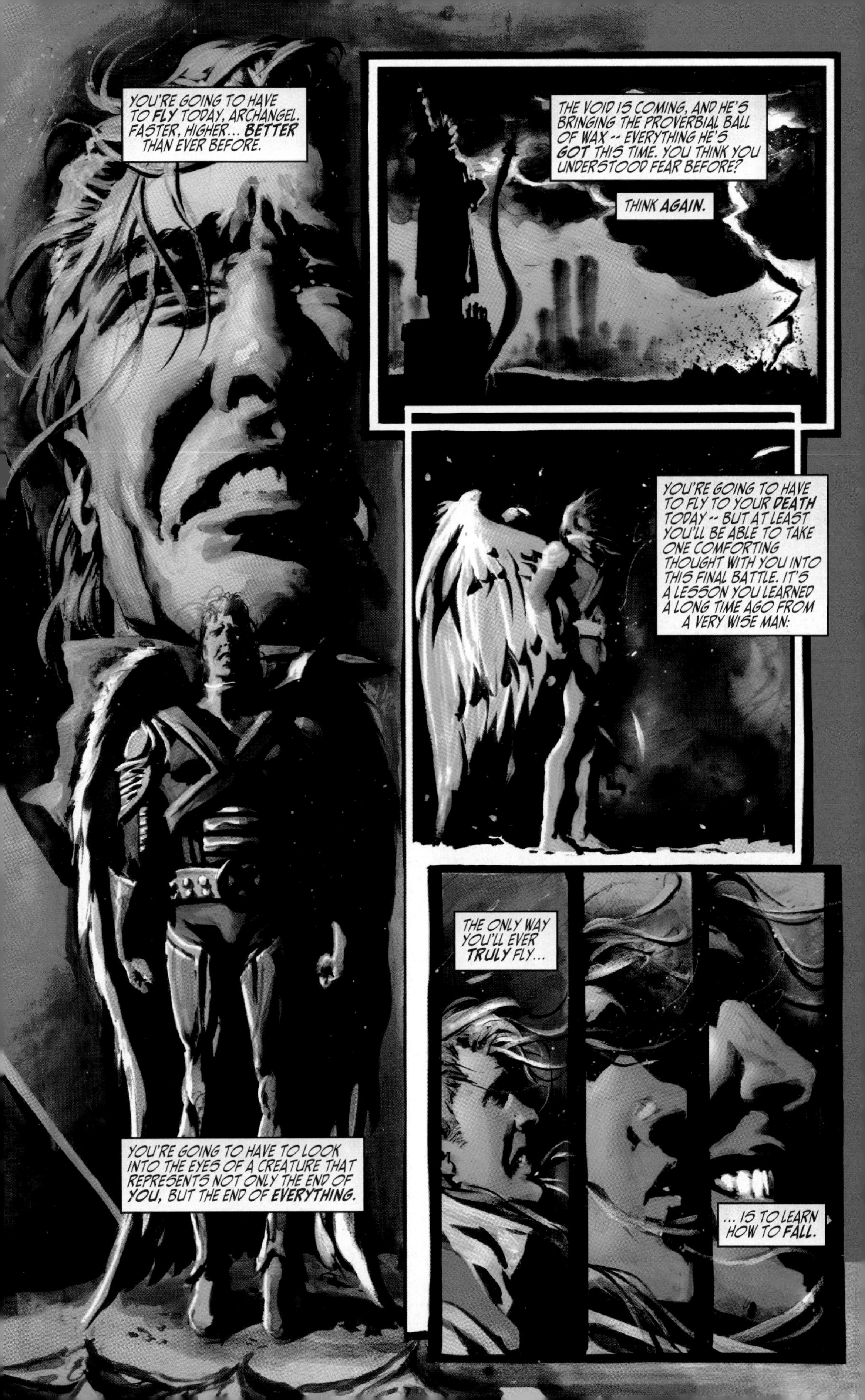
YOU'RE GOING TO HAVE TO FLY TODAY, ARCHANGEL. FASTER, HIGHER... BETTER THAN EVER BEFORE.
THE VOID IS COMING, AND HE'S BRINGING THE PROVERBIAL BALL OF WAX -- EVERYTHING HE'S GOT THIS TIME. YOU THINK YOU UNDERSTOOD FEAR BEFORE?
THINK AGAIN.
YOU'RE GOING TO HAVE TO FLY TO YOUR DEATH TODAY -- BUT AT LEAST YOU'LL BE ABLE TO TAKE ONE COMFORTING THOUGHT WITH YOU INTO THIS FINAL BATTLE. IT'S A LESSON YOU LEARNED A LONG TIME AGO FROM A VERY WISE MAN:
YOU'RE GOING TO HAVE TO LOOK INTO THE EYES OF A CREATURE THAT REPRESENTS NOT ONLY THE END OF YOU, BUT THE END OF EVERYTHING.
THE ONLY WAY YOU'LL EVER TRULY FLY...
...IS TO LEARN HOW TO FALL.

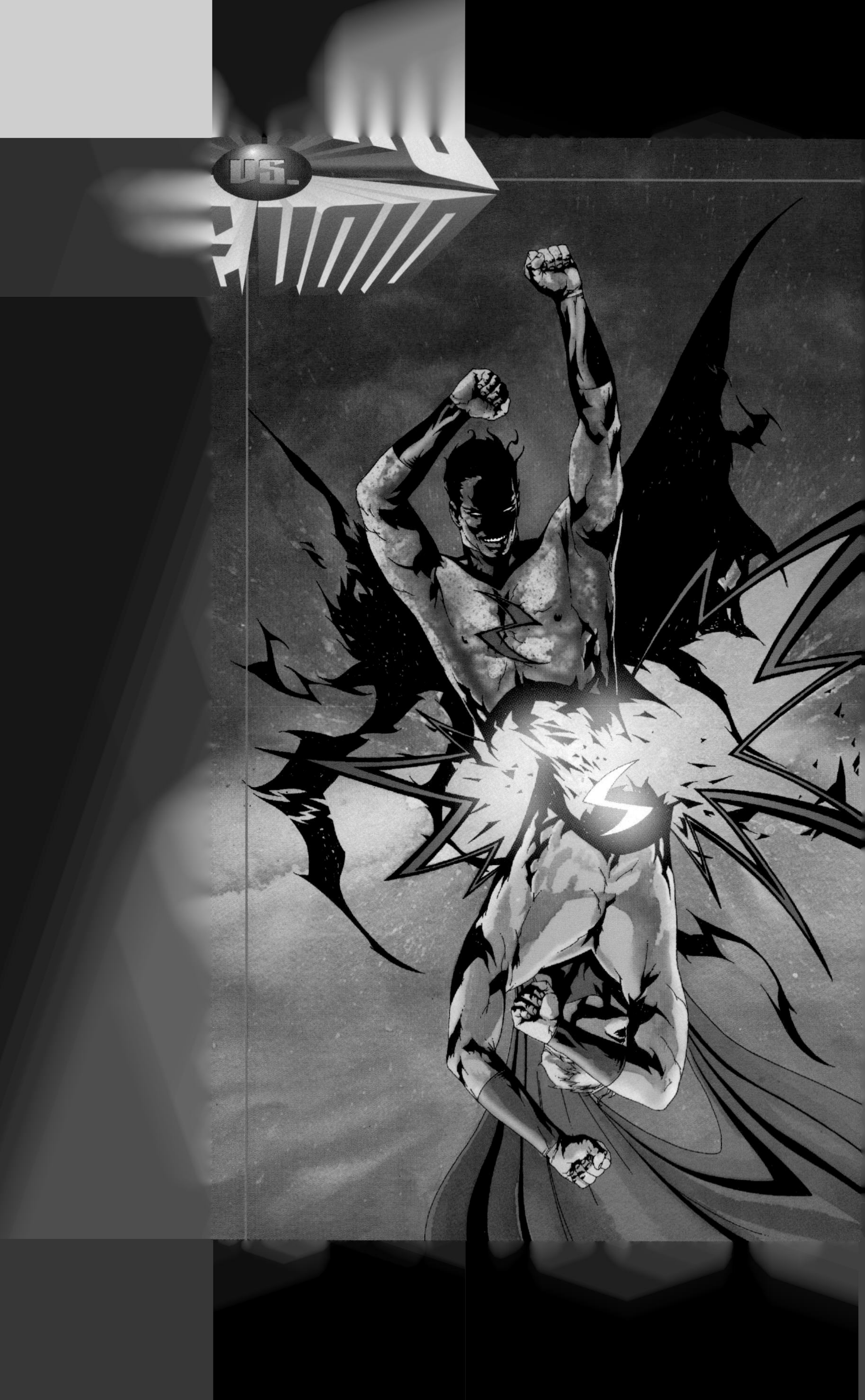
VS.

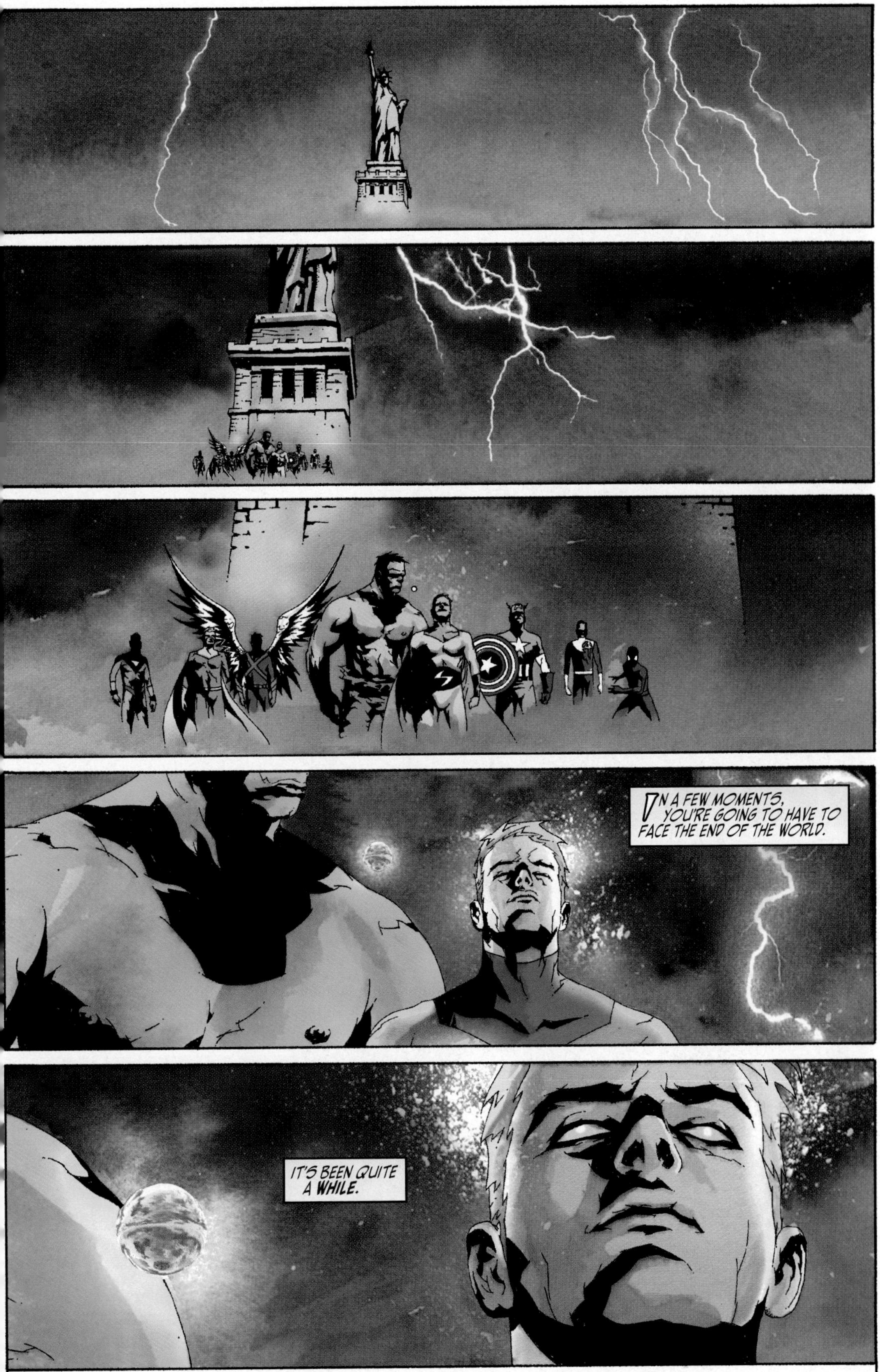
IN A FEW MOMENTS, YOU'RE GOING TO HAVE TO FACE THE END OF THE WORLD.
IT'S BEEN QUITE A WHILE.

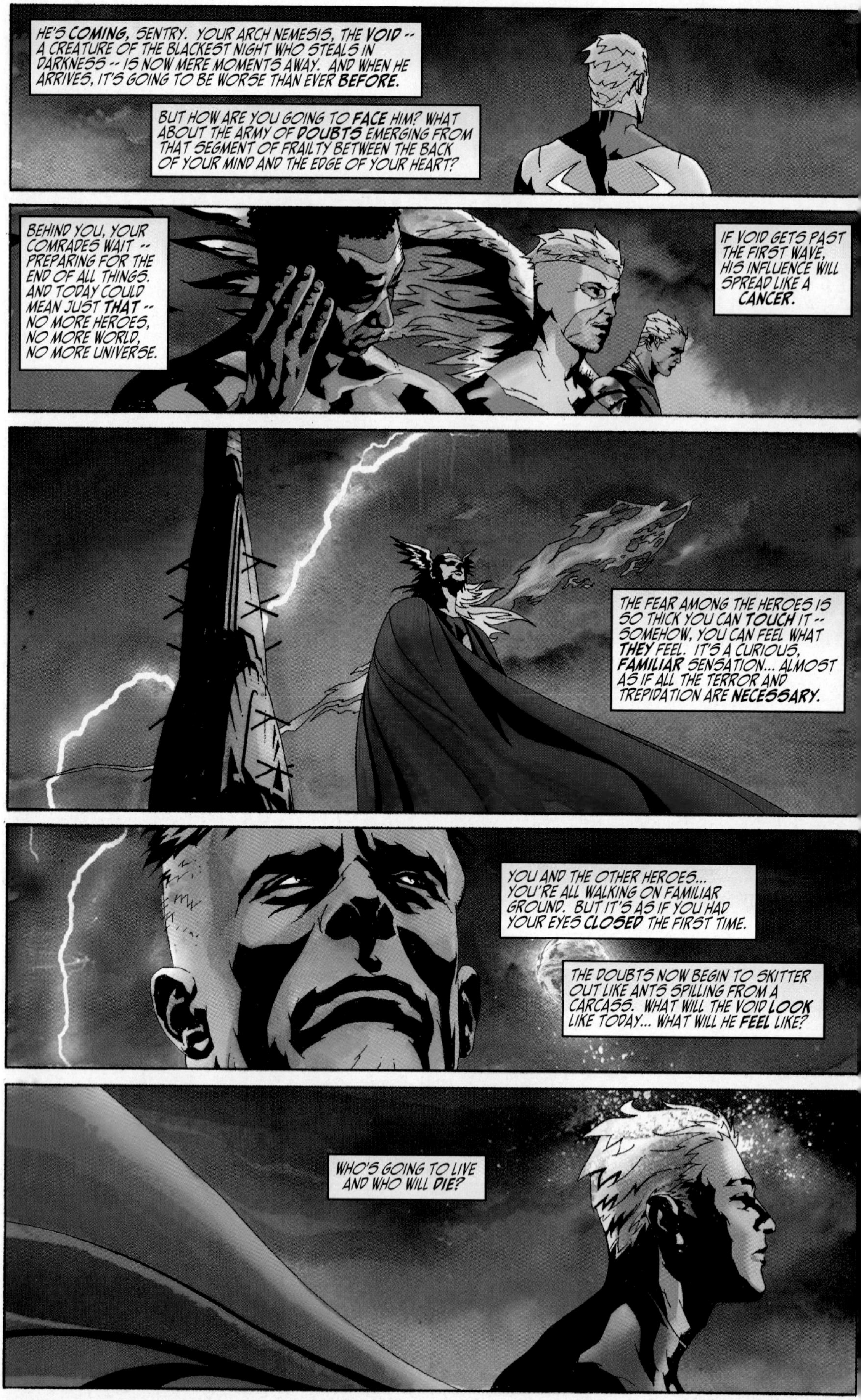
HE'S COMING, SENTRY. YOUR ARCH NEMESIS, THE VOID -- A CREATURE OF THE BLACKEST NIGHT WHO STEALS IN DARKNESS -- IS NOW MERE MOMENTS AWAY. AND WHEN HE ARRIVES, IT'S GOING TO BE WORSE THAN EVER BEFORE.
BUT HOW ARE YOU GOING TO FACE HIM? WHAT ABOUT THE ARMY OF DOUBTS EMERGING FROM THAT SEGMENT OF FRAILTY BETWEEN THE BACK OF YOUR MIND AND THE EDGE OF YOUR HEART?
BEHIND YOU, YOUR COMRADES WAIT -- PREPARING FOR THE END OF ALL THINGS. AND TODAY COULD MEAN JUST THAT -- NO MORE HEROES, NO MORE WORLD, NO MORE UNIVERSE.
IF VOID GETS PAST THE FIRST WAVE, HIS INFLUENCE WILL SPREAD LIKE A CANCER.
THE FEAR AMONG THE HEROES IS SO THICK YOU CAN TOUCH IT -- SOMEHOW, YOU CAN FEEL WHAT THEY FEEL. IT'S A CURIOUS, FAMILIAR SENSATION... ALMOST AS IF ALL THE TERROR AND TREPIDATION ARE NECESSARY.
YOU AND THE OTHER HEROES... YOU'RE ALL WALKING ON FAMILIAR GROUND. BUT IT'S AS IF YOU HAD YOUR EYES CLOSED THE FIRST TIME.
THE DOUBTS NOW BEGIN TO SKITTER OUT LIKE ANTS SPILLING FROM A CARCASS. WHAT WILL THE VOID LOOK LIKE TODAY... WHAT WILL HE FEEL LIKE?
WHO'S GOING TO LIVE AND WHO WILL DIE?

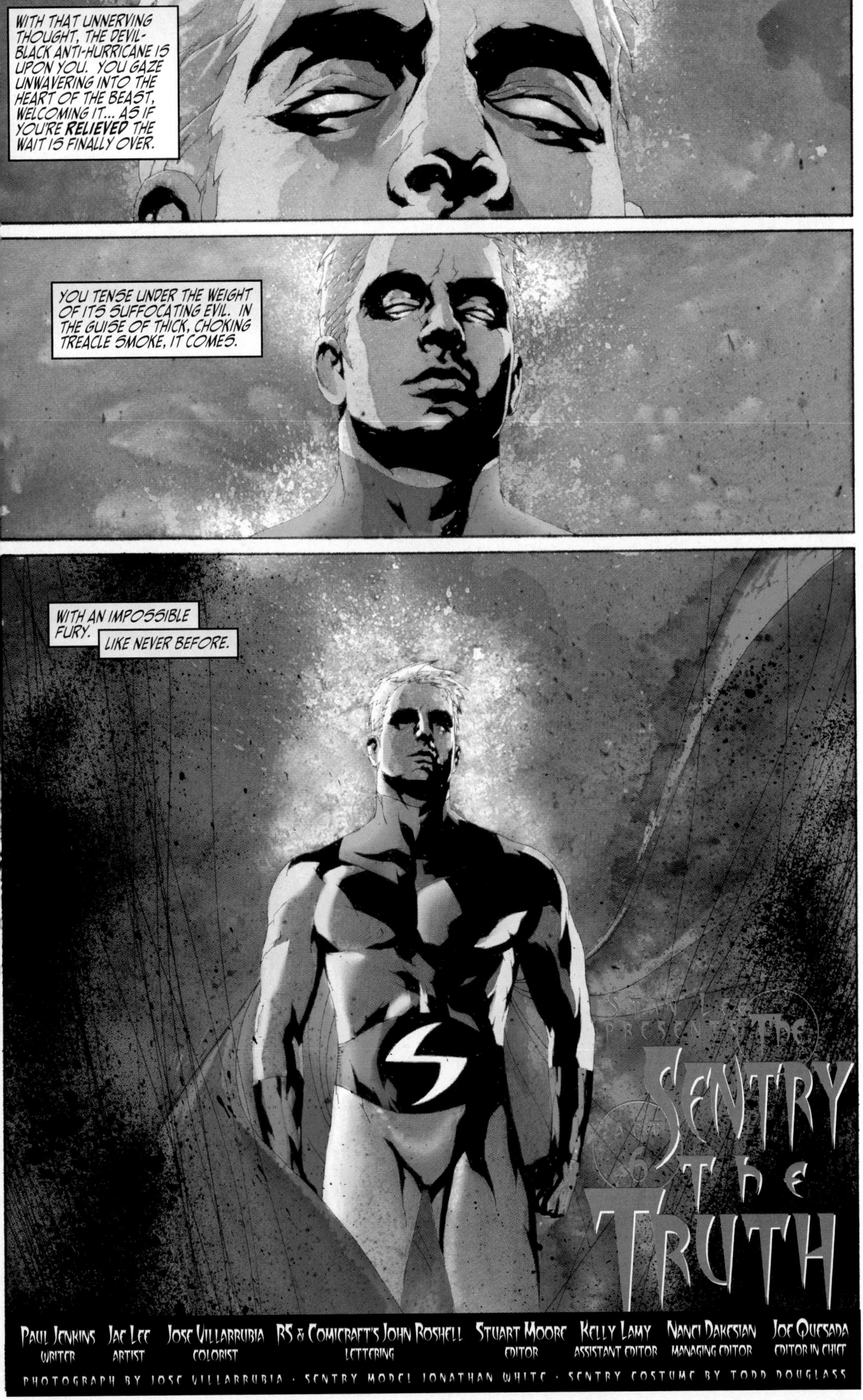
WITH THAT UNNERVING THOUGHT, THE DEVIL-BLACK ANTI-HURRICANE IS UPON YOU. YOU GAZE UNWAVERING INTO THE HEART OF THE BEAST, WELCOMING IT... AS IF YOU'RE **RELIEVED** THE WAIT IS FINALLY OVER.
YOU TENSE UNDER THE WEIGHT OF ITS SUFFOCATING EVIL. IN THE GUISE OF THICK, CHOKING TREACLE SMOKE, IT COMES.
WITH AN IMPOSSIBLE FURY.
LIKE NEVER BEFORE.
STAN LEE PRESENTS THE
SENTRY
6
THE
TRUTH
PAUL JENKINS WRITER
JAE LEE ARTIST
JOSE VILLARRUBIA COLORIST
RS & COMICRAFT'S JOHN ROSHELL LETTERING
STUART MOORE EDITOR
KELLY LAMY ASSISTANT EDITOR
NANCI DAKESIAN MANAGING EDITOR
JOE QUESADA EDITOR IN CHIEF
PHOTOGRAPH BY JOSE VILLARRUBIA · SENTRY MODEL JONATHAN WHITE · SENTRY COSTUME BY TODD DOUGLASS

IN THOSE FIRST FEW **AWFUL** MOMENTS, THE MEMORIES FLOOD BACK TO YOU. OH GOD, YOU THINK... IF ONLY YOU'D BEEN ABLE TO **WARN** THEM.

HOW THE VOID WILL ATTACK WITH ONE INFINITENDRIL CLOSE ENOUGH TO TOUCH YOU, AND YOU'LL PARRY THE BLOW, AND WHILE YOU'RE NOT LOOKING HE'LL REACH BEYOND YOU AND STRIKE AGAIN. AND AGAIN.

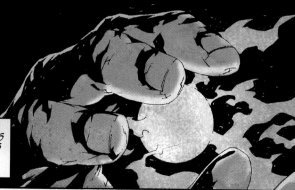

IMMEDIATELY, VOID GOES TO WORK ON THE **HULK**... YOU SUSPECTED HE MIGHT ALL ALONG, BUT THERE WAS NO WAY YOU COULD HAVE FOREWARNED THE POOR BRUTE.

THE BALL OF ENERGY YOU'VE FASHIONED IS ENOUGH TO KEEP HULK ALIVE -- **BARELY.** IT CONTAINS A MEASURE OF YOUR GOLDEN ESSENCE... ENOUGH TO DIVERT VOID'S ATTENTION AS HE REACHES INTO THE WRETCHED CREATURE'S SOUL AND **TWISTS** IT... LIKE WET CLAY IS TWISTED IN THE HANDS OF A CHILD.

BACK WHEN YOU WERE A KID, YOUR DAD DROVE OVER A RACCOON. YOU GOT OUT OF THE CAR TO MAKE SURE IT WAS DEAD, BUT IT **WASN'T**... IT JUST LAY THERE, CRYING, ITS GUTS SPREAD OUT BEHIND IT OUT LIKE A PLATE OF SPAGHETTI. AND YOU DIDN'T HAVE THE HEART TO PUT IT OUT OF ITS MISERY.

ON LIBERTY ISLAND, AMIDST ALL THE CHAOS AND FLYING DEBRIS, THE SPIDER-MAN STANDS FAST AGAINST THE DRIVING RAIN. EVEN WITH ALL HIS STRENGTH AND AGILITY, IT'S ENOUGH FOR NOW TO SIMPLY DODGE THE VOID'S INFINITENDRILS AS THEY TOUCH DOWN ALL AROUND.

IN THE CONFUSION, THE WEBSPINNER NOTICES HIS SPIDER SENSES GOING OFF TEN TO THE DOZEN. TURNING IN SURPRISE, HE REALIZES THE MAN FIGHTING ALONGSIDE HIM IS NONE OTHER THAN THE CRIMINAL KNOWN AS DOCTOR OCTOPUS.

THE TWO MEN HAVE FACED EACH OTHER MANY TIMES BEFORE, BUT NEVER UNDER THESE CIRCUMSTANCES. "GLAD YOU COULD MAKE THE PARTY," JOKES SPIDER-MAN, TRYING TO MASK HIS FEAR.

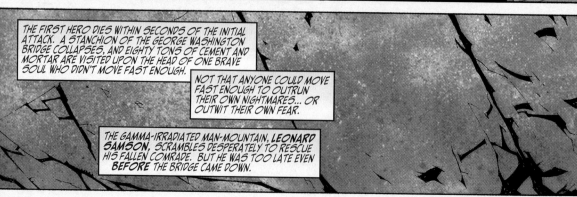

THE FIRST HERO DIES WITHIN SECONDS OF THE INITIAL ATTACK. A STANCHION OF THE GEORGE WASHINGTON BRIDGE COLLAPSES, AND EIGHTY TONS OF CEMENT AND MORTAR ARE VISITED UPON THE HEAD OF ONE BRAVE SOUL WHO DIDN'T MOVE FAST ENOUGH.

NOT THAT ANYONE COULD MOVE FAST ENOUGH TO OUTRUN THEIR OWN NIGHTMARES... OR OUTWIT THEIR OWN FEAR.

THE GAMMA-IRRADIATED MAN-MOUNTAIN, **LEONARD SAMSON,** SCRAMBLES DESPERATELY TO RESCUE HIS FALLEN COMRADE. BUT HE WAS TOO LATE EVEN **BEFORE** THE BRIDGE CAME DOWN.

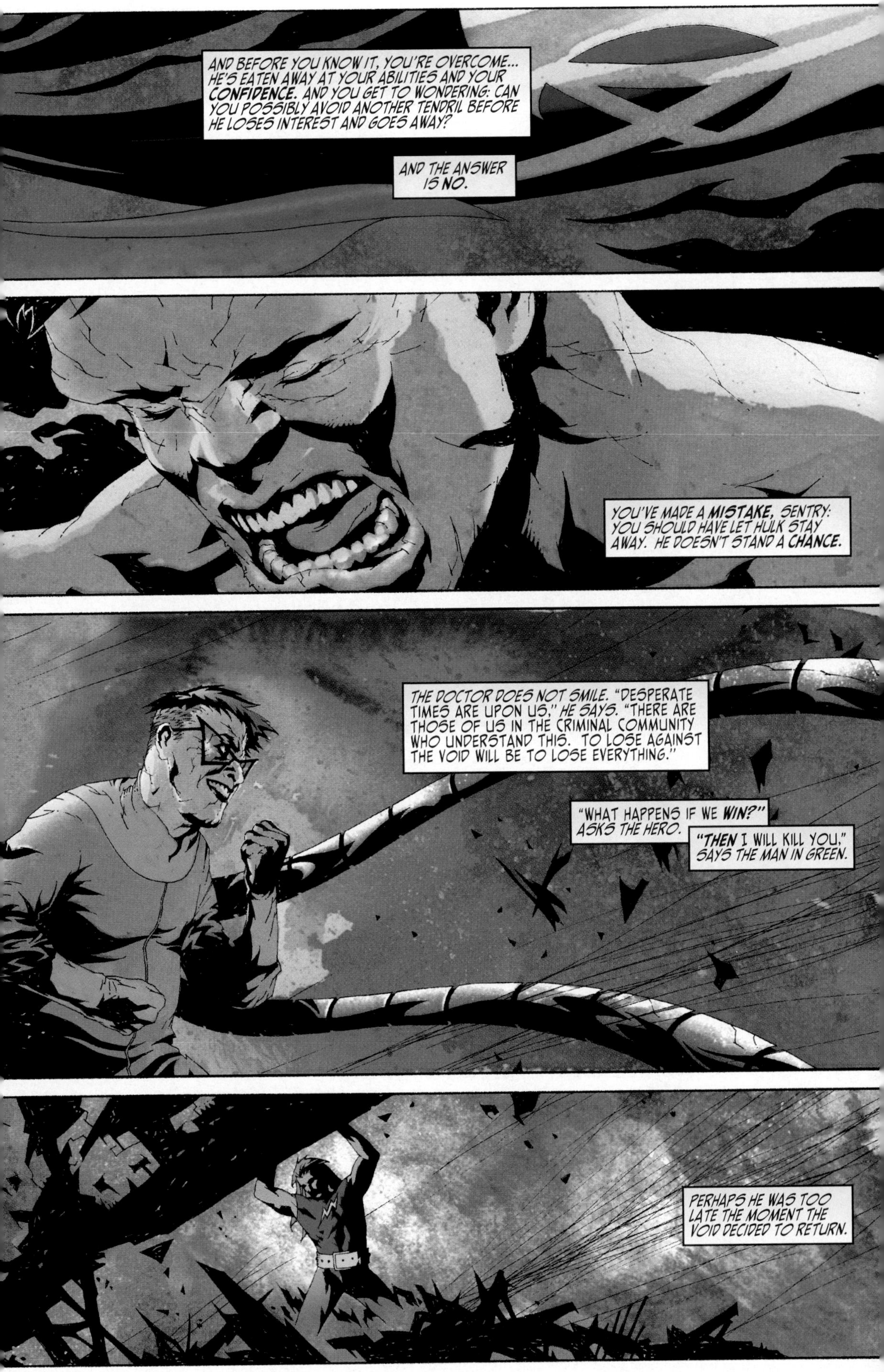
AND BEFORE YOU KNOW IT, YOU'RE OVERCOME... HE'S EATEN AWAY AT YOUR ABILITIES AND YOUR CONFIDENCE. AND YOU GET TO WONDERING: CAN YOU POSSIBLY AVOID ANOTHER TENDRIL BEFORE HE LOSES INTEREST AND GOES AWAY?
AND THE ANSWER IS NO.
YOU'VE MADE A MISTAKE, SENTRY: YOU SHOULD HAVE LET HULK STAY AWAY. HE DOESN'T STAND A CHANCE.
THE DOCTOR DOES NOT SMILE. "DESPERATE TIMES ARE UPON US," HE SAYS. "THERE ARE THOSE OF US IN THE CRIMINAL COMMUNITY WHO UNDERSTAND THIS. TO LOSE AGAINST THE VOID WILL BE TO LOSE EVERYTHING."
"WHAT HAPPENS IF WE WIN?" ASKS THE HERO.
"THEN I WILL KILL YOU," SAYS THE MAN IN GREEN.
PERHAPS HE WAS TOO LATE THE MOMENT THE VOID DECIDED TO RETURN.

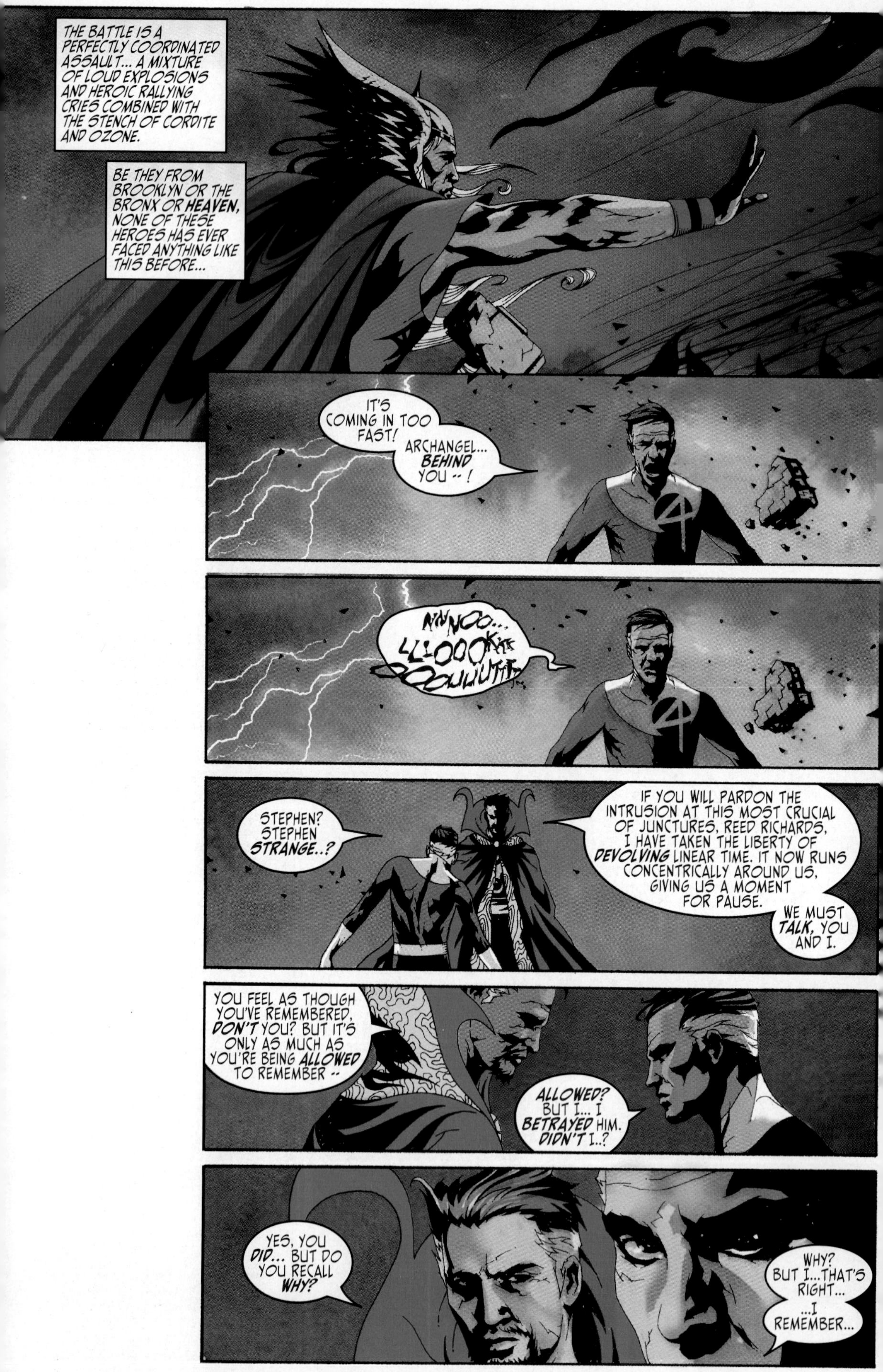

THE BATTLE IS A PERFECTLY COORDINATED ASSAULT... A MIXTURE OF LOUD EXPLOSIONS AND HEROIC RALLYING CRIES COMBINED WITH THE STENCH OF CORDITE AND OZONE.
BE THEY FROM BROOKLYN OR THE BRONX OR HEAVEN, NONE OF THESE HEROES HAS EVER FACED ANYTHING LIKE THIS BEFORE...
IT'S COMING IN TOO FAST!
ARCHANGEL... BEHIND YOU -- !
NNNOO... LLOOOK OOOUUUTT
STEPHEN? STEPHEN STRANGE..?
IF YOU WILL PARDON THE INTRUSION AT THIS MOST CRUCIAL OF JUNCTURES, REED RICHARDS, I HAVE TAKEN THE LIBERTY OF DEVOLVING LINEAR TIME. IT NOW RUNS CONCENTRICALLY AROUND US, GIVING US A MOMENT FOR PAUSE.
WE MUST TALK, YOU AND I.
YOU FEEL AS THOUGH YOU'VE REMEMBERED, DON'T YOU? BUT IT'S ONLY AS MUCH AS YOU'RE BEING ALLOWED TO REMEMBER --
ALLOWED? BUT I... I BETRAYED HIM. DIDN'T I..?
YES, YOU DID... BUT DO YOU RECALL WHY?
WHY? BUT I...THAT'S RIGHT... ...I REMEMBER...

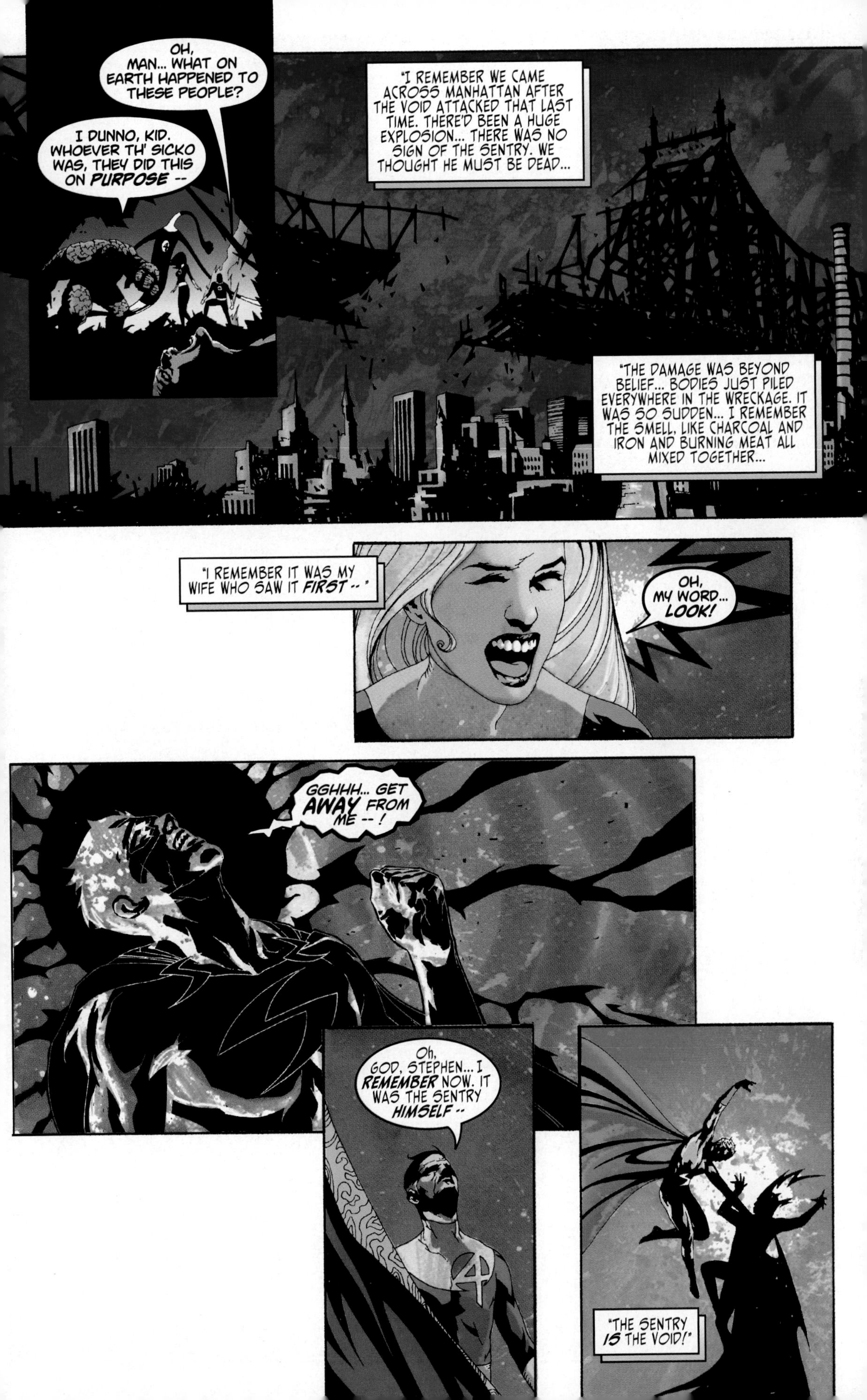
OH, MAN... WHAT ON EARTH HAPPENED TO THESE PEOPLE?
I DUNNO, KID. WHOEVER TH' SICKO WAS, THEY DID THIS ON PURPOSE --
"I REMEMBER WE CAME ACROSS MANHATTAN AFTER THE VOID ATTACKED THAT LAST TIME. THERE'D BEEN A HUGE EXPLOSION... THERE WAS NO SIGN OF THE SENTRY. WE THOUGHT HE MUST BE DEAD...
"THE DAMAGE WAS BEYOND BELIEF... BODIES JUST PILED EVERYWHERE IN THE WRECKAGE. IT WAS SO SUDDEN... I REMEMBER THE SMELL, LIKE CHARCOAL AND IRON AND BURNING MEAT ALL MIXED TOGETHER...
"I REMEMBER IT WAS MY WIFE WHO SAW IT FIRST --"
OH, MY WORD... LOOK!
GGHHH... GET AWAY FROM ME -- !
Oh, GOD, STEPHEN... I REMEMBER NOW. IT WAS THE SENTRY HIMSELF --
"THE SENTRY IS THE VOID!"

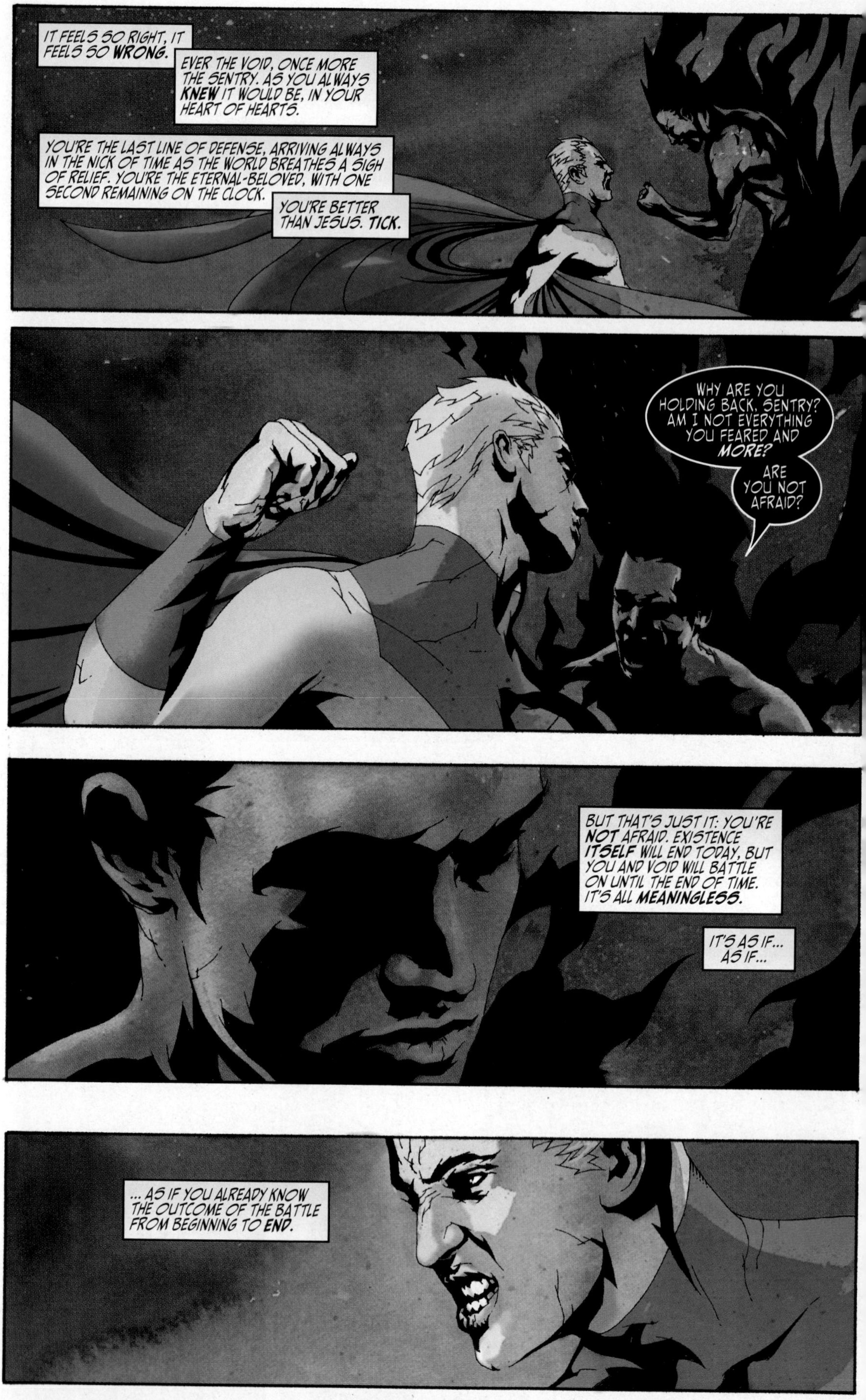
IT FEELS SO RIGHT, IT FEELS SO **WRONG**.
EVER THE VOID, ONCE MORE THE SENTRY. AS YOU ALWAYS **KNEW** IT WOULD BE, IN YOUR HEART OF HEARTS.
YOU'RE THE LAST LINE OF DEFENSE, ARRIVING ALWAYS IN THE NICK OF TIME AS THE WORLD BREATHES A SIGH OF RELIEF. YOU'RE THE ETERNAL-BELOVED, WITH ONE SECOND REMAINING ON THE CLOCK.
YOU'RE BETTER THAN JESUS. **TICK.**
WHY ARE YOU HOLDING BACK, SENTRY? AM I NOT EVERYTHING YOU FEARED AND **MORE?**
ARE YOU NOT AFRAID?
BUT THAT'S JUST IT: YOU'RE **NOT** AFRAID. EXISTENCE **ITSELF** WILL END TODAY, BUT YOU AND VOID WILL BATTLE ON UNTIL THE END OF TIME. IT'S ALL **MEANINGLESS.**
IT'S AS IF... AS IF...
...AS IF YOU ALREADY KNOW THE OUTCOME OF THE BATTLE FROM BEGINNING TO **END**.

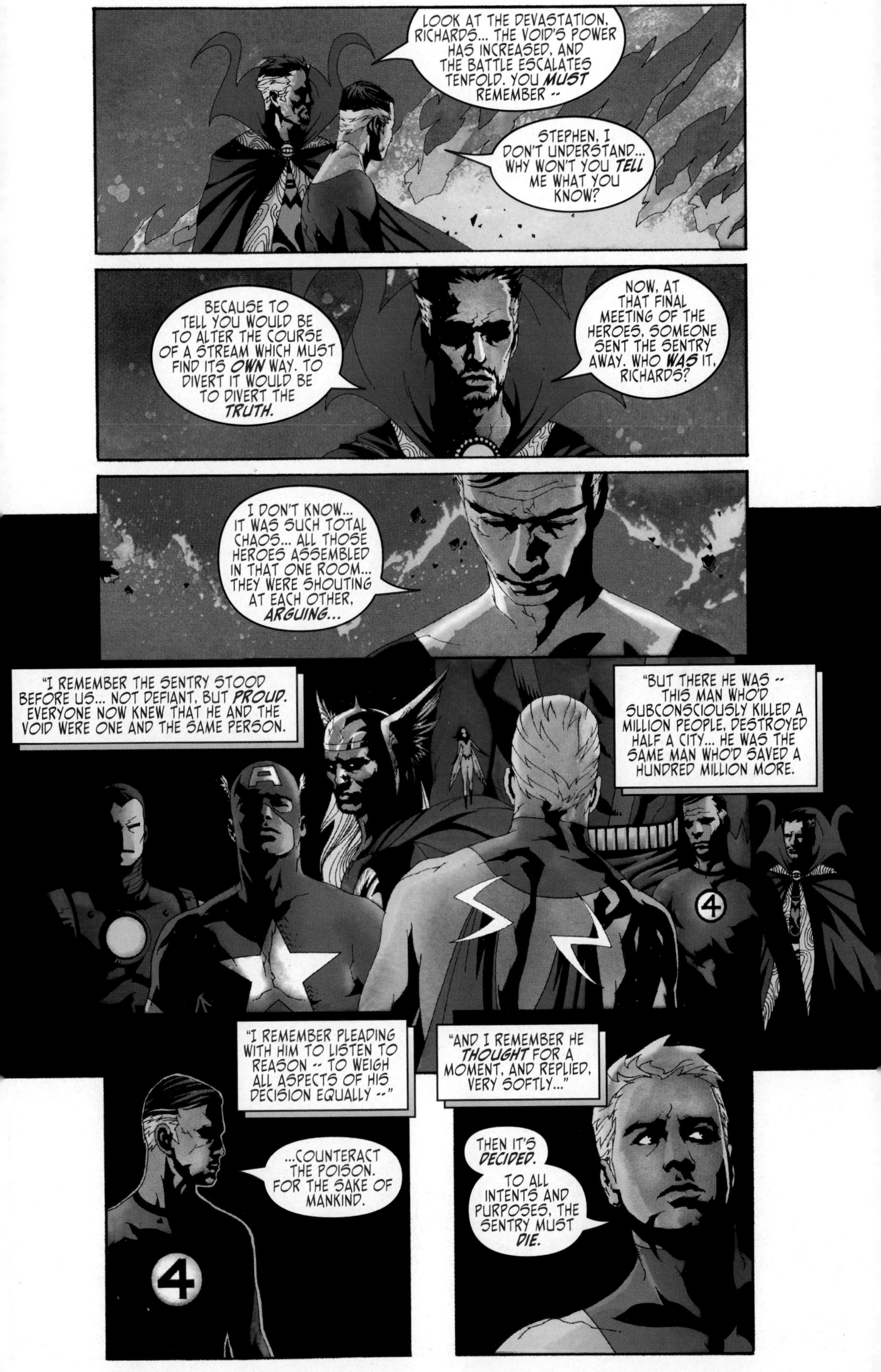

LOOK AT THE DEVASTATION, RICHARDS... THE VOID'S POWER HAS INCREASED, AND THE BATTLE ESCALATES TENFOLD. YOU ***MUST*** REMEMBER --
STEPHEN, I DON'T UNDERSTAND... WHY WON'T YOU ***TELL*** ME WHAT YOU KNOW?
BECAUSE TO TELL YOU WOULD BE TO ALTER THE COURSE OF A STREAM WHICH MUST FIND ITS ***OWN*** WAY. TO DIVERT IT WOULD BE TO DIVERT THE ***TRUTH.***
NOW, AT THAT FINAL MEETING OF THE HEROES, SOMEONE SENT THE SENTRY AWAY. WHO ***WAS*** IT, RICHARDS?
I DON'T KNOW... IT WAS SUCH TOTAL CHAOS... ALL THOSE HEROES ASSEMBLED IN THAT ONE ROOM... THEY WERE SHOUTING AT EACH OTHER, ***ARGUING...***
"I REMEMBER THE SENTRY STOOD BEFORE US... NOT DEFIANT, BUT ***PROUD.*** EVERYONE NOW KNEW THAT HE AND THE VOID WERE ONE AND THE SAME PERSON.
"BUT THERE HE WAS -- THIS MAN WHO'D SUBCONSCIOUSLY KILLED A MILLION PEOPLE, DESTROYED HALF A CITY... HE WAS THE SAME MAN WHO'D SAVED A HUNDRED MILLION MORE.
"I REMEMBER PLEADING WITH HIM TO LISTEN TO REASON -- TO WEIGH ALL ASPECTS OF HIS DECISION EQUALLY --"
...COUNTERACT THE POISON. FOR THE SAKE OF MANKIND.
"AND I REMEMBER HE ***THOUGHT*** FOR A MOMENT, AND REPLIED, VERY SOFTLY..."
THEN IT'S ***DECIDED.***
TO ALL INTENTS AND PURPOSES, THE SENTRY MUST ***DIE.***

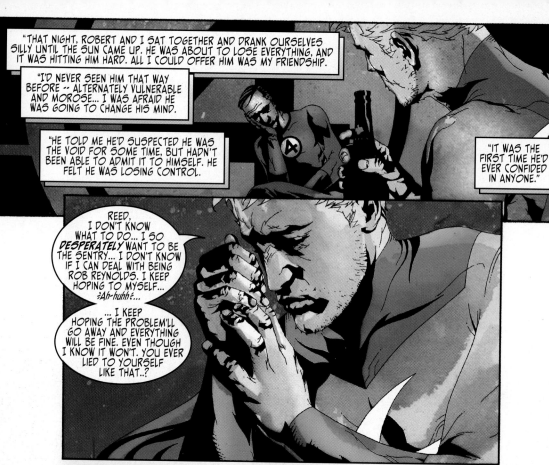

"THAT NIGHT, ROBERT AND I SAT TOGETHER AND DRANK OURSELVES SILLY UNTIL THE SUN CAME UP. HE WAS ABOUT TO LOSE EVERYTHING, AND IT WAS HITTING HIM HARD. ALL I COULD OFFER HIM WAS MY FRIENDSHIP.

"I'D NEVER SEEN HIM THAT WAY BEFORE -- ALTERNATELY VULNERABLE AND MOROSE... I WAS AFRAID HE WAS GOING TO CHANGE HIS MIND.

"HE TOLD ME HE'D SUSPECTED HE WAS THE VOID FOR SOME TIME, BUT HADN'T BEEN ABLE TO ADMIT IT TO HIMSELF. HE FELT HE WAS LOSING CONTROL.

"IT WAS THE FIRST TIME HE'D EVER CONFIDED IN ANYONE."

REED, I DON'T KNOW WHAT TO DO... I SO *DESPERATELY* WANT TO BE THE SENTRY... I DON'T KNOW IF I CAN DEAL WITH BEING ROB REYNOLDS. I KEEP HOPING TO MYSELF... ≠Ah-huhh≠...

... I KEEP HOPING THE PROBLEM'LL GO AWAY AND EVERYTHING WILL BE FINE. EVEN THOUGH I KNOW IT WON'T. YOU EVER LIED TO YOURSELF LIKE THAT..?

WE ALL DO TO SOME EXTENT, ROBERT. LISTEN, DON'T GIVE UP HOPE, OKAY? I THINK I HAVE AN IDEA --

"WE NEEDED TO FIND A WAY FOR EVERYONE TO FORGET THE SENTRY, I SAID... INCLUDING ROBERT HIMSELF. I BEGAN TO JABBER ON ABOUT HYPNOTIC TRANSMITTERS AND POWER SOURCES... I WAS TRYING TO MAKE MYSELF FEEL BETTER AS MUCH AS HIM.

"AND THERE HE SAT, LISTENING PATIENTLY -- MY BEST FRIEND IN ALL THE WORLD -- STRUGGLING TO CONTAIN THE EFFECTS OF THE VOID, TRAPPED BY HIS OWN MORTALITY.

"IT WAS THE FIRST TIME HE'D EVER COME TO TERMS WITH HIS *ADDICTION* -- "

IT'S A GOOD PLAN, REED... BUT IF WE'RE GOING TO MAKE PEOPLE FORGET, YOU'RE GOING TO HAVE TO *BURY* ME FIRST.

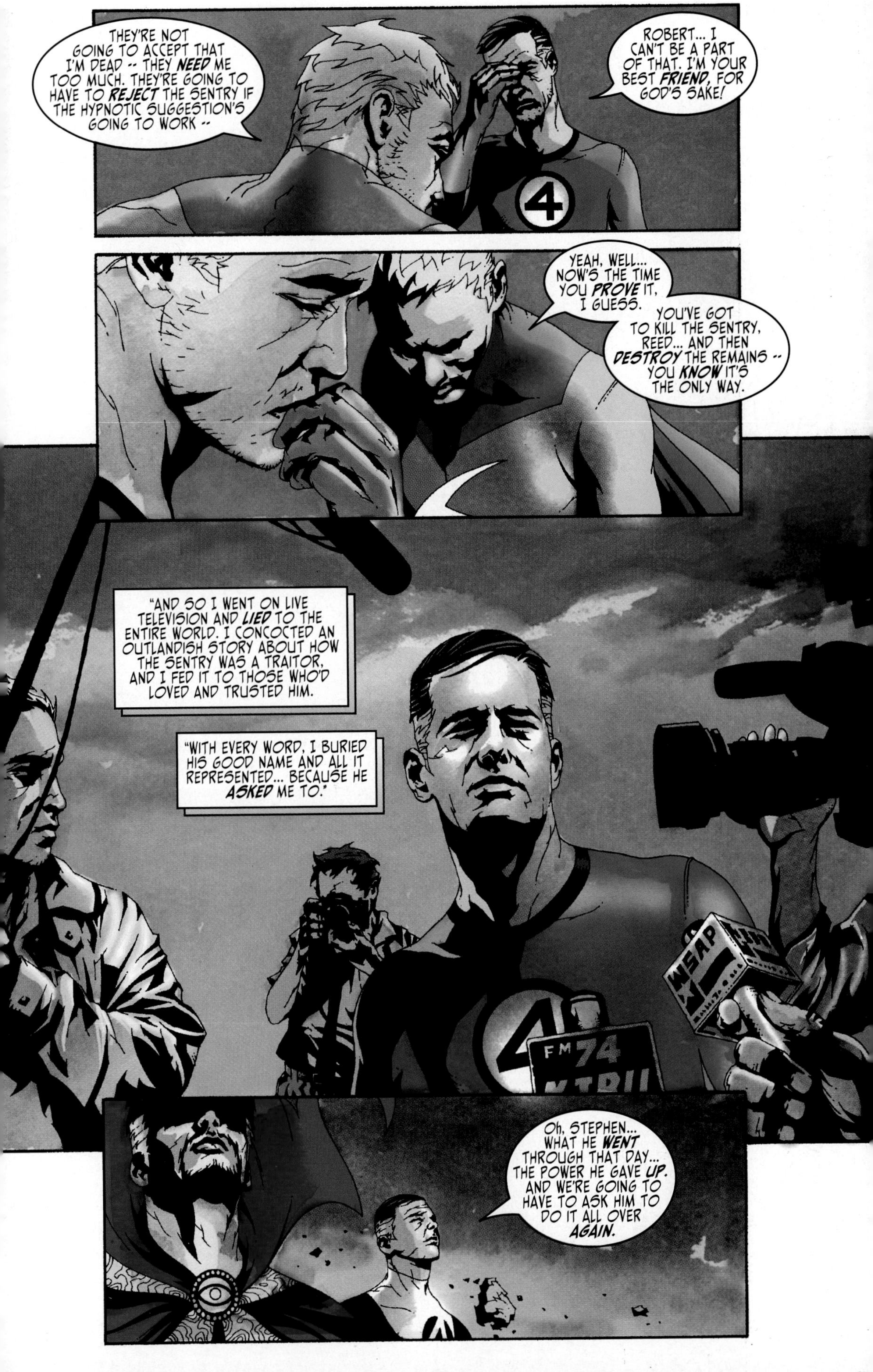
THEY'RE NOT GOING TO ACCEPT THAT I'M DEAD -- THEY NEED ME TOO MUCH. THEY'RE GOING TO HAVE TO REJECT THE SENTRY IF THE HYPNOTIC SUGGESTION'S GOING TO WORK --
ROBERT... I CAN'T BE A PART OF THAT. I'M YOUR BEST FRIEND, FOR GOD'S SAKE!
4
YEAH, WELL... NOW'S THE TIME YOU PROVE IT, I GUESS.
YOU'VE GOT TO KILL THE SENTRY, REED... AND THEN DESTROY THE REMAINS -- YOU KNOW IT'S THE ONLY WAY.
"AND SO I WENT ON LIVE TELEVISION AND LIED TO THE ENTIRE WORLD. I CONCOCTED AN OUTLANDISH STORY ABOUT HOW THE SENTRY WAS A TRAITOR, AND I FED IT TO THOSE WHO'D LOVED AND TRUSTED HIM.
"WITH EVERY WORD, I BURIED HIS GOOD NAME AND ALL IT REPRESENTED... BECAUSE HE ASKED ME TO."
WSAP
FM 74
Oh, STEPHEN... WHAT HE WENT THROUGH THAT DAY... THE POWER HE GAVE UP. AND WE'RE GOING TO HAVE TO ASK HIM TO DO IT ALL OVER AGAIN.

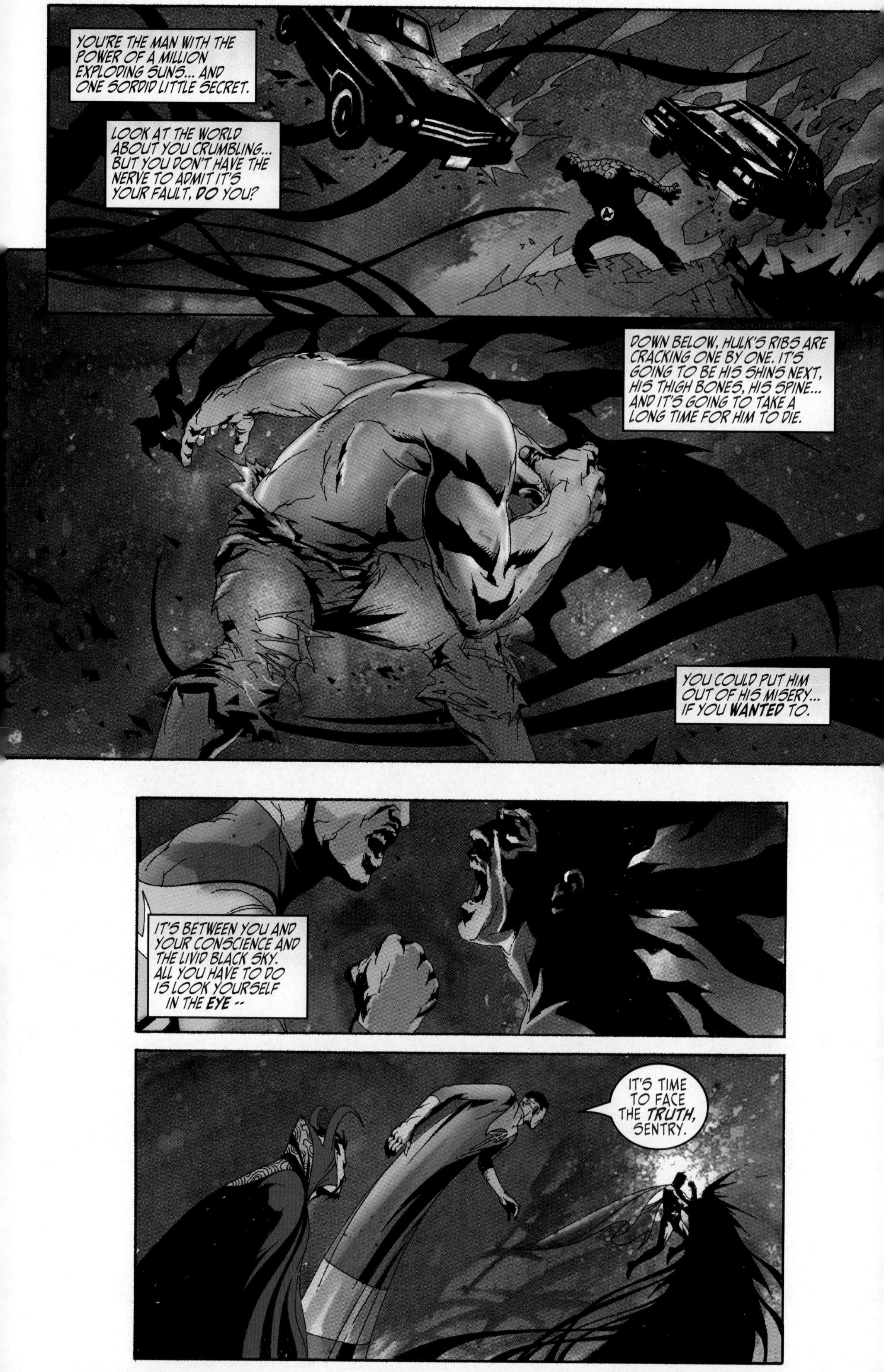
YOU'RE THE MAN WITH THE POWER OF A MILLION EXPLODING SUNS... AND ONE SORDID LITTLE SECRET.
LOOK AT THE WORLD ABOUT YOU CRUMBLING... BUT YOU DON'T HAVE THE NERVE TO ADMIT IT'S YOUR FAULT, DO YOU?
DOWN BELOW, HULK'S RIBS ARE CRACKING ONE BY ONE. IT'S GOING TO BE HIS SHINS NEXT, HIS THIGH BONES, HIS SPINE... AND IT'S GOING TO TAKE A LONG TIME FOR HIM TO DIE.
YOU COULD PUT HIM OUT OF HIS MISERY... IF YOU WANTED TO.
IT'S BETWEEN YOU AND YOUR CONSCIENCE AND THE LIVID BLACK SKY. ALL YOU HAVE TO DO IS LOOK YOURSELF IN THE EYE --
IT'S TIME TO FACE THE TRUTH, SENTRY.

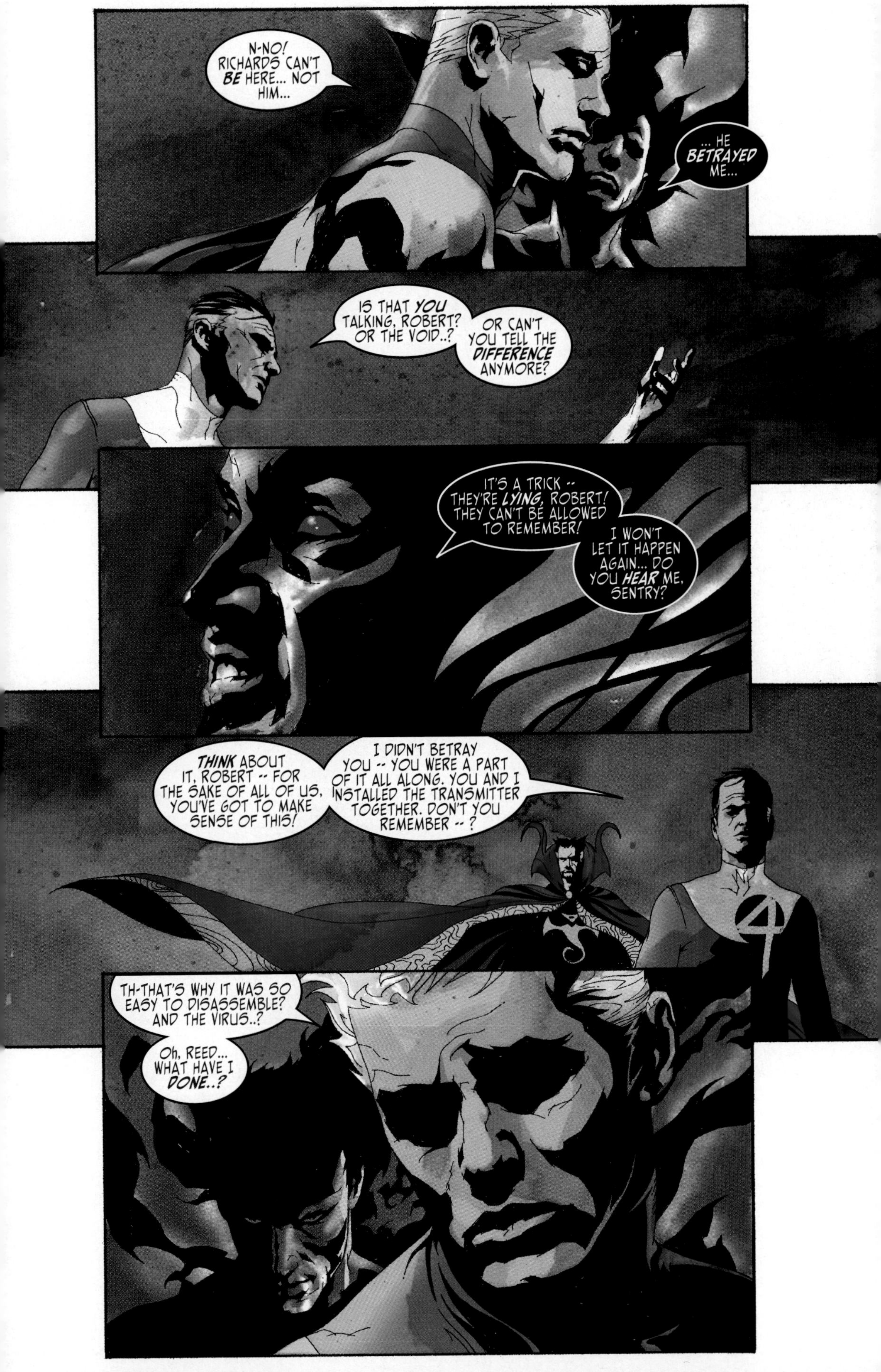
N-NO! RICHARDS CAN'T BE HERE... NOT HIM...
... HE BETRAYED ME...
IS THAT YOU TALKING, ROBERT? OR THE VOID..?
OR CAN'T YOU TELL THE DIFFERENCE ANYMORE?
IT'S A TRICK -- THEY'RE LYING, ROBERT! THEY CAN'T BE ALLOWED TO REMEMBER!
I WON'T LET IT HAPPEN AGAIN... DO YOU HEAR ME, SENTRY?
THINK ABOUT IT, ROBERT -- FOR THE SAKE OF ALL OF US, YOU'VE GOT TO MAKE SENSE OF THIS!
I DIDN'T BETRAY YOU -- YOU WERE A PART OF IT ALL ALONG. YOU AND I INSTALLED THE TRANSMITTER TOGETHER. DON'T YOU REMEMBER --?
TH-THAT'S WHY IT WAS SO EASY TO DISASSEMBLE? AND THE VIRUS..?
Oh, REED... WHAT HAVE I DONE..?

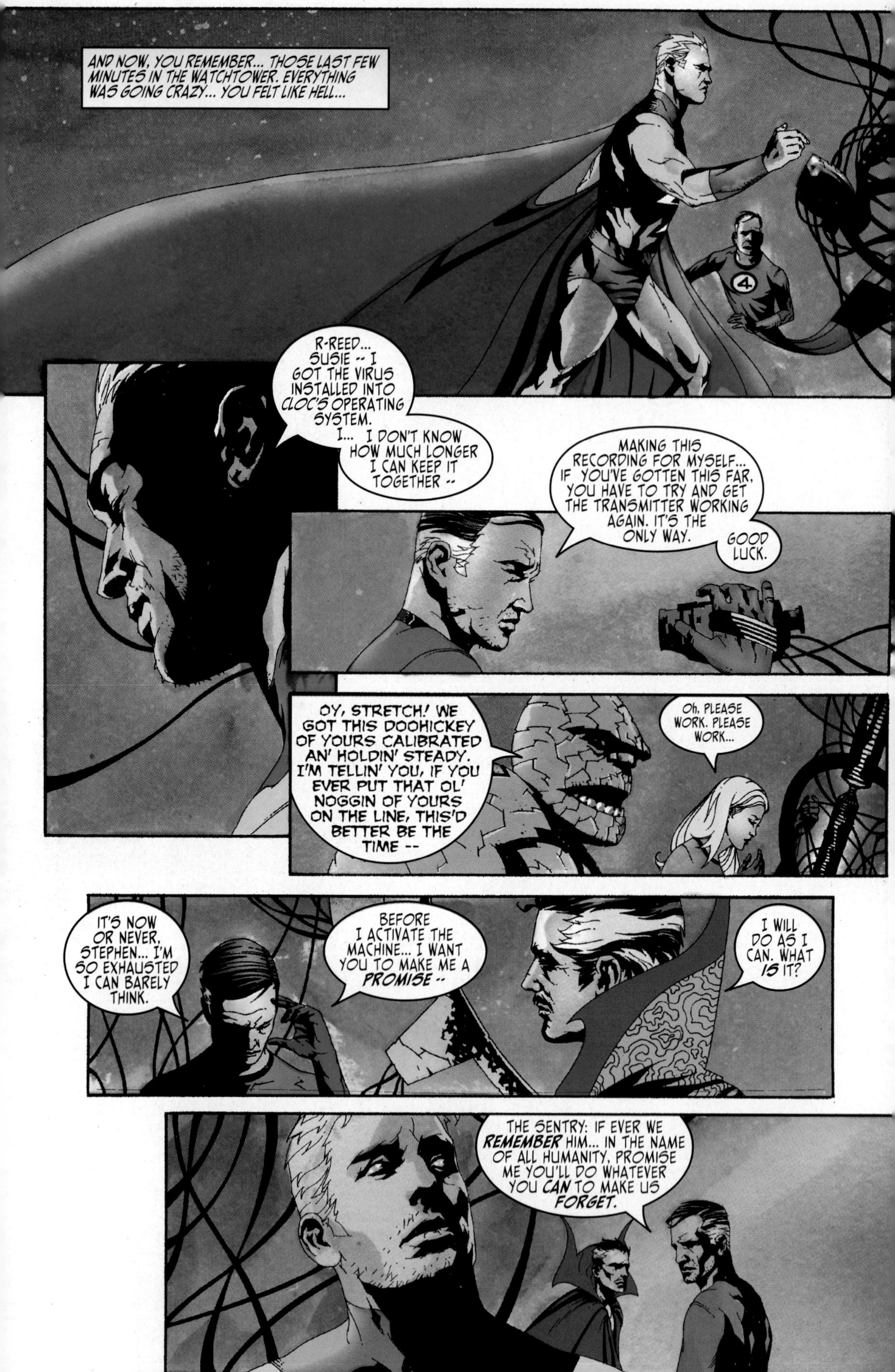
AND NOW, YOU REMEMBER... THOSE LAST FEW MINUTES IN THE WATCHTOWER. EVERYTHING WAS GOING CRAZY... YOU FELT LIKE HELL...
R-REED... SUSIE -- I GOT THE VIRUS INSTALLED INTO CLOC'S OPERATING SYSTEM.
I... I DON'T KNOW HOW MUCH LONGER I CAN KEEP IT TOGETHER --
MAKING THIS RECORDING FOR MYSELF... IF YOU'VE GOTTEN THIS FAR, YOU HAVE TO TRY AND GET THE TRANSMITTER WORKING AGAIN. IT'S THE ONLY WAY.
GOOD LUCK.
OY, STRETCH! WE GOT THIS DOOHICKEY OF YOURS CALIBRATED AN' HOLDIN' STEADY. I'M TELLIN' YOU, IF YOU EVER PUT THAT OL' NOGGIN OF YOURS ON THE LINE, THIS'D BETTER BE THE TIME --
Oh, PLEASE WORK. PLEASE WORK...
IT'S NOW OR NEVER, STEPHEN... I'M SO EXHAUSTED I CAN BARELY THINK.
BEFORE I ACTIVATE THE MACHINE... I WANT YOU TO MAKE ME A PROMISE --
I WILL DO AS I CAN. WHAT IS IT?
THE SENTRY: IF EVER WE REMEMBER HIM... IN THE NAME OF ALL HUMANITY, PROMISE ME YOU'LL DO WHATEVER YOU CAN TO MAKE US FORGET.

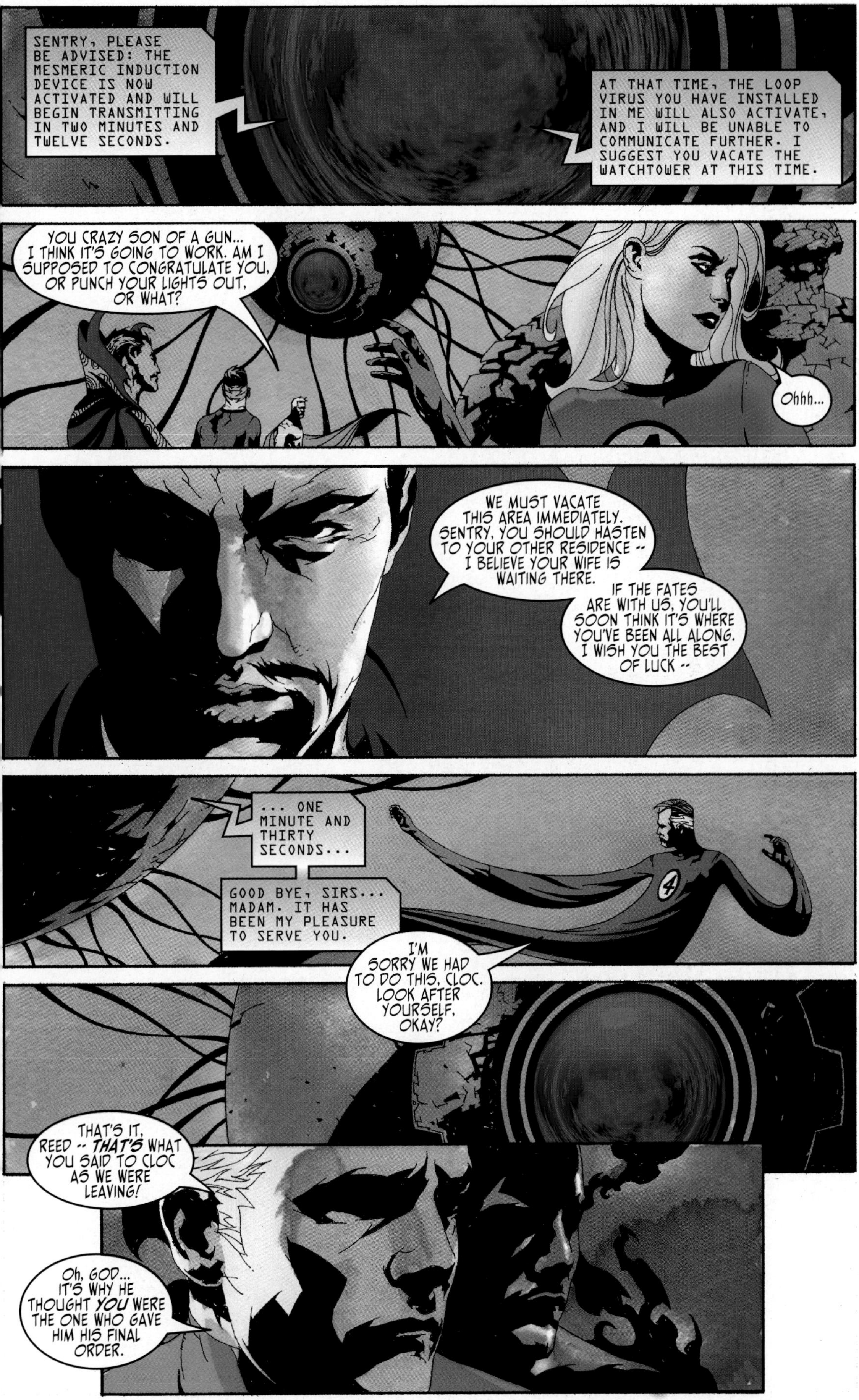
SENTRY, PLEASE BE ADVISED: THE MESMERIC INDUCTION DEVICE IS NOW ACTIVATED AND WILL BEGIN TRANSMITTING IN TWO MINUTES AND TWELVE SECONDS.
AT THAT TIME, THE LOOP VIRUS YOU HAVE INSTALLED IN ME WILL ALSO ACTIVATE, AND I WILL BE UNABLE TO COMMUNICATE FURTHER. I SUGGEST YOU VACATE THE WATCHTOWER AT THIS TIME.
YOU CRAZY SON OF A GUN... I THINK IT'S GOING TO WORK. AM I SUPPOSED TO CONGRATULATE YOU, OR PUNCH YOUR LIGHTS OUT, OR WHAT?
Ohhh...
WE MUST VACATE THIS AREA IMMEDIATELY. SENTRY, YOU SHOULD HASTEN TO YOUR OTHER RESIDENCE -- I BELIEVE YOUR WIFE IS WAITING THERE.
IF THE FATES ARE WITH US, YOU'LL SOON THINK IT'S WHERE YOU'VE BEEN ALL ALONG. I WISH YOU THE BEST OF LUCK --
... ONE MINUTE AND THIRTY SECONDS...
GOOD BYE, SIRS... MADAM. IT HAS BEEN MY PLEASURE TO SERVE YOU.
I'M SORRY WE HAD TO DO THIS, CLOC. LOOK AFTER YOURSELF, OKAY?
THAT'S IT, REED -- THAT'S WHAT YOU SAID TO CLOC AS WE WERE LEAVING!
Oh, GOD... IT'S WHY HE THOUGHT YOU WERE THE ONE WHO GAVE HIM HIS FINAL ORDER.

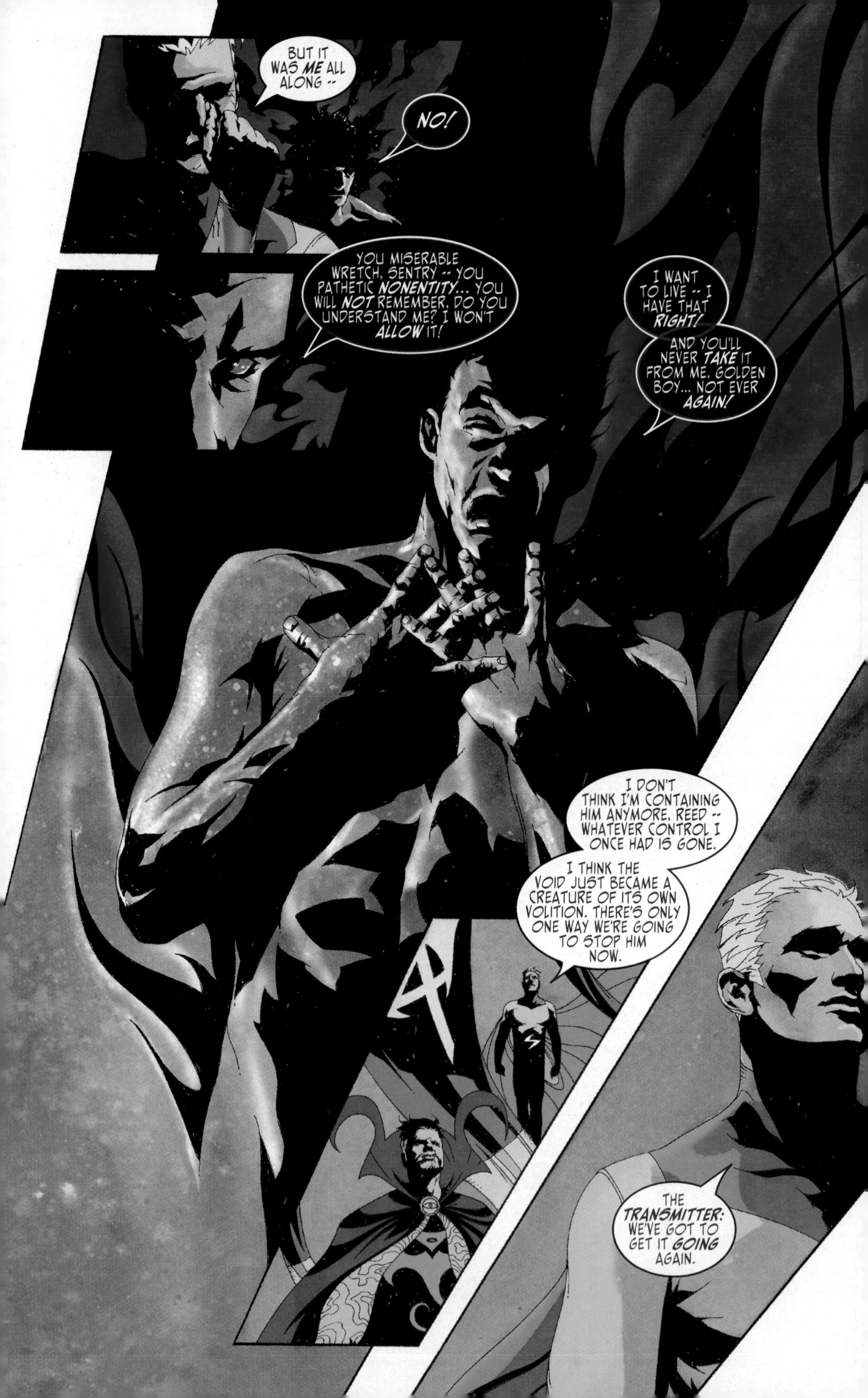
BUT IT WAS ME ALL ALONG --
NO!
YOU MISERABLE WRETCH, SENTRY -- YOU PATHETIC NONENTITY... YOU WILL NOT REMEMBER, DO YOU UNDERSTAND ME? I WON'T ALLOW IT!
I WANT TO LIVE -- I HAVE THAT RIGHT!
AND YOU'LL NEVER TAKE IT FROM ME, GOLDEN BOY... NOT EVER AGAIN!
I DON'T THINK I'M CONTAINING HIM ANYMORE, REED -- WHATEVER CONTROL I ONCE HAD IS GONE.
I THINK THE VOID JUST BECAME A CREATURE OF ITS OWN VOLITION. THERE'S ONLY ONE WAY WE'RE GOING TO STOP HIM NOW.
THE TRANSMITTER: WE'VE GOT TO GET IT GOING AGAIN.

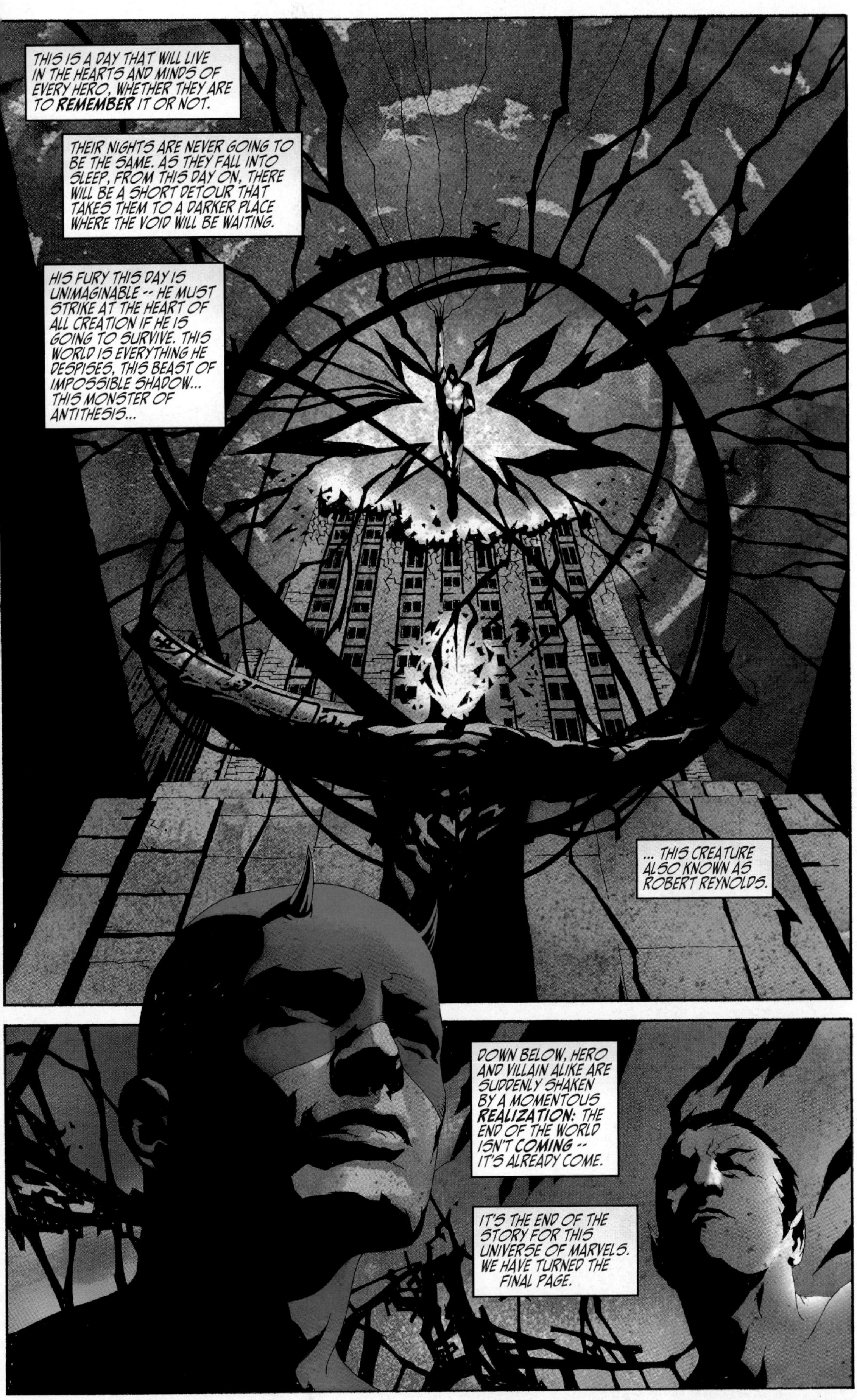
THIS IS A DAY THAT WILL LIVE IN THE HEARTS AND MINDS OF EVERY HERO, WHETHER THEY ARE TO REMEMBER IT OR NOT.
THEIR NIGHTS ARE NEVER GOING TO BE THE SAME. AS THEY FALL INTO SLEEP, FROM THIS DAY ON, THERE WILL BE A SHORT DETOUR THAT TAKES THEM TO A DARKER PLACE WHERE THE VOID WILL BE WAITING.
HIS FURY THIS DAY IS UNIMAGINABLE -- HE MUST STRIKE AT THE HEART OF ALL CREATION IF HE IS GOING TO SURVIVE. THIS WORLD IS EVERYTHING HE DESPISES, THIS BEAST OF IMPOSSIBLE SHADOW... THIS MONSTER OF ANTITHESIS...
... THIS CREATURE ALSO KNOWN AS ROBERT REYNOLDS.
DOWN BELOW, HERO AND VILLAIN ALIKE ARE SUDDENLY SHAKEN BY A MOMENTOUS REALIZATION: THE END OF THE WORLD ISN'T COMING -- IT'S ALREADY COME.
IT'S THE END OF THE STORY FOR THIS UNIVERSE OF MARVELS. WE HAVE TURNED THE FINAL PAGE.

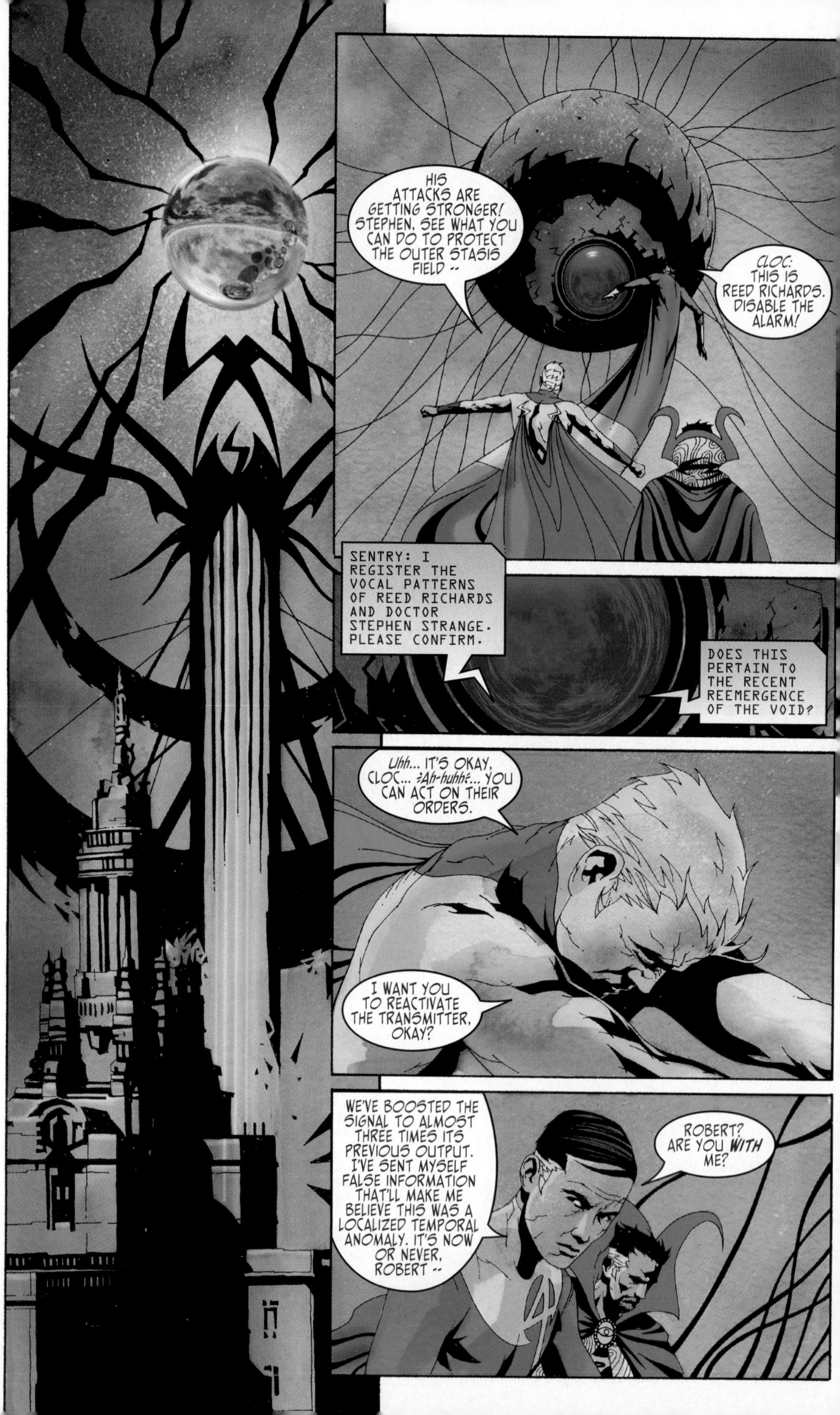
HIS ATTACKS ARE GETTING STRONGER! STEPHEN, SEE WHAT YOU CAN DO TO PROTECT THE OUTER STASIS FIELD --
CLOC: THIS IS REED RICHARDS. DISABLE THE ALARM!
SENTRY: I REGISTER THE VOCAL PATTERNS OF REED RICHARDS AND DOCTOR STEPHEN STRANGE. PLEASE CONFIRM.
DOES THIS PERTAIN TO THE RECENT REEMERGENCE OF THE VOID?
Uhh... IT'S OKAY, CLOC... *Ah-huhh*... YOU CAN ACT ON THEIR ORDERS.
I WANT YOU TO REACTIVATE THE TRANSMITTER, OKAY?
WE'VE BOOSTED THE SIGNAL TO ALMOST THREE TIMES ITS PREVIOUS OUTPUT. I'VE SENT MYSELF FALSE INFORMATION THAT'LL MAKE ME BELIEVE THIS WAS A LOCALIZED TEMPORAL ANOMALY. IT'S NOW OR NEVER, ROBERT --
ROBERT? ARE YOU **WITH** ME?

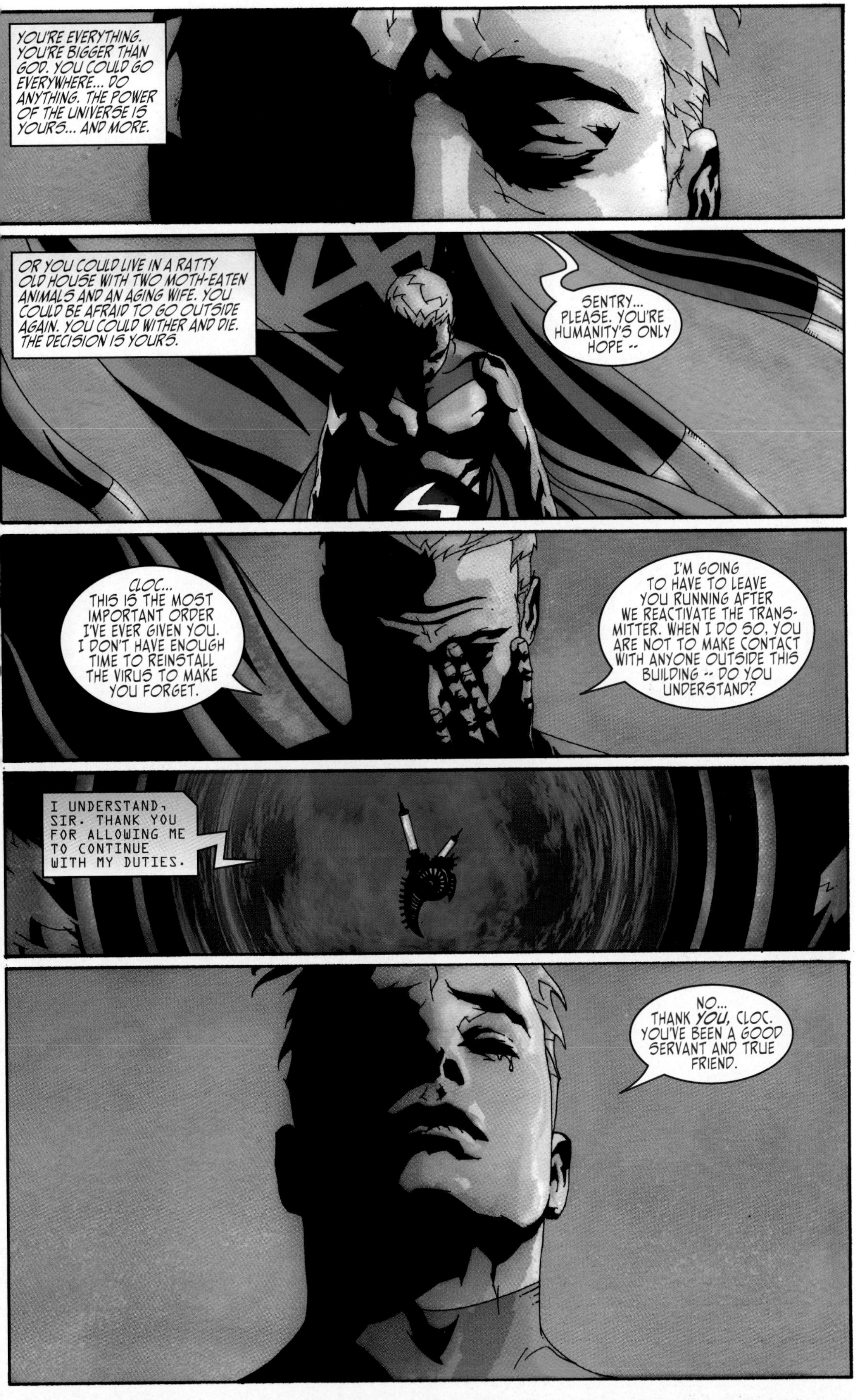
YOU'RE EVERYTHING. YOU'RE BIGGER THAN GOD. YOU COULD GO EVERYWHERE... DO ANYTHING. THE POWER OF THE UNIVERSE IS YOURS... AND MORE.
OR YOU COULD LIVE IN A RATTY OLD HOUSE WITH TWO MOTH-EATEN ANIMALS AND AN AGING WIFE. YOU COULD BE AFRAID TO GO OUTSIDE AGAIN. YOU COULD WITHER AND DIE. THE DECISION IS YOURS.
SENTRY... PLEASE. YOU'RE HUMANITY'S ONLY HOPE --
CLOC... THIS IS THE MOST IMPORTANT ORDER I'VE EVER GIVEN YOU. I DON'T HAVE ENOUGH TIME TO REINSTALL THE VIRUS TO MAKE YOU FORGET.
I'M GOING TO HAVE TO LEAVE YOU RUNNING AFTER WE REACTIVATE THE TRANS-MITTER. WHEN I DO SO, YOU ARE NOT TO MAKE CONTACT WITH ANYONE OUTSIDE THIS BUILDING -- DO YOU UNDERSTAND?
I UNDERSTAND, SIR. THANK YOU FOR ALLOWING ME TO CONTINUE WITH MY DUTIES.
NO... THANK YOU, CLOC. YOU'VE BEEN A GOOD SERVANT AND TRUE FRIEND.

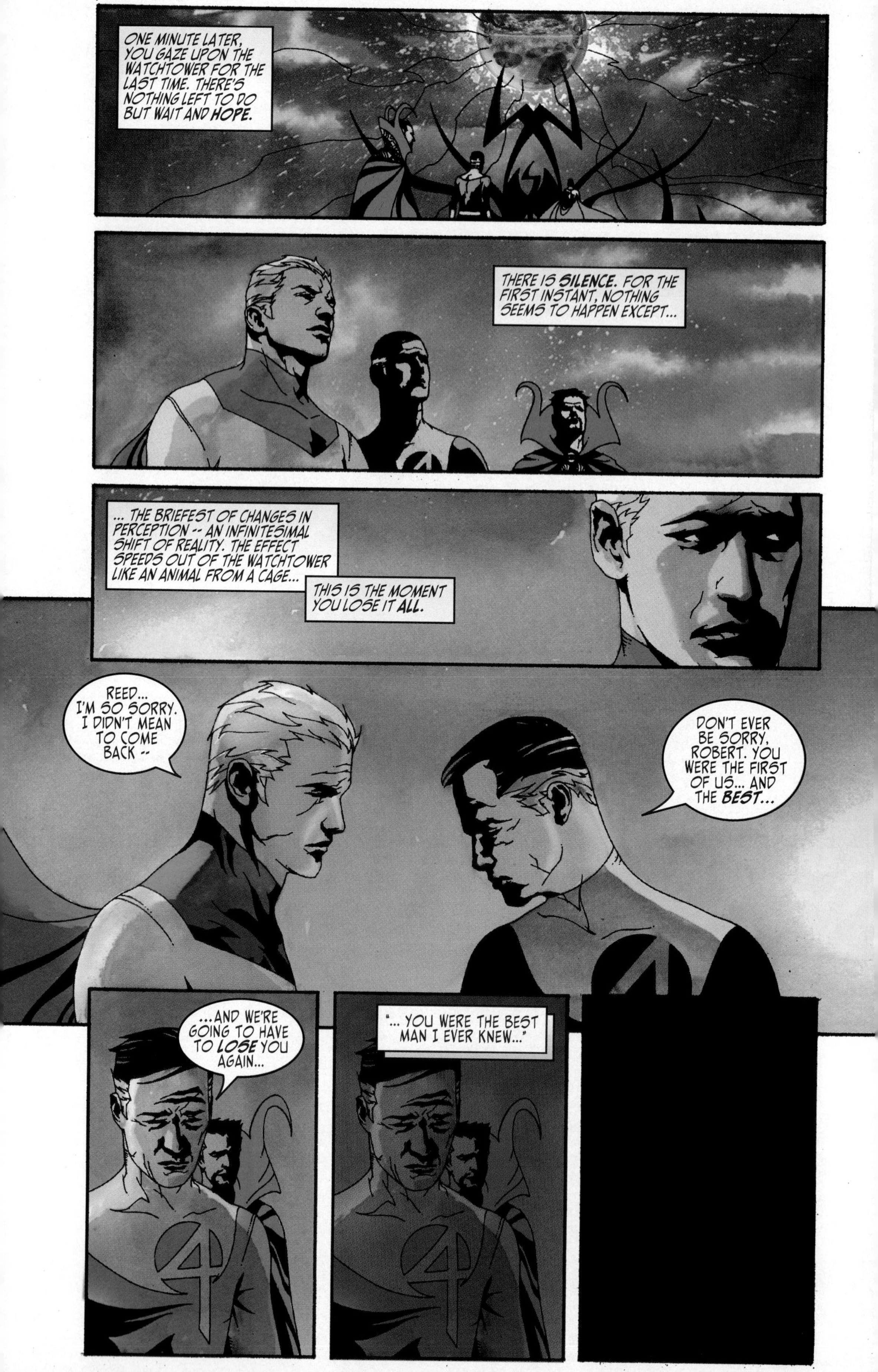
ONE MINUTE LATER, YOU GAZE UPON THE WATCHTOWER FOR THE LAST TIME. THERE'S NOTHING LEFT TO DO BUT WAIT AND HOPE.
THERE IS SILENCE. FOR THE FIRST INSTANT, NOTHING SEEMS TO HAPPEN EXCEPT...
... THE BRIEFEST OF CHANGES IN PERCEPTION -- AN INFINITESIMAL SHIFT OF REALITY. THE EFFECT SPEEDS OUT OF THE WATCHTOWER LIKE AN ANIMAL FROM A CAGE...
THIS IS THE MOMENT YOU LOSE IT ALL.
REED... I'M SO SORRY. I DIDN'T MEAN TO COME BACK --
DON'T EVER BE SORRY, ROBERT. YOU WERE THE FIRST OF US... AND THE BEST...
...AND WE'RE GOING TO HAVE TO LOSE YOU AGAIN...
"... YOU WERE THE BEST MAN I EVER KNEW..."

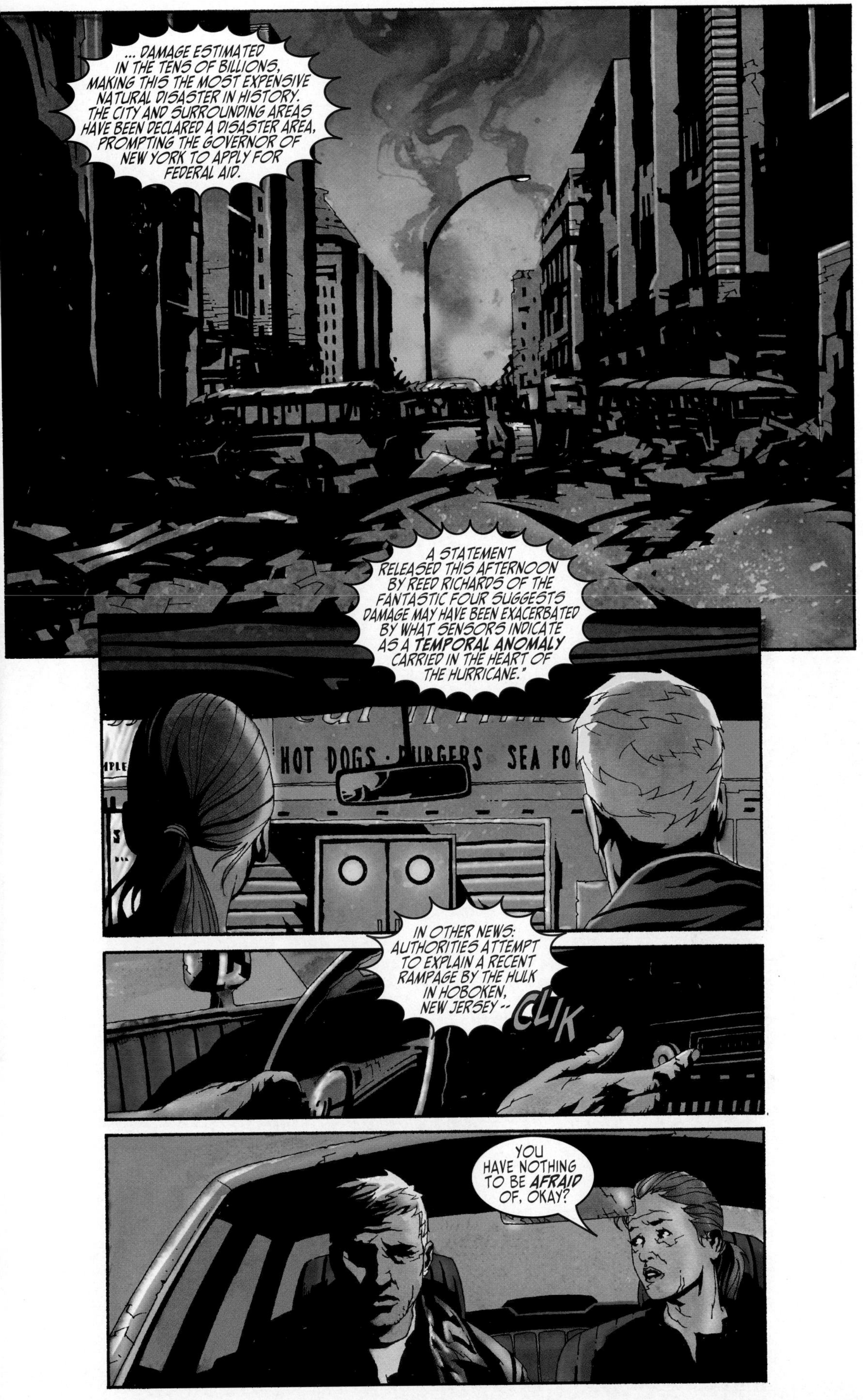

... DAMAGE ESTIMATED IN THE TENS OF BILLIONS, MAKING THIS THE MOST EXPENSIVE NATURAL DISASTER IN HISTORY. THE CITY AND SURROUNDING AREAS HAVE BEEN DECLARED A DISASTER AREA, PROMPTING THE GOVERNOR OF NEW YORK TO APPLY FOR FEDERAL AID.
A STATEMENT RELEASED THIS AFTERNOON BY REED RICHARDS OF THE FANTASTIC FOUR SUGGESTS DAMAGE MAY HAVE BEEN EXACERBATED BY WHAT SENSORS INDICATE AS A TEMPORAL ANOMALY CARRIED IN THE HEART OF THE HURRICANE."
HOT DOGS · BURGERS SEA FO
IN OTHER NEWS: AUTHORITIES ATTEMPT TO EXPLAIN A RECENT RAMPAGE BY THE HULK IN HOBOKEN, NEW JERSEY --
CLIK
YOU HAVE NOTHING TO BE AFRAID OF, OKAY?

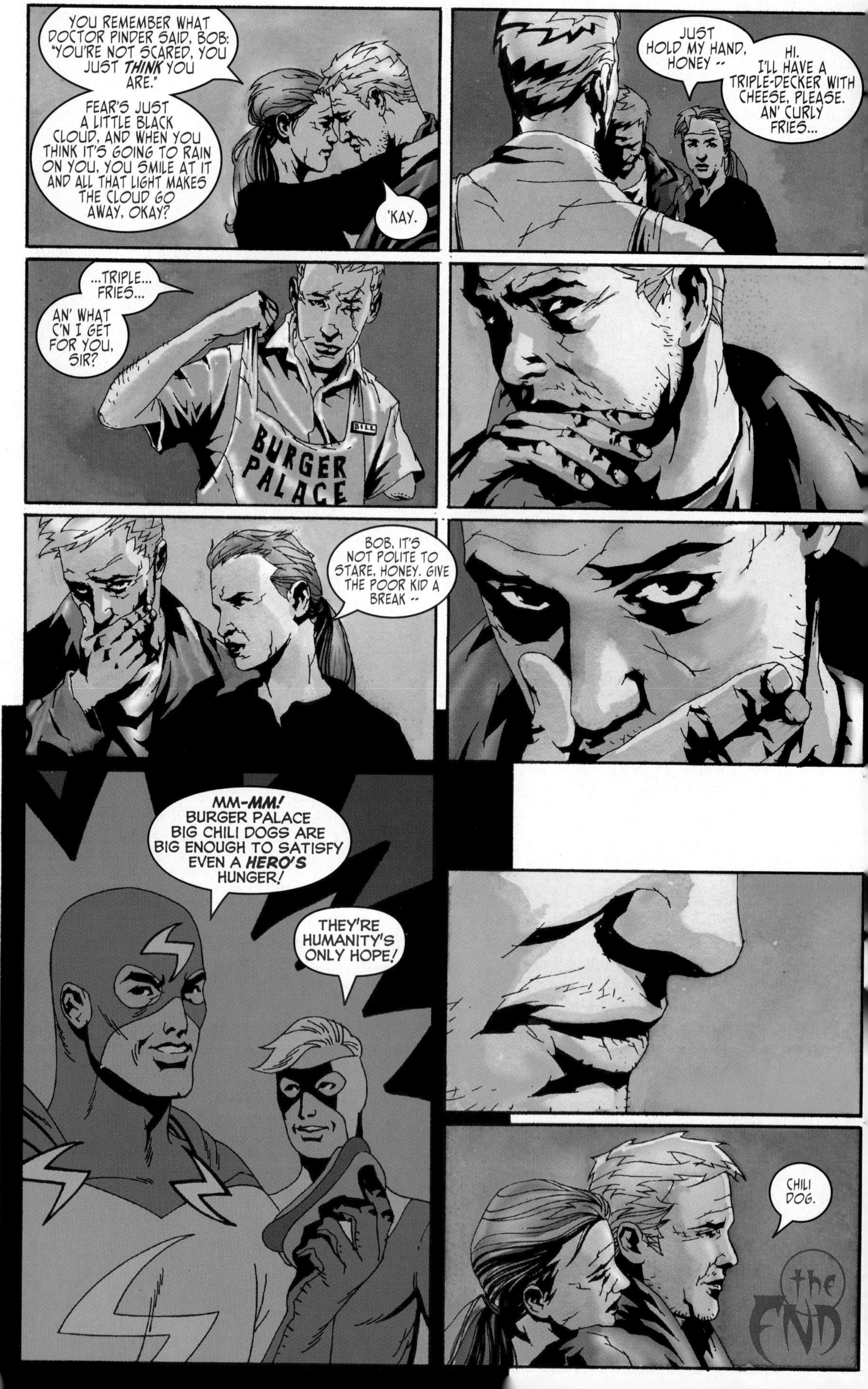
YOU REMEMBER WHAT DOCTOR PINDER SAID, BOB: "YOU'RE NOT SCARED, YOU JUST *THINK* YOU ARE."
FEAR'S JUST A LITTLE BLACK CLOUD, AND WHEN YOU THINK IT'S GOING TO RAIN ON YOU, YOU SMILE AT IT AND ALL THAT LIGHT MAKES THE CLOUD GO AWAY, OKAY?
'KAY.
JUST HOLD MY HAND, HONEY --
HI. I'LL HAVE A TRIPLE-DECKER WITH CHEESE, PLEASE. AN' CURLY FRIES...
...TRIPLE... FRIES...
AN' WHAT C'N I GET FOR YOU, SIR?
BILL
BURGER PALACE
BOB, IT'S NOT POLITE TO STARE, HONEY. GIVE THE POOR KID A BREAK --
MM-MM! BURGER PALACE BIG CHILI DOGS ARE BIG ENOUGH TO SATISFY EVEN A ***HERO'S*** HUNGER!
THEY'RE HUMANITY'S ONLY HOPE!
CHILI DOG.
the END

Stan's Scintillating SENTRY Scoop

part the first:

THERE SHALL COME... A HERO!

The Sentry book you hold in your hand is a comic child of the year 2000. But there's actually a chance that the character was the first-ever Marvel hero, predating even the Fantastic Four. Editor Joe Quesada talks to Marvel's keeper of the flame, Stan Lee, in a five-part interview to get to the bottom of how and why the Sentry came to be.

JOE: The story of how the Sentry was found after all these years reads like a comic itself, Stan. How'd it happen?

STAN: Hey, you know better than I! You tell 'em!

JOE: Well, it's weird circumstance. Paul Jenkins just pulled something off the submission pile and it was this "lost file" of stuff you and artist Artie Rosen had worked on in, it looks like, 1961.

STAN: You know, like I tell everyone, I have a terrible memory for these things. I wrote so many stories and so many strips, there's no way I can remember them all. I must admit the Sentry is just kinda a vague memory to me. He definitely looks like a heroic character, and I know we were looking to go down the super hero path at that point in 1961.

JOE: But this was even before Fantastic Four #1, right?

STAN: Right. We were called Atlas Comics at the time. We were churning out a lot of monster comics then. Incidentally, if I may stroll briefly down memory lane, I gotta tell you I loved some of their names! There was "The Terror of Tim-Boo-Bah!" and of course, Fin Fang Foom! God, they were great. I loved making up those crazy names!

But anyway, to answer your question and desist from this dizzy dash of dissertation, I know that our publisher, Martin Goodman, wanted to try some heroic characters again. I developed the Fantastic Four and assigned Jack Kirby to draw them as part of that project. I may have assigned other artists more new characters to draw. I know I came up with a bunch of ideas right off the bat. The Sentry seems to ring a bell in the deep recesses of what I laughingly call my mind.

JOE: Bob Reynolds, the Sentry character—It looks like he may be crazy, he may be an alcoholic, he may be a super hero. What did you intend him to be?

STAN: Like I said, most of my memories of the character are kinda vague. I figure that I probably intended him to be a great hero. But that also means that I intended him to be a great human. That's part of Marvel and the way we've always done things here. The heroes are just like you and me, with as many pimples and flaws as we have. And sometimes, no matter how strong or powerful they are, their feet of clay quake with fear in their brightly colored little booties!

JOE: Yeah, but an alcoholic super hero?

STAN: Well, we did a very famous story in Iron Man some years after I left the strip that dealt with alcoholism. And Marvel just won an award last year for dealing with alcoholism in Avengers. It's real. It's part of the world. And it makes for an engaging, very human story.

JOE: And what's with the dog sidekick?

STAN: I don't believe we had an idea for a dog sidekick right away. But don't knock the dog! My wife Joan and I have a couple ourselves—Tinkerbell and Pookie. Real macho monikers, right?

NEWS&NOTES

STAN'S SECRET

Did Lee create something before the FF?

Stan Lee may have done it again.

Or rather, before.

The Marvel rumor mill reports the folks at the House of Ideas actually have sketches and story information for a previously unseen hero created by Lee. A source inside Marvel reports one of the sketches includes a date scribbled in ink, a mark which suggests the character may actually have been created prior to the Fantastic Four.

"If it were true—and I am in no way saying it is—it would have a tremendous impact on Marvel's history," Marvel Editor in Chief Bob Harras said. "And on the history of comics in general."

He's not kidding. Such a find would be of enormous value, both for Marvel, which would definitely benefit from the discovery of a "lost" Silver Age Lee character, and for Lee himself. The timing would be extremely beneficial for Lee, who's preparing to officially launch Stan Lee Media, a company that promises to offer online comics involving new heroes created by the legendary writer.

"I'm not at liberty to say anything about it right now," Lee said. "But wouldn't it be great if there had been something before the FF?"

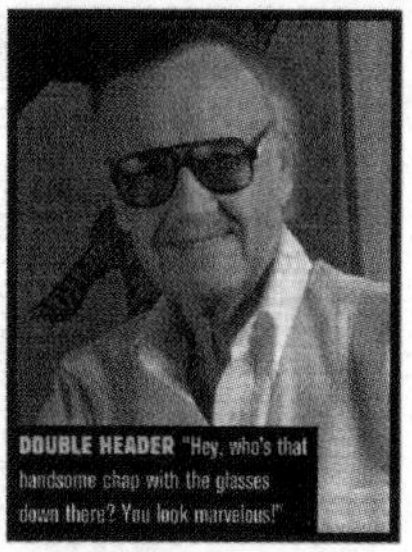

DOUBLE HEADER "Hey, who's that handsome chap with the glasses down there? You look marvelous!"

Sure, Lee worked at Marvel prior to the FF's 1961 introduction, but most of his work immediately preceding *FF* #1 was in the non-superhero genre, and involved a mixture of monster stories, westerns, teenage dramas, war comics and horror tales. All that changed, however, with the debut of the Fantastic Four, the characters ultimately credited with introducing humanity to the world of superhero comics.

But were they really the first? That's a question Lee would like to see answered.

"I'd be more than happy to look at the sketches, to try and help Marvel out in any way I could," Lee offers. "Like I said, I'm not sure what it is they found, but if it really is something I created way back when, I'd at least like to take a look at it." ■ CL

JOE: Did you have the concept for this villain right off the bat? The Void?

STAN: He rings the same kind of bell The Sentry does in my memory. It's only fair, you know. You can't just be a super hero and good-naturedly gallivant across the globe all day. You've got to have someone to confront. And that's how we did the strips back in those days. Very often, the first question I'd ask when I'd sit down with an artist to plot a new issue was, "Okay! So who are we going to have him fight?" That's your starting point.

I seem to recall needing a real close relationship between the Sentry and the Void. I wanted there to be a link, maybe a tragic bond between them, like I later did with Reed Richards and Dr. Doom in Fantastic Four. Reed and Doom are like two sides of the same coin—one went bad and one went good, but both have their own air of nobility about them. When you have a hero and villain that are so close to each other, but yet so far away, you set the stage for grandeur! You can play with the trappings of a Shakespearean tragedy! But don't assume that the Void is pure evil. Give the guy a break! I believe that there's a bit of heroism in every character. I think that's the only true way to write them. I've often said, you see, that there are few villains in the Marvel Universe, mostly fallen heroes.

JOE: Speaking of powers, how did the Sentry get his powers?

STAN: Paul Jenkins, the writer of this strip, seems to have it down as I remember it—Bob Reynolds ingested a secret formula. We did a lot of secret formulas back in those days. It worked for Captain America, right? And if it's good enough for Cap, then it's good enough for the Sentry!

JOE: What are his powers? All we really see is that Bob can somehow "perceive" there's trouble brewing. And at the end, I guess he can fly.

STAN: I'm reluctant to use the term "all-powerful," but remember—this was going to be our first fearless foray back into the hero genre. I wanted a hero that would have colossal power, superior strength, monumental might! I wanted a hero near-omnipotent in scope, who could make any villain we came up with tremble in fear! The Sentry was going to be the centerpiece for a modern comic universe—the little realm that grew up to be the Marvel Universe. He had to be very powerful indeed.

JOE: Sounds big. So why, after all this planning, did the Sentry get set aside and lay undiscovered so long?

STAN: It may have been for the good of us all. I seem to recall that he was too big. He was so powerful, he could very well have destroyed the entire Marvel Universe and everything we were planning. I wish I could remember, but I really can't specifically recall why I didn't continue on with the Sentry. But I'm sure there must have been a very good and very important reason. In fact, this may turn out to be the greatest mystery in the history of comics. Hey, I can live with that!

part the second: STORIES TO STARTLE SOUND SANITY!

With the mystery of the character slowly being revealed in the pages of our story, Joe and Stan try to piece together how and why the Sentry could go missing from publication for almost 40 years.

JOE: Stan, I guess we've been able to determine that the Sentry appeared in a few issues of *Startling Stories*. But I'm a huge Marvel Zombie. How is it that I've never heard of this book?

STAN: [mockingly, and with a smile] Some "True Believer" you are, Quesada! Turn in your F.O.O.M. membership card at the door on your way out!

JOE: Well, I've never even heard anything about it. And it's not even in listings or price guides or whatever. You'd think there would be some mention.

STAN: Well, collectors know an awful lot, but they don't know everything. There's a real fanaticism, almost a religious fervor, that's grown around Marvel Comics over the years, and man, I love it 'cause it's kept me employed and off the welfare rolls for all this time! But there are so many intricate nooks and crannies of the Marvel mythos, I'm sure no one source can catalog them all. By the Hoary Hosts of Irving Forbush! Even I don't know 'em all—And I invented most of 'em!

JOE: I guess we established in this issue that Bob, the Sentry, is an old friend of Reed Richards.

STAN: It stands to reason. That was one of the things that I really wanted to focus on as we built the Marvel Universe—that it would be the first true comicbook universe, with emphasis on the "uni," meaning "one." Everything was part of the one, and everything would take place on the same stage. You might only see some of the actors or part of the play in any given strip, but it was all part of an intricately woven tapestry. What happened in Avengers might have a ripple effect in Tales of Suspense, and the adventures of the Fantastic Four could wreak horrible havoc in Daredevil's life. Everyone knew everyone else in our universe. Sometimes they were friends, sometimes enemies. Sometimes the relationships themselves got rather famous. Spider-Man and the Human Torch had their famed friendly rivalry. The Thing and the Hulk were always mixing it up in a bodacious, bombastic brawl, much to the delight of readers, and, I might add, myself! I loved scripting those pulsating punch-em-ups!

JOE: But the Sentry makes a reference to some sort of conspiracy angle when he's talking to Reed. Does someone not want these stories remembered?

STAN: Well, within the context of the story, I think it's obvious that The Void might be behind some kind of "memory blackout" on everyone's part. If he was defeated in the past, maybe he doesn't want anyone to remember just how it happened. Perhaps he has an Achilles heel, or one fatal flaw that could lay him low. Maybe there's something that beat him before and might defeat him again.

Outside the story and within the context of what I'm forced to call "the real world," I really don't know. I still can't recall much about The Sentry. I even had my able and amiable assistant, Michael Kelly, scrambling through my archives for *Startling Stories*, but he couldn't find any copies. Then again, I have to admit my own personal collection is woefully inadequate. Heck, I'm even missing several issues of Millie the Model, including Queen-Size Millie #1!

JOE: That's a tragic loss. Millie was a hottie. It looks like we move on to a flashback at a wedding in this story.

STAN: Yes, and a big star-studded one at that. It seems the only way to get the heroes out of their brightly colored union suits is to have them put on their tuxes and go to a wedding. Everyone shows up for free food and polka music!

JOE: Is Reed the best man?

STAN: Well, he's a very good man! But I've always been kinda partial to my own scintillatin' self! [chuckles]

JOE: Well, you know what I mean.

STAN: From what Paul Jenkins, the scripter of this series, has done, it sure looks like Reed is the best man here. And there may be a historical precedent for that, too. The Sentry and the Fantastic Four were two of Marvel's earliest pillars of heroism. And like I said earlier, I wanted everyone in the Marvel Universe to be able to interact, to be chummy. It makes good sense that Bob and Reed would have had a close friendship,

JOE: This issue gets really...I don't know? What's the word I'm looking for? Ominous?

that perhaps the Fantastic Four might even have appeared in those lost and lonely issues of *Startling Stories* that I can't seem to find.

JOE: This issue gets really...I don't know? What's the word I'm looking for? Ominous?

STAN: I'd say "ominous" fits about as well as anything, especially at the end. There's a real sense of tension, as if a catastrophic disaster could befall our gallant heroes at the next instant, the next turn of a page! And the real scary part is that it seems as if the only one who can stop the impending doom is Bob, the Sentry. But he has no allies, no one who can help him, because no one believes him. Heck, I'm not even sure if he believes himself at this point!

JOE: Has this always been a problem with Bob? This self-doubt?

STAN: Hey, you'd have doubts too if you hadda go toe-to-toe with tough cookies like this Void guy! That's one of the things that's so important to Marvel storytelling. We all know, as readers of stories, that the good guy usually wins. Doesn't matter if you're reading Edgar Allen Poe or comic books, or if you're watching the latest Schwarzenegger action movie—you know in almost every case the hero is gonna win the day. So I always tried to come up with villains at least as strong and usually stronger than the heroes. It's gotta be a tough fight for the good guy. I want the reader on the edge of his seat, gripping that comic with white knuckles and sweaty palms! If the outcome is in doubt, you introduce real drama, true tension. And remember: In Marvel Comics, the heroes don't always win. Oh, sure, they're always valiant and valorous, always dauntless and daring, but they can't win the day every time. It's because they're human, because they're flawed. They may lose occasionally, but they can still be heroes. Charlie Brown taught us that!

ARTIST ROSEN PASSES AWAY

The comic world's lost one of its elder statesmen. Artie Rosen, the artist best remembered for his work on *Crime Can't Win* for Marvel/Atlas Comics and *Love Experiences*, died January 13, 2000 from heart failure. He was 83.

While the majority of his work was uncredited, Rosen's comic career spanned four decades, from his debut in *Exciting Comics* in 1941 to his final work on Gold Key's *Mod Wheels* in the mid-1970s.

He remained a staunch supporter of the industry following his retirement, and he was a fixture at comic conventions near his home in Brooklyn, New York.

"We were close, years ago, but I hadn't seen or heard from Artie in so many years," said Stan Lee, who worked with Rosen at Marvel. "It came as a big shock to me." ∎ ⊡

JOE: Heavy stuff. On a lighter note, is there any chance we'll be able to get our own copy of that Sentry wedding video?

STAN: [laughs] Well, we've done stranger things. We gave away great gimmicks and dazzling doo-hickeys as part of the Merry Marvel Marching Society once. And we did the same for F.O.O.M.—Friends Of Ol' Marvel. Heck, we even put out an album in the '60s in which the Bullpen sang songs! So it's possible. Provided, of course, I get my share of the profits or, at least, the chance to sing a song!

JOE: I'll buy two of 'em.

STAN: If we live that long. I didn't want to say it earlier, but when Michael Kelly went through my archives, he said it looked like someone purposely took certain books out. Or maybe they were misnumbered or out of sequence. It was real creepy the way he described it—It looked like someone had been very manipulative. Perhaps you were right about this "conspiracy" thing. It's almost as if there is something larger going on, something we can't yet see. I fear there may be a very dire and dangerous reason the story of the Sentry shouldn't be told.

part the third: REUNIONS, REMEMBRANCES AND REVELATIONS!

*B*its and pieces of just who the Sentry is are pieced together, but for each mystery revealed, two more seem to take its place....

JOE: The Sentry sure seems to have a lot of friends, or at least would-be friends—the Hulk, Spider-Man, Doctor Strange, the list just goes on and on.

STAN: Yeah, he sure seems to be quite the social butterfly in this issue. He gallivants around the globe and hob-nobs with almost as many Marvel mainstays as I do in a given day!

JOE: I take it he once had a central place in the Marvel Universe.

STAN: I seem to recall that was the case. The Sentry was going to be a massively powered force, and I wanted to set him up as one of the supporting columns of the mighty House of Ideas that would one day become the Marvel Universe. Hey, you don't think I would've wasted a catchy moniker like "The Golden Guardian of Good" on just any ol' nebbish, do ya?

JOE: [laughs] No, I wouldn't think so. The main problem still seems to be that people have a hard time remembering him, though. But the Hulk recognizes him right off the bat. Why is that?

STAN: Well, I think perhaps there's something tied up in the nature of the Hulk that allows him to remember. The Hulk was always supposed to be about the duality of man, and how we can have these two warring natures inside us—in this case, the reason and intellect of Bruce Banner versus the savagery and mindlessness of the Hulk. One of those natures sure seems to recognize Bob as the Sentry. The other? I guess we don't know yet.

There's obviously something going on here, some forces at play we don't yet see. The Sentry definitely exists and he's always existed. But someone or something is trying to bury all knowledge of him. Maybe if you get down to the level where there is no intellect—only the mindlessness of a Hulk—that's the only level the Sentry can be perceived on...for now.

JOE: Strange that the Hulk is the smartest one in the story at this point.

STAN: [laughs] Yeah! It is kind of funny! But give ol' Jade Jaws his due! I think the two characters share a lot. The Hulk has his dual nature, and the Sentry seems to have one also. On the one hand, the Sentry is this great hero. On the other, he's like a drifter, a man out of time and out of place. And everyone seems to think he's crazy! He's something of an outcast because of that. All that reminds me of the way we portrayed the Hulk back in the 1970s TV series. I think Bob and the Hulk may have a lot more in common than you see on the surface.

They may have some history, too. Way back in the first few issues of *Incredible Hulk*—and when he was with the Avengers—the Hulk was savage, but he was also smart. Naturally, he wasn't a worldly wordsmith of my mighty magnitude, of course [laughs], but he wasn't the "Hulk Smash!" Hulk we later came to know either. I don't think it's ever been explained why he evolved in that direction, but I've got a feeling the Sentry may have had something to do with it. I think I was planning the story of their connection for an old issue of *Incredible Hulk*, or perhaps *Tales to Astonish*. But I don't know if I ever got around to writing that strip.

JOE: Interesting. So what's with this glowing ball Bob gives the Hulk?

STAN: I've got a vague memory in a dusty, seldom-used back corner of my noggin that some of the Sentry's powers had to do with light. He could control light, bend it to his will, and even make constructs out of light.

JOE: What kind of constructs could he make?

STAN: Anything really, if the patchwork quilt I call my memory is working. Weapons, transmitters, a Ronco Pocket Fisherman if he wanted to! I've got a feeling this glowing ball is one of those light constructs, and will play a part again as the story goes on. Bob seems to be giving—or at least trying to give—something to everyone to help them remember. He gave Reed Richards the unicorn last issue and gives Hulk the ball in this one.

JOE: Speaking of Reed, he still seems pretty mystified by all this.

STAN: Well, that's part of his nature. He's always had a hard time whenever things come down to a matter of facts versus feeling. He's really a very passionate man, but the things that he's passionate about are not things of the emotional world—they're things of the scientific world. When he has a feeling that contradicts a fact, his impulse is to go with the fact. That's just what he does as a man of science.

JOE: The Sentry tries to jog Spider-Man's memory too, I guess, with…a photo?

STAN: Yeah, but for whatever reason, Spidey can't see it. Now that's odd. Hey, Bob even said that Spidey—in his secret identity as Peter Parker, of course—was the one who took the photo! You'd think he'd recognize his own handiwork, just like I'd recognize every last word of my sparkling, scintillating scripts!

JOE: Every word?

STAN: Well, I may have forgotten a couple by now. And all the commas start to look the same after a while!

JOE: Now what's this Bob mentions as Spidey swings off? Something about Clarion and Time magazine running out of sequence?

STAN: I wish I knew exactly what that meant, but it sounds like a serious clue that could be the key that unlocks this whole conspiracy. And if I know Spidey at all—and I do consider myself kinda well-acquainted with the ol' Web-Head—I think he'll be following up on it. Probably by next ish! So reserve your copy today!

JOE: Doesn't that whole misnumbering thing sound like something we were talking about earlier?

STAN: Right! Like I said, when I went back to research the Sentry in my old copies of *Startling Stories*, something was definitely amiss. I couldn't locate all the issues, and the ones

I did find were…I don't know, there was just something strange about them. I think some of those issues were numbered out of sequence, too. I know in my mind that I wrote certain stories before others, but when I went back to check, it seemed like the tales had been…reorganized in some sinister fashion. And other stories I'm sure I wrote weren't there at all.

JOE: That's weird. It's almost as if the events of the book are playing themselves out here.

STAN: It would seem that way, wouldn't it? And that's a bit unsettling. Hey, I like our charismatic champions and vile villains to be as real as possible for the readers. But when the strips start to visit themselves upon us in the real world, well…even I gotta admit it has me looking over my shoulder. I just can't shake the feeling of danger I'm getting from this. It's like Doc Strange was right at the end of this issue. If we remember who the Sentry is and what he's all about…it could spell doom for us all.

part the fourth: TICKING TIME AND TREMORS OF TERROR!

*A*s Bob Reynolds, the man who would be The Sentry, continues his odyssey through the Marvel Universe, things get even more ominous. It would appear that the Sentry might be part of the problem, as opposed to part of the solution. It looks like everyone has forgotten him for a very good-- and very important-- reason.

JOE: I gotta admit, Stan. I was about as confused as Reed Richards was at the beginning of this issue. Good thing Doc Strange showed us a flashback.

STAN: At this point, I think Reed *had* to know what was going on, both to understand the problem, *and* just to be Reed Richards! See, Doc nailed him right on the head. Reed is a logical thinker. He's gonna keep picking at a problem until he finally scratches a solution!

JOE: Why is it that Doctor Strange seems to be the only one who knows the full story?

STAN: Well, I'd presume that someone had to be the "gatekeeper" of this knowledge in case the Void ever came back, and it sure looks like he's comin'. I'd postulate that ol' Doc Strange is the kind of guy who could make something like this happen. He's got the ability to cloud the minds of the Marvel Universe and make people forget about the Sentry. And I'd pontificate that Doc can handle this kind of burden. After all, he's tussled with the like of Dormammu, Nightmare and Baron Mordo, and walked away from it. Also he's gazed into the very visage of Eternity! But for all that, even Doc still seems shook up by the gravity of the situation.

JOE: Did you just do all P's there? Presume, pontificate, and… what was the other one? Postulate?

STAN: Only three of them? Sheesh; I must be losing my touch!

JOE: Since Doctor Strange seems to be the Sentry's "gatekeeper," is he in league with the Sentry?

STAN: I wouldn't swear to it. I somehow doubt it. You said previously that Doctor Strange seems to know "the full story."

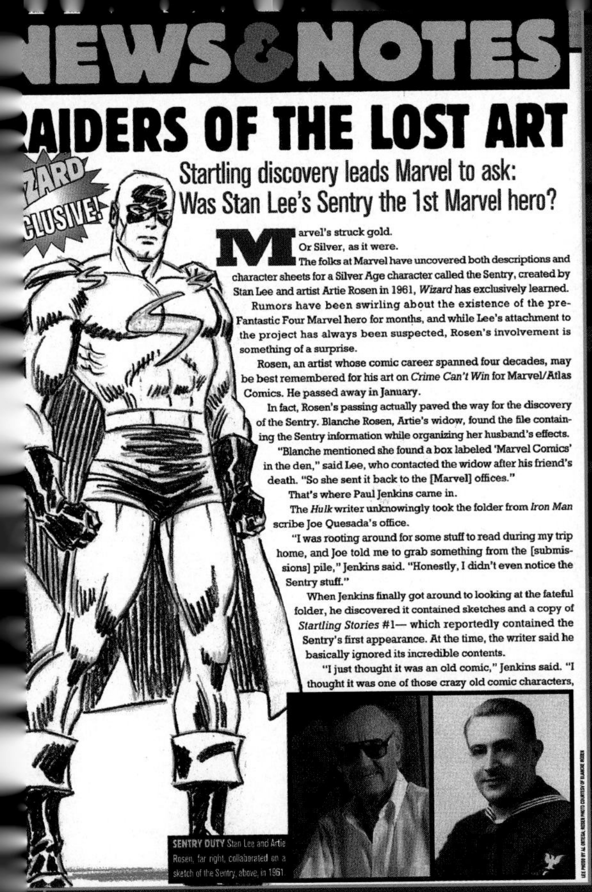

NEWS&NOTES

RAIDERS OF THE LOST ART

ZARD
CLUSIVE!

Startling discovery leads Marvel to ask: Was Stan Lee's Sentry the 1st Marvel hero?

Marvel's struck gold.

Or Silver, as it were.

The folks at Marvel have uncovered both descriptions and character sheets for a Silver Age character called the Sentry, created by Stan Lee and artist Artie Rosen in 1961, *Wizard* has exclusively learned.

Rumors have been swirling about the existence of the pre-Fantastic Four Marvel hero for months, and while Lee's attachment to the project has always been suspected, Rosen's involvement is something of a surprise.

Rosen, an artist whose comic career spanned four decades, may be best remembered for his art on *Crime Can't Win* for Marvel/Atlas Comics. He passed away in January.

In fact, Rosen's passing actually paved the way for the discovery of the Sentry. Blanche Rosen, Artie's widow, found the file containing the Sentry information while organizing her husband's effects.

"Blanche mentioned she found a box labeled 'Marvel Comics' in the den," said Lee, who contacted the widow after his friend's death. "So she sent it back to the [Marvel] offices."

That's where Paul Jenkins came in.

The *Hulk* writer unknowingly took the folder from *Iron Man* scribe Joe Quesada's office.

"I was rooting around for some stuff to read during my trip home, and Joe told me to grab something from the [submissions] pile," Jenkins said. "Honestly, I didn't even notice the Sentry stuff."

When Jenkins finally got around to looking at the fateful folder, he discovered it contained sketches and a copy of *Startling Stories* #1— which reportedly contained the Sentry's first appearance. At the time, the writer said he basically ignored its incredible contents.

"I just thought it was an old comic," Jenkins said. "I thought it was one of those crazy old comic characters,

SENTRY DUTY Stan Lee and Artie Rosen, far right, collaborated on a sketch of the Sentry, above, in 1961.

LEE PHOTO BY AL ORTEGA; ROSEN PHOTO COURTESY OF BLANCHE ROSEN

Well, I'm not sure that Doc, or anyone for that matter, truly knows the *full* story at this point. Not even the Sentry himself.

JOE: What is it with the theme of all the clocks with the Sentry's Watchtower?

STAN: [laughing heartily] Wow, it only took you four issues to notice that, Quesada? I noticed the clock being set back in issue #1 of this merry missive! Well, hey, that's why I get the big bucks-- or would if I did!

JOE: Okay, so I'm not perfect! So... what's up with the clocks?

STAN: Well, it's like the fog is being lifted off my own memory as I read this. But I'm still not 100% certain. As I said earlier, I believe the Sentry has some powers derived from light. I also think he's somehow tied in with time. I don't think he's a time traveler or one who has mastery over time, but I have a vague recollection back in a dusty corner of my noggin that the Sentry is somehow linked to the force we know as time.

JOE: Well, that's about as clear as mud. The Sentry seems a bit miffed by the time he reaches Professor Xavier. He says his existence has been... what's he say? Stolen?

STAN: Hey! That'd be enough to cheese off even a cuddly customer and generous gent like myself! But the thing that really chills me is what the Sentry *himself* has to say-- that even he can't fit all the pieces together. He seems to be the only one who has any inkling of an answer! But if he doesn't know for sure, then who does?

JOE: Well, Peter Parker seems to be getting a little closer. He's piecing together the mystery of the missing or misnumbered issues of *Clarion*, the *Daily Bugle* weekly mag.

STAN: Y'know, that really seems to strike a chord in the sometimes dissonant rhythms of my mind. I seem to recall I wrote a strip in which Peter Parker took a photo of the Sentry that won him the Pulitzer Prize. Or maybe it was a photo that just *could have* won him the Pulitzer Prize. All I know is that wher I went to find the issue that strip was in, I couldn't. I seem tc be suffering the same misnumbering malady that maligns ou mighty masters of musculature! But think about it-- if Pete won a Pulitzer Prize, then he really wouldn't be *Peter Parker* now would he? He wouldn't be the loveable loser we've al come to know as our Friendly Neighborhood Spider-Man That's the kind of event-- winning an award like that-- that car change a person's life. I don't know if the event ever hap pened. Or maybe-- Maybe! --it's been wiped out of existenc to protect us all!

JOE: The Sentry seems to have something of a "why me?" vibe going on this issue. From the start, he looked like he might be a reluctant hero. Now he looks downright con frontational.

STAN: Well, I'm guessing something very, very bad once hap pened. And the collected heroes of Marveldom assembled are even talking about something "discovered" and "severity o measure." It's almost like he's being voted out, as if this was "Survivor" on steroids or some such. It's hard to fully under stand what's going through their minds as they do this. The Sentry seems an ally, but they're almost treating him as if he were the enemy.

JOE: He don't seem to like it much. He really gets in Tony Stark's face. He seems to want to know who did him in.

STAN: Now that's more than a bit troubling, ol' pal. Even The Sentry doesn't seem to have all the pieces of the puzzle as tc who The Void is and how to defeat him, but he seems to have more than most. And we can gather that if The Sentry defeat ed The Void once before, our Golden Guardian of Good mus be one tough cookie. I'll tell ya one thing: I'd want the Sentry on my side in a scrap! But if there's something going on we don't know about yet-- some hidden agenda or some mystery or maybe some close connection Bob has to The Void-- well not even the Hoary Hosts of Hoggoth would be able to help our heroes. I get the feeling the Sentry can be a staunch ally - or the most fearsome enemy you can imagine.

part the fifth:

LO, THERE SHALL COME... A RECKONIN

The table appears to be set for a massive con frontation, as humanity and heroes alike suddenl remember just who The Sentry is. But they alsc remember The Void. And questions remain: Is The Sentry a force for good, or evil? Can even the might o Marvel's assembled heroes defeat a foe as powerful as The Void? And what is Reed Richards' mysterious role in all this? Has he betrayed The Golden Guardian o Good? Perhaps out of jealousy? Or is Reed the only one who knows a terrible secret--that The Sentry jus might represent a horrible menace?

OE: Stan, I gotta tell ya--I read this and I'm a bit shook up. mean, I've accepted that The Sentry is one of the good guys But it looks like Reed Richards has set him up for a fal What's that make Reed?

conflict with Reed Richards. They were friends. They were allies. Heck, Reed was best man at The Sentry's wedding! If there's bad blood between these bosom buddies, well, that's the last veil to fall--the last mystery we need to figure out.

JOE: I know what you mean, Stan. It's like a fog has been lifted from my own memory on The Sentry. But if Reed is a traitor--to someone he says is a traitor--now wouldn't that be a switch?

STAN: Yeah, that's crafty! Reed's always been a very intelligent guy--and Paul Jenkins, who's scripting this yarn, seems to be a pretty swift cookie, too--but I think there's another explanation. Like I said, Reed and The Sentry were allies. There's bound to be a good, logical reason behind all this apparent confusion.

JOE: So…what's the reason?

STAN: I seem to recall that The Sentry had to go away for a while. He became so powerful that he lost his way.

JOE: What's that mean?

STAN: I think, after a fashion, that The Sentry became addicted to his power, and that made him dangerous. There are definitely issues of addiction at play here. Remember, at the beginning of this tremendous and titanic tale, it looked like Bob Reynolds--The Sentry--was an alcoholic. Even the transmitter that was finally disabled, allowing everyone to get their memories back, looks like a syringe. Something tells me that's more than just window dressing--there's something going on here.

JOE: I'd have to agree. But what?

STAN: Well, it's obviously something of dire and distressing

consequence. Look at all the failsafes that were in place to make sure that no one remembered The Sentry. Even The Sentry himself had to outsmart his own computer in his own Watchtower! This whole "memory loss" would seem to be less a conspiracy and more a carefully laid plan now. I think it's the Machiavellian machinations of a core cadre of characters, crafted to make people forget The Sentry for a very good reason. And that's what makes me think Reed Richards is not a betrayer! I think Reed and The Sentry are ultimately in league with each other, and it's their plan.

JOE: Well, The Sentry still looks mighty pissed that Reed betrayed him. If it's all their master plan, why is he so miffed?

STAN: Hey, just 'cause we think that's what 'sup doesn't necessarily mean that's what The Sentry thinks. He might not even be clued in yet, because of all the failsafes. Sometimes, people like Jenkins and me are the only ones with all the answers--'cause we're the ones who make up the stories!

JOE: Is there something else wrong with The Sentry? Lindy mentions his…what was that? Angora sweaters or something?

STAN: [with a laugh] I think the word you're stumbling around for is "agoraphobia." It means "fear of open spaces." People who have this often can't even leave their house. What's the matter, Quesada? Lose your dictionary?

JOE: Well, it's a big word.

STAN: Yeah, I guess I've just got more experience in the word field. Hey, kid—stick in this business as long as I have and even you might become a veritable volume of loquacious lexicography like me!

JOE: Only you, Stan. Only you.

STAN: Well, remember--we build all the Marvel heroes with the same human frailties, foibles and flaws that any ol' nebbish on the street might have--that's what makes 'em interesting characters. That's what makes them human! And roll this pearly nugget of wisdom around your brainpan and see what you come up with--if Bob Reynolds had agoraphobia, wouldn't that help the plan?

JOE: How so?

STAN: Well, early on, Bob had doubts about just who he was. If he has a hard time even leaving the house, then it would be even harder to piece together his identity and learn who he really was. It may very well have been one facet of the master plan.

JOE: Well, it looks like The Sentry's still got a lot of pull. Even though there might be some doubts about who and what he is, everyone turned out when he put out the call for help.

STAN: Yeah, it's a veritable "who's who" of mighty Marveldom! But the thing that I really like about this version is that the first hero to make the scene was the Hulk. He may not be the brightest bulb on the tree, but he's as loyal as a faithful dog--an 800-pound, gamma-irradiated pooch who can juggle Buicks, but a faithful dog nonetheless!

JOE: Yeah, it is a bit on the heartwarming side. The only thing that creeps me out is that the Hulk seems…scared.

STAN: He sure does. And you know that if The Void is someone who can make ol' Jade Jaws tremble in his torn-up purple pants, he's gotta be a high-caliber foe!

JOE: Makes you wonder what's going to happen next. I mean, if all of Marvel's heroes--together!--are scared, we could be witnessing something big. Maybe even the destruction of the Marvel Universe.

STAN: I dunno. I think we need one more chapter to bring it all on home. And I need one more page to explain it all to you--and to the legendary legend of Marveldom Assembled.

---

like the Blue Beetle, that I didn't know anything about.

"I put it to one side, and it just sat there."

Eventually, Jenkins picked up the material again and started to leaf through the descriptions of the Superman-like character. It was then he noticed the name at the top of one of the pages—"Stan Lee."

Intrigued, Jenkins sat down and read through the material in its entirety, coming away fairly impressed.

"I thought, 'Wow, this is pretty cool,' " he said. "I called Jae [Lee], told him about it, then sent him copies of the stuff."

The two men talked about the character, and, as Jenkins recalled, "something clicked." The *Inhumans* artist drew up some new, more modern character sketches and submitted them to Marvel Knights editors Quesada and Jimmy Palmiotti, seeking permission to use the Sentry for their next MK project, bumping their planned *Namor of Atlantis* six-issue limited series.

"People wanted us to do Namor," Jenkins said, "but we thought this was really cool, so we decided to do it."

The Marvel Knights guys had never heard of the Sentry, and despite scouring both the Marvel library and *The Official Handbook of the Marvel Universe*, they came up empty-handed — though both admit their search triggered distant memories of the hero.

Quesada contacted Stan Lee for more information about the character—and to ask if he had any additional *Sentry* comics—but Lee couldn't initially recall having created the character.

"As far as I remember, there never was a Marvel Superman," Lee said. "But the idea sounds vaguely familiar."

Disheartened, the Marvel Knights asked Jenkins for all the contents of the Sentry folder, and only then did they realize the full scope of the discovery.

"The development sketches had Stan and Artie's names on it, and the date 1961," Quesada said. "We couldn't believe it. I mean, this was a Marvel superhero that predated the Fantastic Four."

Fantastic Four #1 hit comic racks in November 1961, introducing humanity into the world of superhero comics and ushering in the Marvel Era.

So could *Startling Stories* #1 come to supplant *FF* #1 as the catalyst for the "classic Marvel tradition"?

Marvel Editor-in-Chief

Bob Harras admitted it's a possibility.

"The very existence of the Sentry runs contrary to everything we know about the origins of what is now the Marvel Universe," Harras said. "This is an incredible thing, a discovery that could very well force us to rewrite the history books."

As such, the character could prove to be a tremendous boon for both the House of Ideas and Lee, who's excited to hear Marvel will revive his "lost" character.

"This is going to be great," the industry legend said. "I have complete faith in Joe, Jimmy, Paul and Jae."

"I'm sure they'll do Artie and me proud."

With Lee's blessing, the Marvel Knights put the project on the fast track, and hope to release the first issue of *The Sentry* in mid-summer.

"I was very excited we'd uncovered some character that had previously fallen by the wayside," Jenkins said. "And, in a way, it's even more exciting that Jae and I will revive this character that people are very, very unfamiliar with."

So does Quesada think he could have any more lost treasures in his office? Some long-unseen drawings by Jack Kirby or John Romita, Sr.?

"Anything's possible, I guess," he laughed. "Whenever somebody sends something blindly to Marvel it has a funny way of getting dropped in my office.

"Never fails." ■ **CHRISTOPHER LAWRENCE**

BACK TO THE FUTURE Jae Lee and Paul Jenkins will launch a new Sentry project this summer.

PART THE SIXTH:

THE ELABORATE ENDGAME!

Well, True Believers—We've come to the terminus of this titanic tale of terror and tribulation! It would appear that the Void has been vanquished, the Golden Guardian of Good has gained victory via his guile and guts...and the Marvel Universe is once again unaware that the greatest hero of all—The Sentry!—walks among us. But just how did this happen? And why? And if the Sentry awoke once before, might he do so again?

Here to hopefully shed light on these dark corners of the saga of the Sentry, Joe Quesada concludes his interview with Marvel founding father Stan Lee.

JOE: Well. As far as endings go, that one was pretty elaborate. And it's a little ironic how things came full circle. In a way, we're right back where we started.

STAN: Yep. But you have to ask yourself—is that truly a good thing? After all, "right back where we started" is where we were when The Void came back to life! That makes me just a little bit edgy!

JOE: You? Wow, that's saying a lot. I mean, you've been there for some pretty mind-bending things, Stan! Well, at least we have some answers now. Everything seems to fit rather nicely, and I guess the answers were there all along.

STAN: Y'know, Arthur Conan Doyle, a pretty fair writer who gave us all those "Sherlock Holmes" tales had a saying. He said something to the effect of, "Once you know who done it, all the clues just seem to jump out at you." That would appear to be the case here. This Paul Jenkins guy had it all laid out for the reader to see—if the reader was swift enough to pick up on the hints.

JOE: Yeah, but I wonder how much of it was planned out and how much of it was planted memory? We talked about the duality of The Sentry and The Void, and they really did turn out to be two sides of the same coin.

STAN: There we were, jawin' about The Sentry and addiction, and it turns out the thing he was really addicted to was his power. He truly wanted to be remembered, to have a lasting legacy leaving him larger than life...kinda like yours truly. I'm the idol of millions, y'know—Sam Millions that is, the guy who runs the deli down the street!

JOE: [laughing] Do you ever stop?

STAN: [with a smile] "Stop?" What does that alien word mean?

JOE: Well, it's rather sad that he didn't get to leave his legacy, to have people remember him.

STAN: Maybe so. But in my eyes, that makes him all the more heroic. The Sentry gave up his legacy, he gave up his power, he gave up a huge portion of his life, for the good of us all. That's sacrifice. That's a hero! In a way, albeit in a different way, that does make him larger than life. Reed Richards said it himself. The Sentry was the best of them all.

JOE: Yeah, I guess so. It does become a bigger sacrifice, especially seeing as how his "normal" life as Bob Reynolds isn't all that easy.

STAN: Yes. Bob has his agoraphobia, his fear of open spaces.

JOE: Doesn't it seem a bit...cruel to force him back into that life?

STAN: Maybe. But things happen to these characters all the time. Sometimes, it's in front of the readers' eyes as they read our elegant little epics. Sometimes, it's "off panel." I've got a good feeling that Bob Reynolds is just a little bit more than your average Joe on the street. On some level, deep down inside at the core of his being, he's still a hero—he's still The Sentry. If there's one man who can beat back adversity and conquer affliction, I've gotta believe it's Bob Reynolds. Heck, I'd bet my Merry Marvel Marching Society membership card and a stack of No-Prizes that stretches from here to Kalamazoo on it!

JOE: Well, Stan, if you're betting then I guess the odds are pretty good! One part I really dug, just 'cause it was so different, was Dr. Octopus teaming up with the heroes...and Spider-Man!

STAN: Well, ol' Otto Octavius isn't the nicest guy you're liable to meet, but he's nobody's fool. Doc Ock tends a bit toward the anti-social side, but that doesn't make him an idiot. He knows that if the Void were to win, everyone else would lose—himself included. He may not like Spider-Man, but he's making the practical choice, the intelligent choice. Hey, we don't call 'em criminal "masterminds" for nothin'!

JOE: The ending was pretty choice, too. "Chili dog." What a walk-away line. I mean, what a way to end a story.

STAN: [laughing] Well, it's no "Rosebud," but it'll do.

JOE: There's one question that's still bugging me, one thing I don't quite understand. Look at that last page and the "Burger Palace" flashback. Then look at Bob smile in the next panel. Do you think he remembers he's The Sentry?

STAN: I doubt it. After all, the fail-safes were put back in place by Reed Richards himself. And he's a pretty complete customer! When Reed puts his stamp on the job, that's better than the Good Housekeeping Seal of Approval to me!

JOE: But Stan, come on! There's a way out here! CLOC knows. Doesn't that leave the door open?

STAN: [smiles] Is the door ever really closed? I don't know that there is such a thing as a closed door in the Marvel Universe. And ask yourself: Should there be? The only thing that can present a boundary to us is the limit on the imaginations of our sturdy scripters and pulse-pounding pencilers. And last I checked, there were no limits there. Anyway, now that you're running the show in my old seat as the editor-in-chief, it's your job to make sure things stay that way, Quesada! So nose to the grindstone! Get back to work!

JOE: Come on, Stan, level with me. Level with us all. DOES Bob remember? Will The Sentry return?

STAN: [sighs] Hey, face it, Joe—it's not for me to decide. It's not for you, either. 'Cause these titillating tales with their titanic tussles and draconian dramas are done for the readers. This much we know: The rest of the Marvel Universe has forgotten The Sentry. They're back in the dark, just like they were in The Sentry #1 or Amazing Spider-Man #192 or *Night Nurse* #4. And we on the inside will soon forget too, as it has to be. And that's fine. I think the only people who can decide if Bob knows and the only people who can remember the whole tale—really, the only people whom it's appropriate to have that power—are the readers. After all, we do it all for them. I don't mind letting them in on a secret that the rest of us have forgotten. Provided, that is, that they don't go and blab it all to Reed Richards.

So, if you choose, True Believers, you can let the memory linger. But be sure to buy the sequel—if we dare put one out!

Now, c'mon, Quesada, all this talk of food has made me hungry! I know a great little chili dog stand on the corner!!!

Excitement.

It's what entertainment's all about. Orson Welles knew it, founded a brilliant career on it, in fact. On Halloween, 1938, Welles and a troupe of radio actors broadcast an adaptation of the science fiction novel *The War of the Worlds*. Millions tuned in to hear Welles' unique take on the performance, played out in such a way that it would sound like an actual news account of an invasion from Mars.

As the play continued, a portion—a large portion—of the audience believed it was hearing a real news broadcast, and a panic ensued. People headed to the streets with guns, wrapped their heads in towels to avoid the effects of Martian gas weapons, and hid in their cellars and sheds— unintentionally lending truth to the fictitious story Welles was weaving.

A similar phenomenon swept over popular society in 1999, when *The Blair Witch Project* hit theaters. Bolstered by "fact-filled" Internet sites and a Sci-Fi Channel "documentary" on the witch, audiences believed the filmmaker's supposition that three young people disappeared in the Maryland woods while searching for a mysterious phantom. They believed it to the effect of a $140 million box office gross.

How'd they do it? By making the audience a part of the story. That's exactly what Joe Quesada and Jimmy Palmiotti had in mind when they walked into the Wizard offices to explain their idea for promoting *The Sentry*. The Marvel Knights wanted to give the story—a tale of a forgotten hero—an interesting twist, an instant injection of excitement... something comics had lacked for a while. The Ultimates hadn't yet arrived, and anything that could draw more attention to the medium would be good. Not only for the Knights, not only for The Sentry, but for comics in general.

That in mind, Wizard played along; creating, then killing, fictitious artist Artie Rosen; spreading rumors about a lost project by Stan Lee; lending credence to the myth the Knights were developing. The goal wasn't to mislead anyone or betray anyone, but to get fans to further suspend their disbelief, to lead them to better appreciate the intricacies of Paul Jenkins' plot, to help them have fun.

And there's absolutely nothing wrong with that—especially since no one had to wrap their head in a towel.

—Chris Lawrence
Staff Writer, *Wizard* Magazine

MARVEL FOOLED MILLIONS BY PASSING OFF 'THE SENTRY' AS A FORGOTTEN STAN LEE CLASSIC—AND GOT A SMASH HIT. NOW THE TRUTH CAN BE TOLD...

Big Lie

BY CHRISTOPHER LAWRENCE

Joe Quesada couldn't remember.

Wandering the halls of his suburban New Jersey home, Marvel's future editor-in-chief furrowed his brow and fought to recall last night's dream. Sometime during the wee hours of the morning, he'd had an idea on how to promote the comic pitch he'd just gotten from Paul Jenkins and Jae Lee. The *Sentry* only a few nights before, and hadn't been able to get it off his mind. He found the concept—a forgotten superhero addicted to his amazing powers—engrossing, and wanted to ensure Jenkins and Lee's follow-up to their Eisner Award-winning *Inhumans* would get the attention it deserved. He'd come up with something that fit the bill—he knew he had—he just couldn't recall it. Amid his amnesiac haze, Quesada caught flashes of his idea, fleeting snippets and vague recollections.

"Why can't I remember?" he asked himself.

And then it hit him.

"Maybe I'm not supposed to," Quesada mused.

With that, the Marvel Knight concocted the big lie. An uncanny promotion plan that would entangle Jenkins, Jae Lee, WIZARD magazine and even Marvel Founding Father Stan Lee himself. Together, they would create a 40-year history and an unheard-of artist to turn the Sentry into a Silver Age legend. All for a character that never saw print until the year 2000.

Quesada proposed, because that's the way his "real" creators, Lee and Rosen, decided it had to be. The Marvel Universe, with all of its intrinsically flawed heroes, simply couldn't handle the perfection of the Superman-like Golden Guardian of Good, so the Sentry had to be forgotten. Totally.

But Lee and Rosen did too good a job wiping the Sentry from the consciousness of the Marvel Universe—their efforts seemingly spilled over into our reality. Thus, the lie suggested, no one could recall the hero with the power of a million exploding suns—not even its creators.

Now all the ruse needed was for Stan Lee to play along.

"I didn't know how Stan was going to take the idea," Quesada says, admitting he felt a twinge of nervousness when making the initial call. "But when I pitched it to him, he was absolutely floored."

Describing Jenkins as a "great writer," Lee acknowledges he thought the series—and the hoax—was a phenomenal idea. "I have a very poor memory anyway," the *Fantastic Four* creator laughs. "And as everybody knows, I'm happy to take credit for anything."

The last person Quesada needed to rope in was Sentry co-creator Artie Rosen. That proved easy—he never existed.

THE CONSPIRACY SPREADS

The Knights wasted no time promoting the Sentry's myth, and quickly sent Artie Rosen to meet the 'Devil.'

"We want...all of you to join us in sending off hearty get-well wishes to Artie Rosen and the Rosen family," read an editor's note on the letters page of *Daredevil* #9. "Artie, for you younger readers, was instrumental during Marvel's formative years, providing some of comics' most influential yet least acknowledged pencil and ink work. Artie, you keep inspiring us."

That mention in *DD* was only the tip of the iceberg, however. Moving into Phase Two of their marketing plan, the Knights pitched the Sentry storyline to WIZARD in January 2000, enlisting THE COMIC MAGAZINE's help in spreading the lie. First step—killing off Rosen with a fake obituary in issue #103.

"We were close, years ago, but I hadn't seen or heard from Artie in many years," Stan Lee said, kicking off the first in a

NULL AND VOID The Sentry doesn't know what's worse—his archenemy the Void or his drinking problem.

THE HOAX

The story fed to the general public went a little something like this: Prior to the 1961 release of *Fantastic Four* #1—the comic generally recognized as having kicked off the Marvel Era—Stan Lee collaborated with artist Artie Rosen to create a character called the Sentry.

The Superman-esque, all-powerful hero starred in his own title, but no one—not comic historians, not Marvel employees, not even Lee himself—could remember him.

At least, not until a twist of fate left a long-lost file filled with Sentry information in Jenkins' hands. Rosen, the story had it, died early in 2000, and while sifting through her husband's effects, Blanche Rosen discovered a box labeled "Property of Marvel Comics." Ever the dutiful wife, Mrs. Rosen sent the contents to the Marvel offices, where they were summarily dropped on then-Marvel Knights editor Quesada's desk.

Quesada set it aside, where it sat unnoticed until Jenkins accidentally picked it up amid a stack of comp comics. He opened it weeks later and found some old Sentry comics, along with character descriptions and conceptual sketches. Intrigued, Jenkins sent the folder to Jae Lee and together, the duo agreed the obscure character would be the perfect star for their first post-*Inhumans* project.

After securing Stan Lee's permission to "revive" the hero, the Marvel Knights mini-series *The Sentry* was born.

THE TRUTH—TAKE ONE

The story of the Golden Guardian of Good had been kicking around in Jenkins' head for almost ten years.

"It was one of the first things I wanted to do in comics," he said. "I wanted to write a story about a superhero who might become addicted to their power."

Prior to getting his big break on *Hellblazer*, Jenkins approached Vertigo editor Karen Berger about reviving Hourman—a hero the writer describes as the logical vehicle for his story.

"He had these pills that made him into a superhero for one hour—talk about the biggest rush in history," Jenkins says. "Hourman would be great to write as an addicted hero."

ARTIE'S ART This "Rosen sketch" (left) is really by John Romita Sr.; Jae Lee aped a Silver Age art style in the comic.

But it wasn't meant to be. Barred from using any established DC characters in his story, Jenkins created the Sentry, an addict suffering from delusions of superheroic grandeur.

"Initially, it was going to begin and end with that," Jenkins recounts of his character's hoax-free beginnings. "I was going to do it as a prestige story about a guy who may or may not be a superhero—a guy who has these flashback memories of a superhero life."

Several DC editors expressed interest in the idea, but nothing came of it.

"Every time an editor would get the project, something would stand in their way," Jenkins says. "The editor would leave, they'd find out they just couldn't do it, whatever."

THE TRUTH—TAKE TWO

After his stint on *Hellblazer* ended, Jenkins took some freelance work at Marvel, then pitched them his Sentry proposal. Again, it hit editorial limbo.

Undeterred, Jenkins dug even deeper into the idea he was sure could be a hit and extended it from a one-shot to a mini-series,

grafting a deeper mystery of identity, [a] tale of power and addiction.

He bounced ideas off his frie[nd] *Swamp Thing* artist Rick Veitch, w[ho was] invaluable in fleshing out the sto[ry].

"I owe a great deal of gratitude [to him]," he says. "He's responsible for q[uite an] amount of the ideas you see in T[he Sentry]."

The story continued to evo[lve as] writer and artist's conversations, a[nd got] to the point where the duo conside[red pitch]ing the mini-series together.

Time passed, and the writer n[oticed his] biggest su[...] career—[...] After w[inning an] Eisner Aw[ard, Jenkins] and Jae [Lee found] themselves [sought] by questi[oners about] their col[lab on the] future. [...] Jenkins [decided] to resurre[ct the Sentry.]

After [a talk with Jae it was] okay from [both of them to] carry on w[ith...] the writer [...] "Jae, I've go[t...] It's been t[o...] many differ[ent...] it makes m[e...] cry. I'm go[ing to...] one more s[hot...]

Lee liste[ned to the] proposal and [...]

Together, the *Inhumans* create[d] *The Sentry* into the Marvel Knig[hts...]

"It was a brilliant concept," [says] founder Quesada. "I loved it."

They greenlighted the pr[oject.] Jenkins saw his seven-year qu[est...] umphantly—but with a bitte[r...] couldn't take credit for it. At le[ast...]

THE SET-UP

Quesada's conspiracy concept tu[rned] from the guy who created the S[entry to] a guy who found an old Stan Lee[...] didn't sit too well with Jenkins a[t first.]

"It wasn't part of my deal—[getting] into the whole pulling-the-w[ool-over-]people's-eyes thing," he admits[...] horrible liar." In the end, thoug[h the] powers of persuasion proved [...] and Jenkins agreed to go along w[ith it.]

"The big hype they were p[utting] behind it—where did he come[...] could we possibly have forgott[en won]derful, original hero—that w[ay the] scripts," the scribe relays. "The[...] was a reflection of the story, an[d it made] it all a lot more valid for me."

No one could remember

series of interviews in which he lent credence to the Sentry story. "It [his death] came as a big shock to me." In issue #104, WIZARD ran a story hinting at the existence of a long-lost Lee/Rosen character, and finally an in-depth news item announcing the discovery of the Sentry materials the following month.

The revelatory announcements sparked heated debates on Internet message boards, lengthy conversations in comic-related chatrooms and a slew of letters to the Marvel Knights offices—all to Quesada's delight.

"I couldn't think of a better way to promote a book like this. Call it a publicity stunt, call it whatever you want," he laughs. "It's not the worst thing that's ever been perpetrated on society."

Jenkins was enjoying the hoax, too...though maybe not as much as Quesada.

"You could see me at conventions all last year squirming around, hanging my head in shame because I knew I was lying," he says. "Well, it wasn't really lying—it was fun."

The added attention brought on by the hoax did have a downside, though—added pressure.

"*The Sentry* was the first comic book of mine that I've ever had published where I was nervous," Jenkins says. "The incredible success of *Inhumans* set a certain level of expectation for the Jenkins/Lee team, and that—combined with Jenkins' own eight-year struggle to tell the Sentry story—had the writer wondering, "Are we ever going to be able to capture lightning in a bottle again?"

THE PAYOFF

Jenkins' worries were for naught.

The Sentry debuted in the summer of 2000 to both critical and commercial acclaim, ranking 31st in Diamond Comic Distributor's list of the Top 100 comics.

Each issue of the mini-series featured a Q&A with Stan Lee, conducted by Quesada. Lee—a master marketer in his own right—even managed to out-trick the original trickster. "When you're sitting there talking to Stan about this and he makes it sound so real, you question yourself,"

Quesada says of the pieces where Stan waxed on the Sentry's "origin." "You have a hard time separating the fiction from the reality."

By the time the series wrapped and fans learned that every resident in the Marvel Universe had "forgotten" the Sentry, most fans figured the promotional scheme out. Some still haven't. Now that the truth has been revealed, Quesada says he doesn't expect any backlash from fans.

"We didn't drive fans to pick up a crappy comic book," he offers. "They picked it up because they were curious, and whether they believed the mythology or not, they were hooked."

Marvel's EIC says the marketing campaign—the hoax—added to the overall enjoyment of the series, similar to the way Alan Moore's intricate text supplements functioned in *Watchmen*.

"They weren't necessary for the enjoyment of the book, but they added color to the world," he says. "That's what we tried to do here...create the world of the Sentry—inside the comic and a little bit outside the book."

Jenkins is pleased, too. He's finally told the story he wanted to—and he can proudly reap the credit.

"It all worked," the writer says. "I think people will look at *The Sentry* and say, 'They accomplished something really f–king cool.'"

As for his brilliant hoax, Quesada doesn't think fans will forget how effortlessly they were duped—or how much they enjoyed it—any time soon. "People will still argue it's real," he says. "And you never know—you could have been brainwashed by the Sentry, too."

WIZARD Staff Writer Christopher Lawrence claims to be a

afterword

The scary part about what you've just read is, I'm still not sure it isn't true!

Y'see, I've never been famous for having a great memory. So, when Jocular Joey Quesada called me some time ago and asked if I remembered writing The Sentry, I cautiously mumbled, "Yeah, it does sound kind'a familiar."

Fact is, I've done so much writing over the past few hundred years (at least it seems like that long) that everything sounds familiar to me. Also, since the Sentry is such a great character, I'd like to think I did dream him up.

Wouldn't it be a gas if Marvel's whole batty Bullpen thinks it was just a cool gag, and none of them realize there actually was a Sentry? In fact, it would be even cooler if the Sentry was none other than-- me!

I mean, just think about it. He was there before the Fantastic Four, right? Well, I was there before the FF, wasn't I? And someone took away his memory, right? Well, everyone knows I've always had the world's worst memory. And his greatest enemy was The Void, right? Okay, what's the last letter in "Void?" Uh huh, it's "D." I figure they just didn't wanna make it too obvious by adding a "C" also, but I'm sure you get my drift.

So here's the really mind-blowing part: Paul Jenkins did a truly brilliant job scripting what he thought was a fictional story, and Jae Lee created some of the year's greatest artwork thinking he was just making up all those illustrations. In fact, all of Marveldom Assembled got a great kick out of what they thought was a howlin' hoax, and now they expect you to believe that it was all a maniacal mènage of make-believe.

Well, far be it from me to spoil the fun of editor Quesada and his capricious co-conspirators, but I'd like to leave you with this tantalizing thought-- if it didn't really happen, if there hadn't really been a Sentry, then how come the Void isn't now the ruler of the world?

Sheesh! Next thing y'know, they'll be saying that Ditko and I just made up Spider-Man!

Excelsior!

Stan

Stan Lee